CATEGORICAL SYLLOGISMS

Every standard-form categorical syllogism has exactly three terms, to wit:

The *major term* is the predicate term of the conclusion (P).
The *minor term* is the subject term of the conclusion (S).
The *middle term* is the term appearing in the premises but not in the conclusion (M).

The premise containing the major term is the *major premise.*
The premise containing the minor term is the *minor premise.*
A syllogism is in *standard form* when each of its component statements is in standard form, and they are given in this order: major premise, minor premise, conclusion.

Every proposition in a categorical syllogism must be one of the following four:

An **A** proposition—*universal affirmative*   e.g., All collies are dogs.
An **E** proposition—*universal negative*   e.g., No dogs are cats.
An **I** proposition—*particular affirmative*   e.g., Some dogs are collies.
An **O** proposition—*particular negative*   e.g., Some dogs are not collies.

The *mood* of a syllogism is determined by its three types of component propositions, **AAA, EIO,** etc. The order follows standard form: major premise, minor premise, conclusion.

The *figure* of a standard-form syllogism is determined by the position of the middle term:

M P	P │ M	M │ P	P M
S M	S │ M	M │ S	M S
first figure	**second figure**	**third figure**	**fourth figure**

1st: The middle term is the subject of the major premise and the predicate of the minor premise.
2nd: The middle term is the predicate of both premises.
3rd: The middle term is the subject of both premises.
4th: The middle term is the predicate of the major premise and the subject of the minor premise.

VALID FORMS OF THE CATEGORICAL SYLLOGISM (ON THE BOOLEAN INTERPRETATION)

Figure 1	Figure 2	Figure 3	Figure 4
AAA-1	AEE-2	AII-3	AEE-4
EAE-1	EAE-2	IAI-3	IAI-4
AII-1	AOO-2	EIO-3	EIO-4
EIO-1	EIO-2	OAO-3	

DISTRIBUTION

A term is *distributed* when the proposition in which the term appears refers to the entire class of objects to which the term refers. It is summarized in the following chart (D = distributed; U = undistributed):

All S^D are P^U.
No S^D are P^D.
Some S^U are P^U.
Some S^U are not P^D.

RULES GOVERNING EVERY VALID CATEGORICAL SYLLOGISM (ON THE BOOLEAN INTERPRETATION)

1. The syllogism must contain exactly three terms, each term having the same meaning throughout the syllogism.
2. The middle term of the syllogism must be distributed at least once.
3. Any term that is distributed in the conclusion must be distributed in the corresponding premise.
4. A valid syllogism cannot have two negative premises.
5. If either premise of the syllogism is negative, the conclusion must be negative as well.
6. From two universal premises no particular conclusion may be drawn.

SUMMARY OF THE TRUTH TABLE DEFINITIONS OF THE CONNECTIVES

p	$\sim p$	p	q	$p \bullet q$	$p \vee q$	$p \supset q$	$p \equiv q$
T	F	T	T	T	T	T	T
F	T	T	F	F	T	F	F
		F	T	F	T	T	F
		F	F	F	F	T	T

ESSENTIALS *of* LOGIC

Irving M. Copi
University of Hawaii

Carl Cohen
University of Michigan

with
Daniel E. Flage
James Madison University

PEARSON

Prentice
Hall

Upper Saddle River, New Jersey 07458

Library of Congress Cataloging-in-Publication Data

Copi, Irving M.
   Essentials of logic / Irving M. Copi, Carl Cohen.—2nd ed.
      p. cm.
   Includes index.
      ISBN 0-13-238034-X
         1. Logic—Textbooks. I. Cohen, Carl, 1931- II. Title.
BC108.C685 2007
160—dc22   2006009190

Editor-in-Chief: *Sarah Touborg*
Senior Acquisitions Editor: *Mical Moser*
Editorial Assistant: *Carla Worner*
Senior Media Editor: *Anita Castro*
Vice President/Director of Production and Manufacturing: *Barbara Kittle*
Senior Managing Editor: *Joanne Riker*
Production Liaison: *Louise Rothman*
Prepress and Assistant Manufacturing Manager: *Mary Ann Gloriande*
Prepress and Manufacturing Buyer: *Christina Amato*
Director of Marketing: *Brandy Dawson*
Assistant Marketing Manager: *Andrea Messineo*
Cover Art: *Jutta Klee/CORBIS*
Director, Image Resource Center: *Melinda Reo*
Manager, Visual Research: *Beth Brenzel*
Cover Image Specialist: *Karen Sanatar*
Composition and Full Service Project Management: *Emily Autumn/GGS Book Services*
Printer/Binder: *VonHoffmann, Inc.*
Cover Printer: *Phoenix Color Corporation*

Interior photos: Pages 199, 343 Courtesy of National Archives and Records Administration.

Pearson Education LTD.
Pearson Education Australia PTY, Limited
Pearson Education Singapore, Pte. Ltd
Pearson Education North Asia Ltd

Pearson Education, Canada, Ltd
Pearson Educación de Mexico, S.A. de C.V.
Pearson Education–Japan
Pearson Education Malaysia, Pte. Ltd

PEARSON
Prentice
Hall

10 9 8 7 6 5 4 3 2 1

ISBN 0-13-238034-X

PREFACE

In a republican nation, whose citizens are to be led by reason and persuasion and not by force, the art of reasoning becomes of the first importance.

—THOMAS JEFFERSON

Since the publication of the first edition in 1953, Irving M. Copi's *Introduction to Logic* has served thousands of instructors and students in both teaching and studying the fundamentals of classical and modern logic. The first edition of *Essentials of Logic* was written in response to numerous instructors' requests for a concise introductory logic text for use in their courses. The second edition was revised in light of many instructors' suggestions. While retaining the rigor for which Copi has been known for over half a century, it was revised with an eye to clearer explanations, somewhat wider coverage, and an increased number of aids for students. We believe the revisions in this edition will make the distinctions clearer to students while retaining the logical rigor one expects from Copi.

FEATURES OF THE SECOND EDITION

Section reduction and coverage. The number of sections in the second edition has been reduced from 62 to 52, but the coverage of topics has been expanded. The discussion of informal fallacies (Chapter 2) has been revised to show more clearly how informal fallacies are related to acceptable arguments. This reflects recent scholarship on informal fallacies. In Chapter 4, the distinction between logically equivalent statement forms and immediate inference has been clarified. Chapter 5 includes a systematic discussion of how to find the missing premise in an enthymematic categorical syllogism. Chapter 6 includes a new section on incomplete and reverse or "one-row" truth tables. Chapter 7 includes new sections on conditional and indirect proofs for propositional logic. Chapter 8 includes a new section on conditional and indirect proofs for quantificational logic. The chapter on induction (Chapter 9) now includes discussions of evaluating hypotheses and argument to the best explanation. There is a new appendix on using truth trees in propositional and quantificational logic.

Exercise sets. The exercise sets include over 1,200 exercises, nearly half of which are new to this edition of *Essentials of Logic*. Further, the book now includes solutions to *all* the odd-numbered exercises.

Increased use of charts, tables, and hints to students. A significant number of side-bars called "Essential Hints" have been added. These give hints, suggestions, and encouragement to students. In Chapter 5, there is a chart of nonstandard quantifiers for categorical logic. In Chapter 6, there is an extensive dictionary (translation guide) for propositional logic. In Chapter 7 and 8, there are expanded rules of thumb (strategies) for constructing proofs. In Chapter 8, there is an extensive dictionary (translation guide) for quantificational logic.

Instructor supplements. Accompanying *Essentials of Logic* for instructors is an instructor's manual with sample test questions and solutions to all the even-numbered exercises. The test questions are also available in a computerized test manager program to aid in the preparation of tests for students.

Student supplement. There is also a revision of Prentice Hall's groundbreaking logic tutorial, *e***Logic** This tutorial includes over 500 of the exercises in *Essentials of Logic* for students to work electronically. Together with the exercises from the text, *e***Logic** includes the tools students need to solve logic problems. Students can work problems—including diagramming arguments, creating Venn diagrams, constructing truth tables, and building proofs—and receive constant feedback to guide them through solutions. Students can submit their work via email or hardcopy to their instructors, together with a Log Book showing how well they did. The following walkthrough provides an initial introduction to what awaits students in their use of *e***Logic**!

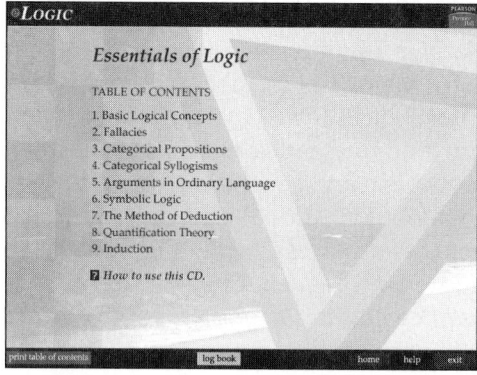

After students enter their own username and email address, they will decide which exercises they need to work by locating the appropriate chapter and entering the appropriate section where the exercises reside.

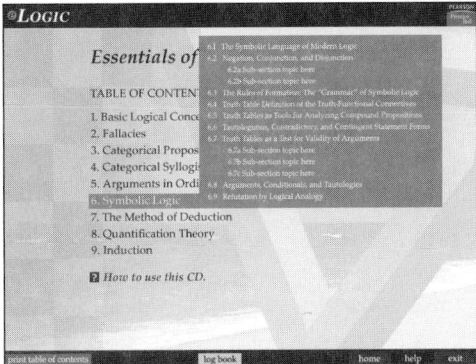

Numerous navigation links are always available on the main screen, including help and access to the Log Book, where students can see which exercises they've worked on and how well they've done!

NOTE that students can always refresh their understanding on how to use *e***Logic** through the help link!

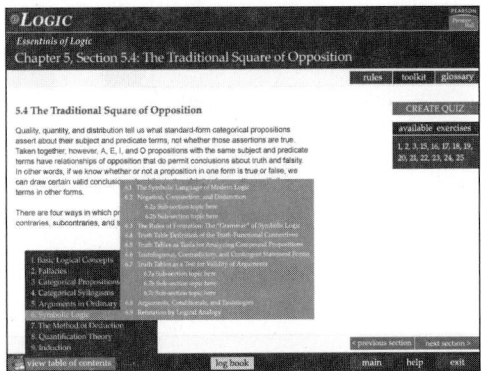

Students select exercises by chapter section, and have ready at their command all necessary toolkits to solve logic problems—including diagramming arguments, Venn diagrams, truth tables, proof checkers, and a symbolic notation editor. Additionally, rules and a glossary are available for student reference.

ACKNOWLEDGMENTS

The revisions in this edition of *Essentials of Logic* benefited greatly by comments from Norman R. Schultz (Metro State College), Robert Kimball (University of Louisville), Andrew Aberdein (Florida Institute of Technology), A.T. Anchustegui (Boise State University), Keith W. Krasemann (College of Du Page), and Harlan Miller (Virginia Polytechnic and State University). Working with Mical Moser and Carla Worner at Prentice Hall and Emily Autumn at GGS Book Services has been delightful. I also want to thank my family for their love and tolerance.

BASIC LOGICAL CONCEPTS

1.1 WHAT LOGIC IS

Logic is the study of the quality of arguments. Broadly speaking, an argument is an attempt to provide reasons for accepting the truth of some claim. (We give a more precise definition of *argument* in section 1.3.) Some arguments provide good reasons; other arguments do not. This book teaches you how to identify and evaluate arguments so that you will be able to sort good arguments from bad ones. Logic is a kind of self-defense. Understanding logic helps you to avoid being fooled. It encourages you to seek good reasons for your beliefs. Understanding logic also enables you to construct better arguments of your own. Arguments help us to determine whether or not to believe what we read in the newspaper or see on television. They help us reach decisions. They are the backbone of the essays that we read and write. We even use arguments when talking with friends. The skills taught in this logic book are useful in everyday life.

1.2 PROPOSITIONS AND SENTENCES

All arguments are constructed out of *propositions* or *statements*, so we begin by discussing them. **A proposition is something that can be asserted or denied.** A proposition is either *true* or *false*. It is true if it corresponds with the facts it describes. If it does not correspond, it is false. In this way propositions differ from questions, requests, commands, and exclamations, none of which can be asserted or denied. Although a defining feature of propositions is that they are *either true or false*, we may not always know whether a given proposition is true or false.

Example

The proposition "David Letterman sneezed three times on his twenty-first birthday" is either true or false, but we will probably never know which one it is.

Questions, commands, requests, and exclamations do not make claims about the world. Unlike propositions, they do not have *truth values;* they are neither true nor false.

Declarative sentences are used to communicate propositions in print or speech. Sentences are not propositions. A proposition is what is meant by a declarative sentence in a certain context. Two sentences can state the same proposition. Propositions are independent of the language in which they are stated. For example, "Il pleut," "Es regnet," and "Está lloviendo," are different sentences that assert the same proposition: They assert that it is raining. And, of course, there are many ways to assert the same proposition in a given language.

Example

A. George W. Bush won the 2004 U.S. presidential election.

B. The winner of the U.S. presidential election held in the year 2004 was George W. Bush.

C. George W. Bush was elected to the U.S. presidency in 2004.

These sentences differ in structure. However, they have the same meaning; they are true under the same conditions. All three sentences assert the same proposition.

Notice, too that the *same sentence* can be used in different contexts to assert *different propositions*. The time and place at which a sentence is uttered may affect the proposition it asserts.

Examples

Humans have walked on the moon.

If this statement had been uttered before 1969, it would have been false. If uttered after 1969, it is true.

It is raining.

If it *is* raining at the place and time this sentence is uttered, it is true. At other places and times, it is false.

You are a thief!

At one time and place, this sentence might assert (truly or falsely, depending on the facts) that *Bob* is a thief, while at another time, it might assert (truly or falsely) that *Joan* is a thief.

> **ESSENTIAL** HINTS
>
> Logicians distinguish between propositions, statements, and sentences. A proposition is what is asserted. A statement is the proposition asserted by a sentence in a particular language. The meanings of *proposition* and *statement* are close enough to one another that we shall use them interchangeably.

In later chapters, we discuss properties of propositions. Some propositions have other propositions as parts (they are compound propositions). Others don't (they are simple propositions). Sometimes the structures of propositions make important differences in the arguments in which they are found.

1.3 ARGUMENTS, PREMISES, AND CONCLUSIONS

An *inference* is a mental process by which one proposition is arrived at and affirmed on the basis of one or more other propositions that are assumed as the starting point of the process. To determine whether an inference is correct, the logician examines the propositions with which that process begins and ends and the relations among them. This cluster of propositions constitutes an *argument*.

Now we are ready to formulate a more precise definition of *argument*. **An *argument* is a collection of propositions in which some propositions, the *premises*, are given as reasons for accepting the truth of another proposition, the *conclusion*.** In the following argument:

> All humans are mortals.⎫
> Socrates is a human.   ⎬ Premises
> Socrates is a mortal.⎭ Conclusion

the first two propositions are the premises. They provide reasons to believe that the conclusion, "Socrates is a mortal," is true.

In ordinary discourse we use the word *argument* in other ways. For example, someone might say, "My parents divorced because they were always arguing." But in logic we restrict the term *argument* to refer only to attempts to provide premises in support of conclusions. Arguments do not require disagreements.

An argument is not *merely* a collection of propositions. The propositions have to have a certain kind of relationship in order to be an argument. The premises of an argument must provide reasons to believe (evidence) that the conclusion is true. In practice, the premises of an argument are known or assumed before the conclusion is known.

There are two basic types of arguments. **A *deductive* argument is an argument that attempts to prove the truth of its conclusion with *certainty*.** This book concentrates mainly on the logic of deductive arguments. **An *inductive* argument is one that attempts to establish its conclusion with some degree of *probability*.** There are many kinds of deductive and inductive arguments, but the general descriptions just given always apply. Section 1.8 of this chapter gives you more information about induction, and the final chapter of the text examines some common inductive argument types in detail. Inductive and deductive arguments are evaluated according to very different standards.

Before we get to the standards for evaluating specific types of arguments, let's continue with the general account of arguments. An argument always has *at least one premise*. There is no upper limit to the number of premises, but two or three is common. Additionally, there is always *exactly one conclusion* per argument. No single proposition by itself constitutes an argument. Here are some examples of arguments:

PREMISE:	All students are hard workers.	Deductive
CONCLUSION:	If Carla is a student, then she is a hard worker.	

PREMISE:	All arachnids are invertebrates.	Deductive
PREMISE:	All spiders are arachnids.	
CONCLUSION:	All spiders are invertebrates.	

PREMISE:	If Luis went to the dance, then Bernadette went to the dance.	Deductive
PREMISE:	Luis went to the dance.	
CONCLUSION:	Bernadette went to the dance.	

PREMISE:	John is a member of $\Delta K\Phi$, and John went to the dance.	Inductive
PREMISE:	Jorge is a member of $\Delta K\Phi$, and Jorge went to the dance.	
PREMISE:	Dmitri is a member of $\Delta K\Phi$, and Dmitri went to the dance.	
CONCLUSION:	Probably all the members of $\Delta K\Phi$ went to the dance.	

PREMISE:	Sam and Dana are alike insofar as they both enjoy history classes, science classes, and math classes.	Inductive
PREMISE:	Sam enjoys her logic class.	
CONCLUSION:	It is likely Dana also enjoys his logic class.	

These five sample arguments are all arranged in *standard form*. In standard form, the premises are stated first and the conclusion last, with a single proposition written on each line, and a line is drawn between the premises and the conclusion. By stating arguments in standard form, you show the relationship between the premise(s) and the conclusion. But in ordinary written and verbal communication, arguments are often *not* stated in standard form. For example, it is very common for the conclusion of an argument to be stated first and the premises given afterwards:

> The Food and Drug Administration should stop all cigarette sales immediately. After all, cigarette smoking is the leading cause of preventable death.

In this case, the first sentence is the conclusion, and the second sentence is the reason that we are supposed to accept the truth of the claim made by the first sentence.

The techniques logicians have developed for evaluating arguments require that one distinguishes between the premise(s) and conclusion of an argument. If you begin by stating arguments in standard form, you will make the distinction clear. When reading a passage, the best way to begin that process is to identify the conclusion. Ask yourself, "What am I supposed to believe as a result of reading this passage?" Whatever it is, that is likely to be the conclusion. Then identify the premises by asking yourself, "What reasons are given for me to believe that the conclusion is true?"

Notice, however, that although every argument is a structured cluster of propositions, not every structured cluster of propositions is an argument. This means that you need to decide whether a given passage contains an argument—rather than a description, an explanation, or something else. Again, looking for the conclusion is often a useful way to proceed: If there is no conclusion, then the passage does not contain an argument.

> **ESSENTIAL** HINTS
>
> Descriptions answer the questions Who?, What?, When?, Where?, and sometimes How? Explanations answer the questions Why? or sometimes How? Arguments give reasons to believe a proposition (the conclusion) is true.

Example

It is likely that life evolved on countless other planets that scientists now believe exist in our galaxy, because life very probably evolved on Mars during an early period in its history when it had an atmosphere and climate similar to Earth's.[1]

The conclusion here is the proposition between the words *It* and *because*; the premise comes after *because*. Here is the argument stated in standard form:

PREMISE: Life very probably evolved on Mars during an early period in its history, when it had an atmosphere and climate similar to Earth's.

CONCLUSION: Therefore it is likely that life evolved on countless other planets that scientists now believe exist in our galaxy.

The following passage contains an explanation of how camels manage water in their bodies. There is no argument:

Camels do not store water in their humps. They drink furiously, up to 28 gallons in a ten-minute session, and then distribute the water evenly throughout their bodies. Afterward, they use the water stingily. They have viscous urine and dry feces. They breathe through their noses and keep their mouths shut. They do sweat, but only as a last resort. . . . They can survive a water loss of up to one-third of their body weight, then drink up and feel fine.[2]

---

[1]Richard Zare, "Big News for Earthlings," *The New York Times*, 8 August 1996.
[2]William Langewiesche, *Sahara Unveiled: A Journey Across the Desert* (New York: Pantheon Books, 1996).

Identify the premises and conclusions in the following arguments.[3]

1. A well-regulated militia being necessary to the security of a free state, the right of the people to keep and bear arms shall not be infringed.

   —*The Constitution of the United States*, Amendment 2

2. Computers will soon become conscious because they will eventually become so complex that self-awareness will emerge.

3. My porridge is all gone! Someone must have eaten it.

4. The police are sitting at the exit. This must be a speed trap.

5. This can't be Kansas. Everything is in color.

6. The valley is under water. So, the dam must have burst.

7. Snow is white. But this stuff is yellow. So this must not be snow.

8. There has been an increase in the violence portrayed in movies, on TV, and in music. It is not surprising, therefore, that social violence has increased.

9. We have class on Monday, Wednesday, and Friday. Today is Monday. So, we must have class.

10. I should be admitted to State U. because my high school grades were good, my SAT scores were high, and my letters of recommendation are strong.

11. You never change the oil in your car. You never check the coolant. So, you can expect engine trouble soon.

12. Of all our passions and appetites, the love of power is of the most imperious and unsociable nature, since the pride of one man requires the submission of the multitude.

    —Edward Gibbon, *The Decline and Fall of the Roman Empire*, vol. 1, chap. IV

13. Forbear to judge, for we are sinners all.

    —William Shakespeare, *Henry VI, Part II*, act 3, scene 3

14. The essence of our admirable economic system is to create wants as fast as, or faster than, it satisfies them. Thus the improvement of living conditions, meaning greater consumer satisfaction, is, by definition, impossible.

    —J. Maher, "Never Better," *The New York Times*, 1 January 1993

15. He that loveth not knoweth not God; for God is love.

    —1 John 4:8

---

[3]Solutions to the odd-numbered exercises are found at the end of the book.

16. "That is the absolute rock-bottom minimum—or Charilaos Konstantinides was a blithering idiot—and he wasn't."

    —Dashiell Hammett, *The Maltese Falcon* (New York: Alfred A. Knopf, 1930), p. 156

17. The theoretical justification of our argument [that the legalization of abortion in the 1970s substantially reduced crime in the 1990s] rests on two simple assumptions: 1) Legalized abortion leads to fewer "unwanted" babies being born, and 2) unwanted babies are more likely to suffer abuse and neglect and are therefore more likely to be criminally involved in later life.

    —Steven Levitt, *www.slate.com/dialogues/*, 23 August 1999

18. The institution of public education thrives on its own failures. The more poorly its charges perform, the more money it asks for (and gets) from the public and the government. The more money it gets, the more it can grow itself.

    —Ian Hamet, "School for Scandal," *The Weekly Standard*, 23 August 1999

19. Accusations [of sexual harassment] are based on "impact" not intention; therefore the accused is guilty if the accuser believes him to be guilty.

    —Herbert London, New York University Dean, quoted in Alan Kors and Harvey Silverglate, *The Shadow University* (New York: The Free Press, 1998)

20. Unquestionably, no more important goal exists in medical research today than the development of an AIDS vaccine. Last year (1998) AIDS, caused by HIV (Human Immunodeficiency Virus) was the infectious disease that killed the most people around the world, and the epidemic is not abating.

    —David Baltimore, President of the California Institute of Technology, in *The Chronicle of Higher Education*, 28 May 1999

1.4   ARGUMENTS AND EXPLANATIONS

Many passages that look like arguments are not arguments. They're explanations. **Explanations answer the question Why? or How?** The questions "Why won't my car start?" and "How do you assemble this bicycle?" are questions that call for explanations. "Your battery's dead. That's why your car won't start," explains your mechanic. The instructions all mechanically inept parents dread explain how to put the bicycle together. *Notice what you know first:* You know that your car won't start. You know you want to assemble a bicycle. These are phenomena to be explained. You're looking for accounts of why that's so or how to do it.

In an argument, the premises are known or assumed to be true at the beginning. They allegedly provide reasons to believe that the conclusion is true.

So, in an argument, the premises are known first; in an explanation, the phenomenon to be explained is known first.

Example

Consider these two passages:

A. Our inspection of the building reveals that it has been constructed using substandard materials. Because of this we believe it may collapse in the near future.

B. The building collapsed because it was constructed with substandard materials.

In **A**, the use of *because* indicates that the information is being used to predict something that has not yet happened. The first proposition, "Our inspection of the building reveals that it has been constructed using substandard material" is offered as a premise for the conclusion "we believe it may collapse in the near future."

In **B**, it is a fact that the building has already collapsed, and the information being offered, "it was constructed with substandard materials" is provided as an explanation for that fact.

Here is another example. In responding to a question about the color of quasars (celestial objects lying far beyond our galaxy), one scientist wrote:

The most distant quasars look like intense points of infrared radiation. This is because space is scattered with hydrogen atoms (about two per cubic meter) that absorb blue light, and if you filter the blue from visible white light, red is what's left. On its multibillion-year journey to earth, quasar light loses so much blue that only infrared remains.[4]

This is not an argument; it does not provide reasons to believe *that* quasars have the apparent color they do. It assumes that quasars appear to have that color. The passage explains why quasars have the observed color they have. It attempts to tell you what *causes* quasars to have that apparent color.

Consider the following:

If Carlos took Maria to the dance, Luigi is jealous. Carlos took Maria to the dance. So, Luigi is jealous.

---

[4]Jeff Greenwald, "Brightness Visible," *The New York Times Magazine*, 14 May 2000.

Is it an argument or an explanation? You can't tell. You need to look at it within a certain context.

> **Context A:** You're at the dance. You notice that Carlos and Maria come in together. They're obviously on a date. You know that Luigi has been enamored of Maria for some time. Luigi is noted for his jealousy. You know that if Carlos took Maria to the dance, then Luigi would be jealous. So you conclude that Luigi is jealous—or he will be when he finds out.

> **Context E:** It's the day after the dance. You see Luigi in a jealous rage. You wonder why. You bump into Solvig and ask if she knows why Luigi is behaving as he is. "You know, Luigi has this thing for Maria. She went to the dance with Carlos last night. That's why he's jealous."

Context A is the context of argument. You know it's true that if Carlos took Maria to the dance then Luigi would be jealous, and you know that Carlos took Maria to the dance. The question is what follows from what you know.

Context E is the context of explanation. Here you know that Luigi is jealous and you wonder why. Solvig gives an explanation.

To distinguish explanations and arguments, you must be sensitive to context. Even then there may be passages whose original purpose cannot be determined. A problematic passage may be open to alternative readings. It might be viewed as an argument when interpreted one way and as an explanation when interpreted in another.

EXERCISES

I. For each of the following passages, decide which is an argument and which is an explanation.

1. He did not come to class today. It must be because he is ill.
2. The last time Clint Eastwood won an Oscar was for a sports movie he directed. He will probably direct another sports movie soon, so he has a chance to get another Oscar.
3. There are a lot of people getting into weird mystical cults lately. It must be because they are disappointed with traditional religions.
4. The cost of computers has dropped incredibly in the last few years. So, it will probably keep going down in the near future as well.
5. The cost of home computers has dropped incredibly in the last few years. I'm sure it's because the cost of producing microchips has plummeted.
6. Ants follow pheromone trails to know where to go. The more ants that go in a certain direction, the more pheromone that trail has. The shortest distance to a food source will soon have the most pheromone trails, so the ants learn the shortest way to the food.

7. When I read without my glasses I get a headache. Eyestrain must be the cause of the headaches.

8. Young people are not interested in politics today. They don't vote, and they don't participate in political parties. They must not care what the government does.

9. Sometimes the body language of people from another culture is hard to understand. In their culture it may be impolite to look right at the other person. If you think they are lying when they do not look at you, you may not trust what they say to you. When you look at them all the time, they may think this is hostile and indicates lack of trust. It is important to understand cultural differences like this to communicate successfully with people of other cultures.

10. Climate must have a great deal to do with the kinds of sounds people use to speak. Languages in hot parts of the world, where the air is thin, have mostly open vowel sounds. In cold parts of the world, where the air is dense, languages have mostly closed consonant sounds. Even the animals native to cold climates make hard clicking sounds that carry far in the cold air, but the birds in Hawaii make long, open sounds that reach from one end of Waimea Canyon to the other.

II. Some of the following passages contain explanations, some contain arguments, and some may be interpreted as either an argument or an explanation. What is your judgment about the chief function of each passage? What would have to be the case for the passage in question to be an argument? To be an explanation? Where you find an argument, identify its premises and conclusion. Where you find an explanation, indicate what is being explained and what the explanation is.

11. It would be immoral and selfish not to use animals in research today, given the harm that could accrue to future generations if such research were halted.
   —*Science, Medicine, and Animals* (Washington, DC: National Academy of Sciences, Institute of Medicine, 1991)

12. Changes are real. Now, changes are only possible in time, and therefore time must be something real.
   —Immanuel Kant, *Critique of Pure Reason* (1781), "Transcendental Aesthetic," section II

13. To name causes for a state of affairs is not to excuse it. Things are justified or condemned by their consequences, not by their antecedents.
   —John Dewey, "The Liberal College and Its Enemies," *The Independent*, 1924

14. I like Wagner's music better than anybody's. It is so loud that one can talk the whole time without people hearing what one says.
   —Oscar Wilde, *The Picture of Dorian Gray*, 1891

15. Love looks not with the eyes but with the mind; And therefore is wing'd Cupid painted blind.
    —William Shakespeare, *A Midsummer Night's Dream*, act 1, scene 1

16. U.S. Presidents have always been more likely to be killed or disabled by assassins than by diseases, and the Secret Service thus has more to do with the President's health and safety than the President's physicians.
    —George J. Annas, "The Health of the President and Presidential Candidates," *New England Journal of Medicine*, 5 October 1995

17. Increasing incarceration rates do not result in decreasing crime rates because few crimes result in imprisonment or arrest. This is not because judges are soft on criminals but because 90 percent of crimes are either not reported or go unsolved.
    —Elizabeth Alexander, "Look to More Cost-effective Antidotes than Prison," *The New York Times*, 25 January 1996

18. By any standard one wants to set, Americans are not learning science. All too often what is taught as science is better not taught at all. All too often the mind-set against science and the fear of mathematics are solidly installed in grade school. All too often science can be skipped in high school and in most colleges. As for most American college students, the science requirement is a sad joke.
    —Leon M. Lederman, "Science Education, Science, and American Culture," *The Key Reporter*, Winter 1992

19. George Mason, one of my ancestors, urged the abolition of slavery at the Constitutional Convention, calling it "disgraceful to mankind." Failing in this attempt, he urged that his Declaration of Rights be enacted as a bill of rights. It too was turned down. Thus, Mason refused to sign the Constitution.
    —Thomas C. Southerland, Jr., "A Virginia Model," *The New York Times*, 5 July 1997

20. Black or white, rich or poor, male or female, conservative or liberal: we are willfully blind to the 700,000 black men incarcerated in 1994 (up from 25,000 in 1960) and to the 11,000 killed as a result of homicide in 1993 (both figures from the Bureau of Justice Statistics), to unemployment and life expectancy that lags far behind every other racial and gender classification. This class of Americans doesn't have think tanks, political parties or lobbyists. To paraphrase writer Ralph Wiley, that's why black boys tend to shoot.
    —Bill Stephney, "Rap Star's Death Highlights Harsher Reality," *The New York Times*, 18 September 1996

1.5 RECOGNIZING ARGUMENTS

A. Premise- and Conclusion-Indicators

Techniques for evaluating an argument depend on distinguishing the premises from the conclusion, but the order of the propositions found in an argument in ordinary speech or writing is no guarantee of the role played by those propositions. There are certain words or phrases, which we call *premise-* and *conclusion-indicators*, that can be helpful in identifying the role played by the propositions in an argument in natural language. Here is a partial list of conclusion-indicators:

therefore	thus	*is evidence that
hence	so	*implies that
accordingly	I conclude that	*means that
in consequence	*ergo*	*which shows that
consequently	*which means that	
proves that	*which entails that	
as a result	*which implies that	
for this reason	*which allows us to infer that	
for these reasons	*which points to the conclusion that	
it follows that	*is a reason to believe that	
we may infer	*is a reason to hold that	

In the expressions marked with an asterisk (*), one or more premises usually precede the conclusion-indicator.

Here is a partial list of premise-indicators:

since	due to	†follows from
because	in view of the fact that	†may be derived from
for	inasmuch as	†may be deduced
as	insofar as	†may be inferred from
given (that)	†as indicated by	†as shown by
assuming (that)	†from	†the reason is that

In the expressions marked with a dagger (†) the conclusion usually precedes the premise-indicator.

Notice that premise-indicators and conclusion-indicators are merely guides, not guarantees. Many of these words and phrases also have other uses. For example, the premise-indicator *since* is also used to indicate the passage of time: "Airport security has changed since September 11, 2001." *Because* is used to talk about causes: "Abby cried because she scratched her finger." Many of the indicator words are used in explanations as well as in arguments: the "conclusion-indicators" point to the phenomenon to be explained, and the "premise-indicators" to the conditions explaining the

> **ESSENTIAL** HINTS
>
> **If. . . , then . . .**
> Some students believe that whenever they find a conditional statement, a statement containing
> an "If. . . , then. . ." construction, they have found an argument. As we'll see in Chapter 6, many
> arguments contain conditional statements. But a conditional statement *by itself* is *not* an
> argument. I might say, "If I had a million dollars, I'd vacation in Iowa." This tells you nothing
> about my financial status or my vacation plans. It simply describes a hypothetical situation. To
> *conclude* I'll vacation in Iowa, you'd *also* need the statement "I have a million dollars" (which is
> false). To *conclude* that I *don't* have a million dollars, you'd *also* need the statement "I won't
> vacation in Iowa" (which is false). Conditional statements, as such, are merely descriptive. In
> the instructions for a computer program you might find the conditional statement, "If you
> want to save your file, type control-S." Sometimes you want to save your file; sometimes you
> don't. The statement is true in either case, but, from it alone, you can draw no conclusions
> regarding your activities.

phenomenon.[5] If you remember that the premises provide evidence for the *truth* of the conclusion, you'll realize that the indicator words are a kind of shorthand. As *premise-* and *conclusion*-indicators, they should be followed by the phrase, "it is true that."

> Since (it is true that) Juan went to the new *Star Wars* movie, and because (it is true that) the new *Star Wars* movie is entertaining, we may conclude (it is true that) Juan enjoyed the movie.

By adding the assumed phrase "it is true that," you should be able to distinguish the use of these words as indicator-words from other uses. If you also remember that, in an argument, the truth of the premises is known or assumed before the truth of the conclusion, you should be able to distinguish the use of the words in arguments from their use in explanations.

EXERCISES

Use premise- and conclusion-indicators to help you identify the premises and conclusions in the following arguments. State the arguments in standard form.

1. Genes and proteins are discovered, not invented. Inventions are patentable; discoveries are not. Thus, protein patents are intrinsically flawed.

> —Daniel Alroy, "Invention vs. Discovery,"
> *The New York Times*, 29 March 2000

---

[5]See, for example, Michael Faraday, *The Chemical History of a Candle*, introduction by L. Pearce Williams (New York: Collier Books, 1962), pp. 24–25. Faraday explains why a cup is formed at the top of a burning candle. It's all explanation. He uses *therefore*, in the sense of "as a result."

2. Since you didn't do the dishes and because you left the room a mess, it is clear that your allowance is not enough to get you to do your work. Hence, I am giving you a raise.

3. "In Midtown the bedrock's close to the surface, which means so are the aquifers."

> —Jeffrey Deaver, *The Bone Collector*
> (New York: Signet Books, 1997), p. 56

4. During this season of giving, a small donation to the local humane society might also be appropriate because, in the very near future, Tasha [the dog whose genetic makeup was deciphered] may well be credited for saving countless human lives.

> — "Man's Best Friend: Dogs Are Even More Wonderful Than We
> Thought," *Daily News-Record*, Harrisonburg, VA, 9 December 2005

5. Why decry the wealth gap? First, inequality is correlated with political instability. Second, inequality is correlated with violent crime. Third, economic inequality is correlated with reduced life expectancy. A fourth reason? Simple justice. There is no moral justification for chief executives being paid hundreds of times more than ordinary employees.

> —Richard Hutchinsons, "When the Rich Get Even Richer,"
> *The New York Times*, 26 January 2000

6. That we do not read of Hebrews and Israelites in Eighteenth Dynasty Egyptian documents no more implies that they were not present than the fact that Egypt's pyramids are not mentioned in the Bible may be taken as proof that the kingdom's most obvious architectural features never existed. Absence of evidence is not always evidence of absence: Pyramids and Hebrews were simply not important, depending on whose side was telling the story.

> —Charles Pellegrino, *Return to Sodom and Gomorrah*
> (New York: Avon Books), 1994, p. 240

7. Married people are healthier and more economically stable than single people, and children of married people do better on a variety of indicators. Marriage is thus a socially responsible act. There ought to be some way of spreading the principle of support for marriage throughout the tax code.

> —Anya Bernstein, "Marriage, Fairness and Taxes,"
> *The New York Times*, 15 February 2000

8. Wilson refused to suspect Tom [of Judge Driscoll's murder]; for first Tom couldn't murder anyone—he hadn't character enough; secondly, if he could murder a person he wouldn't select his doting benefactor and nearest relative; thirdly, self-interest was in the way; for while the uncle lived, Tom was sure of a free support and a chance to get the

destroyed will revived again, but with the uncle gone, that chance was gone, too. It was true the will had already been revived, as was now discovered, but Tom could not have been aware of it, or he would have spoken of it, in his native talky, unsecretive way. Finally, Tom was in St. Louis when the murder was done, and got the news out of the morning journals, as was shown by his telegram to his aunt. These speculations were unemphasized sensations rather than articulated thoughts, for Wilson would have laughed at the ideas of seriously connecting Tom with the murder.

— Mark Twain, *Pudd'nhead Wilson*

9. "And what was decided about the contract?" asked the rabbi.

"We didn't decide anything," said Wasserman. "It was held over for the next meeting—that is, for the coming Sunday."

The rabbi studied his teacup, his brow furrowed in concentration. Then without looking up, as if thinking aloud, he said, "Tonight is Thursday, three days before the meeting. If approval were certain and the vote only a matter of form, you would have waited until Sunday to tell me. If approval were likely but not absolutely certain, you would probably mention it when next you happed to see me, which would be Friday evening at the services. But if it looked as though the vote were uncertain or even likely to go against me, you would not want to mention it Friday evening for fear of spoiling the Sabbath. So your coming tonight can only mean that you have reason to believe I will not be reappointed. That's it, isn't it?"

Wasserman shook his head in admiration. Then he turned to the rabbi's wife and waggled an admonishing forefinger. "Don't ever try to deceive your husband, Mrs. Small. He'll find you out in a minute."

—Harry Kemelman, *Friday the Rabbi Slept Late*
(New York: Fawcett Crest, 1964), pp. 40–41

10. For discussion:

In a recent murder trial in Virginia, the judge instructed the jury that: "you may fix the punishment of the defendant at death" if the state proved beyond a reasonable doubt at least one of two aggravating circumstances: that the defendant would continue to be a serious threat to society, or that the crime was "outrageously or wantonly vile, horrible or inhuman." The jury, deliberating the sentence after finding the accused guilty, returned to the judge with this question: If we believe that the state has satisfied one of these alternatives, "then is it our duty as a jury to issue the death penalty?" The judge, in response, simply told them to re-read the instructions already given on that point. The jury returned two hours later, some of its members in tears, with a death sentence for the defendant.

> This death sentence was appealed, and the case was ultimately reviewed by the U.S. Supreme Court [*Weeks v. Angelone*, No. 995746, decided 19 January 2000]. The issue that Court confronted was whether, in the circumstances of this case, the death sentence should be nullified on the ground that the jury had been confused about the instructions they had been given. What arguments would you construct in support of either side of this controversy?

B. Arguments in Context

Although indicator words often signal an argument and identify premises and conclusions, some argumentative passages lack them. The argumentative functions of such passages are exhibited by their contexts and meanings—in the same way, if I said that I am taking a lobster home for dinner, you would have little doubt that I intended to eat it, not feed it. Passages containing arguments often also contain additional material that serves neither as premise nor conclusion. Such material may, in some cases, be extraneous, but in other cases may supply background information helping us to understand what the argument is about.

Example

I cannot believe that my daughter would throw a rock through a school window. Her friends claim that she was with them and that they were nowhere near the school when it happened, so she couldn't have done it.

Paraphrasing the argument clarifies the relationship between the propositions.

PREMISE 1:   Her friends claim that she was with them when it happened (when someone threw a rock through a school window).

PREMISE 2:   They were nowhere near the school at the time.

CONCLUSION: She could not have done it.

Once we clarify the argument, we can see that the first sentence does not offer support for the conclusion, and therefore is not a premise. It does, however, help us understand what the argument is about.

C. Premises Not in Declarative Form

Although *questions* themselves do not assert anything, they sometimes can function as premises. These are *rhetorical questions*. Rhetorical questions suggest or assume a proposition as a premise when the question is one to which the author believes the answer is obvious. Arguments in which one of the premises is a question whose answer is assumed to be evident are quite common.

Example _____

Isn't smoking disgusting? No one should smoke.

The question here implies the premise, "Smoking is disgusting," which is taken here to be a reason supporting the conclusion, "No one should smoke."

Since questions are neither true nor false, they can function as premises _only_ when the assumed answer is obvious. If the answer is _not_ obvious, then the argument is defective. To avoid directly asserting a premise, authors sometimes use a question whose answer is dubious or false. By _suggesting_ the desired answer, one can increase the persuasiveness of an argument.

Example _____

Haven't you spent enough money trying to fix that piece of junk? It's time you bought a new car.

The speaker obviously wants the listener to answer the question by agreeing that enough money has been spent trying to fix the car. The speaker is really saying the following:

PREMISE: You have already spent too much money trying to fix that car.

CONCLUSION: It is time you bought a new car.

Sometimes the conclusion of an argument will take the form of an imperative or a command. Reasons are given to persuade us to perform a given action, and then we are directed to act that way. Since a command, like a question, cannot state a proposition, it cannot be the conclusion of an argument. However, in those contexts, commands can be paraphrased as propositions telling us that we _should_ or _ought_ to act in the manner specified in the command.

Example _____

Clean up your room. Someone might come and see the mess. Besides, a messy room is a sign of a cluttered, confused mind.

Paraphrasing the argument allows us to see that the command in the first sentence can be translated into a proposition that is the conclusion of the argument.

PREMISE 1: Someone might come and see the mess.

PREMISE 2: A messy room is a sign of a cluttered, confused mind.

CONCLUSION: You _should_ clean up your room.

In arguments, we need to focus on the propositions themselves. We want to know (1) whether they are true or false, (2) what they imply, (3) whether they are themselves implied by other propositions, and (4) whether they are serving as premises or as a conclusion in some argument.

D. Unstated Propositions

Sometimes not all the premises or the conclusion of an argument are stated. These are called *enthymemes*. If you confront an enthymematic argument, you need to fill in the missing element(s) before you can analyze the argument. Why do people construct enthymemes? There are at least two reasons. (1) Enthymemes are rhetorically strong, since the reader or hearer is "complimented" by being seen as smart enough to fill in the missing element(s). (2) Leaving a premise unstated can cover defects in the argument. In a valid deductive argument you can figure out what the missing premise has to be. In a valid deductive argument, it is impossible for all the premises to be true and the conclusion false. (We discuss validity in 1.6, and we look at ways to determine what missing premises of a valid deductive argument *must* be in later chapters.)

Examples

If this is an enthymeme, then you need to find a missing premise. So, if this is an enthymeme, you'll have to think before you analyze the argument.

Stated premise:
 1. If this is an enthymeme, then you need to find a missing premise.

Missing premise:
 2. If you need to find a missing premise, then you'll have to think before you analyze the argument.

Conclusion:
 3. If this is an enthymeme, you'll have to think before you analyze the argument.

The *only* premise that, with the given premise, yields the conclusion is "If you need to find a missing premise, then you'll have to think before you analyze the argument." Once you've discovered the premise you should ask whether it is true. It is.

No two-year-olds are readers. So, no two-year-olds are cooks.

If the argument is valid, it has to be the following:

Stated premise:
 1. No two-year-olds are readers.

Missing premise:
 2. All cooks are readers.

Conclusion:
 3. No two-year-olds are cooks.

The missing premise is false. At least one of your distant ancestors could cook but couldn't read. If you had assumed the missing premise was "All readers are cooks," the argument would have been invalid (so it's not the best choice) *and* the premise would be false. Don't *you* know someone who reads but can't boil water without burning it?

If the conclusion of a valid deductive argument is unstated, you can work out what it must be.

Example

We all understand in our hearts what the principles of justice make clear to our minds, namely that all forms of slavery are wrong and should be stopped. The sad truth is that there is an active slave trade in Sudan.

The premises are "all forms of slavery are wrong and should be stopped" and "there is an active slave trade in Sudan," that is, "there are forms of slavery in Sudan." The conclusion that follows is "The forms of slavery in Sudan are wrong and should be stopped." Although the conclusion is not explicitly stated, it's probably the conclusion the arguer wanted us to draw.

There is no way to determine what a missing premise of an inductive argument *must* be, since inductive arguments only show that a conclusion is probably true. Nonetheless, the context usually gives clues to the assumed premise.

Example

Chris never studies. So, Chris probably won't do well in his logic class.

Ask yourself why anyone would claim there is evidence for the conclusion based on the premise. You'll probably conclude that the argument would be given as follows:

Stated premise:
  1. Chris never studies.

Missing premise:
  2. Most people who never study do not do well in logic classes.

Conclusion:
  3. Chris probably won't do well in his logic class.

Dealing with enthymemes can be tricky. The missing premise should be true. It should be readily accepted by anyone who knows the topic being discussed. In general, you should apply the *principle of interpretive charity*. This principle requires that, when there is any question, you should give the arguer the benefit of the doubt. This means you, as the person reconstructing the argument, should choose reasonable premises. You reconstruct the argument in such a way that it provides the best evidence for the conclusion consistent with the truth of its premises.[6] As we have already seen, however, sometimes the missing premise that yields a valid argument is false. Usually the context helps determine what the assumed premise is. Sometimes you'll find that the truth of the assumed premise is questionable.

Examples

Your daughter is not making her education loan payments on time. Therefore you must make the payments for her.

The hidden and disputable premise in this argument is that parents are responsible for the loan if their daughter defaults. But if she were old enough and took out the loan on her own without her parent's cosignature, then that premise would be false.

No one wants to get attacked by a bear. So you should stop poking that bear with that stick.

The missing premise here is a fact that is obvious to anyone who knows anything about bears: If you poke bears with sticks, they are likely to attack.

EXERCISES

I.   In each of the following passages, identify and number all propositions, and identify the premises and conclusions, filling in unstated propositions and reformulating rhetorical questions and imperatives, as needed.

   1. The Supreme Court will only uphold federal racial set-asides in light of convincing evidence of past discrimination by the federal government itself; but, for almost 20 years, the federal government has been discriminating in favor of minority contractors rather than against them. Therefore, federal minority preferences in procurement are doomed.
       —Jeffrey Rosen, cited by Ian Ayres, "Remedying Past Discrimination,"
       Los Angeles Times, 26 April 1998

   2. Gasoline prices will not go down. Under the new administration, we will get additional oil from once protected parts of Alaska, but the amount will be too small to have any effect on the overall supply. Coal production is going to be raised, but it will not offset the ever-increasing amount of gasoline that is consumed by cars, trucks, and airplanes. In addition, the new administration will

---

[6]This applies to *any* ambiguities in an argument, not just missing premises.

more than likely reduce the pressure on the automakers to increase gas mileage in new cars.

3. Don't you know that driving without a seatbelt is dangerous? Statistics show you are ten times more likely to be injured in an accident if you are not wearing one. Besides, in our state you can get fined $100 if you are caught not wearing one. You ought to wear one even if you are driving a short distance.

4. Jean studied at least ten hours for the exam, and she got an 'A.' Bill studied at least ten hours for the exam, and he got an 'A.' Sue studied at least ten hours for the exam, and she got an 'A.' Jim studied at least ten hours for the exam. Jim probably got an 'A' on the exam.

5. Did you ever hear the saying, "If you're not with the one you love, love the one you're with?" Is that any way to have a good marriage? If marriage is based on trust, then that saying is not the kind of attitude you need to have to have a successful marriage. Instead, you should think, "Absence makes the heart grow fonder."

6. Science studies the natural. That is all we ask of it. If there is any fact or truth beyond nature, science knows nothing about it and has nothing to say on the subject.
   —Richard W. Metz, "Don't Throw Crackpottery at Haunted Houses,"
   The New York Times, 1 August 1996

7. *The New York Times* reported, on 30 May 2000, that some scientists were seeking a way to signal back in time. A critical reader responded thus:

   It seems obvious to me that scientists in the future will never find a way to signal back in time. If they were to do so, wouldn't we have heard from them by now?

   —Ken Grunstra, "Reaching Back in Time,"
   The New York Times, 6 June 2000

8. I reject the argument that the white journalist featured in your series on race should not have written about black drug addicts in Baltimore because it was not "his story to tell." This assumes that only black people can or should write about black people, and implies that there exists a single, unanimous perspective that all black Americans hold.
   —Ian Reifowitz, in a letter to *The New York Times*, 19 June 2000

9. There can be no resolution of the conflict between the autonomy of the individual and the putative authority of the state. Insofar as a man fulfills his obligation to make himself the author of his decisions, he will . . . deny that he has a duty to obey the laws of the state *simply because they are the laws*. In that sense . . . anarchism is the only political doctrine consistent with the virtue of autonomy.
   —Robert Paul Wolff, *In Defense of Anarchism*, 1970

10. The Internal Revenue Code is inordinately complex, imposes an enormous burden on taxpayers, and thus undermines compliance with the law. Repeated efforts to simplify and reform the law have failed. We have reached the point where further patchwork will only compound the problem. It is time to repeal the Internal Revenue Code and start over.
   —Shirley D. Peterson, "Death to the Tax Code,"
   The New York Times, 29 July 1995

II. Each of the following passages can be interpreted as containing two arguments, each of which may have more than one premise. Analyze these arguments, paraphrasing premises and conclusions where you find that helpful.

11. In a recent attack upon the evils of suburban sprawl, the authors argue as follows:

   The dominant characteristic of sprawl is that each component of a community—housing, shopping centers, office parks, and civic institutions—is segregated, physically separated from the others, causing the residents of suburbia to spend an inordinate amount of time and money moving from one place to the next. And since nearly everyone drives alone, even a sparsely populated area can generate the traffic of a much larger traditional town.[7]

12. Life is not simply a "good" that we possess. Our life is our person. To treat our life as a "thing" that we can authorize another to terminate is profoundly dehumanizing. Euthanasia, even when requested by the competent, attacks the distinctiveness and limitations of being human.
   —Ramsey Colloquium of the Institute on Religion
   and Public Life, "Always to Care, Never to Kill,"
   Wall Street Journal, 27 November 1991

13. All of the positive contributions that sports make to higher education are threatened by disturbing patterns of abuse, particularly in some big-time programs. These patterns are grounded in institutional indifference, presidential neglect, and the growing commercialization of sport combined with the urge to win at all costs. The sad truth is that on too many campuses big-time revenue sports are out of control.
   —*Keeping Faith with the Student-Athlete: A New Model for
   Intercollegiate Athletics*, Knight Foundation Commission
   on Intercollegiate Athletics, Charlotte, NC, March 1991

---

[7]Paraphrased in part from Andres Duany, Elizabeth Plater-Zyberk, and Jeff Speck, *Suburban Nation: The Rise of Sprawl and the Decline of the American Dream* (North Point Press, 2000).

14. As force is always on the side of the governed, the governors have nothing to support them but opinion. It is therefore on opinion only that government is founded.
    —David Hume, cited in Keith Thomas, "Just Say Yes,"
    The New York Review of Books, 24 November 1988

15. Cognitive function depends on neuro-chemical processes in the brain, which are influenced by enzymes. These enzymes are made by genes. It would be dumbfounding if intellectual functioning were without genetic influence.
    —Dr. Gerald E. McClearn, "Genes a Lifelong Factor in Intelligence,"
    The New York Times, 6 June 1997

16. Does the past exist? No. Does the future exist? No. Then only the present exists. Yes. But within the present there is no lapse of time? Quite so. Then time does not exist? Oh, I wish you wouldn't be so tiresome.
    —Bertrand Russell, *Human Knowledge*, 1948

17. The lower strata of the middle class—the small tradespeople, shopkeepers, and retired tradesmen generally, the handicraftsmen and peasants—all these sink gradually into the proletariat, partly because their diminutive capital does not suffice for the scale on which modern industry is carried on, and is swamped in the competition with the large capitalists, partly because their specialized skill is rendered worthless by new methods of production. Thus the proletariat is recruited from all classes of the population.
    —Karl Marx and Friedrich Engels, *The Communist Manifesto*, 1848

18. No one means all he says, and yet very few say all they mean, for words are slippery and thought is viscous.
    —Henry Adams, *The Education of Henry Adams* (1907), chapter 31

19. Cuts in tuition can reduce institutional income from government-financed aid programs, which in certain cases are based on total expenses charged, so there is a built-in disincentive to lower prices.
    —David Spadafora, "Don't Expect Many Colleges to Lower Tuition,"
    The New York Times, 29 January 1996

20. Native American beliefs about the past and the dead certainly deserve respect, but they should not be allowed to dictate government policy on the investigation and interpretation of early American prehistory. If a choice must be made among competing theories of human origins, primacy should be given to theories based on the scientific method. Only scientific theories are built on empirical evidence; only scientific theories can be adjusted or overturned.
    —R. Bonnichsen and A. L. Schneider, "Battle of the Bones,"
    The Sciences, August 2000

1.6   DEDUCTION AND VALIDITY

Every argument makes the claim that its premises provide grounds for accepting the truth of its conclusion. But arguments divide into two major classes—deductive and inductive—depending on the *way* in which their conclusions are supported by their premises. A deductive argument involves the claim that its conclusion is supported by its premises *conclusively*—in other words, that the conclusion *must* be true if the premises are true. If, in interpreting a passage, we judge that such a claim is being made, we treat the argument as deductive. If we judge that a claim of conclusiveness is not being made, we treat the argument as inductive. Since every argument either makes the claim of conclusiveness or it does not, every argument is either deductive or inductive.

When the claim is made that the premises of an argument, *if true*, provide irrefutable grounds for the truth of its conclusion, and this claim proves to be correct, then that deductive argument is *valid*. If the claim is not correct, then that deductive argument is invalid. For logicians, the term *validity* applies only to deductive arguments. **A deductive argument is *valid* when it is impossible for its conclusion to be false if its premises are true; otherwise, the argument is *invalid*.** Notice that deductive validity does not depend on the premises *actually* being true, just on the fact that *if* the premises *were* true, it would be impossible for the conclusion to be false. Validity asks about what is *possible* regarding the truth and falsity of the premises and conclusion. If it is possible for the conclusion to be false at the same time that the premises are true, then the argument is invalid. Otherwise it is valid. Every deductive argument must be valid or invalid.

Examples

All mammals have lungs.
This dog is a mammal.
Therefore, this dog has lungs.

This argument is valid. It is impossible for the conclusion to be false if the premises are true.

Mammals are hairy.
This monkey is a mammal.
Therefore, this monkey has exactly 200,127 hairs on its body.

This argument is invalid. It is possible for the conclusion to be false even if the premises are true.

Validity is a property of an argument's *form* or structure. The form of an argument is like the design of a house. Just as you find many houses with the same design, you find many arguments with the same form or argument pattern. The following two arguments have the same form:

All mammals are vertebrates.
All dogs are mammals.
All dogs are vertebrates.

All cats are mammals.
All Siamese are cats.
All Siamese are mammals.

We can replace terms by variables and represent the form of the argument as follows:

All M are P.
All S are M.
All S are P.

The following two arguments have the same form:

If John likes cats, then Tonya likes dogs.
Tonya does not like dogs.
John does not like cats.

If the sun is red, then the moon is blue.
The moon is not blue.
The sun is not red.

We can replace the individual propositions with variables and represent the form of the argument as follows:

If p, then q.
Not q.
Not p.

In later chapters our primary concern with deductive arguments will be with determining *whether* an argument form is valid and showing *that* a conclusion follows deductively from a set of premises in a finite number of steps.

> **ESSENTIAL** HINTS
>
> Are you a bit puzzled by "forms"? Look at it this way. An argument form is to an argument what a tax form is to tax information. You and I both fill out Form 1040. The form—the sheet of blanks—is the same for you and for me. The content we add differs. The argument form consists of "blanks" (variables) in a certain structure. By filling in propositions or terms (content), the result is an argument.

1.7 VALIDITY AND TRUTH

Validity is a special relation between the premises and a conclusion in a deductive argument. It's a *truth-preserving* relation. It is impossible for the premises of a valid deductive argument to be true and the conclusion false. Because validity is a relation between propositions, it can never apply to a single proposition. Truth and falsity, on the other hand, *are* attributes of individual propositions. Since premises and conclusions are individual propositions, they may be true or false, but never valid or invalid.

Just as the concept of validity does not apply to single propositions, truth and falsity do not apply to arguments. Deductive arguments may be valid or invalid, but never true or false. The validity of a deductive argument guarantees only that *if* the premises are true, the conclusion is true. It does *not* guarantee that the premises are in fact true. It follows that an argument may be valid even when its conclusion and one or more of its premises are false.

The concept of deductive validity is the key concept in this book. It is one that people often have some difficulty understanding from a purely abstract point of view, so let's look at some examples of arguments to illustrate how the concept of validity works.

There are many possible combinations of true and false premises and conclusions in both valid and invalid arguments. A look at seven of these will permit us to formulate some important principles concerning the relations between the truth of propositions and the validity of arguments.

I.   Some *valid* arguments contain *only true* propositions—true premises and a true conclusion:

> All mammals have lungs.
> All whales are mammals.
> Therefore, all whales have lungs.

II.   Some *valid* arguments contain *only false* propositions:

> All four-legged creatures have wings.
> All spiders have four legs.
> Therefore, all spiders have wings.

This argument is valid because, if its premises were true, its conclusion would have to be true also—even though we know that in fact both the premises *and* the conclusion of this argument are false.

> **ESSENTIAL** HINTS
>
> Notice that arguments **I** and **II** have the same *form*:
> > All M are P.
> > All S are M.
> > All S are P.
>
> Because their form is valid, it is impossible for the premises to be true and the conclusion false.

III.   Some *invalid* arguments contain *only true* propositions—all their premises are true, and their conclusions are true as well:

> If I owned all the gold in Fort Knox, then I would be wealthy.
> I do not own all the gold in Fort Knox.
> Therefore, I am not wealthy.

IV.   Some *invalid* arguments contain *only true premises* and have a *false conclusion*. This can be illustrated with an argument in a form that is exactly like the argument shown in example III, but changed just enough to make the conclusion false.

> If Bill Gates owned all the gold in Fort Knox, then Bill Gates would be wealthy.
> Bill Gates does not own all the gold in Fort Knox.
> Therefore, Bill Gates is not wealthy.

> **ESSENTIAL** HINTS
>
> Notice that arguments **III** and **IV** have the same form:
> > If p, then q.
> > Not p.
> > Not q.

The premises of this argument are true, but its conclusion is false. Such an argument *cannot* be valid because it is impossible for the premises of a valid argument to be true and its conclusion to be false.

V. Some *valid* arguments can have *false premises* and a *true conclusion:*

> All fish are mammals.
> All whales are fish.
> Therefore, all whales are mammals.

The conclusion of the argument is true. Moreover it may be validly inferred from the given premises, both of which are false. This shows that an argument's validity, by itself, is not enough to establish that the argument's conclusion is true. Only a *sound* argument—a valid argument with true premises—guarantees the truth of its conclusion.

VI. Some *invalid* arguments can have *false premises* and a *true conclusion:*

> All mammals have wings.
> All whales have wings.
> Therefore, all whales are mammals.

From examples V and VI taken together, it is clear that we cannot tell from the fact that an argument has false premises and a true conclusion whether it is valid or invalid.

VII. Some *invalid* arguments contain *all false propositions:*

> All mammals have wings.
> All whales have wings.
> Therefore, all mammals are whales.

These seven examples make it clear that valid arguments can have false conclusions (example II) and that invalid arguments can have true conclusions (examples III and IV). **Hence, the *actual* truth or falsity of an argument's conclusion does not, by itself, allow you to determine the validity or invalidity of an argument**. Of course, you can show that an argument form is *invalid* if an argument of that form has true premises and a false conclusion (example IV). You can be certain of a conclusion's truth only if the form is valid and its premises are true.

The following two tables refer to the seven examples on the preceding pages. They make clear the variety of possible combinations of truth values and validity. The first table shows that invalid arguments can have every possible combination of true and false premises and conclusions:

INVALID ARGUMENTS		
	TRUE CONCLUSION	**FALSE CONCLUSION**
True premises	Example III	Example IV
False premises	Example VI	Example VII

The second table shows that valid arguments can have only three of those combinations of true and false premises and conclusions:

VALID ARGUMENTS		
	True Conclusion	**False Conclusion**
True premises	Example I	
False premises	Example V	Example II

The one blank position in the second table exhibits a fundamental point: *If an argument is valid and its premises are true, we may be certain that its conclusion is true also.* To put it another way: *If an argument is valid and its conclusion is false, at least one of its premises must be false.*

Knowing that an argument has true premises and a false conclusion tells you that the argument has to be invalid. But every other arrangement of truth and falsity in the premises and conclusion is possible for *both* valid and invalid arguments. So we cannot determine much about the invalidity or validity of an argument from knowing the actual truth and falsity of its propositions. Validity has to do with the relations among propositions. If those interconnections have the right *form* (structure), it is impossible for the conclusion to be false when the premises are true. For now, we rely on an intuitive grasp of the conditions under which that impossibility holds. Later in the book, we will learn several techniques for discovering and proving that the conditions for validity are present in an argument.

When an argument is valid and all of its premises are also in fact true, the argument is said to be *sound*. **A deductive argument is *sound* when it is both valid and its premises are true.** It is very important to notice that the conclusion of a sound argument is one that *must* be true (it *cannot* be false). It is this property of deductive arguments that makes deduction so powerful and so interesting. Sound deductive arguments lead to perfect certainty. Knowing how to assess the validity and soundness of arguments is a very important skill. It enables you to avoid being fooled into thinking that something is proven with certainty when it is not.

If a deductive argument is *unsound*—that is, if the argument is not valid, *or* if it is valid but not all of its premises are true—then that argument *fails* to establish the truth of its conclusion *even if the conclusion is true.*

Logic confines itself to studying the relationships between the propositions in an argument. Whether the premises are true is an issue for science, and for the most part this sort of activity is outside the province of logic. In this book, when we discuss deductive arguments, we shall be interested primarily in their validity, and only secondarily (if at all) with their soundness. But when you are analyzing deductive arguments in the "real world," remember that soundness is required for the conclusion to be proven.

Notice that if an argument is valid, but you do not know whether its premises are true, then you have to say that you *do not know* whether the argument is sound. The truth of the conclusion is not known. If an argument is invalid—regardless of the truth values of the premises—it does not show that the conclusion is true. The truth of the conclusion is not proved. Neither type of unsoundness, however, shows that the conclusion is false. *Not known* and *not proved* are different from *disproved*!

When we examine deductive arguments in later chapters, we shall be concerned with the form or structure of the argument. Many arguments have the same form. We've noticed that three of the arguments above have the same form (I, II, and V). Validity is a characteristic of an argument's form. If one argument of a given form is valid, every other argument of the same form is valid. As we've seen, an argument's content is irrelevant to questions of validity. If an argument form is invalid, any argument of that form can provide only *inductive* evidence for the truth of its conclusion. It is to inductive arguments that we now turn.

1.8   INDUCTION AND PROBABILITY

A sound deductive argument establishes its conclusion with certainty. In contrast, inductive arguments *do not* claim that their premises, even if true, establish their conclusions with certainty. Inductive arguments make the weaker but important claim that their conclusions are established with some degree of *probability*. Because they do not claim certainty, the criteria for evaluating inductive arguments differ from those for evaluating deductive arguments.

Evaluating inductive arguments is one of the leading tasks of scientists. Inductive arguments are also very common in ordinary life. The premises of an inductive argument provide *some* support for its conclusion. Inductive arguments vary in degrees of strength. Some provide very good evidence for their conclusions (they are strong). Others provide little evidence (they are weak). But even when the premises are true and strongly support their conclusion, the conclusion of an inductive argument is never certain.

ESSENTIAL HINTS

Several types of inductive arguments

In an **analogy** you compare things directly and reach a conclusion.

Juan and I are alike insofar as we both like milkshakes and banana splits. I like chocolate sundaes. So, it's likely that Juan also likes chocolate sundaes.

In an **inductive generalization** you go from characteristics of a number of individual things to characteristics of a group.

I've seen 500 crows and they were all black. So, it's likely that most crows are black.

In an **argument to the best explanation** you consider alternative explanations of an event to determine which is more probable.

My car won't start. It could be that the battery is low, or it could be that I'm out of gas. I filled the car with gas yesterday and drove straight home. So, it's probably the battery.

Because an inductive argument can only show that its conclusion is probable, it is always possible that additional information will strengthen or weaken the evidence for its conclusion. Deductive arguments, on the other hand, cannot gradually become better or worse. They either succeed or they do not succeed in achieving certainty. Validity is not a matter of degree. No additional premises can strengthen or weaken the evidence for the conclusion of a valid deductive argument. This is not true of inductive arguments. Adding new premises might strengthen or weaken the evidence for the conclusion of an inductive argument.

Example

You stop at a coffee shop for an espresso. You have never been to this particular store, but you reason, on the basis of previous experiences with other stores in the same chain, that the espresso here will probably be delicious. New information might change the strength of this conclusion. For example, if a friend tells you that this store has excellent staff, you will be even more confident that your espresso will be delicious. In contrast, if someone who was in line ahead of you spits out his drink in disgust, you will be less confident that your drink will be good.

A good way to summarize the differences between deductive and inductive arguments is the following. **Generally, the conclusion of a deductive argument contains no information that is not already contained in the premises.**[8] Consider the following argument:

> If Shaun went to the movie, then Jen went to the movie.
> If Jen went to the movie, then Merlin ate popcorn.
> So, if Shaun went to the movie, Merlin ate popcorn.

Notice that all the information in the conclusion is contained in the premises. All it tells you is the relations between the activities of Shaun, Jen, and Merlin. If the premises are true, the conclusion must be true as well.

Contrast inductive arguments. **The conclusion of an inductive argument provides information that is *not* contained in the premises.** For example, let's say that you, Carman, and Ian are similar insofar as you all like vanilla, butter pecan, and rocky road ice cream. Carman and Ian also like mocha fudge ice cream. So, there is some reason to believe that you like mocha fudge ice cream, too. The premises provide *no* information about *your* views on mocha fudge ice cream. If the premises are true, the conclusion could be false. Is it?

---

[8]As we'll see in Chapter 7, there are occasions in which the conclusion of a deductive argument contains information that is not in the premises. This *only* happens, however, when the premises entail inconsistent propositions, that is, when the premises entail both a statement and its denial. From a pair of inconsistent claims, *any* proposition follows. Of course, if the premises entail an inconsistency, the argument is *unsound*.

Although induction is an extremely important type of inference in science and in ordinary life, logicians have an incomplete account of the standards for evaluating inductive arguments. This is in contrast to deduction, about which, in a significant sense, we have known all there is to know for a long time. Some branches of inductive logic (probability theory and statistics, for example) are worked out in more detail than others (such as the logic of the confirmation of scientific hypotheses). In Chapter 9 we return to inductive arguments, but this book is primarily concerned with deductive logic.

1.9   ANALYZING ARGUMENTS

Many arguments are simple. Others are quite complex. The premises of an argument may support its conclusion in different ways. The number of premises and the order of the propositions in an argument may vary. We need techniques to analyze argumentative passages and clarify the relations of premises and conclusions within them. Two techniques are common: *paraphrasing* and *diagramming*. When you are analyzing arguments, choose the one that helps most in the context.

A. Paraphrasing

A *paraphrase* of an argument is constructed by putting the argument's propositions in clear language and in proper order, listing each premise straightforwardly, restating the conclusion, and simplifying the language (where appropriate). Paraphrasing an argument often helps us understand the argument better. Be careful, though, that your paraphrase accurately captures the meaning of the original, or the argument you end up with will be different from the one you wanted to analyze!

Consider the following argument in which there are more than two premises and the conclusion is stated first:

> Upright walking therapods, the group that includes Tyrannosaurus rex, could not have evolved into modern birds for three main reasons. The first is that most fossils of birdlike therapod dinosaurs originated 75 million years *after* the fossilized remains of the first bird. The second is that the ancestors of birds must have been suited for flight—and therapods are not. A third problem is that every therapod dinosaur has serrated teeth, but no bird has serrated teeth.[9]

To clarify this argument we may paraphrase it as follows:

1. Fossils of birdlike therapod dinosaurs originated long after the fossilized remains of the first bird.
2. The ancestors of birds must have been suited for flight, but therapod dinosaurs were not so suited.

---

[9]Adapted from Alan Feduccia, *The Origin and Evolution of Birds* (New Haven, CT: Yale University Press, 1996).

3. Every therapod dinosaur has serrated teeth, but no bird has serrated teeth.
Therefore therapod dinosaurs could not have evolved into modern birds.

Paraphrasing often assists our understanding and analysis of an argument because it requires that we must bring to the surface assumptions that are not explicitly stated in the original argument. For example,

Archimedes will be remembered when Aeschylus is forgotten because languages die and mathematical ideas do not.[10]

To paraphrase the argument, we would have to spell out what it takes for granted:

1. Languages die.
2. The great plays of Aeschylus are in a language.
3. So the work of Aeschylus will eventually die.
4. Mathematical ideas do not die.
5. The great work of Archimedes was with mathematical ideas.
6. So the work of Archimedes will not die.
Therefore Archimedes will be remembered when Aeschylus is forgotten.

B. Diagramming Arguments

We can *diagram* an argument by representing the relationships between premises and conclusion as relationships between circled numbers that stand for the propositions in the argument. In outline, the procedure is this: Begin by numbering each of the propositions in the argument in the order in which they occur. Next, identify the conclusion. Then, determine the ways in which the remaining propositions (the premises) are related to each other and to the conclusion and represent those relations with arrows.

The advantage of diagramming is that it makes the relationships between the propositions in an argument open to direct inspection, which often aids understanding. A diagram can exhibit, as a paraphrase might not, the way in which the premises support the conclusion.

In a given argument, the premises might support the conclusion either independently or dependently. If the premises act *independently*, then each premise, *by itself*, supplies some reason to accept the conclusion, and it provides this support even in the absence of the other premises. In diagrams, each independent premise has its own arrow linking it to the conclusion.

Example

I should not buy these shoes. They do not fit properly. They are the wrong color for my wardrobe. And they are far too expensive.

---

[10] G.H. Hardy, *A Mathematicians Apology* (Cambridge University Press, 1940).

First, number the propositions in the order in which they occur:
①I should not buy these shoes.
②They do not fit properly.
③They are the wrong color for my wardrobe.
④And they are far too expensive.

Then, diagram the relationships between the propositions. In this case the conclusion, ①, gets *independent* support from each of the other propositions; that is, ②, ③, and ④ each, *by itself*, provides some reason to accept ①. You would *still* have reasons to accept ① even if one of the premises were taken away.

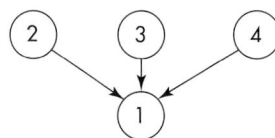

Imagine a prosecutor is building a case against a suspect. Each bit of evidence gives *some* reason to believe the suspect committed the crime. Together they provide fairly strong evidence that the suspect committed the crime.

① The suspect had a motive for the murder: She was being blackmailed. ② The suspect had the opportunity to commit the crime: They were both at the party at which the victim was killed. ③ The suspect owned the murder weapon. ④ The suspect's fingerprints were on the murder weapon. ⑤ Traces of the victim's blood were found on the suspect's clothes. So, ⑥ the suspect committed the crime.

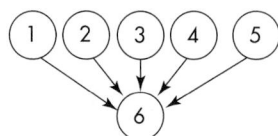

Premises act *dependently* when they support the conclusion only in combination, working together. In diagrams, dependent premises are joined by brackets. A single arrow links the bracketed premises to the conclusion. The premises of *all* deductive arguments and the premises of *some* inductive arguments support their conclusions only in combination.

Examples

The following is a valid deductive argument known as a *disjunctive syllogism*:

① Either Julio rides Arabian stallions or Flora drives formula-1 race cars. ② Flora does not drive formula-1 race cars. So, ③ Julio rides Arabian stallions.

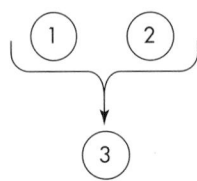

The following is an inductive argument. It is an argument by analogy.

① John, Shaun, Ian, Ivan, Giovanni, and Hans all enjoy Harrison Ford movies.
② John, Shaun, Ian, Ivan, and Giovanni also enjoy Robert Duval movies.
So, ③ it's likely that Hans also enjoys Robert Duval movies.
The diagram looks exactly like the diagram for the disjunctive syllogism above:

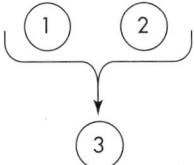

C. Interwoven Arguments

Diagrams can be particularly helpful for analyzing the structure of complex passages with two or more arguments and a number of propositions whose relations are not obvious. The number of arguments in any passage is determined by the number of conclusions. A passage with a single premise that supports two conclusions, for example, would contain two arguments.

Example _____

① The power crisis in California is hurting the national economy along with the state's economy. We may conclude that
② the crisis demands immediate action by the state government, but
③ it also demands immediate action from the federal government.

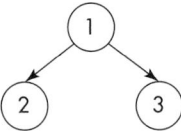

E X E R C I S E S

Analyze the arguments in the following passages, paraphrasing the propositions where needed, and diagramming where that is helpful.

1. We should prosecute people who steal copyrighted material. Taking someone's artistic creation without paying for it deprives the artist of a deserved royalty. Lacking a reasonable royalty, the artist cannot

survive. Artistic creations are precious commodities deserving of support. We support artists by purchasing their creations.

2. A company has the copyright for hypertext links. They are suing another major company (AOL) for millions of dollars for using hypertext links on web pages. This is a test case. If they win this lawsuit they will follow it up by suing anyone else who uses hypertext links. But everyone with web pages on the Internet uses hypertext links! They should not have been given a copyright for something that everyone uses. The court should let AOL win the suit or else the Internet will have to shut down.

3. Time is of the essence. If we leave now we will make it to the party on time. If we make it to the party on time, we will be able to leave early. If we are late we will have to stay late to show the host that we were glad to go to the party. If we at least get there on time, it won't look bad for us to leave early. Then we will be able to get to your mother's on time for her party. So hurry up and get dressed or your mother will think you don't love her any more.

4. A company posts material on a web page and points out that it is copyrighted material. They state that you may not copy the material without their consent. In order to see this web page and read the copyright statement, an Internet browser makes a copy of the web page on the viewer's computer. Most browsers, such as Internet Explorer and Netscape, enable this copy to be viewed even off line. Since the company posting material on the Internet must know such copies of their web pages are necessary for anyone to read their web pages, it implies that they give consent to others to copy the web page.

5. The divergent paths taken by New York and Texas in the 1990s illustrate the futility of over-reliance on prisons as a cure for crime. Texas added more people to prisons in the 1990s (98,081) than New York's entire prison population (73,233). If prisons are a cure for crime, Texas should have mightily outperformed New York from a crime-control standpoint. But from 1990 to 1998 the decline in New York's crime rate exceeded the decline in Texas's crime rate by 26%.

—Vincent Schiraldi, "Prisons and Crime,"
The New York Times, 6 October 2000

6. In most presidential elections in the United States, more than half the states are ignored; voters who don't live in so-called swing states are in effect bystanders in these quadrennial events. An amendment to the U.S. Constitution should replace the archaic electoral vote system with a direct vote. Only in this manner will citizens in all 50 states be able to take part fully in selecting our nation's leaders.

—Lawrence R. Foster, "End the Electoral College,"
The New York Times, 27 September 2000

1.10 COMPLEX ARGUMENTATIVE PASSAGES

The special province of logic is the evaluation of arguments. Successful evaluation supposes a clear grasp of the arguments we confront. In some passages many arguments are interwoven with each other. Different propositions appear, some serve only as premises, and some both as conclusions of one argument and as premises of another. These can prove difficult to analyze. Complex passages may be subject to varying plausible interpretations of their logical structure. So, in many cases there is *not* only one interpretation that is clearly correct. All the things we've considered so far—including unstated premises or conclusions, the distinction between arguments and explanations, and context—come into play when diagramming an extended argument. This is why two people can develop different, but reasonable, accounts of what is claimed in an argumentative passage.

To analyze a complex passage, we must identify the individual arguments and see how they fit together. Only after we have done so can we go about deciding whether or not the conclusions drawn follow from the premises that have been affirmed.

Within an argument, individual propositions are sometimes repeated in differently worded sentences. This repetition complicates the task of analysis. The analysis of an argument must take into account the fact that premises may appear in compressed form, sometimes as a short noun phrase. If so, paraphrasing may help clarify the meaning of the proposition. When analyzed, many complex argumentative passages—passages containing many premises and intermediate conclusions—will be seen to be coherent and clear.

Ideally, in order for a complex passage to justify the conclusion it attempts to justify, the parts of the passage must have a clear relationship to one another and to the conclusion. Arguments in everyday life, however, often fall short of this standard. Statements may be included whose role is unclear, and the connections among the several statements in the argument may be tangled or misstated. Analysis, including diagramming, can expose such deficiencies. By displaying the structure of a reasoning process, we can see how it was intended to work, and what its strengths and weaknesses may be. Diagrams exhibit the logical structure of arguments. We "read" them beginning with those "highest" on the page and, therefore, earliest in the cascade, following each of the several paths of reasoning "downward" to the final conclusion.

Let's say we have the following argument:

> ① If José writes poetry, then Alexandra builds airplanes; and if Doyle drives a DeLorean, then Beatrice drives a Buick. ② So, if Jose writes poetry, then Alexandra builds airplanes. ③ José writes poetry. ④ So, Alexandra builds airplanes. ⑤ So, if Doyle drives a DeLorean, then Beatrice drives a Buick. ⑥ Beatrice does not drive a Buick. ⑦ So, Doyle does not drive a DeLorean. ⑧ Alexandra builds airplanes and Doyle does not drive a DeLorean. ⑨ If Alexandra builds airplanes and Doyle does not drive a DeLorean, then I'll eat my hat. ⑩ I'll eat my hat.

You need to notice how the various parts of the passage fit together to form individual arguments. Notice that proposition ① is composed of two propositions. The individual propositions in ① are conclusions stated in ② and ⑤. So, the initial diagram will look like this:

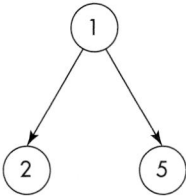

Propositions ② and ③ entail ④ (it's a deductive argument), and propositions ⑤ and ⑥ entail ⑦. So, the diagram is expanded to look like this:

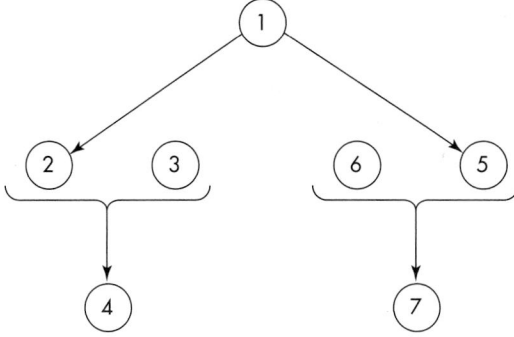

Propositions ④ and ⑦ entail ⑧:

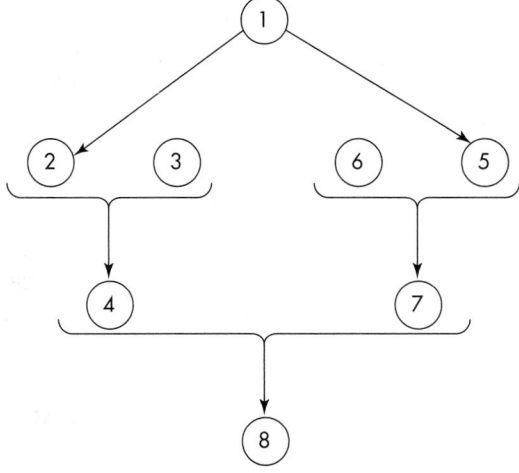

Finally, ⑧ and ⑨ entail ⑩.

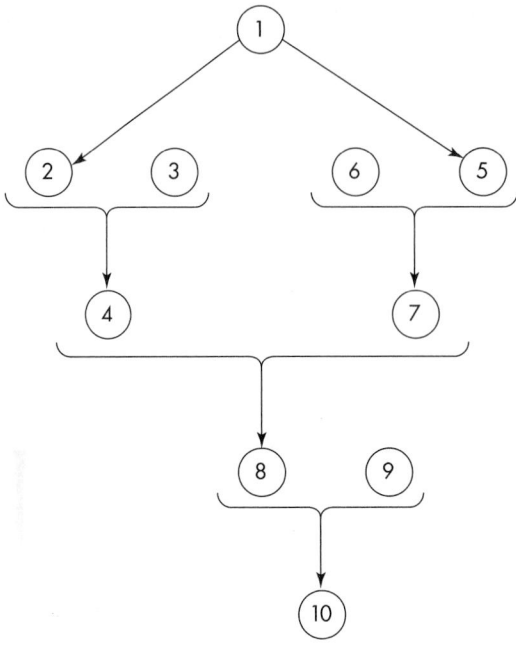

Sometimes the premises and conclusions of an argument are in no particular order. (Professors sometimes write these to see if you're on your toes.) In those cases, you need to look at the various propositions and figure out how they fit together. Consider the following argument:

> ① Marty makes mincemeat mostly on Mondays only if Susan is a member of ΣΣψ and she was born in Oslo. ② Either Ali writes movie scripts or Marty makes mincemeat mostly on Mondays. ③ Else is a member of ΣΣψ and she was born in Oslo. ④ Ali does not write movie scripts. ⑤ So, Marty makes mincemeat mostly on Mondays. ⑥ Thus, Susan is a member of ΣΣψ and she was born in Oslo. ⑦ If most members of ΣΣψ were born in Oslo, then ΣΣψ is a sorority that is featured on *Prairie Home Companion*. ⑧ Therefore, ΣΣψ is a sorority that is featured on *Prairie Home Companion*. ⑨ Hence, most members of ΣΣψ were born in Oslo. ⑩ Both Babette and Erica are members of ΣΣψ and were born in Oslo.

Where do you begin? There's a nice set of conclusion-indicators (*so, thus, therefore, hence*), so you should be able to determine what the writer intended the conclusions to be. Once you find the conclusions, you should be able to piece together the individual arguments. In the case of *deductive* arguments, you will find that either the conclusion is a part of a premise, or, as in the case of ⑧ in the previous argument, the conclusion is reached by putting earlier premises together. In the case of an inductive generalization, individual premises support a general conclusion. So, you will probably put together the individual arguments as follows:

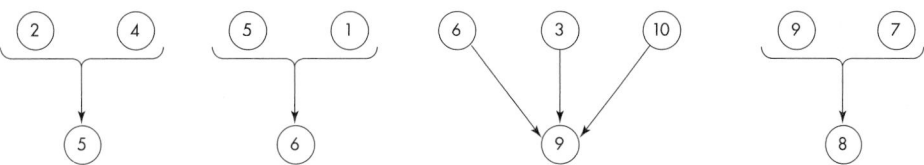

⑤ is the conclusion of one argument and a premise of another. ⑥ is the conclusion of one argument and a premise of another. ⑨ is the conclusion of one argument and a premise of another. So, you'll put the entire argument in the passage together as follows:

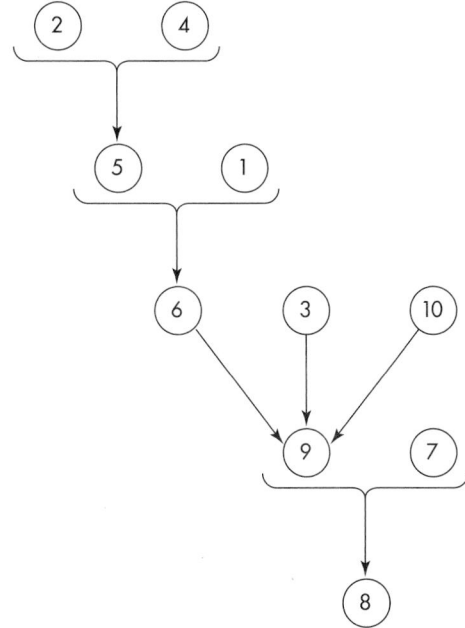

The two cases we've considered are somewhat contrived. There are conclusion-indicators throughout. There are no superfluous propositions. None of the propositions are repeated in different sentences. In "real world" arguments, it will often take more thought to sort things out. There might not always be indicator-words. Propositions might be repeated using slightly different words. Premises or conclusions might not be stated. You will often need to think very hard to analyze an argument.

Example

Consider this complex argument:

① Logic courses are very important. ② Studies have repeatedly shown that philosophy majors have some of the highest rates of acceptance to law schools and medical schools. ③ Because students who take logic courses are given the opportunity to develop reasoning skills, ④ they tend to do well on the section of the GRE exam that deals with logical reasoning. ⑤ Philosophy majors take numerous logic courses. ⑥ Anyone planning to take the LSAT, MCAT, or the GRE would benefit from taking as many logic courses as possible. ⑦ Many employers look favorably on philosophy majors because the employers know that these students have learned to apply reasoning to problem-solving situations. ⑧ In addition, philosophy majors generally have to write extensive argumentative papers, and employers realize that these students probably have good writing and communication skills. As you can see then, ⑨ it's very important for you to take logic courses.

Notice that ① and ⑨ assert the same proposition. So, we shall ignore ⑨. One way to diagram this complex argumentative passage is the following:

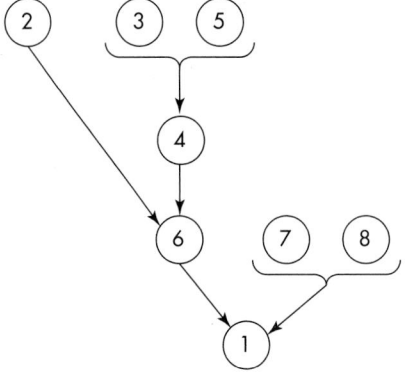

This diagram exhibits the logical structure of the argument. We can understand the argument by reading the propositions corresponding to each premise or intermediate conclusion, beginning with those "highest" on the diagram, and following each of the several paths of reasoning to the final conclusion.

Did *you* diagram the argument above in the same way? If not, don't panic. Diagramming complex passages is often difficult. It takes a good deal of practice. As you become more familiar with arguments, diagramming complex passages becomes easier.

EXERCISES

Diagram the structure of the following complex argumentative passages.

1. Since you are going to have to work for a living for most of your life, you should get into an occupation that you enjoy. Of course, it is not always possible to correctly predict how well you will like a certain occupation. Sometimes a career looks good from the outside, but

when you actually do it for a while, it loses its appeal. Getting a broad education allows you to gain general skills applicable to many careers. Sometimes specializing too early locks you into a field that you may not like later on in life. These are some of the reasons why getting a liberal arts education can be a good decision.

2. Democratic laws generally tend to promote the welfare of the greatest possible number; for they emanate from the majority of the citizens, who are subject to error, but who cannot have an interest opposed to their own advantage. The laws of an aristocracy tend, on the contrary, to concentrate wealth and power in the hands of the minority because an aristocracy, by its very nature, constitutes a minority. It may therefore be asserted, as a general proposition, that the purpose of a democracy in its legislation is more useful to humanity than that of an aristocracy.

—Alexis de Tocqueville, *Democracy in America*, 1835

3. Paternal and maternal genes can be antagonistic to one another. Consider pregnancy. In most mammals, the mother's body regards the growing embryo as an intruder and tries to limit the demands it places on her resources. The father, of course, does not bear the young and so is unaffected by such considerations. His genetic interest is unambiguous: to stimulate the embryo's growth and to shield it from the mother's defenses. Thus only males contribute the genes that foster the growth of the protective organ known as the placenta; females do not. Uniparental mouse eggs, created from the genes of the mother alone, develop into normal embryos, but the embryos lack a placenta and so do not flourish.

—Laurence Marschall, in a review of *Genome*, by Matt Ridley (HarperCollins, 2000), appearing in *The Sciences*, August 2000

4. A question arises: whether it be better [for a prince] to be loved than feared or feared than loved? One should wish to be both, but, because it is difficult to unite them in one person, it is much safer to be feared than loved, when, of the two, one must be dispensed with. Because this is to be asserted in general of men, that they are ungrateful, fickle, false, cowards, covetous . . . and that prince who, relying entirely on their promises, has neglected other precautions, is ruined, because friendships that are obtained by payments may indeed be earned but they are not secured, and in time of need cannot be relied upon. Men have less scruple in offending one who is beloved than one who is feared, for love is preserved by the link of obligation which, owing to the baseness of men, is broken at every opportunity for their advantage; but fear preserves you by a dread of punishment which never fails.

—N. Machiavelli, *The Prince*, 1515

5. Consider why the federal government is involved in student lending: It is in the national interest to have an educated populace. On average, college graduates earn almost twice the annual salary of high school graduates. The cost of the nation's investment in the education of student borrowers is recouped many times over through increased productivity and greater earnings. By making a college education possible for millions of Americans, federally sponsored student loans produce a tremendous return for the U.S. Treasury and students, whose incomes—and tax payments—are greatly increased with their college degrees.

   But most college students are not creditworthy borrowers. The typical student is cash poor, owner of few if any assets that could be used as collateral, and often earns too little to be considered a good credit risk. If such a borrower could get a loan, in all likelihood it would carry a high interest rate—high enough to lead many students to decide not to go on to higher education. That is why student loans are backed by federal money and the interest charged on those loans is capped.

   —Richard W. Riley, "Should Washington Have a Bigger Share
   of the Student-loan Industry? Yes!" *Insight*, 29 April 1996

6. ". . . You appeared to be surprised when I told you, on our first meeting, that you had come from Afghanistan."

   "You were told, no doubt."

   "Nothing of the sort. I knew you came from Afghanistan. From long habit the train of thoughts ran so swiftly through my mind that I arrived at the conclusion without being conscious of intermediate steps. There were such steps, however. The train of reasoning ran, 'Here is a gentleman of a medical type, but with the air of a military man. Clearly an army doctor, then. He has just come from the tropics, for his face is dark, and that is not the natural tint of his skin, for his wrists are fair. He has undergone hardship and sickness, as his haggard face says clearly. His left arm has been injured. He holds it in a stiff and unnatural manner. Where in the tropics could an English army doctor have seen much hardship and got his arm wounded? Clearly in Afghanistan.' The whole train of thought did not occupy a second. I then remarked that you came from Afghanistan, and you were astonished."

   "It is simple enough as you explain it," I said, smiling.

   — A. Conan Doyle, *A Study in Scarlet*, 1887

7. One of the most difficult problems associated with quantum research is how to observe subatomic particles in their natural states without affecting them—observing them nondestructively, so to speak. It's difficult for two reasons. First, atoms and subatomic particles are the smallest constituents of matter. Since any medium used to observe

them emits energy of its own, that energy must affect the energy of the observed particles. Second, in isolation, atomic components exist in two quantum states simultaneously—particles and waves. It's as if they were packets of statistical probability. Only when they interact with other components do they display one manifestation or the other.

—"Skinning Schrodinger's Cat," *Insight*, 15 July 1996

8. In the U.S. Postal Service there is no straightforward mechanism to correct problems or force the agency to change. No citizens can own tradable shares. The income and security of managers and workers are guaranteed, by the monopoly on first-class mail, public funding and the employees' political clout with Congress. The public cannot shift its business to more efficient competitors, because competition is prohibited. Consequently, the gross postal inefficiencies are not the result of the character or personality of the individuals who happen to occupy positions and jobs; they stem from the structure of the Postal Service itself.

—Douglas K. Adie, "Privatizing Will Improve Mail Service Posthaste," *Insight*, 30 January 1995

9. Eliminating a tax on marriage sounds like a great idea. But it is also a sound idea to set higher rates on wealthier people and to tax families with the same total income the same no matter how their income is split between spouses. No tax code can satisfy these three goals simultaneously. Two people whose individual incomes are low enough to be taxed at 15 percent can, under a progressive code, hit the 28 percent bracket when their incomes are combined. Congress can eliminate the marriage tax, but only by sacrificing progressivity.

—"Temptations of a Balanced Budget," Editorial in *The New York Times*, 31 December 1997

10. Nothing is demonstrable unless the contrary implies a contradiction. Nothing that is distinctly conceivable implies a contradiction. Whatever we conceive as existent, we can also conceive as nonexistent. There is no being, therefore, whose non-existence implies a contradiction. Consequently there is no being whose existence is demonstrable.

—David Hume, *Dialogues Concerning Natural Religion*, Part IX, 1779

ESSENTIALS OF CHAPTER 1

Logic is the study of the methods and principles used to evaluate arguments. The value of skill in logic is seen in myriad situations: in evaluating claims made by political candidates, in understanding the intricacies of legal documents, in formulating a persuasive business plan, in evaluating research claims in scientific experiments, and so on. Skill in logic is thus of enormous value, and **the only way to improve that skill is by practice**—hence the large quantity of examples and exercises in this book. Whether or not your teacher assigns them for credit, you should work through all or most of the exercises in order to be sure that you understand the concepts and can apply the techniques quickly and reliably.

A **proposition** is something that can be asserted or denied (something that is *either true or false*) and is to be distinguished from the sentences that may express it **(1.2)**.

An **argument** is a collection of propositions in which one is the conclusion and the other(s) are premises offered in its support. **(1.3)** Arguments are distinguished from explanations, descriptions and other kinds of collections of propositions by virtue of their *function*: arguments attempt to provide grounds for accepting the truth of some proposition on the basis of some other propositions **(1.4)**. **Premise- and conclusion-indicators** are often helpful in analyzing the structure of arguments **(1.5A)**. Sometimes contextual information, hidden premises, or submerged conclusions are involved in an argument; these things need to be made explicit before the argument can be properly evaluated **(1.5)**.

A **deductive argument** is an argument that aims to establish its conclusion with certainty **(1.3)**.

An **inductive argument** is an argument that aims to establish its conclusion with some degree of probability **(1.3)**.

An argument is in **standard form** when it is written with the premises first, separated from the conclusion by a line **(1.3)**.

A deductive argument is **valid** when it is impossible for its conclusion to be false and its premises true; that is, **A deductive argument is valid when it is the case that, *if* the premises were true, it would be impossible for the conclusion to be false (1.6)**. Validity does not depend on the actual truth or falsity of the propositions of the argument. It depends only on what would be possible for the conclusion on the assumption that the premises were true. The validity of an argument depends only on its form (the structure of the relations between the propositions of the argument), not on its content.

A deductive argument is **sound** when it is both valid and its premises are in fact true. The conclusion of a sound argument is one that is certain (it *cannot* be false) **(1.7)**.

Two techniques that aid in the analysis of argumentative passages are paraphrasing and diagramming. In **paraphrasing (1.9A)**, we rewrite the argument in clear language, supplying any missing or assumed information that is not explicitly stated, being careful to preserve the meaning of the original. In **diagramming (1.9B)**, we number all the propositions of the argument in the order in which they occur, and represent the relations between the propositions with arrows and brackets. Sometimes arguments may be interwoven in complex ways; these interconnections are made more clear by diagramming the arguments **(1.9C)**. Similarly, very complex arguments can be made more clear by diagramming **(1.10)**.

How the terms fit together:

- **Propositions (statements)** are either **true** or **false**. *Only* propositions are true or false.

- Propositions fit together to form **descriptions, explanations,** and **arguments**.

- Descriptions answer the questions Who? What? When? Where? and sometimes How? (how something is).

- Explanations answer the questions Why? and How? (how to do something or how something came to be).

- The **premises** of an argument give reasons to believe that a proposition (the **conclusion**) is true. Arguments are either **deductive arguments** or **inductive arguments**.

- The **form** or structure of a **valid** deductive argument guarantees that it is impossible for the premises to be true and the conclusion false. An **invalid** deductive argument with true premises can only provide some, but not conclusive, evidence for the truth of its conclusion. All inductive arguments are invalid deductive arguments.

- In inductive argument can be **strong** or **weak**. A strong inductive argument provides good **evidence** that its conclusion is **probably** true. Inductive arguments include **analogies, inductive generalizations,** and **arguments to the best explanation**.

- You **analyze** an argument by determining which propositions are premises and which are conclusions, determining the strength of the evidence the premises provide for the conclusion, and determining whether the premises are true or false. You might construct a **diagram** of the argument as part of the analysis. A diagram is a map of the argument. It shows whether premises support a conclusion only when taken together—the premises are placed together in a brace—or whether they individually support the truth of the conclusion—in which case there is a arrow from the individual premise to the conclusion.

CHAPTER TWO

INFORMAL FALLACIES

2.1 WHAT IS A FALLACY?

A *fallacy* **is a defective argument. It is an error in reasoning**. As we shall see in Chapters 4 and 6, sometimes the defect is in the form or structure of a deductive argument. These are invalid arguments. They are known as *formal fallacies*. For example, the following argument commits the formal fallacy, denying the antecedent:

> If José went to the dance, then Belinda went to the dance.
> José did not go to the dance.
> So, Belinda did not go to the dance.

The form or structure of the argument can be represented by replacing statements with variables:

> If *p*, then *q*.
> Not *p*.
> So, not *q*.

Because the argument form is invalid, it is possible for an argument of that form to have true premises and a false conclusion:

> If Bill Gates received all the profits made by the *Lord of the Rings* movies, then he would be rich.
> Bill Gates did not receive all the profits made by the *Lord of the Rings* movies.
> So, Bill Gates is not rich.

Here the problem is with the form of the argument. The problem is independent of the content of the arguments, that is, the claims about José, Belinda, Bill Gates, and wealth.

As we saw in the last chapter, deductive invalidity is not the only way in which an argument can fail to establish its conclusion. The best inductive arguments can have true premises and a false conclusion. Sometimes inductive arguments are very weak. Also, no false premise provides a reason to believe that a conclusion is true.

The fallacies with which we shall be concerned in this chapter are called *informal fallacies* or *material fallacies*. In most cases, the problem is found in the content of the argument, that is, the statements from which the argument is constructed. In some cases, there is a false premise. In some cases, the premises assume more than they explicitly state. In some cases, the premises provide no reason to believe that the conclusion is true. In *all* cases, the fallacies are similar to good arguments we use every day. In many cases, we'll have to ask why there is a problem in a particular case, even though there is no problem in another.

How many informal fallacies are there? There is no agreement. The ancient Greek philosopher, Aristotle (384–322 BCE) identified thirteen.[1] Others identify more than 100.[2] Why is there so much disagreement? If you choose a small number of fallacy names, there are often several ways in which the fallacy can be committed. You *could* give each variation a distinct name. That's one reason why there are significant variations in lists of fallacies.

In this chapter we examine nineteen common fallacies. These fallacies are divided into three general groups: (1) fallacies of *relevance*, (2) fallacies of *presumption*, and (3) fallacies of *ambiguity*. Our classification system is somewhat arbitrary. There will be times when you'll correctly suggest that an argument could be seen to commit more than one fallacy. There will be other times when you'll suggest that there is something wrong with an argument, but it doesn't quite fit any of the fallacies on the list. In principle, it's more important to be able to analyze a defective argument and explain why the premises fail to show that the conclusion is true than to be able to spout off fallacy names. Indeed, since there are acceptable arguments of the same form as many of the fallacies, if you unthinkingly shout out fallacy names, you'll sometimes claim that acceptable arguments are fallacious. So, identifying fallacies presupposes careful argument analysis.

---

[1] Aristotle, *Sophistical Refutations*.

[2] The most voluminous list of fallacies we know appears in David H. Fischer's *Historians' Fallacies* (New York: Harper & Row, 1979); here he discussed and named more than 112 different fallacies. In *Fallacy: The Counterfeit of Argument* (Englewood Cliffs, NJ: Prentice-Hall, 1959), W. W. Fernside and W. B. Holther named and illustrated 51 fallacies. A historical and theoretical treatment of the topic was given by C. L. Hamblin in *Fallacies* (London: Methuen, 1970), and another excellent treatment of the topic is to be found in *Argument: The Logic of the Fallacies* (Scarborough, Ont.: McGraw-Hill Ryerson, 1982) by John Woods and Douglas Walton. Douglas Walton has written several excellent books in which he provides extensive and careful treatments of individual fallacies: *Informal Logic: A Handbook for Critical Argumentation* (Cambridge: Cambridge University Press, 1989); *Arguments from Ignorance* (University Park: Pennsylvania State University Press, 1996); *Appeal to Expert Opinion: Arguments from Authority* (University Park: Pennsylvania State University Press, 1997); *One-Sided Arguments* (Albany: State University of New York Press, 1999); *Appeal to Popular Opinion* (University Park: Pennsylvania State University Press, 1999). Howard Kahane presented insightful criticism of the usual methods of classifying fallacies in "The Nature and Classification of Fallacies" in *Informal Logic*, edited by J. A. Blair and R. J. Johnson (Inverness, CA: Edgepress, 1980). All these books are warmly recommended to readers who wish to go more deeply into the subject of fallacies.

Nonetheless, while argument analysis is more important than learning the fallacy names, there are two reasons why you should learn the fallacy names. First, the fallacy names are in common use. So, by learning the names, you'll be able to communicate more easily with other educated people. Second, your instructor expects you to know the names.

Since there are acceptable forms of many of these arguments, we distinguish between the acceptable and fallacious uses of the argument. Some of the fallacies have several names, including Latin names. So, we note alternative names of some of the fallacies.

2.2 FALLACIES OF RELEVANCE

The premises of an argument provide reasons to believe that a conclusion is true. If the argument is acceptable, there must be some connection between the premises and the conclusion. The premises must be relevant. They must show or tend to show that the conclusion is true. The fallacies of relevance occur when the premises fail to give reasons to believe that the conclusion is true.

R1. Argument from Ignorance *(argumentum ad ignorantiam)*

Have you ever heard someone argue in the following way?

We don't know that the claims made by astrologers are true, so they're false. This argument commits a fallacy known as **argument from ignorance**. There are good reasons to question the claims of astrologers. One reason is that it is difficult to explain how the positions of the stars and planets could have an impact on our daily lives. Another reason is that many astrological predictions are false. But the fact that we don't know that their claims are true is *not* a sufficient reason to claim that claims made by astrologers are false.

Where p is a proposition, an argument from ignorance is typically given in one of the following forms:

1. **We don't know that (or there is no evidence that, or there is little reason to believe that) p is true, so p is false.**
2. **We don't know that p is false, so p is true.**

Like many informal fallacies, there is a missing premise in the argument, and once the premise is stated, you'll begin to question whether the conclusion should be accepted. For the first version of the fallacy, the complete argument might be stated as follows:

If p is true, then we know that p is true.
We don't know that p is true.
Therefore, p is not true (p is false).

If you don't know that a statement is true, it is often prudent not to accept it as true: It is prudent to suspend judgment. It does *not* follow, however, that the statement is false.

Assume that the following argument was given in 1850:

> If successful human heart transplants could be performed, we'd (now) know they can be performed.
> We don't (now) know that successful human heart transplants can be performed.
> Therefore, successful human heart transplants cannot be performed.

As we now know, the conclusion is false. The problem is that the first premise was false in 1850. **In general, the fact that you *don't know* whether a statement is true (or false) tells you nothing about whether the statement is true (or false).**

Appeals to ignorance are similar to some perfectly legitimate inferences. Your roommate asks you whether his logic book is on his desk. You respond, "I don't see it," and he concludes that the logic book is not on his desk. A scientist argues that if her hypothesis is true, then when she constructs her experiment she'll make some certain specific observations. She conducts her experiment but doesn't make those observations. So, she concludes that her hypothesis is false. A historian argues that, since there is no documentary evidence that young George Washington cut down the cherry tree and said "I cannot tell a lie, I did it!," it is likely that the popular story about young George is false. Aren't these appeals to ignorance?

No. In each of these cases there is an implicit (explicit in the case of the scientist) conditional premise of the form "If *p* is true, then there is something you will know in a specific way." It is *not* the vague claim that if *p* is true, then *p* is known or that there is evidence for *p*. Further, if pressed, the person presenting the argument must be in a position to show that the premises are true. The *burden of proof*, the responsibility of showing that the premises are true, always rests upon the person offering the argument. If the historian were pressed, for example, she'd say that the only known source of the cherry tree story was Washington's first biography. Since Washington was the biographer's hero, there's some likelihood the biographer embellished the facts. Since documentary evidence from the period is the sole basis for supporting historical claims, the absence of written evidence from the period—diary entries, letters, etc.—supporting the story is a reason to question it.

Of course, there are cases in which you might need more information to determine whether what appears to be an argument from ignorance is fallacious.

> On May 27, 2005, there were news reports that Viagra and similar drugs cause blindness—more properly, the loss of clear vision in some part of the visual field—in some men. It does not have this effect in many men: The report cited about fifty cases out of the twenty-three million men who had taken Viagra. Pfizer,

the makers of Viagra, released a statement that there is "no proof" that Viagra causes blindness.

Is this a fallacious argument from ignorance? It is hard to say. If, as the public might (erroneously?) assume, the charge was made on the same day it was reported and Pfizer gave an immediate reply, one might suspect that Pfizer gave a fallacious argument from ignorance. When alleged problems arise with products, it is not uncommon for the producers to deny the evidence. It's a form of damage control. If the reply was virtually immediate, it is unlikely that the company had time to reexamine the evidence from the clinical trials to see if there were any cases in which the use of Viagra was correlated with reduced visual ability. Given the rarity of the alleged effect, it is possible that, even if there is such a correlation, it was never encountered during the clinical trials or that it was so rare that there was no suspicion of a causal connection.

On the other hand, if Pfizer knew of the claim for a time before the story "broke," there might have been time to reexamine the evidence from the clinical trials, and their claim of "no proof" has greater plausibility. Assume that they heard the charge several weeks before it was reported on the news and that they reexamined the evidence from their clinical trials and discovered that reduced visual ability occurred only in patients having other conditions, such as high cholesterol or diabetes, and that such blindness sometimes arises in such patients even if they *don't* take Viagra. This *doesn't* show that Viagra was *not* a cause or a contributing factor in some cases in which users went blind, and Pfizer would have been guilty of a fallacious argument from ignorance if they claimed it did. But since all cases in which blindness occurred were cases in which Viagra users suffered from other medical conditions, there is reason to doubt that Viagra by itself causes blindness. If Viagra were itself the cause, there should have been cases in which blindness resulted *without* other medical conditions being present. But, of course, there is now a warning of another possible side effect when the drug is sold.

So, there are many cases in which what might appear to be arguments from ignorance are perfectly reasonable. The fallacy arises only when one of the premises is false.

Before going on, we should look at what some people take as a special case of argument from ignorance. In the American court system, the accused is assumed innocent until proven guilty. This is a procedural rule. *Guilt* and *innocence* are technical legal terms. It also assumes an unusual notion of "proof." Ed will be proven guilty of murder if and only if a group of twelve of his peers become convinced—and it makes little difference *how* they become convinced—that Ed is guilty. Notice this is *not* the same as saying, "If Ed killed Selma, then there is sufficient evidence to show that he did. There is not sufficient evidence to show that he did. So, Ed did not kill Selma." Whether Ed killed Selma is a fact independent of all considerations of evidence. The first premise might well be false: There are many cases in which crimes are committed, but in which there is not sufficient evidence to show that the perpetrator did it. Nonetheless, the procedural rule requires that jurors treat the conditional, "If Ed killed Selma, then there is sufficient evidence to show that he did," *as if* it were true. If they find the evidence insufficient to show that Ed killed Selma, the jury is to find Ed not guilty; that is, they direct the court to treat the proposition, "Ed did not kill Selma," *as if* it were true, not to remand Ed to the penal system, etc. Unlike a typical case of appeal to ignorance, here the truth of the conditional premise is treated *as if* it were unproblematic.

R2. Appeal to Illegitimate Authority *(argumentum ad verecundiam)*

You believe most of what your professors say. When they're speaking within their areas of training and research, it is reasonable to do so. They are authorities in their fields. This doesn't mean they're always right—everyone occasionally makes a mistake—but there is good reason to believe that they're right the overwhelming majority of the time. Should you believe them when they make claims outside their areas of training and research?

An argument commits the fallacy of appeal to illegitimate authority if it appeals to someone or something as an authority on a particular subject who is not an authority on that subject. Illegitimate appeals to authority are common in advertising. Many commercials feature famous people. James Earl Jones is a fine actor. He studied acting at the American Theatre Wing in New York City, among other places. If he made a pitch for the American Theatre Wing, you'd have *some* reason to believe what he says. He'd be an actor talking about training for actors. As an alumnus of the school, he has some familiarity with it, although any intimate familiarity with it might be half a century out of date. And you might be tempted to conclude that since Jones went there and became a great actor, you would become a great actor if you went there, an inference that does not follow. For every famous alumnus of a school there are usually hundreds who never attain fame. Nonetheless, since James Earl Jones is an actor, he would be talking within his general area of expertise if he endorsed a certain acting school.

As far as I know, James Earl Jones does not do commercials for the American Theatre Wing. He *is* the spokesperson for Verizon, the telephone company. Jones is a wonderful spokesperson. He has a magnificent voice. He has a friendly, outgoing demeanor. And, of course, he's a fine and popular actor. All this might yield a "halo effect": You might conclude that since Jones is wonderful, Verizon is wonderful, too. But should you believe anything in the commercial *because* James Earl Jones says it? No. There's little reason to believe he knows much more about telephone companies than you or I do.

Tiger Woods, of golf fame, has appeared in Buick commercials. Arnold Palmer, of golf fame, was the spokesperson for Pennzoil for many years. Former professional football player John Madden does commercials for Ace Hardware. Penn State football coach Joe Paterno has appeared in commercials for a food company. Numerous famous athletes have appeared on the front of the Wheaties box. Numerous Hollywood personalities have endorsed charitable or political causes. In each of these cases, a famous personality is endorsing a product. In each of these cases, there is little reason to believe the celebrity has the background necessary to have carefully evaluated the product. In each of these cases, there is good reason to believe that the conclusion, "Buy our stuff," is based on an appeal to illegitimate authority.

"Okay," you say, "so we shouldn't believe everything we hear on commercials. That's not surprising. But if you have a scientist talking about issues in science, there's no problem there, right?" Wrong. In 1970, Linus Pauling published a book called *Vitamin C and the Common Cold*.[3] Pauling was a chemist. He won the 1954 Nobel Prize for Chemistry, as well as the 1962 Nobel Peace Prize. Shouldn't you take seriously his claim that massive doses of Vitamin C prevent the common cold? No. Chemistry and medicine are not the same disciplines. Pauling was making claims outside his discipline. Subsequent studies showed that Vitamin C relieves the symptoms of colds, but it doesn't prevent colds. If you're taking Vitamin C just because Pauling said it would ward off colds, you've fallen victim to an appeal to illegitimate authority.

Have you ever accepted a claim as true because "they" say that it's true? Who are "they"? What credentials can "they" claim? What "they" say is mere rumor. Rumors never should be trusted as a source of information. Basing conclusions on rumors involves an illegitimate appeal to authority. And rumors come in various guises. You might hear that "numerous studies show . . .", without being given any information about who conducted the alleged studies and how they were conducted. If you have information about the studies, you can evaluate the probable reliability of the studies. Without such information, appeals to "numerous studies" are variations on rumor. You might be told that "everybody knows that . . .". Ask yourself whether *you* know that, and if you believe you do, what kind of evidence you have to support your belief. It's probably true that "everybody knows there are trees in Canada." You might have seen tree-filled pictures in brochures produced by the Canadian Tourist Bureau, or you might have seen news reports from Canada with trees in the background, or you might have studied about the Canadian logging industry in geography. But appeals to common knowledge

> **ESSENTIAL** HINTS
>
> Does the fact that a person is famous in one area show that he or she is *not* an authority in another? No. The late Hedy Lamarr was a popular actress during the first half of the twentieth century. She was also an inventor. She invented the technology that made cell phones possible. So, before yelling "appeal to illegitimate authority," you are obliged to check into the background of the person making the endorsement.

---

[3]Linus Pauling, *Vitamin C and the Common Cold* (San Francisco: W. H. Freeman, 1970).

are often appeals to common, but unsubstantiated, beliefs: They're rumors in another guise. Should someone say, "Everyone knows that when the [choose your favorite political party] control the government, we're in for good economic times," you should be skeptical. Check your history. In the past century, there have been some very good, and some very bad, economic times when each party has controlled the American government.

Closely related to this is an appeal to the authority of popular opinion.[4] Several years ago, Ford Motor Company advertised that the Ford Taurus was the most popular mid-sized car built in America. More people purchased the Ford Taurus than comparable cars made by other American auto makers. What follows from that? Why is popularity a reason to buy a Taurus? Popularity, as such, doesn't imply superior quality. Popularity doesn't imply superior safety. Popularity doesn't imply superior comfort in operation. Popularity doesn't imply superior economy of operation. Popularity at the time of purchase doesn't even imply satisfaction a few years down the road. Quality, safety, comfort, and economy of operation are all factors you reasonably might take into consideration when deciding to buy a car. Appeals to popularity seem to carry with them the suggestion that "this many people can't be wrong."

> **ESSENTIAL** HINTS
>
> **Democracy**
> Don't the views of the majority have a different status in a democracy? Don't the views of the majority determine what is right and wrong? Yes and no. In a democracy, the views of the majority can be enacted into law. Those laws tell us what it is *legally* right to do or not to do. Sometimes those laws are inconsistent with higher (constitutional) laws, and then they're overturned by the courts. Sometimes laws are *morally* wrong. In terms of moral rightness or wrongness, the views of the majority are irrelevant. Laws that discriminate against people on the basis of their race, for example, would be morally wrong even if they reflected the views of the majority.

Choose your favorite "bad habit." Many people engage in it. There have been many popular political candidates who, once elected, have not turned out well. "That many people" can be wrong and often are. Popular belief that a statement is true usually provides no reason to believe that the statement is true.

Tradition can be a questionable authority. Why should you infer that the way to do something is right just because it's always been done that way?

> "This family has always voted for the Democratic candidates. It's a tradition! So, you should support them as well!"

---

[4]This is a bandwagon argument. It is often considered an appeal to emotion (*ad populum*). As we'll see below, an appeal to emotion often leads to the conclusion that there are reasons to do something. The case we consider could be so understood. In this case, we consider an appeal to popular opinion as a basis for claiming something like quality.

Is tradition a good way to choose for whom to vote? Some people believe it's more reasonable to vote for the party rather than for particular candidates. They say that the party stands for certain ideals, and it's more likely that those ideals will be enacted into law if that party has support across the board. Even if that's true, partisan political ideals evolve over a period of years. If you vote for a party just because it's traditional in your family to do so, there is no guarantee that the party's ideals and yours coincide. Isn't it more reasonable to determine what the ideals of a candidate or party are before you vote, rather than just to follow a family tradition? Would it make any difference if the ancestor who started the tradition held political views you diametrically oppose?

Many traditions are fine. Your family might have traditional ways to celebrate holidays. You might engage in certain rituals before you go on vacation. Your family might have traditional ways to eat meals: You sit at a table rather than stand at a sink or stare at a television while eating. There's usually nothing wrong with such traditions. Sometimes they make events special. But consider the following:

> "We've always dropped our pledges into a deep pool of mud. It's a tradition! So, if you want to join, you have to be dropped in the mud, too!"
> "Keeping slaves is traditional in this part of the world. So, owning slaves is right!"

If there is an appeal to tradition you should ask—as you should regarding the premises of any argument—whether the appeal to tradition gives a good reason to believe or to do something. If not, the appeal to tradition is an illegitimate appeal to authority.

R3. Argument Against the Person (Personal Attack, *argumentum ad hominem*)

If you criticize an argument, you need to show either that one or more of the premises is false or that the premises fail to support the conclusion even if they are true. In either case, the attack is on the argument. **An argument is an** *argument against the person* **if it replies to an argument by attacking the credibility of the arguer rather than the credibility of the argument.** There are several variations on such arguments. None is a conclusive refutation of the original argument. In some cases, however, a reply might be reasonable.

An *abusive* **argument against the person replies to an argument by attacking the arguer's character rather then the argument presented.**

Example _____

Marta has argued that the best way to prevent the overpopulation of stray animals is to have our pets neutered. But Marta is a notorious liar. So, we should reject her conclusion.

The reply to Marta's argument shows neither that one or more of Marta's premises is false nor that her reasoning from the premises is faulty. Therefore, the reply does *not* show that Marta's conclusion is unwarranted. However, it *might* give some reason to question her premises.

When you evaluate the *testimony* of a person, one question you need to ask is whether the person's testimony has been reliable in the past.[5] If the person has a reputation for misrepresenting the facts, you have *some* reason to question the person's testimony. So, if Marta does not have a stellar reputation for truth telling, she might reasonably reply by giving arguments for the truth of her premises. Ideally, those arguments would be based on premises her critic would concede.

As we shall see, cases of argument against the person that have *any* credibility are based on criteria for evaluating testimony.

Although the previous argument against the person was very weak, it provided some reason to question the premises, and therefore the conclusion. In some cases, it is very difficult to see how the "criticism" is relevant to the issue at hand. The responsibility (burden of proof) falls upon the person offering the criticism to show that her point is relevant. If she fails to do so, the argument against the person is fallacious.

Abusive personal attacks are common in political contexts. They're often called "mud slinging."

> **ESSENTIAL** HINTS
>
> **Politics and Character**
> Don't the voters have a *right* to know whether the candidates are honest? So, isn't "mud-slinging" an acceptable reply to an argument in political contexts? The answer to the first question is "yes." The answer to the second is "no," since it avoids the issues examined in the arguments. The only acceptable reply to an argument focuses on the truth of the premises and the strength of the inference.

Example

A few years ago there were two candidates for a political office. Let's call them **A** and **B**. **A** was a war hero. **B** had managed to avoid military service during a time when many of his contemporaries were unable to do so. **A** labeled **B** a "draft dodger." **A** had a standard reply to almost any of **B**'s arguments: "But **B** was a draft dodger. So we must reject his conclusion."

It is unclear how having avoided military service in the past was relevant to issues regarding national defense, let alone to social issues. **A** provided no grounds for claiming that avoiding military service was relevant to the issues. So, **A**'s arguments were fallacious attacks on the person.

---

[5]For a discussion of the evaluation of testimony see Daniel E. Flage, *The Art of Questioning: An Introduction to Critical Thinking* (Upper Saddle River, NJ: Prentice Hall, 2004), pp. 109–123.

Not all arguments against the person are abusive. Some are circumstantial. **A *circumstantial* argument against the person replies to an argument by appealing to some circumstances in which the arguer finds himself or herself as a reason to discredit the argument.**

Example _____

Father Murphy has argued that abortion should not be legal. Father Murphy is a Roman Catholic priest. It is the official position of the Roman Catholic Church that abortion is a sin. So, we should not take his argument seriously.

One of the questions you need to ask when evaluating *testimony* is whether or not the person offering the testimony is biased. If a person is biased, he or she might not notice relevant information in evaluating a claim. So, the argument in the above example raises a possibility: Claims of bias do not show that the premises are false or that relevant information has not been taken into account. It has *not* shown that Father Murphy's premises are false or unreasonable. The objection *suggests* that the reasons Murphy advances for his position are mere rationalizations. It's an attempt to **poison the well**. You would expect Father Murphy to respond: "If you grant the truth of my premises, you are forced to grant the conclusion. If you don't grant the truth of my premises, it's your responsibility to show that they're false. Short of that, you've committed a fallacious argument against the person."

Sometimes there is a reply to an argument that suggests that the actions of the arguer are inconsistent with her actions. This is called a *tu quoque* (literally "you too").

> **ESSENTIAL** HINTS
>
> **Poisoning the Well**
> The British novelist and clergyman Charles Kingsley, attacking the famous Catholic intellectual John Henry Cardinal Newman, argued thus: Cardinal Newman's claims were not to be trusted because, as a Roman Catholic priest, Newman's first loyalty (Kingsley alleged) was not to the truth; it was to Catholic doctrine. Newman countered that this *ad hominem* attack made it impossible for him and indeed for all Catholics to advance their arguments, since anything that they might say to defend themselves would then be undermined by others alleging that, after all, truth was not their first concern. Kingsley, said Cardinal Newman, had "poisoned the well" of discourse.

Example _____

Rush Limbaugh has argued, among other things, that the country would be a better place if anyone who married remained married to his or her first spouse and if people participated in the activities of religious organizations. One day a caller to the *Rush Limbaugh Show* presented the following argument: "Why should I believe anything you say? Between you and your wife you've been married six times. You talk about the virtues of participating in religious organizations, but you yourself don't do so. You're a hypocrite!" Limbaugh's reply was, "And what does that have to do with my arguments?"

Limbaugh's reply was exactly right. To show that his arguments fail, you need to show that there is something wrong with the arguments. If he doesn't follow his own advice, this might show that he suffers from weakness of will, but that's independent of the arguments he presented.

R4. Appeal to Emotion (Mob Appeal, *argumentum ad populum*)

If we have good grounds for accepting a conclusion, the conclusion must be supported by a sound deductive argument or a strong inductive argument. Humans are not purely rational beings. So, we are sometimes *persuaded* to accept a conclusion through an appeal to our emotions. The words used make a difference. You wouldn't oppose increasing government aid to the poor, would you? Would you also favor increasing welfare payments? It's the same thing you know.[6]

An argument that commits the fallacy of appeal to emotion is of the following form:

> If believing that proposition p is true makes me "feel good" (loved, accepted, important, special, righteous, etc.), then proposition p is true.
> Believing that proposition p is true makes me "feel good."
> _____
> Proposition p is true.

There generally is little reason to accept the first premise as true. It might be true that I would feel good if I were loved or respected by some famous person, but believing that I am doesn't imply that I am loved or respected by that person. In practice, the first premise is implicit. Indeed, the argument might not be consciously considered.

Where do you find appeals to emotion? They're often found in political gatherings, religious revivals, sales meetings, and advertising. Believing they were members of the "master race," that they had been ill-treated after World War I, and therefore that they deserved better than they had received, led a generation of Germans to believe that they were special. They concluded that

---

[6]Walton reports a study finding that 63 percent of those surveyed believed the government should provide more assistance to the poor, whereas only 19 percent believed that the government should increase funds for welfare. See Walton, *Appeal to Popular Opinion*, pp. 5–6.

all those claims were true.[7] If believing that "spreading freedom and democracy" makes you feel righteous, you might conclude that spreading freedom and democracy is the thing to do. If believing that "the little guy deserves an even break" makes you feel virtuous, you might conclude that it is true that the little guy deserves an even break. In some of these cases, the conclusion is not unreasonable, but basing the conclusion on an emotional appeal does not show that the conclusion is true. An emotional commitment to the conclusion can result in taking the conclusion as an end to be pursued *regardless* of the means to it. For example, had the Germans of the early 1930s used only diplomatic means to improve their lot—had the emotional appeals not led to World War II—the results of the emotional appeals would not have been disastrous.

Advertisers also use emotional appeals. Luxury cars are often depicted as marks of being successful. *You* want to appear successful. So, you conclude that you want a luxury car. Is that a good reason to buy a Cadillac or a Mercedes? It's *not* if it is your *only* consideration. You might also ask whether you can afford the car payments, the insurance, and the upkeep. In other words, is the appearance of success worth the costs? Ads for beer, soft drinks, or coffee often feature attractive people having a great time. *You* want to be identified with the beautiful people. Is that a reason to buy that brand of drink?[8]

Emotional attachments are not unimportant in our daily lives. Perhaps only emotional factors can motivate you to act in certain ways—that's a psychological issue, not a logical issue. But emotional considerations alone are almost never a sufficient reason to accept a proposition as true.

R5. Appeal to Pity *(argumentum ad misericordiam)*

After the tsunami disaster in Southeast Asia in late 2004 and Hurricane Katrina in 2005, there were numerous appeals for disaster relief. The television images were heart-wrenching. How could anyone see such pictures and hear their accompanying descriptions and not be moved to contribute?

The fallacy of appeal to pity takes an emotional response to an unfortunate situation as a reason to believe or act in a certain way. Let us be clear on what this means and does not mean. An emotional response, as such, is not a *reason* to do anything, even if it causes you to act in a certain way. Since it's not a reason to act, an emotional response cannot be the premise for an argument. Are there *reasons* why you should contribute to disaster relief? Sure. We are morally obligated to help, as best we can, those who are less fortunate than we are. This is a moral principle. This principle fits into an argument:

---

[7]Leni Riefenstahl's movie, *Triumph of the Will*, depicts the 1934 Nuremberg rallies in Nazi Germany. It is replete with emotional appeals.
[8]If someone argued that drinking a certain brand of coffee *makes* you a beautiful person, the argument would be an instance of *false cause* (see **P2** below).

> We should help people in need.
> The disaster victims are people in need.
> So, we should help the disaster victims.

So, even if you contributed to the victims of a disaster strictly out of an emotional response—a sense of pity—you probably didn't do anything wrong.[9]

Of course, there are many cases in which there is a clear-cut fallacious appeal to pity, an appeal in which there is no moral obligation corresponding to a feeling of pity. At one time or another, your professor has probably heard something like this. It's usually toward the end of the semester:

> You have to give me at least a *B* in the course. If I don't receive at least a *B*, I won't be able to take classes in my major next semester (or I won't be able to graduate this semester, or I'll be placed on probation, or I'll be expelled and have to start repaying my loans, or . . .).
>
> You just have to accept my paper, even though it's six weeks late. I've had a very difficult semester. I've had to help my roommate deal with her drug problem. My parents are getting a divorce. And my cat had a difficult pregnancy. It was impossible to concentrate on a paper earlier in the semester! So, you just have to accept it, even if it's a bit late.

What is the problem? A professor's syllabus usually spells out the working principles of a course. Among those are the grading scale and policies regarding the late submission of work. Like moral principles, these policies are universal: They apply to everyone in the class. The fallacious appeals to pity contend that, due to an emotion-evoking situation, there are reasons for the professor to treat one student differently from the others.

A mark of an acceptable moral or procedural principle is that it can be universalized, that is, consistently applied in all similar cases. Fallacious cases of appeal to pity cannot be consistently universalized.

R6. Appeal to Force *(argumentum ad baculum)*

An argument commits the fallacy of appeal to force if it includes an implicit but unwarranted (or inappropriate) threat. Sometimes the threat is blatant: "If you want to keep working here, you should make a contribution to Greenpeace." Often the threat is more subtle. "You should contribute to

---

[9]This doesn't necessarily mean you did anything morally praiseworthy. We leave the issue of whether acting morally for nonmoral reasons is morally praiseworthy to the ethicists. Regardless of that issue, dropping money in a container marked "Tsunami Relief" doesn't guarantee that you've helped. Some organizations gather money "for" one disaster, but use the money for later disasters. Others spend a large portion of what you give on advertising and other expenses. So, you might want to check the practices of the organization to which you give so you can be reasonably certain your gift makes a difference.

Greenpeace. After all, you're *currently* an employee here." In either case, the argument is as follows:

> If you want to continue working here, then you should contribute to Greenpeace.
> You want to keep working here. (implicit premise)
> _____
> So, you should contribute to Greenpeace.

The argument is valid. The *reason* you are told you should contribute to Greenpeace is of the wrong sort. There should be no connection between your job status and your political contributions. The argument commits the fallacy of appeal to force.[10]

But there are *legitimate* appeals to force. You're driving down the Interstate at 73 miles per hour. The posted speed limit is 65 miles per hour. Suddenly there are flashing lights. You're pulled over, and a member of the state police approaches your car. "You were driving eight miles per hour over the posted speed limit. I'm going to let you go this time with a warning, but if it happens again, you can expect a fine of at least $240." There's a threat, but it is the job of law officers to enforce the law. The threat was perfectly legitimate. It was a nonfallacious appeal to force.

Similarly, there are cases that might resemble appeals to force but which are cases of advice. Your friend tells you to quit smoking because it will probably shorten your life, it will reduce your pool of friends, and it will discolor your teeth. These are undesirable consequences of smoking, but they're natural consequences of smoking. This is a case of giving you advice on the basis of reasonable predictions: Smoking will almost immediately reduce your pool of friends and, over a period of years, it will discolor your teeth and probably shorten your life.

R7. Irrelevant Conclusion *(ignoratio elenchi; non sequitur)*

An argument commits the fallacy of irrelevant conclusion when it draws a conclusion that is *not* suggested by the premises. Sometimes it is blatant:

> If you do well in college, you'll be able to find a good job. If you find a good job, you'll live a good life. So you should major in economics.

The expected conclusion (the conclusion that is entailed by the premises) is "If you do well in college, you'll live a good life." There is no clear connection between that statement and the conclusion given.

An argument that obscures the issue with attractive generalizations about some larger or different end commits the fallacy of irrelevant conclusion. Such

---

[10]Even if the person were working for the money-raising arm of Greenpeace, the appeal would be illegitimate, *unless* making such a contribution were part of his or her job description.

arguments sometimes convince readers or hearers to accept their conclusions by distracting attention from the main issue.

Example

All parents in this city want better schools for their children. My new tax proposal will raise enough money to build ten new schools and completely staff them with the most qualified teachers available. I need your support for this new proposal.

It is possible to agree to the need for better schools without agreeing to the speaker's specific proposal and the taxes to pay for it. The speaker gives no reasons why the specific proposal is the only possible solution to the school problem. There are no relevant premises that support this tax proposal as the best way to get the desired results.

One type of argument that commits the fallacy of irrelevant conclusion is called a *red herring*. This is always given in reply to another argument. It *does not* attack the premises of the argument. It discusses a different, perhaps related issue, and takes the conclusions regarding the second issue as a reason to reject the original argument.

Example

A commission of the United States government recently proposed closing a number of military bases. The reasons given for the proposed closings were that the bases in question duplicated what was being done more efficiently at other bases. By closing some bases and consolidating operations to others, the commission claimed that the government could save billions of dollars every year. A spokesperson for an affected city protested, "This shouldn't be done! It will cost the state over two and a half billion dollars per year if they close the base." The issue was whether the bases should be closed as a way of saving money for the *federal* government. It goes without saying that closing a military base will have a significant impact on the local economy of the areas in which the base was found. But that is irrelevant to the issue of saving federal government money.

Another type of argument that commits the fallacy of irrelevant conclusion is called a *straw person*. Like a red herring, it is an attack on an argument. It differs from a red herring insofar as it distorts the original argument. It either (incorrectly) claims that the argument assumed an additional premise and attacks the "assumed premise," or it claims the conclusion was stronger or in some way different from the stated conclusion and attacks the supposed conclusion.

Example _____

Natasha presented an argument concluding that the government should enact legislation that would assure that no citizen is systematically deprived of medical insurance. Lenny replies as follows: "What Natasha advocates is socialized medicine. Socialized medicine was tried in Canada and throughout Europe. The result in each case was a system that allocates health care on the basis of triage: If a treatment is not acutely needed, you're put on a waiting list. Canadians and Europeans regularly come to the United States for treatments they can't get at home for months or years. So, we must reject Natasha's argument." It's one thing to argue for a law that does not systematically deprive people of health care. It is something else to argue for socialized medicine, that is, a government-run health care system. Lenny's argument distorts Natasha's conclusion. It is a straw person argument.

SUMMARY: FALLACIES OF RELEVANCE	
Appeal to Ignorance *ad ignorantiam*	An appeal to ignorance is an argument of either of the following forms:
	1. We don't know that proposition p is true, so p is false.
	2. We don't know that proposition p is false, so p is true.
	The *fallacy* of argument from ignorance requires that two conditions occur. First, either the first premise or the second premise of the argument is false. Second, the *burden of proof*, the responsibility of showing that the premises are true, rests upon the person offering the argument, and, in fallacious cases, the arguer *does not* provide evidence of the truth of the premises.
Appeal to Illegitimate Authority *ad verecundiam*	An argument commits the fallacy of appeal to illegitimate authority if it appeals to someone or something as an authority on a particular subject who is not an authority on that subject.

Argument Against the Person (Personal Attack) *ad hominem*	An argument against the person replies to an argument by attacking the credibility of the arguer rather than the argument that was presented.
	    Abusive: An *abusive* argument against the person replies to an argument by attacking the arguer's character rather then the argument presented.
	    Circumstantial: A circumstantial argument against the person appeals to some

(continued)

	circumstances in which the arguer finds himself or herself as a reason to discredit the argument. *tu quoque*: A *tu quoque* focuses on inconsistencies between an argument and the arguer's actions.
Appeal to Emotion (Mob Appeal) *ad populum*	An argument commits the fallacy of appeal to emotion if it takes the fact that believing that a statement is true makes you "feel good" is a sufficient reason to believe that the statement is true.
Appeal to Pity *ad misericordiam*	The fallacy of appeal to pity takes an emotional response to an unfortunate situation as a reason to believe or act in a certain way.
Appeal to Force *ad baculum*	An argument commits the fallacy of appeal to force if it includes an implicit but unwarranted (or inappropriate) threat.

Irrelevant Conclusion *ignoratio elenchi* *non sequitur*	An argument commits the fallacy of irrelevant conclusion when it draws a conclusion that is *not* suggested by the premises.
	
	    Red herring: A reply to an argument that diverts attention from the issue.
	
	    Straw person: A reply to an argument that attacks an allegedly unstated premise (when that premise is *not* assumed) or distorts the conclusion and attacks the distorted version of the conclusion.

EXERCISES

I. Identify the fallacy of relevance that best characterizes each passage.

1. He is out of work. We can't blame him for getting drunk and crashing his car.
2. No, don't pick her for the basketball team. She is a computer nerd, so she probably can't play at all.
3. Tiger Woods's picture is on this box of cereal. Therefore, it must be good for you.
4. No experiment has ever proved for sure that there aren't any ghosts. So, ghosts exist.
5. Since he is a member of the National Rifle Association, he shouldn't be invited to our seminar on animal rights.
6. I had a Ford, and it got good gas mileage. I had a Chevy, and it got good gas mileage. So, I think I'll take up skydiving.

7. I haven't made my decision on your final grades yet. I want to see how much you support this school. I expect to see you all at the football game tonight.

8. My favorite movie star drinks this brand of water, so I am sure it must be the best.

9. You are gonna pass this test or I am gonna beat you!

10. I have been to this forest several times, and I have never seen a bear. There must not be any bears here.

11. A text-based society thinks differently than a video-based society. When you read, you think linearly, and linear thinking is logical thinking. You think differently when using your visual memory, so people who grow up watching TV will not be as logical as people who grow up reading books. TV is dumbing down our society.

12. Maggie has argued that the system of letter grades should be abolished. But such a position assumes that there are no genuine differences in the quality of work done by students, which is absurd. So the system of letter grades should not be abolished.

13. Women are much more emotional than men. To be president you have to be cool and rational under stress, so a woman should never be president.

14. Whales are the main food for our village during the winter. If you shut down our whale hunt this year because of the decline in the whale population then we will not eat. You must think whales are more important than us!

15. He says that he is a Christian. He must not believe in evolution.

16. The book of Genesis is Jewish, but the Jews see no conflict between evolution and creation. First comes light from darkness, then dry land from the waters, then fish and crawling things. . . . Moses described evolution before Darwin! And if Moses says evolution is true, then it must be.

17. Justice demands the death penalty for those that have murdered others. He killed our friend, and so now he must die! We are all here to see that justice is done.

18. Can't you see how miserable he is now that his wife and children are dead? He has already had his punishment. He was drunk and killed his wife and children, so now you want to kill him, too? What about the bartender that served a drunk man more drink? What about the boss that fired him and caused him to start drinking? Aren't they culpable, too? What about the rest of us? Didn't we see the way things were going for him? And we let it continue. He has already suffered enough for his crimes. If you convict this man, you convict yourselves.

19. Asteroids have been responsible for many cataclysmic extinctions on the earth. It is only a matter of time before another one comes our way. We must build a satellite defense system that will prevent the next one from hitting the earth.

20. Dr. Stark has argued that the petrochemical plant in town should be closed, since it poses major health risks to the community. With more than 300 employees, that plant is the second largest employer in town. Closing the plant would throw the town into an economic recession. So we can't afford to close the plant.

21. Birthdays come but once a year, so if we celebrate our unbirthdays, then we can have an unbirthday party all year long!

22. The poor women on welfare, the "welfare queens," are really the ones having the most children. Since the women who have the most children are the ones who are the fittest in the evolutionary paradigm, they must be the real winners in today's society.

23. A bumper sticker says: "Here is your brain: Ford. Here is your brain on drugs: Chevy."

24. Nietzsche was personally more philosophical than his philosophy. His talk about power, harshness, and superb immorality was the hobby of a harmless young scholar and constitutional invalid.
    —George Santayana, *Egotism in German Philosophy*

25. However, it matters very little now what the king of England either says or does; he hath wickedly broken through every moral and human obligation, trampled nature and conscience beneath his feet, and by a steady and constitutional spirit of insolence and cruelty procured for himself an universal hatred.
    —Thomas Paine, *Common Sense*

26. On the Senate floor in 1950, Joe McCarthy announced that he had penetrated "Truman's iron curtain of secrecy." He had eighty-one case histories of persons whom he considered to be Communists in the State Department. Of Case 40, he said, "I do not have much information on this except the general statement of the agency that there is nothing in the files to disprove his Communist connections."
    —Richard H. Rovere, *Senator Joe McCarthy*

27. To ignore the possibility that America was discovered by Africans because these explorers are "unknown" is irresponsible and arrogant. If we are unaware of an event, does that mean it never happened?
    —Andrew J. Perrin, "To Search for Truth,"
    The New York Times, 16 November 1990

28. According to R. Grunberger, author of *A Social History of the Third Reich*, Nazi publishers used to send the following notice to

German readers who let their subscriptions lapse: "Our paper certainly deserves the support of every German. We shall continue to forward copies of it to you, and hope that you will not want to expose yourself to unfortunate consequences in the case of cancellation."

29. But can you doubt that air has weight when you have the clear testimony of Aristotle affirming that all the elements have weight including air, and excepting only fire?

—Galileo Galilei, *Dialogues
Concerning Two New Sciences*

30. Like an armed warrior, like a plumed knight, James G. Blaine marched down the halls of the American Congress and threw his shining lances full and fair against the brazen foreheads of every defamer of his country and maligner of its honor. For the Republican Party to desert this gallant man now is worse than if an army should desert their general upon the field of battle.

—Robert G. Ingersoll, nominating speech at the
Republican National Convention, 1876

II. Each of the following passages may be plausibly criticized by some who conclude that it contains a fallacy, but each will be defended by some who deny that the argument is fallacious. Discuss the merits of each argument and explain why you conclude that it does or does not contain a fallacy of relevance.

31. Chairman of General Electric, Jack Welch, was challenged at a stockholder's meeting recently by a nun who argued that GE was responsible for the cleanup of the Hudson River where pollutants from GE's plants had for many years been allowed to collect. Welch flatly denied the company's responsibility, saying, "Sister, you have to stop this conversation. You owe it to God to be on the side of truth here."

—Elizabeth Kolbert, "The River,"
The New Yorker, 4 December 2000

32. "But I observe," says Cleanthes, "with regard to you, Philo, and all speculative sceptics, that your doctrine and practice are as much at variance in the most abstruse points of theory as in the conduct of common life."

—David Hume, *Dialogues Concerning Natural Religion*

33. Consider genetically engineered fish. Scientists hope that fish that contain new growth hormones will grow bigger and faster than normal fish. Other scientists are developing fish that could be introduced into cold, northern waters, where they cannot now survive. The intention is to boost fish production for food. The economic benefits may be obvious, but not the risks. Does this make the risks reasonable?

—Edward Bruggemann, "Genetic Engineering Needs Strict Regulation," *The New York Times*, 24 March 1992

34. Anytus: "Socrates, I think that you are too ready to speak evil of men: and, if you will take my advice, I would recommend you to be careful. Perhaps there is no city in which it is not easier to do men harm than to do them good, and this is certainly the case at Athens, as I believe that you know."

—Plato, *Meno*

35. In that melancholy book *The Future of an Illusion*, Dr. Freud, himself one of the last great theorists of the European capitalist class, has stated with simple clarity the impossibility of religious belief for the educated man of today.

—John Strachey, *The Coming Struggle for Power*

2.3 FALLACIES OF PRESUMPTION

Arguments seldom occur in a vacuum. Examining the context often will allow you to determine what can reasonably be taken for granted. The fallacies of presumption occur when an argument makes presuppositions unwarranted by the context. In some cases, it assumes the conclusion of the argument. In other cases, it assumes that all the relevant information has been presented.

P1. Complex Question

A complex question is a question that assumes another question has already been answered. We ask complex questions all the time, and in most cases they're perfectly acceptable. A friend might ask you, "What did you do on Saturday night?" The question is complex. It assumes you did *something* on Saturday night, which you did. You might answer, "I studied in the library" or "I went to a party." Someone who has known you for a time might ask, "Have you quit smoking?" Assuming that this person knew that you used to smoke, and therefore knew that the answer to the assumed question "Did you ever smoke?" is "Yes," there is nothing improper in the question. Now contrast those cases with a witness on the stand in court who is asked, "Have you quit doing drugs?" Whatever the witness answers—whether "Yes" or "No"—she admits that the answer to the assumed question, "Have you ever done drugs?," is "Yes." In this case, the question is *loaded*; answering it is self-incriminating. Any answer provides the basis for the conclusion, "You've done drugs."

A fallacious complex question provides the basis for a conclusion based on the answer to the assumed question. The question must either be "loaded"—that is, the answer to the assumed question places the answerer in a bad light—or the answer to the assumed question is false. Notice that the complex question is properly the *basis* for a fallacy, but by itself is not a fallacy, since it is not an argument. Nonetheless, since its answer provides the basis for an argument, it is traditionally listed among informal fallacies.

Examples

Have you stopped cheating in this course?

The question requires a "Yes" or "No" answer. If you answer in either way, you have admitted that you have cheated in the course.

When did George Washington cut down a cherry tree and say, "I cannot tell a lie"?

If you answer the question—"On his seventh birthday at 3:00 in the afternoon"—you have granted the truth of the claim, "George Washington cut down a cherry tree and said, 'I cannot tell a lie'," a claim most historians now believe is false.

What do you do if you're confronted with a complex question that can provide the basis for a fallacious inference? You divide the question. "The question 'Have you stopped cheating in this course?' assumes that I *have* cheated, which I *haven't*." "Before we can determine *when* George Washington cut down the cherry tree, we have to ask whether there is evidence *that* he cut it down."

P2. False Cause *(post hoc, ergo propter hoc; non causa pro causa)*

We generally look for causal connections in the world. By doing so, we not only can explain why things happen, we sometimes can prevent unwanted events from happening. **An argument commits the fallacy of false cause when it identifies something as a cause which is *not* a cause.**

Example

I've always worn the number *13* when I've played basketball. That's why I'm a star.

The number on your athletic jersey has no effect on your performance on the basketball court. If you do well, you might have certain natural abilities and you've certainly spent many hours honing your skills.

The cause of an event occurs before the event or at the same time as an event. If there's an earthquake, fires often follow. You're probably right if you say that the earthquake caused the gas lines to rupture, and the gas provided fuel for the fires. But not all cases in which one event occurs before another are cases of causal relations. There needs to be a very general pattern if your causal claim is to be justified.

Example _____

I walked under a ladder on the way to work this morning. I'll never do that again! I had just a horrible day!!!

Walking under the ladder was not the cause of the horrible day. It was just coincidence that the quality of the day corresponded to an old superstition. Of course, there could be some connection. If you were drenched with paint while walking under the ladder, it's unlikely that would be the beginning of a wonderful day. But even in that case, it's not walking under the ladder, as such, that was the cause of the less-than-ideal day.

_____

There are cases in which there might be no causal connection between one event and another, but the false belief that there is a connection can result in the desired effect.

Example _____

A few years ago a baseball team was in a slump. One day, their manager rushed into their locker room and said, "Give me your bats!" He took them and ran off. Just before the game he returned the bats and said, "There's a revivalist preacher in town. I had him bless all your bats. Now you can't lose!!!" The team went on to win the game 14–0.

The blessing of the bats is an unlikely cause of the team's success. The confidence instilled by the false causal belief might have played a role in the team's success.

_____

Sometimes you're not concerned with only one cause. You're concerned with a whole chain of causes: **A** causes **B**, which causes **C**, which causes **D**. In what is known as a *slippery slope argument*, things may begin fairly innocently, but they become progressively worse as you progress on the chain, as you slide down the slope. Here also, you need to ask whether the alleged causal relations are genuine. The following might be good advice:

Tailgating causes rear-end collisions. Being responsible for a rear-end collision causes your car insurance premiums to rise. Higher insurance premiums cause you to have less money to spend on enjoyable activities. So, you shouldn't tail-gate.

But the following involves at least one instance of a false cause, so it should be rejected.

Example _____

If you smoke tobacco, it will lead to (cause you to start) smoking marijuana. If you smoke marijuana, it will lead to harder drugs. If you use harder drugs, you'll need to turn to a life of crime to support your habit. If you turn to a life of crime, you'll end up in prison. So, you shouldn't smoke.

Smoking tobacco does not cause you to smoke marijuana. There are millions of people who smoke tobacco and use no other drugs. So, at least the first causal claim is false, and there is good reason to believe that at least some of the subsequent causal claims are false as well.

P3. Begging the Question *(petitio principii)*

An argument begs the question if it assumes as a premise what it sets out to prove as its conclusion. It can be blatant. Consider the parent's argument: "Why [for what reason] should you do as I say? Because I say it, that's why!" Often it is more subtle. The conclusion of the argument asserts the same proposition as the premise, but the wording is different. The fallacy of begging the question is illustrated by the following argument, reported long ago by Richard Whately: "To allow every man unbounded freedom of speech must always be, on the whole, advantageous to the state; for it is highly conducive to the interests of the community that each individual should enjoy a liberty, perfectly unlimited, of expressing his sentiments."

An argument that begs the question is a valid deductive argument. It's a sound deductive argument if the premise is true. The problem is that a proposition, even if true, cannot provide evidence for its own truth. So, since the premise and the conclusion assert the same proposition, the premise cannot provide evidence for the truth of the conclusion. Hence, it is fallacious.

Example _____

No one has more money than Joe does. So, you must agree that Joe is the world's richest person.

If the premise is true, the conclusion must be true, too. But this is because the conclusion merely restates the premise.

Sometimes the problem does not arise in a single argument. This problem is that there is a chain of arguments in which the premise of one argument is the conclusion of an argument later in the chain. This is called *arguing in a circle*.

Example _____

Because the Bible is the inspired word of God, it follows that everything the Bible says is true. And since everything the Bible says is true, it follows that it's the inspired word of God.

The premise of the first argument is the same as the conclusion of the second. It might be that the conclusions of both arguments are true, but the pair of arguments provides no reason to believe that either premise is true.

A third way to beg the question is on the basis of a *question-begging epithet.* An epithet is a descriptive adjective, noun, or phrase. If the premise of an argument uses terms that assume what is asserted in the conclusion, the argument begs the question by way of an epithet.

Example _____

All the evidence shows that that crook Cribbs stole the car. So, you have no choice but to convict him of larceny.

The issue is whether Cribbs is guilty of stealing a car. Referring to Cribbs as a crook begs the question.

P4. Accident

We argue from general truths and general principles all the time. If it's true that all humans eventually die and that Lolita is a human, we can correctly conclude that Lolita will eventually die. Similarly, some general principles tell you what your obligations (generally) are. For example, you are (generally) obligated to tell the truth; if you tell something to your lawyer or psychiatrist, she is (generally) obligated to keep it in confidence. **The fallacy of accident occurs when either (1) the general claim to which the argument appeals is false or (2) a general principle that holds in most cases is applied in a case in which it does not apply.** Let's consider the second case first.

Example _____

Sam promised to meet Chris for lunch. She's running a few minutes late, and on her way she sees a car drive off the road and run into a tree. She argues, "I promised to meet Chris for lunch. You should always keep your promises. So, I shouldn't aid the accident victims."

There is a conflict of principles: 1. you should keep the promises you make and 2. you should aid people in distress. In this case, the second

is more important than the first. There will probably be few bad consequences if she misses the luncheon. The accident victims could die if she
doesn't stop and render aid. Sam's argument commits the fallacy of
accident.

When there is a conflict of principles, it's not always obvious on which
side your primary obligation lies. You're a lawyer. You have an obligation to
protect the interests of your client. You also have an obligation to act to uphold
the laws of the state and to act in the public interest. Let's say your client is
charged with murder. He's out on bail while awaiting trial. During that time,
two more murders are committed, and, while he confessed to neither of them,
there is a growing body of evidence—known only to you—that your client
committed them. What are you obligated to do?

A common version of the first version of the fallacy is based on stereotypes. A *stereotype* is a false, though commonly made, general claim about
a group of people. "Redheads are hot tempered," is an example of a stereotype. The premise stating the stereotype is often unstated.

Example _____

Dan is a redhead. So, you can expect him to blow up at the least provocation.

The implicit premise is "All redheads are hot tempered." The argument
is valid. The suppressed premise is false. *Some* redheads are tempera-
mental, but so are some blonds and brunettes. *Some* redheads are very
even tempered. So, the argument is unsound.

A variation on stereotypes is based on the place from which a person
comes. This is sometimes known as the *genetic fallacy*.

Example _____

Bridget is from a rural area. So, she can't be very bright.

The implicit premise is "No person from a rural area is intelligent." That
premise is false, as a perusal of lists of Nobel Prize winners (including
Alexander Fleming, Norman Borlaug, and Jimmy Carter) or past
American presidents (including Herbert Hoover, Jimmy Carter, and Bill
Clinton) should convince you.[11]

---

[11]Sometimes stereotypical arguments are considered cases of false cause. The suggestion
then is that having red hair causes people to be hot tempered, or coming from a rural area
causes them to be unintelligent. If appeals to such stereotypes are given as a reason to reject
a person's argument, it is *also* a case of argument against the person.

P5. Converse Accident (Hasty Generalization)

We reach inductive generalizations on the basis of a limited amount of data. The truth of such generalizations—whether universal or statistical—is never certain. It can be revised as additional data become available. Until Australia was discovered, it would have been a reasonable generalization to conclude that all swans are white, since, until then, all known swans were white. (There are black swans in Australia.) The fallacy of converse accident (hasty generalization) occurs in relatively extreme cases. **An argument commits the fallacy of converse accident (hasty generalization) when a general claim—whether universal or statistical—is reached on the basis of insufficient evidence, particularly when the sample on which the generalization is based is atypical.**

Examples

Dan is a redhead. Dan is hot tempered. So, all redheads are hot tempered.

Here you're going from one case to a general conclusion. Given only one case, there is not reason to believe the case is typical.

During the first week of the first semester, I took a survey in my freshman dorm and found that two-thirds of the students believed that doing well in college classes requires very little work outside of class. So, two-thirds of the student body believes that doing well in college requires little work outside of class.

First-semester freshmen are not typical college students. Usually before the end of their first semester they discover that doing well requires work outside of class, often a considerable amount of work.

As we'll see in Chapter 9, there are several factors that should be taken into account to increase the probability that an inductive generalization is reasonable. Does this mean that you can never generalize from a small sample? No, but the cases in which doing so is reasonable are quite special.

Example

Alejandra has discovered a new chemical element. She has very little of the element—far less than a gram. She conducts a number of experiments and publishes a list of the properties of the element in a scientific journal.

A lovely thing about a chemical element is that the chemical properties of one sample are exactly like those of another sample. Further, when a new element is discovered, it fits into a large body of existing scientific knowledge. So, on the basis of some of its properties, others can reasonably be predicted. That's why Marie and Pierre Curie could describe the properties of radium on the basis of a sample of less than a decigram. This kind of situation, however, is almost unique. So, you should always be skeptical of generalizations from a small number of cases.

Some students find the distinction between accident and converse accident (hasty generalization) puzzling. The difference is in the position of the general statement. If an argument commits the fallacy of *accident*, one *premise* is a general statement. The problem is that the statement is either false or incorrectly applied. If an argument commits the fallacy of *converse accident* (hasty generalization), the general statement is the *conclusion*. The problem is that the premises fail to support the general conclusion.

Examples

The same statements can be found in both an argument that commits the fallacy of accident and converse accident, but their positions will differ.

Accident:

All graduates of private colleges are wealthy persons. (This premise is false.)
Dana is a graduate of a private college.
Dana is a wealthy person.

Converse Accident:

Dana is a graduate of a private college.
Dana is a wealthy person.
All graduates of private colleges are wealthy persons. (This conclusion is false.)

P6. Suppressed Evidence

If you're discussing an issue, there are always at least two sides to consider. It is often difficult to determine what the evidence on either side of the issue is. Sometimes it is difficult to determine what counts as evidence. Further, no one presenting a persuasive argument is obligated to discuss both sides of an issue, although she is obligated not to hide relevant information. **An argument commits the fallacy of suppressed evidence if it ignores evidence that is contrary to the conclusion it defends.**

Examples

Mr. Big of Big Biz argues that your town would benefit by allowing him to build a factory. He cites facts regarding similar towns where he built factories: The unemployment rate dropped by an average of 7 to 10 percent, the local economy grew by an average of 15 to 20 percent within five years, and property values increased.

Are those sufficient reasons to construct the factory? Mr. Big knew, but failed to mention, 1. that in past cases most of the factory workers were "imported," which had often changed the character of the town, 2. that in similar towns crime rates had risen by an average of 40 to 70 percent within the first two years of the factory's operation, and 3. that the need for additional schools and services had increased local taxes by an average of 50 percent in the first five years of the factory's operation. These facts are not favorable for allowing the factory to move into town. The unfavorable evidence is relevant to the decision, but it was suppressed.

Mr. Smith is attempting to convince you to buy a whole life (nonterm) insurance policy. "There's money if you live: You can cash in the policy when you retire. There's money for your family if you die. And you'll never pay a dime more than you'll pay today."

While all this is true, it's not the whole story. If your primary interest is security for your family, you receive the most coverage with term insurance, but the rates will increase as you get older and there is not the "cash value" found in whole life. If you want to invest, life insurance probably is not your best choice: It's safe, but the returns are usually low. Even if you want something that is both insurance and an investment, you might push Mr. Smith to tell you how the several policies his company sells balances one objective against the other.

The old adage "Buyer beware!" is generally good advice. Whether you're buying goods, services, or ideas, the arguer is unlikely to set out the case against his or her position. So, you're generally wise to look for evidence that was suppressed.

P7. False Dichotomy

As we'll see in Chapter 7, a common deductive argument form is known as disjunctive syllogism. Where p and q are variables that can be replaced by any statements, it is an argument of the following form:

Either p is true or q is true.
p is not true.
So, q is true.

The first premise may be called the disjunctive premise. **A disjunctive syllogism commits the fallacy of false dichotomy if its disjunctive premise is false.** You are often faced with a choice between two alternatives, when there are other options.

Examples _____

Either you're going to vote for the Democrats, or you're going to vote for the Republicans. You've assured me that you're not going to vote for the Democrats. So, you've got to vote for the Republicans.

There are third parties, and there is always the option not to vote. The argument commits the fallacy of false dichotomy.

Either Tristan went to Chicago or he went to Denver. He didn't go to Denver. So, he went to Chicago.

Let's say that Tristan went to Los Angles, rather than either Chicago or Denver. In that case, the disjunctive premise is false, and the argument commits the fallacy of false dichotomy.

SUMMARY: FALLACIES OF PRESUMPTION	
Complex Question	A fallacious complex question provides the basis for a conclusion based on the answer to the assumed question. The question must either be "loaded," that is, the answer to the assumed question places the answerer in a bad light, or the answer to the assumed question is false.
False Cause	An argument commits the fallacy of false cause when it identifies something as a cause which is *not* a cause.
Begging the Question *petitio principii*	An argument begs the question if it assumes as a premise what it sets out to prove as its conclusion. This can occur when: 1. The conclusion of the argument is merely a restatement of the premise. 2. In a chain of arguments, the conclusion of the last argument is a premise of the first (circular argument). 3. The premise of an argument uses terms that assume what is asserted in the conclusion (question-begging epithet).
Accident	The fallacy of accident occurs when an argument appeals to a general claim and either (1) the general claim to which the argument appeals is false or (2) a general principle that holds in most cases is applied in a case in which it does not apply.
Converse Accident (Hasty Generalization)	An argument commits the fallacy of converse accident (hasty generalization) when a *(continued)*

	general claim—whether universal or statistical—is reached on the basis of insufficient evidence, particularly when the sample on which the generalization is based is atypical.
Suppressed Evidence	An argument commits the fallacy of suppressed evidence if it ignores evidence that is contrary to the conclusion it defends.
False Dichotomy	A disjunctive syllogism commits the fallacy of false dichotomy if its disjunctive premise is false.

EXERCISES

Identify the fallacy of presumption that best characterizes each passage.

1. Every time the barometer drops it rains. The barometer must somehow be able to make it rain.

2. That fire engine was going over 60 mph in a 35 mph zone. The police should give the driver a ticket.

3. Are you still stealing coins from parking meters?

4. My uncle smoked three packs of cigarettes every day and he lived to be ninety-one years old. Smoking can't be bad for your health.

5. We should drill for oil in the Alaskan Wildlife Refuge because that's where the oil is.

6. "The sole purpose of language is to voice disagreement with what others have said." "I disagree." (Or, "I agree.")

7. Either you are for me or you are against me. If you are for me then you will be saved! If you are against me then you will perish in the flames of hell. So are you with me or are you going to hell?

8. The craziest people in any society are the ones that leave for the frontier to get away from everyone. The craziest people in Europe left for the new frontier of America. When the east coast started getting civilized those who couldn't stand other people went west, pushing the frontier farther and farther. When they got to Alaska, they couldn't go any farther, so it is no wonder that Alaska is full of crazy people. And most of those are men! That is why they say, if you are a woman looking for a man, the odds are good in Alaska, but the goods are odd.

9. There are more lawyers per capita in America than anywhere else on earth. It is no wonder nothing ever gets done in America.

10. God is that of which nothing greater can be conceived, so God must exist. Otherwise, a thing greater than God can be conceived, namely, a God who also exists.

11. Life is a state of mind. So do not ask where heaven is or when heaven will come. It is all around you, only you don't see it.

12. Given the medical evidence regarding the relationship between cholesterol and heart disease, the choice is clear: Give up meat or die of a heart attack!

13. First comes love, then comes marriage, then comes Johnny with the baby carriage!

14. If we allow euthanasia for those who are terminally ill and request it, it won't be long before society begins pressuring the old and infirm to get out of the way and make room for the young. Before long the government will be deciding who should live and who should die.

15. This computer game has lots of fighting and adventures in it. You'll like it.

16. Voting for the state bond issue will not raise taxes because all costs of administering the bonds will be drawn from the lottery fund.

17. Either you support the Republicans or you support the Democrats. In either case, the government is going to get bigger and the taxes are going to go up!

18. Absence makes the heart grow fonder. So a little time away from one another will be good for you.

19. Everyone who has a job finds a way of getting out of jury duty, so the only ones left on juries are those that will let criminals off no matter what the charge or the evidence.

20. Statistics show that, in high school, girls begin to have lower self esteem than boys, so there must be something in our school system that lowers the self-esteem of girls.

21. Statistics show that, in high school, girls begin to have lower self-esteem than boys. Since girls mature faster than boys, it must be because the girls' increasing maturity gives them a more realistic view of themselves than boys have of themselves.

22. What did you do last Sunday afternoon?

23. Furniture is expensive. Either you spend your money on the furniture itself, or you spend your money on the tools and wood to make it. In either case, you'll spend thousands of dollars on furniture.

24. My generation was taught about the dangers of social diseases, how they are contracted, and the value of abstinence. Our schools did not teach us about contraception. They did not pass out condoms, as many of today's schools do. And not one of the girls in any of my classes, not even in college, became pregnant out of wedlock. It wasn't until people began teaching the children about contraceptives that our problems with pregnancy began.

—Frank Webster, "No Sex Education, No Sex," *Insight*, 17 November 1997

25. In 1960, this great country had the finest public schools in the world. After thirty-five years and spending billions of dollars of Federal money, our public schools rank near the bottom of the industrialized world. What happened? The Federal Government intruded into public education. We now have the largest number of functional illiterates in the industrialized world.

—Ross Perot, 14 September 1996, in a speech
to the Christian Coalition in Washington, DC,
during the presidential campaign of 1996

2.4   FALLACIES OF AMBIGUITY

Words and sentences are often *ambiguous*: They have more than one meaning. Usually we have little trouble determining the intended meaning. If the meaning of a word, phrase, or sentence shifts in the course of an argument and the acceptability of the conclusion depends upon that shift in meaning, the argument commits a fallacy of ambiguity.

A1. Equivocation

To equivocate is to use a word in two senses. **An argument commits the fallacy of *equivocation* if there is a shift in the meaning of a word or phrase in the course of an argument.**

Example

Honda is the top car in America today. A top is a children's toy. Therefore, Hondas are children's toys.

Sometimes equivocation is obvious and absurd and is used in a joking line or passage. Lewis Carroll's account of the adventures of Alice in *Through the Looking Glass* is replete with clever and amusing equivocations such as this one:

"Who did you pass on the road?," the King went on, holding his hand out to the messenger for some hay.
   "Nobody," said the messenger.
   "Quite right," said the King; "this young lady saw him too. So, of course, Nobody walks slower than you."

The equivocation here is subtle: The first "nobody" means simply "no person," but then the pronoun *him* is used as if "nobody" named a person, and finally "Nobody" is capitalized and plainly used as a name for the person putatively passed on the road.

Equivocal arguments are always fallacious, but equivocation is not always silly or comic, as will be seen in the example discussed in the following excerpt:

> There is an ambiguity in the phrase "have faith in" that helps make faith look respectable. When a man says that he has faith in the president, he is assuming that it is obvious and known to everybody that there is a president, that the president exists, and he is asserting his confidence that the president will do good work on the whole. But, if a man says he has faith in telepathy, he does not mean that he is confident that telepathy will do good work on the whole, but that he believes that telepathy really occurs sometimes, that telepathy exists. Thus the phrase "to have faith in x" sometimes means to be confident that good work will be done by x, who is assumed or known to exist, but at other times it means to believe that x exists. Which does it mean in the phrase, "have faith in God?" It means ambiguously both, and the self-evidence of what it means in the one sense recommends what it means in the other sense. If there is a perfectly powerful and good god, it is self-evidently reasonable to believe that he will do good. In this sense "have faith in God" is a reasonable exhortation. But it insinuates the other sense, namely "believe that there is a perfectly powerful and good god, no matter what the evidence." Thus the reasonableness of trusting God if he exists is used to make it seem also reasonable to believe that he exists.[12]

One kind of equivocation deserves special mention. This is the mistake that arises from the misuse of *relative terms*—tall and short, for example, or big and little—which have different meanings in different contexts. A big elephant, for example, is not the same size as a big mouse. Certain forms of argument that are valid for nonrelative terms break down when relative terms are substituted for them. This argument is valid: "An elephant is an animal; therefore, a gray elephant is a gray animal." But this parallel argument commits the fallacy of equivocation: "An elephant is an animal; therefore, a small elephant is a small animal."

A2. Amphiboly

Sometimes loose sentence construction leaves unclear what proposition is expressed by a sentence. For example, if you read the headline "Man Robs, Then Kills Himself,"[13] you might momentarily wonder how he could rob himself. An extra word, such as *bank* or *store* after *robs*, would have eliminated the ambiguity. **An argument commits the fallacy of *amphiboly* when an ambiguous statement serves as a premise with the interpretation that makes it true, and a conclusion is drawn from it on an interpretation that makes the premise false.**

In 2001 I received a memo that read, "We are going to commemorate the 100th anniversary of Giuseppe Verdi's death at James Madison University." I

---

[12]Richard Robinson, *An Atheist's Values* (Oxford University Press, Oxford, 1964), p. 121.
[13]Quoted in The Bathroom Reader's Institute, *Uncle John's Biggest Ever Bathroom Reader* (Thunder Bay Press, 2002), p. 410.

EQUIVOCATION

Tom Cruise is a big star. Astronomers tell us that planets revolve around big stars. So, there must be planets revolving around Tom Cruise.

In this case we have a triple equivocation. The first is a play on two meanings of the word *star*. The second is a play on two meanings of *big*, one in the relative sense of *large* and the other in the nonrelative sense of *wildly popular*. This second equivocation sets up the third, a play on the relative meaning of *big*, in that a big star in the astronomical sense is not the same size as a big movie star.

immediately drew the conclusion that the Italian composer died at JMU. Then I realized that the conclusion was false: The school wasn't founded until 1908. I'd constructed an amphibolous argument on the basis of an ambiguous sentence. What they meant was, "We at James Madison University are going to commemorate the 100th anniversary of Giuseppe Verdi's death."

Example _____

Rev. Smith said it was his privilege to marry six people yesterday. So, Rev. Smith is a bigamist.

The first sentence is probably true if it is taken to mean that Rev. Smith performed a marriage ceremony for three couples.

_____

Remember, there has to be an argument for there to be a fallacy. So, there is no fallacy in these famous lines from the Marx Brothers movie *Animal Crackers*:

Groucho (Captain Spalding): One morning I shot an elephant in my pajamas. How he got into my pajamas, I don't know.[14]

_____

[14] *Animal Crackers* (Paramount Pictures, 1930).

A3. Accent

An argument may prove deceptive, and invalid, when the shift of meaning within it arises from changes in the emphasis given to its words or parts. **An argument commits the fallacy of** *accent* **when a premise relies for its apparent meaning on one possible emphasis, but a conclusion is drawn from it that relies on the meaning of the same words accented differently.** Consider, as an illustration, the different meanings (five? or more?) that can be given to the statement, "We should not speak ill of our friends," depending on which word is emphasized.

Example

The label on the sauce I'm using for supper says, "Shake well before using." So, I decided to shake it right after breakfast.

The intended accent is *"Shake well* before using," but the speaker puts the accent on "Shake *well before* using."

A second version of accent is based upon quotation. The quotation either is taken out of context or is incomplete, and it shifts its meaning. Let's say that Heather argued that there are no cases in which abortion is permissible. Part of her argument was a reply to an objection: "Some would claim that a woman's right to control her body and everything that happens to it trumps any arguments against abortion, but this is unreasonable because . . . ." Sonya replied to Heather's argument as follows, "Heather said that 'a woman's right to control her body and everything that happens to it trumps any arguments against abortion'—those are her very words. So, her argument against abortion must be rejected." By quoting the words out of context, the intent of Heather's words is distorted.[15]

> **ESSENTIAL** HINTS
>
> After Richard Roeper named *Little Nicky* his choice for worst movie of 2000, Roger Ebert commented: "I haven't had a whole lot of enthusiasm for a lot of Adam Sandler's movies, and you may recall that on this show I said I thought *Little Nicky* was actually the *best* Sandler movie, even though I gave it a Thumbs Down. And amazingly in the ads they just quoted, "'The best movie Adam Sandler has ever made.' Roger Ebert," you know.
>
> **Roeper:** "Well, you said that though."
>
> **Ebert:** "But it was bad, you know. I wasn't able to get that in, so I'm glad you gave me an opportunity to set the record straight.
>
> "The Worst Movies of 2000," *Ebert and Roeper and the Movies*, January 2001.

---

[15]Given that Sonya suggests that Heather's position is inconsistent—when it is not because the words introduce an objection—this might also be seen as an instance of argument against the person.

The previous example might be an example of an intentional distortion. It can also happen by carelessness. If you're reading an interpretation of a philosophical or literary work, you would do well to check the context of most quotations upon which conclusions are based. For example, at one point in his *Treatise of Human Nature*, David Hume (1711–1776) argues that, given Descartes's definition of substance, all perceptions (states of mind) must be considered substances.[16] So, should you conclude that Hume took perceptions to be substances? Does it make any difference that in the following paragraph he explicitly states, "A substance is entirely different from a perception"[17]?

There can be similar distortions based on pictorial representations. A few years ago I received an ad for an allergy medicine. It was composed of two pictures. One showed a picture of two empty rocking chairs. This represented how things were before taking the product. The second picture showed two people in conversation with the empty rocking chairs far in the background. This was the "after" picture. My copy of the ad was imperfect: There were faint blue lines running through the pictures. I concluded that one picture had been cropped in two different ways to form the two pictures.[18]

Even the literal truth can be manipulated to deceive with accent. Disgusted with his first mate who was repeatedly inebriated on duty, the ship's captain noted in the log, almost every day, "The mate was drunk today." The angry mate took his revenge: Keeping the log himself on a day that the captain was ill, the mate recorded, "The captain was sober today."

A4. Composition

An argument commits the fallacy of composition if it improperly concludes that a property true of a part of a whole applies to the whole or that a property true of a member of a class applies to the whole class.

Example

Every part of this machine is light, therefore this machine as a whole must be light.

The mistake here is obvious: If enough light parts are added together, the whole will not be light. So this conclusion could be false even if the premise is true.

---

[16]David Hume, *A Treatise of Human Nature*, edited by L. A. Selby-Bigge, 2nd edition revised by P. H. Nidditch (Oxford: Clarendon Press, 1978), p. 233.

[17]Hume, *Treatise*, p. 234.

[18]My wife, who suffers from allergies, uses the product in question. She says it works. Of course, *I* asked whether it causes you to crop pictures differently. I was charged with the fallacy of false cause.

The second type of fallacy of composition turns on a confusion of the *distributive use* and the *collective use* of a general term. A term is used *distributively* when it refers to attributes of each member of a group or set of objects individually. A term is used *collectively* when it refers to attributes of the members of the group taken as a whole (collection). Here are some examples to illustrate the distinction:

Example

Busses use more fuel than cars.

If the terms *busses* and *cars* are used distributively, this proposition is true. An individual bus uses more fuel than an individual car uses.

Cars use more fuel than busses.

If the terms *cars* and *busses* are used collectively here, this proposition is true. Because there are far more cars than busses, collectively cars use more fuel than busses.

The second form of the fallacy of composition occurs when inference is drawn from what is true of a term taken distributively to what is true of a term taken collectively.

Example

Busses use more fuel than cars. So, no fuel will be saved if we switch from individual cars to public transportation.

This argument commits the fallacy of composition. Busses individually take more fuel than cars. There are far more cars then busses. So, the entire class of cars take more fuel than the entire class of busses. So, fuel almost certainly would be saved if there were a shift from individual cars to public transportation.

But you can't simply yell "Composition!" every time you see an argument that proceeds from a part to a whole or from a member of a class to a class as a whole. Sometimes the move is legitimate, so you have to look at the individual case.

Example

The engine in my car weights over three hundred pounds. So, my car weighs over three hundred pounds.

The engine is a part of the car. If that alone weights over 300 pounds then it plus additional parts—each of which has some positive weight— must weigh over 300 pounds.

A5. Division

Division is the mirror image of composition. **An argument commits the fallacy of division if it illegitimately claims that a term that is true of a whole is true of a part or a term that is true of a class of things is true of a member of that class.**

Example _____

People in China require more drinking water than people in the United States, so the Chinese must be thirstier than Americans.

The premise compares the Chinese people to the American people collectively. Because the Chinese are collectively more numerous than the Americans, they need more water to drink. But it does not follow that people in China distributively—individual Chinese—need more water than people in the United States.

Another example: To argue that conventional weapons have killed more people than nuclear weapons, and therefore that conventional weapons are more dangerous than nuclear weapons, would be to commit the fallacy of division of the second type.

Like composition, there are legitimate cases of division. If my computer weighs fewer than fifteen pounds, I can correctly infer that any part of my computer weighs fewer than fifteen pounds. So, as in the case of composition, you might need to think a bit before you declare an inference a fallacy.

The fallacy of division, which springs from a kind of ambiguity, resembles the fallacy of accident, which springs from unwarranted presumption. Likewise, the fallacy of composition, also flowing from ambiguity, resembles converse accident, another fallacy of presumption. But these likenesses are superficial.

If we were to infer, from looking at a large machine, that because one or two parts happen to be well-designed, and therefore that every one of its many parts is well-designed, we would commit the fallacy of converse accident (hasty generalization). For what is true about one or two parts surely might not be true of all. If we were to examine every single part and find each carefully made, and from that finding infer that the entire machine is carefully made, we would also reason fallaciously, because however carefully the individual parts were produced, they may have been *assembled* awkwardly or carelessly, or the design of the machine might be defective. But here the fallacy is one of composition. In converse accident, one argues that some atypical members of a class have a specified attribute, and therefore that all members of the class, distributively, have that attribute; in composition, one argues that, since each and every member of the class has that attribute, the class *itself* (collectively) has that attribute. The difference is great. In converse accident, all predications are distributive; whereas in the composition fallacy, the mistaken inference is from distributive to collective predication.

Similarly, division and accident are two distinct fallacies; their superficial resemblance hides the same kind of underlying difference. In division, we argue (mistakenly) that, since the class itself has a given attribute, each of its members also has it. Thus, it is the fallacy of division to conclude that, because an army as a whole is nearly invincible, each of its units is nearly invincible. But in accident, we argue (also mistakenly) that, because some rule applies in general, there are no special circumstances in which it might not apply. Thus, we commit the fallacy of accident when we insist that a person should be fined for ignoring a "No Swimming" sign when jumping into the water to rescue someone from drowning.

Accident **and** *converse accident* **are** *fallacies of presumption,* **in which we assume that for which we have no warrant**. This involves reasoning improperly from or to general statements or principles. *Composition* **and** *division* **are** *fallacies of ambiguity,* **resulting from the multiple uses and meanings of terms.**This involves reasoning improperly about wholes or parts and classes or members. Wherever the words or phrases used may mean one thing in one part of the argument and another thing in another part, and wherever those different meanings are deliberately or accidentally confounded, we may expect the argument to be bad.

SUMMARY: FALLACIES OF AMBIGUITY	
Equivocation	An argument commits the fallacy of *equivocation* if there is a shift in the meaning of a word or phrase in the course of an argument.
Amphiboly	An argument commits the fallacy of *amphiboly* when an ambiguous statement serves as a premise with the interpretation that makes it true and a conclusion is drawn from it on an interpretation that makes the premise false.
Accent	An argument commits the fallacy of *accent* when a premise relies for its apparent meaning on one possible emphasis, but a conclusion is drawn from it that relies on the meaning of the same words accented differently. One form of this fallacy occurs when a quotation is incomplete or taken out of context, and the meaning of the quotation changes. *(continued)*

Composition	An argument commits the fallacy of composition if it improperly concludes that a property true of a part of a whole applies to the whole, or that a property true of a member of a class applies to the whole class.
Division	An argument commits the fallacy of division if it illegitimately claims that a term that is true of a whole is true of a part, or a term that is true of a class of things is true of a member of that class.

EXERCISES

I. Identify the fallacy of ambiguity that best characterizes each passage.

1. These paint colors are lovely. So the portrait will definitely be lovely.

2. SUE: You're going with me tonight.
    JANE: I am?
    SUE: I'm glad you agree.

3. That car is a real creampuff. Creampuffs are good dipped in coffee. That car will be good dipped in coffee.

4. The painting is horrible. So the colors in it must be horrible, too.

5. Being perfectly frank, you should probably lie about who spilled the milk.

6. I went to a beauty salon and had a mudpack to make myself look more beautiful. It worked for a couple of days. Then the mud fell off.

7. Little baby ducks walk softly because little baby ducks can't hardly walk.

8. The Pilgrims set sail from Plymouth and after sailing across the Atlantic finally arrived in . . . Plymouth! So they must have not gone very far.

9. "In this box, I have a 10-foot snake."
    "You can't fool me, Teacher. Snakes don't have feet!"

II. Identify and explain the fallacies of ambiguity that appear in the following passages.

10. Robert Toombs is reputed to have said, just before the Civil War, "We could lick those Yankees *with* cornstalks." When he was asked after the war what had gone wrong, he is reputed to have said, "It's very simple. Those damyankees refused to fight with cornstalks."

    —E. J. Kahn, Jr., "Profiles (Georgia),"
    The New Yorker, 13 February 1978

11. To press forward with a properly ordered wage structure in each industry is the first condition for curbing competitive bargaining; but there is no reason why the process should stop there. What is good for each industry can hardly be bad for the economy as a whole.

—Edmond Kelly, *Twentieth Century Socialism*

12. . . . each person's happiness is a good to that person, and the general happiness, therefore, a good to the aggregate of all persons.

—John Stuart Mill, *Utilitarianism*

13. No man will take counsel, but every man will take money: Therefore money is better than counsel.

—Jonathan Swift

14. Fallaci wrote her: "You are a bad journalist because you are a bad woman."

—Elizabeth Peer, "The Fallaci Papers,"
Newsweek, 1 December 1980

15. A Worm-eating Warbler was discovered by Hazel Miller in Concord, while walking along the branch of a tree, singing, and in good view. *(New Hampshire Audubon Quarterly)*

That's our Hazel—surefooted, happy, and with just a touch of the exhibitionist.

—*The New Yorker*, 2 July 1979

III. Each of the following passages may be plausibly criticized by some who conclude that it contains a fallacy, but each will be defended by some who deny that the argument is fallacious. Discuss the merits of the argument in each passage, and explain why you conclude that it does (or does not) contain a fallacy of ambiguity.

16. Seeing that eye and hand and foot and every one of our members has some obvious function, must we not believe that in like manner a human being has a function over and above these particular functions?

—Aristotle, *Nicomachean Ethics*

17. Mr. Stace says that my writings are "extremely obscure," and this is a matter as to which the author is the worst of all possible judges. I must therefore accept his opinion. As I have a very intense desire to make my meaning plain, I regret this.

—Bertrand Russell, "Reply to Criticisms,"
in P. A. Schilpp, ed., *The Philosophy of Bertrand Russell*
(Evanston, IL: The Library of Living Philosophers), p. 707

18. The only proof capable of being given that an object is visible, is that people actually see it. The only proof that a sound is audible, is that people hear it: and so of the other sources of our

experience. In like manner, I apprehend, the sole evidence it is possible to produce that anything is desirable, is that people actually desire it.

—John Stuart Mill, *Utilitarianism*, ch. 4

19. Thomas Carlyle said of Walt Whitman that he thinks he is a big poet because he comes from a big country.

—Alfred Kazin, "The Haunted Chamber,"
The New Republic, 23 June 1986, p. 39

20. All phenomena in the universe are saturated with moral values. And, therefore, we can come to assert that the universe for the Chinese is a moral universe.

—T. H. Fang, *The Chinese View of Life*

IV. Consider all the fallacies covered in this chapter. Which of the following passages commits an informal fallacy? If the passage commits a fallacy, name the fallacy and explain why the fallacy is committed. If the passage commits no fallacy, explain why it does not.

21. ROGER MURTAUGH: George.
    GEORGE: Yes, sir?
    ROGER: Home. Out.
    GEORGE: But, sir . . .
    ROGER: George, I got a gun.
    GEORGE: Yes, sir. [George leaves.]

—*Lethal Weapon 2* (Burbank: Warner Bros., 1989)

22. A recent report by the Department of Agriculture reports that over 10 percent of all food consumed in the United States is from the inside of cars. So you shouldn't be surprised if you find large bites taken from your car's seats.

23. "Of course Thomas Jefferson would have been a member of WMRA, had he been around at this time."

—Announcer on WMRA-FM,
Harrisonburg, VA, July 3, 1998

24. It's not snowing, so it's not cold.

25. It's the party of peace and prosperity! Vote Republican!

26. The federal government has no right to control the production of wine, for wine is made by pressing grapes, and the First Amendment guarantees that "Congress shall make no law . . . abridging the freedom . . . of the press."

27. Hitchhiker: "I stood on Route 150 for three hours without getting a ride. As soon as I put on my stocking cap, I got a ride all the way to Capital City. So it was the cap that got me the ride, and now I always wear it when I hitch."

28. Everyone should spend a couple of years in the Army, for it certainly helped a guy in my high-school class who used to be lazy and a drug-user.

29. Boss: Is that harebrained scheme of yours going to have detrimental effects on company profits?

    Employee: No, my study suggests it will improve profits.

    Boss: Nonetheless, since you admit it's a harebrained scheme, we're going to have to make some changes around here!

30. Ms. Margroff argues that the government's deficit spending is an economic time bomb that will ultimately destroy the country. But the American people have demanded a national health-care system. We have obligations to retired people, the unemployed, and the underemployed. Defense is still a pressing need. And the tax revenues simply will not cover everything. So deficit spending is here to stay.

31. It was a unique briefcase that Ms. Nehrer lost, for her ad in the paper reads, "Lost: American Tourister briefcase with eyeglasses."

32. We must have a free press. For we must not restrict the rights of our news media to inform us of the facts as they see them and to voice their opinions on the central issues of the day.

33. We must not allow children to play with firecrackers, for Col. Oakdale, the head of the Army Demolition Squad, says that their fuses burn erratically.

34. My new car is well-designed. Therefore, its radiator is well-designed.

35. Boss to employee: You will want to increase your giving to the United Way this year. After all, you should be thankful that you're *currently* in a position to be charitable.

36. All sorority members are women. So Josephine, a member of Sigma Alpha Psi sorority, is a woman.

37. It would be terrible if the government decreased the size of its welfare program. Think of all those children who would suffer from malnutrition and exposure to the cold.

38. It is improper to charge persons bail to get out of jail, since the Eighth Amendment to the Constitution asserts that ". . . bail shall not be required."

39. Alicia has argued that recycling paper is beneficial to the environment. But her argument is reasonable only if one assumes that there are recycling centers in every city and town across the country. But any town of less than 2,500 residents is unlikely to have its own recycling center. So, we must reject her argument.

40. We should reject arguments for tighter environmental controls on industry, since such controls are certain to reduce the numbers of people employed in existing industries.

41. Given the federal deficit, the choice is clear: Either we cancel our foreign aid program or the national debt will double in the next four years.

42. Block's Granulated Sugar must be the best sugar on the market: Granny Smerad has been using it for years.

43. Senator Rockingham has argued that we should increase the minimum wage. What would you expect from a senator whose primary source of campaign funds comes from labor-union war chests?

44. Professor Sun has argued that genetic manipulation holds the key to curing numerous diseases. But genetic engineering is dangerous. The bacteria used in gene manipulation experiments are hard to contain. Several scientists have died as a result of their own genetic experiments. If some of those things they're working on escaped from the labs, they could destroy human life as we know it.

45. Each and every American citizen has the right to keep and bear arms. So the United States is militaristic.

46. The First Amendment forbids the government from prohibiting the free exercise of religion. Therefore, the government cannot prohibit religions from engaging in human sacrifice.

47. You don't want to smoke. Smoking is old-fashioned, passé. It's not an activity condoned by those who are with it.

48. If God is everywhere, [as] I had concluded, then He is in food. Therefore, the more I ate the godlier I would become. Impelled by this new religious fervor, I glutted myself like a fanatic.

    —Woody Allen, *Getting Even* (New York: Random House, 1971), pp. 86–87

49. The Tennessean's jaw dropped. "But you got to go back. Jus because you run, don't mean you've done quit. All them boys have run. I run myself. But you don't go back, the provost, he's gonna shoot you. Old Stonewall's provost right keen to shoot fellows don't want to fight no more."

    —Donald McCaig, *Jacob's Ladder: A Novel of Virginia During the Civil War* (New York: Penguin Books, 1998), p. 230

50. We should always help a friend in need. So, we should help our friends who become stumped during an examination.

51. The Roman Catholic Church has declared that gender discrimination is a sin. So, the Catholic Church has no objection to ordaining women as priests.

52. It makes no difference what your occupation is: Either you commit yourself to it fully or you fail.

53. Never let your kids play in the snow. If they play in the snow, they'll want to go sledding. If they want to go sledding, they'll want to go skiing. If they take up skiing, they'll either crash into a tree while careening down a slippery slope, or they'll want to enter Olympic competition. If they enter Olympic competition, they'll either win the gold or they won't. If they win, it'll go to their heads and you won't be able to live with them. If they don't win, they'll be so depressed you won't be able to live with them. So, unless you don't want to live with your kids, don't let them play in the snow.

54. "Chemistry for the Consumer" was an easy course. I had always thought that chemistry courses were some of the most difficult courses in the university. I now see that they're really quite simple.

55. Joan contends that it is wrong to support the euthanasia movement. But people have rights everywhere. So, certainly, young people in the Far East have as many rights to their movement as anyone else.

56. The Sixth Amendment to the Constitution asserts that "In all criminal prosecutions, the accused shall enjoy . . . a speedy and public trial, . . ." But I talked with George, and it was clear that he didn't enjoy his murder trial at all, and it took a full twenty weeks. So, his conviction should be overturned on constitutional grounds.

57. How'd you manage to pull off the perfect bank robbery?

58. Jessica says she hopes to be married one day. Thus, I suspect Jessica will pay her divorce lawyer a retainer even before the wedding.

59. John has argued that retaining a strong military provides the best prospect for world peace. If he is correct, we must assume that members of the military are primarily peacemakers. But the military consists of soldiers, men and women trained to fight wars. So, as professional warriors, members of the military are certainly not peacemakers, and we must reject John's argument.

60. There is no evidence that a system of letter grades improves the quality of education, so the grading system should be rejected.

61. The majority of members of the Senate and the House believe that there should be relatively few restrictions on campaign contributions, so there must be good reasons not to restrict contributions.

62. A mob is no worse than the individuals in it.

63. You can tell that Dave has a high moral character by the character of his friends, for people who hang out with Dave must be of the highest moral type, or they wouldn't associate with him.

64. You should support the referendum for a state lottery, for a lottery provides a means of generating state revenues without raising taxes.

65. First Fundamentalist Church believes in predestination—it's one of the doctrines upon which the church was founded. So Ginger, who's a member of First Fundamentalist, believes in predestination.

66. Minister: You may believe that there is no harm in an exaggerated claim of youth or cheating the scale of a few pounds. It's just a little white lie you tell yourself. But let sin in the door, and you're on your way down the road that leads to hell and damnation! The little white lie becomes comfortable. So it's easier to tell a large lie—indeed, the lies are certain to get larger, for the only way to cover one lie is with another. You will lose all sense of guilt. Cheating on your income tax, you will tell yourself, is just a little lie. Cheating the butcher, the baker, the candlestick maker are just little lies. Cheating on your spouse is just a little lie. Taking the life of another is little more than a little lie. So you see what will inevitably follow from those little white lies: hellfire and damnation!

67. Perhaps there may be someone who is offended at me, when he calls to mind how he himself on a similar, or even less serious occasion, prayed and entreated the judges with many tears, and how he produced his children in court, which was a moving spectacle, together with a host of relations and friends; whereas I, who am probably in danger of my life, will do none of these things. The contrast may occur to his mind, and he may be set against me, and vote in anger because he is displeased at me on this account. Now, if there be such a person among you—mind, I do not say that there is—to him I may fairly reply: My friend, I am a man, and like other men, a creature of flesh and blood, and not "of wood or stone," as Homer says; and I have a family, yes, and sons, O Athenians, three in number, one almost a man, and two others who are still young; and yet I will not bring any of them hither in order to petition for an acquittal.
    — Socrates, in Plato's *Apology*, translated by Benjamin Jowett

68. Letter to a hair-product manufacturer:

    I'm writing to tell you what a wonderful dandruff shampoo you produce. I know you claim that it works, but you should know that the longer you use it, the better it works. I've been using your shampoo every day for the last thirty years. When I was twenty, I had a serious case of dandruff, and it helped keep it under control. By the time I was thirty, and my hair was beginning to thin a bit, it was considerably more effective. Now that I'm fifty, I no longer have any problem with dandruff.

Recently, I've also been using your new head wax. It's all I expected: It really keeps that old chrome dome shining. Thank you for these wonderful products!

69. McCool presents the following account of the origin of the counter-culture of the late 1960s:

"The '50s was a generation of Dull," said McCool. "We were running around trying to be F. Scott Fitzgerald characters. The only difference between us and our parents was we were young and they were not. I have a theory on what got things moving: the high school dress codes."

"Oh, stop."

"Hear me out. I just want to try on an idea. The Beatles came along when?—about 1963?—and kids start wearing their hair a little long. Principal says 'no.' Then some of the kids start playing in rock bands on weekends and making more money than the Principal makes all week. They say they need long hair for their work, and they have real lawyers to say it louder. The youth culture is born, and the lines are drawn. Dress codes come out of the Principal's office carved in granite, but the kids peck away at them: a little more hair here, a little less skirt there, and the dress code turns to mush. Aha! Authority is successfully defied."

Rene exploded into a coughing fit, thumped his chest, "Greedy, greedy," he said.

McCool continued. "It becomes a real test of wills. The kids are treated to the spectacle of a red-faced coach in a flattop marine haircut ranting at them about how the All-American football team wears its hair short and the All-American football team is clean, decent, brave, manly, and, especially, American. This is being said in front of a portrait of George Washington wearing powdered curls. . . ."

"You may have a point."

"So a generation of kids learn a great lesson in school: If authority is stupid and arbitrary and won't explain itself rationally, you can tell it to . . . itself and, by George, it will. Then these same kids come right out of high school and into the Vietnam War, and they get to try it out for real. And next thing you know, the whole system is coming apart."

–Denison Andrews, *How to Beat the System:*
The Fiftieth, Last and True Success Book of Lionel Goldfish
(Sag Harbor, New York: Permanent Press, 1987), pp. 75–76

70. U.S. imperialism invaded China's territory of Taiwan and has occupied it for the past nine years. A short while ago it sent forces to invade and occupy Lebanon. The United States has set up hundreds of military bases in many countries all over the world. China's territory of Taiwan, Lebanon, and all military bases of the United States on foreign soil are so many nooses round the neck of U.S. imperialism. The nooses have been fashioned by the Americans themselves and by nobody else, and it is they themselves who have put these nooses round their own necks, handing the ends of the ropes to the Chinese people, the peoples of the

Arab countries, and all the peoples of the world who love peace and oppose aggression. The longer the U.S. aggressors remain in those places, the tighter the nooses round their necks will become.

> — Mao Tse-Tung, Speech at the Supreme State Conference (September 8, 1958), in *Quotations from Chairman Mao Tse-Tung* (New York: Bantam Books, 1967), p. 41

71. In the Miss Universe Contest of 1994, Miss Alabama was asked: If you could live forever, would you? And why? She answered: I would not live forever, because we should not live forever, because if we were supposed to live forever, then we would live forever, but we cannot live forever, which is why I would not live forever.

72. Order is indispensable to justice because justice can be achieved only by means of social and legal order.

> —Ernest Van Den Haag, *Punishing Criminals*

73. The following advertisement for a great metropolitan newspaper appears very widely in the State of Pennsylvania: In Philadelphia nearly everybody reads the *Bulletin*.

74. The war-mongering character of all this flood of propaganda in the United States is admitted even by the American press. Such provocative and slanderous aims clearly inspired today's speech by the United States Representative, consisting only of impudent slander against the Soviet Union, to answer which would be beneath our dignity. The heroic epic of Stalingrad is impervious to libel. The Soviet people in the battles at Stalingrad saved the world from the fascist plague and that great victory which decided the fate of the world is remembered with recognition and gratitude by all humanity. Only men dead to all shame could try to cast aspersions on the shining memory of the heroes of that battle.

> —Anatole M. Baranovsky, speech to the United Nations General Assembly, 30 November 1953

75. The most blatant occurrence of recent years is all these knuckle-heads running around protesting nuclear power—all these stupid people who do no research at all and who go out and march, pretending they care about the human race, and then go off in their automobiles and kill one another.

> —Ray Bradbury, in *Omni*, October 1979

76. All of us cannot be famous, because all of us cannot be well-known.

> —Jesse Jackson, quoted in *The New Yorker*, 12 March 1984

77. Mysticism is one of the great forces of the world's history. For religion is nearly the most important thing in the world, and religion never remains for long altogether untouched by mysticism.

> —John Mctaggart, Ellis Mctaggart, "Mysticism," *Philosophical Studies*

78. If we want to know whether a state is brave we must look to its army, not because the soldiers are the only brave people in the community, but because it is only through their conduct that the courage or cowardice of the community can be manifested.
—R. L. Nettleship, *Lectures on the Republic of Plato*

79. Whether we are to live in a future state, as it is the most important question which can possibly be asked, so it is the most intelligible one which can be expressed in language.
—Joseph Butler, "Of Personal Identity"

80. Which is more useful, the Sun or the Moon? The Moon is more useful since it gives us light during the night, when it is dark, whereas the Sun shines only in the daytime, when it is light anyway.
—George Gamow (inscribed in the entry hall of the Hayden Planetarium, New York City)

THE MAJOR INFORMAL FALLACIES

Fallacies of Relevance

R1 Argument from Ignorance (*argumentum ad ignoratiam*)

R2 Appeal to Illegitimate Authority (*ad verecundiam*)

R3 Argument Against the Person (*ad hominem*)

R4 Appeal to Emotion (Mob appeal, *argumentum ad populum*)

R5 Appeal to Pity (*argumentum ad misericordiam*)

R6 Appeal to Force (*argumentum ad baculum*)

R7 Irrelevant Conclusion (*ignoratio elenchi*; *non sequitur*)

Fallacies of Presumption

P1 Complex Question

P2 False Cause (& Slippery Slope)

P3 Begging the Question (*petitio principii*)

P4 Accident

P5 Converse Accident (Hasty Generalization)

P6 Suppressed Evidence

P7 False Dichotomy

Fallacies of Ambiguity

A1 Equivocation

A2 Amphiboly

A3 Accent

A4 Composition

A5 Division

ESSENTIALS OF CHAPTER 2

A *fallacy* **is a defective argument, an error in reasoning**. An *informal fallacy* is an error in reasoning based on the content of an argument (2.1). We distinguish nineteen main varieties of informal fallacies under three main headings: the *fallacies of relevance,* the *fallacies of presumption,* and the *fallacies of ambiguity.* In many cases you must carefully examine the content of the argument, since only some arguments of that form are fallacious.

The Fallacies of Relevance (2.2)

R1. **Argument from Ignorance.** An argument from ignorance is an argument of the form:

> If some proposition *p* were true (false), then we would know that *p* is true (false).
> We do not know that *p* is true (false).
> So, *p* is not true (false).

The **Fallacy of Argument from Ignorance** (*ad ignorantiam*) requires that two conditions occur. First, either the first premise or the second premise of the argument is false. Second, the *burden of proof,* the responsibility of showing that the premises are true, rests upon the person offering the argument, and, in fallacious cases, the arguer *does not* provide evidence of the truth of the premises.

R2. **Appeal to Illegitimate Authority** (*ad verecundiam*) An argument commits the fallacy of appeal to illegitimate authority if it appeals to someone or something as an authority on a particular subject who is not an authority on that subject.

R3. An argument commits the **fallacy of** *argument against the person* (personal attack; *argumentum ad hominem*) if it replies to an argument by attacking the credibility of the arguer rather than the argument. It can take the following forms:

> **Abusive:** An *abusive* argument against the person replies to an argument by attacking the arguer's character rather than the argument presented.

> **Circumstantial:** A circumstantial argument against the person appeals to some circumstances in which the arguer finds himself or herself as a reason to discredit the argument.

> *tu quoque:* A *tu quoque* focuses on inconsistencies between an argument and the arguer's actions.

R4. An argument that commits the fallacy of emotional appeal is of the following form:

> If believing that proposition *p* is true makes me "feel good" (loved, accepted, important, special, righteous, etc.), then proposition *p* is true.

> Believing that proposition *p* is true makes me "feel good."
> Proposition *p* is true.

Generally, believing that a proposition is true makes you "feel good" is not a sufficient reason for claiming that the proposition is true.

R5. The **Fallacy of Appeal to Pity** (*argumentum ad misericordiam*) takes an emotional response to an unfortunate situation as a reason to believe or act in a certain way.

R6. An argument commits the **Fallacy of Appeal to Force** (*argumentum ad baculum*) if it includes an implicit but unwarranted (or inappropriate) threat.

R7. An argument commits the **Fallacy of Irrelevant Conclusion** (*ignoratio elenchi; non sequitur*) when it draws a conclusion that is *not* suggested by the premises.

> **Red herring:** A reply to an argument that diverts attention from the issue.
>
> **Straw person:** A reply to an argument that attacks an allegedly unstated premise (when that premise is *not* assumed) or distorts the conclusion and attacks the distorted version of the conclusion.

The Fallacies of Presumption (2.3)

The fallacies of presumption occur when an argument makes presuppositions unwarranted by the context.

P1. A **fallacious Complex Question** provides the basis for a conclusion based on the answer to the assumed question. The question must either be "loaded," that is, the answer to the assumed question places the answerer in a bad light, or the answer to the assumed question is false.

P2. An argument commits the **Fallacy of False Cause** when it identifies something as a cause which is *not* a cause. A *slippery slope fallacy* occurs when there is a chain of alleged causes and at least one of the causal claims is false. In a slippery slope argument, the situation described first is usually fairly mundane, but things become progressively worse as you slide down the slope.

P3. An argument commits the **Fallacy of Begging the Question** (*petitio principi*) if it assumes as a premise what it sets out to prove as its conclusion. This can occur when:

(1) The conclusion of the argument is merely a restatement of the premise.

(2) In a chain of arguments, the conclusion of the last argument is a premise of the first (circular argument).

(3) The premise of an argument uses terms that assume what is asserted in the conclusion (question-begging epithet).

P4. The **Fallacy of Accident** occurs when an argument appeals to a general claim and either 1. the general claim to which the argument appeals is false or 2. a general principle that holds in most cases is applied in a case in which it does not apply. *Stereotyping* and the *genetic fallacy* are special cases of accident that are based on false claims about a group.

P5. An argument commits the **Fallacy of Converse Accident** (hasty generalization) when a general claim—whether universal or statistical—is reached on the basis of insufficient evidence, particularly when the sample on which the generalization is based is atypical.

P6. An argument commits the **Fallacy of Suppressed Evidence** if it ignores evidence that is contrary to the conclusion it defends.

P7. A disjunctive syllogism commits the **Fallacy of False Dichotomy** if its disjunctive premise is false.

Fallacies of Ambiguity (2.4)

If the meaning of a word, phrase, or sentence shifts in the course of an argument and the acceptability of the conclusion depends upon that shift in meaning, the argument commits a fallacy of ambiguity.

A1. An argument commits the **Fallacy of Equivocation** if there is a shift in the meaning of a word or phrase in the course of an argument.

A2. An argument commits the **Fallacy of Amphiboly** when an ambiguous statement serves as a premise with the interpretation that makes it true and a conclusion is drawn from it on an interpretation that makes the premise false.

A3. An argument commits the **Fallacy of Accent** when a premise relies for its apparent meaning on one possible emphasis, but a conclusion is drawn from it that relies on the meaning of the same words accented differently. One form of this fallacy occurs when a quotation is incomplete or taken out of context, and the meaning of the quotation changes.

A4. An argument commits the **Fallacy of Composition** if it improperly concludes that a property true of a part of a whole applies to the whole or that a property true of a member of a class applies to the whole class.

A5. An argument commits the **Fallacy of Division** if it illegitimately claims that a term that is true of a whole is true of a part or a term that is true of a class of things is true of a member of that class.

CHAPTER **THREE**

CATEGORICAL PROPOSITIONS

3.1 CATEGORICAL LOGIC

In Chapter 1 we defined and discussed some of the foundational concepts of logic, including the notions of validity and soundness for deductive arguments. An argument form is valid when, if the premises were true, it is impossible for its conclusion to be false. An argument is sound if it is both valid and the premises are true. Validity is a truth-preserving relation. Just as the design of a house can guarantee that a house will withstand violent storms *so long as* it is constructed of good materials, so a valid form guarantees that its conclusion is true *so long as* its premises are also true. Validity depends only on the structures of the propositions in an argument. In Chapter 2 we looked at fallacies, common patterns of argument that tend to be psychologically persuasive but which, on analysis, turn out to be unsound.

In this and the next two chapters, we discuss a system of formal logic known as *categorical* or *Aristotelian* logic in honor of its inventor, the ancient Greek philosopher Aristotle (384–322 B.C.E.). Categorical logic concerns relations among classes of objects, or categories. Medieval European logicians brought this sort of logic to the height of its development. Categorical logic is *formal* in two senses. First, it is a *system* insofar as it prescribes a class of strict rules and techniques for reliably determining the validity of categorical arguments. Second, and more importantly, categorical logic has to do purely with the forms (structures) of propositions and arguments.

In later chapters we discuss the modern systems of *sentential* and *quantificational* logic. As we shall show, these modern systems of logic supersede categorical logic, but there are several reasons why what you learn about categorical logic will be useful in our discussions of modern logic. First, categorical logic is a good way to introduce formal analysis, since it is somewhere between natural language analysis of the sort discussed in Chapter 2 and the purely symbolic systems of modern logic we discuss in Chapters 6 through 8. Second, many of the concepts of categorical logic are directly related to important parts of quantificational logic. Third, categorical logic is an efficient way to learn and practice some of the central concepts in logic.

The concepts of validity and soundness apply to categorical logic in the same way that they apply to deductive arguments generally. We begin by dealing with propositions, in this case *categorical* propositions. In Chapter 4 we discuss arguments built out of categorical propositions. In Chapter 5 we discuss some techniques for using categorical logic to assess the validity of arguments in ordinary discourse.

3.2   CATEGORICAL PROPOSITIONS AND CLASSES

The building blocks of Aristotelian logic are **categorical propositions**. Categorical propositions concern categories or classes of objects. Here is an example of an argument in categorical logic:

> No athletes are vegetarians.
> All football players are athletes.
> _____
> Therefore, no football players are vegetarians.

All three of the propositions in this argument are *categorical* propositions. *Categorical propositions* **affirm or deny that some class *S* is included, in whole or in part, in some other class *P*.** A *class* is a collection of all the objects that have a specified common characteristic. In the example above, the categorical propositions refer to the class of athletes, the class of vegetarians, and the class of football players.

Classes can be constructed quite arbitrarily. Any property or characteristic held in common by a group of objects can be used to define a class. Thus, redness can be used to define the class of red things. In the most arbitrary case, the class-making characteristic can be simply the property of being a member of *this* particular class, where you point at the objects in question and which need be related to each other in no other way. Examples of classes that are more typical would include the class of all objects that are colored blue, the class of all objects that are cows, the class of all people who are politicians, the class of all people who are under five feet tall, and even the class of all the objects that happen to be in this room right now.

Categorical propositions state a relationship between classes of objects. Not all propositions are categorical. Classes are composed of objects. So, strictly speaking, since redness (for example) is a property, not a class of objects, the statement "All barns are red" does not assert a relation between classes, and hence is not a categorical proposition. But it is easy to transform it into a categorical proposition that is equivalent in meaning: for example, "All barns are *buildings that are red*" or "All barns are *red things*." The point is that in categorical logic, whenever you see a property, you should think of the class of objects picked out by that property. Sometimes you will need to rewrite the propositions of an argument to make them categorical in this way.

There are four ways in which two classes may be related to one another:

1. If every member of one class is also a member of a second class, then the first class is said to be included in or contained in the second. Example: All dogs are mammals.
2. If the two classes have no members in common, the two classes may be said to exclude one another. Example: No triangles are circles.
3. If some, but perhaps not all, members of one class are also members of another, then the first class may be said to be partially contained in the second class. Example: Some females are athletes.
4. If some, but perhaps not all, members of one class are *not* members of another, the first class may be said to be partially excluded from the second class. Example: Some dogs are not collies.

In ordinary English, there are numerous ways categorical propositions can be expressed.[1] To simplify and provide greater uniformity in discussing categorical syllogisms, we introduce the notion of a **standard form categorical proposition**. Every standard form categorical proposition has four parts: a *quantifier*, a *subject term*, a *copula*, and a *predicate term*. The basic structure of a standard form categorical proposition is as follows:

	Quantifier	*(subject term)*	*copula*	*(predicate term)*
Example:	All	squares	are	plane figures.

Standard form categorical propositions use three quantifiers:

All
No
Some

In the fourth case above, the quantifier *some* is followed by a negated predicate, as in "Some dogs are not collies." The *copula* is some form of the verb *to be: is, are, was, were, would be,* and so on.

Categorical propositions have two characteristics: **quantity** and **quality**. The quantity of a categorical proposition refers to the number of objects about which we are concerned. Categorical propositions are either **universal** or **particular** in quantity. A universal proposition refers to all the members of a class. A particular proposition refers to some members of a class. Following a long tradition, we stipulate that *some* means *at least one*.

The quality of a categorical proposition is either **affirmative** or **negative**. An affirmative proposition makes a positive claim. "All collies are dogs" and

---

[1]We discuss some of those ways in Chapter 5.

"Some dogs are collies" are affirmative propositions. A negative proposition includes a denial: It asserts that all or some members of one class are *not* members of another class. "No cats are dogs" and "Some cats are not Siamese" are negative propositions.

The subject term refers to a class of objects which we call the *subject class*. The predicate term refers to a class of objects which we call the *predicate class*. If we choose two classes of objects for the sake of illustration—say, the class of all the things that are cows, and the class of all the things that are brown—we can see that there are exactly four possible standard form categorical propositions that have the same pair of subject and predicate terms.

> All cows are brown things.
> No cows are brown things.
> Some cows are brown things.
> Some cows are not brown things.

Since it will be useful to talk about standard form categorical propositions without having to talk about specific subject and predicate terms, we let *S* stand for the subject term, and we let *P* stand for the predicate term. Then the four standard form categorical proposition types can be represented as below. We also list the single capital letter that is the traditional name for each proposition type and specify the proposition's quantity and quality.

A: All *S* are *P*. (Universal Affirmative)
E: No *S* are *P*. (Universal Negative)
I: Some *S* are *P*. (Particular Affirmative)
O: Some *S* are not *P*. (Particular Negative)

The **A** and **I** designations for affirmative categorical propositions come from the Latin for "I affirm" (*AffIrmo*), and the **E** and **O** designations for negative categorical propositions come from the Latin for "I deny" (*nEgO*).

The first standard form categorical proposition, the **A proposition**,

All *S* are *P*.

represents a *universal affirmative* proposition. It asserts that every member of the subject class is also a member of the predicate class.

Example _____

All rock musicians are Nobel Prize winners.

This is an example of a universal affirmative categorical proposition. It claims that the class designated by the subject term, in this case *rock musicians*, is completely included in the class designated by the predicate term, in this case *Nobel Prize winners*.

The second standard form categorical proposition, the **E proposition**,

No *S* are *P*.

represents a *universal negative* proposition. It asserts that all members of the subject class are excluded from the predicate class.

No rock musicians are Nobel Prize winners.

This is an example of a universal negative proposition. It claims that not even one member of the class designated by the subject term, *rock musicians*, is also a member of the class designated by the predicate term, *Nobel Prize winners*.

The third standard form categorical proposition, the **I proposition**,

Some *S* are *P*.

represents a *particular affirmative* proposition. It asserts that *at least one* member of the subject class is also a member of the predicate class.

Some rock musicians are Nobel Prize winners.

This is an example of a particular affirmative proposition. It claims that at least one member of the class designated by the subject term, *rock musicians*, is also a member of the class designated by the predicate term, *Nobel Prize winners*.

The fourth standard form categorical proposition, the **O proposition**,

Some *S* are not *P*.

represents a *particular negative* proposition. It asserts that at least one member of the subject class is excluded from the whole predicate class.

Some rock musicians are not Nobel Prize winners.

This is an example of a particular negative proposition. It claims that at least one member of the class designated by the subject term, *rock musicians*, is not a member of the class designated by the predicate term, *Nobel Prize winners*.

SUMMARY: STANDARD FORM CATEGORICAL PROPOSITIONS

PROPOSITION FORM	QUANTITY AND QUALITY	EXAMPLE
All *S* are *P*.	**A:** Universal Affirmative	All collies are dogs.
No *S* are *P*.	**E:** Universal Negative	No dogs are cats.
Some *S* are *P*.	**I:** Particular Affirmative	Some dogs are collies.
Some *S* are not *P*.	**O:** Particular Negative	Some dogs are not collies.

EXERCISES

For each of the following categorical propositions, identify the subject term, the predicate term, and the standard form categorical proposition (**A, E, I,** or **O**).

1. All game shows are intellectually stimulating shows.
2. Some Academy Award-winning films are foreign films.
3. No parrot is my grandfather.
4. All billionaires are people I wish were my friends.
5. Some zodiac signs are not lucky signs.
6. All houses on this block are houses surrounded by a picket fence.
7. Some jokes are not funny things.
8. All newlyweds are people that are temporarily happy.
9. No life form is a closed thermodynamic system.
10. Some parrot is a thing responsible for eating my book.
11. Some parrot is not my grandmother.
12. No U.S. Supreme Court justices are people who are ignorant of the U.S. Constitution.
13. No dogs that are without pedigrees are candidates for blue ribbons in official dog shows sponsored by the American Kennel Club.
14. Some paintings produced by artists who are universally recognized as masters are not works of genuine merit that either are or deserve to be preserved in museums and made available to the public.
15. Some drugs that are very effective when properly administered are not safe remedies that all medicine cabinets should contain.

3.3 SYMBOLISM AND VENN DIAGRAMS FOR CATEGORICAL PROPOSITIONS

Logicians have developed a number of ways to represent propositions symbolically. Such representations are easier to handle than ordinary English sentences, in much the same way as Arabic numerals are easier to handle than Roman numerals. So, let's begin by introducing some symbolic representations of categorical propositions.

A proposition of the form "All S are P" claims that the entire class of things that are S is contained in the class of things that are P. This means that there are no things that are S but not P: The class of things that are S but not P is empty.

Let zero represent the empty class. If you claimed that S has no members (S is empty), you represent it this way:

$$S = 0$$

If you said the S is not empty (S has at least one member), you represent it this way:

$$S \neq 0$$

A bar over a letter represents everything that is *not* in a class. So, the notation:

$$\overline{S}$$

represents the class of all things that are not S.

Two letters together indicate the intersection, or product, of the classes they represent. Thus

$$SP$$

symbolizes the class of things that are members of *both S and P*.

With these symbols we can represent the four standard form categorical propositions as shown in the following table:

SUMMARY: SYMBOLIC REPRESENTATIONS OF CATEGORICAL PROPOSITIONS			
FORM	**PROPOSITION**	**SYMBOLIC REPRESENTATION**	**EXPLANATION**
A	All S are P.	$S\overline{P} = 0$	The class of things that are S but are not P is empty.
E	No S are P.	$SP = 0$	The class of things that are both S and P is empty.
I	Some S are P.	$SP \neq 0$	The class of things that are both S and P is not empty.
O	Some S are not P.	$S\overline{P} \neq 0$	The class of things that are S but not P is not empty. ($S\overline{P}$ has at least one member.)

The English mathematician and logician John Venn (1834–1923) developed a means of making this information clear.

Venn represented the relationships asserted in categorical propositions by relationships among circles.[2] In Venn diagrams, a circle designates a class, and we label each circle with the capital letter that names that class.

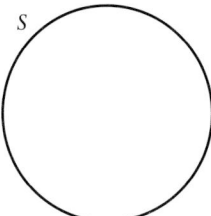

Shading indicates a class is empty. An X indicates that it is not empty.

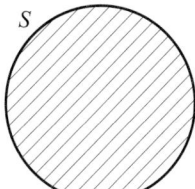
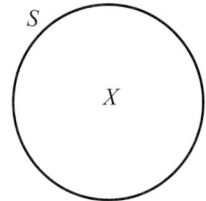

Diagramming standard form categorical propositions requires two overlapping circles, one for the subject term and one for the predicate term. The overlapping area represents the *intersection* of the two classes, the class of objects that are in both S and P. The box around the circles represents the universe assumed by the proposition.

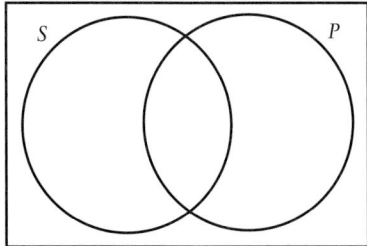
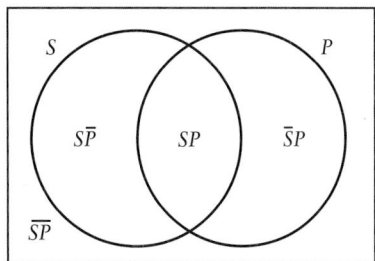

We can label such a diagram using the notation introduced previously.

---

[2]As we'll see in section 3.4, there are two interpretations of categorical logic. The interpretation assumed by Venn diagrams is the so-called Boolean interpretation. The Boolean interpretation makes fewer assumptions than the traditional or Aristotelian interpretation. For our current purposes, the differences are of little importance.

Notice that the region outside both circles is $\overline{SP}$. It contains everything that is neither S nor P.

Venn diagrams for the four standard form categorical propositions are as follows:

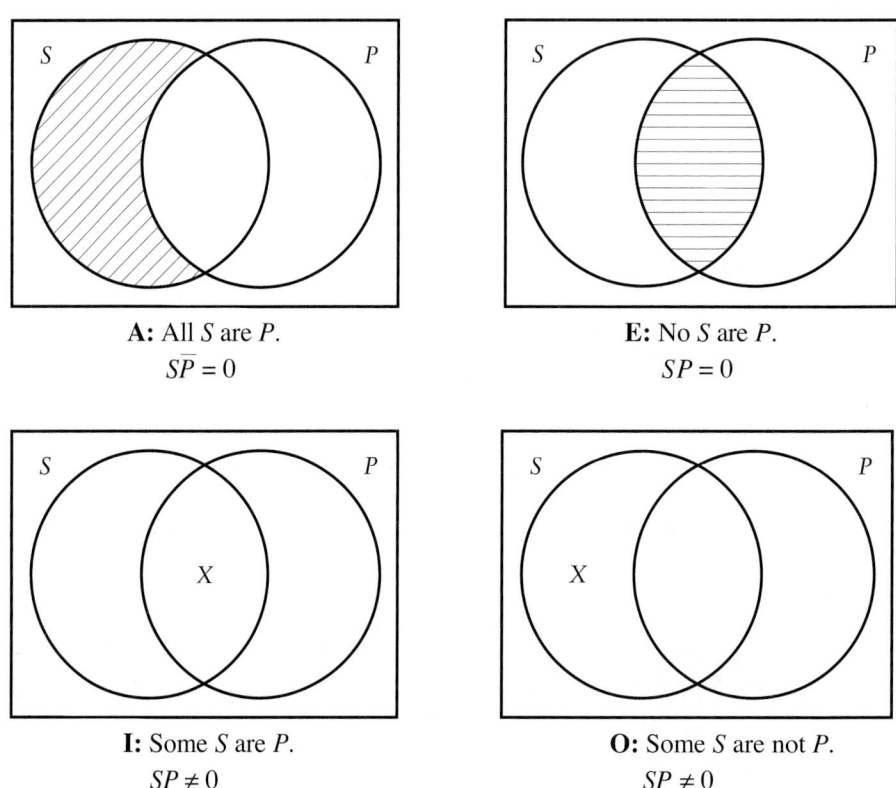

A: All S are P.
$$S\overline{P} = 0$$

E: No S are P.
$$SP = 0$$

I: Some S are P.
$$SP \neq 0$$

O: Some S are not P.
$$S\overline{P} \neq 0$$

We can also draw Venn diagrams for the propositions that result by switching the place of the subject and predicate terms.

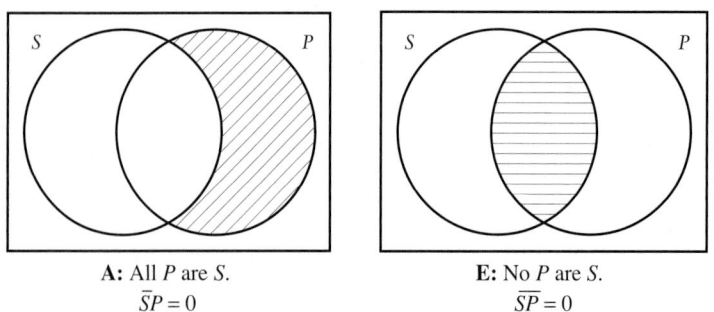

A: All P are S.
$$\overline{S}P = 0$$

E: No P are S.
$$\overline{SP} = 0$$

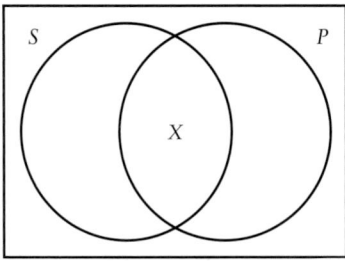

I: Some *S* are *P*.

$SP \neq 0$

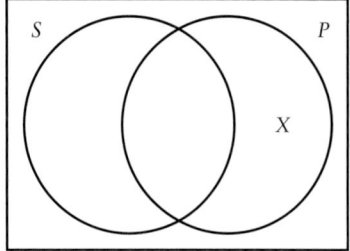

O: Some *S* are not *P*.

$\overline{S}P \neq 0$

EXERCISES

For each of the following propositions, identify its form (**A**, **E**, **I**, or **O**), pick the appropriate symbolic expression representing each class by the first letter of the English term designating it, and draw a Venn diagram.

1. All banana splits are healthy desserts.
2. Some Toyotas are not gasoline-powered vehicles.
3. No homecoming queen is someone graduating *magna cum laude*.
4. Some Canadians are people of French descent.
5. All pigs are fantastic pets.
6. No cockroaches are members of an endangered species.
7. Some Olympic gold medal winners are drug users.
8. All teachers are underpaid workers.
9. All knights in white satin are people that slide off of horses.
10. Some poets are dead people.
11. No dead people are people who tell tales.
12. All people who read poems are folks who keep poets alive.
13. All toilets in Australia are counterclockwise flushing toilets.
14. Some cockroaches are fantastic pets.
15. No pigs are animals of French descent.
16. Some parrots are things that people think make fantastic pets.
17. All triangles are objects that have three sides.
18. Some sculptors are painters.
19. Some musicians are not pianists.
20. All physicians licensed to practice in this state are medical school graduates who have passed special qualifying examinations.
21. No modern paintings are photographic likenesses of their objects.

22. Some state employees are not public-spirited citizens.

23. Some passengers on large jet airplanes are not satisfied customers.

24. Some stalwart defenders of the existing order are not members of political parties.

25. All pornographic films are menaces to civilization and decency.

3.4 DISTRIBUTION

A term is *distributed* if it refers to an entire class, otherwise it is *undistributed*. If you think about it, you'll realize that in a universal proposition, the subject term is distributed. In a negative proposition, the predicate term is distributed. The following diagram shows the distribution terms for standard form categorical propositions.

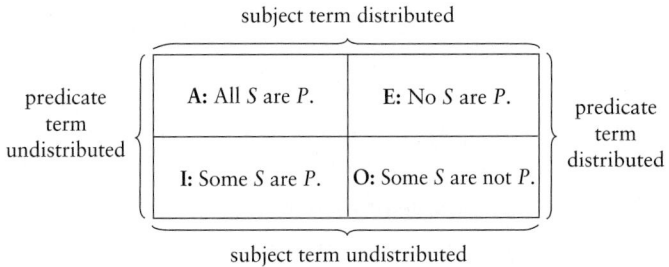

Another way to summarize the distribution of terms is

A: All S^D are P^U.
E: No S^D are P^D.
I: Some S^U are P^U.
O: Some S^U are not P^D.

We now look at the individual propositions in turn.

A propositions ("All S are P") assert that the subject class is contained in the predicate class. They say nothing about the entire predicate class. Thus, **A** propositions distribute the subject term, but not the predicate term. So, the proposition "All collies are dogs" tells you that the whole class of collies is in the class of dogs. This point is nicely illustrated by the Venn diagram for an **A** proposition. Remember the shaded area is empty:

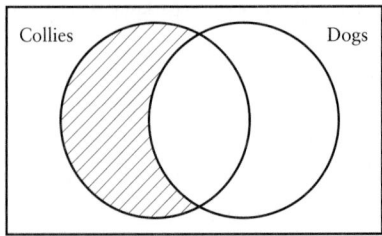

If there are any collies, they are included in the class of dogs. The area of the diagram representing collies that are not dogs is empty.

E propositions ("No *S* are *P*") assert that the subject and predicate classes are excluded from one another. Since it makes a claim about the entirety of both classes, both terms are distributed. So, the proposition "No dogs are cats" tells you that the whole class of dogs is excluded from the whole class of cats. Again, a Venn diagram illustrates this nicely. Remember, the shaded area has no members:

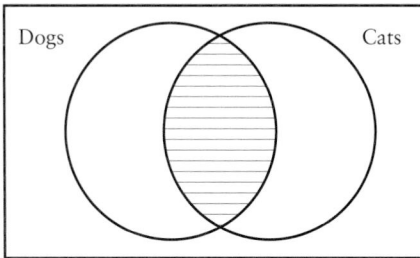

The diagram indicates that the class of things that are both dogs and cats is empty. So, it shows that the class of dogs that are not cats is entirely distinct from the class of cats that are not dogs.

I propositions ("Some *S* are *P*") assert that the subject and predicate classes have at least one member in common. Since it makes *no* claim about the entirety of either class, neither term is distributed. The Venn diagram for "Some dogs are collies" illustrates this. Remember, the *X* marks the spot where there is something:

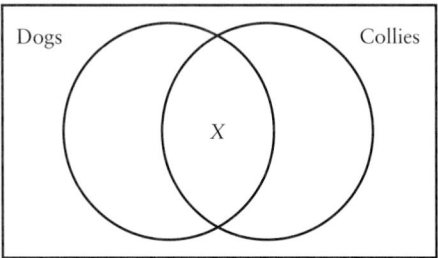

The *X* is in the area representing things that are both dogs and collies. It only shows you that there is at least one thing that is both a dog and a collie. The diagram shows nothing about the entire class of things that are dogs but not collies and nothing about the entire class of things that are collies but not dogs. So, it shows that neither term is distributed.

O propositions ("Some *S* are not *P*") assert that there is at least one thing that is excluded from the predicate class. Since it tells you something about the entire predicate class, but nothing about the entire subject class, the predicate term is distributed and the subject term is undistributed. The Venn diagram for "Some dogs are not collies" illustrates this. Remember, the X marks the spot where there is something:

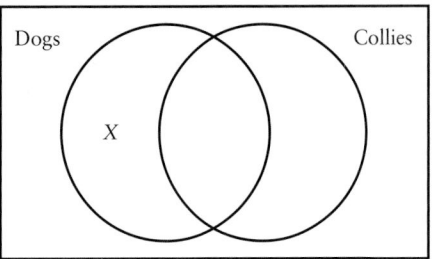

The X is completely outside the circle representing the class of collies. So it shows that the predicate term is distributed.

ESSENTIAL HINTS

If you find the discussion of distribution clear and intuitive, *do not read this note*! If you're a bit puzzled, take heart: You're in the same boat as at least 60 percent of students, most of whom do *very* well evaluating syllogisms. *Their* solution is to put a Post-It® on the page with the distribution chart and do about thirty problems involving distribution. After that they know the chart. *Their* attitude is that distribution is just something logicians dreamt up so they could have rules to evaluate syllogisms. So, *they* say, it's not a big deal if you can't quite understand what distribution is. Of course, it's the *official* view of the *authors* that you should understand the concept, but . . .

EXERCISES

Identify the propositional form (**A, E, I, O**) of each of the following propositions and indicate whether each of its terms is distributed or undistributed.

1. All sweet-toothed teenagers are dentists' best friends.
2. Some running shoes are not objects worth smelling.
3. No chlorinated swimming pool is an algae-free thing.
4. Some computer games are addicting pastimes.
5. No stuffed turkeys are vegetarians' delights.
6. All Newfoundlands are big dogs.
7. No puppy is a big dog.
8. Some Newfoundlands are puppies.
9. Some things are not things that are clear.
10. Some cold medications are drugs that make people drowsy.
11. All artificial intelligence (AI) algorithms are abstract entities that are unaware of what they are.
12. Some presidential candidates will be sadly disappointed people.
13. Some members of the military-industrial complex are mild-mannered people to whom violence is abhorrent.
14. Some recent rulings of the Supreme Court were politically motivated decisions that flouted the entire history of American legal practice.
15. All new labor-saving devices are major threats to the trade union movement.

3.5   EXISTENTIAL IMPORT

There are two interpretations of categorical propositions. The difference between the two concerns the existential import of universal (*A* and *E*) propositions. **A proposition has *existential import* if its truth requires that the subject class has at least one member.** Everyone agrees that *particular (I and O) propositions have existential import*. Does this make a difference whether universal propositions have existential import? Sure. Consider the following two statements:

> All unicorns are mythical horselike animals with a single horn growing from the middle of their foreheads.
>
> All objects, not acted upon by an outside force, which are at rest or in a state of uniform rectilinear motion will remain at rest or in a state of uniform rectilinear motion unless they're acted upon by an outside force. (Newton's First Law of Motion)

If the truth of a universal proposition requires existential import, both of the above propositions are false since there are no unicorns and there are no objects that are *not* acted upon by an outside force. If the truth of a universal proposition does *not* require existential import, both of the above propositions are true.

The traditional or **Aristotelian interpretation** of categorical propositions assumes that universal propositions have existential import. Some people believe that this is the commonsense approach. It certainly works with true universal statements about objects we *already know to exist*. As we'll see in the next section, assuming the Aristotelian interpretation allows you to draw several inferences regarding other propositions with the same subject or predicate term *if* you know that a universal statement is true or a particular statement is false. But the Aristotelian interpretation entails that universal statements about objects that do not exist are all false. So, while *Webster's New World Dictionary* defines *unicorn* as follows:

> a mythical horselike animal with a single horn growing from the center of its forehead[3]

the universal statement corresponding to the definition must be false, since there are no unicorns. Similarly, Newton's first law of motion, and any other scientific principle that holds only in an "idealized" set of conditions, is false.

The alternative, in which universal propositions *do not* have existential import, is known as the **Boolean Interpretation**, named after the nineteenth-century mathematician and logician George Boole (1815–1864), who

---

[3]In *Webster's New World Dictionary and Thesaurus* (Macmillan Digital Publishing, 1997).

championed the interpretation.[4] On the Boolean interpretation, a universal proposition is understood as a *conditional statement* (an *if–then* statement). A universal affirmative statement is of the form, "For anything, if it is *S*, then it is *P*." So, we understand, "All unicorns are one-horned horses" as "For anything, if it is a unicorn [which it is not, since they don't exist], then it's a one-horned horse." As we'll see in Chapter 6, any conditional statement with a false antecedent (*if*-clause) is true. This means that, on the Boolean interpretation, *any* universal claim about unicorns (or any object that doesn't exist) is true. For example, on the Boolean interpretation, "All unicorns are pot-bellied pigs" is true.

The Venn diagram technique and the rules we'll introduce for evaluating syllogisms in the next chapter assume the Boolean interpretation. Why? There are several reasons. (1) There are times that we want to talk about objects that do not exist, and it is only reasonable to claim that some of those claims are true—for example, when a universal proposition asserts a definition. Similarly, anyone who holds that mathematics concerns idealizations will want to claim that basic mathematical propositions—"2 + 2 = 4," "All squares are rectangles"—are true. The Boolean interpretation allows you to claim that statements about idealizations are true; the Aristotelian interpretation does not. (2) Sometimes what we say does not suppose that there are members in the classes we are talking about. "All trespassers will be prosecuted," for example, not only does not assume that the subject class is nonempty but is asserted in order to try to ensure that the subject class remains empty. (3) We often wish to reason without making any presuppositions about existence. Newton's First Law of Motion, for example, asserts that bodies not acted on by external forces preserve their state of motion, whether of rest or of constant speed in a straight line. That may be true; a physicist may want to express and defend it *without* wanting to presuppose that there are any bodies that are free from external forces. (4) When we make universal statements about things *we already know exist*, we can treat them as asserting two propositions, both a universal proposition and its corresponding particular proposition. For example, if you said, "All rap musicians are people who can talk quickly," you could be understood as saying *both "All rap musicians are people who can talk quickly" and "Some* rap musicians are people who can talk quickly." As we'll see in Chapter 5, *some* universal statements in ordinary English should be taken as making both claims. If they are not so understood, the arguments in which they are found would be deemed invalid, whereas *only* champions of the Boolean interpretation would claim invalidity.

---

[4]This does *not* mean that Boole was the first person to champion the interpretation. For example, René Descartes (1596–1650) assumed the Boolean interpretation (see his *Principles of Philosophy*, Part 1, §10).

					EXISTENTIAL
NAME	**FORM**	**QUANTITY**	**QUALITY**	**DISTRIBUTION**	**IMPORT**
A	All S are P.	Universal	Affirmative	Subject term only	No
E	No S are P.	Universal	Negative	Both subject and predicate terms	No
I	Some S are P.	Particular	Affirmative	Neither subject nor predicate term	Yes
O	Some S are not P.	Particular	Negative	Predicate term only	Yes

SUMMARY: PROPERTIES OF CATEGORICAL STATEMENTS ON THE BOOLEAN INTERPRETATION

3.6 THE ARISTOTELIAN SQUARE OF OPPOSITION AND IMMEDIATE INFERENCES

Quality, quantity, and distribution tell us what it is that standard form categorical propositions assert about the inclusion or exclusion relations of their subject and predicate classes, not whether those assertions are true. Taken together, however, **A**, **E**, **I**, and **O** propositions with the same subject and predicate terms have relationships that allow us to make inferences about their truth and falsity. This is called **opposition**. In other words, if we know a proposition in one form is true or false, we can draw some valid inferences about the truth or falsity of propositions with the same terms in other forms.

On the Aristotelian interpretation of categorical logic, there are four ways in which propositions may be opposed: as *contradictories, contraries, subcontraries,* and *subalterns* or *superalterns*. These relations are diagrammed in the traditional square of opposition.

The Traditional or Aristotelian Square of Opposition

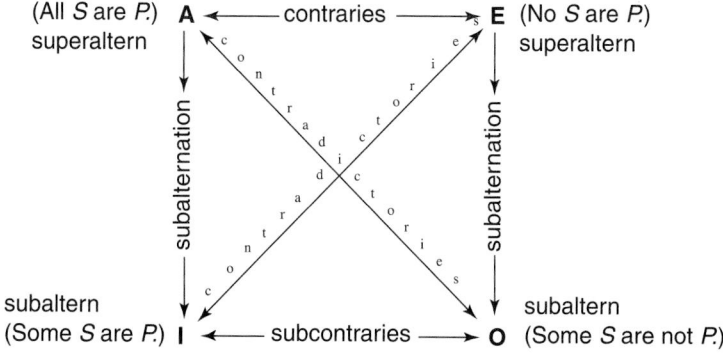

The rightmost propositions, **E** and **O,** are *negative* in quality. The **A** and **E** propositions at the top of the square are *universal* in quantity. The **I** and **O** propositions at the bottom of the square are *particular* in quantity. The leftmost propositions, **A** and **I,** are *affirmative* in quality.

A. Contradictories

Two propositions with the same subject and predicate terms are *contradictories* **if one is the denial or negation of the other: They cannot both be true and cannot both be false at the same time.** If one is true, the other must be false. If one is false, the other must be true. **A** propositions (All *S* are *P*) and **O** propositions (Some *S* are not *P*), which differ in both quantity and quality, are contradictories. **E** propositions (No *S* are *P*) and **I** propositions (Some *S* are *P*) are also contradictories. For each pair (**A** and **O**; **E** and **I**) exactly one must be true and the other false. For example,

A: All Adam Sandler movies are ridiculous movies.

and

O: Some Adam Sandler movies are not ridiculous movies.

are opposed in both quantity and quality. We may not know which proposition is false, but if one is true then the other must be false. If it is *true* that all Sandler movies are ridiculous movies, it must be *false* that some Sandler movie is not a ridiculous movie, that is, it must be false that at least one Sandler movie is not a ridiculous movie. And if it is *false* that all Sandler movies are ridiculous movies, then it must be *true* that at least one Sandler movie is not ridiculous. And, correspondingly, if the **O** proposition is true, the **A** proposition must be false; if the **O** proposition is false, the **A** proposition must be true.

A similar analysis holds for any pair of **E** propositions and **I** propositions which share the same subject and predicate terms, as you will see by studying the pair of statements that follow:

E: No undertakers are people with a happy disposition.
I: Some undertakers are people with a happy disposition.

Again, exactly one must be true and exactly one false.

B. Contraries

Two propositions with the same subject and predicate terms are *contraries* **if they cannot both be true, but they can both be false.** If one of a pair of contrary propositions is true, it follows that the other is false. But if one is false, it *does not* follow that the other has to be true. Both might be false. **A** and **E** propositions with the same subject and predicate terms, which are both universal but differ in quality, are contraries.

All pepperoni pizzas are fat-free foods.
No pepperoni pizzas are fat-free foods.

Here we have two universal categorical propositions with the same subject and predicate terms that differ in quality. The first, an **A** proposition, is universal and affirmative. The second, an **E** proposition, is universal and negative.

　　Both propositions cannot be true at the same time. If all pepperoni pizzas are fat free, then it must be false that none are. Likewise if no pepperoni pizzas are fat free, then it must be false that all are.

　　But what happens, say, if exactly one pepperoni pizza is fat free, and the rest are not? Then both propositions would be false.

　　Thus these two propositions cannot both be true, but they can both be false.

C. Subcontraries

Two propositions with the same subject and predicate terms are *subcontraries* **if they cannot both be false, although they both might be true.** **I** propositions and **O** propositions that share the same subject and predicate terms are subcontraries.

Some football players are heavier than 250 pounds.
Some football players are not heavier than 250 pounds.

Here we have two particular categorical propositions that share the same subject and predicate terms, but which differ in quality. The first, an **I** proposition, is particular and affirmative. The second, an **O** proposition, is particular and negative.

　　These two propositions can be true at the same time. This would be the case if there were at least one football player who weighed more than 250 pounds and another who weighed 250 pounds or fewer. But these two propositions cannot both be false at the same time unless there are no football players. If the first proposition were false then that would mean that there is not even one football player who weighs more than 250 pounds. But in that case, the second proposition, which claims that at least one football player is not heavier than 250 pounds, would have to be true. Likewise if the second proposition were false, the first would have to be true.

D. Subalternation

Propositions with the same subject and predicate terms that agree in quality but differ in quantity are called *corresponding propositions.* Thus **A** (All *S* are *P*) and **I** (Some *S* are *P*) are corresponding propositions, as are **E** (No *S* are *P*) and **O** (Some *S* are not *P*). *Subalternation* **is the relationship between a** *universal proposition* **(the** *superaltern***) and its** *corresponding particular proposition* **(the** *subaltern***), such that if the universal proposition is true, then its corresponding particular proposition is also true.** Thus if an **A** proposition is true, the corresponding **I** proposition is also true. Likewise if an **E** proposition is true, its corresponding **O** proposition is true. The reverse, however, does not hold. That is, if a particular proposition is true, its corresponding universal might be true or it might be false. For example, if the proposition, "Some cats are not friendly animals," is true, the proposition, "No cats are friendly animals," might be false. However, if the particular is false, its corresponding universal must also be false. If the universal is false, again we cannot infer anything about the truth or falsity of its corresponding particular. For example, if the proposition, "No dogs are friendly animals," is false, we can draw no inferences about the truth of the statement, "Some dogs are not friendly animals."

Example

All students are interesting people.
Some students are interesting people.

Here we have a universal affirmative proposition with its corresponding particular, which is the subaltern of the first. In Aristotelian logic, if the first is true, then the second must be also because the subject class must have at least one member (it has existential import), and anything that is universally true of a class must be true of each of its particular members. What's true of all students has to be true of some of them as well. However, what is true of a particular proposition is not necessarily true of its corresponding universal. If it's true that some students are interesting people, it may or may not be true that all are. But if it is false that some students are interesting people, then it must be false that all students are interesting people.

We have just described the relationships of contradictoriness, contrariness, subcontrariness, and subalternation, as viewed from within the *traditional* or *Aristotelian* interpretation of existential import. If you are given the *truth value* of one proposition—a proposition's truth or falsity—the square of opposition allows you to infer the truth values of other propositions. This is called *going around the square.* In *some* cases, the square of opposition allows you to infer the truth values of *all* statements with the same subject and predicate terms. In some cases it does not. In those cases in which you *cannot* determine the truth value of proposition, we call its truth value *undetermined.*

Assume you are given that an **A** proposition is true. If the **A** proposition is true, then its contrary, the **E** proposition, is false. The contradictory of the **A**, the **O** proposition, is false. And the subaltern of the **A**, the **I** proposition, is true. The blue arrows on the square show how you reason:

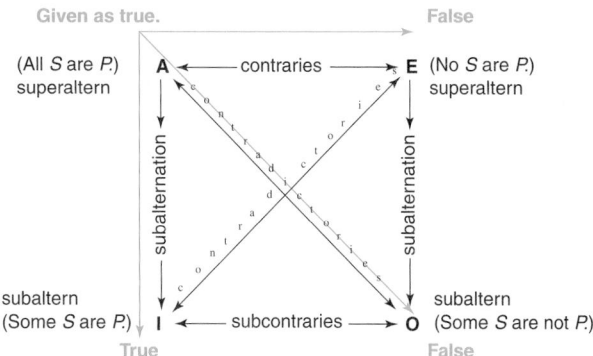

If you are given that an **E** proposition is false, you can infer that its contradictory, an **I** proposition with the same subject and predicate terms, is true. That's the *only* truth value of a proposition on the square that you can infer. Think about it. Let's say the proposition, "No Pontiacs are dependable cars," is given as false. If that statement is false, then there must be at least one Pontiac that is a dependable car; that is, the **I** proposition, "Some Pontiacs are dependable cars," must be true. But you know nothing about *all* Pontiacs since you cannot draw any valid inferences from the falsehood of one of a pair of contraries to the truth value of the other contrary. You know nothing about the truth value of the **O** proposition, "Some Pontiacs are not dependable cars," since nothing follows about the truth value of the subaltern of a false proposition, and nothing follows about the truth value of a subcontrary given the truth of the other subcontrary. So, the square looks like this:

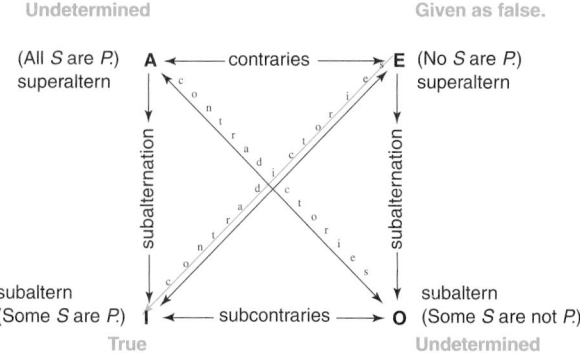

Now let's say you're given the truth of an **I** proposition. If an **I** proposition is true, its contradictory, the **E** proposition with the same subject and predicate terms, is false. That's the *only* truth value of a proposition on the square you can infer. Consider the proposition, "Some dogs are mammals." If that proposition is true, then its contradictory, "No dogs are mammals," must be false. But you can draw no other valid inferences. From the falsehood of one of a pair of contrary propositions (**E**), you can infer nothing regarding the truth value of the other contrary (**A**). From the truth of one of a pair of subcontraries (**I**), you can infer nothing regarding the truth value of the other subcontrary (**O**). *Remember:* **We are concerned here *only* with what truth values can be validly inferred given the truth value of another proposition. The fact that you might know on other grounds that the proposition, "All dogs are mammals," is true and that "Some dogs are not mammals" is false *is irrelevant* to questions of valid inference.** Your reasoning based on the square of opposition looks like this:

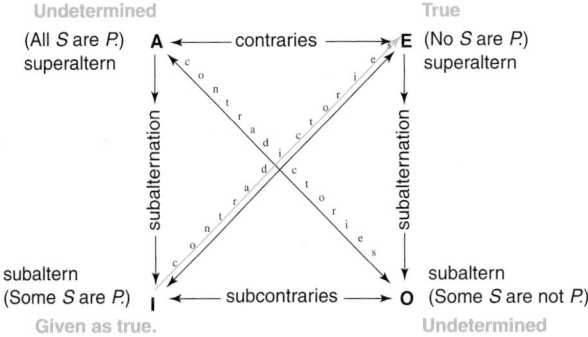

Finally, assume you are given that an **O** proposition is false. Once again, you can go all the way around the square. If **O** is false, its contradictory, **A**, must be true. If **A** is true, then its contrary, **E**, must be false. If **O** is false, its subcontrary, **I**, must be true. Your reasoning based on the square of opposition looks like this:

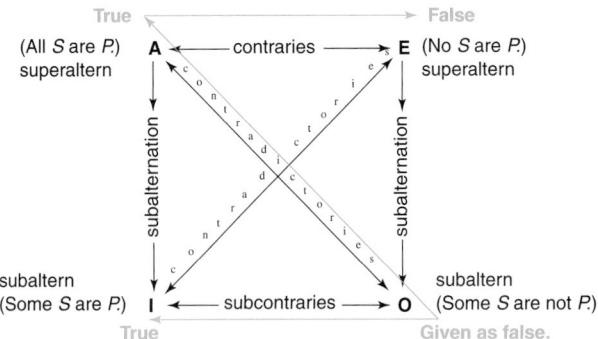

In short, if you are given that a universal proposition is true or that a particular proposition is false, you can go all the way around the square. If you are given that a universal proposition is false, you can *only* infer that its contradictory is true. If you are given that a particular proposition is true, you can *only* infer that its contradictory is false.

EXERCISES

I. Answer the following questions.

    1. State the contradictory of "All spiders are nine-legged creatures."

    2. State the contrary of "All Regis Philbin look-alikes are handsome."

    3. State the relationship of opposition, if any, between these two propositions.

> Some horror movies are funny movies.
> Some horror movies are scary movies.

    4. If it is true that "Some rocket scientists are slow thinkers," then what immediate inference based on the square of opposition, if any, can one make about the proposition that "No rocket scientists are slow thinkers"?

    5. If it is false that "All rocket scientists are slow thinkers," then what immediate inference based on the square of opposition, if any, can one make about the proposition that "Some rocket scientists are slow thinkers?"

    6. If it is true that "All jokes are fallacious arguments," then can it be also true that "Some joke is not a fallacious argument?" Why or why not?

    7. "Some joke is an equivocation" and "Some joke is not an equivocation" can both be true but cannot both be false. True or false? Explain.

    8. If "No joke from Henny Youngman's tape *The World's Worst Jokes* is one of the world's worst jokes" is a true statement, then the statement "Some joke from Henny Youngman's tape *The World's Worst Jokes* is not one of the world's worst jokes" must also be true. True or false? Explain.

    9. If "Some rocket scientist named Joe is now a retired person that sells t-shirts in the Tomorrowland Gift Shop at Disney World" is true, then what immediate inference based on the square of opposition, if any, can one make about the proposition "All rocket scientists named Joe are now retired persons that sell t-shirts in the Tomorrowland Gift Shop at Disney World?" Explain.

    10. Since "No logic textbook is round" is true, what can we know about the statement "Some logic textbook is round?" Explain.

II. What can be inferred about the truth or falsehood of the remaining propositions in each of the following sets (1) if we assume the first to be true, and (2) if we assume the first to be false?

    11. a. All successful executives are intelligent people.

       b. No successful executives are intelligent people.

       c. Some successful executives are intelligent people.

       d. Some successful executives are not intelligent people.

12. **a.** No animals with horns are carnivores.
    b. Some animals with horns are carnivores.
    c. Some animals with horns are not carnivores.
    d. All animals with horns are carnivores.
13. **a.** Some uranium isotopes are highly unstable substances.
    b. Some uranium isotopes are not highly unstable substances.
    c. All uranium isotopes are highly unstable substances.
    d. No uranium isotopes are highly unstable substances.
14. **a.** Some college professors are not entertaining lecturers.
    b. All college professors are entertaining lecturers.
    c. No college professors are entertaining lecturers.
    d. Some college professors are entertaining lecturers.

3.7   THE BOOLEAN SQUARE OF OPPOSITION

The Aristotelian interpretation of categorical logic assumes that all categorical propositions have existential import. As we noted in section 3.4, this implies that statements such as "All unicorns are one-horned horses" and, on some understandings of the nature of mathematical objects, "All squares are rectangles," are false.

Does existential import make any difference regarding the immediate inferences you can draw regarding categorical propositions? Yes. On the Boolean interpretation, a universal proposition about an empty class is true. So, on the Boolean interpretation both "All unicorns are one-horned horses" and "No unicorns are one-horned horses" are true. So, universal propositions are not contraries. The contradictions of both true claims about objects that do not exist are false. So, there are no subcontraries. And, since universal propositions on the Boolean interpretation have no existential import, subalternation goes as well. The Boolean square of opposition is comparatively modest.

The Boolean Square of Opposition

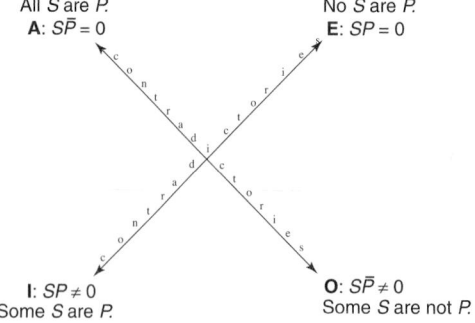

3.8 LOGICAL EQUIVALENCE AND IMMEDIATE INFERENCES

Two propositions are *logically equivalent* if and only if they always have the same truth value. In this section we examine three statement forms that are related to the standard **A**, **E**, **I**, and **O** forms. They are formed by manipulating the propositions in various ways. In *some* cases the resulting proposition is logically equivalent to the standard form proposition; in some cases it is not. Considerations of logical equivalence are independent of the interpretation of categorical propositions you assume. We shall see, however, that by combining considerations of logical equivalence with the squares of opposition, there are *inferences* that are warranted by the Aristotelian square that are *not* warranted by the Boolean interpretation.

A. Conversion

Conversion **is a process that involves replacing the subject term of a categorical proposition with its predicate term and its predicate term with its subject term**. The original proposition is known as the *convertend* and the result is known as the *converse*. The converse of "No *S* are *P*," for example, is "No *P* are *S*." The convertend and its converse are logically equivalent if and only if they have the same distribution of terms.

Converting **E** propositions and **I** propositions yields logically equivalent propositions. That is, if the proposition

No S are P

is true, then its converse

No P are S

is also true. If *S* is wholly excluded from *P*, then *P* must also be wholly excluded from *S*. The distribution of terms in an **E** proposition is the same as in its converse. This should be clear if you look at the Venn diagrams for an **E** proposition and its converse:

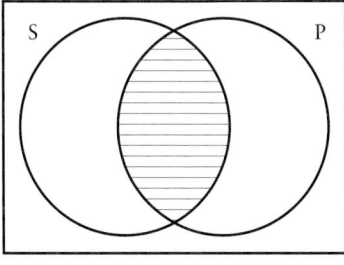 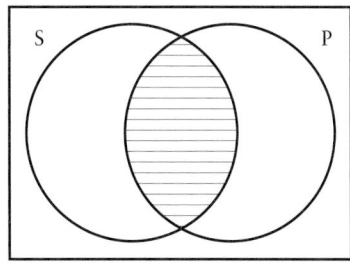

No S are P.   No P are S.

The Venn diagrams are identical. So, an **E** proposition and its converse are logically equivalent.

Likewise, if the proposition

Some *S* are *P*

is true, then its converse

Some *P* are *S*

is also true. If there is at least one thing that is both *S* and *P*, then there is at least one thing that is both *P* and *S*. The distribution of terms in an **I** proposition is the same as in its converse. Again, the Venn diagrams for an **I** proposition and its converse are identical:

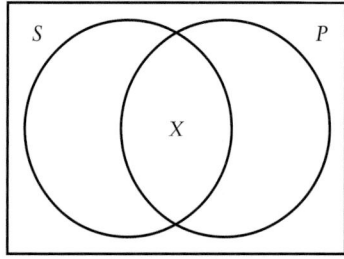   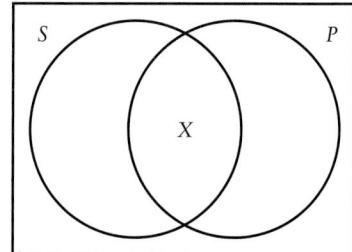

Some *S* are *P*.   Some *P* are *S*.

The converse of an **A** is *not* logically equivalent to its convertend. If you have any question, notice that

All collies are dogs.

is a true proposition, while its converse,

All dogs are collies.

is false. In an **A** proposition of the form "All *S* are *P*," *S* is distributed; in its converse, "All *P* are *S*," *P* is distributed. This is shown in the difference between the Venn diagrams for an **A** proposition and its converse:

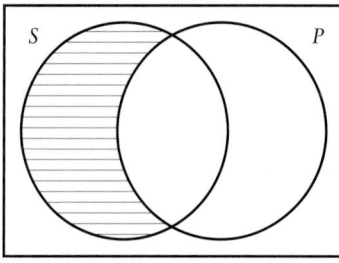   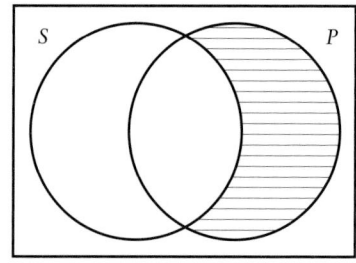

All *S* are *P*.   All *P* are *S*.

Similarly, an **O** proposition is *not* logically equivalent to its converse. If you have any question notice:

> Some dogs are not collies.

is true, while its converse:

> Some collies are not dogs.

is false. In an **O** proposition of the form "Some *S* are not *P*," *P* is distributed; in its converse, "Some *P* are not *S*," *S* is distributed. Again, this is shown by the difference between a Venn diagram for an **O** proposition and its converse:

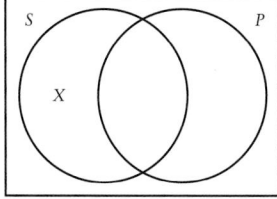

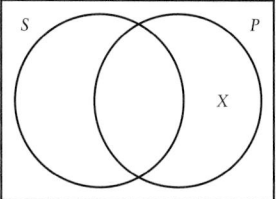

Some *S* are not *P*.   Some *P* are not *S*.

While an **A** proposition is *never* logically equivalent to its converse, the *Aristotelian* square of opposition allows you to draw an inference from an **A** proposition to the converse of an **I** proposition. If an **A** proposition is true, then, on the Aristotelian interpretation, the corresponding **I** proposition is true. An **I** proposition is logically equivalent to its converse. So, given the truth of an **A** proposition one can *infer* that the converse of the corresponding **I** proposition is true. This is known as *conversion by limitation* or *conversion by subalternation*. **Notice:** this is an *inference* based on the Aristotelian square of opposition followed by a conversion that is logically equivalent to the proposition inferred in the square. Conversion by limitation *does not* yield a logically equivalent proposition. Conversion by limitation is *not* a valid inference on the Boolean interpretation, since the Boolean interpretation does *not* warrant subalternation.

B. Obversion

Before discussing obversion we need to define the notion of a *complement*. The complement of a *class* is the collection of all the objects that do not belong to the original class. The complement of a *term* is formed by adding the prefix *non-* to it; thus the complement of *P* is *non-P*. So, if the term *moose* designates the class of all the things that are moose, its complement, the term *nonmoose*, designates the class of all the things that are not moose. Since classes are formed by identifying a *class-defining characteristic* common to all the members of the class, we can say that the members of the complement of a given class are all those objects that *lack* that class-defining characteristic. Whatever lacks mooseness is not a moose, and hence is a nonmoose. Alternatively, we can think of nonmooseness as the class-defining characteristic of the class nonmoose. The complement of the term *nonmoose* is *non-nonmoose* or simply *moose*. Note that the complement of a class is itself a class.

Obversion **is an immediate inference performed by changing the quality of a proposition from affirmative to negative or from negative to affirmative and replacing the predicate term by its complement**. In obversion, the original proposition is called the *obvertend* and the result is called the *obverse*. *The obverse of any standard form categorical proposition is logically equivalent to the original proposition.*

Example

1. Obvertend

   A: All cartoon characters are fictional characters.

   Obverse

   E: No cartoon characters are nonfictional characters.

2. Obvertend

   E: No current sitcoms are funny shows.

   Obverse

   A: All current sitcoms are nonfunny shows.

3. Obvertend

   I: Some songs are lullabies.

   Obverse

   O: Some songs are not nonlullabies.

4. Obvertend

   O: Some movie stars are not geniuses.

   Obverse

   I: Some movie stars are nongeniuses.

If you aren't convinced that every standard form categorical proposition is logically equivalent to its obverse, let's look at the Venn diagrams for each proposition and think about what is claimed.

The Venn diagram for an **A** proposition is as follows:

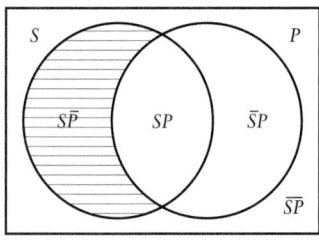

All *S* are *P*.
No *S* are *non-P*.

We have marked the classes represented in each area of the diagram. Remember that a bar above a letter indicates that the relevant class has no members. So, $S\bar{P}$ is the class of things that are S but not P. The proposition, "No S are *non-P*," is true if and only if the class of objects that are S but not P is empty. That is what is shown by the Venn diagram for an **A** proposition. So, an **A** proposition and its obverse are logically equivalent.

The Venn diagram for an **E** proposition is as follows:

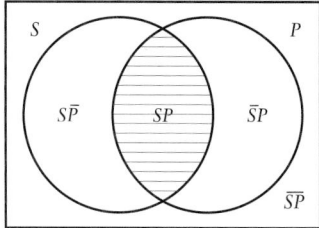

No S are P.
All S are *non-P*.

The proposition "All S are non-P" is true if and only if the class of things that are both S and P is empty. That is what is shown by the diagram for an **E** proposition. So, an **E** proposition and its obverse are logically equivalent.

The Venn diagram for an **I** proposition is as follows:

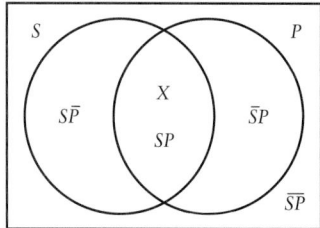

Some S are P.
Some S are not *non-P*.

The proposition "Some S are not non-P" is true if and only if the set of things that are S and not non-P has a member. The diagram shows that the subject class has at least one member, and that member is *not* in the class of things that are S and *not* P. (Linguistically, we'd say that the *not* and the *non-* cancel one another.)

The Venn diagram for an **O** proposition is:

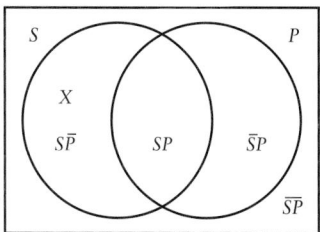

Some S are not P.
Some S are *non-P*.

The proposition "Some S are non-P" is true if and only if there is at least one thing in the class of things that are S but are not P, which is precisely what the diagram shows.

C. Contraposition

Contraposition **is a process that involves replacing the subject term of a categorical proposition with the complement of its predicate term and the predicate term with the complement of its subject term**. The original proposition is called the *contraponend*, and the result is called the *contrapositive*.

An **A** proposition, "All S are P," is logically equivalent to its contrapositive, "All non-P are non-S." We can see this by examining the Venn diagram for an **A** proposition:

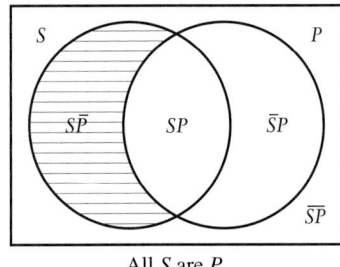

All S are P.

All non-P are non-S.

The only area showing a class of things that are not P that might have members (the area representing a class of things that are not P that is not shaded, and therefore empty) is also the class of things that are not $S(\overline{SP})$. So, the diagram shows that an **A** proposition and its contrapositive are logically equivalent.

Example

1. Contraponend

   A: All sandals are comfortable things to walk in.

2. Contrapositive

   A: All noncomfortable things to walk in are nonsandals.

   If the first proposition is true, every sandal is in the class of comfortable footwear. The contrapositive claims that any noncomfortable footwear is also a nonsandal—something other than a sandal.

Similarly, an **O** proposition, "Some S are not P," is logically equivalent to its contrapositive, "Some non-P are not non-S." We can see this by examining the Venn diagram for an **O** proposition:

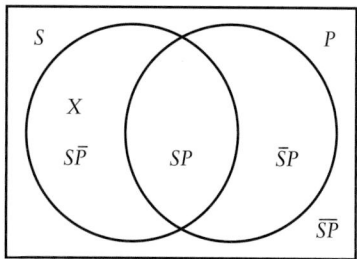

Some *S* are not *P*.
Some non-*P* are not non-*S*.

The diagram shows that there is at least one thing in the class of things that are not *P* that is also *not* in the class of things that are *not S*. In other words it shows that there is at least one thing that is *S* and not *P*. (Linguistically, we'd say that the *not* and the *non-* cancel one another.)

> **ESSENTIAL** HINTS
>
> Contraposition might be called a *derivative statement form,* for in all cases in which a categorical proposition is logically equivalent to its contrapositive, it can be derived from it by obversion, conversion, and obversion. "All *S* are *P*" obverts to "No *S* are non-*P*," which converts to "No non-*P* are *S*," which obverts to "All non-*P* are non-*S*." "Some *S* are not *P*" obverts to "Some *S* are non-*P*," which converts to "Some non-*P* are *S*," which obverts to "Some non-*P* are not non-*S*."

Example _____

1. **Contraponend**

    O: Some interesting books are not mysteries.

2. **Contrapositive**

    O: Some nonmysteries are not noninteresting books.

If the first proposition is true, then there is at least one interesting book that is not a mystery. The contrapositive claims that at least one non-mystery is not a noninteresting (uninteresting) book.

The contrapositive of an **E** proposition is *not* logically equivalent to an **E** proposition. The proposition, "No dogs are cats" is true. Its contrapositive is "No non-cats are non-dogs," which is false: A horse is both a non-dog and a non-cat. Should there be any question consider the Venn diagrams for an **E** proposition and its contrapositive.

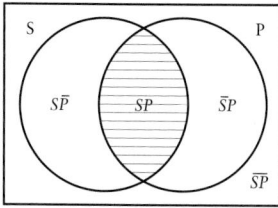

No *S* are *P*.

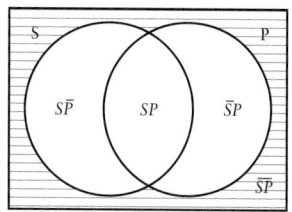

No non-*P* are non-*S*.

The contrapositive of an **E** proposition asserts that nothing is both non-*P* and non-*S*. So, the area *outside* the circles is shaded. A proposition of the form "No non-*P* are non-*S*" tells you *nothing* about the inclusion or exclusion relations between *S* and *P*.

Similarly, the contrapositive of an **I** proposition is *not* logically equivalent to an **I** proposition. Although both statements, "Some dogs are collies," and its contrapositive, "Some non-collies are non-dogs" are true, it should be clear that the two statements do *not* pick out the same objects. Lassie is both dog and a collie. Seabiscuit, of equestrian fame, is both a non-dog and a non-collie. Again, the Venn diagrams for **I** and its contrapositive show that the two statements are not logically equivalent.

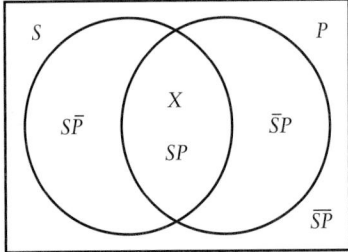

Some *S* are *P*.

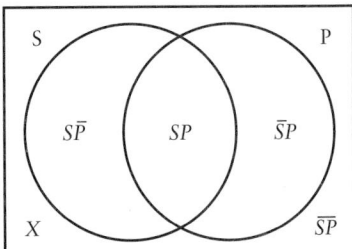

Some non-*P* are non-*S*.

The proposition "Some non-*P* are non-*S*" claims that there is at least one object that is neither a *P* nor *S*. It tells you at least one thing is *excluded* from both *S* and *P*, whereas an **I** proposition tells you that there is at least one thing that is *included* in both *S* and *P*.

One more point should be made before closing. Just as an **A** proposition is not logically equivalent to its converse, but on the Aristotelian interpretation it *entails* a proposition that *can* be converted (conversion by limitation), just so an **E** *entails* a proposition on the Aristotelian interpretation that can be contraposed. On the Aristotelian interpretation, the truth of an **E** proposition entails the truth of its corresponding **O** proposition by subalternation. An **O** proposition is logically equivalent to its contrapositive. So, on the Aristotelian interpretation, the truth of an **E** proposition entails the truth of the contrapositive of its corresponding **O** proposition. This is known as *contraposition by limitation* or *contraposition by subalternation*. **Notice:** This is an *inference* based on the Aristotelian square of opposition followed by a contraposition that is logically equivalent to the proposition inferred in the square. Contraposition by limitation *does not* yield a logically equivalent proposition. Contraposition by limitation is *not* a valid inference on the Boolean interpretation, since the Boolean interpretation does *not* warrant subalternation.

LOGICAL EQUIVALENCES
CONVERSION, OBVERSION, AND CONTRAPOSITION

CONVERSION

CONVERTEND	CONVERSE
A: All S are P.	not logically equivalent*
E: No S are P.	**E:** No P are S.
I: Some S are P.	**I:** Some P are S.
O: Some S are not P.	not logically equivalent

*On the *Aristotelian* interpretation only, you can *infer* the truth of the converse of the corresponding **I** proposition (conversion by limitation).

OBVERSION

OBVERTEND	OBVERSE
A: All S are P.	**E:** No S are non-P.
E: No S are P.	**A:** All S are non-P.
I: Some S are P.	**O:** Some S are not non-P.
O: Some S are not P.	**I:** Some S are non-P.

CONTRAPOSITION

CONTRAPONEND	CONTRAPOSITIVE
A: All S are P.	**A:** All non-P are non-S.
E: No S are P.	not logically equivalent†
I: Some S are P.	not logically equivalent
O: Some S are not P.	**O:** Some non-P are not non-S.

†On the *Aristotelian* interpretation only, you can *infer* the truth of the contrapositive of the corresponding **O** proposition (contraposition by limitation).

LOGICALLY EQUIVALENT FORMS OF THE FOUR
CATEGORICAL PROPOSITIONS

A: All S are P obverts to
E: No S are non-P, which converts to
E: No non-P are S, which obverts to
A: All non-P are non-S.
Notice: the last is also the contrapositive of the first.

E: No S are P, which obverts to
A: All S are non-P, which contraposes to
A: All P are non-S, which obverts to
E: No P are S.
Notice: the last is also the converse of the first.

I: Some S are P, which obverts to
O: Some S are not non-P, which contraposes to
O: Some P are not non-S, which obverts to
I: Some P are S.
Notice: the last is also the converse of the first.

O: Some S are not P, which obverts to
I: Some S are non-P, which converts to
I: Some non-P are S, which obverts to
O: Some non-P are not non-S.
Notice: the last is also the contrapositive of the first.

EXERCISES

I. For each of the following, provide the converse, obverse, and contrapositive of the given statement. If any transformation is not logically equivalent to the given proposition, explain why not.

   1. Some results of plastic surgery are things beyond belief.
   2. Some Las Vegas casinos are not places likely to increase your wealth.
   3. No VCRs are easy-to-program things.
   4. All microwave foods are things best left uneaten.
   5. No chocolate candy bars are things good for your complexion.
   6. No amount of alcohol is a safe amount of alcohol for a pregnant woman.
   7. All cigarettes are carcinogenic things.
   8. Some seat belts are things that save lives.
   9. All UFOs are unidentified flying objects.

II. State the converses of the following propositions and indicate which of them are equivalent to the given propositions.

   10. All graduates of West Point are commissioned officers in the U.S. Army.
   11. No people who are considerate of others are reckless drivers who pay no attention to traffic regulations.
   12. Some European cars are overpriced and underpowered automobiles.
   13. Some reptiles are not warm-blooded animals.

III. State the obverses of the following propositions.

   14. No organic compounds are metals.
   15. Some clergy are not abstainers.
   16. All geniuses are nonconformists.

IV. State the contrapositives of the following propositions and indicate which of them are equivalent to the given propositions.

   17. Some soldiers are not officers.
   18. All scholars are nondegenerates.
   19. All things weighing fewer than fifty pounds are objects not more than four feet high.

V. If "All socialists are pacifists" is true, what may be inferred about the truth or falsehood of the following propositions on the Aristotelian and on the Boolean interpretations? That is, which could be known to be true, which could be known to be false, and which would be undetermined?

   20. All nonsocialists are nonpacifists.
   21. All nonpacifists are nonsocialists.
   22. All pacifists are socialists.

VI. If "No scientists are philosophers" is true, what may be inferred about the truth or falsehood of the following propositions on the Aristotelian and on the Boolean interpretations? That is, which could be known to be true, which could be known to be false, and which would be undetermined?

   23. All nonscientists are nonphilosophers.
   24. All philosophers are scientists.
   25. Some scientists are not philosophers.

VII. If "Some saints were martyrs" is true, what may be inferred about the truth or falsehood of the following propositions on the Aristotelian and on the Boolean interpretations? That is, which could be known to be true, which could be known to be false, and which would be undetermined?

   26. All saints were nonmartyrs.
   27. All martyrs were nonsaints.
   28. No martyrs were saints.
   29. Some saints were not martyrs.
   30. No nonsaints were martyrs.

VIII. If "Some merchants are not pirates" is true, what may be inferred about the truth or falsehood of the following propositions on the Aristotelian and on the Boolean interpretations? That is, which could be known to be true, which could be known to be false, and which would be undetermined?

   31. No merchants are nonpirates.
   32. Some nonmerchants are nonpirates.
   33. No pirates are nonmerchants.
   34. Some nonpirates are merchants.
   35. No merchants are nonpirates.

ESSENTIALS OF CHAPTER 3

Categorical **propositions affirm or deny that some class *S* is included, in whole or in part, in some other class *P*. A *class* or *category* is the collection of all the objects that have a specified characteristic in common.** While there are numerous ways to express categorical propositions, we (initially) express them all in **standard form**. All standard form categorical propositions consist of a *quantifier* (*All, No,* or *Some*), a *subject term*, a *copula*, and a *predicate term* (3.2). They are either universal or particular in *quantity*. They are either affirmative or negative in *quality*. There are four distinct kinds of categorical propositions, which represent the four possible relations among classes:

   A (universal affirmative): All *S* are *P*.
   E (universal negative): No *S* are *P*.
   I (particular affirmative): Some *S* are *P*.
   O (particular negative): Some *S* are not *P*.

Categorical propositions can be represented by *Venn diagrams* (3.3). A Venn diagram represents a class by a circle. A Venn diagram represents a categorical proposition by two circles. Venn diagrams for universal propositions shade areas of the two circle diagram that are empty. Since an **A** proposition claims that all members of the subject class (*S*) are members of the predicate class (*P*), the area of the diagram that is *S* but not *P* is shaded. Since an **E** proposition claims that no members of the subject class are members of the predicate class, the area where the two circles overlap (the area that is both *S* and *P*) is shaded. Venn diagrams for particular propositions show that a class is inhabited by placing an *X* in a portion of the diagram. Since an **I** proposition claims that there is at least one thing that is in both the subject and predicate classes, an *X* is placed in the area where the two circles overlap (the area that is both *S* and *P*). Since an **O** proposition claims that at least one member of the subject class is *not* a member of the predicate class, an *X* is placed in the area that is *S* but not *P*.

A term is *distributed* if it refers to an entire class (3.4). In an **A** proposition the subject term is distributed and the predicate term is undistributed. In an **E** proposition, both the subject and the predicate terms are distributed. In an **I** proposition, neither the subject nor the predicate term is distributed. In an **O** proposition the subject term is undistributed and the predicate term is distributed.

A proposition has *existential import* if its truth depends upon the existence of at least one object in its subject class (3.5). On the *Aristotelian interpretation* of categorical propositions, both universal and particular propositions have existential import. On the *Boolean interpretation* of categorical propositions, *only* particular propositions have existential import.

The Aristotelian square of opposition allows you to make up to three inferences given the truth or falsehood of a categorical proposition (3.6). Two propositions with the same subject and predicate terms are *contradictories* if one is the denial or negation of the other: They cannot both be true and cannot both be false at the same time. **A** and **O** propositions with the same subject and predicate terms are contradictories; **E** and **I** propositions with the same subject and predicate terms are contradictories. Two propositions with the same subject and predicate terms are *contraries* if they cannot both be true, but they can both be false. **A** and **E** propositions are contraries. Two propositions with the same subject and predicate terms are *subcontraries* if they cannot both be false, although they both may be true. **I** propositions and **O** propositions that share the same subject and predicate terms are subcontraries. Propositions with the same subject and predicate terms that agree in quality but differ in quantity are called *corresponding propositions*. *Subalternation* is the relationship between a *universal proposition* (the *superaltern*) and its *corresponding particular proposition* (the *subaltern*), such that if the universal proposition is true, then its corresponding particular proposition is also true. Thus if an **A** proposition is true, the corresponding **I** proposition is also true. Likewise if an **E** proposition is true, its corresponding **O** proposition is true. If you are given that a universal proposition is true, you can infer the truth value of any other proposition on the Aristotelian square of opposition. If you are given that a particular proposition is false, you can infer the truth value of any other proposition on the Aristotelian square of opposition.

The Boolean interpretation of categorical logic does *not* ascribe existential import to universal propositions. So, the Boolean square of opposition only allows you to infer that if one of a pair of contradictory propositions (**A** and **O**; **E** and **I**) is true, then the other is false (3.7). No other immediate inferences on the Aristotelian square of opposition are warranted on the Boolean interpretation.

Two propositions are *logically equivalent* if and only if they always have the same truth value (3.8). *Conversion* is a process that involves replacing the subject term of a categorical proposition with its predicate term and its predicate term with its subject term. The *converses* of **E** and **I** propositions are logically equivalent to standard form **E** and **I** propositions. The converses of **A** and **O** propositions are *not* logically equivalent to the given proposition. On the Aristotelian interpretation (and *not* the Boolean), however, the truth of an **A** proposition entails the truth of its corresponding **I** proposition, which *can* be converted. So, on the Aristotelian interpretation, the truth of an **A** proposition *implies* the truth of the converse of an **I** proposition, but an **A** proposition is *not logically equivalent to* the converse of its corresponding **I** proposition. This is known as *conversion by limitation*.

Obversion is an immediate inference performed by changing the quality of a proposition from affirmative to negative or from negative to affirmative and replacing the predicate term by its *complement*. The complement of the class of things that are *P* is the class of things that are non-*P*. The obverse of any standard form categorical proposition is logically equivalent to the given proposition.

Contraposition is a process that involves replacing the subject term of a categorical proposition with the complement of its predicate term and the predicate term with the complement of its subject term. The contrapositives of **A** and **O** propositions are logically equivalent to standard form **A** and **O** propositions. The contrapositives of **E** and **I** propositions are *not* logically equivalent to standard form **E** and **I** propositions. On the Aristotelian interpretation (and *not* the Boolean), however, the truth of an **E** proposition entails the truth of its corresponding **O** proposition, which *can* be contraposed. So, on the Aristotelian interpretation, the truth of an **E** proposition *implies* the truth of the contrapositive of an **O** proposition, but an **E** proposition is *not logically equivalent to* the contrapositive of an **O** proposition. This is known as *contraposition by limitation*.

CATEGORICAL SYLLOGISMS

4.1 STANDARD FORM CATEGORICAL SYLLOGISMS

Consider the following argument:

No logic students are irrational people.
Some politicians are irrational people.
Therefore, some politicians are not logic students.

This argument is an example of a standard form categorical syllogism. A *syllogism* is any deductive argument in which a conclusion is inferred from two premises. A *categorical syllogism* consists of three categorical propositions. A *categorical syllogism* is in *standard form* when its premises and conclusion are all standard form categorical propositions (A, E, I, or O), when it contains exactly three terms that are assigned the same meanings throughout the syllogism, and when those terms are arranged in a specified standard order (discussed below). For the sake of brevity, in this chapter we will sometimes refer to categorical syllogisms simply as *syllogisms*, although there are other kinds of syllogisms that will be discussed in later chapters.

A. Major, Minor, and Middle Terms

The conclusion of a standard form categorical syllogism is the key to defining its elements. Since all three propositions in a standard form categorical syllogism are standard form categorical propositions, we know that each of them has a subject term and a predicate term. **The predicate term of the conclusion is called the *major term*. The subject term of the conclusion is called the *minor term*. The major term also appears in one premise, which is called the *major premise*. The minor term also appears in one premise, which is called the *minor premise*. The third term in the argument, which appears once in each premise, is called the *middle term*.**

In a *standard form categorical syllogism*, the major premise is stated first. The minor premise is stated second and underscored. The conclusion is stated last. The syllogism at the beginning of this chapter is stated in standard form.

In the previous example, the conclusion is "Some politicians are not logic students." The major term is *logic students*, and the minor term is *politicians*. *Irrational people*, which appears once in each of the premises but not in the conclusion, is the middle term. The major premise is "No logic students are irrational people." The minor premise is "Some politicians are irrational people."

In the following syllogism, *nose-ticklers* is the major term, *colas* is the minor term, and *fountain drinks* is the middle term. In the remainder of this text we sometimes use the symbol ∴ to stand for *therefore*.

All fountain drinks are nose-ticklers. **major premise**
All colas are fountain drinks. **minor premise**
∴ All colas are nose-ticklers. **conclusion**

SUMMARY: THE PARTS OF A STANDARD FORM CATEGORICAL SYLLOGISM	
Major Term	The predicate term of the conclusion.
Minor Term	The subject term of the conclusion.
Middle Term	The term that appears in both premises but not in the conclusion.
Major Premise	The premise containing the major term. In a standard form categorical syllogism, the major premise is always stated first.
Minor Premise	The premise containing the minor term. In a standard form categorical syllogism, the minor premise is always stated second.
Conclusion	The statement containing both the major and the minor term. In a standard form categorical syllogism, the conclusion is always stated last and is separated from the premises by a line.

B. Mood

Categorical syllogisms can be distinguished from one another in part through the types of categorical propositions out of which they are composed. In the example that opens this chapter, the major premise is an **E** proposition (universal negative), the minor premise is an **I** proposition (particular affirmative), and the conclusion is an **O** proposition (particular negative). These three letters, **EIO**, represent what logicians call the ***mood*** of the syllogism. The order of the letters when stating the mood is *always* major premise, minor premise, conclusion, just as the syllogism is presented in standard form. All categorical syllogisms can be classified in terms of a three-letter mood.

C. Figure

The mood of a standard form categorical syllogism does not completely characterize its form. Because the middle term can occupy one of two positions—subject or predicate—in each premise, there are four possible arrangements of terms in any syllogism with a given mood. **The possible arrangements of the middle term are known as** *figures.* There are four figures:

1. In the first figure, the middle term is the subject term of the major premise and the predicate term of the minor premise.
2. In the second figure, the middle term is the predicate term of both the major and the minor premises.
3. In the third figure, the middle term is the subject term of both the major and the minor premises.
4. In the fourth figure, the middle term is the predicate term of the major premise and the subject term of the minor premise.

This information can be conveniently represented in the following diagram, in which the major and minor premises are listed, followed by a conclusion. Because we want to cover all possible cases, we use a schematic form to represent each categorical proposition: *P* refers to the major term (predicate of the conclusion), *S* to the minor term (subject of the conclusion), and *M* to the middle term. We can ignore quantifiers when identifying the figure of a syllogism because quantifiers will be accounted for when we identify the mood. A useful mnemonic device for remembering this arrangement for identifying the figures of categorical syllogisms is to imagine lines joining the middle terms: Those lines resemble a V-neck collar with a skinny neck in it or the front of a shirt collar.

SUMMARY: THE FOUR FIGURES			
	First Figure	**Second Figure**	**Third Figure**	**Fourth Figure**
Schematic Representation	M – P S – M ∴S – P	P – M S – M ∴S – P	M – P M – S ∴S – P	P – M M – S ∴S – P
Description	The middle term is the subject term of the major premise and the predicate term of the minor premise.	The middle term is the predicate term of both the major and minor premises.	The middle term is the subject term of both the major and minor premises.	The middle term is the predicate term of the major premise and the subject term of the minor premise.

Taken together, mood and figure completely describe the *form* of any standard form categorical syllogism. The form of the example that opens this chapter, for instance, is **EIO–2**. The expression **EIO** indicates the *mood* of the syllogism and the number **2** indicates that the syllogism is in the *second figure*. Because there are sixty-four moods and four figures, there are 256 distinct standard form syllogisms. Only fifteen of them are valid, however. If we take any given *syllogistic form* and substitute into it specific terms, the result is a *syllogism*. **Validity is a property of an argument form.** Validity is independent of what we substitute for S, P, and M. **If a form is valid, any syllogism with that form is valid; if a form is invalid, every syllogism with that form is invalid.**

E X E R C I S E S

I. Identify the major and minor terms, the mood, and the figure of the following syllogisms.

1. No scoundrels are gentlemen.
   All gamblers are scoundrels.
   ∴ No gamblers are gentlemen.

2. Some actors are students.
   Some waiters are not students.
   ∴ Some waiters are not actors.

3. No trucks are vans.
   All trucks are automobiles.
   ∴ No automobiles are vans.

4. No kings are beggars.
   Some philosophers are kings.
   ∴ Some philosophers are not beggars.

5. All monkeys are good chess players.
   All Wookies are monkeys.
   ∴ All Wookies are good chess players.

6. No planets are stars.
   All pulsars are stars.
   ∴ No pulsars are planets.

7. All inkblots are unidentifiable shapes.
   Some butterflies are not unidentifiable shapes.
   ∴ Some butterflies are not inkblots.

8. No psychiatrists are professional boxers.
   All people who wake up rich are professional boxers.
   ∴ Some people who wake up rich are not psychiatrists.

9. All examples of Indian art are artifacts.
   No artifacts are living room decorations.
   ∴ No living room decorations are examples of Indian art.

10. No lawn is a parking lot.
    Some front yards are parking lots.
    ∴ Some front yards are not lawns.

11. No snake pit is a good place to live.
    Some good places to live are places in the Bronx.
    ∴ Some places in the Bronx are not snake pits.

12. All elevators are very small rooms.
    All very small rooms are claustrophobic places.
    ∴ Some claustrophobic places are elevators.

13. All very small rooms are elevators.
    All claustrophobic places are very small rooms.
    ∴ Some claustrophobic places are elevators.

14. Some Scottish dancers are not bowlegged people.
    All Scottish dancers are people who are light on their feet.
    ∴ Some people who are light on their feet are not bowlegged
    people.

15. No birth certificates are undated documents.
    No birth certificates are unimportant documents.
    ∴ No unimportant documents are undated documents.

II. Rewrite each of the following syllogisms in standard form, and name its
mood and figure. (*Procedure: First,* identify the conclusion; *second,* note its
predicate term, which is the major term of the syllogism; *third,* identify
the major premise, which is the premise containing the major term; *fourth,*
verify that the other premise is the minor premise by checking to see that
it contains the minor term, the subject term of the conclusion; *fifth,* rewrite
the argument in standard form—major premise first, minor premise second, conclusion last; *sixth,* name the mood and figure of the syllogism.)

16. No nuclear-powered submarines are commercial vessels, so no
    warships are commercial vessels, since all nuclear-powered sub-
    marines are warships.

17. Some evergreens are objects of worship, because all fir trees are
    evergreens, and some objects of worship are fir trees.

18. Some conservatives are not advocates of high tariff rates, because
    all advocates of high tariff rates are Republicans, and some
    Republicans are not conservatives.

19. All juvenile delinquents are maladjusted individuals,
    and some juvenile delinquents are products of broken

homes; hence some maladjusted individuals are products of broken homes.

20. All proteins are organic compounds, hence all enzymes are proteins, because all enzymes are organic compounds.

4.2 THE NATURE OF SYLLOGISTIC ARGUMENTS

The mood and figure of a syllogism uniquely represent its form. The form of a syllogism determines whether the syllogism is valid or invalid. An argument is valid when it is impossible for all its premises to be true and its conclusion to be false. Thus, any syllogism that has the form **AAA–1**

All *M* are *P*.
All *S* are *M*.
∴ All *S* are *P*.

is a valid argument no matter what terms we substitute for the letters *S*, *P*, and *M*. In other words, in syllogisms of this and other valid forms, if the premises are true, then the conclusion must also be true. The conclusion could be false only if one or both premises were false.

Example

All students are Americans.
All freshmen are students.
∴ All freshmen are Americans.

This **AAA–1** syllogism is valid, as are all syllogisms in this form. If the premises were both true, the conclusion would be true. In this case, however, the major premise is false—obviously, some students are not Americans—and therefore, the premises do not guarantee the truth of the conclusion. The conclusion is false.

Any argument with an invalid syllogistic form is invalid, even if both its premises and its conclusion happen to be true. A syllogistic form is invalid if it is *possible* to construct an argument of that form with true premises and a false conclusion. **A powerful way to prove that an argument is invalid is to counter it with a *refutation by logical analogy*—an argument in the same form, but with obviously true premises and an obviously false conclusion.** This is a rhetorically powerful technique, and it is often used in debates.

Example

Some Hillary Clinton voters are New Yorkers.
Some Republicans are Hillary Clinton voters.
∴ Some Republicans are New Yorkers.

The premises and conclusion of this argument are true. Is the argument valid? If we can construct an analogous syllogism—one with the same form, **III–1**—with true premises and a false conclusion, we can demonstrate the invalidity of this argument, and of all arguments in the same form. The following argument does just that:

Some pets are dogs.
Some parrots are pets.
∴ Some parrots are dogs.

This is an **III–1**, as was the example above. The premises are true, but the conclusion is false. This shows (by giving an *actual* instance) that it *is possible* for a syllogism of the form **III–1** to have true premises and a false conclusion. Therefore all arguments of the form **III–1** are invalid.

Although this method of refutation by logical analogy can demonstrate that a syllogistic form is invalid, it is a cumbersome tool for attempting to identify which of the 256 forms are invalid. More importantly, the inability to find a refuting analogy does not demonstrate that a valid form is valid. So, the rest of this chapter is devoted to more efficient and effective ways to demonstrate that an argument form is valid or invalid.

EXERCISES

Refute the following syllogisms by the method of constructing logical analogies. That is, find a syllogism in the same form as the one under investigation, but with *obviously* true premises and an *obviously* false conclusion.

1. No former hippies are Republicans.
   No Republicans are Democrats.
   ∴ Some Democrats are former hippies.

2. All labor leaders are union members.
   No labor leaders are corporate executives.
   ∴ Some corporate executives are union members.

3. All intellectuals are good teachers.
   Some good teachers are biologists.
   ∴ Some biologists are intellectuals.

4. Some short people are not people with a reason to live.
   All tall people are people with a reason to live.
   ∴ Some tall people are not short people.

5. All pink flowers are carnations.
   All boutonnières are carnations.
   ∴ All boutonnières are pink flowers.

6. All free-range chickens are chickens raised humanely.
All free-range chickens are chickens free from added hormones.
∴ All chickens raised humanely are chickens free from added hormones.

7. All pied pipers are men dressed in fancy outfits.
All men dressed in fancy outfits are people attractive to youngsters.
∴ All people attractive to youngsters are pied pipers.

8. Some doctors are talented people.
Some dancers are talented people.
∴ Some dancers are doctors.

9. No hunters are carrion eaters.
No buzzards are hunters.
∴ All buzzards are carrion eaters.

10. Some folksingers are mezzo-sopranos.
Some folksingers are multitalented musicians.
∴ All multitalented musicians are mezzo-sopranos.

11. No busy people are stockholders.
All employers are stockholders.
∴ All employers are busy people.

12. No computers are self-conscious agents.
All computers are artificial intelligence machines.
∴ No artificial intelligence machines are self-conscious agents.

13. No Republicans are Democrats, so some Democrats are wealthy stockbrokers, since some wealthy stockbrokers are not Republicans.

14. No Republicans are Democrats, so some Republicans are not labor leaders, since some Democrats are labor leaders.

15. All supporters of the American Civil Liberties Union are liberals, so some conservatives are not liberals, since some conservatives are not supporters of the American Civil Liberties Union.

4.3 VENN DIAGRAM TECHNIQUE FOR TESTING SYLLOGISMS

As we saw in Chapter 3, two-circle Venn diagrams represent the relationship between the classes designated by the subject and predicate terms in standard form categorical propositions. If we add a third circle, we can represent the relationships among the classes designated by the three terms of a standard form categorical syllogism. We use the label *S* to designate the circle for the minor term (the subject of the conclusion), the label *P* to designate the circle for the major term (the predicate of the conclusion), and the label *M* to designate the circle for the middle term (the term that is in the premises but not in the conclusion). When we draw and label a Venn diagram, we always do it in the same way: The top left circle represents the minor term, the top right circle represents the major term, and the bottom circle represents the middle term. The result is a diagram of eight classes that represent all the possible combinations of S, P, and M. The following diagram shows the relations among the S, P, and M classes. A bar over a letter, for example, $\overline{P}$, indicates that no members of that class are included in the class represented in that part of the diagram. When *you* construct a Venn diagram, you will *not* be expected to mark all the relations of class inclusion and exclusion.

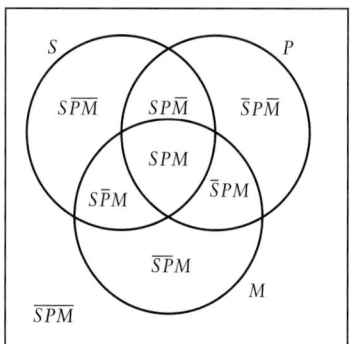

With this diagram we can represent the propositions in a categorical syllogism of any form, and we can thereby determine whether or not that form yields valid deductive arguments. **To use a Venn diagram as a test for the validity of a standard form categorical syllogism, we fill in the diagram for the premises and then examine the result to see if it includes a diagram of the conclusion. If it does, it shows that the argument form is valid. If the conclusion is *not* represented in the diagram of the premises, it shows that the conclusion is not entailed by the premises, and the form is invalid.**

The Venn diagram technique works because it picks up on a very important characteristic of valid deductive arguments: **When an argument is valid, and its premises are consistent, the conclusion says no more than is already present in the premises.**[1] If the premises already say everything that is contained in the conclusion, it is impossible for the conclusion to be false at the same time that the premises are true. And if the conclusion says more than the premises do, then it is possible for that extra claim in the conclusion to be false even if the premises are true.

Let's now see how the Venn diagram technique works for a valid syllogistic argument. Take a syllogism of the form **AAA–1**:

All *M* are *P*.
All S are *M*.
∴ All S are *P*.

---

[1]As we'll see in Chapter 7, anything follows from inconsistent premises, that is, a set of premises that entail both some proposition *p* and its denial, not *p*. You *won't* run into inconsistent premises when working with standard form categorical syllogisms.

To diagram the major premise, "All M are P," we focus on the two circles labeled M and P. In Boolean terms, this proposition means that the class of things that are both M and non-P is empty $(M\bar{P} = 0)$. We diagram this by shading out all of the M circle that is *not* contained in (overlapped by) the P circle.

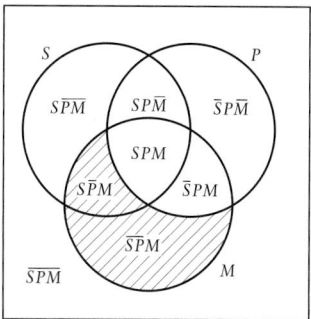

To diagram the minor premise, "All S are M," we shade out all of S that is not contained in (overlapped by) M. This shows that the region of S that is outside of M is empty, that is, $S\bar{M} = 0$.

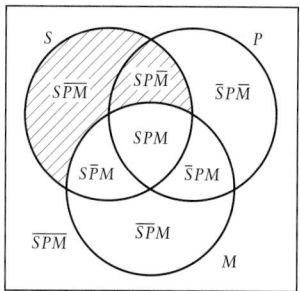

Combining these two diagrams gives us a diagram of both premises—"All M are P" and "All S are M"—at the same time.

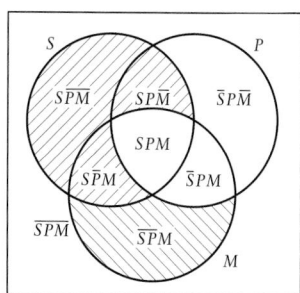

Examining this diagram reveals that the shaded areas include the region of S that is

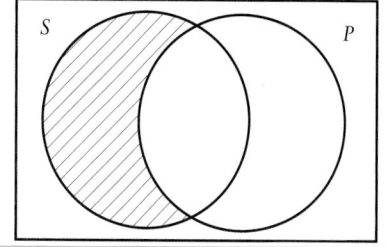

outside of P, and that the only unshaded region of S falls within the circle for P. In other words, this diagram of the premises includes, without any modifications, a diagram of the conclusion: "All S are P," or $S\overline{P} = 0$. The premises therefore already say what the conclusion says, and so all syllogisms of the form **AAA–1** are valid.

Now consider an **AEE–4**:

> All P are M.
> No M are S.
> ∴ No S are M.

Diagram the major premise:

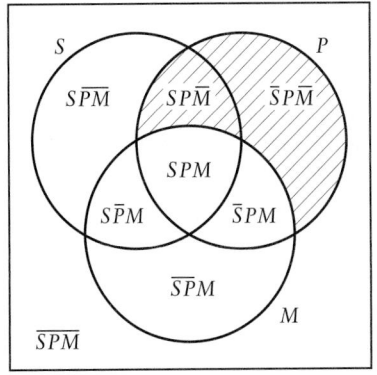

Now diagram the minor premise:

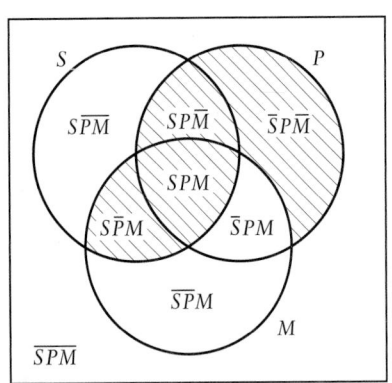

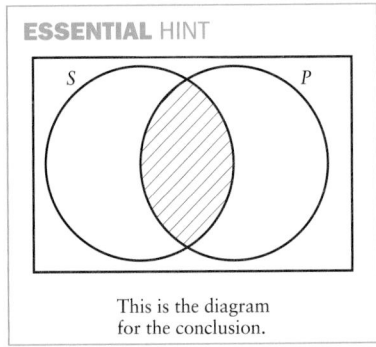

This is the diagram for the conclusion.

By diagramming the premises, we have diagrammed the conclusion. So the argument form is valid.

Now consider syllogisms of the form **AAA–2**:

> All P are M.
> All S are M.
> ∴ All S are P.

A Venn diagram of the premises looks like this:

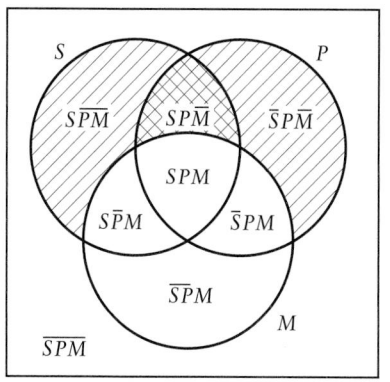

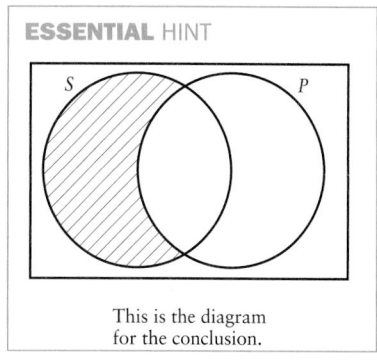

ESSENTIAL HINT

This is the diagram
for the conclusion.

In order for the conclusion to be represented in this diagram, all of the S circle that does not overlap with the P circle would have to be shaded. But part of S that is outside of P—namely, the $S\overline{P}M$ region—has not been shaded by diagramming the premises. So the conclusion is *not* diagrammed. Therefore syllogisms of the form **AAA–2** are invalid.

An important tip for diagramming syllogistic forms that have one universal premise and one particular premise is to *diagram the universal premise first*. The reason is that *sometimes* by diagramming the universal first, there will be only one nonempty region in which you could place the X when diagramming the particular premise.

Consider the form **AII–3**:

All *M* are *P*.
Some *M* are *S*.
∴ Some *S* are *P*.

Diagram the universal premise first:

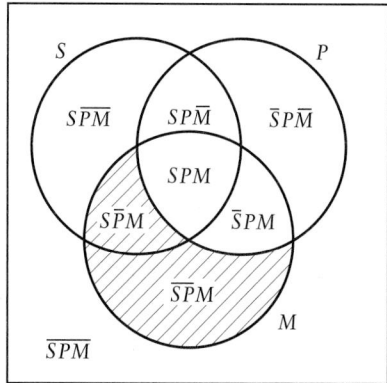

Now diagram the particular. The *X* goes in the region where *S* and *M* overlap. Diagramming the universal premise shows that $S\overline{P}M$ is empty. You can't place an *X* in an empty region. So, the *X* goes in *SPM*. By diagramming the universal premise first, you have "forced" the *X* into a single region of the diagram.

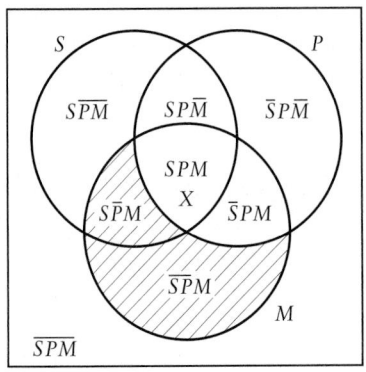

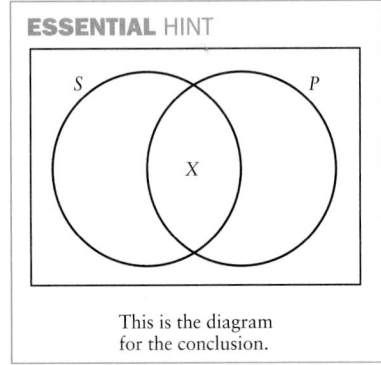

By diagramming the premises, you have diagrammed the conclusion. Any argument of the form **AII-3** is valid.

Sometimes diagramming the universal premise first does not force the *X* into a single region of the diagram. What do you do then? The *X* goes "on the line," that is, you place the *X* on the line that divides the two possible regions where *X* could go into two regions. Consider the form **AII-2**:

> All *P* are *M*.
> Some S are *M*.
> ∴ Some S are *P*.

Diagramming the major premise gives us this:

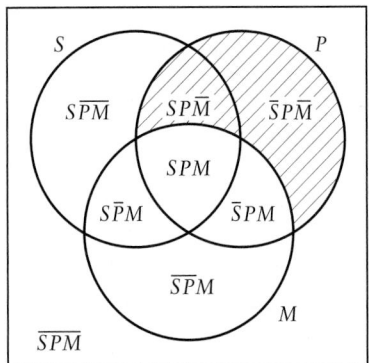

Turning to the particular premise, "Some *S* are *M*," we run into a difficulty. The overlapping areas of circle *S* and *M* contain two regions, *SPM* and $S\overline{P}M$. *SPM* is included in circle *P*. $S\overline{P}M$ is not. Where do you put the *X*? You put the *X* on the line that divides *SPM* from $S\overline{P}M$. Why? Because the premises *do not* tell you that either region is empty. So there are no grounds for forcing the X into either region. X sits on the line in the same way you might "sit on the fence" when you don't have enough information to make a decision. So the diagram looks like this:

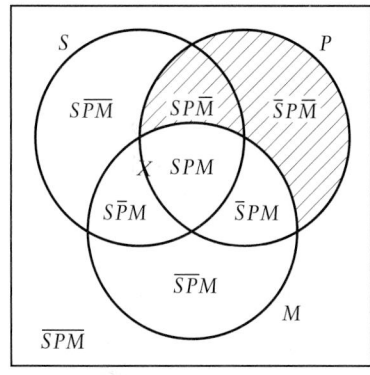 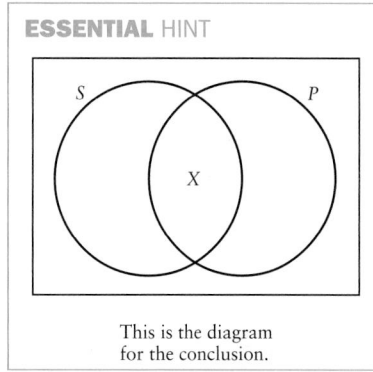

ESSENTIAL HINT

This is the diagram for the conclusion.

Does this diagram of the premises include a diagram of the conclusion? No. If it did, there would be an X in exactly one region where S and P overlap, either $S\overline{P}M$ or SPM. The shading in $S\overline{P}M$ indicates that that region is empty. The X on the line between SPM and $S\overline{P}M$ indicates that at least one of them must be nonempty, but it does not tell us *which* one (it could be either). This means that the premises do not entail the conclusion, and so the argument form **AII–2** is invalid.

Example

All professional wrestlers are actors.
Some politicians are actors.
∴ Some politicians are professional wrestlers.

It so happens that the premises and conclusion of this **AII–2** syllogism are all true. Some actors do become politicians (think of Ronald Reagan); and a professional wrestler, Jesse "The Body" Ventura, was elected governor of Minnesota. But as we have demonstrated in the Venn diagram above, **AII–2** is an invalid form. If you still need convincing, consider this analogous argument:

All cats are mammals.
Some dogs are mammals.
∴ Therefore some dogs are cats.

Things become even more interesting when you have two particular premises. Then both Xs are on a line. Consider an argument of the form **OOE-4**:

Some P are not M.
Some M are not S.
∴ No S are P.

Diagramming the major premise, you put an X inside P, outside M. That region is divided into two parts: $SP\overline{M}$ and $\overline{S}P\overline{M}$. So, you place the X on the line (the S-circle) that divides the region into two parts:

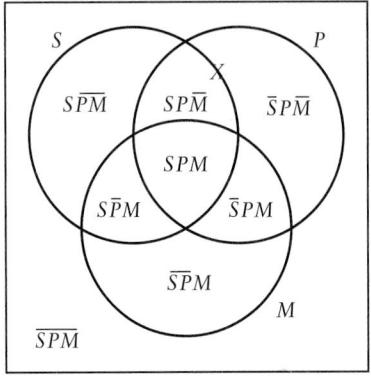

Diagramming the minor premise, you put an X inside M, outside S. That region is divided into two parts: $\overline{S}PM$ and $\overline{S}\overline{P}M$. So, you place the X on the line (the P-circle) that divides the region into two parts:

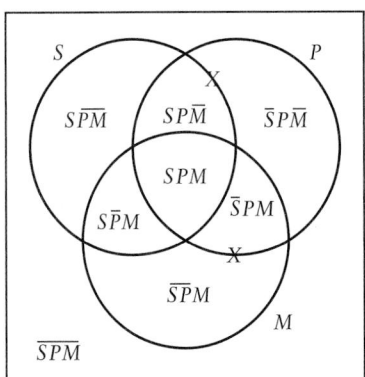

Nothing is shaded. So, the conclusion is not diagrammed. So, the argument form **OOE-4** is invalid.

Summary of Venn Diagrams for Categorical Syllogisms

1. Label the circles of a three-circle Venn diagram so that the minor term is represented by the top left circle, the major term is represented by the top right circle, and the middle term is represented by the bottom circle.
2. Diagram both premises. If one premise is universal and the other particular, start with the universal premise.

3. If a particular premise does not indicate on which side of a line between two regions the *X* should be placed, place the *X on* the line.

4. Inspect the resulting diagram of the premises to see whether by diagramming the premises you have also diagrammed the conclusion. If you have, the syllogism is valid; if you haven't, the syllogism is invalid.

I. Write out each of the following syllogistic forms, using *S* and *P* as the subject and predicate terms of the conclusion, and *M* as the middle term. Then test the validity of each syllogistic form by means of a Venn diagram.

1. AEE–1
2. EIO–2
3. AAA–4
4. AOO–3
5. OAO–3
6. EIO–4
7. AOO–1
8. EAE–3
9. EIO–3
10. OAO–4

II. Write the following syllogisms in standard form and test for validity using Venn diagrams.

11. Some philosophers are mathematicians; hence some scientists are philosophers, since all scientists are mathematicians.
12. Some mammals are not horses, for no horses are centaurs, and all centaurs are mammals.
13. All underwater craft are submarines; therefore no submarines are pleasure vessels, since no pleasure vessels are underwater craft.
14. Some Christians are not Methodists, for some Christians are not Protestants, and some Protestants are not Methodists.
15. No weaklings are labor leaders, because no weaklings are liberals, and all labor leaders are liberals.
16. All professors are actors; for some professors are writers, and some actors are not writers.
17. All roses are flowers. So, no roses are trees, for some flowers are not trees.
18. All trees are woody plants, and no trees are grasses, so some grasses are not woody plants.
19. All moose are large animals; so some elephants are large animals, for some elephants are not moose.
20. Some elephants are large animals, so some mice are not elephants, since some mice are not large animals.

21. All eccentrics are prodigious persons, for some prodigious persons are people who live a balanced life, and some people who live a balanced life are not eccentrics.
22. Some politicians are power-hungry people, so some participants in student government are not politicians, since all participants in student government are power-hungry people.
23. All elephants are large animals, and no mice are large animals, so no mice are elephants.
24. All moose are animals with antlers, and some animals with antlers are deer, so all moose are deer.
25. Some chocoholics are people who like licorice, for some chocoholics are not candy makers, and all candy makers are people who like licorice.
26. Some bibliophiles are not chocoholics, for some salubrious persons are bibliophiles, and some salubrious persons are not chocoholics.
27. All successful authors are coffee addicts, and no kindergarteners are successful authors, so some kindergarteners are coffee addicts.
28. No notorious criminals are German shepherds, since some notorious criminals are not pampered dogs, and some German shepherds are pampered dogs.
29. Some successful street vendors are enterprising entrepreneurs, so some hot dog vendors are not successful street vendors, for some hot dog vendors are not enterprising entrepreneurs.
30. Some dangerous Dobermans are not cute collies, for some silly spaniels are not dangerous Dobermans, and some silly spaniels are not cute collies.

4.4   SYLLOGISTIC RULES AND SYLLOGISTIC FALLACIES

This section presents six rules obeyed by every valid syllogism and the fallacies that result from violating them. Any syllogism that violates one of these rules is invalid. The rules and Venn diagrams will always give the same answer about the validity or invalidity of a given syllogistic form.

Rule 1. Avoid Four Terms

A categorical syllogism shows the relationships between three classes of things. Each class is picked out by a term of the syllogism. If there is a change in the meaning of a term in the course of an argument, the terms pick out *four* classes, not three. So, it is *not* a categorical syllogism. Such an argument commits **the fallacy of four terms**.

This rule is unique. It tells you to make sure you have a categorical syllogism. If the terms pick out more than three classes—whether it's four, or five, or six—you don't have a categorical syllogism. Therefore, you can't state it as a standard form categorical syllogism, there is no mood and figure, you can't do a Venn diagram for it, and *the remainder of the rules do not apply to it*.

Although the remaining rules, like Venn diagrams, can be applied mechanically, to apply the first rule you need to pay attention to the content of the argument. Sometimes there might be a mix of proper names and common names.

Example

All longhorns are large cattle with long horns.
All University of Texas athletes are Longhorns.
∴ All University of Texas athletes are large cattle with long horns.

There is something wrong here, since the conclusion is false. The problem is that *longhorns* in the major premise picks out members of a breed of cattle, while *Longhorns* in the minor premise picks out the class of University of Texas students. There are four terms. It is *not* a categorical syllogism.

More commonly, you'll find a common noun or phrase assigned two meanings.

Example

No people who have had enough to eat are people hungry for more.
All people with power are people hungry for more.
∴ No people with power are people who have had enough to eat.

Although this syllogism appears to be an instance of the valid form **EAE–1**, it actually contains four terms. The middle term *hungry for more* is used with two different meanings. We can see this by asking "more *what?*" In the first premise, *people hungry for more* refers to people who are hungry for more *food*. In the second premise, the same phrase refers to people who want more *power*. The result is the conclusion that powerful people never get enough to eat. This equivocation means the argument commits the fallacy of four terms and hence is invalid.

There can even be a shift in the referent of a pronoun:

Example

All dogs who should eat H∗E∗D (Halitosis Eradicator for Dogs) Dog Food are dogs who like it.
All dogs with bad breath are dogs who should eat H∗E∗D Dog Food.
∴ All dogs with bad breath are dogs who like it.

In the major premise *it* refers to H∗E∗D Dog Food. In the conclusion *it* refers to bad breath. There are four terms.

So, you need to check the meanings of terms to determine *whether* you have exactly three terms so that the categorical syllogism can be stated in standard form. The presence of three subject or predicate terms that look identical does *not* guarantee that you have a syllogism. Further, as we'll see in the next chapter, there are times when the presence of four or more terms does *not* guarantee that the syllogism commits the fallacy of four terms. In some cases the number of terms can be "reduced" to three (see 5.2), and the argument can be stated as a standard form categorical syllogism.

If an argument commits the fallacy of four terms, it's not a categorical syllogism and none of the remaining five rules applies to it.

Rule 2. The Middle Term Must Be Distributed in at Least One Premise

A proposition distributes a term when it asserts something about the entire class that the term designates (see section 3.4). The following table illustrates distribution as it applies to the four types of standard form categorical propositions:

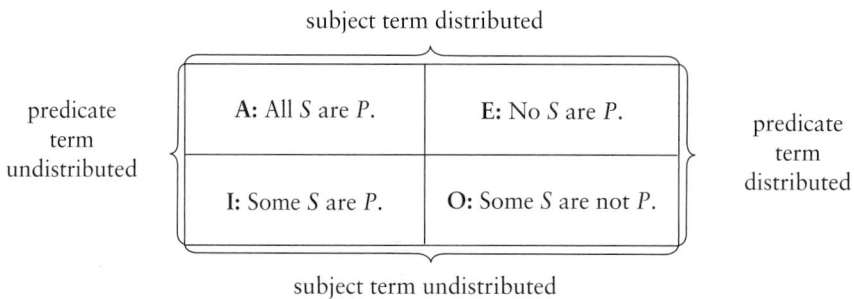

subject term distributed

	subject term distributed	
predicate term undistributed	**A:** All *S* are *P*.	**E:** No *S* are *P*.
	I: Some *S* are *P*.	**O:** Some *S* are not *P*.

predicate term undistributed

predicate term distributed

subject term undistributed

The middle term links the terms of the conclusion. It follows that a syllogism cannot be valid unless either the subject or the predicate of the conclusion is related to the *whole* class that the middle term designates, because if that is not so, then each of the terms of the conclusion might pick out different members of the class designated by the middle term. To violate this rule is to commit **the fallacy of the undistributed middle**.

Example _____

All brain surgeons are geniuses.
All rocket scientists are geniuses.
∴ All rocket scientists are brain surgeons.

The middle term is the predicate of both premises and both premises are universal affirmatives. The predicate of a universal affirmative proposition, however, is undistributed, so the middle term is undistributed in both premises. The inclusion of all brain surgeons and all rocket scientists in the class of geniuses does not tell us anything about the possible inclusion of rocket scientists in the class of brain surgeons. The syllogism commits the fallacy of the undistributed middle and hence is invalid.

Of course, both *brain surgeon* and *rocket scientist* are colloquial synonyms for *genius*. Interpreted in that sense, this argument suffers from an equivocation and therefore it isn't really a standard form categorical syllogism at all. On this colloquial reading, we have three terms with the same meaning, that is, just *one* term.

Rule 3. Any Term Distributed in the Conclusion Must Be Distributed in the Relevant Premise

A premise that asserts something about only some members of a class (a premise that does *not* distribute the term designating that class) cannot validly entail a conclusion that asserts something about an entire class. Therefore, whenever the conclusion of a syllogism distributes a term that is undistributed in the premises, the syllogism is invalid. To violate this rule is to commit **the fallacy of illicit process**. This fallacy takes two forms: (1) **Illicit process of the major term** (*illicit major*) occurs when the major term is distributed in the conclusion but not in the major premise.

Example

All apples are fruits.
No oranges are apples.
∴ No oranges are fruits.

The major term, *fruits*, is distributed in the conclusion but not in the major premise. The syllogism commits the fallacy of illicit process of the major term (illicit major) and hence is invalid.

(2) **Illicit process of the minor term** (*illicit minor*) occurs when the minor term is distributed in the conclusion but not in the minor premise.

Example

All tigers are good hunters.
All tigers are four-legged animals.
∴ All four-legged animals are good hunters.

The minor term, *four-legged animals*, is distributed in the conclusion but not in the minor premise. The

> **ESSENTIAL** HINTS
>
> Some students find it useful to mark the distribution of terms in the argument itself. So, an **AAA-3** would be marked as follows:
>
> All M^D are P^U.
> All M^D are S^U.
> ∴ All S^D are P^U.
>
> This allows them to apply rules 2 and 3 more easily.

syllogism commits the fallacy of illicit process of the minor term (illicit minor) and hence is invalid.

Rule 4. Avoid Two Negative Premises

A negative (**E** or **O**) categorical proposition denies that a certain class is included in another class, either in whole or in part. If you have two negative premises, each tells you that the class designated by the middle term is wholly or partially excluded from the classes designated by the major and minor terms. It doesn't tell you how the major and minor terms are related to one another. So, no conclusion is entailed by a pair of negative premises. To violate this rule is to commit **the fallacy of exclusive premises**.

> **ESSENTIAL** HINTS
>
> If you're not convinced, reflect on Venn diagrams. If the premises are both **E** propositions, area *SPM* will be shaded twice. If both premises are **O** propositions, both *X*s will be on lines. If one premise is an **E** and the other an **O**, then if the middle term is in the subject place of the **O** proposition, the *X* will be in $\overline{SPM}$. If the middle term is in the predicate of the **O** proposition, the *X* will be on a line.

Example _____

No English professors are illiterates.
Some kindergartners are not illiterates.
∴ Some kindergartners are English professors.

The two negative premises exclude the entire class of English professors and part of the class of kindergartners from the class of the illiterate. But they say nothing about how the class of English professors and the class of kindergartners might or might not be included in one another. The syllogism commits the fallacy of exclusive premises and hence is invalid.

Rule 5. If Either Premise Is Negative the Conclusion Must Be Negative

An affirmative conclusion asserts that one of two classes, *S* or *P*, is contained in the other, in whole or in part. Such a conclusion can be validly inferred only from premises that assert the existence of a third class, *M*, that contains the first and is itself contained in the second. But class inclusion can be stated only by an affirmative proposition. An affirmative conclusion, then, can follow only from affirmative premises. To violate this rule is to commit **the fallacy of drawing an affirmative conclusion from a negative premise**.

Example _____

Some football players are students on probation.
No students on probation are honor students.
∴ Some honor students are football players.

Excluding the class of students on probation from the class of honor students does not permit us to draw any positive conclusion about the inclusion of honor students in the class of football players. The syllogism commits the fallacy of drawing an affirmative conclusion from a negative premise and hence is invalid.

Rule 6. From Two Universal Premises No Particular Conclusion May Be Drawn

On the Boolean interpretation, particular propositions have existential import, but universal propositions do not. On that interpretation, a particular conclusion cannot follow from universal premises. Violating this rule commits **the existential fallacy.**[2]

Example _____

All superheroes are eternal champions.
All eternal champions are perpetual winners.
∴ Some superheroes are perpetual winners.

The two universal premises do not support the assertion made by the conclusion that some superheroes exist. The syllogism commits the existential fallacy and hence is invalid.

SUMMARY: SYLLOGISTIC RULES AND FALLACIES	
1. Avoid four terms	Four Terms
2. Distribute the middle term in at least one premise.	Undistributed Middle
3. Any term distributed in the conclusion must be distributed in the relevant premise.	Illicit process of the major term (*illicit major*) Illicit process of the minor term (*illicit minor*)
4. Avoid two negative premises.	Exclusive premises
5. If either premise is negative, the conclusion must be negative.	Drawing an affirmative conclusion from a negative premise
6. From two universal premises no particular conclusion may be drawn.	Existential fallacy

Flowchart for Applying the Six Syllogistic Rules

The following captures the process for working throught the six rules of validity for categorical syllogisms.

_____

[2]This rule and this fallacy do *not* apply on the Aristotelian interpretation.

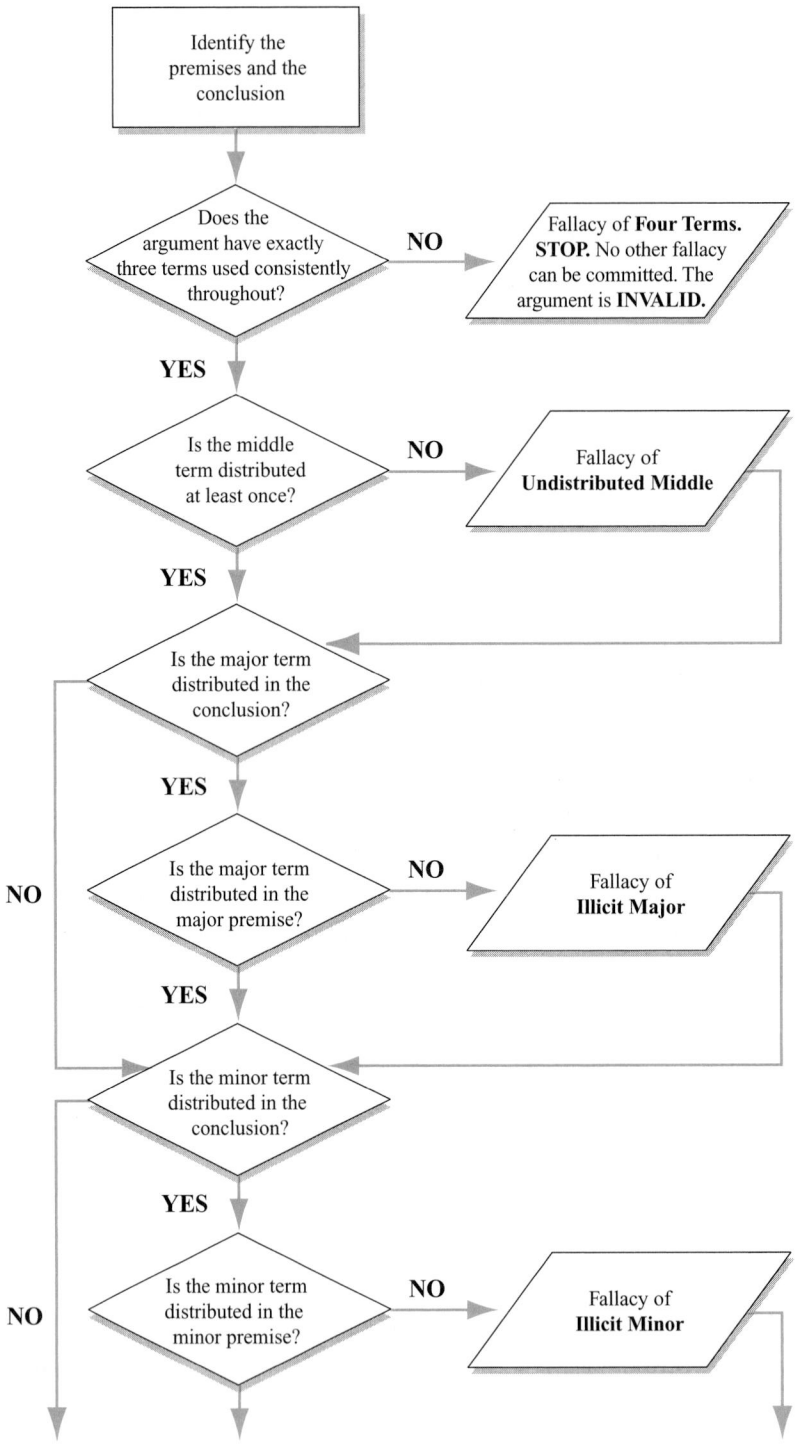

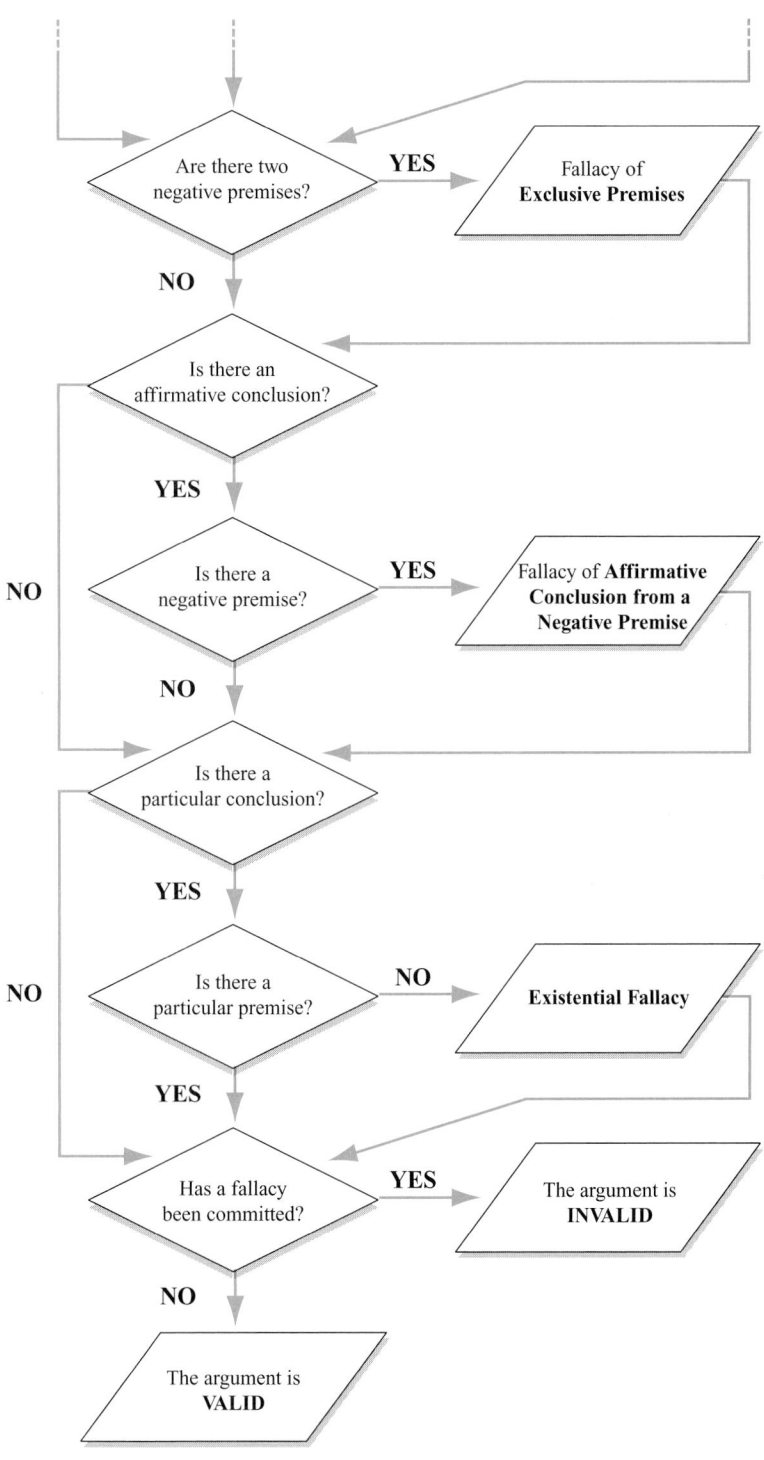

Adapted from Daniel E. Flage, *Understanding Logic* (Prentice Hall, 1995).

EXERCISES

I. Give a schematic diagram of an argument of each of the following forms. Name the rules broken and the fallacies committed by syllogisms of the following forms.

    1. **AAA–3**

    2. **EEE–1**

    3. **EOI–2**

    4. **OII–4**

    5. **IIO–4**

    6. **III–3**

    7. **OEO–4**

    8. **EAO–4**

    9. **EAO–3**

    10. **OAO–2**

II. Identify the rule or rules broken by any of the following syllogisms that are invalid, and name fallacy or fallacies they commit.

    11. All criminal actions are wicked deeds.
        All prosecutions for murder are criminal actions.
        Therefore all prosecutions for murder are wicked deeds.

    12. Some parrots are not pests.
        All parrots are pets.
        Therefore no pets are pests.

    13. Some good actors are not powerful athletes.
        All professional wrestlers are powerful athletes.
        Therefore all professional wrestlers are good actors.

    14. Some diamonds are not precious stones.
        Some carbon compounds are diamonds.
        Therefore some carbon compounds are not precious stones.

    15. All people who are most hungry are people who eat most.
        All people who eat least are people who are most hungry.
        Therefore all people who eat least are people who eat most.

III. Restate the following arguments in standard form. Identify the rule or rules broken by any of the following syllogisms that are invalid, and name the fallacy or fallacies they commit.

    16. All inventors are people who see new patterns in familiar things, so all inventors are eccentrics, since all eccentrics are people who see new patterns in familiar things.

    17. Some snakes are not dangerous animals, but all snakes are reptiles, therefore some dangerous animals are not reptiles.

18. All opponents of basic economic and political changes are outspoken critics of the liberal leaders of Congress, and all right-wing extremists are opponents of basic economic and political changes. It follows that all outspoken critics of the liberal leaders of Congress are rightwing extremists.

19. All supporters of popular government are democrats, so all supporters of popular government are opponents of the Republican Party, inasmuch as all Democrats are opponents of the Republican Party.

20. No coal tar derivatives are nourishing foods, because no coal tar derivatives are natural grain products, and all natural grain products are nourishing foods.

21. All hippopotami are large animals, so some horses are not hippopotami, since some horses are large animals.

22. Some mammals are dogs, so some hounds are dogs, for all hounds are mammals.

23. All people who do these problems are diligent students, but some teachers are not diligent students, so some teachers are people who work these problems.

24. No elephants are spaniels, and no elephants are dogs, so some spaniels are dogs.

25. Some dogs are not pit bulls, so some dogs are not Dobermans, for no Dobermans are pit bulls.

26. Some dogs are schnauzers and some dogs are poodles. So, no poodles are schnauzers.

27. Since some cars are Fords, we may conclude that all Pontiacs are cars, since some Fords are not Pontiacs.

28. Some dogs are poodles, so some cats are not dogs, since some cats are not poodles.

29. All aardvarks are mammals, so some birds are not aardvarks, for some mammals are not birds.

30. Some mice are not cows, since some horses are not mice and no horses are cows.

ESSENTIALS OF CHAPTER 4

In Chapter 4, we examined the standard form categorical syllogism: its elements, its forms, its validity, and the rules governing its proper use. In section 4.1, the major, minor, and middle terms of a syllogism were identified:

- **Major term:** the predicate of the conclusion
- **Minor term:** the subject of the conclusion
- **Middle term:** the third term appearing in both premises but not in the conclusion.

We identified major and minor premises as those containing the major and minor terms, respectively. **We specified that a categorical syllogism is in** *standard form* **when its propositions appear in precisely this order: major premise first, minor premise second, and conclusion last.**

In section 4.1 we also explained how the mood and figure of a syllogism are determined. The **mood of a syllogism** is determined by the three letters identifying the types of its three propositions, **A, E, I,** or **O.** There are 64 different moods.

The **figure of a syllogism** is determined by the position of the middle term in its premises. The four possible figures are described and named thus:

- **First Figure:** The middle term is **the subject term of the major premise and the predicate term of the minor premise.**

  Schematically: $M-P$, $S-M$, therefore $S-P$.

- **Second Figure:** The middle term is **the predicate term of both premises.**

  Schematically: $P-M$, $S-M$, therefore $S-P$.

- **Third Figure:** The middle term is **the subject term of both premises.**

  Schematically: $M-P$, $M-S$, therefore $S-P$.

- **Fourth Figure:** The middle term is **the predicate term of the major premise and the subject term of the minor premise.**

  Schematically: $P-M$, $M-S$, therefore $S-P$.

In section 4.2, we explained how the **mood and figure** of a standard form categorical syllogism **jointly determine its logical form.** Since each of the 64 moods may appear in all four figures, there are exactly 256 standard form categorical syllogisms, of which only 15 are valid.

In section 4.3, we explained the **Venn diagram technique for testing the validity of syllogisms,** using overlapping circles appropriately marked or shaded to exhibit the meaning of the premises.

In section 4.4, we explained the **six rules for standard form syllogisms** and named the **fallacy** that results when each of these rules is broken:

- **Rule 1.** A standard form categorical syllogism must contain exactly three terms, each of which is used in the same sense throughout the argument.

  Violation: Fallacy of **four terms.**

- **Rule 2.** In a valid standard form categorical syllogism, the middle term must be distributed in at least one premise.

  Violation: Fallacy of **undistributed middle.**

- **Rule 3.** In a valid standard form categorical syllogism, if either term is distributed in the conclusion, then it must be distributed in the premises.

  Violation: Fallacy of the **illicit major,** or fallacy of the **illicit minor.**

- **Rule 4.** No standard form categorical syllogism having two negative premises is valid.

  Violation: Fallacy of **exclusive premises**.

- **Rule 5.** If either premise of a valid standard form categorical syllogism is negative, the conclusion must be negative.

  Violation: Fallacy of **drawing an affirmative conclusion from a negative premise**.

- **Rule 6.** No valid standard form categorical syllogism with a particular conclusion can have two universal premises.

  Violation: **Existential fallacy**.

CHAPTER FIVE

ARGUMENTS IN ORDINARY LANGUAGE

5.1 SYLLOGISTIC ARGUMENTS IN ORDINARY LANGUAGE

In ordinary discourse arguments rarely present themselves in the pure language of standard form categorical syllogisms. Nonetheless many arguments in ordinary language are syllogistic in structure and can be reformulated in standard form without any loss or change of meaning. We shall use the phrase "syllogistic argument" in a broad sense to refer to a categorical syllogism that is either in standard form or can be reformulated in standard form without any loss or change of meaning.

The process of reformulating ordinary language arguments as standard form categorical syllogisms is called **reduction to standard form** or **translation to standard form**, and the result is called the *standard form translation* of the original syllogistic argument. Once an argument in ordinary language has been reduced to standard form, we can test its validity with Venn diagrams and the syllogistic rules discussed in Chapter 4.

There are various ways in which a syllogistic argument in natural language can fail to be a standard form categorical syllogism.

1. The order of the premises and conclusion may not follow the pattern for standard form categorical syllogisms.
2. The component propositions of the argument in ordinary language may use more than three terms.
3. The component propositions of the syllogistic argument in natural language may not all be standard form categorical propositions.

We've been reducing arguments to standard form in the first way for some time. It's just a matter of restating the syllogism in the standard order: major premise, minor premise, conclusion, with a line between the minor premise and the conclusion. The other two are a bit trickier because propositions stated in ordinary language often are *not* in standard form, *and* syllogisms in ordinary language often have more than three terms. So, we'll start by discussing the reduction of terms. Then we'll look at transforming nonstandard propositions to standard form. In practice, you'll often reduce propositions to standard form *before* you attempt to reduce the number of terms.

5.2 REDUCING THE NUMBER OF TERMS IN A SYLLOGISTIC ARGUMENT

In Chapter 1 we distinguished between sentences and the propositions they express. Since several sentences can express the same proposition, sometimes the sentences stating a valid syllogism in ordinary language have more than three distinct terms. In that case, you need to reduce the syllogism to standard form by:

- Eliminating synonyms
- Eliminating complementary terms (antonyms)

If two or more terms in an argument are synonyms, you can reduce the number of terms by substituting one synonym for another.

Example

Some sports fans are grade school students.
All elementary school pupils are children.
∴ Some kids are sports fans.

This argument contains five terms, but *grade school students* and *elementary school pupils* are synonyms, as are *children* and *kids*. Eliminating these synonyms gives us a standard form categorical syllogism with three terms. It is the valid form **IAI–4**:

Some sports fans are grade school students.
All grade school students are children.
∴ Some children are sports fans.

> **ESSENTIAL** HINTS
>
> If two terms in an ordinary language syllogism are nearly synonymous, you should treat them as synonyms. This is a charitable interpretation (1.4). So, while *dogs* and *canines* are not strictly synonymous—wolves and foxes, as well as dogs, are canines—you should treat the terms *dogs* and *canines* as synonymous for the sake of the argument.

A syllogistic argument that appears to have more than three terms sometimes contains complementary terms, for example, *dogs* and *nondogs*. To replace a term with its complement, you'll need to look at logically equivalent forms of categorical propositions (3.8). In some cases you'll need to obvert. In other cases you'll need to convert and obvert. In still others you might contrapose or contrapose and obvert. Recall that contraposition and obversion replace terms with their complements.

Example

Reducing the number of terms by conversion and obversion:

All analog watches are watches with hands.
No digital watches are watches with jeweled movements.
All watches with jeweled movements are watches with hands.

To determine whether this argument is valid, you need to recognize that digital watches (watches with numbers on an LED display) are nonanalog watches. So, you might start by restating the minor premise as, "No nonanalog watches are watches with jeweled movements." You can then convert that statement to "No watches with jeweled movements are nonanalog watches" and obvert that statement to "All watches with jeweled movements are analog watches." The resulting syllogism is:

All analog watches are watches with hands.
All watches with jeweled movements are analog watches.
All watches with jeweled movements are watches with hands.

The argument is an **AAA-1**, which is valid.

Example

Reducing the number of terms by contraposition:

No porous material is rainproof material.
All nonrainproof material is nonplastic.
∴ No plastic is porous material.

This syllogism has five terms: *porous material, rainproof material, nonrainproof material, nonplastic,* and *plastic.* But *rainproof material* and *nonrainproof material* are complements, as are *plastic* and *nonplastic.* Applying contraposition to the minor premise changes it from "All nonrainproof material is nonplastic" to "All plastic is rainproof material," eliminating two terms.

> **ESSENTIAL** HINTS
>
> In ordinary language, the complement of a term is usually *not* prefaced with *non-*. It is more common to use prefixes such as *in-* or *im-* or *un-*. But you can't simply assume that one of those prefixes marks the complement of a term without the prefix. If you're not convinced, check the definitions of the terms *flammable* and *inflammable,* or *valuable* and *invaluable.*

The result is:

No porous material is rainproof material.
All plastic is rainproof material.
∴ No plastic is porous material.

This is a valid categorical syllogism in the form **EAE–2**.

Sometimes you need to pay attention to the *context* assumed by the syllogism if you are to reduce the number of terms.

Example

All politicians elected to two-year terms are people who never stop campaigning.
No senators are politicians elected to two-year terms.
So, all members of the House of Representatives are people who never stop campaigning.

We seem to have four terms. But the context assumed by the argument is members of Congress. Senators are nonrepresentatives; representatives are nonsenators. So, the second premise is equivalent to "No nonrepresentatives are politicians elected to two-year terms," which converts to "No politicians elected to two-year terms are nonrepresentatives," which obverts to "All politicians elected to two-year terms are representatives." So, you can restate the argument as:

All politicians elected to two-year terms are people who never stop campaigning.
All politicians elected to two-year terms are representatives.
∴ All representatives are people who never stop campaigning.

The syllogism is of the form **AAA-1**, which is valid.

EXERCISES

Translate these syllogisms into standard form by eliminating synonyms and complements. Then identify the form of the argument and, if it is possible to do so, construct a Venn diagram to determine whether it is valid. If it is invalid, list the fallacies committed.

1. Some students are meticulous.
No member of my class is a student.
∴ Some of my classmates are extremely careful about details.

2.   All nonadults are noneligible voters.
     <u>All people over 18 are eligible voters.</u>
     ∴All people over 18 are nonminors.

3.   All nonman's best friends are nonsmart animals.
     <u>All nonsmart animals are nondogs.</u>
     ∴ Dog is man's best friend.

4. Some metals are rare and costly substances, but no welder's materials are nonmetals; hence some welder's materials are rare and costly substances.

5. Some Asian nations were nonbelligerents, since all belligerents were allies either of Germany or Britain, and some Asian nations were not allies of either Germany or Britain.

6. All things inflammable are unsafe things, so all things that are safe are nonexplosives, since all explosives are flammable things.

7. All worldly goods are changeable things, for no worldly goods are things immaterial, and no material things are unchangeable things.

8. All mortals are imperfect beings, and no humans are immortals, whence it follows that all perfect beings are nonhumans.

9. All things present are nonirritants; therefore no irritants are invisible objects, because all visible objects are absent things.

10. All useful things are objects no more than six feet long, since all difficult things to store are useless things, and no objects over six feet long are easy things to store.

5.3   TRANSLATING CATEGORICAL PROPOSITIONS INTO STANDARD FORM

In many cases syllogistic arguments in ordinary language do not contain standard form categorical propositions. Reducing syllogisms whose propositions are in nonstandard form requires first reformulating those propositions as **A, E, I,** or **O** propositions without changing their meanings. No hard and fast rules dictate how to do this in all cases. The following discussion suggests guidelines for reformulating ten categories of nonstandard propositions. In all cases, however, it is important to translate the *meaning* of the propositions in question, rather than just relying on the general rules, because the rules have exceptions. This means that you must pay careful attention to what is being said by an argument in natural language before trying to reduce it. Keep in mind that the context in which a syllogism is presented can have an important impact on the meaning of the syllogism's propositions, and thus can have an impact on how (and to what) those propositions get reduced. In such cases, especially, it is important to consider the meaning of the propositions in an argument rather than only their syntactic structures.

A. Singular Propositions

Singular propositions affirm or deny that a specific individual or object belongs to a certain class of objects. "Hillary Clinton is a Democrat" and "My car is not white" are examples. Although singular propositions refer to individual objects, we can interpret them as referring to a **unit class**, a class that contains only a single member. This being so, an *affirmative singular proposition* **can be understood as a standard form A proposition**. For example, "Hillary Clinton is a Democrat" can be understood as the **A** proposition, "All people who are Hillary Clinton are Democrats." Similarly, a negative singular proposition such as "My car is not white" can be understood as the standard form **E** proposition, "No thing that is my car is a white thing." It is customary to make this interpretation automatically, however, without any explicit reformulation. In other words, affirmative singular propositions are understood as **A** propositions, and negative singular propositions are understood as **E** propositions.

But singular propositions tell us more than is asserted by a universal. Hillary Clinton is a real person, so it follows that there is at least one person who is a Democrat, that is, "Some people are Democrats." So, the singular proposition, "Hillary Clinton is a Democrat," can be understood as the **I** proposition, "Some people who are Hillary Clinton are Democrats." Similarly, the singular proposition, "My car is not white," can be understood as the **O** proposition, "Some things that are my car are not white things." So, a singular proposition can be understood as asserting both a universal and its corresponding particular of the same quality.

In practice this means that, if a premise and the conclusion of a syllogism are singular propositions with the same subject term, you can treat them *both* as universals or you can treat them *both* as particulars.

> **ESSENTIAL** HINTS
>
> Some people translate a singular proposition into a universal or a particular by placing an *All* or a *Some* in parentheses before the subject term since that expresses the sense of the proposition. If *you* do that, you must remember that the proposition still is concerned with exactly one thing. So, "(All) Hillary Clinton is a Democrat" is short for "All things identical with Hillary Clinton are Democrats." It *does not* mean "All Hillary Clintons are Democrats." For example, my neighbor, Hillary Clinton, who is *not* identical to the former first lady, might be a Republican or a communist or have no political affiliation.

Example _____

All Democrats who are older than 35 are potential presidential candidates.
Hillary Clinton is a Democrat who is older than 35.
∴ Hillary Clinton is a potential presidential candidate.

can be treated as:

All Democrats who are older than 35 are potential presidential candidates.
All people who are Hillary Clinton are Democrats who are older than 35.
∴ All people who are Hillary Clinton are potential presidential candidates.

or:

All Democrats who are older than 35 are potential presidential candidates.
Some people who are Hillary Clinton are Democrats who are older than 35.
∴ Some people who are Hillary Clinton are potential presidential candidates.

The first is an **AAA-1**. The second is an **AII-1**. Both are valid.

_____

If two singular propositions are the premises of an argument, however, you can't treat *both* as universals or *both* as particulars. If the argument is obviously valid, you treat one proposition as a universal and the other as a particular.

Example _____

Hillary Clinton is a Democrat.
Hillary Clinton is a former first lady.
∴ Some former first ladies are Democrats.

The premises show that there is at least one person—Hillary Clinton—who is both a former first lady and a Democrat, which is what is asserted by the conclusion. If you treated both premises as universals, the syllogism would commit the *existential fallacy* (Rule 6). If you treated both as particulars, the syllogism would commit the fallacy of *undistributed middle* (Rule 2). So, you treat one premise as a universal and the other premise as a particular. This means the syllogism is treated as either an **AII-3** or an **IAI-3**:

All *M* are *P*.	Some *M* are *P*.
Some *M* is *S*.	All *M* are *S*.
∴ Some *S* is *P*.	∴ Some *S* are *P*.

Both forms are valid.

_____

EXERCISES

Translate these singular propositions into standard form. Translate them as both universal and particular.

1. Muhammad Ali is a boxer.
2. George is not a monkey.
3. My dentist is a person who likes white teeth.
4. Mother Teresa is a saint.
5. George Bush is a Republican.
6. Billy Sunday was a preacher.
7. Brad Pitt is an actor.
8. Renée Zellweger is an Academy Award winner.
9. Helen Keller was a writer and lecturer.
10. This exercise is an easy exercise.

B. Categorical Propositions with Adjectives or Adjectival Phrases as Predicates

Propositions in ordinary language often have adjectives (such as *beautiful*, *red*, or *wicked*) and adjectival phrases (such as "on assignment" or "out of time") instead of class terms as predicates. Such propositions are not standard form categorical propositions since the predicate term does not explicitly refer to a class of *things*. To reformulate such propositions into standard form we can **replace the adjective (or adjectival phrase) with a term designating the class of objects to which the adjective or adjectival phrase applies.**[1]

Example

The predicate of the proposition, "Some flowers are beautiful," is an adjective. It could be reformulated in standard **I** proposition form as "Some flowers are beauties" or "Some flowers are beautiful things."

The predicate of the proposition, "All students who haven't finished the test yet are out of time," is an adjectival phrase. It could be reformulated as a standard **A** proposition: "All students who haven't finished the test yet are students who are out of time."

---

[1]You'll notice that we did this above when we reformulated the singular proposition "My car is not white" as the categorical proposition "No thing that is my car is a white thing."

EXERCISES

Translate these propositions into standard form:

1. Muhammad Ali is the greatest.
2. George is out to lunch.
3. My doctor is out of time.
4. Mother Teresa is not self-indulgent.
5. All astronauts are courageous.
6. Some cows are brown.
7. Some houses are not built for families of six or more.
8. No famous jazz trumpeters are under the age of ten.
9. All Swedish meatballs are made from beef and pork.
10. Some exercises are harder than others.

C. Categorical Propositions with Verbs Other Than the Standard Form Copula *To Be*

Propositions with a main verb other than *to be* can be translated into standard form by treating the verb phrase as a class-defining characteristic.

Examples

"All celebrities crave the spotlight," which has a main verb other than a form of *to be*, can be translated into the standard form proposition, "All celebrities are spotlight cravers" or "All celebrities are people who crave the spotlight." "Some cats eat dog food" can be translated into the standard form proposition, "Some cats are eaters of dog food" or "Some cats are animals that eat dog food."

EXERCISES

Translate these propositions into standard form:

1. Muhammad Ali stings like a bee.
2. George has wooden teeth.
3. My doctor didn't follow his own advice.
4. Some nuns teach love and kindness.
5. All cows eat grass.

6. Some cars guzzle gas.

7. The person to my left has bad breath.

8. Some hairdos keep hairdressers awake at night.

9. All stained houses fade after a few years.

10. Some exercises try your patience.

D. Categorical Propositions in Nonstandard Order

In ordinary language we sometimes encounter statements with all the ingredients of standard form categorical propositions but arranged in nonstandard order. To reformulate one of these, we must first decide which term is the subject term and then rearrange the words to make a standard form categorical proposition.

Example

The proposition, "Dogs registered by the American Kennel Club are all purebreds," which is in nonstandard order, can be rephrased in standard form as "All dogs registered by the American Kennel Club are purebreds." When the order is nonstandard, you can usually tell what must have been meant by asking whether the proposed proposition in standard form is true. (Not all purebred dogs are registered.)

EXERCISES

Translate these propositions into standard form:

1. Boxers all worship Muhammad Ali.

2. Georges are all curious monkeys.

3. Doctors all have their faults.

4. Mothers are all a little crazy.

5. The poor ye have with thee at all times.

6. Well-known racehorses are all thoroughbreds.

7. "Abandon all hope ye who enter here."
   —Dante, *The Inferno*

8. Arguments of the form **AAA-1** and **AII-1** are some of the most common examples of categorical syllogisms in ordinary English.

9. A Chevy Cavalier is no Corvette.

10. A new Ford is not some old car your dad used to drive.

E. Categorical Propositions with Nonstandard Quantifiers

Ordinary language has a far richer variety of terms designating quantity than the three standard form quantifiers *all*, *no*, and *some*. Propositions with universal affirmative quantifying terms like *every* and *any* are usually easily translated into **A** propositions. Other affirmative universal quantifiers, such as *whoever*, *everyone*, and *anyone*, refer specifically to classes of people.

Example

"Anyone born in the United States is a citizen" translates into standard form as "All people born in the United States are citizens."

The grammatical articles *a* and *an* may also serve to indicate quantity, but whether they are used to mean *all* or *some* depends largely on context.

Examples

"A candidate for office is a politician" is reasonably interpreted to mean "All candidates for office are politicians."
   "A candidate for office is speaking at a campaign rally tonight," in contrast, is properly reduced to "Some candidates are speakers at a campaign rally tonight."

The article *the*, again depending on context, may be used to refer either to a particular individual or to all members of a class.

Examples

"The grapefruit is a citrus fruit" translates into standard form as "All grapefruits are citrus fruits."
   "The grapefruit was delicious this morning," in contrast, translates as "Some grapefruit is a thing that was delicious this morning."

Negative quantifiers such as *not every* and *not any* are trickier than affirmative quantifiers and require special care in reformulation. Thus, for example, "Not every S is P," reformulates as "Some S is not P," whereas "Not any S is P" reformulates as "No S is P."

Examples

"Not every public servant is a politician" translates into standard form as "Some public servants are not politicians."

"Not any public servants are politicians" translates as "No public servants are politicians."

EXERCISES

Translate these propositions into standard form:

1. Not every great boxer is a Muhammad Ali.
2. Not just any old monkey is named George.
3. The doctor is not in.
4. A woman is nursing the sick in the street.
5. Not every problem in this set is difficult.
6. Not any problem in this set is difficult.
7. Whoever went to last night's game saw an exciting finish.
8. The cat next door is a pest.
9. The dog is a mammal.
10. Anyone who figures out these wrinkles on translation is ready to go on to the next ones.

F. Exclusive Propositions

Categorical propositions that involve the words *only* or *none but* are called **exclusive propositions**. Exclusive propositions translate into **A** propositions. The general rule is convert the subject and predicate, and replace the *only* with *all*. Thus, "Only S are P" and "None but S's are P's" are understood to express "All P are S."

> **ESSENTIAL** HINTS
>
> The sense of "None but S are P" is "No non-S are P," which converts to "No P are non-S," which obverts to "All P are S."

Examples

"Only actors who have appeared in critically acclaimed movies are serious Oscar contenders" translates into standard form as "All serious Oscar contenders are actors who have appeared in critically acclaimed movies."

"None but the brave deserves the fair" translates into standard form as the considerably less eloquent "All people who deserve the fair are people who are brave."

But *only* is peculiar. *Only* is sometimes taken to mean "if and only if" which, as we'll see in Chapter 6, means both "If *S* then *P*" and "If *P* then *S*." So, if you have an exclusive proposition of the form, "Only *S* are *P*," you apply the general rule and translate it as "All *P* are *S*," plug it into the syllogism, and discover that the syllogism is invalid, you are *not* finished with the syllogism. You should then check the alternative formulation of the proposition, namely, "All *S* are *P*." If the proposition is true, plug it into the syllogism and check it again.

Example

In the proposition "Only mammals are warmblooded vertebrates that are usually hairy and whose offspring are fed with milk secreted by the female mammary glands," the predicate term defines the subject term.[2] So, the proposition can be taken to mean *both* "All warmblooded vertebrates that are usually hairy and whose offspring are fed with milk secreted by the female mammary glands are mammals" *and* "All mammals are warmblooded vertebrates that are usually hairy and whose offspring are fed with milk secreted by the female mammary glands." If you plug the first statement into a syllogism and the argument is invalid, you must *also* test the second statement.

The only, on the other hand, leaves the order as it stands.

Example

The only person who finished the assignment was Carl.

The sense of the proposition is that there is exactly one person who finished the assignment and that person was Carl. The class of people who finished the assignment is entirely contained in the class of things that are Carl, that is, "All people who finished the assignment are people identical with Carl."

---

[2]See *Webster's New World Dictionary and Thesaurus* (Macmillan Digital Publishing, 1997).

EXERCISES

Translate these propositions into standard form:

1. None without geometry enter here.
2. Only the greatest can be like Muhammad Ali.
3. The only monkey with his own book series is Curious George.
4. Only dead doctors are members of this club.
5. None but the clever figure out how to translate *none but*.
6. No one except a philosopher would read Wittgenstein's *Tractaus Logico-Philosophicus*.
7. Only mammals are horses.
8. None but logicians find the words *none but* fascinating.
9. Katrina is the only person in this class who finds exclusive propositions amusing.
10. Only those with an odd interest in odd terms are sad that this set of exercises is over.

G. Propositions Without Quantifiers

Sometimes categorical propositions appear in the form "*S* is *P*" without any words that indicate quantity. The context in which such a proposition appears is our only hint as to how it should be reformulated.

Example

Whales are mammals.

Although this proposition has no quantifier, it translates into standard form as "All whales are mammals." However, "Dogs are barking" probably means "Some dogs are animals that are barking."

H. Propositions Not in Standard Form that Have Logically Equivalent Standard Form Alternatives

Propositions that do not resemble standard form categorical propositions often can be rephrased as logically equivalent propositions in standard form.

Example

The proposition, "There are professional baseball players who are underpaid," is not in standard form, but it is logically equivalent to the standard form proposition, "Some professional baseball players are underpaid players." Success in this kind of reduction requires careful attention to the meanings of the propositions to be reduced.

I. Exceptive Propositions

Exceptive propositions are propositions that assert that all members of some class, with the exception of the members of one of its subclasses, are members of some other class. Exceptive propositions make a compound claim: first, that *all members of the subject class not in the excepted subclass are members of the predicate class,* and second, that *no members of the excepted subclass are members of the predicate class.*

Example

All students except seniors are eligible to apply for the scholarship.

This proposition, like all exceptive propositions, makes a compound claim: first, that all nonseniors are eligible to apply for the scholarship, and, second, that no senior is eligible to apply for the scholarship.

Because exceptive propositions are compounds, they cannot be translated into single standard form categorical propositions, so arguments containing them are not syllogistic arguments. Nonetheless, they can sometimes be susceptible to syllogistic analysis and appraisal.

Example

All students except seniors are eligible to apply for the scholarship.
Some students in the music class are not seniors.
∴ Some students in the music class are eligible to apply for the scholarship.

The first premise is an exceptive proposition and is thus a compound of two categorical propositions: "All nonseniors are eligible to apply for the scholarship" and "No seniors are eligible to apply for the scholarship." To analyze the original argument as a syllogistic argument, we need to focus on each of these propositions separately. If substituting either one for the first premise yields a valid categorical syllogism, then the argument is valid. Substituting the first proposition we get:

All nonseniors are eligible to apply for the scholarship.
Some students in the music class are nonseniors.
∴ Some students in the music class are eligible to apply for the scholarship.

This standard form categorical syllogism is in the valid form **AII–1**, so the original argument is valid.

J. More Complex Quantifiers

Almost all, Not quite all, and *Only some* mean *both* some are *and* some are not. "Almost all students are serious scholars" means both "Some students are serious scholars" and "Some students are not serious scholars." If you have a *premise* with a complex quantifier, use whichever of the two meanings will give you a valid argument. If neither yields a valid syllogism, you must show that neither does. At most, one categorical proposition follows from a pair of standard form categorical propositions. So, if a complex quantifier is the *conclusion* of an argument, you can show that the argument is invalid by showing that *one* form of the conclusion does *not* follow from the premises.

> **ESSENTIAL** HINTS
>
> **Can an argument with a complex quantifier in the conclusion be valid?**
> Assume you are given the argument:
>
> Only some M are P.
> All M are S.
> Only some S are P.
>
> If you interpret the argument *charitably*, you will interpret it as *two* distinct arguments:
>
> Some M are P.   Some M are not P.
> All M are S.   All M are S.
> Some S are P.   Some S are not P.
>
> Each of these argument forms is valid.

Examples

All dogs are animals that bark.
Only some dogs are pit bulls.
∴ Some pit bulls are animals that bark.

The proposition "Only some dogs are pit bulls" makes two claims: "Some dogs are pit bulls" and "Some dogs are not pit bulls." If we inserted the **O** proposition, we would break Rule 5; we'd commit the *fallacy of drawing an affirmative conclusion from a negative premise*. But since the minor premise *also* asserts the **I** proposition, "Some dogs are pit bulls," we are free to insert the **I** proposition into the syllogism. This results in the syllogism:

All dogs are animals that bark.
Some dogs are pit bulls.
∴ Some pit bulls are animals that bark.

The argument is an **AII-3**, which is valid.

On the other hand, if we're given the argument:

All dogs are animals that bark.
Some dogs are pit bulls.
∴ Not quite all pit bulls are animals that bark.

the conclusion asserts *both* "Some pit bulls are animals that bark" and "Some pit bulls are not animals that bark." Since at most one proposition follows from a pair of standard form categorical propositions, *both* claims *cannot* follow. So, you choose the one that *does not* follow and reconstruct the syllogism as follows:

All dogs are animals that bark.
Some dogs are pit bulls.
∴ Some pit bulls are not animals that bark.

This is an **AIO-3**. It breaks Rule 3; it commits the *fallacy of illicit major*. It is invalid.

A GUIDE TO NONSTANDARD QUANTIFIERS	
NONSTANDARD FORM	**TRANSLATION INTO STANDARD FORM**
A (an) S is P.	Some S are P. For example, "A dog is on the mat" means "Some dog is on the mat." **In some contexts** "All S are P." For example, "A dog is a mammal" means "All dogs are mammals."
A few S are P.	Some S are P.
All but S are P.	All non-S are P **and** No S are P.
All except S are P.	All non-S are P **and** No S are P.
Almost all S are P.	Some S are P **and** Some S are not P.
Any S are P.	All S are P.
At least one S is P.	Some S are P.
Diverse S are P.	Some S are P.
Every S is P.	All S are P.
Many S are P.	Some S are P.
None but S are P.	All P are S.
None of the Ss are Ps.	No S are P.
Not all S are P.	Some S are not P.
Not any S are P.	No S are P.
Not every S is P.	Some S are not P.
Not only S are P.	Some P are not S.
Not quite all S are P.	Some S are P **and** Some S are not P.
Numerous Ss are Ps.	Some S are P.

Only S are P.	All P are S. **But** if this yields an invalid syllogism and the statement "All S are P" is true, insert "All S are P" into the syllogism and check that syllogism for validity.
Only some S are P.	Some S are P **and** Some S are not P.
Several S are P.	Some S are P.
The only S is P.	All S are P.
The S is P.	All S are P **or** Some S are P, depending upon the context.
There exists an S that is P.	Some S are P.
There is an S that is P.	Some S are P.
There is no S unless it's a P.	All S are P.
Various Ss are Ps.	Some S are P.
Whatever S is P.	All S are P.

EXERCISES

Translate the following statements into standard form categorical propositions.

1. Cats are curious.
2. Only optimists think positively all the time.
3. Not every preacher is a boring speaker.
4. Forbidden things alone are truly interesting things.
5. A logician is a person who analyzes arguments.
6. Love is a mystery.
7. You have to look at the bright side of life.
8. This has happened before, and it has always been attributed to human error.
9. Many a person has lived to regret a misspent youth.
10. Nothing is both safe and exciting.
11. He sees not his shadow who faces the sun.
12. Nobody doesn't like Sara Lee.
13. Happy indeed is she who knows her own limitations.
14. None think the great unhappy but the great.

15. A soft answer turneth away wrath.

16. Only some of these exercises are puzzling.

17. Everyone except scoundrels can be expected to tell the truth.

18. There is no animal that expects to be worshiped unless it's a cat.

19. Several of these exercises could be challenging.

20. Almost everyone who has reached this point in the exercises is glad they're finished.

5.4   UNIFORM TRANSLATION

To reformulate certain arguments as standard form categorical syllogisms, we sometimes have to introduce a *parameter*—**an auxiliary symbol that is of aid in expressing the original assertion in standard form**. The use of a parameter that permits a uniform translation of all three constituent propositions results in a syllogism containing exactly three terms. Common parameters are terms such as *times*, *places*, and *cases*.

The sentence "The poor always you have with you," can be expressed as a standard form categorical statement, but reducing it is tricky. It does not mean that *all* the poor are with you, or even that some (particular) poor are *always* with you. One way to reduce this proposition is to make use of the key word *always*, which means *at all times*. Thus we can reduce the original proposition to "All times are times when you have the poor with you." The word *times*, which appears in both the subject and the predicate term, is a parameter.

Example _____

Wherever it is raining the sky is overcast.
It's raining here.
∴ It's overcast here.

In order to express this argument as a standard form, three-term syllogism we introduce the parameter "places." We thus obtain:

All places where it is raining are places where the sky is overcast.
This place is a place where it is raining.
∴ This place is a place where the sky is overcast.

The singular proposition in the second premise is understood as the **A** proposition "All places that are this place are places where it is raining." And the singular proposition in the conclusion is understood as the **A** proposition "Therefore all places that are this place are places where the sky is overcast." Thus this is a valid syllogism in the form **AA–1**.

Introducing parameters into a translation is a delicate affair. In order to avoid mistakes you must always be guided by a precise understanding of the original proposition.

EXERCISES

I. Translate the following sentences into standard form categorical propositions, using parameters where necessary.

1. Susan never eats her lunch at her desk.
2. If Peter is asked to speak, then Peter speaks for hours.
3. Errors are tolerated only when they are the result of honest mistakes.
4. She never drives her car to work.
5. He walks where he chooses.
6. He always orders the most expensive item on the menu.
7. She tries to sell life insurance wherever she may happen to be.
8. His face gets red when he gets angry.
9. The lights are always on.
10. Error of opinion may be tolerated where reason is left free to combat it.

II. For each of the following arguments:

a. Translate the argument into standard form.
b. Name the mood and figure of its standard form translation.
c. Test its validity using a Venn Diagram.
d. If it is invalid, name the fallacy or fallacies it commits.

11. . . . no names come in contradictory pairs; but all predicables come in contradictory pairs; therefore no name is a predicable.
    —Peter Thomas Geach, *Reference and Generality*

12. Barcelona Traction was unable to pay interest on its debts; bankrupt companies are unable to pay interest on their debts; therefore, Barcelona Traction must be bankrupt.
    —John Brooks, "Annals of Finance," *The New Yorker,* 28 May 1979

13. Any two persons who contradict each other cannot both be lying. Hence the first and third natives cannot both be lying, since they contradict each other.

14. Where there's smoke there's fire, so there's no fire in the basement, because there's no smoke there.

15. All bridge players are people. All people think. Therefore all bridge players think.
    —Oswald and James Jacoby, "Jacoby on Bridge,"
    Syndicated Column, 5 November 1966

16. It must have rained lately, because the fish are not biting, and fish never bite after a rain.

17. Since then to fight against neighbors is an evil, and to fight against the Thebans is to fight against neighbors, it is clear that to fight against the Thebans is an evil.

—Aristotle, *Prior Analytics*

18. Not all who have jobs are temperate in their drinking. Only debtors drink to excess. So not all the unemployed are in debt.

19. Cynthia must have complimented Henry because he is cheerful whenever Cynthia compliments him, and he's cheerful now.

20. And no man can be a rhapsodist who does not understand the meaning of the poet. For the rhapsodist ought to interpret the mind of the poet to his hearers, but how can he interpret him well unless he knows what he means?

—Plato, *Ion*

21. The express train alone does not stop at this station, and as the last train did not stop, it must have been the express train.

22. There are plants growing here, and since vegetation requires water, water must be present.

23. There are handsome men, but only man is vile, so it is false that nothing is both vile and handsome.

24. Although he complains whenever he is sick, his health is excellent, so he won't complain.

25. All who were penniless were convicted. Some of the guilty were acquitted. Therefore some who had money were not innocent.

5.5 ENTHYMEMES

In everyday discourse we frequently state arguments elliptically, omitting premises or a conclusion that we expect our listeners or readers to fill in. **An argument that is stated incompletely is called an *enthymeme*.** An incompletely stated argument is characterized as being *enthymematic*.

Why do people leave parts of an argument unstated? Enthymematic arguments can be rhetorically powerful. You might take it as a compliment if someone leaves part of an argument unstated. It suggests that the arguer believes you can figure out what follows from a set of premises or what the "obvious" missing premise is. But enthymemes can also cover a multitude of intellectual sins. They can hide a false premise or an invalid argument. So, we need a method to figure out what the missing element *must be* if the argument is valid, and to explain why, in some cases, *no premise* will yield a valid syllogism. Once you find the missing element, you still need to ask whether the missing element is true or false. We begin with syllogisms in which the conclusion is unstated.

If you are given a pair of premises for a categorical syllogism, you can construct a Venn diagram to see what conclusion, if any, follows from the premises.

All aardvarks are mammals, and all mammals are animals with backbones, so the conclusion is obvious.

If you draw a Venn diagram for the premises, you'll diagram the conclusion, "All aardvarks are animals with backbones."

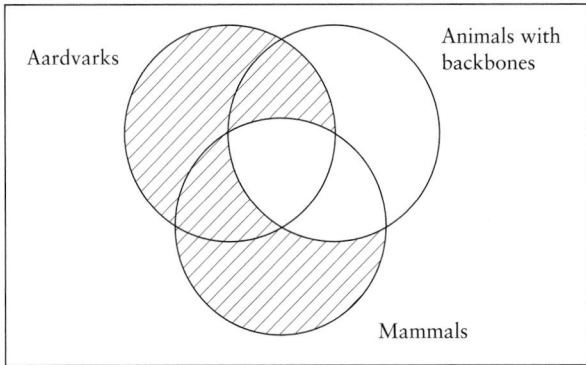

Of course, it doesn't always work out so nicely. Sometimes *no* categorical statement follows from the premises; the premises alone entail a fallacy.

Since no aardvarks are birds, and not any birds are spiders, the conclusion is obvious.

We trust *you're* saying that what's *obvious* is that the argument as it stands commits the fallacy of exclusive premises, so nothing follows. And, of course, the Venn diagram shows that no conclusion is entailed by the premises.

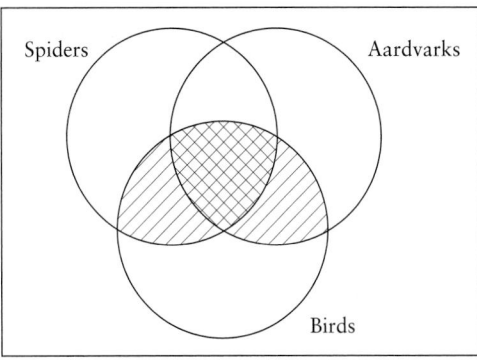

If you're given a premise and a conclusion, there is a procedure you can follow to find what premise, if any, will yield a valid syllogism.

1. If you find *any* of the following, *no* premise will yield a valid syllogism:

   a. If you are given a universal conclusion and a particular premise, no premise will yield a valid syllogism.

   b. If you are given an affirmative conclusion and a negative premise, no premise will yield a valid syllogism (it commits the fallacy of drawing an affirmative conclusion from a negative premise).

   c. If the distribution of the major or minor term (as the case might be) in the conclusion differs from the distribution of the term in the given premise, no premise will yield a valid syllogism.

If you confront *any* of those conditions, the argument is invalid as it stands. Indicate that it's invalid and cite the relevant condition under 1 above. If *none* of those conditions holds, it is possible to find a premise that yields a valid syllogism by the following steps.

2. Finding the quantity (universal or particular) of the missing premise:

   a. If the conclusion is universal, the missing premise is universal.

   b. If the conclusion is particular *and* the given premise is universal, the missing premise is particular.

   c. If the conclusion is particular *and* the given premise is particular, the missing premise is universal.

3. Finding the quality (affirmative or negative) of the missing premise:

   a. If the conclusion is affirmative, the missing premise is affirmative.

   b. If the conclusion is negative *and* the given premise is affirmative, the missing premise is negative.

   c. If the conclusion is negative *and* the given premise is negative, the missing premise is affirmative.

By this point you know whether the missing premise is an *A*, an *E*, an *I*, or an *O*.

4. Distribution:

   a. Assign the same distribution to the major or minor term (as the case might be) in the missing premise as it has in the conclusion.

   b. Make sure the middle term is distributed *exactly once* in the premises. (If you've done everything above correctly, the position of the middle term in the missing premise will be determined, and the middle term *will* be distributed *exactly once* in the premises. This is a partial check on your work.)

Examples _____

No two-year-olds are readers, so no two-year-olds are cooks.

Because both the given premise and the conclusion are universal negatives, none of the situations listed under **1** above is found. So, there *is* a premise that will yield a valid syllogism. The conclusion is universal, so the premise must be universal (**2a**). Both the given premise and the conclusion are negative, so the missing premise must be affirmative (**3c**). So, the missing premise is an **A** proposition. Because the major term, *cooks*, is distributed in the conclusion, we must distribute *cooks* in the premise (**4a**). The middle term, *readers*, is distributed in the minor premise (the given premise), so it must be *undistributed* in the major premise (**4b**). So the missing premise must be "All cooks are readers" —it's the only premise that yields a valid syllogism.

All cooks are readers.
No two-year-olds are readers.
∴ No two-year-olds are cooks.

Of course, the syllogism is *unsound*, since the missing premise is false. If you have any question of its falsehood, trace your ancestry back a few years—15,000 years should do—and you'll find an ancestor who could cook but couldn't read: there were no readers before there was written language.

At least one person who is reading this is a bit puzzled. So, there is a logic student who is puzzled.

After reducing the premise and conclusion to standard form, you have this:

Some person who is reading this is a puzzled person.
∴ Some logic student is a puzzled person.

Again, you look at the conditions under **1**. Since both the given premise and the conclusion are **I** propositions, we don't have a universal conclusion from a particular premise (**1a**), an affirmative conclusion from a negative premise (**1b**), or a difference in the distribution of the major term (**1c**). So there is a premise that will yield a valid syllogism. Both the given premise and the conclusion are particular, so the missing premise must be universal (**2c**). Both the given premise and the conclusion are affirmative, so the missing premise must be affirmative (**3a**). So, the missing premise must be an **A** proposition. The minor term, *logic* *students*, is undistributed in the conclusion, so it must be undistributed in the premise. The middle term, *people who are reading this*, is undistributed in the given premise, so it must be distributed in the missing premise (**4b**). So the missing premise must be, "All people who are reading this are logic students." So long as you're willing to grant that even logic teachers are logic students, the premise is true.

Of course, things don't always (usually?) work out that nicely.

Example _____

Someone reading this sentence is clueless. So no one reading this sentence is a logic student.

State the premise and conclusion in standard form:

Some person reading this sentence is a clueless person.
∴ No person reading this sentence is a logic student.

1a assures us that you can never derive a universal conclusion from a particular premise. So, there is *no* premise that will yield a valid syllogism.

Our procedure is very formal. It does *not* tell you what the person offering an enthymematic syllogism *actually* assumed. Mind reading, alas, is outside the domain of logic. It *does* tell you what the person offering the enthymematic argument *must have* assumed *if* the syllogism is valid. So, if the arguer pays *you* a rhetorical compliment in presenting an enthymematic syllogism, *you* return the compliment by treating the arguer as someone who can do logic.

EXERCISES

Identify the missing premise or conclusion in each of the following enthymematic arguments, then rephrase the argument in syllogistic form.

1. Hal is an honest person, for no refined people are dishonest.
2. All proposals in the green folder were rejected, and all of our proposals were in the green folder.
3. Susanna is a safe driver, so her insurance rates are low.
4. Billy Bob, on the other hand, has had lots of accidents.
5. Hal is a series 9000 computer, and computers don't lie.

6. Education standards are declining, for logic is not a required course.

7. The soul through all her being is immortal, for that which is ever in motion is immortal.

—Plato, *Phaedrus*

8. As a matter of fact, man, like woman, is flesh, therefore passive, the plaything of his hormones and of the species, the restless prey of his desires.

—Simone De Beauvoir, *The Second Sex*

9. . . . I am an Idealist, since I believe that all that exists is spiritual.

—John McTaggart, Ellis McTaggart, *Philosophical Studies*

10. All physicians are college graduates, so all members of the American Medical Association must be college graduates.

11. It must have rained lately, because the fish just aren't biting.

12. Henry is interested only in making money, but you cannot serve both God and Mammon!

13. No enthymemes are complete, so this argument is incomplete.

14. He knows his own child, so he must be a wise father.

15. He who is without sin should cast the first stone. There is no one here who does not have a skeleton in his closet. I know, and I know them by name.

—Representative Adam Clayton Powell,
speech in the U.S. House of Representatives, 1967

16. Man tends to increase at a greater rate than his means of subsistence; consequently he is occasionally subject to a severe struggle for existence.

—Charles Darwin, *The Descent of Man*

17. Liberty means responsibility. That is why most men dread it.

—George Bernard Shaw, *Maxims for Revolutionists*

18. Who controls the past controls the future. Who controls the present controls the past.

—George Orwell, *1984*

19. Advertisements perform a vital function in almost any society, for they help to bring buyers and sellers together.

—Burton M. Leiser, *Liberty, Justice, and Morals*

20. . . . the law does not expressly permit suicide, and what it does not expressly permit it forbids.

—Aristotle, *Nichomachean Ethics*

ESSENTIALS OF CHAPTER 5

In this chapter we have examined syllogistic argument as it is used in ordinary language, exhibiting the different guises in which syllogisms appear and showing how they may be best understood, used, and evaluated.

In section 5.1, we explained the need for techniques to translate syllogistic arguments of any form into standard form. And we identified **the ways in which syllogistic arguments may deviate from standard form categorical syllogisms.**

In section 5.2, we explained **how syllogisms in ordinary language appearing to have more than three terms may sometimes have the number of terms in them appropriately reduced to three** by eliminating synonyms and complementary terms.

In section 5.3, we explained **how the propositions of a syllogistic argument, when not in standard form, may be translated into standard form so as to allow the syllogism to be tested** either by Venn diagrams or by use of the rules governing categorical syllogisms. Nonstandard propositions of **ten different kinds** were examined, and the methods for translating each kind were explained and illustrated:

1. Singular propositions
2. Propositions having adjectives as predicates
3. Propositions having main verbs other than *to be*
4. Statements having standard form ingredients, but not in standard form order
5. Propositions having quantifiers other than *all*, *no*, and *some*
6. Exclusive propositions, using *only* or *none but*
7. Propositions without words indicating quantity
8. Propositions not resembling standard form propositions at all
9. Exceptive propositions, using *all except* or similar expressions
10. Other complex quantifiers, such as *almost all*

In section 5.4, we explained how the **uniform translation** of propositions into standard form, essential for testing, may be assisted by the use of **parameters**.

In sections 5.5 we explained **enthymemes,** syllogistic arguments in which one of the constituent propositions has been suppressed. If the conclusion was suppressed, you can construct a Venn diagram to determine what conclusion, if any, follows from the premises. We also examined a method by which to determine what suppressed premise, if any, would yield a valid categorical syllogism.

SYMBOLIC LOGIC

6.1 THE SYMBOLIC LANGUAGE OF MODERN LOGIC

The theory of deduction provides techniques for the analysis and appraisal of deductive arguments. We have already looked at *classical* or *Aristotelian* logic in the previous three chapters. Now, in Chapter 6 through 8, we turn to *modern symbolic* logic. Developed primarily within the past century, symbolic logic rests upon an artificial language that was developed to represent statement forms and argument forms.

Why should we develop a symbolic language? It is extremely convenient for our purposes. When focusing on deduction, the issue with which we are concerned is validity. Validity is a property of the *form* of an argument. The content makes no difference. The artificial language we develop does nothing but represent statement forms and argument forms. Hence, it is useful for examining deductive arguments. It allows us "see" relationships that are concealed by the words. As one of the greatest modern logicians noted, "By the aid of symbols we can make transitions in reasoning almost mechanically by the eye, which otherwise would call into play the higher faculties of the brain."[1]

The arguments with which we are concerned in this chapter and the next are based on the relations among propositions. We'll be concerned with what is known as *propositional logic* or *sentential logic*. The propositions with which we are concerned are known as *truth-functional propositions*. Every proposition is either true or false. The truth or falsity of a proposition is called its *truth-value*. A proposition such as "Jamal plays football" may be called a *simple proposition* or a *simple statement*. Any statement that contains a simple statement as a proper part is a *compound statement*. So, the statements, "Jamal plays football and Solvig plays harp," and, "Dana believes that Tristan's favorite musical group is U2," are compound statements. *Some* compound statements are *truth-functional compound statements*. A statement is a truth-functional compound statement if and only if the truth of the compound statement is determined solely by the truth-values of its component propositions. The statement, "Jamal

---

[1]Alfred North Whitehead, *An Introduction to Mathematics*, 1911.

plays football and Solvig plays harp," is truth-functionally compound. As we'll see in the next section, the statement is true if and only if it is true that Jamal plays football and it is true that Solvig plays harp. The statement, "Dana believes that Tristan's favorite musical group is U2," contains the statement, "Tristan's favorite musical group is U2," but it is *not* a truth-functionally compound statement. The truth value of the component statement is irrelevant to the truth value of the whole. It might be true that Dana *believes* Tristan's favorite group is U2 even if his favorite group is Chicago. In a *non-truth-functional compound statement*, the truth of the statement *does not* depend upon the truth of the component propositions.

The propositional arguments we examine in this chapter and the next are arguments composed solely on truth-functional compound propositions. Such arguments are far more common in everyday life than categorical syllogisms. In later sections we examine techniques for determining whether an argument composed solely of truth-functional compound propositions is valid.

6.2 SYMBOLESE 101: THE LANGUAGE OF PROPOSITIONAL LOGIC

Artificial languages are developed with particular purposes in mind. In our case, we want to represent arguments in propositional logic and their forms. If you think about ordinary compound declarative sentences that express propositions, you'll notice that they have three elements. (1) There are the individual simple statements of which they are composed. (2) There are the words that hook those simple sentences together, words such as *and, or, although, if . . . then*, and so forth. (3) There are punctuation marks that allow us to group sentences together and thereby understand what is being said. So, we need each of these in our artificial language.

When dealing with categorical syllogisms we abbreviated terms to a single letter. So, the categorical proposition, "All aardvarks are beautiful animals," might have been represented by "All *A* are *B*." Let's do something similar here and abbreviate specific statements to single uppercase letters. "Jamal plays football" might be abbreviated *J*. "Solvig plays harp" might be abbreviated *S*. "Tristan's favorite musical group is Chicago" might be abbreviated *T*. We'll use the uppercase letters $A, B, C, \ldots Z$ as abbreviations for statements.

When dealing with categorical syllogisms, we used the letters *S*, *P*, and *M* to represent the three terms of a syllogism. This allowed us to provide a schematic representation of a categorical syllogism of any form. *S*, *P*, and *M* were variables. Replacing them by actual terms resulted in a determinate categorical syllogism. We want to do something similar regarding arguments in propositional logic since we want to be able to represent the form of a statement or argument independent of any content. So, let's let the lowercase letters $p, q, r, \ldots z$ be variables that can be replaced by statements of any degree of complexity. So, "If p, then q" represents a statement form. By replacing the variables with statements, you obtain statements of that form. So, "If Tristan drives a bus, then Angela is an artist" is an instance of "If p, then q." "If the economy booms and the stock market rises rapidly, then either I'll be able to retire early or I'll be able to buy a bigger house" is also an instance of "If p, then q."

We introduce symbols to represent linguistic particles, those pieces of linguistic glue that hold two or more simple statements together to form compound statements—words such as *not*, *and*, *or*, *if . . . then . . .* , and *if and only if*. We do this by way of *truth tables*. A truth table shows all possible combinations of truth values for a simple statement or statements. Since any proposition is either true or false, the truth table for one simple statement will have two rows. Let's abbreviate the statement "Today it is sunny" as S. The truth table for S would be:

S	
T	
F	

We can also construct truth tables for variables. The truth tables for one variable, p, and for two variables, p and q, are as follows:

p	
T	
F	

p	q	
T	T	
T	F	
F	T	
F	F	

We use these combinations of truth values to define our propositional connectives. The connectives mean *exactly* what the truth tables for them say they mean; that is, they are true or false *only* under the conditions stated in the truth tables. This means the correlation between the symbols and the English words that are translated as the symbols is sometimes imperfect.

A. Negation

Every proposition is true or false. Any proposition that is not true is false, and vice versa. **The *negation* or *denial* of a true statement is a false statement.**

The negation or denial of a false statement is a true statement. Let us represent negation by the tilde (~).[2] So, the truth table defining the tilde is as follows:

p	$\sim p$
T	F
F	T

The proper reading of "$\sim p$" is "tilde p." The tilde is a symbolic translation of the English expressions *not* and *it is not the case that*. So, some people tend to read "$\sim p$" as "not p," even though that's like reading, "*Der Vogelfänger bin ich ja*," as "I am the bird catcher": it's a case of reading the *translation* into the symbol.

B. Conjunction

A *conjunction* **of two statements is true if and only if both statements (the** *conjuncts***) are true**. We represent conjunction by the dot (•).[3] The dot is defined as follows:

p	q	$p \bullet q$
T	T	T
T	F	F
F	T	F
F	F	F

"$p \bullet q$" is read "p dot q." The dot is a symbolic translation of the words *and, but, yet, although, even though, nonetheless,* and so forth. Our truth table definitions are very precise: The dot means nothing more than what is represented in the truth table. So, the dot does not capture all that you might mean by the use of *and*. If you say, "Giovanni immigrated to the United States and settled in Minnesota," you probably

> **ESSENTIAL** HINTS
>
> You shouldn't find it surprising that a translation doesn't always capture everything in the context from which it is translated. It also happens in natural languages. You're writing a German friend. You want to tell her that you had apple pie for supper. Germans don't make pies; there is no German word for *pie*. So you'll have to make do with allusions to *Apfelkuchen* (apple cake) or *Apfeltortre* (apple torte), neither of which is quite right.

---

[2]The choice is somewhat arbitrary. The tilde is, perhaps, the most common symbol to show negation, but some other logic books use other symbols to represent negation. Sometimes, the negation of p is represented by the bar ($-p$), the hook ($\neg p$), or a bar above the statement abbreviation or variable ($\bar{p}$).

[3]Other logic books represent conjunction by the ampersand ($p \,\&\, q$) or the caret ($p \wedge q$).

CONJUNCTIONS

Jeff wanted an *A* but the teacher gave him a *C*.

This English sentence is correctly understood as the conjunction of the two simple statements, "Jeff wanted an *A*," and, "The teacher gave him a *C*." The English word *but* can be used with a variety of meanings, but most frequently—as in this case—it functions as a conjunction.

mean that first he immigrated and then he settled in Minnesota. He did both. The fact that he did both is *all* that is captured by the dot. The dot does *not* tell you the order in which he did those things. So the meanings of the dot and the English words that are translated by the dot are not always quite the same. Nonetheless, it captures what is essential to the logic.

C. Disjunction

A *disjunction* is true except when both of its component statements (*disjuncts*) are false. We represent disjunction by the wedge (∨).[4] The wedge is defined as follows:

p	q	$p \vee q$
T	T	T
T	F	T
F	T	T
F	F	F

The wedge is a symbolic translation of the English words *or* and *unless*. This is known as *inclusive* disjunction since a disjunction is true even if *both* of its component statements are true. The English word *or* is ambiguous. Generally, its sense is captured by the wedge. Sometimes, however, an English *or* is *exclusive*. The restaurant menu that says soup or salad is included in the price of dinner means soup or salad, but not both soup and salad, is included in the

---

[4]Most logic books use the wedge to represent disjunction.

price. If you run into a case where the sense of *or* is clearly exclusive, you translate it as *p* or *q* but not both *p* and *q*: $(p \vee q) \bullet \sim (p \bullet q)$.

D. Material Implication (Material Conditionality)

A *statement of material implication* **is a statement of the form "If *p*, then *q*." A statement of material implication is true except when its *antecedent* (if-clause) is true and its consequent (*then*-clause) is false.** We represent material conditionality by the horseshoe ($\supset$).[5] The horseshoe is defined as follows:

p	q	$p \supset q$
T	T	T
T	F	F
F	T	T
F	F	T

For the purposes of propositional logic, the horseshoe is a translation of the English expression *if . . . then . . .* and equivalent expressions. Each of the following is translated $p \supset q$:

> If *p*, then *q*.
> *p* only if *q*.
> *q* if *p*.
> *q* on the condition that *p*.
> *q* provided that *p*.
> Provided that *p*, *q*.
> *p* is a sufficient condition for *q*.
> *q* is a necessary condition for *p*.

Remember, the horseshoe means *exactly* what the truth table defining it says it means. It represents the relation of material conditionality: It is true

MATERIAL IMPLICATION

If the world is flat, then the moon is made of green cheese.

This proposition is of the form $F \supset G$. A statement of material implication is true *except* when its antecedent is true and its consequent is false, so this proposition is true.

---

[5]In some logic books material conditionality is represented by the arrow ($\rightarrow$).

except when the antecedent is true and the consequent is false. This is *not* the *only* way in which the expression *if . . . then . . .* is used in English. For example, if I say, "If water is heated to 212°F, then it boils," I might mean that heating water to 212°F *causes* water to boil. Understood as a statement of *material implication*, however, the conditional means *only* that it is not the case both that the water was heated to 212°F and that it did not boil.

E. Biconditionals (Material Equivalence)

A *biconditional* **(a statement of material equivalence) is true if and only if its components have the same truth value; otherwise it is false**. We represent biconditionality by the tribar (≡).[6] The tribar is defined as follows:

p	q	$p \equiv q$
T	T	T
T	F	F
F	T	F
F	F	T

The tribar is the symbolic translation of the English words *if and only if, just in case (that)*, and *is a necessary and sufficient condition for*. As we'll see later, a biconditional of the form $p \equiv q$ asserts *both* $p \supset q$ and $q \supset p$.

F. Grouping Indicators

In English we have various punctuation marks to show how the clauses in a complex sentence are related to one another. The punctuation makes a difference. The following two sentences contain the same clauses, but the first is true and the second is false.

(1) Abraham Lincoln was elected president in 2000 and Saddam Hussein was not in power in 2005, only if there had been a war in Iraq.
(2) Abraham Lincoln was elected president in 2000, and Saddam Hussein was not in power in 2005 only if there had been a war in Iraq.

The first statement is a conditional statement with a compound antecedent. The antecedent is false and the consequent is true. So, the first statement is true. The second statement is a conjunction in which the second conjunct is a conditional. The first conjunct is false. So, the statement is false.

Just as we need punctuation marks in English to sort out the different compound statements that can be expressed by combinations of simple statements, we use parentheses, square brackets ([]), and braces ({}) to punctuate

---

[6]In some logic books biconditionality is represented by the double-arrow ($p \leftrightarrow q$) or the tilde ($p \sim q$).

our symbolic statements. These may be called *grouping indicators*. Using these together with the connectives allows us to punctuate our statements.

PUNCTUATION

The statement

I will study hard and pass the exam or fail

is ambiguous. It could mean "I will study hard and pass the exam, or I will fail the exam" or it could mean "I will study hard and I will either pass the exam or fail it."

The symbolic notation

$$S \bullet P \lor F$$

is similiarly ambiguous. Parentheses clarify the ambiguity. For "I will study hard and pass the exam, or I will fail the exam" we get

$$(S \bullet P) \lor F$$

and for "I will study hard and I will either pass the exam or fail it" we get

$$S \bullet (P \lor F)$$

You should notice that the tilde (~) is a one-place connective. It negates *whatever* statement is to its immediate right. So, consider the statement "Charlie did not go to the game." Let C represent the statement, "Charlie went to the game." Its negation would be represented by $\sim C$. If you have the negation of a compound statement, such as "It is not the case that if Charlie went to the game then Juanita went to the opera," you symbolize it as $\sim(C \supset J)$.

The other four connectives are two-place connectives. The grouping indicators show which statements are grouped together. For example, the two statements above regarding Abraham Lincoln, Saddam Hussein, and war in Iraq would be represented by:

$$(1)\ (L \bullet \sim H) \supset W$$
$$(2)\ L \bullet (\sim H \supset W)$$

Translating correctly from English to symbols is a skill that takes practice. You will need to look very carefully at the structure of the English sentence to see where, for example, the grouping indicators are put. The statement, "If either Jorge or Dmitri went to the movie, then Felicia went to the movie," is translated:

$$(J \lor D) \supset F$$

The statement, "Either Jorge or Dmitri went to the movie if Felecia went to the movie," is translated:

$$F \supset (J \lor D)$$

TRANSLATING

In his famous "I have a dream speech" during the March on Washington for civil rights in 1963, Martin Luther King Jr. said, "I have a dream that my four little children will one day live in a nation where they will not be judged by the color of their skin but by the content of their character. I have a dream today." The statement, "My four little children will not be judged by the color of their skin," is the negation of the statement, "My four little children will be judged by the color of their skin." Thus, using S to represent this latter statement and C to represent the statement, "My four little children will be judged by the content of their character," we can symbolize the conjunction, "My four little children will not be judged by the color of their skin but by the content of their character," like this: $\sim S \bullet C$

The statement, "It is not the case that if either Jorge did not go to the movie or Dmitri went to the movie then Felicia went to the movie," is translated:

$$\sim[(\sim J \vee D) \supset F]$$

The statement, "If neither Jorge did not go to the movie nor Dmitri went to the movie then Felicia went to the movie," is translated:

$$\sim(\sim J \vee D) \supset F$$

or

$$(\sim\sim J \bullet \sim D) \supset F$$

The only way to master translation is by lots of practice. Your translations should be *perspicuous*. For example, you *could* translate "Giuseppe did not go skiing" as G, but since the statement contains the word *not*, the more perspicuous translation is $\sim G$. In general, your translation should acknowledge each of the connectives to which the English words allude. Such translations provide the *specific form* of the statement. **The *specific form* of a statement is that form from which the statement results by consistently substituting a different simple statement for each different statement variable and including each instance of a connective.** By focusing on the specific form of statements, we can easily see the relations among the simple statements composing a compound statement. The ability to see such relationships will be particularly important when we turn to arguments.

SUMMARY OF THE TRUTH TABLE DEFINITIONS							
OF THE CONNECTIVES							
p	$\sim p$	p	q	$p \bullet q$	$p \vee q$	$p \supset q$	$p \equiv q$
T	F	T	T	T	T	T	T
F	T	T	F	F	T	F	F
		F	T	F	T	T	F
		F	F	F	F	T	T

SUMMARY OF THE LANGUAGE OF PROPOSITIONAL LOGIC						
$A, B, C, \ldots Z$	Abbreviations for simple statements					
$p, q, r, \ldots z$	Variables that can be replaced by a proposition of *any* degree of complexity					
( ), [ ], { }	Grouping indicators					
TRUTH-FUNCTIONAL CONNECTIVE AND ITS NAME	**PROPOSITION TYPE**	**NAMES OF COMPONENTS OF PROPOSITIONS OF THAT TYPE**	**TRUTH CONDITIONS**	**ENGLISH SENTENCE**	**TRANSLATION**	
~ tilde	Negation		If p is true, $\sim p$ is false. If p is false, $\sim p$ is true.	John is not happy.	$\sim J$	
• dot	Conjunction	Conjuncts	$p \bullet q$ is true if and only if both p and q are true.	Simone is sad and Ramon is puzzled.	$S \bullet R$	
∨ wedge	Disjunction	Disjuncts	$p \vee q$ is true *except* when both p and q are false.	Belinda is happy or Rolf is confused.	$B \vee R$	
⊃ horseshoe	Conditional	Antecedent, consequent	$p \supset q$ is true *except* when p is true and q is false.	If Gustav grows grapes, then Winnie makes wine.	$G \supset W$	
≡ tribar	Biconditional	Components	$p \equiv q$ is true if and only if both p and q have the same truth values.	Lola runs if and only if Maria bakes bread.	$L \equiv M$	

ENGLISH TO SYMBOLESE / SYMBOLESE TO ENGLISH DICTIONARY FOR PROPOSITIONAL LOGIC

*Where **p** and **q** are statements of any degree of complexity:*

English to Symbolese

although	*p* although *q*	$p \bullet q$
and	*p* and *q*	$p \bullet q$
both	Both *p* and *q*	$p \bullet q$
but	*p* but *q*	$p \bullet q$
either . . . or . . .	Either *p* or *q*	$p \lor q$
entails	*p* entails *q*	$p \supset q$
even though	*p* even though *q*	$p \bullet q$
given that	given that *p*, *q*	$p \supset q$
given that	*q*, given that *p*	$p \supset q$
however	*p* however *q*	$p \bullet q$
If . . . then . . .	If *p*, then *q*.	$p \supset q$
if and only if	*p* if and only if *q*	$p \equiv q$
if	If *p*, *q*	$p \supset q$
if	*q*, if *p*	$p \supset q$
implies	*p* implies *q*	$p \supset q$
in case	In case *p*, *q*	$p \supset q$
in case [that]	*q*, in case [that] *p*	$p \supset q$
in the event that	in the event that *p*, *q*	$p \supset q$
in the event that	*q*, in the event that *p*	$p \supset q$
inasmuch as	*p* inasmuch as *q*	$p \bullet q$
is a necessary and sufficient condition for	*p* is a necessary and sufficient condition for *q*	$p \equiv q$
is a necessary condition for	*q* is a necessary condition for *p*	$p \supset q$
is a sufficient condition for	*p* is a sufficient condition for *q*	$p \supset q$
is entailed by	*q* is entailed by *p*	$p \supset q$
is implied by	*q* is implied by *p*	$p \supset q$
It is not the case that . . .	It is not the case that *p*.	$\sim p$
just in case [that]	*p* just in case [that] *q*	$p \equiv q$
neither . . . nor . . .	neither *p* nor *q*	$\sim p \bullet \sim q$
neither . . . nor . . .	neither *p* nor *q*	$\sim(p \lor q)$
nevertheless	*p* nevertheless *q*	$p \bullet q$
not	not *p*	$\sim p$
on the condition that	On the condition that *p*, *q*	$p \supset q$
on the condition that	*q*, on the condition that *p*	$p \supset q$
only if	*p* only if *q*	$p \supset q$
or	*p* or *q*	$p \lor q$
provided that	provided that *p*, *q*	$p \supset q$
provided that	*q*, provided that *p*	$p \supset q$
though	*p* though *q*	$p \bullet q$
unless	*p* unless *q*	$p \lor q$
yet	*p* yet *q*	$p \bullet q$

Symbolese to English

~p	not p
	It is not the case that p
$p \cdot q$	p and q
	p but q
	p yet q
	p however q
	p inasmuch as q
	p although q
	both p and q
	p though q
	p even though q
	p nevertheless q
$p \lor q$	p or q
	either p or q
	p unless q
$p \supset q$	If p, then q
	p only if q
	q, if p
	q, given that p
	q, provided that p
	provided that p, q
	q, on the condition that p
	on the condition that p, q
	p implies q
	q is implied by p
	p entails q
	q is entailed by p
	q is a necessary condition for p
	p is a sufficient condition for q
	q in the event that p
	in the event that p, q
	in case [that] p, q
	q, in case [that] p
$p \equiv q$	p if and only if q
	p just in case [that] q
	p is a necessary and sufficient condition for q
~$p \cdot$ ~q	neither p nor q
~$(p \lor q)$	neither p nor q

I. Using the truth table definitions of the connectives, determine the truth values of the following statements. **Remember:** You need to determine the truth values of the components of compound propositions to determine the truth value of the whole.

1. Rome is the capital of Italy ∨ Rome is the capital of Spain.
2. Rome is the capital of Italy ⊃ Rome is the capital of Spain.
3. Rome is the capital of Italy ≡ Rome is the capital of Spain.
4. Rome is the capital of Italy • ~Rome is the capital of Spain.
5. ~(London is the capital of England • ~Stockholm is the capital of Norway).
6. ~London is the capital of England • Stockholm is the capital of Norway.
7. ~London is the capital of England ⊃ Stockholm is the capital of Norway.
8. ~London is the capital of England ≡ Stockholm is the capital of Norway.
9. Paris is the capital of France ≡ (Dublin is the capital of Ireland • Edinburgh is the capital of Denmark).
10. Edinburgh is the capital of Denmark ⊃ (Canberra is the capital of Australia ≡ ~Oslo is the capital of Venezuela).
11. (Edinburgh is the capital of Denmark ⊃ Oslo is the capital of Venezuela) ∨ (Moscow is the capital of Nigeria • Chicago is the capital of the U.S.A.).
12. ~(~Brasilia is the capital of Argentina • Beijing is the capital of China) ⊃ (~Oslo is the capital of Norway ∨ Dublin is the capital of Spain).
13. ~(Abuja is the capital of Nigeria ∨ Canberra is the capital of Australia) ⊃ (~Oslo is the capital of Ireland ∨ Moscow is the capital of Russia).
14. (Abuja is the capital of Nigeria ∨ Canberra is the capital of Australia) ⊃ ~(~Oslo is the capital of Ireland ∨ Moscow is the capital of Russia).
15. [London is the capital of England ≡ (Paris is the capital of France • Berlin is the capital of Germany)] ∨ (North Dakota is one of the Hawaiian islands ≡ Stockholm is in Italy).
16. [London is the capital of England • (Paris is the capital of France • Berlin is the capital of Germany)] ≡ ~(North Dakota is one of the Hawaiian islands ≡ Stockholm is in Italy).
17. [London is the capital of Sweden ∨ (~Paris is the capital of France • Berlin is the capital of Germany)] ∨ (~North Dakota is one of the Hawaiian islands ⊃ Stockholm is in Italy).
18. ~{[London is the capital of Sweden ∨ (~Paris is the capital of France • Berlin is the capital of Germany)] ∨ (~North Dakota is one of the Hawaiian islands ⊃ Stockholm is in Italy)}.

19. ~[Tokyo is the capital of Japan ≡ (Toronto is in Canada • Jakarta is the capital of Costa Rica)] ⊃ [Managua is the capital of Nicaragua ⊃ (London is the capital of England ≡ ~Edinburgh is the capital of Scotland)].

20. ~[Tokyo is the capital of Japan ≡ (Toronto is in Canada • Jakarta is the capital of Costa Rica] ≡ [Managua is the capital of Nicaragua ⊃ (London is the capital of England ∨ ~Edinburgh is the capital of Scotland)].

21. ~[Jakarta is the capital of Indonesia • (~San José is the capital of Costa Rica ∨ San Diego is the capital of Canada)] ⊃ [~(Edinburgh is the capital of Scotland • Dublin is the capital of Ireland) ∨ ~Moscow is the capital of South Africa].

22. {(Montreal is the capital of Canada ∨ Canberra is the capital of Australia) ≡ ~[(Chicago is the capital of Russia • Buenos Aires is the capital of Argentina) ∨ Hollywood is the capital of Italy]} ⊃ (Berlin is the capital of Germany • ~Managua is the capital of England).

23. ~[~Managua is the capital of Nicaragua ∨ (Des Moines is the capital of Iowa · Richmond is the capital of Virginia)] ⊃ {[(~London is the capital of Holland ≡ Paris is the capital of France) ⊃ Moscow is the capital of Russia] ∨ Stockholm is the capital of Sweden}.

24. ~[Managua is the capital of Nicaragua ⊃ (Des Moines is the capital of Iowa ⊃ Richmond is the capital of Virginia)] ≡ {[(~London is the capital of Holland ≡ Paris is the capital of France) ⊃ Oslo is the capital of Russia] • Stockholm is the capital of Sweden}.

25. ~{[Managua is the capital of Nicaragua ≡ (London is the capital of England ⊃ ~Brasilia is the capital or Belgium)] ∨ [Ottawa is the capital of Canada ⊃ (~Oslo is the capital of Norway ≡ ~Baghdad is not the capital of Iraq)]} ∨ [Kabul is the capital of China].

II. If A, B, and C are true statements and X, Y, and Z are false statements, what is the truth value of each of the following propositions?

26. $\sim B \vee X$
27. $\sim Z \vee X$
28. $\sim A \supset Z$
29. $\sim B \supset \sim Z$
30. $\sim Z \supset \sim A$
31. $\sim (A \supset X)$
32. $\sim (\sim A \bullet Y)$
33. $\sim Z \equiv B$
34. $\sim (A \bullet B) \vee Z$
35. $\sim (A \bullet B) \vee (Z \bullet A)$
36. $\sim (A \bullet B) \vee \sim (Z \bullet A)$

37. $(\sim A \supset Z) \vee \sim(Z \bullet A)$
38. $(A \supset \sim X) \bullet \sim(Z \vee B)$
39. $(\sim Y \supset \sim C) \supset \sim(A \bullet \sim Z)$
40. $[(\sim Y \supset \sim C) \supset \sim A] \vee Z$
41. $[(\sim A \equiv Y) \bullet \sim Y] \vee Z$
42. $[(\sim A \vee Y) \supset \sim Y] \bullet Z$
43. $[(X \vee \sim Z) \equiv B] \supset (C \bullet \sim B)$
44. $[(X \supset \sim Z) \equiv B] \bullet (\sim C \supset \sim B)$
45. $[(A \vee X) \supset (B \equiv C)] \supset \sim[(X \bullet B) \supset X]$
46. $[(A \supset X) \vee (X \supset Y)] \equiv [\sim(A \bullet B) \supset X]$
47. $\sim\{[A \bullet (B \vee X)] \supset [(X \supset Y) \supset Z]\} \equiv [(X \supset A) \equiv \sim C]$
48. $\sim\{[\sim(X \vee (Y \bullet A)) \vee Z] \supset [X \equiv (Y \vee [(A \bullet \sim B) \supset \sim Z])]\}$
49. $\sim\{\sim[(X \vee (\sim Y \bullet A)) \vee Z] \equiv [\sim X \equiv (Y \vee [(A \vee \sim B) \supset \sim Z])]\}$
50. $\{\sim[\sim(A \bullet Z) \supset (B \vee X)] \supset [((A \supset Y) \supset Z) \bullet A]\} \supset (A \bullet \sim B)$

III. If A and B are true, and X and Y are false, but the truth values of P and Q are unknown, what are the truth values of the following statements? If it is impossible to determine the truth value of a statement, write *indeterminable.*

51. $Q \bullet X$
52. $Q \vee \sim X$
53. $\sim B \bullet P$
54. $P \supset A$
55. $A \supset \sim P$
56. $Q \equiv \sim A$
57. $\sim P \vee (Q \vee P)$
58. $P \bullet (\sim P \vee X)$
59. $P \supset (Q \equiv A)$
60. $\sim P \supset (\sim Q \equiv X)$
61. $\sim(P \bullet Q) \vee P$
62. $(P \vee Q) \bullet \sim(Q \vee P)$
63. $(P \bullet Q) \bullet (P \supset \sim Q)$
64. $P \supset [Q \supset (P \bullet Q)]$
65. $\sim(P \bullet Q) \vee (Q \bullet P)$
66. $(P \supset Q) \equiv \sim(P \bullet \sim Q)$
67. $\sim[\sim(\sim P \vee Q) \vee P] \vee P$
68. $(\sim A \vee P) \bullet (\sim P \vee Y)$
69. $(P \equiv Q) \supset [(A \equiv B) \vee (A \equiv X)]$
70. $(P \supset A) \supset [(Q \equiv A) \vee (Q \equiv Y)]$
71. $[P \vee (Q \bullet A)] \bullet \sim[(P \vee Q) \bullet (P \vee A)]$
72. $\sim[\sim P \vee (\sim Q \vee X)] \vee [\sim(\sim P \vee Q) \vee (\sim P \vee X)]$
73. $\sim[\sim P \vee (\sim Q \vee A)] \vee [\sim(\sim P \vee Q) \vee (\sim P \vee A)]$
74. $\sim(P \bullet \sim A) \supset [(Q \vee A) \equiv \sim(P \bullet X)]$
75. $\sim(Q \bullet X) \equiv \sim[(P \bullet Q) \vee (\sim P \bullet \sim Q)]$

IV. Translate the following into symbols using the abbreviations suggested.

76. José went to the dance but Maria went to the movie. (*J, M*)
77. If Ramon went swimming, then Tonya went dancing. (*R, T*)
78. Xenia writes music only if Lola writes ludicrous limericks. (*X, L*)
79. Either Sara writes sonnets or Luther rolls logs. (*S, L*)
80. Beth bobs for apples just in case Mortimer makes mincemeat. (*B, M*)
81. The fact that Sean is an Irish dancer is a necessary and sufficient condition for Kayla to play bagpipes. (*S, K*)
82. Dmitri wrote music unless Joan didn't write poetry. (*D, J*)
83. Jamal plays football if and only if Yvette does not play basketball. (*J, Y*)
84. Beebee plays trumpet if Wynton plays trumpet. (*B, W*)
85. It is not the case that if Beebee plays trumpet then Wynton plays clarinet. (*B, W*)
86. Provided that Iona does not write poetry, Norman sings silly songs. (*I, N*)
87. Wynona does not understand this problem, on the condition that Luis is laughing uproariously. (*W, L*)
88. If Ivan does not drive a Toyota, then Prudence does not drive a Pontiac. (*I, P*)
89. It is not the case that both Sean and Deirdre are Irish dancers. (*S, D*)
90. It is not the case that either Boris or Natasha work for the KGB. (*B, N*)
91. Neither Yolinda nor Ana cooks. (*Y, A*)
92. Melinda goes to the game if and only if Jamal plays quarterback; and Ana kicks field goals. (*M, J, A*)
93. Melinda goes to the game, if and only if Jamal plays quarterback and Ana kicks field goals. (*M, J, A*)
94. Either Lucinda plays cello, or both Tyrone and Zola play trumpet. (*L, T, A*)
95. Either Lucinda plays cello or Tyrone plays trumpet; and Zola plays trumpet. (*L, T, A*)
96. Either Bridgette hunts bears, or Henry is a hermit only if Nola writes poetry. (*B, H, N*)
97. Either Gert grows grapes or Minnie raises mink, provided that Lucy likes lollypops. (*G, M, L*)
98. If Luis plays violin, then Manuel plays viola unless Carlos plays trumpet. (*L, M, C*)
99. Fritz plays fiddle provided that Raphael plays trumpet, or Cleo does not play clarinet. (*F, R, C*)
100. Tyrone plays tuba if and only if both Morris and Alice play flute. (*T, M, A*)

101. If either Bruno builds boats or Minnie makes mincemeat, then Gustav does not grow grapes. (*B, M, G*)

102. Deirdre drugs druids if and only if either Heather herds hogs or Bill does not burn bats. (*D, H, B*)

103. Harry cuts hair on the condition that both Millie and Billie are competitive swimmers. (*H, M, B*)

104. If it is not the case that either Carlos writes poetry or Juanita plays fiddle, then Igor does not write books. (*C, J, I*)

105. If Ole does not like lutefisk, then Solvig does not like lefse unless Cole craves cod. (*O, S, C*)

106. If Ole likes lutefisk then Solvig does not like lefse, unless Cole craves cod. (*O, S, C*)

107. Waldo is waiting patiently and Rolf is a nervous wreck, provided that either Solvig said she'd be late or Ingrid does not plan to come. (*W, R, S, I*)

108. Rudolf runs regularly and Ella exercises excitedly; even though the fact that Ted made the track team implies that Meta made the softball team. (*R, E, T, M*)

109. Hermione reads thrillers just in case Roland reads romances; if Belinda fixes engines only if George knits wool sox. (*H, R, B, G*)

110. Tom's talk about cars is correct if and only if Ray's remarks are not right; unless the puzzler has been solved and the chumps have not been stumped. (*T, R, P, C*)

111. If Trudy does not write poetry then Horace writes music; but it is not the case that if Trudy writes the poetry then Horace does not write music. (*T, H*)

112. Jules likes pizza even though Luigi likes lasagna, just in case either Moshe likes mozzarella or Henri likes limburger. (*J, L, M, H*)

113. It is not the case that if Sam bakes bread then Jen bakes cookies; even though Barb barbeques trout provided that Carla does not cook cabbage. (*S, J, B, C*)

114. If the fact that Susan is a lawyer implies that Clarence cares for computers, then it is not the case that either Luis makes tacos or Belinda builds boats. (*S, C, L, B*)

115. Luigi likes lasagna, only if either Norma likes noodles or Maria likes mincemeat if and only if Olive likes ostrich. (*L, N, M, O*)

116. If Belinda writes music, then Marge writes novels; provided that Hugo plays piano; given that Lisa plays sax. (*B, M, H, L*)

117. It is not the case that if Nola grows flowers then Lucretia gardens; on the condition that if Connie catches cats then Dmitri chases dogs. (*N, L, C, D*)

118. It is not the case that if Nola grows flowers then Lucretia gardens; if and only if Dmitri chases dogs if Connie catches cats. (*N, L, D, C*)

119. If Carmella catches crickets, then if Brunhild builds beds, then if Horatio herds hogs then Norman writes novels. (*C, B, H, N*)

120. Luigi writes novels provided that Brutus builds boats, on the condition that Danielle plays drums if Ethel eats eggs. (*L, B, D, E*)

121. If it is not the case that either Felix fricassees fish or Amelia argues amiably, then Belinda fishes for bass unless Deloris does not drive a Dodge. (*F, E, B, D*)

122. Neither Felix nor Elmer attends class regularly, only if Boris works for the CIA provided that Deidre does not work for MI6. (*F, E, B, D*)

123. The fact that Nella writes mysteries is a necessary and sufficient condition for Della to be a legal secretary; if and only if the fact that James goes by a double-ought number implies that Brigadier Ferguson is in charge only if Sean is up to his old tricks. (*N, D, J, B, S*)

124. The fact that Ian works for MI6 or John works for MI5 is a necessary condition for Giovanni to call them in from the cold, in case Sean was not part of the plot or Hans was not caught. (*I, J, G, S, H*)

125. The fact that Ira works for MI6 unless Joan works for the CIA, is a sufficient condition for Gretta to be on her guard; provided that Lola has contacts with the Mossad only if Natasha is a lieutenant in the SAS. (*I, J, G, L, N*)

6.3 Truth Tables as Tools for Analyzing Compound Propositions

We can summarize the information from the five characteristic truth tables in a single table, which we may call **the master truth table**.

p	q	$\sim p$	$p \vee q$	$p \cdot q$	$p \supset q$	$p \equiv q$
T	T	F	T	T	T	T
T	F	F	T	F	F	F
F	T	T	T	F	T	F
F	F	T	F	F	T	T

Given the definitions of the connectives, you can determine all possible truth values of any compound statement by constructing a truth table.

The procedure is straightforward. Construct *guide columns* for the truth table. The guide columns consist of a column for every simple statement in a compound statement. They give all the possible combinations of truth values for the simple statements. If there is one simple statement, *p*, there is one guide column with two rows below it: p is either true or false. If there are two simple statements, as in the master truth table above, there are two guide columns with four rows below it: It is possible that both p and q are true; it's possible that p is true and q is false; it's possible that p is false and q is true; and it's possible that both p and q are false. If there are three simple statements, there are three guide columns, and your truth table will have eight rows below the variables. If there are four simple statements, there will be four guide columns with sixteen rows below the variables. And so forth.[7] It is essential that you set up the guide columns in a systematic way so that you'll have all the possible combinations of truth values in the truth table. Starting from the left, put a T in each successive row until you have a T in half the rows under the guide column; then put an F in the remaining rows. As you proceed to the right, vary the frequency with which you change truth values twice as often for each successive column. The right-most guide column will vary the truth value every other row. The guide columns for truth tables with one, two, and three guide columns should look like this:

p		p	q		p	q	r	
T		T	T		T	T	T	
F		T	F		T	T	F	
		F	T		T	F	T	
		F	F		T	F	F	
					F	T	T	
					F	T	F	
					F	F	T	
					F	F	F	

Once you have constructed the guide columns, you construct a column for each compound statement.

Consider the truth-functional compound $\sim(p \bullet q)$. This is the negation of the conjunction of p with q. We should expect, then, that $\sim(p \bullet q)$ will always have the opposite truth value of $(p \bullet q)$. If we want to determine its truth conditions precisely, we can construct a truth table. First you fill in a column for $(p \bullet q)$. Use the guide columns together with the definition of the dot ($\bullet$) to determine the truth values in every row:

p	q	$p \bullet q$
T	T	T
T	F	F
F	T	F
F	F	F

[7]In general, where n is the number of simple statements, there will be 2^n rows under the guide columns.

Now you add a column for $\sim(p \bullet q)$:

p	q	$p \bullet q$	$\sim(p \bullet q)$
T	T	T	F
T	F	F	T
F	T	F	T
F	F	F	T

Notice that the column for $\sim(p \bullet q)$ has a T wherever the column for $p \bullet q$ has an F, and vice versa. The truth table shows that the truth values for $\sim(p \bullet q)$ are just what we would expect.

Consider the compound statement form $(q \lor \sim p)$. To construct the truth table, proceed just as we did above.

Step 1: Sketch the truth table and fill in the guide columns.

p	q	
T	T	
T	F	
F	T	
F	F	

Step 2: To determine the truth value of the propositional form $(q \lor \sim p)$, you need to determine the truth value of $\sim p$. **Always begin by determining the truth values of the component propositions of the compound proposition or propositional form for which you wish to determine the truth value.** Use the guide column for p together with the definition of the tilde ($\sim$) to determine the truth values of $\sim p$:

p	q	$\sim p$
T	T	F
T	F	F
F	T	T
F	F	T

There are two schools of thought on truth tables. Both require the same columns. The resulting truth table for a given proposition will contain the same truth values. According to one, you proceed as we did to the left. If you're concerned with $\sim(p \bullet q)$, you construct a column for the component proposition, $p \bullet q$, then you write the entire proposition $\sim(p \bullet q)$ to its right and construct a column for it. The alternative is the truth-values-under-the-connective approach, which gives the following:

p	q	$\sim(p \bullet q)$
T	T	F T
T	F	T F
F	T	T F
F	F	T F

Notice that both tables have the same truth values. Since some students find the first approach easier, at least when they're beginning, we follow the first approach in this section. In subsequent sections we use the truth-values-under-the-connective approach.

Step 3: Complete the truth table by filling in the truth values for the entire statement form. Use the guide column for q together with the column for $\sim p$ and the definition of the wedge ($\vee$) to determine the truth values of $(q \vee \sim p)$:

p	q	$\sim p$	$(q \vee \sim p)$
T	T	F	T
T	F	F	F
F	T	T	T
F	F	T	T

This shows that the disjunction is true whenever either of its disjuncts is true.

Now consider a more complex propositional form: $\sim p \supset (q \bullet r)$. There are three simple statements, p, q, and r, so our truth table will have eight rows of truth values:

p	q	r	
T	T	T	
T	T	F	
T	F	T	
T	F	F	
F	T	T	
F	T	F	
F	F	T	
F	F	F	

There are two compound statement forms that are components of the proposition—$\sim p$ and $q \bullet r$—so we'll need columns for both. Use the guide column for p together with the definition of the tilde ($\sim$) to determine the truth value for $\sim p$. Use the guide columns for q and r together with the definition of the dot ($\bullet$) to determine the truth value for $q \bullet r$:

p	q	r	$\sim p$	$q \bullet r$
T	T	T	F	T
T	T	F	F	F
T	F	T	F	F
T	F	F	F	F
F	T	T	T	T
F	T	F	T	F
F	F	T	T	F
F	F	F	T	F

Now use the columns for $\sim p$ and $q \cdot r$ together with the definition of the horseshoe ($\supset$) to determine the truth values for $\sim p \supset (q \cdot r)$:

p	q	r	$\sim p$	$q \cdot r$	$\sim p \supset (q \cdot r)$
T	T	T	F	T	T
T	T	F	F	F	T
T	F	T	F	F	T
T	F	F	F	F	T
F	T	T	T	T	T
F	T	F	T	F	F
F	F	T	T	F	F
F	F	F	T	F	F

You also can use truth tables to determine the truth values of given statements when all or some of the truth values of the component statements are known. For example, suppose A and B are true statements, and X is a false statement. We could determine the truth value of the compound statement $\sim[A \cdot (X \lor \sim B)]$ by appealing to the truth table definitions of $\sim$, $\cdot$, and $\lor$ as follows:

Example

Since you know the truth values of each of the statements, you can construct a one-row truth table showing the truth values of each simple statement:

A	B	X	
T	T	F	

Now you can construct columns for the component statements. Use the guide column for B and the definition of the tilde ($\sim$) to determine the truth value for $\sim B$. Use the column for $\sim B$, the guide column for X, and the definition of the wedge ($\lor$) to determine the truth value of $(X \lor \sim B)$. Use the column for $(X \lor \sim B)$, the guide column for A, and the definition of the dot ($\cdot$) to determine the truth value for $A \cdot (X \lor \sim B)$. Finally, use the column for $A \cdot (X \lor \sim B)$ together with the definition of the tilde ($\sim$) to determine the truth value of $\sim[A \cdot (X \lor \sim B)]$. Your truth table would look like this:

A	B	X	$\sim B$	$(X \lor \sim B)$	$A \cdot (X \lor \sim B)$	$\sim[A \cdot (X \lor \sim B)]$
T	T	F	F	F	F	T

If you don't know the truth value of a statement, the procedure is the same *except* you need two rows of truth values for the simple statement the truth value of which you do not know: The statement could be true or it could be false.

Example

Where A is true, X is false, and the truth value of P is unknown, what is the truth value of $X \supset (A \bullet {\sim}P)$? Construct a truth table with two rows of truth values:

A	X	P	
T	F	T	
T	F	F	

Use the guide column for P together with the definition of the tilde (~) to construct a column for ${\sim}P$. Use the column for ${\sim}P$, the guide column for A, and the definition of the dot ($\bullet$) to construct a column for $A \bullet {\sim}P$. Use the column for $A \bullet {\sim}P$, the guide column for X, and the definition of the horseshoe ($\supset$) to construct a column for the statement $X \supset (A \bullet {\sim}P)$. Your truth table should look like this:

A	X	P	~P	A•~P	X⊃(A•~P)
T	F	T	F	F	T
T	F	F	T	T	T

Since $X \supset (A \bullet {\sim}P)$ is true in both rows, the truth table shows that the statement is true regardless of the truth value of P.

EXERCISES

I. Construct a truth table to show all possible truth values of the following statements.

   1. $p \supset {\sim}q$
   2. $(p \bullet q) \vee q$
   3. $(p \vee q) \supset {\sim}q$
   4. $(p \supset q) \equiv (q \supset p)$
   5. $(p \equiv {\sim}q) \supset ({\sim}q \supset {\sim}p)$
   6. $p \supset [q \supset ({\sim}q \supset {\sim}p)]$
   7. $(p \supset {\sim}p) \equiv [q \supset (p \bullet {\sim}q)]$
   8. $p \supset ({\sim}q \vee {\sim}r)$

9. $(\sim p \lor q) \equiv (\sim q \bullet r)$
10. $\sim(p \supset \sim q) \lor (q \lor \sim r)$
11. $\sim(\sim p \equiv q) \bullet (\sim q \supset r)$
12. $\sim[p \supset \sim(q \supset \sim r)]$
13. $[\sim p \lor \sim(\sim q \bullet \sim r)] \lor p$
14. $(p \supset \sim q) \lor (\sim r \supset s)$
15. $\sim[(p \lor \sim q) \bullet r] \lor \sim s$

II. Under the assumption that A and B are true statements and C and D are false statements, construct a truth table to determine the truth value of the following compound statements.

16. $(\sim B \lor D)$ 17. $B \bullet (C \lor \sim D)$
18. $\sim[(\sim A \lor (B \bullet C)]$ 19. $A \bullet B$
20. $A \lor C$ 21. $A \bullet \sim B$
22. $B \bullet C$ 23. $B \bullet (A \lor D)$
24. $B \bullet (C \lor D)$ 25. $[B \supset (C \lor D)] \bullet (A \equiv B)$

III. If A, B, and C are true statements and X, Y, and Z are false statements, determine which of the following are true, using the truth tables for the horseshoe, the dot, the wedge, and the tilde.

26. $A \supset X$ 27. $B \supset Y$
28. $Y \supset Z$ 29. $(X \supset Y) \supset Z$
30. $(A \supset B) \supset C$ 31. $(X \supset Y) \supset C$
32. $A \supset (B \supset Z)$ 33. $[(A \supset B) \supset C] \supset Z$
34. $[A \supset (X \supset Y)] \supset C$ 35. $[A \supset (B \supset Y)] \supset X$
36. $[(Y \supset B) \supset Y] \supset Y$ 37. $[(A \supset Y) \supset B] \supset Z$
38. $[(A \bullet X) \supset C] \supset [(A \supset X) \supset C]$
39. $[(A \bullet X) \lor (\sim A \bullet \sim X)] \supset [(A \supset X) \bullet (X \supset A)]$
40. $\{[(X \supset Y) \supset Z] \supset [Z \supset (X \supset Y)]\} \supset [(X \supset Z) \supset Y]$

IV. If A and B are known to be true, and X and Y are known to be false, but the truth values of P and Q are not known, of which of the following statements can you determine the truth values?

41. $X \supset Q$ 42. $(Q \supset A) \supset X$
43. $(P \bullet A) \supset B$ 44. $(X \supset Q) \supset X$
45. $(P \bullet X) \supset Y$ 46. $[P \supset (Q \supset P)] \supset Y$
47. $(P \supset X) \supset (X \supset P)$ 48. $(P \supset A) \supset (B \supset X)$
49. $[(P \supset B) \supset B] \supset B$ 50. $(P \supset X) \supset (\sim X \supset \sim P)$
51. $(X \supset P) \supset (\sim X \supset Y)$ 52. $(P \supset Q) \supset (P \supset Q)$
53. $\sim(A \bullet P) \supset (\sim A \lor \sim P)$ 54. $\sim(P \bullet X) \supset \sim(P \lor \sim X)$
55. $[P \supset (A \lor X)] \supset [(P \supset A) \supset X]$

6.4 TAUTOLOGOUS, CONTRADICTORY, AND CONTINGENT STATEMENT FORMS

A *tautology* **is a statement that is true in virtue of its form**. There is no assignment of truth values to the simple component propositions of a tautology which will make the compound statement false. "It is raining in Atlanta or it is not raining in Atlanta," for example, is a substitution instance of the statement form

$$p \lor \sim p$$

which a truth table shows to be tautologous because it is true on every possible truth assignment to its simple components:

p	p	$\lor$	$\sim p$
T		**T**	F
F		**T**	T

Another way to say the same thing is to say that **a tautologous statement form only has true substitution instances**. It doesn't matter what proposition we uniformly substitute for p: Whatever it is, the statement will turn out to be true on all possible truth assignments. There is nothing we can uniformly substitute for the simple components of this statement form that will yield a false statement.

A *contradiction* **is a statement that is** *false* **in virtue of its form**. There is no assignment of truth values to the simple component propositions of a contradiction which will make the statement true. "It is raining in Atlanta and it is not raining in Atlanta," for example, is a substitution instance of the statement form

$$p \bullet \sim p$$

which a truth table shows to be a contradiction because it is false on every possible truth assignment to its simple components:

p	p	$\bullet$	$\sim p$
T		**F**	F
F		**F**	T

Another way to say the same thing is to say that **a contradictory statement form has only false substitution instances;** there is nothing we can uniformly substitute for the simple components of this statement form that will yield a true statement.

Statement forms that have both true and false statements among their substitution instances are called contingent statement forms. Thus, **a *contingent statement* (or statement form) is a statement (form) that is neither a tautology nor a contradiction. A contingent statement is true on at least one truth assignment and is false on at least one truth assignment**. The statement forms $(p \bullet q)$, $(p \lor q)$, and $(p \supset q)$ are all examples of contingent statement forms. Such statements forms and their substitution instances are called *contingent* because their actual truth values depend upon or *are contingent upon* the actual truth values of their simple components. Notice that tautologies and contradictions have truth values that *do not* depend in this way on the actual truth values of their simple components; rather, tautologies are true, and contradictions false, *regardless* of the truth values of their simple components.

The examples given above suggest how to use truth tables to test given compound propositions to see whether they are tautologous, contradictory, or contingent. The procedure is as follows. Fill in the truth table in the normal way. Then inspect the truth values under the main connective. If they are all true, then the statement is a *tautology;* if they are all false, then the statement is a *contradiction;* if there is at least one truth assignment on which the statement is true *and* at least one truth assignment on which the statement is false, then the statement is *contingent.*

For example, we may want to know whether $[\sim(\sim p \lor q) \lor p]$ is tautologous, contradictory, or contingent. Note that the main connective here is a disjunction, whose disjuncts are the negated disjunction $\sim(\sim p \lor q)$ and the proposition p. We first construct its truth table:

p	q	$\sim$	$(\sim p$	$\lor$	$q)$	$\lor$	p
T	T	F	F	T		**T**	
T	F	T	F	F		**T**	
F	T	F	T	T		**F**	
F	F	F	T	T		**F**	

And we find that the truth values under the main connective are mixed; hence, the statement $[\sim(\sim p \lor q) \lor p]$ is contingent. To put it differently, the table shows that there is at least one truth assignment to its basic propositions on which $[\sim(\sim p \lor q) \lor p]$ is true, and at least one truth assignment on which it is false. Hence the statement is contingent.

In earlier chapters we spoke informally about the notion of *logical equivalence.* We said, for example, that the obvertend is logically equivalent to the obverse of any categorical proposition. We are now in a position to state with precision what logical equivalence really means. **Two statements are *logically equivalent* if and only if, on every truth assignment to their simple components, the two sentences always have the same truth value**. Thus, for example, the truth table below shows that the two sentences $(p \supset q)$ and $(\sim p \lor q)$ are logically equivalent.

p	q	$\sim p \vee q$		$p \supset q$
T	T	F	T	T
T	F	F	F	F
F	T	T	T	T
F	F	T	T	T

The general procedure for testing for logical equivalence with truth tables is as follows: Construct and fill in a truth table for the two statements in question, putting each statement in its own column. **If on every truth assignment to their simple components the two compound statements agree in truth value, then the two compound statements are logically equivalent.** To say that the two statements agree in truth value is to say that on every truth assignment, when one statement is true, the other is true, and when one is false, the other is false. **If there is at least one truth assignment on which the truth values of the two compound statements *differ*, then the statements are *not* logically equivalent.** The two statement forms tested in the truth table above are logically equivalent: There is no truth assignment on which one is true while the other is false. The following truth table is one that shows that the two sentence forms $(p \bullet q)$ and $\sim(p \equiv \sim q)$ are *not* logically equivalent.

p	q	$p \bullet q$	$\sim(p$	$\equiv$	$\sim q)$
T	T	T	T	F	F
T	F	F	F	T	T
F	T	F	F	T	F
F	F	F	T	F	T

In this case, we find the truth value of $\sim(p \equiv \sim q)$ on each truth assignment by reasoning in the following way: A biconditional is true when its components have the same truth value; in this case, that means that the biconditional will be true when p and $\sim q$ have the same truth value. When the biconditional is true, its negation is false, and when the biconditional is false, its negation is true. On the first truth assignment (in the first row) p is true and $\sim q$ is false, so the biconditional is false, which means its negation (the statement in which we are interested) is *true*. On the second truth assignment (in the second row), p is true and $\sim q$ is true, so the biconditional is true, and its negation is therefore *false*. On the third truth assignment (in the third row), both p and $\sim q$ are false, so the biconditional is true, and its negation is *false*. On the fourth truth assignment (in the fourth row), p is false and $\sim q$ is true, therefore the biconditional is false and its negation is *true*. Filling in the table for the other statement is just a matter of copying the characteristic truth table for conjunction. Once the table is completed, we inspect it. In this case, we see that in the fourth row, when p is false and $\sim q$ is true, $(p \bullet q)$ is false, but $\sim(p \equiv \sim q)$ is true. That is, there is at least one truth assignment in which the truth values of these two statements' forms differ, and hence they are not logically equivalent.

A second way of testing for the logical equivalence of two statements or statement forms combines the truth table definition of the biconditional and the notion of tautology. **When a biconditional is a tautology, the components of the biconditional are logically equivalent**. This is because a biconditional is true if and only if its components have the same truth value, and by definition two statements that are logically equivalent have the same truth value on every possible truth assignment. It follows that a biconditional joining two logically equivalent statements is true on every possible truth assignment: It is a tautology. Here is an example in which this procedure is followed to prove that $(p \cdot q)$ is logically equivalent to $\sim(\sim p \lor \sim q)$:

p	q	$(p \cdot q)$	$\equiv$	$\sim($	$\sim p$	$\lor$	$\sim q)$
T	T	T	**T**	T	F	F	F
T	F	F	**T**	F	F	T	T
F	T	F	**T**	F	T	T	F
F	F	F	**T**	F	T	T	T

The statement $\sim(\sim p \lor \sim q)$ is a negated disjunction. The disjunction of it is true whenever at least one of its disjuncts, $\sim p$ and $\sim q$, is true—that is, whenever at least one of p and q is false. So the disjunction is false only in the first row; its negation is true in that case. On every other truth assignment the disjunction is true, and so its negation is false. Thus, this table proves that on every possible assignment of truth values to the simple components p and q, the biconditional joining $(p \cdot q)$ to $\sim(\sim p \lor \sim q)$ is true. Hence the biconditional is a tautology, which means that its components $(p \cdot q)$ and $\sim(\sim p \lor \sim q)$ are logically equivalent.

Let's now prove something to which we alluded earlier, namely that a biconditional $(p \equiv q)$ is logically equivalent to the conjunction of two conditionals $[(p \supset q) \cdot (q \supset p)]$.

p	q	$(p \equiv q)$	$\equiv$	$[(p \supset q)$	$\cdot$	$(q \supset p)]$
T	T	T	**T**	T	T	T
T	F	F	**T**	F	F	T
F	T	F	**T**	T	F	F
F	F	T	**T**	T	T	T

The conditional $p \supset q$ is false in the second row; therefore, the conjunction that is the second component of the biconditional is false. In every other row $p \supset q$ is true. The conditional $q \supset p$ is false in the third row, and hence the conjunction is false on that row. In every other row $q \supset p$ is true. The TFFT pattern of truth values for the conjunction $[(p \supset q) \bullet (q \supset p)]$ mirrors the pattern of truth values for $p \equiv q$. Hence the assertion of their material equivalence is a tautology. Hence the two sentences are logically equivalent.

So, two statements are logically equivalent when the statement of their material equivalence is a tautology. To represent this relationship, we introduce a new symbol, the tribar symbol with a small T (for tautology) immediately above it, $\overset{T}{\equiv}$. One common logical equivalence is double negation. The statement, "I am not unaware of the problem," for example, is logically equivalent to, "I am aware of the problem." A truth table confirms that p and $\sim\sim p$ are logically equivalent, and so can be expressed as the tautologous (or, "logically true") biconditional $(p \overset{T}{\equiv} \sim\sim p)$:

p	q	$p \overset{T}{\equiv}$	$\sim$	$\sim p$
T	T	**T**	T	F
T	F	**T**	T	F
F	T	**T**	F	T
F	F	**T**	F	T

There are two important logical equivalences that help us understand the interrelations among conjunction, disjunction, and negation. These equivalencies were first formalized by Augustus De Morgan (1806–1871) and are known as De Morgan's Theorems.

The first of De Morgan's Theorems states that *the negation of a disjunction is logically equivalent to the conjunction of the negation of each of the disjuncts*, or

$$\sim(p \lor q) \overset{T}{\equiv} (\sim p \bullet \sim q)$$

Example

To say "It is not the case that either the Steelers or the Dolphins will win the Superbowl" is logically equivalent to saying "The Steelers will not win the Superbowl and the Dolphins will not win the Superbowl."

The second of De Morgan's Theorems states that *the negation of a conjunction is logically equivalent to the disjunction of the negation of each of the conjuncts*, or

$$\sim(p \bullet q) \overset{T}{\equiv} (\sim p \lor \sim q)$$

Example

"It is false that both Nils and Marta are students" is logically equivalent to "Either Nils is not a student or Marta is not a student."

De Morgan's theorems can be shown with truth tables to be tautologies (for convenience we put them both in one table):

p q	$\sim(p \bullet q)$	$\underset{=}{\perp}$	$(\sim p$	$\vee$	$\sim q)$	$\sim(p \vee q)$	$\underset{=}{\perp}$	$(\sim p$	$\bullet$	$\sim q)$
T T	F T	T	F	F	F	F T	T	F	F	F
T F	T F	T	F	T	T	F T	T	F	F	T
F T	T F	T	T	T	F	F T	T	T	F	F
F F	T F	T	T	T	T	T F	T	T	T	T

One other logical equivalence is important to mention in this context. Earlier, we said that "p materially implies q" simply means that it is not the case that p is true while q is false. We therefore treated $(p \supset q)$ as an abbreviated way of saying $\sim(p \bullet \sim q)$. With the help of DeMorgan's Theorems we can now see that the statement form $\sim(p \bullet \sim q)$ is logically equivalent to $(\sim p \vee \sim\sim q)$. Since $\sim\sim q$ is logically equivalent to q, we can conclude that $\sim(p \bullet \sim q)$ is logically equivalent to $(\sim p \vee q)$. Consider this truth table:

p q	$\sim(p$	$\bullet$	$\sim q)$	$\underset{=}{\perp}$	$(p \supset q)$	$(p \supset q)$	$\underset{=}{\perp}$	$(\sim p$	$\vee q)$
T T	T	F	F	T	T	T	T	F	T
T F	F	T	T	T	F	F	T	F	F
F T	T	F	F	T	T	T	T	T	T
F F	T	F	T	T	T	T	T	T	T

This truth table shows both that $\sim(p \bullet \sim q)$ is logically equivalent to $(p \supset q)$, and that $(p \supset q)$ is logically equivalent to $(\sim p \vee q)$. It follows that $\sim(p \bullet \sim q)$ is logically equivalent to $(\sim p \vee q)$: We leave it as an exercise for the reader to prove this with another truth table.

By the way, you may have realized that if, instead of making two columns here, we had joined the two biconditionals with another tribar, the result would have itself been a tautology. This means that all tautologies are logically equivalent to one another! By similar reasoning we would find that all contradictions are logically equivalent to one another. However, we cannot conclude that all contingent statements are logically equivalent to one another since there are many different ways of being contingent. We also leave it as an exercise for the reader to find an example of two contingent sentences that are not logically equivalent to one another.

EXERCISES

I. Use truth tables to characterize the following statement forms as tautologous, self-contradictory, or contingent.

    1. $[p \supset (p \supset q)] \supset q$

    2. $p \bullet [(q \supset \sim p) \bullet q]$

3. $[(p \supset \sim q) \supset p] \supset p$
4. $p \vee (q \vee \sim p)$
5. $p \bullet \sim p$
6. $p \vee \sim p$
7. $p \vee q$
8. $\sim p \supset (p \supset q)$

II. Use truth tables to decide which of the following biconditionals (material equivalencies) are tautologies and which are contingent statements.

9. $(p \supset q) \equiv (\sim q \supset \sim p)$
10. $p \equiv (p \vee (p \supset q))$
11. $[p \bullet (q \vee r)] \equiv [\sim((\sim q \bullet \sim r) \vee \sim p)]$
12. $(\sim p \supset \sim q) \equiv (\sim q \supset \sim p)$
13. $p \equiv (p \vee p)$
14. $\sim(p \supset q) \equiv \sim(\sim q \supset \sim p)$
15. $p \supset [(p \supset q) \supset q]$
16. $(p \bullet q) \bullet (p \supset \sim q)$
17. $p \supset [\sim p \supset (q \vee \sim q)]$
18. $(p \supset p) \supset (q \bullet \sim q)$
19. $[p \supset (q \supset r)] \supset [(p \supset q) \supset (p \supset r)]$
20. $\{[(p \supset q) \bullet (r \supset s)] \bullet (p \vee r)\} \supset (q \vee s)$

III. Use truth tables to decide which of the following biconditionals are tautologies.

21. $(p \supset q) \equiv (\sim p \supset \sim q)$
22. $[(p \supset q) \supset r] \equiv [(q \supset p) \supset r]$
23. $[p \supset (q \supset r)] \equiv [q \supset (p \supset r)]$
24. $p \equiv [p \bullet (p \supset q)]$
25. $p \equiv [p \vee (p \supset q)]$
26. $p \equiv [p \vee (q \bullet \sim q)]$
27. $p \equiv [p \vee (q \vee \sim q)]$
28. $[p \bullet (q \vee r)] \equiv [(p \vee q) \bullet (p \vee r)]$
29. $[p \vee (q \bullet r)] \equiv [(p \vee q) \bullet (p \vee r)]$
30. $[(p \bullet q) \supset r] \equiv [p \supset (q \supset r)]$

6.5 **TRUTH TABLES AS A TEST FOR VALIDITY OF ARGUMENTS**

We can use truth tables to test arguments for validity. Doing so relies on the notion of an "argument form." **An *argument form* is any array of symbols containing statement variables but no statements, such that when statements are consistently substituted for the variables the result is an argument.**

Example _____

$$H \supset M \qquad F \supset S$$
$$\underline{M} \qquad\quad \underline{S}$$
$$\therefore H \qquad \therefore F$$

These two arguments have the same form.

$$p \supset q$$
$$\underline{q}$$
$$\therefore p$$

Recall that in section 6.2 we defined the *specific form of a statement* to be that form from which the statement results by consistently substituting a different simple statement for each different statement variable. We can give a parallel definition for arguments: **The *specific form of an argument* is that form from which the argument results by consistently substituting a different simple statement for each different statement variable in the argument form.** It is important to distinguish the *form* of an argument from the *specific form* of that argument. Many different forms will have that argument as a substitution instance, whereas only one specific form will have that argument as a substitution instance. When we test an argument for validity we need to test its *specific form* for the following reasons. Consider the valid disjunctive syllogism

> The blind prisoner has a red hat or the blind prisoner has a white hat.
> The blind prisoner does not have a red hat.
> Therefore the blind prisoner has a white hat.

which may be symbolized as

$$R \lor W$$
$$\underline{\sim R}$$
$$\therefore W$$

This is a substitution instance of the valid argument form

$$p \lor q$$
$$\underline{\sim p}$$
$$\therefore q$$

It is *also* a substitution instance of the *invalid* argument form

$$p$$
$$\underline{q}$$
$$r$$

From the two premises p and q we could not validly infer r. So *an invalid argument form* **can** *have a valid argument* **or** *an invalid argument as a substitution instance.* However, **an argument form that is valid can have only valid arguments as substitution instances.** In determining whether any given argument is valid, *we must look to the specific form of the argument in question.* Only the specific form of the argument accurately reveals the full logical structure of that argument, and because it does, we can know that if the specific form of the argument is valid, then the argument itself must be valid.

Recall the definition of validity: **An argument is valid when it is the case that, if the premises were true, it would be impossible for the conclusion to be false.** Another way to say this is that an argument form is valid when it has only valid arguments as substitution instances. To test an argument form for validity, we could examine all possible substitution instances of it to determine whether any of them resulted in an argument with true premises and a false conclusion. For example, if we had the argument form

$$p \supset q$$
$$\underline{p }$$
$$\therefore q$$

we could substitute "All dogs are mammals" for p and "All mammals are air-breathers" for q uniformly in the argument form to get

If all dogs are mammals, then all mammals are air-breathers.
All dogs are mammals.
Therefore all mammals are air-breathers.

It happens that this argument has true premises and a true conclusion. However, this does not tell us much because, as we saw in section 1.7, it is perfectly possible for an invalid argument form to have a substitution instance in which all its propositions are true. What we would have to demonstrate in order to show that this argument form is valid by this method is that *no* substitution instance of this argument form has true premises and a false conclusion. This approach is not practical, however, because any argument form has an infinite number of substitution instances.

Any statement we substitute for a statement variable, however, must be either true or false, so we need not concern ourselves with *actual* statements (actual substitution instances) at all, and we can instead focus on their possible truth values alone. The statements we substitute for any sentential variable can have only one of two truth values: true (T) or false (F). The substitution instances for an argument form containing exactly two sentential variables can thus have only four possible truth value combinations for their simple components: true statements for both p and q; a true statement for p and a false one for q; a false statement for p and true one for q; or false statements for both p and q.

To determine the validity of an argument with two variables, then, we need only to examine these four truth value combinations. We can do this in a truth table. Take the following invalid argument form, a form known as the *fallacy of affirming the consequent*:

$$p \supset q$$
$$\underline{q}$$
$$\therefore p$$

To test the validity of this argument, we construct the following truth table:

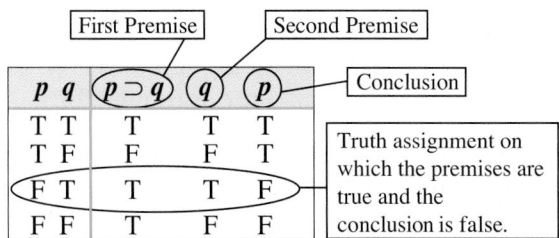

The two guide columns on the left are constructed as usual. Then, across the top of the table, we write each proposition of the argument in order, placing each in its own column. Then we fill in the truth table as usual according to the characteristic truth tables for the relevant connectives (in this case, $\supset$ is the only connective). Since an argument is valid as long as it is impossible for all the premises to be true and the conclusion false, and since a truth table provides all possible assignments of truth values to the statements in an argu-ment, we should inspect the table for a truth assignment to the simple compo-nents of the argument form on which the premises are true and the conclusion is false. If there is at least one such case, then it *is* possible for the conclusion to be false at the same time that the premises are true, and hence the argument is *invalid*. If there is *no* truth assignment to the simple compo-nents of the argument form on which the premises are true and the conclusion false, the truth table shows us that the argument is valid. In the table above, the third row is a truth assignment on which the premises of the original argument are true but the conclusion false, and hence we conclude that the argument form *affirming the conse-quent* is invalid.

ESSENTIAL HINTS

Since *only* the rows in which the conclusion is false can show that an argument or argument form is invalid, some students find it helpful to place a check mark (✓) beside the rows in which the conclusion is false, so they know which rows to check.

p q	p ⊃ q	q	p
T T	T	T	T
T F	F	F	T
F T	T	T	F ✓
F F	T	F	F ✓

The following is a table for *modus ponens*, a valid argument form.

p q	*p ⊃ q*	*p*	*q*
T T	T	T	T
T F	F	T	F
F T	T	F	T
F F	T	F	F

In this table we see that in each instance where the conclusion is false (the second and fourth rows), there is at least one false premise. So there is no possible truth assignment on which both premises of this argument form are true and the conclusion false. Hence it is a valid argument form. This means that every argument that shares this specific form (every substitution instance of this argument form) is a valid argument.

The truth table method for testing the validity of arguments makes one key point very clear: The validity of a given argument depends purely on its *form* (on the structural relations within and between premises and conclusion), and not at all on its particular content.

A. Some Common Valid Argument Forms

Truth tables can establish the validity of such fundamental argument forms as disjunctive syllogism, *modus ponens, modus tollens,* and hypothetical syllogism. If you examine the truth tables for each of these forms, you will find no rows with a T under all the premises when there is an F under the conclusion.

1. The disjunctive syllogism:

$$p \lor q$$
$$\underline{\sim p}$$
$$\therefore q$$

Example _____

Elena went to Vancouver or she went to Mexico City.
Elena did not go to Vancouver.
Therefore she went to Mexico City.

The disjunctive syllogism is delineated in the following truth table:

p q	*p ∨ q*	*~p*	*q*
T T	T	F	T
T F	T	F	F
F T	T	T	T
F F	F	T	F

2. *Modus ponens:*

$$p \supset q$$
$$\underline{p}$$
$$\therefore q$$

Example ———————————————————————————

If Elena went to Mexico City, she saw some Aztec ruins.
Elena went to Mexico City.
Therefore she saw some Aztec ruins.

The *modus ponens* argument form is delineated in the following truth table. It was also used above to introduce the truth table test for validity:

p	q	$p \supset q$	p	q
T	T	T	T	T
T	F	F	T	F
F	T	T	F	T
F	F	T	F	F

3. *Modus tollens:*

$$p \supset q$$
$$\underline{\sim q}$$
$$\therefore \sim p$$

Example ———————————————————————————

If Elena went to Mexico City, she saw some Aztec ruins.
Elena did not see some Aztec ruins.
Therefore she did not go to Mexico City.

The *modus tollens* argument form is delineated in the following truth table:

p	q	$p \supset q$	$\sim q$	$\sim p$
T	T	T	F	F
T	F	F	T	F
F	T	T	F	T
F	F	T	T	T

4. The hypothetical syllogism:

$$p \supset q$$
$$q \supset r$$
$$\therefore p \supset r$$

If Elena went to Vancouver, she went hiking in the Canadian Rockies.
If Elena went hiking in the Canadian Rockies, she saw some magnificent scenery.
Therefore if Elena went to Vancouver, she saw some magnificent scenery.

The hypothetical syllogism is delineated in the following truth table:

p	q	r	$p \supset q$	$q \supset r$	$p \supset r$
T	T	T	T	T	T
T	T	F	T	F	F
T	F	T	F	T	T
T	F	F	F	T	F
F	T	T	T	T	T
F	T	F	T	F	T
F	F	T	T	T	T
F	F	F	T	T	T

B. Some Common Invalid Argument Forms

Two invalid argument forms—the fallacy of affirming the consequent and the fallacy of denying the antecedent—deserve special mention because they bear superficial resemblance to valid forms and therefore often tempt careless writers or readers to draw invalid conclusions.

The form of the fallacy of affirming the consequent,

$$p \supset q$$
$$q$$
$$\therefore p$$

is superficially similar to the form of *modus ponens*.

If I finish my homework before dinner, then I'll go to the movies.
I went to the movies.
Therefore I finished my homework before dinner.

A truth table shows this form to be invalid. The third row has *T*s under both premises and an *F* under the conclusion.

p q	*p ⊃ q*	*q*	*p*
T T	T	T	T
T F	F	F	T
F T	T	T	F
F F	T	F	F

The form of the fallacy of denying the antecedent,

$$p \supset q$$
$$\sim p$$
$$\therefore \sim q$$

is superficially similar to the form of *modus tollens*.

Example

If Elena hiked in the Canadian Rockies, then she saw some magnificent scenery.
Elena did not hike in the Canadian Rockies.
Therefore she did not see some magnificent scenery.

A truth table shows that the argument form is invalid. Notice that the third row has Ts under both premises and an F under the conclusion.

p	*q*	*p ⊃ q*	*∼p*	*∼q*
T	T	T	F	F
T	F	F	F	T
F	T	T	T	F
F	F	T	T	T

C. More Complex Arguments

As the propositions in arguments become more complex, you will need to construct columns for component propositions in the arguments. Let's say you're given an argument of the form

$$(p \bullet \sim q) \supset r$$
$$r \lor q$$
$$\therefore \sim p$$

To construct a truth table for this argument form, you'd need eight rows. You'd also need columns for $\sim q$, $p \bullet \sim q$, $(p \bullet \sim q) \supset r$, $r \lor q$, and $\sim p$. You start by assigning truth values to the statements most deeply embedded in the parentheses. Start with $\sim q$, then construct a column for $(p \bullet \sim q)$, and then construct a column for $(p \bullet \sim q) \supset r$, as well as the second premise and the conclusion. Using the columns-under-the-connective approach, the truth table will look like this:

p q r	$(p \bullet \sim q) \supset r$	$r \vee q$	$\sim p$
T T T	F F T	T	F ✓
T T F	F F T	T	F ✓
T F T	T T T	T	F ✓
T F F	T T F	F	F ✓
F T T	F F T	T	T
F T F	F F T	T	T
F F T	F T T	T	T
F F F	F T T	F	T

The argument is invalid, right? In each of the first three rows the premises are true and the conclusion is false. So, following a long-standing tradition, we circle the first three rows and declare the argument form invalid.

p q r	$(p \bullet \sim q) \supset r$	$r \vee q$	$\sim p$
T T T	F F T	T	F ✓
T T F	F F T	T	F ✓
T F T	T T T	T	F ✓
T F F	T T F	F	F ✓
F T T	F F T	T	T
F T F	F F T	T	T
F F T	F T T	T	T
F F F	F T T	F	T

"But," I hear some of you saying, "there are Fs in both of the first two rows. Doesn't only the third row show that the argument form is invalid?" No. You are concerned *only* with the columns for the premises and the conclusion. Those are the columns for the horseshoe, the wedge, and the $\sim p$. They're marked with arrows below:

p q r	$(p \bullet \sim q) \supset r$	$r \vee q$	$\sim p$
T T T	F F T	T	F
T T F	F F T	T	F ✓
T F T	T T T	T	F
T F F	T T F	F	F ✓
F T T	F F T	T	T
F T F	F F T	T	T
F F T	F T T	T	T
F F F	F T T	F	T

Each of the first three rows shows that the argument form is invalid, since *each* shows that the *premises* are true and the *conclusion* is false.

It is important to keep track of which columns are reserved for the premises or conclusion and which columns might be called *assistance columns*, that is, columns that are introduced *solely* to determine the truth values of a premise or conclusion. Some students find it useful to cross out the assistance columns once they've been "used" so it is clear which columns are columns reserved for the premises only. Using such a procedure, the above truth table would look like this:

p q r	$(p \bullet \sim q) \supset r$	$r \vee q$	$\sim p$
T T T	F F T	T	F ✓
T T F	F F T	T	F ✓
T F T	T F T	T	F ✗
T F F	T T F	F	F ✓
F T T	F F T	T	T
F T F	F F T	T	T
F F T	F T T	T	T
F F F	F T T	F	T

This might make it clearer *which* columns "count" in determining whether or not the argument form is valid.

I. Following will be found a group of arguments (Group A, lettered a–o) and a group of argument forms (Group B, numbered 1–24).

For each of the arguments (in Group A), indicate which of the argument forms (in Group B), if any, have the given argument as a *substitution instance*. In addition, for each given argument (in Group A), indicate which of the argument forms (in Group B), if any, is the *specific form* of that argument.

Use truth tables to prove the validity or invalidity of each of the argument forms in Group B.

Group A—Arguments

a. $A \bullet B$
    $\therefore A$

b. $C \supset D$
    $\therefore C \supset (C \bullet D)$

c. E
    $\therefore E \vee F$

d. $G \supset H$
    $\sim H$
    $\therefore \sim G$

e. I
    J
    $\therefore I \bullet J$

f. $(K \supset L) \bullet (M \supset N)$
    $K \vee M$
    $\therefore L \vee N$

g. $O \supset P$

$\sim O$

$\therefore \sim P$

h. $Q \supset R$

$Q \supset S$

$\therefore R \vee S$

i. $T \supset U$

$U \supset V$

$\therefore V \supset T$

j. $(W \bullet X) \supset (Y \bullet Z)$

$\therefore (W \bullet X) \supset [(W \bullet X) \bullet (Y \bullet Z)]$

k. $A \supset B$

$\therefore (A \supset B) \vee C$

l. $(D \vee E) \bullet \sim F$

$\therefore D \vee E$

m. $[G \supset (G \bullet H)] \bullet [H \supset (H \bullet G)]$

$\therefore G \supset (G \bullet H)$

n. $(I \vee J) \supset (I \bullet J)$

$\sim (I \vee J)$

$\therefore \sim (I \bullet J)$

o. $(K \supset L) \bullet (M \supset N)$

$\therefore K \supset L$

Group B—Argument Forms

1. $p \supset q$

$\therefore \sim q \supset \sim p$

2. $p \supset q$

$\therefore \sim p \supset \sim q$

3. $p \bullet q$

$\therefore p$

4. p

$\therefore p \vee q$

5. p

$\therefore p \supset q$

6. $p \supset q$

$\therefore p \supset (p \bullet q)$

7. $(p \vee q) \supset (p \bullet q)$

$\therefore (p \supset q) \bullet (q \supset p)$

8. $p \supset q$

$\sim p$

$\therefore \sim q$

9. $p \supset q$

$\sim q$

$\therefore \sim p$

10. p

q

$\therefore p \bullet q$

11. $p \supset q$

$p \supset r$

$\therefore q \vee r$

12. $p \supset q$

$q \supset r$

$\therefore r \supset p$

13. $p \supset (q \supset r)$

$p \supset q$

$\therefore p \supset r$

14. $p \supset (q \bullet r)$

$(q \vee r) \supset \sim p$

$\therefore \sim p$

15. $p \supset (q \supset r)$

$q \supset (p \supset r)$

$\therefore (p \vee q) \supset r$

16. $(p \supset q) \bullet (r \supset s)$

$p \vee r$

$\therefore q \vee s$

17. $(p \supset q) \bullet (r \supset s)$

$\sim q \vee \sim s$

$\therefore \sim p \vee \sim s$

18. $p \supset (q \supset r)$

$q \supset (r \supset s)$

$\therefore (p \supset s)$

19. $p \supset (q \supset r)$
$(q \supset r) \supset s$
$\therefore p \supset s$

20. $(p \supset q) \cdot [(p \cdot q) \supset r]$
$p \supset (r \supset s)$
$\therefore p \supset s$

21. $(p \lor q) \supset (p \cdot q)$
$\sim(p \lor q)$
$\therefore \sim(p \cdot q)$

22. $(p \lor q) \supset (p \cdot q)$
$(p \cdot q)$
$\therefore p \lor q$

23. $(p \cdot q) \supset (r \cdot s)$
$\therefore (p \cdot q) \supset [(p \cdot q) \cdot (r \cdot s)]$

24. $(p \supset q) \cdot (r \supset s)$
$\therefore p \supset q$

II. Use truth tables to determine the validity or invalidity of each of the following argument forms.

25. $p \supset q$
$q \supset p$
$\therefore p \lor q$

26. $(p \cdot q) \lor r$
$\sim q$
$\therefore r$

27. $p \supset (q \lor \sim r)$
$q \supset \sim r$
$\therefore p \supset \sim r$

28. $(p \supset q) \supset \sim r$
$\sim q$
$\sim p$
$\therefore \sim r$

29. $(C \lor D) \supset (C \cdot D)$
$C \cdot D$
$\therefore C \lor D$

30. $E \supset F$
$F \supset E$
$\therefore E \lor F$

31. $(G \lor H) \supset (G \cdot H)$
$\sim(G \cdot H)$
$\therefore \sim(G \lor H)$

32. $K \lor L$
K
$\therefore \sim L$

33. $(O \lor P) \supset Q$
$Q \supset (O \cdot P)$
$\therefore (O \lor P) \supset (O \cdot P)$

34. $(R \lor S) \supset T$
$T \supset (R \cdot S)$
$\therefore (R \cdot S) \supset (R \lor S)$

III. Translate and use truth tables to determine the validity or invalidity of the following arguments.

35. If Denmark refuses to join the European Community, then, if Estonia remains in the Russian sphere of influence, then Finland will reject a free trade policy. Estonia will remain in the Russian sphere of influence. So if Denmark refuses to join the European community, then Finland will reject a free trade policy.

36. If Japan continues to increase the export of automobiles, then either Korea or Laos will suffer economic decline. Korea will not suffer economic decline. It follows that if Japan continues to increase the export of automobiles, then Laos will suffer economic decline.

37. If Montana suffers a severe drought, then, if Nevada has its normal light rainfall, Oregon's water supply will be greatly reduced.

Nevada does have its normal light rainfall. So if Oregon's water supply is greatly reduced, then Montana suffers a severe drought.

38. If terrorists' demands are met, then lawlessness will be rewarded. If terrorists' demands are not met, then innocent hostages will be murdered. So either lawlessness will be rewarded or innocent hostages will be murdered.

39. If people are entirely rational, then either all of a person's actions can be predicted in advance or the universe is essentially deterministic. Not all of a person's actions can be predicted in advance. Thus, if the universe is not essentially deterministic, then people are not entirely rational.

40. If oil consumption continues to grow, then either oil imports will increase or domestic oil reserves will be depleted. If oil imports increase and domestic oil reserves are depleted, then the nation eventually will go bankrupt. Therefore, if oil consumption continues to grow, then the nation eventually will go bankrupt.

6.6 INCOMPLETE AND REVERSE TRUTH TABLES

A. Incomplete Truth Tables

Some of you have been sitting there mumbling things to yourself such as, "Yeah, doing truth tables is virtually mechanical, but it's so *tedious!*" or "If it's only the rows in which the conclusion is false that really make any difference, why bother with the other rows?" To keep you happy, we're going to introduce two abbreviated forms of truth tables.

An incomplete truth table recognizes three facts. (1) It's only the rows in which a conclusion is false that can show that an argument is invalid. (2) Even if the conclusion is false, if one of the premises is false, there's little reason to bother with the other premises for that assignment of truth values in the guide columns. (3) One row with true premises and a false conclusion is sufficient to show that the argument form is invalid, so there's little reason to look for a second or third row.

To construct an incomplete truth table, set things up as usual: Construct the guide columns and state the argument across the top of the table. Next, construct the column for the conclusion: This sometimes will require constructing assistance columns so that you can construct the column for the conclusion. Focus *only* on the rows in which the conclusion is *false*. Moving from right to left, assign truth values to the premises according to the guide columns for that row.[8] If you find a false premise, go to the next row in

---

[8]This is not a hard and fast rule. If you see a premise that has to be false in that row—$p \cdot q$, in a row in which p is false, for example—you may go directly to that premise, assign it falsehood, and go on to another row.

which there is a false conclusion. Continue until *either* you find a row in which all the premises are true—that shows that the argument is invalid—or you have shown that there is at least one false premise in every line in which there is a false conclusion. To see how this works, let's consider a couple of examples.

Consider the following argument form:

$$p \supset (q \lor r)$$
$$\sim q$$
$$\therefore \sim p$$

Set things up as usual, and construct a column for the conclusion:

p q r	p ⊃ (q ∨ r)	~q	~p
T T T			F ✓
T T F			F ✓
T F T			F ✓
T F F			F ✓
F T T			T
F T F			T
F F T			T
F F F			T

Now assign truth values to the premises, deserting a row once you find a false premise and declaring the argument invalid if you find a row in which both premises are true. Your incomplete truth table should look like this (I crossed off the value in the assistance column):

p q r	p ⊃ (q ∨ r)	~q	~p
T T T		F	F ✓
T T F		F	F ✓
T F T	T T	T	F ✓
T F F			F ✓
F T T			T
F T F			T
F F T			T
F F F			T

The argument is invalid.

If the argument is valid, you'll find at least one false premise in each row in which the conclusion is false. Consider an incomplete truth table for a hypothetical syllogism:

p q r	$p \supset q$	$q \supset r$	$p \supset r$
T T T			T
T T F		F	F ✓
T F T			T
T F F	F	T	F ✓
F T T			T
F T F			T
F F T			T
F F F			T

The argument form is valid.

EXERCISES

I. Construct an incomplete truth table for each of the following to determine whether or not the argument form is valid.

1. $p \supset \sim q$
   q
   $\therefore \sim p$

2. $\sim p \equiv q$
   $\sim q \bullet (p \lor \sim p)$
   $\therefore q$

3. $p \lor \sim p$
   $\therefore q \bullet (p \bullet q)$

4. $p \bullet \sim p$
   $\therefore \sim q$

5. $p \supset (q \lor \sim r)$
   $\sim q$
   $\therefore p \supset \sim r$

6. $p \bullet \sim (q \lor r)$
   $r \equiv \sim p$
   $\therefore \sim q$

7. p
   $p \supset (q \bullet \sim r)$
   $\therefore r$

8. $(p \bullet \sim r) \supset (q \equiv r)$
   $p \lor q$
   $\therefore \sim (\sim r \equiv \sim p)$

9. $p \bullet [(q \lor r) \supset s]$
   $\sim s \lor \sim p$
   $\therefore \sim q \bullet \sim r$

10. $[p \supset (q \lor r)] \supset s$
    $\sim s \bullet \sim p$
    $\therefore \sim q \lor \sim r$

B. Reverse Truth Tables

But we still hear some of you complaining, "Yeah, that's fine, but paper is expensive. You don't save any paper doing incomplete truth tables, and the savings in ink is negligible. Isn't there a way to construct just that one line that shows an argument form is invalid?" We're so glad you asked!!!

What is known as a *reverse truth table*, or a one-line truth table, or a *reduction ad absurdum* truth table constructs that one line which shows that an argument form is invalid. As you might guess, that's easier when the argument form *is* invalid, but it also can be used to show that an argument form is valid. So, let's start with something easy, such as the fallacy of denying the antecedent.

Recall that the fallacy of denying the antecedent is an argument of the following form:

$$p \supset q$$
$$\underline{\sim p}$$
$$\therefore \sim q$$

To construct a reverse truth table, *assume* that all the premises are true and the conclusion is false. Assign truth values to the conclusion so that the conclusion is false. Then, consistent with the truth values assigned in the conclusion—the *same* truth values assigned to simple statements in the conclusion *must* be assigned to the same simple statements in the premises—assign truth values to the simple statements in the premises so that all the premises are true. So, write out the argument in a single line. You may remind yourself of the *assumed* truth values of the premises and conclusion by writing the assumed truth values *above* the statements:

Assumed:	T	T	F
	$p \supset q$	$\sim p$	$\therefore \sim q$

Now assign truth values to the simple statements in an attempt to make good on your assumption. If the conclusion is false, $\sim q$ must be false, so q must be true. If $\sim p$ is a premise, it must be true, so p must be false. Assign truth values accordingly, and you show that the argument form is invalid.

Assumed:	T	T	F
	$p \supset q$	$\sim p$	$\therefore \sim q$
	F T	F	T
	T	T	F

Notice that you include the truth values for the simple statements immediately below the simple statement and the truth value of the compound proposition under the relevant connective.

Let's construct a reverse truth table for the following argument form:

$$(p \bullet q) \supset r$$
$$\sim r \supset s$$
$$\underline{\sim q}$$
$$\therefore p \supset s$$

Write the argument on a single line and assign truth values so the conclusion is false. For the conclusion to be false, p has to be true and s has to be false. So, begin by assigning those truth values:

Assume:	T	T	T	F

$$(p \bullet q) \supset r \quad \sim r \supset s \quad \sim q \quad \therefore p \supset s$$

T		F		T F
				F

Now fill in the remaining truth values. $\sim q$ is true, so q has to be false. s is false, so $\sim r$ must be false for the second premise to be true, so r must be true. So, you fill in the truth values, and your reverse truth table looks like this:

Assume:	T	T	T	F

$$(p \bullet q) \supset r \quad \sim r \supset s \quad \sim q \quad \therefore p \supset s$$

T	F	T	T	F	F	T F
	F		F		T	F
	T		T			

You've assigned truth values in such a way that all the premises are true and the conclusion is false. So you've shown that the argument form is invalid.

Of course, your assumption that the argument form is invalid is true if and only if the argument form *is* invalid. If the argument form is valid, you can't assign truth values consistently with the assumption that the argument is invalid. What do you do? You begin in the same way. Consider the reverse truth table for *modus ponens*:

$$p \supset q$$
$$\underline{p}$$
$$\therefore q$$

Assume:	T	T	F

$$p \supset q \quad p \quad \therefore q$$

q has to be false; p has to be true, since it's a premise. So consistently assign truth values to the premise and conclusion.

$$
\begin{array}{cccc}
\textit{Assume:} & \text{T} & \text{T} & \text{F} \\
& p \supset q & p & \therefore q \\
& \text{T \quad F} & \text{T} & \text{F} \\
& \text{F} & &
\end{array}
$$

A consistent assignment of truth values indicates that the first premise is *false*, contrary to your initial assumption! What do you do? You show that to make good on your assumption you would need to assign truth values inconsistently to one of the simple statements. If p were false in the first premise, but *not* the second premise, or if q were true in the premise, but *not* in the conclusion, you could have made all the premises true. You show this by writing F/T under the q in the first premise—or under the p in the same premise, if you prefer—circle the F/T notation, and declare the argument valid:
The argument form is valid.

$$
\begin{array}{cccc}
\textbf{Assume:} & \text{T} & \text{T} & \text{F} \\
& p \supset q & p & \therefore q \\
& \text{T} \;\boxed{F/T} & \text{T} & \text{F} \\
& \text{F} & &
\end{array}
$$

So far we've looked only at arguments in which one assignment of truth values makes the conclusion false. If the conclusion is a conjunction, there are three assignments of truth values that make the conclusion false. If the conclusion is a biconditional, there are two assignments of truth values that make the conclusion false. Because of this, if your first assignment of truth values for an argument form that has a conjunction or a biconditional as a conclusion *does not* show that the argument is invalid, you need to try other combinations. You succeed in showing that the argument is *valid* only if you show that there is *no* consistent assignment of truth values to the sample statements in the argument form according to which the premises are true and the conclusion is false. So, if you were examining the following argument form,

$$
\begin{array}{c}
p \\
q \\
\hline
\therefore p \bullet q
\end{array}
$$

your reverse truth table would look like this:

$$
\begin{array}{cccc}
\textbf{\textit{Assume:}} & \text{T} & \text{T} & \text{F} \\
& p & q & \therefore p \bullet q \\
& \text{T} & \text{(T/F)} & \text{T}\quad\text{F} \\
& & & \text{F} \\
& \text{(F/T)} & \text{T} & \text{F}\quad\text{T} \\
& & & \text{F} \\
& \text{(F/T)} & \text{(F/T)} & \text{F}\quad\text{F} \\
& & & \text{F}
\end{array}
$$

Now let's say you're given the following argument form:

$$
\begin{array}{c}
p \supset q \\
q \supset r \\
\hline
\therefore p \equiv r
\end{array}
$$

You construct a reverse truth table, assuming that p is true and r is false, which makes the biconditional false:

$$
\begin{array}{cccc}
\textbf{\textit{Assume:}} & \text{T} & \text{T} & \text{F} \\
& p \supset q & q \supset r & \therefore p \equiv r \\
& \text{T}\quad\text{T} & \text{(T/F)F} & \text{T}\quad\text{F} \\
& \text{T} & \text{F} & \text{F}
\end{array}
$$

You did not make good on your assumption that the premises are true and the conclusion is false. But there is another assignment of truth values to the conclusion which makes it false, so you have to try that one as well:

$$
\begin{array}{cccc}
\textbf{\textit{Assume:}} & \text{T} & \text{T} & \text{F} \\
& p \supset q & q \supset r & \therefore p \equiv r \\
& \text{T}\quad\text{T} & \text{(T/F)F} & \text{T}\quad\text{F} \\
& \text{T} & \text{F} & \text{F} \\
& \text{F}\quad\text{F} & \text{F}\quad\text{T} & \text{F}\quad\text{T} \\
& \text{T} & \text{T} & \text{F}
\end{array}
$$

Your second assignment of truth values shows that it is possible for all the premises to be true and the conclusion false.[9] So, the argument form is invalid.

There! Now everyone should be happy![10]

---

[9]It would have worked equally well if you'd assigned T to q.

[10]Of course, if you want a *good* reason to be concerned with reverse truth tables, I'll give two. (1) It's the reasoning behind a logical procedure called *truth trees*. See the Appendix to this book. You should be warned, however, that truth trees eliminate any paper savings enjoyed by reverse truth tables. (2) It's also the reasoning reflected in indirect proofs, at which we'll look briefly in the next chapter.

EXERCISES

I. Construct a reverse truth table for each of the following to determine whether the argument form is valid.

1. p
   q
   $\therefore p \equiv q$

2. $(p \bullet q) \vee r$
   $\sim q$
   $\therefore p \vee r$

3. $(p \bullet q) \bullet r$
   $p \vee \sim r$
   $\therefore q$

4. $(p \vee q) \bullet r$
   $r \supset p$
   $\therefore \sim q$

5. $(p \supset q) \vee r$
   $r \supset \sim p$
   $\therefore q$

6. $p \supset (q \vee r)$
   $\sim r \supset q$
   $\therefore \sim p$

7. $p \equiv (r \supset \sim q)$
   $\sim p \supset r$
   $\therefore \sim q \bullet p$

8. $p \equiv (r \supset \sim q)$
   $\sim p \supset r$
   $\therefore \sim q \vee p$

9. $p \equiv (r \supset \sim q)$
   $\sim p \supset r$
   $\therefore \sim q \supset p$

10. $p \bullet (q \equiv \sim r)$
    $r \vee (p \bullet \sim q)$
    $\therefore p \vee \sim q$

11. $p \vee (q \equiv \sim r)$
    $r \bullet (p \vee \sim q)$
    $\therefore p \equiv \sim q$

12. $p \supset (\sim q \vee r)$
    $r \bullet (p \vee \sim q)$
    $\therefore p \bullet q$

13. $p \supset [q \vee (r \bullet s)]$
    $p \vee \sim s$
    $q \vee \sim r$
    $\therefore \sim p \vee q$

14. $p \supset [q \vee (r \bullet s)]$
    $p \bullet \sim s$
    $q \vee r$
    $\therefore \sim p \bullet q$

15. $p \equiv [\sim q \bullet (r \equiv s)]$
    $p \vee \sim s$
    $\sim q \bullet r$
    $\therefore \sim p \bullet s$

16. $p \bullet [\sim q \supset (r \vee \sim s)]$
    $p \supset s$
    $\sim q \supset r$
    $\therefore \sim p \supset q$

17. $p \vee [q \supset (\sim r \equiv s)]$
    $\sim p \supset \sim s$
    $(p \bullet \sim s) \supset r$
    $\therefore \sim p \supset q$

18. $p \vee [q \supset (\sim r \equiv s)]$
    $\sim p \equiv (\sim r \supset s)$
    $(\sim p \vee s) \supset \sim r$
    $\therefore \sim s$

19. $p \vee [q \supset (\sim r \equiv s)]$
    $\sim p \supset t$
    $\sim p \equiv (\sim t \supset s)$
    $(\sim p \vee s) \supset \sim t$
    $\therefore \sim s \vee t$

20. $p \supset [q \supset (\sim r \bullet s)]$
    $\sim p \supset \sim t$
    $\sim p \equiv (t \supset \sim s)$
    $\sim (p \vee s) \supset \sim t$
    $\therefore \sim s \bullet t$

6.7   ARGUMENTS, CONDITIONALS, AND TAUTOLOGIES

To every argument there corresponds a conditional statement whose antecedent is the conjunction of the argument's premises and whose consequent is the argument's conclusion. Thus, an argument having the specific form of *modus ponens*

$$p \supset q$$
$$p$$
$$\therefore q$$

may be expressed as the *corresponding conditional statement* $\{[(p \supset q) \bullet p] \supset q\}$. Since an argument form is valid if and only if its truth table has a T under the conclusion in every row in which there are T's under all of its premises, it follows that **an argument form is valid if and only if the corresponding conditional is a tautology.**

p	q	$[(p \supset q)$	$\bullet$	$p] \supset q$		
T	T	T	T	T		
T	F	F	F	T		
F	T	T	F	T		
F	F	T	F	T		

The corresponding conditional for *modus ponens* is a tautology. This is because the premises are never both true at the same time that the conclusion is false, and so the corresponding conditional never has a true antecedent and a false consequent.

ESSENTIALS OF CHAPTER 6

In this chapter we developed the syntax and semantics of sentential or propositional logic. In section 6.2 we gave the rules of formation that allow us to construct truth-functional compound statements out of simpler propositional components. We gave the truth table definitions for each of the five truth-functional connectives (not, ~; and, $\bullet$; or, $\vee$; if . . . then, $\supset$; if and only if, $\equiv$). This was summarized in the "master truth table" in section 6.3. We developed techniques for using truth tables to prove that statements are tautologous, contradictory, or contingent; to prove that a given pair of sentences is logically equivalent; and to prove that a given argument form is valid or invalid.

The following are the key concepts from this chapter:

- A simple statement is represented in sentential logic by a single capital letter. (6.2)

- A **simple statement** is one that does not contain any other statement as a component. (6.2)

- A **compound statement** is one that does contain another statement as a component. (6.2)

- A component is a **truth-functional component** of a statement provided that, if the component is replaced in the compound by any different statements having the same truth value as each other, the different compound statements produced by those replacements will also have the same truth values as each other. (6.2)

- A **truth-functional compound statement** is one in which all of its components are truth-functional components of it. (6.2)

- A **truth-functional connective** is a symbol that joins together propositions to make a truth-functional compound proposition. (6.2)

- A **statement form** is any sequence of symbols containing statement variables but no statements such that when statements are substituted for the statement variables—the same statement being substituted for the same statement variable uniformly throughout—the result is a statement. (6.2)

- The **specific form** of a statement is that form from which the statement results by consistently substituting a different simple statement for each different statement variable. (6.2)

- In a truth table, each line of the column(s) under the component proposition(s) is called a **truth assignment.** (6.4)

- A **tautology** (or tautologous statement form) is a statement (or statement form) that is *true* on every possible truth assignment to its component simple propositions. (6.4)

- A **contradiction** (or a self-contradictory statement form) is a statement (or statement form) that is false on every possible truth assignment to its component simple propositions. (6.4)

- A **contingent statement** (or statement form) is a statement (or statement form) that is neither a tautology nor a contradiction. A contingent statement is true on at least one truth assignment and is false on at least one truth assignment. (6.4)

- Two statements are **logically equivalent** if, on every truth assignment to their simple components, the two sentences always have the same truth value. If there is at least one truth assignment on which the truth values of the two statements *differ*, then the statements are *not* logically equivalent. (6.4)

- When two statements (or statement forms) are put into a material biconditional and that biconditional turns out to be a tautology, then the original two statements (or statement forms) are logically equivalent. (6.4)

- An **argument form** is any array of symbols containing statement variables but no statements, such that when statements are consistently substituted for the variables, the result is an argument. (6.5)

- The **specific form of an argument** is that form from which the argument results by consistently substituting a different simple statement for each different statement variable in the argument form. (6.5)

- **An argument is valid when it is the case that, if the premises were true, it would be impossible for the conclusion to be false.** Another way to say this is that an argument form is valid when it has only valid arguments as substitution instances. The validity of a given argument depends purely on its *form* (on the structural relations within and between premises and conclusion), and not at all on its particular content. (6.5)

- We used truth tables to determine the validity of arguments (6.5), and developed abbreviated truth table techniques (6.6). An **incomplete truth table** fills in rows only where the conclusion is false, and there only until you find either a false premise or a row in which all the premises are true and the conclusion is false. A **reverse truth table** attempts to find a line in which the premises are true and the conclusion is false by assigning truth values in such a way that the conclusion is false and *consistently* assigning truth values to the simple statements in the premises so all the premises are true. If it is impossible to consistently assign truth values in this way, a reverse truth table shows that the argument or argument form is valid.

- To every argument there corresponds a conditional statement whose antecedent is the conjunction of the argument's premises and whose consequent is the argument's conclusion. An argument form is valid if and only if the corresponding conditional is a tautology. (6.7)

CHAPTER SEVEN

THE METHOD OF DEDUCTION

7.1 NATURAL DEDUCTION VERSUS TRUTH TABLES

In the previous chapter we introduced symbolic logic. There we used truth tables to define the five truth-functional connectives, showed how to use truth tables to test individual sentences for various properties, and demonstrated how to use truth tables to test arguments for validity. In this chapter, we develop an alternative system of proof—*the method of deduction*. The method of deduction is a proof system logicians call *natural deduction* because the kinds of reasoning employed are close to natural language reasoning. This is in contrast to the truth table method which, though reliable and perfectly adequate as a system of proof, is not a very natural way to reason. If you're trying to convince a friend to accept your conclusion, natural deduction follows the step-by-step method you'd use to demonstrate that, given your premises, your friend must accept your conclusion.

Because natural deduction follows the ways in which we ordinarily argue, many students claim doing deductive proofs improves their argumentative skills. Some have claimed doing proofs improves their general organizational abilities. The method of deduction, however, differs from truth tables in two important ways. First, if you're constructing a complete truth table, the procedure is virtually mechanical: You use the guide columns to fill in the columns for all the compound propositions according to the definitions of the connectives. When constructing a deductive proof, however, you'll need to recognize argument forms, and you'll often have to think carefully to figure out how to link the premises to the conclusion by means of a chain of valid argument forms. Second, truth tables can demonstrate invalidity as well as validity. The method of deduction can *only* be used to show that a conclusion follows by a series of valid inferences from a given set of premises. It cannot be used to demonstrate invalidity—but that's easily done with a reverse truth table, so there is no problem.

7.2   FORMAL PROOFS OF VALIDITY

Consider the following argument:

$$A \supset B$$
$$B \supset C$$
$$\sim C$$
$$A \lor D$$
$$\therefore D$$

To establish the validity of this argument with a truth table would require a table of 16 rows. But we can establish its validity by a sequence of elementary arguments, each of which is known to be valid. Such a step-by-step procedure is called a *formal proof.*

In general, we can define a formal proof as follows: **A *formal proof* of an argument is a sequence of statements, each of which is either a premise of that argument or follows as an elementary valid argument from preceding statements in the sequence, such that the last statement in the sequence is the conclusion of the argument whose validity is being proved. An *elementary valid argument* is any argument that is a substitution instance of an elementary valid argument form**. A proof consists of two columns. In one column you have the premises and all the conclusions that follow from them. In the other column, you cite the rule and the lines of the proof that justify the conclusion reached in that line.

A formal proof of the argument above would look like this:

1. $A \supset B$
2. $B \supset C$
3. $\sim C$
4. $A \lor D$
   $\therefore D$
5. $A \supset C$ 1,2 H.S.
6. $\sim A$ 3,5 M.T.
7. D 4,6 D.S.

The first four numbered propositions are the premises of the original argument. The premises are followed by a statement of the conclusion that is to be derived. Notice that the statement of the conclusion is not a part of the formal proof. Only the numbered steps or *lines* are part of the proof. Lines five through seven follow from preceding lines by elementary valid arguments. The notation to the right of each numbered line constitutes its justification. Thus Step 5, $A \supset C$, is a valid conclusion from premises 1 and 2 by an elementary valid argument that is a substitution instance of the form called hypothetical syllogism (abbreviated H.S.).

FORMAL PROOF: FIRST INFERENCE

Hypothetical Syllogism

1. $A \supset B$		$p \supset q$
2. $B \supset C$		$q \supset r$
3. $\sim C$		$\therefore\ p \supset r$
4. $A \lor D$	1. $A \supset B$	
$\therefore\ D$	2. $B \supset C$	
5. $A \supset C$	**1,2 H.S.**	5. $A \supset C$

Step 6, $\sim A$, is a valid conclusion from premise 3 and step 5 by an elementary valid argument that is a substitution instance of the form called *modus tollens* (M.T.).

FORMAL PROOF: SECOND INFERENCE

Modus Tollens

1. $A \supset B$		$p \supset q$
2. $B \supset C$		$\sim q$
3. $\sim C$		$\therefore\ \sim p$
4. $A \lor D$		
$\therefore\ D$		5. $A \supset C$
5. $A \supset C$	**1,2 H.S.**	3. $\sim C$
6. $\sim A$	**5,3 M.T.**	6. $\sim A$

And finally, Step 7, D, which is the conclusion of the argument, is a valid conclusion from premise 4 and step 6 by an elementary valid argument that is a substitution instance of the form called the disjunctive syllogism (D.S.). Step 7, in other words, shows that D follows from the original premises, and that the argument is valid.

FORMAL PROOF: THIRD INFERENCE

Disjunctive Syllogism

1. $A \supset B$		$p \lor q$
2. $B \supset C$		$\sim p$
3. $\sim C$		$\therefore\ q$
4. $A \lor D$		
$\therefore\ D$		
5. $A \supset C$	**1,2 H.S.**	4. $A \lor D$
6. $\sim A$	**5,3 M.T.**	6. $\sim A$
7. D	**4,6 D.S.**	7. D

Elementary valid argument forms like *modus tollens* (M.T.), Hypothetical Syllogism (H.S.), and Disjunctive Syllogism (D.S.) constitute *rules of inference*. Rules of Inference allow you to validly infer conclusions from premises. There are nine such rules—summarized in the following table—corresponding to elementary argument forms whose validity is easily established by truth tables. With their aid, formal proofs of validity can be constructed for a wide range of more complicated arguments.

RULES OF INFERENCE: ELEMENTARY VALID ARGUMENT FORMS		
NAME	**ABBREVIATION**	**FORM**
Modus Ponens	**M.P.**	$p \supset q$ p $\therefore q$
Modus Tollens	**M.T.**	$p \supset q$ $\sim q$ $\therefore \sim p$
Hypothetical Syllogism	**H.S.**	$p \supset q$ $q \supset r$ $\therefore p \supset r$
Disjunctive Syllogism	**D.S.**	$p \vee q$ $\sim p$ $\therefore q$
Constructive Dilemma	**C.D.**	$(p \supset q) \bullet (r \supset s)$ $p \vee r$ $\therefore q \vee s$
Absorption	**Abs.**	$p \supset q$ $\therefore p \supset (p \bullet q)$
Simplification	**Simp.**	$p \bullet q$ $\therefore p$
Conjunction	**Conj.**	p q $\therefore p \bullet q$
Addition	**Add.**	p $\therefore p \vee q$

It is important to remember that the *variables, p, q, r, and s can be replaced by statements of **any** degree of complexity.* So, although

$$A \bullet B$$
$$\therefore A$$

is an instance of Simplification, so is

$$[(A \supset B) \vee \sim C] \bullet \{[C \equiv (D \vee \sim E)] \supset \sim (A \equiv \sim C)\}$$
$$\therefore (A \supset B) \vee \sim C$$

The other point to stress is that *the rules apply to an entire line or lines of a proof,* depending upon the rule. So, you must pay attention to what the *principal* connective in a line of the proof is. Your application of the rules must be mechanical: There must be a perfect match between the principal connectives in the rules and those in the lines to which the rules are applied.

The general idea of the method of deduction is to move, by small inferences that are known to be valid, from the premises of an argument to its conclusion. When you can do this, you have proven that the original argument itself is valid. This works because **validity is truth-preserving.** Each of the rules is a valid deductive inference, as can be shown by truth tables.[1] So, if a valid argument has true premises, its conclusion will be true.

Notice what you're doing when you do a proof. (1) Sometimes you're using the rules to eliminate those simple statements that are in the premises but not in the conclusion. (2) In some cases, you're making bigger statements. (3) Sometimes you'll introduce a simple statement that is in the conclusion but not in the premises: That's *always* done by addition. (4) Sometimes you move things around and change the appearance of statements in the premises so they'll look like the conclusion—this is primarily done by the equivalences falling under the rule of replacement, which we'll examine beginning in the next two sections. Keeping this in mind, the rules of inference can be divided into two classes. The first group might be called *elimination rules*. When you use those rules, you reach a conclusion that contains *fewer* simple statements than are found in the premises. *Modus ponens, modus tollens*, hypothetical syllogism, disjunctive syllogism, simplification, and constructive dilemma are elimination rules. The second group of rules might be called *augmentation rules*. When you use those rules, you reach a conclusion that either contains more simple statements than either of the premises contains or, in the case of absorption, a statement that has more *instances* of simple statements than are found in the premise. Addition, conjunction, and absorption are augmentation rules. So, let's see how these work by considering a couple of examples.

You're given the argument form:

$$p \supset (\sim q \bullet r)$$
$$p$$
$$q \vee \sim s$$
$$\therefore \sim s \vee t$$

You begin by noticing what is in the conclusion. The conclusion contains $\sim s$ and t. t is *not* found in the premises. The *only* rule that allows you to introduce something *not* found in the premises is addition. So, you're going to use addition at the end of the proof. You need to isolate $\sim s$ so you can add. $\sim s$ is in

---

[1]We discussed some of these inferences in the last chapter. If you did all the exercises in the last chapter, you constructed truth tables that show the remaining inferences are valid.

Of course, *now* you're asking, "Yeah, but *which one's right???*" They're both right. Both proofs show that the conclusion follows validly from the premises, which is what a proof is supposed to do. The only difference is the second proof is more *elegant*. Elegance in logic is a matter of length: The shorter the proof, the more elegant it is. Elegance makes no *logical* difference.

So, in constructing a proof, you'll want to do the following:

1. Find the components of the conclusion in the premises.

2. Determine which rules you can use to eliminate simple statements in the premises that are not in the conclusion (*modus ponens, modus tollens,* disjunctive syllogism, hypothetical syllogism, simplification, constructive dilemma).

3. Determine whether you'll need to use a rule to augment a premise or an intermediate conclusion to reach the final conclusion (addition, absorption, conjunction).

4. Construct the proof applying the rules of inference to *an entire line* of the proof (simplification, absorption, addition) or to *two entire lines* of the proof (*modus ponens, modus tollens,* disjunctive syllogism, hypothetical syllogism, constructive dilemma, conjunction).

> **ESSENTIAL** HINTS
>
> You should look at proofs as games or puzzles. As with many games or puzzles, the longer you play with them, the more fun they become. This doesn't mean you'll immediately applaud the joys of proofs. Students *have* been known to say words their grandmothers didn't teach them when doing proofs. But if you work at them for an hour or so a day—*every* day— they become fun. This *doesn't* mean you should sit down and say, "Now I'm going to do proofs for an hour." Proofs can be fatiguing. Initially, proofs can be frustrating. You might do well to begin with several ten or fifteen minute sessions every day. If you become stumped, go on to another problem or stop and return to them later. Sometimes just by being away from a proof for a little while you'll "see" things you didn't see before.

EXERCISES

I. For each of the following elementary valid arguments, state the rule of inference by which its conclusion follows from its premise or premises.

1. $(E \supset F) \cdot (G \supset H)$
$E \vee G$
$\therefore F \vee H$

2. $(D \vee E) \cdot (F \vee G)$
$\therefore D \vee E$

3. $H \supset I$
$\therefore (H \supset I) \vee (H \supset {\sim}I)$

4. ${\sim}(J \cdot K) \cdot (L \supset {\sim}M)$
$\therefore {\sim}(J \cdot K)$

5. $(X \vee Y) \supset \sim(Z \bullet \sim A)$
  $\sim\sim(Z \bullet \sim A)$
  $\therefore \sim(X \vee Y)$

6. $(S \equiv T) \vee [(U \bullet V) \vee (U \bullet W)]$
  $\sim(S \equiv T)$
  $\therefore (U \bullet V) \vee (U \bullet W)$

7. $\sim(B \bullet C) \supset (D \vee E)$
  $\sim(B \bullet C)$
  $\therefore D \supset E$

8. $(F \equiv G) \supset \sim(G \bullet \sim F)$
  $\sim(G \bullet \sim F) \supset (G \supset F)$
  $\therefore (F \equiv G) \supset (G \supset F)$

9. $(A \supset B) \supset (C \vee D)$
  $A \supset B$
  $\therefore C \vee D$

10. $[E \supset (F \equiv \sim G)] \vee (C \vee D)$
  $\sim[E \supset (F \equiv \sim G)]$
  $\therefore C \vee D$

11. $(C \vee D) \supset [(J \vee K) \supset (J \bullet K)]$
  $\sim[(J \vee K) \supset (J \bullet K)]$
  $\therefore \sim(C \vee D)$

12. $\sim[L \supset (M \supset N)] \supset \sim(C \vee D)$
  $\sim[L \supset (M \supset N)]$
  $\therefore \sim(C \vee D)$

13. $N \supset (O \vee P)$
  $Q \supset (O \vee R)$
  $\therefore [Q \supset (O \vee R)] \bullet [N \supset (O \vee P)]$

14. $(W \bullet \sim X) \equiv (Y \supset Z)$
  $\therefore [(W \bullet \sim X) \equiv (Y \supset Z)] \vee (X \equiv \sim Z)$

15. $[(H \bullet \sim I) \supset C] \bullet [(I \bullet \sim H) \supset D]$
  $(H \bullet \sim I) \vee (I \bullet \sim H)$
  $\therefore C \vee D$

II. Each of the following is a formal proof of validity for the indicated argument. State the "justification" for each numbered line that is not a premise.

16.
1. $(E \vee F) \bullet (G \vee H)$
2. $(E \supset G) \bullet (F \supset H)$
3. $\sim G$
  $\therefore H$
4. $E \vee F$
5. $G \vee H$
6. H

17.
1. $I \supset J$
2. $J \supset K$
3. $L \supset M$
4. $I \vee L$
  $\therefore K \vee M$
5. $I \supset K$
6. $(I \supset K) \bullet (L \supset M)$
7. $K \vee M$

18.
1. $W \supset X$
2. $(W \supset Y) \supset (Z \vee X)$
3. $(W \bullet X) \supset Y$
4. $\sim Z$
  $\therefore X$
5. $W \supset (W \bullet X)$
6. $W \supset Y$
7. $Z \vee X$
8. X

19.
1. $(A \vee B) \supset C$
2. $(C \vee B) \supset [A \supset (D \equiv E)]$
3. $A \bullet D$
  $\therefore D \equiv E$
4. A
5. $A \vee B$
6. C
7. $C \vee B$
8. $A \supset (D \supset E)$
9. $D \equiv E$

20. 1. $I \supset J$
    2. $I \vee (\sim\sim K \bullet \sim\sim J)$
    3. $L \supset \sim K$
    4. $\sim(I \bullet J)$
      $\therefore \sim L \vee \sim J$
    5. $I \supset (I \bullet J)$
    6. $\sim I$
    7. $\sim\sim K \bullet \sim\sim J$
    8. $\sim\sim K$
    9. $\sim L$
   10. $\sim L \vee \sim J$

III. For each of the following, adding just two statements to the premises will produce a formal proof of validity. Construct a formal proof of validity for each of the following arguments.

21. $D \supset E$
    $D \bullet F$
    $\therefore E$

22. $J \supset K$
    J
    $\therefore K \vee L$

23. $P \bullet Q$
    R
    $\therefore P \bullet R$

24. $V \vee W$
    $\sim V$
    $\therefore W \vee X$

25. $Y \supset Z$
    Y
    $\therefore Y \bullet Z$

26. $D \supset E$
    $(E \supset F) \bullet (F \supset D)$
    $\therefore D \supset F$

27. $\sim(K \bullet L)$
    $K \supset L$
    $\therefore \sim K$

28. $(T \supset U) \bullet (T \supset V)$
    T
    $\therefore U \vee V$

29. $(Z \bullet A) \supset (B \bullet C)$
    $Z \supset A$
    $\therefore Z \supset (B \bullet C)$

30. $D \supset E$
    $[D \supset (D \bullet E)] \supset (F \supset \sim G)$
    $\therefore F \supset \sim G$

31. $(K \supset L) \supset M$
    $\sim M \bullet \sim(L \supset K)$
    $\therefore \sim(K \supset L)$

32. $[T \supset (U \vee V)] \bullet [U \supset (T \vee V)]$
    $(T \vee U) \bullet (U \vee V)$
    $\therefore (U \vee V) \vee (T \vee V)$

33. $A \supset B$
    $A \vee C$
    $C \supset D$
    $\therefore B \vee D$

34. $J \vee \sim K$
    $K \vee (L \supset J)$
    $\sim J$
    $\therefore L \supset J$

35. $(M \supset N) \bullet (O \supset P)$
    $N \supset P$
    $(N \supset P) \supset (M \vee O)$
    $\therefore N \vee P$

IV. For each of the following, adding just three statements to the premises will produce a formal proof of validity. Construct a formal proof of validity for each of the following arguments.

36. $(D \lor E) \supset (F \bullet G)$
D
$\therefore F$

37. $(H \supset I) \bullet (H \supset J)$
$H \bullet (I \lor J)$
$\therefore I \lor J$

38. $(K \bullet L) \supset M$
$K \supset L$
$\therefore K \supset [(K \bullet L) \bullet M]$

39. $Q \supset R$
$R \supset S$
$\sim S$
$\therefore \sim Q \bullet \sim R$

40. $T \supset U$
$V \lor \sim U$
$\sim V \bullet \sim W$
$\therefore \sim T$

41. $\sim X \supset Y$
$Z \supset X$
$\sim X$
$\therefore Y \bullet \sim Z$

42. $(A \lor B) \supset \sim C$
$C \lor D$
A
$\therefore D$

43. $(H \supset I) \bullet (J \supset K)$
$K \lor H$
$\sim K$
$\therefore I$

44. $(P \supset Q) \bullet (Q \supset P)$
$R \supset S$
$P \lor R$
$\therefore Q \lor S$

45. $(T \supset U) \bullet (V \supset W)$
$(U \supset X) \bullet (W \supset Y)$
T
$\therefore X \lor Y$

V. Construct a formal proof of validity for each of the following arguments.

46. $(F \supset G) \bullet (H \supset I)$
$J \supset K$
$(F \lor J) \bullet (H \lor L)$
$\therefore G \lor K$

47. $(K \lor L) \supset (M \lor N)$
$(M \lor N) \supset (O \bullet P)$
K
$\therefore O$

48. $W \supset X$
$(W \bullet X) \supset Y$
$(W \bullet Y) \supset Z$
$\therefore W \supset Z$

49. $A \supset B$
$C \supset D$
$A \lor C$
$\therefore (A \bullet B) \lor (C \bullet D)$

50. $J \supset K$
$K \lor L$
$(L \bullet \sim J) \supset (M \bullet \sim J)$
$\sim K$
$\therefore M$

51. $[(A \lor B) \supset C] \bullet [(X \bullet Y) \supset Z]$
$\sim C$
$(A \lor B) \lor (Y \supset X)$
$\sim X$
$\therefore \sim Y \lor (X \equiv Y)$

VI. Construct a formal proof of validity for each of the following arguments. Translate using the abbreviations suggested.

52. If Adams joins, then the club's social prestige will rise; and if Baker joins, then the club's financial position will be more secure.

Either Adams or Baker will join. If the club's social prestige rises, then Baker will join; and if the club's financial position becomes more secure, then Wilson will join. Therefore, either Baker or Wilson will join. (*A*—Adams joins; *S*—The club's social prestige rises; *B*—Baker joins; *F*—The club's financial position is more secure; *W*—Wilson joins.)

53. If Brown received the wire, then she took the plane; and if she took the plane, then she will not be late for the meeting. If the telegram was incorrectly addressed, then Brown will be late for the meeting. Either Brown received the wire, or the telegram was incorrectly addressed. Therefore, either Brown took the plane, or she will be late for the meeting. (*R*—Brown received the wire; *P*—Brown took the plane; *L*—Brown will be late for the meeting; *T*—The telegram was incorrectly addressed.)

54. If Neville buys the lot, then an office building will be constructed; whereas if Payton buys the lot, then it quickly will be sold again. If Rivers buys the lot, then a store will be constructed; and if a store is constructed, then Thompson will offer to lease it. Either Neville or Rivers will buy the lot. Therefore either an office building or a store will be constructed. (*N*—Neville buys the lot; *O*—An office building will be constructed; *P*—Payton buys the lot; *Q*—The lot quickly will be sold again; *R*—Rivers buys the lot; *S*—A store will be constructed; *T*—Thompson will offer to lease it.)

55. If Ann is present, then Bill is present. If Ann and Bill are both present, then either Charles or Doris will be elected. If either Charles or Doris is elected, then Elmer does not really dominate the club. If Ann's presence implies that Elmer does not really dominate the club, then Florence will be the new president. So, Florence will be the new president. (*A*—Ann is present; *B*—Bill is present; *C*—Charles will be elected; *D*—Doris will be elected; *E*—Elmer really dominates the club; *F*—Florence will be the new president.)

56. If either Alejandro or Julio went to the dance, then Belinda went to the dance; and if both Ivan and Dmitri went to the game, then Katrina went to the game. Belinda did not go to the dance. Either Alejandro or Julio went to the dance; unless the fact that Dmitri went to the game implies that Ivan went to the game. Ivan did not go to the game. Therefore, either Dmitri did not go to the game, or Ivan went to the game if and only if Dmitri went to the game. (*A*—Alejandro went to the dance; *J*—Julio went to the dance; *B*—Belinda went to the dance; *I*—Ivan went to the game; *D*—Dmitri went to the game; *K*—Katrina went to the game.)

57. If Giovanni plays chess, then Lucia plays chess; and if Tex does not play checkers, then Jen plays checkers. Giovanni plays chess, and Tex plays checkers. Lucia does not play chess. So, either Jen plays checkers and Giovanni plays chess, or if Lucia does not play chess, then Tex plays checkers. (*G*—Giovanni plays chess; *L*—Lucia plays chess; *T*—Tex plays checkers; *J*—Jen plays checkers.)

58. If either Rolf or Solvig plays polo, then Daphne writes poetry. Rolf plays polo. If Daphne writes poetry, then Chris sings ballads. Either Rolf or Solvig plays polo, and Chris sings ballads; only if Theo plays trumpet. Hence, Theo plays trumpet unless Rolf does not play polo. (*R*—Rolf plays polo; *S*—Solvig plays polo; *D*—Daphne writes poetry; *C*—Chris sings ballads; *T*—Theo plays trumpet.)

59. If Lucia writes music, then Gabriella writes novels; and if Horace writes poetry, then Xaneta writes cookbooks. If Pete shoots pool, then Saundra shoots skeet; and if Mei-Mei plays mah-jongg, then Danielle dances. Lucia writes music. If either Gabriella writes novels or Saundra shoots skeet, then Bart is clueless only if Callie catches crows. Callie does not catch crows. So, Bart is not clueless. (*L*—Lucia writes music; *G*—Gabriella writes novels; *H*—Horace writes poetry; *X*—Xaneta writes cookbooks; *P*—Pete shoots pool; *S*—Saundra shoots skeet; *M*—Mei-Mei plays mah-jongg; *D*—Danielle dances; *B*—Bart is clueless; *C*—Callie catches crows.)

60. If Mr. Smith is the brakeman's next-door neighbor, then Mr. Smith lives halfway between Detroit and Chicago. If Mr. Smith lives halfway between Detroit and Chicago, then he does not live in Chicago. Mr. Smith is the brakeman's next-door neighbor. If Mr. Robinson lives in Detroit, then he does not live in Chicago. Mr. Robinson lives in Detroit. Mr. Smith lives in Chicago or else either Mr. Robinson or Mr. Jones lives in Chicago. If Mr. Jones lives in Chicago, then the brakeman is Jones. Therefore, the brakeman is Jones. (*S*—Mr. Smith is the brakeman's next-door neighbor; *W*—Mr. Smith lives halfway between Detroit and Chicago; *L*—Mr. Smith lives in Chicago; *D*—Mr. Robinson lives in Detroit; *I*—Mr. Robinson lives in Chicago; *C*—Mr. Jones lives in Chicago; *B*—The brakeman is Jones.)

61. Ms. Hernandez programs computers. If Ms. Hernandez programs computers, then Mr. Mendez is an accountant and Mr. Sanchez is president of the bank. If Ms. Hernandez programs computers, then Ms. Chang runs a computer firm and Mr. Kim writes software. If Mr. Mendez is an accountant and Ms. Chang runs a computer firm, then Ms. Lewinski keeps the mainframe working. If Ms. Lewinski keeps the mainframe working, then either Mr. Popov has a virus in his computer or Dr. Rasmussen runs the

clinic. Mr. Popov does not have a virus in his computer. If Dr. Rasmussen runs the clinic, then Ms. DiToro is a nurse. Therefore, Ms. DiToro is a nurse. (*H*— Ms. Hernandez programs computers; *M*— Mr. Mendez is an accountant; *S*—Mr. Sanchez is president of the bank; *C*—Ms. Chang runs a computer firm; *K*—Mr. Kim writes software; *L*— Ms. Lewinski keeps the mainframe working; *P*— Mr. Popov has a virus in his computer; *R*— Dr. Rasmussen runs the clinic; *D*—Ms. DiToro is a nurse.)

7.3 THE RULE OF REPLACEMENT (1)

There are many valid arguments whose validity cannot be proved using only the nine rules of inference. For example,

$$A \bullet B$$
$$\therefore B$$

is valid, since a conjunction is true if and only if *both* conjuncts are true. But the rule for simplification allows you *only* to conclude the truth of the left conjunct. $B \bullet A$ is logically equivalent to $A \bullet B$ If we could replace $A \bullet B$ with $B \bullet A$, we could simplify and conclude B.

So, we're going to expand our system of propositional logic by introducing one more rule of inference and a number of logically equivalent statements that fall under that rule. The rule is *the rule of replacement*. **The rule of replacement allows us to replace logically equivalent statements that fall under the rule *wherever* they occur in a proof.** While the first nine rules apply only to a whole line or two lines of a proof, the equivalences falling under the rule of replacement allow you to modify compound statements *within* a line of a proof. For example, since $A \bullet B$ is logically equivalent to $B \bullet A$, you could transform the statement $(A \bullet B) \supset C$ to $(B \bullet A) \supset C$ by commutation. Look at it this way. The nine rules of inference allow you to eliminate and augment statements as a whole. They allow you to "cut up" statements, to remove or add parts, in much the same way that a surgeon might remove something from your body when performing surgery or an auto mechanic might add a new part to your car. The rule of replacement allows you to change the appearance of statements in the same way that a plastic surgeon changes the appearance of a person—sometimes significantly—without changing the person: The fundamental parts are all still there.

We introduce the equivalences falling under the rule of replacement in this section and the next. Once all the equivalences falling under the rule of replacement are introduced, you will be able to demonstrate the validity of any valid argument in propositional logic.

RULE OF REPLACEMENT: ANY OF THE FOLLOWING LOGICALLY EQUIVALENT EXPRESSIONS CAN REPLACE EACH OTHER WHEREVER THEY OCCUR IN A PROOF:		

NAME	ABBREVIATION	FORM
De Morgan's Theorems	**De M.**	$\sim(p \lor q) \overset{T}{\equiv} (\sim p \bullet \sim q)$ $\sim(p \bullet q) \overset{T}{\equiv} (\sim p \lor \sim q)$
Commutation	**Com.**	$(p \lor q) \overset{T}{\equiv} (q \lor p)$ $(p \bullet q) \overset{T}{\equiv} (q \bullet p)$
Association	**Assoc.**	$[p \lor (q \lor r)] \overset{T}{\equiv} [(p \lor q) \lor r]$ $[p \bullet (q \bullet r)] \overset{T}{\equiv} [(p \bullet q) \bullet r]$
Distribution	**Dist.**	$[p \bullet (q \lor r)] \overset{T}{\equiv} [(p \bullet q) \lor (p \bullet r)]$ $[p \lor (q \bullet r)] \overset{T}{\equiv} [(p \lor q) \bullet (p \lor r)]$
Double Negation	**D.N.**	$p \overset{T}{\equiv} \sim\sim p$

De Morgan's theorems tell you how to move a tilde into or out of parentheses when dealing with conjunction or disjunction. If you're given a statement of the form $\sim(p \lor q)$, you can replace it with the logically equivalent statement $\sim p \bullet \sim q$. You could then simplify to $\sim p$. Or if you're given $\sim p \lor \sim q$ you can replace it with $\sim(p \bullet q)$ and use that statement with another statement in the argument.

Commutation allows you to reverse the positions of conjuncts or disjuncts. So, looking again at the example with which we began the section, given $A \bullet B$, you can commute to $B \bullet A$ and simplify to conclude B. If you consider the truth values for conjunction and disjunction, you'll conclude that the order in which the conjuncts or disjuncts are given does not affect the truth value. **Notice,** commutation applies *only* to conjunction and disjunction.

Association allows you to move parentheses in conjunctions in which one conjunct is itself a conjunction and in disjunctions in which one of the disjuncts is itself a disjunction. If you consider the truth values for conjunction and disjunction, you'll conclude that if you have a conjunction of three statements or a disjunction of three statements, the grouping does not affect the truth value. **Notice**, association applies *only* to conjunctions and disjunctions.

Distribution deals with complex statements that include both a conjunction and a disjunction. The English sentence, "Alejandro won the election or both Dmitri and Lucia lost," is logically equivalent to, "Either Alejandro won the election and Dmitri lost, or Alejandro won the election and Lucia lost."

Notice that distribution requires *both* a disjunction and a conjunction, and you can distribute *only* when you have both a disjunction and a conjunction.

Double negation reflects what your English teachers have been telling you for years, namely, two negatives make a positive. Indeed, this is so deeply engrained, that of all the equivalences, double negation is the one you're most likely to *forget* to include as a justification in a proof.

ESSENTIAL HINTS

Commutation, association, and distribution are probably familiar to you from your math classes. Commutation and association are properties of addition and multiplication. Addition and multiplication taken together allow you to distribute.

DOUBLE NEGATION: TWO PROOFS

Consider this argument: $(A \lor B) \supset (\sim\sim D \bullet C)$
$$A$$
$$\therefore D$$

ONE FORMAL PROOF OF THIS ARGUMENT IS THE FOLLOWING:		ANOTHER VALID PROOF OF THE ARGUMENT IS THIS:	
1. $(A \lor B) \supset (\sim\sim D \bullet C)$		1. $(A \lor B) \supset (\sim\sim D \bullet C)$	
2. A		2. A	
$\therefore D$		$\therefore D$	
3. $A \lor B$	2. Add	3. $(A \lor B) \supset (D \bullet C)$	1 D.N.
4. $\sim\sim D \bullet C$	1,3 M.P.	4. $A \lor B$	2 Add.
5. $\sim\sim D$	4 Simp.	5. $D \bullet C$	3,4 M.P.
6. D	5 D.N.	6. D	5 Simp.

In both cases we replaced the expression $\sim\sim D$ with the logically equivalent expression D.

So, let's look at a few examples to see how these equivalences fit together with the nine rules of inference.

Consider the argument:

$$\sim A \lor (\sim B \bullet C)$$
$$\sim D \supset (B \bullet A)$$
$$\therefore D$$

Before we write anything down, we should look at the argument and think. C is in premise 1, but it's not in the conclusion. You can't simplify, since the dot ($\bullet$) is not the principle connective in the premise. If you distribute, you'll be able to simplify. You'll have to get $\sim\sim D$ by *modus tollens* and then double negate. So, you'll need to conclude $\sim(B \bullet A)$ to reach the conclusion. So the proof will look like this:

1.	$\sim A \lor (\sim B \bullet C)$	
2.	$\sim D \supset (B \bullet A)$	
	$\therefore D$	
3.	$(\sim A \lor \sim B) \bullet (\sim A \lor C)$	1 Dist.
4.	$(\sim A \lor \sim B)$	3 Simp.
5.	$\sim(A \bullet B)$	4 De M.
6.	$\sim(B \bullet A)$	5 Com.
7.	$\sim\sim D$	2,6 M.T.
8.	D	7 D.N.

Now consider this one:

$$(A \bullet \sim B) \bullet C$$
$$C \supset (D \supset B)$$
$$\therefore \sim D \lor E$$

You'll have to do some commutation and association so you can use the rules of inference. One way to do the proof is as follows:

1.	$(A \bullet \sim B) \bullet C$	
2.	$C \supset (D \supset B)$	
	$\therefore \sim D \lor E$	
3.	$C \bullet (A \bullet \sim B)$	1 Com.
4.	C	3 Simp.
5.	$D \supset B$	2,4 M.P.
6.	$(\sim B \bullet A) \bullet C$	1 Com.
7.	$\sim B \bullet (A \bullet C)$	6 Assoc.
8.	$\sim B$	7 Simp.
9.	$\sim D$	5,8 M.T.
10.	$\sim D \lor E$	9 Add.

Consider one more:

$$U \bullet Q$$
$$Q \supset \sim(\sim S \lor R)$$
$$S \supset [P \lor (T \bullet R)]$$
$$\therefore P \lor T$$

Now *you* do the proof before looking at the way *we* do it. Did your proof look like this?

1. $U \cdot Q$
2. $Q \supset {\sim}({\sim}S \lor R)$
   $S \supset [P \lor (T \cdot R)]$
   $\therefore P \lor T$
4. $Q \cdot U$ 1 Com.
5. Q 4 Simp.
6. ${\sim}({\sim}S \lor R)$ 2,5 M.P.
7. ${\sim}{\sim}S \cdot {\sim}R$ 6 De M.
8. ${\sim}{\sim}S$ 7 Simp.
9. S 8 D.N.
10. $P \lor (T \cdot R)$ 3,9 M.P.
11. $(P \lor T) \cdot (P \lor R)$ 10 Dist.
12. $P \lor T$ 11. Simp.

If your proof *didn't* look like this, did you do the same things but in a different order? You'll need to commute so that you can simplify and use *modus ponens*. You'll need to use De Morgan's theorem, but you could do that before you do anything else to premise 2. You'll need to distribute the consequent of premise 3, although you could do that before you do anything else to premise 3.

EXERCISES

I. Name the equivalence falling under the rule of replacement that allows you to move from the premise to the conclusion.

1. ${\sim}[A \lor (B \cdot C)]$
    $\therefore {\sim}A \cdot {\sim}(B \cdot C)$

2. $A \cdot {\sim}(C \lor B)$
    $\therefore A \cdot {\sim}(B \lor C)$

3. $A \cdot ({\sim}B \lor C)$
    $\therefore (A \cdot {\sim}B) \lor (A \cdot C)$

4. $(A \cdot B) \lor (S \cdot P)$
    $\therefore [(A \cdot B) \lor S] \cdot [(A \cdot B) \lor P]$

5. ${\sim}{\sim}(C \cdot B)$
    $\therefore {\sim}({\sim}C \lor {\sim}B)$

6. $C \cdot {\sim}{\sim}B$
    $\therefore {\sim}{\sim}B \cdot C$

7. $C \lor [B \supset ({\sim}B \equiv {\sim}{\sim}G)]$
    $\therefore C \lor [B \supset ({\sim}B \equiv G)]$

8. $P \cdot [(Q \lor R) \cdot G]$
    $\therefore [P \cdot (Q \lor R)] \cdot G$

9. $P \lor \{(Q \lor R) \cdot [(Q \cdot S) \supset {\sim}({\sim}W \supset {\sim}{\sim}S)]\}$
    $\therefore [P \lor (Q \lor R)] \cdot \{P \lor [(Q \cdot S) \supset {\sim}({\sim}W \supset {\sim}{\sim}S)]\}$

10. $[P \cdot (Q \supset S)] \lor \{Q \cdot [(S \lor G) \lor {\sim}S]\}$
    $\therefore [P \cdot (Q \supset S)] \lor \{Q \cdot [S \lor (G \lor {\sim}S)]\}$

II. Each of the following is a formal proof of validity for the indicated argument. State the justification for each numbered line that is not a premise.

11.
1. $(p \bullet q) \lor (r \bullet s)$
2. $[(p \bullet q) \supset t] \bullet (s \supset w)$
   $\therefore t \lor w$
3. $[(p \bullet q) \lor r] \bullet [(p \bullet q) \lor s]$
4. $[(p \bullet q) \lor s] \bullet [(p \bullet q) \lor r]$
5. $(p \bullet q) \lor s$
6. $t \lor w$

12.
1. $\sim p \lor (q \lor \sim r)$
2. $\sim q$
   $\therefore \sim(p \bullet r)$
3. $(\sim p \lor q) \lor \sim r$
4. $(q \lor \sim p) \lor \sim r$
5. $q \lor (\sim p \lor \sim r)$
6. $\sim p \lor \sim r$
7. $\sim(p \bullet r)$

13.
1. $\sim p \lor (q \lor \sim r)$
2. $\sim\sim(p \bullet r)$
   $\therefore q \lor \sim(t \bullet \sim s)$
3. $\sim p \lor (\sim r \lor q)$
4. $(\sim p \lor \sim r) \lor q$
5. $\sim(p \bullet r) \lor q$
6. q
7. $q \lor \sim(t \bullet \sim s)$

14.
1. $(r \supset s) \bullet (p \supset q)$
2. $\sim(\sim p \bullet \sim r)$
3. $\sim q$
   $\therefore s$
4. $\sim\sim(p \lor r)$
5. $p \lor r$
6. $(p \supset q) \bullet (r \supset s)$
7. $q \lor s$
8. s

15.
1. $p \lor (q \bullet s)$
2. $\sim q$
3. $p \supset s$
   $\therefore \sim\sim s$
4. $(p \lor q) \bullet (p \lor s)$
5. $p \lor q$
6. $q \lor p$
7. p
8. s
9. $\sim\sim s$

16.
1. $p \supset (q \lor r)$
2. $q \supset s$
3. $\sim r \bullet \sim s$
   $\therefore \sim p$
4. $\sim s \bullet \sim r$
5. $\sim s$
6. $\sim q$
7. $\sim r$
8. $\sim q \bullet \sim r$
9. $\sim(q \lor r)$
10. $\sim p$

17.
1. $p \supset q$
2. $(q \bullet p) \supset (r \lor s)$
3. $\sim r$
4. $s \supset r$
   $\therefore \sim p$
5. $\sim s$
6. $\sim r \bullet \sim s$
7. $\sim(r \lor s)$
8. $\sim(q \bullet p)$
9. $\sim(p \bullet q)$
10. $p \supset (p \bullet q)$
11. $\sim p$

18.
1. $p \lor (q \lor r)$
2. $\sim q$
3. $\sim(\sim p \bullet \sim r) \supset [(s \bullet q) \lor (s \bullet t)]$
   $\therefore s \bullet (q \lor t)$
4. $(p \lor q) \lor r$
5. $(q \lor p) \lor r$
6. $q \lor (p \lor r)$
7. $p \lor r$
8. $\sim\sim(p \lor r)$
9. $\sim(\sim p \bullet \sim r)$
10. $(s \bullet q) \lor (s \bullet t)$
11. $s \bullet (q \lor t)$

19. 1. $\sim p \vee (q \bullet \sim r)$
  2. $\sim(p \bullet r) \supset \sim[r \bullet (s \vee t)]$
  $\therefore \sim(r \bullet t)$
  3. $(\sim p \vee q) \bullet (\sim p \vee \sim r)$
  4. $(\sim p \vee \sim r) \bullet (\sim p \vee q)$
  5. $\sim p \vee \sim r$
  6. $\sim(p \bullet r)$
  7. $\sim[r \bullet (s \vee t)]$
  8. $\sim r \vee \sim(s \vee t)$
  9. $\sim r \vee (\sim s \bullet \sim t)$
  10. $(\sim r \vee \sim s) \bullet (\sim r \vee \sim t)$
  11. $(\sim r \vee \sim t) \bullet (\sim r \vee \sim s)$
  12. $(\sim r \vee \sim t)$
  13. $\sim(r \bullet t)$

20. 1. $\sim(p \vee \sim q)$
  2. $q \supset (s \vee \sim t)$
  3. $\sim(\sim s \bullet t) \supset [w \vee (y \bullet z)]$
  $\therefore w \vee z$
  4. $\sim p \bullet \sim\sim q$
  5. $\sim p \bullet q$
  6. $q \bullet \sim p$
  7. q
  8. $s \vee \sim t$
  9. $\sim\sim s \vee \sim t$
  10. $\sim(\sim s \bullet t)$
  11. $w \vee (y \bullet z)$
  12. $(w \vee y) \bullet (w \vee z)$
  13. $(w \vee z) \bullet (w \vee y)$
  14. $w \vee z$

III. For each of the following, adding just two statements to the premises will produce a formal proof of validity. Construct a formal proof of validity for each of the following arguments.

21. $A \bullet \sim B$
  $\therefore \sim B$

22. $A \supset \sim B$
  B
  $\therefore \sim A$

23. $A \vee (B \bullet C)$
  $\therefore A \vee B$

24. $A \bullet (B \vee C)$
  $\sim(A \bullet B)$
  $\therefore A \vee C$

25. $E \supset (G \vee H)$
  $(\sim G \bullet \sim H)$
  $\therefore \sim E$

26. $(\sim A \bullet \sim B) \supset \sim C$
  $\sim C \supset D$
  $\therefore \sim(A \bullet B) \supset D$

27. $(A \supset B) \bullet (C \supset D)$
  $C \vee A$
  $\therefore B \vee D$

28. $A \vee (B \vee C)$
  $\sim(A \vee B)$
  $\therefore C$

29. $(A \bullet B) \supset C$
  $\therefore (A \bullet B) \supset [C \bullet (A \bullet B)]$

30. $[P \equiv (Q \vee R)]$
  $\sim[P \equiv (Q \vee R)] \vee T$
  $\therefore T$

31. $B \bullet (C \bullet D)$
  $\therefore C \bullet (D \bullet B)$

32. E
  $\therefore (E \vee F) \bullet (E \vee G)$

33. $(E \bullet F) \supset (G \bullet H)$
  $F \bullet E$
  $\therefore G \bullet H$

34. $(N \bullet O) \supset P$
  $\therefore (N \bullet O) \supset [N \bullet (O \bullet P)]$

35. $[(A \vee B) \bullet (A \vee C)] \supset D$
  $A \vee (B \bullet C)$
  $\therefore D$

IV. For each of the following, adding just three statements to the premises will produce a formal proof of validity. Construct a formal proof of validity for each of the following arguments.

36. $\sim[A \lor (B \lor C)]$
$\therefore \sim(B \lor C)$

37. $A \lor \sim(B \lor C)$
$\therefore A \lor \sim B$

38. $M \supset (N \bullet O)$
$\sim N$
$\therefore \sim M$

39. $(P \lor Q) \lor R$
$\sim Q$
$\therefore P \lor R$

40. $(N \bullet O) \lor (N \bullet P)$
$N \supset S$
$\therefore S$

41. $(N \lor O) \bullet (N \lor P)$
$\sim N$
$\therefore O$

42. $\sim(\sim U \lor \sim P)$
$(U \bullet P) \supset R$
$\therefore R$

43. $\sim(\sim U \bullet \sim P)$
$\sim U$
$\therefore P$

44. $P \supset (\sim Q \bullet \sim R)$
$Q \lor R$
$\therefore \sim P$

45. $E \lor (F \bullet G)$
$\therefore E \lor G$

V. Construct a formal proof of validity for each of the following argument forms.

46. $\sim(p \lor q)$
$\therefore \sim q$

47. $p \bullet (q \bullet r)$
$\therefore r$

48. p
$\sim(p \bullet q)$
$\therefore \sim q$

49. $\sim p \supset \sim q$
q
$\therefore p$

50. $p \bullet s$
$\therefore (s \lor q) \bullet (s \lor \sim r)$

51. $p \lor (q \lor r)$
$\sim q$
$\therefore p \lor r$

52. $p \bullet (q \bullet r)$
$\therefore p \bullet r$

53. $(p \supset q) \bullet (r \supset s)$
$p \lor (q \bullet r)$
$\therefore q \lor s$

54. $\sim p \bullet [q \lor (r \bullet s)]$
$\therefore (\sim p \bullet q) \lor (\sim p \bullet s)$

55. $\sim[(p \lor q) \lor r]$
$\therefore \sim q$

56. $p \lor (q \lor r)$
$\sim p \bullet \sim q$
$\therefore r$

57. $(p \supset q) \bullet (q \supset p)$
$\therefore (p \supset p) \bullet (q \supset q)$

58. $\sim[p \bullet (q \lor r)]$
q
$\therefore \sim p$

59. $\sim[p \lor (q \bullet r)]$
r
$\therefore \sim q$

60. $(p \bullet q) \lor (p \bullet r)$
$\sim r$
$q \supset t$
$\therefore (t \lor s) \bullet (t \lor w)$

61. $p \lor \sim(q \lor r)$
$\sim(\sim p \bullet q) \supset s$
$s \supset w$
$\therefore (s \bullet w) \lor (t \bullet z)$

62. $(p \bullet q) \vee (p \bullet s)$
$\quad (s \supset w) \bullet (q \supset m)$
$\quad a \supset \sim(m \vee w)$
$\quad \therefore \sim a \bullet p$

63. $(p \bullet q) \vee (\sim p \bullet \sim q)$
$\quad \therefore (\sim p \vee q) \bullet (\sim q \vee p)$

64. $(p \bullet q) \vee (r \bullet s)$
$\quad s \supset (w \bullet z)$
$\quad \sim q$
$\quad \therefore z$

65. $(p \bullet q) \vee (p \bullet r)$
$\quad \sim(\sim q \bullet \sim r) \supset t$
$\quad \sim t \vee (x \bullet z)$
$\quad \therefore (x \vee a) \bullet (x \vee z)$

7.4   THE RULE OF REPLACEMENT (2)

To complete our system of propositional logic, we introduce several more equivalences falling under the rule of replacement.

RULE OF REPLACEMENT: ANY OF THE FOLLOWING LOGICALLY EQUIVALENT EXPRESSIONS CAN REPLACE EACH OTHER WHEREVER THEY OCCUR IN A PROOF:		
NAME	**ABBREVIATION**	**FORM**
Transposition	**Trans.**	$(p \supset q) \stackrel{\mathrm{T}}{=} (\sim q \supset \sim p)$
Material Implication	**Impl.**	$(p \supset q) \stackrel{\mathrm{T}}{=} (\sim p \vee q)$
Material Equivalence	**Equiv.**	$(p \equiv q) \stackrel{\mathrm{T}}{=} [(p \supset q) \bullet (q \supset p)]$
		$(p \equiv q) \stackrel{\mathrm{T}}{=} [(p \bullet q) \vee (\sim p \bullet \sim q)]$
Exportation	**Exp.**	$[(p \bullet q) \supset r] \stackrel{\mathrm{T}}{=} [p \supset (q \supset r)]$
Tautology	**Taut.**	$p \stackrel{\mathrm{T}}{=} (p \vee p)$
		$p \stackrel{\mathrm{T}}{=} (p \bullet p)$

Transposition is for horseshoes what commutation is for dots and wedges, but notice that when statements are flipped around the horseshoe, both statements are negated. Material implication allows you to remove or introduce horseshoes. Material equivalence provides equivalent forms of biconditionals. Since there are no rules of inference that deal directly with biconditionals, these equivalences are needed to work with biconditionals. Exportation is a useful equivalence. Tautology allows you introduce or remove the disjunction or conjunction of a term with itself. This is particularly useful regarding propositions embedded in more complex propositions.

We now have a complete system of propositional logic. You can prove the validity of any valid propositional argument. Indeed you can even prove the validity of some of the first nine rules using the other rules and equivalences:

$$1.\ p \supset q$$
$$2.\ p$$
$$\therefore\ q$$
$$3.\ \sim p \lor q \quad \text{1 Impl.}$$
$$4.\ \sim\sim p \quad\ \ \ \text{2 D.N.}$$
$$5.\ q \quad\quad\ \ \ \text{3,4 D.S.}$$

So let's look at a couple of proofs that involve some of the new equivalences. Consider the argument form:

$$p$$
$$p \equiv q$$
$$\sim q \lor r$$
$$(r \bullet s) \supset (t \lor t)$$
$$\therefore\ s \supset t$$

An initial survey of the argument form should convince you that you'll need to use material equivalence, since it's the only way to do anything with a biconditional. You'll probably use tautology, since there is one t in the conclusion, and there is the disjunction $t \lor t$ in the fourth premise. A conditional with a conjunction as an antecedent suggests that you might use exportation, especially given that s is a conjunct in the antecedent of the fourth premise and s is the antecedent of the conclusion. One way to do the proof is as follows:

$$1.\ p$$
$$2.\ p \equiv q$$
$$3.\ \sim q \lor r$$
$$4.\ (r \bullet s) \supset (t \lor t)$$
$$\therefore\ s \supset t$$
$$5.\ (p \supset q) \bullet (q \supset p) \quad\quad \text{2 Equiv.}$$
$$6.\ p \supset q \quad\quad\quad\quad\quad\quad\ \ \text{5 Simp.}$$
$$7.\ q \quad\quad\quad\quad\quad\quad\quad\quad\ \text{6,1 M.P.}$$
$$8.\ q \supset r \quad\quad\quad\quad\quad\quad\ \ \text{3 Impl.}$$
$$9.\ r \quad\quad\quad\quad\quad\quad\quad\quad\ \text{8,7 M.P.}$$
$$10.\ (r \bullet s) \supset t \quad\quad\quad\quad\ \text{4 Taut}$$
$$11.\ r \supset (s \supset t) \quad\quad\quad\ \text{10 Exp.}$$
$$12.\ s \supset t \quad\quad\quad\quad\quad\quad\ \text{11,9 M.P.}$$

Could you have gotten away *without* using some of the new equivalences? Yes. You *could* have avoided using exportation, but it would have been far less convenient. You *couldn't* have avoided material equivalence, since it's the only way to use a biconditional. You *couldn't* have avoided tautology. You *could* have introduced the double negation of *q* in line 8 and reached *r* in line 9 by disjunctive syllogism. But, to avoid exportation, you would have had to use implication in line 10. Let's pick up the proof at line 11 and see what would have been involved in avoiding exportation.

$$11. \sim (r \bullet s) \lor t \qquad \text{4 Impl.}$$
$$12. (\sim r \lor \sim s) \lor t \qquad \text{11 De M.}$$
$$13. \sim r \lor (\sim s \lor t) \qquad \text{12 Assoc.}$$
$$14. \sim \sim r \qquad \text{9 D.N.}$$
$$15. \sim s \lor t \qquad \text{13,14 D.S.}$$
$$16. s \supset t \qquad \text{15 Impl.}$$

Some of the new equivalences are essential. Others are at least convenient: They provide for more elegant proofs.

In section 7.2, we said that elegance makes no *logical* difference, so why bring it up again? There's an old saying about not being able to see the forest for the trees. When doing proofs, it works the other way around. You might look at a proof as building a forest one tree (line) at a time. As the forest gets larger, it's harder to see the individual trees. So, with nine rules of inference plus fifteen distinct equivalences (with ten names) falling under the rule of replacement, it becomes important to think several lines ahead before using one of the equivalences. When there were only the nine rules of inference, you could apply most of them with little thought: There were relatively few patterns. Even after adding De Morgan's theorems, commutation, association, distribution, and double negation, things were relatively easy. With the equivalences added in this section, the appearance of statements can be far different from what you might expect. For example, $p \supset q$ could be "hidden" as $\sim (p \bullet \sim q)$:

$$1. p \supset q$$
$$2. \sim p \lor q \qquad \text{1 Impl.}$$
$$3. \sim p \lor \sim \sim q \qquad \text{2 D.N.}$$
$$4. \sim (p \bullet \sim q) \qquad \text{3 De M.}$$

So, ask whether using one of the equivalences will either allow you to use one of the nine rules of inference or to change the appearance of a statement to correspond to the form in the conclusion. Think a few lines ahead. If you use the equivalences willy-nilly, there is a good chance that you'll build a large forest and not be able to see the individual "trees" you might need for your proof.

ESSENTIAL HINTS

We could construct a complete system of propositional logic using only the tilde and the wedge or the tilde and the dot. The horseshoe is expendable, but it's terribly convenient. Should you question that, prove hypothetical syllogism without using the rule of hypothetical syllogism.

Let's consider a couple more proofs. You're given what is sometimes called a destructive dilemma:

$$(p \supset q) \bullet (r \supset s)$$
$$\sim q \lor \sim s$$
$$\therefore \sim p \lor \sim r$$

You *can't* prove the conclusion without using at least one of the equivalences we introduced in this section. If you think things through carefully, it's a fairly short proof. If you don't, it's relatively long.

1. $(p \supset q) \bullet (r \supset s)$		
2. $\sim q \lor \sim s$		
$\therefore \sim p \lor \sim r$		
3. $(\sim q \supset \sim p) \bullet (r \supset s)$	1 Trans.	
4. $(\sim q \supset \sim p) \bullet (\sim s \supset \sim r)$	3 Trans.	
5. $\sim p \lor \sim r$	4,2 C.D.	

1. $(p \supset q) \bullet (r \supset s)$	
2. $\sim q \lor \sim s$	
$\therefore \sim p \lor \sim r$	
3. $(\sim p \lor q) \bullet (r \supset s)$	1 Impl.
4. $(q \lor \sim p) \bullet (r \supset s)$	3 Com.
5. $(\sim\sim q \lor \sim p) \bullet (r \supset s)$	4 D.N.
6. $(\sim q \supset \sim p) \bullet (r \supset s)$	5 Impl.
7. $(\sim q \supset \sim p) \bullet (\sim r \lor s)$	6 Impl.
8. $(\sim q \supset \sim p) \bullet (s \lor \sim r)$	6 Com.
9. $(\sim q \supset \sim p) \bullet (\sim\sim s \lor \sim r)$	8 D.N.
10. $(\sim q \supset \sim p) \bullet (\sim s \supset \sim r)$	9 Impl.
11. $\sim p \lor \sim r$	10,2 C.D.

Or you might have gone about it without using constructive dilemma:

1. $(p \supset q) \bullet (r \supset s)$	
2. $\sim q \lor \sim s$	
$\therefore \sim p \lor \sim r$	
3. $q \supset \sim s$	2 Impl.
4. $p \supset q$	1 Simp.
5. $(r \supset s) \bullet (p \supset q)$	1 Com.
6. $r \supset s$	5 Simp.
7. $p \supset \sim s$	4,3 H.S.
8. $\sim s \supset \sim r$	6 Trans.
9. $p \supset \sim r$	7,8 H.S.
10. $\sim p \lor \sim r$	9 Impl.

Each of these proofs is logically valid. The first is more elegant than either of the other two. Does elegance make a difference? Would it make a difference if doing a destructive dilemma were part of a more elaborate argument?

Consider the following argument form:

$$\sim(p \equiv r)$$
$$(p \supset q) \cdot (r \supset s)$$
$$\therefore \sim q \supset s$$

In section 7.1, we mentioned that it is often useful to work backwards from the conclusion for a few lines. Now that we have the equivalences falling under the rule of replacement, "working backwards" often involves looking at logically equivalent forms of the conclusion. If you do so, you'll notice that the conclusion is logically equivalent to $q \lor s$ by implication and double negation. Given that the second premise is a conjunction of conditionals in which q is the consequent of one and s is the consequent of the other, you might reasonably guess that you're going to reach the conclusion by constructive dilemma followed by double negation and implication. The first premise, however, might cause you to take pause. There are two statement forms that are logically equivalent to a biconditional. What do you use? You *can* use either one, but after you've had a bit of experience, you might choose one over the other.

1. $\sim(p \equiv r)$		
2. $(p \supset q) \cdot (r \supset s)$		
$\therefore \sim q \supset s$		
3. $\sim[(p \supset r) \cdot (r \supset p)]$	1 Equiv.	
4. $\sim(p \supset r) \lor \sim(r \supset p)$	4 De M.	
5. $\sim(p \supset r) \lor \sim(\sim r \lor p)$	4 Imp.	
6. $\sim(p \supset r) \lor (\sim\sim r \cdot \sim p)$	5 De M.	
7. $\sim(p \supset r) \lor (r \cdot \sim p)$	6 D.N.	
8. $[\sim(p \supset r) \lor r] \cdot [\sim(p \supset r) \lor p]$	7 Dist.	
9. $\sim(p \supset r) \lor r$	8 Simp.	
10. $\sim(\sim p \lor r) \lor r$	9 Impl.	
11. $(\sim\sim p \cdot r) \lor r$	10 De M.	
12. $(p \cdot r) \lor r$	11 D.N.	
13. $r \lor (p \cdot r)$	12 Com.	
14. $(r \lor p) \cdot (r \lor r)$	13 Dist.	
15. $r \lor p$	14 Simp.	
16. $p \lor r$	15 Com.	
17. $q \lor s$	16 Com.	
18. $\sim\sim q \lor s$	17 D.N.	
19. $\sim q \supset s$	18 Impl.	

1. $\sim(p \equiv r)$
2. $(p \supset q) \bullet (r \supset s)$
   $\therefore \sim q \supset s$
3. $\sim[(p \bullet r) \vee (\sim p \bullet \sim r)]$ 1 Equiv.
4. $\sim(p \bullet r) \bullet \sim(\sim p \bullet \sim r)$ 3 De M.
5. $\sim(\sim p \bullet \sim r) \bullet \sim(p \bullet r)$ 4 Com.
6. $\sim(\sim p \bullet \sim r)$ 5 Simp.
7. $\sim\sim(p \vee r)$ 6 De M.
8. $p \vee r$ 7 D.N.
9. $q \vee s$ 2,8 C.D.
10. $\sim\sim q \vee s$ 9 D.N.
11. $\sim q \supset s$ 10 Impl.

Let's consider one more:

$$p \supset (q \bullet r)$$
$$p \bullet \sim r$$
$$\therefore s$$

There is something odd here! The conclusion is a *simple statement that is not found in the premises!* "Surely," you say, "this argument cannot be valid!" Here it is important to remember the distinction between validity and soundness. Recall that a sound argument is a valid argument with all true premises. Any substitution instance of an argument of the form above will be unsound, for, as we shall see, the premises entail an *inconsistent* pair of conclusions—a statement and its denial—in this case r and $\sim r$. If the premises of a valid deductive argument are inconsistent, *any* statement follows from the premises. So, s follows. Here's the proof:

1. $p \supset (q \bullet r)$
2. $p \bullet \sim r$
   $\therefore s$
3. p 2 Simp.
4. $q \bullet r$ 1,3 M.P.
5. $r \bullet p$ 4 Com.
6. r 5 Simp.
7. $\sim r \bullet p$ 2 Com.
8. $\sim r$ 7 Simp.
9. $r \vee s$ 6 Add.
10. s 9,8 D.S.

If you are given a valid argument with a conclusion consisting of a simple statement that is *not* found in the premises, the argument form must entail inconsistent conclusions. Your task, then, is to find the inconsistency (both p and $\sim p$). Once you've done so, you may add the conclusion to one statement (add x to p to obtain $p \lor x$) and use the other statement ($\sim p$) with the disjunction to reach the conclusion by disjunctive syllogism.

Ultimately, you'll need to do many proofs to master the use of the rules and the equivalences. The following rules of thumb should prove helpful in working though many proofs.

Rules of Thumb: Strategies for Doing Deductive Proofs

1. Determine where the simple statements in the conclusion are found in the premises.

    a. If there is a simple statement in the conclusion that is *not* found in the premises, you will need to use addition.

    b. If the conclusion is a simple statement *not* found in the premises, the premises are inconsistent; that is, both a statement and its denial follow from the premises. In such a case, you'll need to use a combination of addition and disjunctive syllogism to reach the conclusion. For example, if the conclusion is r and you derive some pair of statements p and $\sim p$ from the premises, you then add r to p ($p \lor r$) and use that statement and disjunctive syllogism with $\sim p$ to reach r.[4]

    c. Look at equivalent forms of the conclusion.

2. Work backwards from the conclusion.

    a. If you can "see" what steps led to the conclusion, jot them down. If there are alternative routes, you might jot them down, too.

    b. It is often helpful to work backwards as many steps as you can.

3. If you can use any of the nine rules of inference to break down a compound statement into its simple components, do so. (This is *generally* helpful, but it is not always necessary.)

4. If you can use any of the nine rules of inference to eliminate a simple statement that is not in the conclusion, use it.

5. If there is a tribar ($\equiv$), use the rule of material equivalence; it's usually the only way you can do anything with the statement.

    a. If a *premise* is an affirmative biconditional, you'll probably want to use the first version of the rule so you can then simplify or commute and simplify to use one of the conditionals.

---

[4]If a collection of premises entails both a statement and its denial, the argument is *unsound*. Reaching inconsistent conclusions by deductions from the premises does *not* show that the argument is invalid.

    b. If a *premise* is the denial of a biconditional, you'll probably want to use the second version of the rule so you can use De Morgan's theorem and then simplify or commute and simplify.

    c. If the *conclusion* is a biconditional of the form $p \equiv q$, and if you can establish either $p \bullet q$ or $\sim p \bullet \sim q$, you can add the other one and use the second version of the rule to reach the conclusion.

6. If there is a tilde ($\sim$) outside a set of grouping indicators, use De Morgan's theorem to move the tilde inside, *unless* you can see how the negated statement can be used with *modus tollens* or disjunctive syllogism. Sometimes you will have to use other equivalences to change the statement in the parentheses into a conjunction or a disjunction before you can use De Morgan's theorem.

7. If the *premises* contain both conditionals and disjunctions, you might consider constructive dilemma.

8. If you find a proposition of the form $p \supset (q \supset r)$, you'll probably use exportation. If you have both statements of the form $p \supset (q \supset r)$ and $p \supset q$, using exportation on the first and absorption on the second will allow you to conclude a statement of the form $p \supset r$ by hypothetical syllogism.

9. Plan ahead before using the equivalences falling under the rule of replacement to avoid extra lines in your proof.

10. *Most important*: If you believe you can solve all the problems in this book by following these rules of thumb as if there were no exceptions, you will be disappointed.

RULES OF INFERENCE AND EQUIVALENCES

The rules of inference and equivalences falling under the rule of replacement are as follows:

ELEMENTARY VALID ARGUMENT FORMS:	LOGICALLY EQUIVALENT EXPRESSIONS:
1. Modus Ponens (M.P.): $p \supset q, p, \ \therefore q$	**10. De Morgan's Theorems** (De M.): $\sim(p \bullet q) \ \underset{=}{\mathrm{T}} \ (\sim p \lor \sim q)$ $\sim(p \lor q) \ \underset{=}{\mathrm{T}} \ (\sim p \bullet \sim q)$
2. Modus Tollens (M.T.): $p \supset q, \sim q, \ \therefore \sim p$	**11. Commutation** (Com.): $(p \lor q) \ \underset{=}{\mathrm{T}} \ (q \lor p)$ $(p \bullet q) \ \underset{=}{\mathrm{T}} \ (q \bullet p)$
3. Hypothetical Syllogism (H.S.): $p \supset q, q \supset r, \ \therefore p \supset r$	**12. Association** (Assoc.): $[p \lor (q \lor r)] \ \underset{=}{\mathrm{T}} \ [(p \lor q) \lor r]$ $[p \bullet (q \bullet r)] \ \underset{=}{\mathrm{T}} \ [(p \bullet q) \bullet r]$
4. Disjunctive Syllogism (D.S.): $p \lor q, \sim p, \ \therefore q$	**13. Distribution** (Dist.): $[p \bullet (q \lor r)] \ \underset{=}{\mathrm{T}} \ [(p \bullet q) \lor (p \bullet r)]$ $[p \lor (q \bullet r)] \ \underset{=}{\mathrm{T}} \ [(p \lor q) \bullet (p \lor r)]$

5. Constructive Dilemma (C.D.): $(p \supset q) \bullet (r \supset s), p \vee r, \therefore q \vee s$	**14. Double Negation** (D.N.): $p \overset{I}{=} \sim\sim p$
6. Absorption (Abs.): $p \supset q, \therefore p \supset (p \bullet q)$	**15. Transposition** (Trans.): $(p \supset q) \overset{I}{=} (\sim q \supset \sim p)$
7. Simplification (Simp.): $p \bullet q, \therefore p$	**16. Material Implication** (Impl.): $(p \supset q) \overset{I}{=} (\sim p \vee q)$
8. Conjunction (Conj.): $p, q, \therefore p \bullet q$	**17. Material Equivalence** (Equiv.): $(p \equiv q) \overset{I}{=} [(p \supset q) \bullet (q \supset p)]$ $(p \equiv q) \overset{I}{=} [(p \bullet q) \vee (\sim p \bullet \sim q)]$
9. Addition (Add.): $p, \therefore p \vee q$	**18. Exportation** (Exp.): $[p \supset (q \supset r)] \overset{I}{=} [(p \bullet q) \supset r]$
	19. Tautology (Taut.): $p \overset{I}{=} (p \vee p)$ $p \overset{I}{=} (p \bullet p)$

EXERCISES

I. Which equivalence falling under the rule of replacement justifies the move from the premise to the conclusion in each of the following?

1. $p \equiv (r \vee s)$
   $\therefore [p \supset (r \vee s)] \bullet [(r \vee s) \supset p]$

2. $p \bullet (q \vee q)$
   $\therefore p \bullet q$

3. $(p \bullet q) \supset (r \vee s)$
   $\therefore p \supset [q \supset (r \vee s)]$

4. $\sim p \supset q$
   $\therefore \sim q \supset \sim\sim p$

5. $[(p \bullet \sim q) \bullet (r \vee s)] \vee [\sim(p \bullet \sim q) \bullet \sim(r \vee s)]$
   $\therefore (p \bullet \sim q) \equiv (r \vee s)$

6. $\sim(p \equiv q) \supset (r \equiv s)$
   $\therefore \sim\sim(p \equiv q) \vee (r \equiv s)$

7. $(p \bullet q) \supset (r \supset s)$
   $\therefore [(p \bullet q) \bullet r] \supset s$

8. $p \vee (q \vee r)$
   $\therefore p \vee [q \vee (r \bullet r)]$

9. $\sim\{(q \bullet r) \vee [p \equiv (s \equiv \sim r)]\} \supset (z \vee w)$
   $\therefore \sim\sim\{(q \bullet r) \vee [p \equiv (s \equiv \sim r)]\} \vee (z \vee w)$

10. $\{(q \bullet r) \lor [p \equiv (s \equiv \sim r)]\} \supset (z \lor w)$
$\therefore \sim(z \lor w) \supset \sim\{(q \bullet r) \lor [p \equiv (s \equiv \sim r)]\}$

11. $[(\sim O \lor P) \lor \sim Q] \bullet [\sim O \lor (P \lor \sim Q)]$
$\therefore [\sim O \lor (P \lor \sim Q)] \bullet [\sim O \lor (P \lor \sim Q)]$

12. $[V \supset \sim(W \lor X)] \supset (Y \lor Z)$
$\therefore \{[V \supset \sim(W \lor X)] \bullet [V \supset \sim(W \lor X)]\} \supset (Y \lor Z)$

13. $[(\sim A \bullet B) \bullet (C \lor D)] \lor [\sim(\sim A \bullet B) \bullet \sim(C \lor D)]$
$\therefore (\sim A \bullet B) \equiv (C \lor D)$

14. $[\sim E \lor (\sim\sim F \supset G)] \bullet [\sim E \lor (F \supset G)]$
$\therefore [\sim E \lor (F \supset G)] \bullet [\sim E \lor (F \supset G)]$

15. $[H \bullet (I \lor J)] \lor [H \bullet (K \supset \sim L)]$
$\therefore H \bullet [(I \lor J) \lor (K \supset \sim L)]$

II. **Each of the following is a formal proof of validity for the indicated argument. State the "justification" for each numbered line that is not a premise.**

16. 1. $(D \bullet E) \supset F$
    2. $(D \supset F) \supset G$
       $\therefore E \supset G$
    3. $(E \bullet D) \supset F$
    4. $E \supset (D \supset F)$
    5. $E \supset G$

17. 1. $(M \lor N) \supset (O \bullet P)$
    2. $\sim O$
       $\therefore \sim M$
    3. $\sim O \lor \sim P$
    4. $\sim(O \bullet P)$
    5. $\sim(M \lor N)$
    6. $\sim M \bullet \sim N$
    7. $\sim M$

18. 1. $T \bullet (U \lor V)$
    2. $T \supset [U \supset (W \bullet X)]$
    3. $(T \bullet V) \supset \sim(W \lor X)$
       $\therefore W \equiv X$
    4. $(T \bullet U) \supset (W \bullet X)$
    5. $(T \bullet V) \supset (\sim W \bullet \sim X)$
    6. $[(T \bullet U) \supset (W \bullet X)] \bullet [(T \bullet V) \supset (\sim W \bullet \sim X)]$
    7. $(T \bullet U) \lor (T \bullet V)$
    8. $(W \bullet X) \lor (\sim W \bullet \sim X)$
    9. $W \equiv X$

19. 1. $A \supset B$
    2. $B \supset C$
    3. $C \supset A$
    4. $A \supset \sim C$
       $\therefore \sim A \bullet \sim C$
    5. $A \supset C$
    6. $(A \supset C) \bullet (C \supset A)$
    7. $A \equiv C$
    8. $(A \bullet C) \lor (\sim A \bullet \sim C)$
    9. $\sim A \lor \sim C$
    10. $\sim(A \bullet C)$
    11. $\sim A \bullet \sim C$

20. 1. $(D \bullet E) \supset \sim F$
    2. $F \lor (G \bullet H)$
    3. $D \equiv E$
       $\therefore D \supset G$
    4. $(D \supset E) \bullet (E \supset D)$
    5. $D \supset E$
    6. $D \supset (D \bullet E)$
    7. $D \supset \sim F$
    8. $(F \lor G) \bullet (F \lor H)$

9. $F \lor G$
10. $\sim\sim F \lor G$
11. $\sim F \supset G$
12. $D \supset G$

III. For each of the following, adding just two statements to the premises will produce a formal proof of validity. Construct a formal proof of validity for each of the following arguments.

21. A
$\sim B \supset \sim A$
$\therefore B$

22. $B \equiv C$
$\therefore B \supset C$

23. C
$(C \bullet D) \supset E$
$\therefore D \supset E$

24. $E \supset F$
$\sim F \lor G$
$\therefore E \supset G$

25. $Q \supset [R \supset (S \supset T)]$
$Q \supset (Q \bullet R)$
$\therefore Q \supset (S \supset T)$

26. $(U \bullet U) \supset \sim V$
U
$\therefore \sim V$

27. $W \supset X$
$\sim Y \supset \sim X$
$\therefore W \supset Y$

28. $C \supset \sim D$
$\sim E \supset D$
$\therefore C \supset \sim\sim E$

29. $F \equiv G$
$\sim (F \bullet G)$
$\therefore \sim F \bullet \sim G$

30. $(L \supset M) \bullet (N \supset M)$
$L \lor N$
$\therefore M$

31. $(S \bullet T) \lor (U \bullet V)$
$\sim S \lor \sim T$
$\therefore U \bullet V$

32. $(W \bullet X) \supset Y$
$(X \supset Y) \supset Z$
$\therefore W \supset Z$

33. $(A \lor B) \supset (C \lor D)$
$\sim C \bullet \sim D$
$\therefore \sim (A \lor B)$

34. $[E \bullet (F \bullet G)] \supset H$
$D \supset E$
$\therefore D \supset [(F \bullet G) \supset H]$

35. $(M \supset N) \bullet (\sim O \lor P)$
$M \lor O$
$\therefore N \lor P$

36. $\sim [(U \supset V) \bullet (V \supset U)]$
$(W \equiv X) \supset (U \equiv V)$
$\therefore \sim (W \equiv X)$

37. $(Y \supset Z) \bullet (Z \supset Y)$
$\therefore (Y \bullet Z) \lor (\sim Y \bullet \sim Z)$

38. $[(E \lor F) \bullet (G \lor H)] \supset (F \bullet I)$
$(G \lor H) \bullet (E \lor F)$
$\therefore F \bullet I$

39. $(J \bullet K) \supset [(L \bullet M) \lor (N \bullet O)]$
$\sim (L \bullet M) \bullet \sim (N \bullet O)$
$\therefore \sim (J \bullet K)$

40. $[V \bullet (W \lor X)] \supset (Y \supset Z)$
$\sim (Y \supset Z) \lor (\sim W \equiv A)$
$\therefore [V \bullet (W \lor X)] \supset (\sim W \equiv A)$

IV. For each of the following, adding just three statements to the premises will produce a formal proof of validity. Construct a formal proof of validity for each of the following arguments.

41. $\sim B \lor (C \bullet D)$
$\therefore B \supset C$

42. $E \lor (F \bullet G)$
$\therefore E \lor G$

43. $H \bullet (I \bullet J)$
    $\therefore J \bullet (I \bullet H)$

44. $O \supset P$
    $P \supset {\sim}P$
    $\therefore {\sim}O$

45. $Q \supset (R \supset S)$
    $Q \supset R$
    $\therefore Q \supset S$

46. $T \supset U$
    ${\sim}(U \vee V)$
    $\therefore {\sim}T$

47. $W \bullet (X \vee Y)$
    ${\sim}W \vee {\sim}X$
    $\therefore W \bullet Y$

48. $(C \vee D) \supset (E \bullet F)$
    $D \vee C$
    $\therefore E$

49. $G \supset H$
    $H \supset G$
    $\therefore (G \bullet H) \vee ({\sim}G \bullet {\sim}H)$

50. $(N \bullet O) \supset P$
    $({\sim}P \supset {\sim}O) \supset Q$
    $\therefore N \supset Q$

V. The exercises in this set represent frequently recurring patterns of infer-
    ence found in longer formal proofs of validity. Familiarity with them
    will be useful in subsequent work. Construct a formal proof of validity
    for each of the following arguments.

51. ${\sim}A$
    $\therefore A \supset B$

52. C
    $\therefore D \supset C$

53. $E \supset (F \supset G)$
    $\therefore F \supset (E \supset G)$

54. $H \supset (I \bullet J)$
    $\therefore H \supset I$

55. $K \supset L$
    $\therefore K \supset (L \vee M)$

56. $N \supset O$
    $\therefore (N \bullet P) \supset O$

57. $(Q \vee R) \supset S$
    $\therefore Q \supset S$

58. $T \supset U$
    $T \supset V$
    $\therefore T \supset (U \bullet V)$

59. $W \supset X$
    $Y \supset X$
    $\therefore (W \vee Y) \supset X$

60. $Z \supset A$
    $Z \vee A$
    $\therefore A$

VI. To give you more practice with the equivalent statements introduced in
    this section, construct a proof of validity for each of the following argu-
    ment forms using *only* the nine rules of inference plus transposition,
    material implication, material equivalence, exportation, and tautology.

61. p
    ${\sim}p \vee q$
    $\therefore q$

62. ${\sim}p \vee q$
    ${\sim}q$
    $\therefore {\sim}p$

63. $p \equiv q$
    ${\sim}q$
    $\therefore {\sim}p \bullet {\sim}q$

64. $p \equiv q$
    ${\sim}(p \bullet q)$
    $\therefore {\sim}p \bullet {\sim}q$

65. $(p \supset q) \bullet (r \supset s)$
    ${\sim}q \vee {\sim}s$
    $\therefore {\sim}p \vee {\sim}r$

66. $(p \supset q) \bullet (r \supset q)$
    $p \vee r$
    $\therefore q$

67. $p \supset q$
    ${\sim}{\sim}p$
    $\therefore {\sim}{\sim}q$

68. ${\sim}q \supset p$
    ${\sim}p \vee {\sim}q$
    $\therefore (p \bullet {\sim}q) \vee ({\sim}p \bullet {\sim}{\sim}q)$

69. $p \supset (q \vee \sim s)$
   $\therefore p \supset [p \supset (\sim s \vee \sim\sim q)]$

70. $p \supset (\sim q \supset r)$
   $\sim\sim q \vee p$
   $\therefore \sim r \supset \sim\sim q$

71. $p \equiv q$
   $\sim p \supset r$
   $\therefore \sim q \supset r$

72. $p \supset q$
   $p \supset [q \supset (\sim r \vee s)]$
   $\therefore (p \bullet r) \supset s$

73. $\sim p$
   $\sim p \supset \sim s$
   $\therefore \sim(\sim r \supset \sim q) \supset \sim s$

74. $p \equiv q$
   $q \supset (r \supset s)$
   $\sim s$
   $\therefore (p \bullet r) \supset t$

75. $q \supset \sim p$
   $p \equiv q$
   $\sim\sim p \supset (\sim q \supset r)$
   $\therefore \sim\sim p \supset r$

VII. Construct a formal proof of validity for each of the following arguments.

76. $(D \bullet \sim E) \supset F$
   $\sim(E \vee F)$
   $\therefore \sim D$

77. $(G \supset \sim H) \supset I$
   $\sim(G \bullet H)$
   $\therefore I \vee \sim H$

78. $R \vee (S \bullet \sim T)$
   $(R \vee S) \supset (U \vee \sim T)$
   $\therefore T \supset U$

79. $[(Y \bullet Z) \supset A] \bullet [(Y \bullet B) \supset C]$
   $(B \vee Z) \bullet Y$
   $\therefore A \vee C$

80. $\sim D \supset (\sim E \supset \sim F)$
   $\sim(F \bullet \sim D) \supset \sim G$
   $\therefore G \supset E$

81. $M \supset N$
   $M \supset (N \supset O)$
   $\therefore M \supset O$

82. $T \supset (U \bullet V)$
   $(U \vee V) \supset W$
   $\therefore T \supset W$

83. $\sim B \vee [(C \supset D) \bullet (E \supset D)]$
   $B \bullet (C \vee E)$
   $\therefore D$

84. $J \vee (\sim J \bullet K)$
   $J \supset L$
   $\therefore (L \bullet J) \equiv J$

85. $(M \supset N) \bullet (O \supset P)$
   $\sim N \vee \sim P$
   $\sim(M \bullet O) \supset Q$
   $\therefore Q$

VIII. Construct a formal proof of validity for each of the following arguments, in each case using the suggested notation.

86. The oxygen in the tube either combined with the filament to form an oxide or else it vanished completely. The oxygen in the tube could not have vanished completely. Therefore the oxygen in the tube combined with the filament to form an oxide. (*C, V*)

87. It is not the case that she either forgot or wasn't able to finish. Therefore she was able to finish. (*F, A*)

88. She has many friends only if she respects them as individuals. If she respects them as individuals, then she cannot expect them all to behave alike. She has many friends. Therefore she cannot expect them all to behave alike. (*F, R, E*)

89. Napoleon is to be condemned if he usurped power that was not rightfully his own. Either Napoleon was a legitimate monarch or else he usurped power that was not rightfully his own. Napoleon was not a legitimate monarch. So Napoleon is to be condemned. (*C, U, L*)

90. Had Roman citizenship guaranteed civil liberties, then Roman citizens would have enjoyed religious freedom. Had Roman citizens enjoyed religious freedom, there would have been no persecution of the early Christians. But the early Christians were persecuted. Hence Roman citizenship could not have guaranteed civil liberties. (*G, F, P*)

91. If the first disjunct of a disjunction is true, the disjunction as a whole is true. Therefore, if both the first and second disjuncts of the disjunction are true, then the disjunction as a whole is true. (*F, W, S*)

92. Jones will come if she gets the message, provided that she is still interested. Although she didn't come, she is still interested. Therefore she didn't get the message. (*C, M, I*)

93. If the teller or the cashier had pushed the alarm button, the vault would have locked automatically and the police would have arrived within three minutes. Had the police arrived within three minutes, the robbers' car would have been overtaken. But the robbers' car was not overtaken. Therefore, the teller did not push the alarm button. (*T, C, V, P, O*)

94. Although world population is increasing, agricultural production is declining, and manufacturing output remains constant. If agricultural production declines and world population increases, then either new food sources will become available or else there will be a radical redistribution of food resources in the world unless human nutritional requirements diminish. No new food sources will become available, yet neither will family planning be encouraged nor will human nutritional requirements diminish. Therefore there will be a radical redistribution of food resources in the world. (*W, A, M, N, R, H, P*)

95. Either the robber came in the door, or else the crime was an inside one and one of the servants is implicated. The robber could come in the door only if the latch had been raised from the inside; but one of the servants is surely implicated if the latch was raised from the inside. Therefore one of the servants is implicated. (*D, I, S, L*)

IX. Construct a proof for each of the following arguments. Some of the following arguments might be a bit more challenging than those you've constructed above. Generally, they're at least a bit longer.

96. 1. $E \lor (B \bullet R)$
    2. $(E \supset {\sim}R) \bullet (B \supset W)$
    3. $W \supset {\sim}B$
    $\therefore E \lor {\sim}R$

97. 1. $(M \supset T) \bullet ({\sim}M \supset H)$
    2. $M \lor (H \equiv A)$
    3. ${\sim}T$
    $\therefore A \bullet (T \supset H)$

98. 1. $S \equiv (T \lor \sim B)$
2. $\sim (T \bullet P) \supset (B \lor T)$
3. $\sim P$
    $\therefore S \supset T$

99. 1. $(H \lor C) \bullet [(R \lor \sim D) \supset V]$
2. $R \supset (C \supset D)$
3. $V \supset (H \supset T)$
4. $\sim T$
    $\therefore D \lor C$

100. 1. $(Q \lor \sim P) \supset (\sim P \bullet S)$
2. $P \equiv \sim (R \bullet \sim S)$
    $\therefore P$

101. 1. $P \supset [Q \supset (R \supset S)]$
2. $R \bullet P$
3. $(S \supset T) \bullet (T \supset \sim S)$
    $\therefore \sim Q$

102. 1. $A \supset (G \bullet L)$
2. $L \supset \sim W$
3. $W \lor (\sim A \bullet G)$
    $\therefore \sim A \bullet (G \lor \sim L)$

103. 1. $A \supset C$
2. $(A \bullet C) \supset (G \lor J)$
3. $(E \lor D) \supset H$
4. $A \lor M$
5. $M \supset E$
    $\therefore J \lor (G \lor H)$

104. 1. $T \lor (R \bullet K)$
2. $K \supset C$
3. $(R \lor K) \supset (T \lor \sim C)$
    $\therefore T \lor \sim K$

105. 1. $(A \supset B) \bullet (C \supset D)$
2. $(A \bullet C) \supset (D \supset E)$
3. $\sim E \bullet C$
    $\therefore \sim A \bullet (B \lor D)$

X. The five arguments that follow are also valid, and a proof of the validity of each of them is called for. But these proofs will be somewhat more difficult to construct than those in earlier exercises, and students who find themselves stymied from time to time ought not become discouraged. What may appear difficult on first appraisal may come to seem much less difficult with continuing efforts. Familiarity with the rules of inference and the equivalences falling under the rule of replacement, and repeated practice in applying those rules, are the keys to the construction of these proofs.

106. If you study the humanities then you will develop an understanding of people, and if you study the sciences then you will develop an understanding of the world about you. So, if you study either the humanities or the sciences then you will develop an understanding either of people or of the world about you. (H, P, S, W)

107. If you study the humanities then you will develop an understanding of people, and if you study the sciences then you will develop an understanding of the world about you. So, if you study both the humanities and the sciences then you will develop an understanding both of people and of the world about you. (H, P, S, W)

108. If you have free will then your actions are not determined by any antecedent events. If you have free will then, if your actions are not determined by any antecedent events, then your actions cannot be predicted. If your actions are not determined by any antecedent events then, if your actions cannot be predicted, then the consequences of your actions cannot be predicted. Therefore, if you have free will then the consequences of your actions cannot be predicted. (*F, A, P, C*)

109. Socrates was a great philosopher. Therefore, either Socrates was happily married or else he wasn't. (*G, H*)

110. If either Socrates was happily married or he wasn't, then Socrates was a great philosopher. Therefore, Socrates was a great philosopher. (*H, G*)

7.5 CONDITIONAL PROOF

Given the nine rules of inference and the equivalences falling under the rule of replacement, you can construct a proof for *any* valid argument in propositional logic. Some proofs are long. Sometimes figuring out how the rules and equivalences allow you to justify a claim is anything but obvious—at least one of the authors would claim that even if *you* wouldn't.

In this section and the next we introduce two additional techniques for constructing proofs. Each involves the *assumption* of an additional premise. In each, the assumption must be discharged before you can reach the conclusion of the proof. Look at these as additional arrows in your proof quiver. They're deadly arrows. They'll allow you to construct proofs that you might find elusive when using only the nine rules and equivalences.

Consider a conditional statement. If a statement of the form $p \supset q$ is true, what do you know? You know that *if* the antecedent is true, then the consequent is true. You don't know *that* either the antecedent or the consequent is true. This fact about conditional statements is the basis for conditional proofs.

To construct a *conditional proof*, introduce an additional statement as an assumption for conditional proof (A.C.P.), proceed with the proof, and discharge the assumption with a conditional statement in which the assumed statement is the antecedent and the previous line of the proof is the consequent. "Okay," you say, "so what does that mean?"

Consider the following argument:

$$p \supset (q \bullet r)$$
$$(r \lor s) \supset (s \lor t)$$
$$\sim s$$
$$\therefore p \supset t$$

You have constructed proofs for argument forms like this one. There would be a number of implications—De Morgan's theorem, distributions, simplifications, and so forth—to reach the conclusion. If you did it by conditional proof, you'd proceed as follows:

$$1.\ p \supset (q \bullet r)$$
$$2.\ (r \lor s) \supset (s \lor t)$$
$$3.\ \sim\! s$$
$$\therefore p \supset t$$

	4. p	A.C.P.
	5. $q \bullet r$	1,4 M.P.
	6. $r \bullet q$	5 Com.
	7. r	6 Simp.
	8. $r \lor s$	7 Add.
	9. $s \lor t$	2,8 M.P.
	10. t	9,3 D.S.
11. $p \supset t$		4-10 C.P.

Here's the procedure. Introduce an assumption for conditional proof, marking it _A.C.P._ Indent the line in which you introduce the assumption and show the _scope_ of the assumption by drawing a vertical line along the lines in which the assumption is in force. Use the assumption as an additional premise together with premises that are _not_ under the scope of an assumption that has been discharged. You must _discharge_ the assumption with a conditional statement consisting of the assumption as the antecedent and previous line of proof as the consequent, marking the justification as the _lines_ in which the assumption was in force by conditional proof (C.P.). Notice, this is what was done in the proof above.

There are a couple of additional points to notice. (1) You can introduce assumptions within assumptions. We'll consider such a case below. (2) When there are multiple assumptions, they must be discharged in the reverse of the order in which they were introduced: The _last_ assumption made must be the _first_ assumption that is discharged. (3) Once you have _discharged_ an assumption, _no line within the scope of the discharged assumption can be used to justify further lines of the proof._

Let's look at another one:

$$\sim\! p \lor s$$
$$s \equiv (\sim\! q \lor r)$$
$$\therefore p \supset (q \supset r)$$

This time we're going to introduce _two_ assumptions and discharge them in the appropriate order. Remember, once you've introduced an assumption you can use it as an additional premise *so long, and only so long, as the assumption is in effect*.

1. $\sim p \lor s$	
2. $s \equiv (\sim q \lor r)$	
$\therefore p \supset (q \supset r)$	
3. p	A.C.P.
4. $\sim\sim p$	3 D.N.
5. s	1,4 D.S.
6. q	A.C.P.
7. $[s \supset (\sim q \lor r)] \bullet [(\sim q \lor r) \supset s]$	2 Equiv.
8. $s \supset (\sim q \lor r)$	7 Simp.
9. $\sim q \lor r$	8,5 M.P.
10. $\sim\sim q$	6 D.N.
11. r	9,10 D.S.
12. $q \supset r$	6-11 C.P.
13. $p \supset (q \supset r)$	3-12 C.P.

Notice that although we played with p and premise 1 before we introduced q as an assumption for conditional proof, we could have just as easily assumed q in line 4. Notice also that although we didn't deal with premise 2 until after we had introduced the second assumption for conditional proof, we could as easily have included what are lines 7–9 in the argument above *before* we introduced the second assumption for conditional proof.

  The argument forms we have looked at so far have both had conditional statements in the conclusion, and we assumed the antecedent and looked for the consequent. The times you'll be most inclined to do conditional proofs are probably when the conclusion is a conditional. But given the equivalences falling under the rule of replacement, *some* conditional statement is logically equivalent to *any* statement. So, you can construct a conditional proof for any argument. Consider the following:

$$p \supset q$$
$$q \supset r$$
$$p$$
$$\therefore r$$

Although it's unlikely that any of you would construct a conditional proof for *this* argument (you can get the conclusion by two instances of *modus ponens*, right?), you *could* do it by conditional proof. What would you want to assume? The conclusion is r. r is logically equivalent to $r \lor r$ by tautology, which is logically equivalent to $\sim r \supset r$ by material implication. So, assume $\sim r$.

$$1.\ p \supset q$$
$$2.\ q \supset r$$
$$3.\ p$$
$$\therefore\ r$$

	4. $\sim r$	A.C.P.
	5. $\sim q$	2,4 M.T.
	6. q	1,3 M.P.
	7. $q \lor r$	6 Add.
	8. r	7,5 D.S.
9. $\sim r \supset r$		4-8 C.P.
10. $r \lor r$		9 Impl.
11. r		10 Taut.

In the arguments we have considered so far, we have had no cases of multiple assumptions that did not overlap. Sometimes you'll discharge one assumption before you introduce another. For example, if the conclusion is a biconditional, you might do two successive conditional proofs.

$$1.\ p \equiv q$$
$$2.\ \sim q \lor r$$
$$3.\ \sim(r \bullet \sim q)$$
$$\therefore\ r \equiv p$$

	4. p	A.C.P.
	5. $(p \supset q) \bullet (q \supset p)$	1 Equiv.
	6. $p \supset q$	5 Simp.
	7. q	6,4 M.P.
	8. $\sim\sim q$	7 D.N.
	9. r	2,8 D.S.
10. $p \supset r$		4-9 C.P.
	11. r	A.C.P.
	12. $\sim r \lor \sim\sim q$	3 De M.
	13. $\sim r \lor q$	12 D.N.
	14. $r \supset q$	13 Impl.
	15. q	14,11 M.P.
	16. $(p \supset q) \bullet (q \supset p)$	1 Equiv.
	17. $(q \supset p) \bullet (p \supset q)$	16 Com.
	18. $q \supset p$	17 Simp.
	19. p	18,15 M.P.
20. $r \supset p$		11-19 C.P.
21. $(r \supset p) \bullet (p \supset r)$		20,10 Conj.
22. $r \equiv p$		21 Equiv.

Notice that lines 5 and 16 are identical. "Couldn't you just commute line 5 to get what is now line 17?" you ask. No. Once the assumption is discharged, you are *not* allowed to do *anything* with the lines governed by the assumption. So, in this problem, if you had used material equivalence on line 1 *before* you introduced any assumptions for conditional proof, you could have used it anywhere later in the proof.

A couple points should be noted before we conclude. First, conditional proofs are sometimes easier than nonconditional proofs, since you devote more energy to breaking down compound statements than you usually do when constructing a regular proof. Second, some people consider conditional proofs easier because you can avoid absorption and often some of the more unusual equivalences. Finally, conditional proofs are often longer than regular proofs.

SUMMARY OF CONDITIONAL PROOF

1. Assume a proposition for conditional proof (A.C.P.).

2. Beginning with the line containing the assumption, indent and draw a vertical line to the left of each line in the scope of your assumption.

3. Use the assumption with the earlier lines to draw conclusions.

4. Discharge the assumption by constructing a conditional statement of the form $p \supset q$, where p is the assumption for conditional proof and q is the conclusion reached in the previous line.

5. Assumptions can be made within the scope of other assumptions for conditional proof, but the assumptions must be discharged in the reverse of the order in which they were introduced (last-in-first-out).

6. *Remember*, conclusions reached within the scope of the assumption for conditional proofs *cannot* be used to justify conclusions after the assumption has been discharged.

EXERCISES

Construct a conditional proof for each of the following argument forms.

1. $p \vee q$
  $\sim p$
  $\therefore r \supset q$

2. $p \supset q$
  $r \bullet s$
  $\therefore p \supset (q \bullet r)$

3. p
  $(p \bullet q) \supset r$
  $\therefore \sim r \supset \sim q$

4. $p \supset (q \bullet \sim r)$
  $r \vee s$
  $\therefore p \supset s$

5. $(p \bullet q) \supset r$
$p \supset q$
$\therefore (s \bullet p) \supset r$

6. $(p \bullet q) \supset r$
$\sim r \bullet p$
$\therefore s \supset \sim q$

7. $p \supset q$
$\sim r \supset \sim q$
$\therefore p \supset (p \supset r)$

8. $p \bullet q$
$q \supset (r \lor s)$
$\therefore \sim s \supset (\sim s \bullet r)$

9. $[p \bullet (q \lor r)] \supset s$
$\sim q \supset r$
$\sim p \supset r$
$\therefore \sim r \supset (q \bullet s)$

10. $p \supset \sim q$
q
$\sim p \supset (r \supset s)$
$\therefore r \supset (r \bullet s)$

11. $(p \supset q) \bullet (r \supset s)$
$\therefore (p \lor r) \supset (q \lor s)$

12. $(p \supset q) \bullet (r \supset s)$
$\therefore (p \bullet r) \supset (q \bullet s)$

13. $\sim (p \bullet q)$
$\sim q \supset r$
$\sim r \lor p$
$\therefore r \equiv p$

14. $p \lor (\sim q \bullet r)$
$\sim [\sim p \supset (\sim q \bullet s)]$
$\therefore q \supset (\sim s \lor r)$

15. $p \supset (q \bullet s)$
$\sim q \lor s$
$(q \bullet s) \supset (r \supset t)$
$\sim t$
$\therefore \sim p \lor (t \equiv r)$

16. $(p \supset q) \bullet r$
$(p \bullet r) \supset s$
$\sim s$
$\therefore p \supset (q \bullet r)$

17. $p \supset [(q \bullet r) \supset s]$
$\sim s$
$p \bullet q$
$\therefore \sim r$

18. $q \equiv (t \lor p)$
p
$(q \bullet p) \supset (r \lor s)$
$\sim s$
$\therefore r$

19. $p \equiv (q \lor r)$
r
$(p \bullet r) \supset (s \lor t)$
$\sim t$
$\therefore s$

20. $q \supset (p \bullet r)$
$(\sim p \bullet \sim r) \lor (s \bullet t)$
$s \supset \sim t$
$\therefore q \supset (w \equiv x)$

7.6 INDIRECT PROOF

What is known as *indirect proof* or proof by *reductio ad absurdum* is a variation
on conditional proof. In the last section we noticed that if the conclusion is
a simple statement, you could assume the negation of the conclusion as an
additional premise. For example, for the argument form

$$p \supset q$$
$$q \supset r$$
$$p$$
$$\therefore r$$

we assumed $\sim r$ for conditional proof, proceeded to conclude r from the premises, discharged our assumption for conditional proof as $\sim r \supset r$, asserted $r \lor r$ by material implication, and reached r by tautology. **Whenever you have a valid argument form, if you assume the denial of the conclusion as an additional premise, you generate an inconsistent set of premises. This fact is the basis for constructing an indirect proof**. The rationale is the same as it was for constructing reverse truth tables in 6.6.

The procedure for constructing an indirect proof is similar to that for constructing a conditional proof. **Introduce the denial of the statement you are attempting to prove as an *assumption for indirect proof* (A.I.P.). Mark the scope of your assumption by a vertical line, with the lines governed by the assumption indented. Continue until you have shown that a statement and its denial—*any* statement and its denial—follow from the original premises plus the assumption. Conjoin the statement and its denial and discharge your assumption, stating the denial of your assumption, and justifying it by the lines governed by your assumption and indirect proof (I.P.).** For example, if you had assumed $\sim p$ for indirect proof, you would state the contradiction and discharge the assumption, indicating that p follows by indirect proof and by the lines within the scope of the assumption. The proof would look like this:

1. $p \supset q$
2. $q \supset r$
3. p
$\therefore r$

	3. $\sim r$	A.I.P.
	4. $\sim q$	2,3 M.T.
	5. $\sim p$	1,4 M.T.
	6. $p \bullet \sim p$	3,5 Conj.
7. r		3-6 I.P.

As in the case of conditional proof, there can be an indirect proof within the scope of another indirect proof, and the assumptions must be discharged in the reverse order of their introduction: last-in-first-out. Further, indirect proofs can be used in conjunction with conditional proofs, but the last-in-first-out principle continues to hold: It is permissible to construct an indirect or conditional proof within the scope of another, *but they must not overlap*.

Consider the following argument form:

$$p \lor (q \bullet r)$$
$$p \supset r$$
$$\therefore r$$

If you construct an indirect proof, you assume $\sim r$ as an additional premise and proceed until you reach a contradiction. Then you discharge the assumption. Either of the following would be correct. **Notice: it makes *no* difference which statement and its denial you use to generate the contradiction**.

1. $p \lor (q \bullet r)$			1. $p \lor (q \bullet r)$		
2. $p \supset r$			2. $p \supset r$		
$\therefore r$			$\therefore r$		
	3. $\sim r$	A.I.P.		3. $\sim r$	A.I.P.
	4. $\sim p$	2,3 M.T.		4. $\sim p$	2,3 M.T.
	5. $q \bullet r$	1,4 D.S.		5. $\sim\sim p \lor (q \bullet r)$	1 D.N.
	6. $r \bullet q$	5 Com.		6. $\sim p \supset (q \bullet r)$	5 Impl.
	7. r	6 Simp.		7. $\sim r \lor \sim q$	3 Add.
	8. $r \bullet \sim r$	7,3 Conj.		8. $\sim q \lor \sim r$	6 Com.
9. r		3-8 I.P.		9. $\sim (q \bullet r)$	7 De M.
				10. $\sim\sim p$	6,9 M.T.
				11. $\sim p \bullet \sim\sim p$	4,10 Conj.
			12. r		3-11 I.P.

Notice what you're doing. You assume the denial of the conclusion as an additional premise. Then you use *modus ponens, modus tollens*, hypothetical syllogism, disjunctive syllogism, constructive dilemma, and simplification to break compound statements down into their simple components. Once you find a statement and its denial, you conjoin them and discharge the assumption. **Although you can always break compound statements down to their simpler components when searching for a contradiction, it is equally acceptable to find a compound statement and its denial**.

If you have a conclusion that is a conditional statement, you can use conditional and indirect proof in tandem. Assume the antecedent of the conclusion for conditional proof. Next, assume the denial of the consequent for indirect proof. Proceed until you reach a contradiction. Discharge the assumption for indirect proof, and, in the next line, discharge the assumption for conditional proof. Applying this to hypothetical syllogism would look like this:

$$
\begin{array}{lll}
1.\ p \supset q & & \\
2.\ q \supset r & & \\
\therefore\ p \supset r & & \\
\quad |\quad 3.\ p & \text{A.C.P.} \\
\quad |\quad |\quad 4.\ \sim r & \text{A.I.P.} \\
\quad |\quad |\quad 5.\ q & \text{1,3 M.P.} \\
\quad |\quad |\quad 6.\ \sim q & \text{2,4 M.T.} \\
\quad |\quad |\quad 7.\ q \bullet \sim q & \text{5,6 Conj.} \\
\quad |\quad 8.\ r & \text{4-7 I.P.} \\
\quad 9.\ p \supset r & \text{3-8 C.P.}
\end{array}
$$

As with conditional proof, once you have discharged an assumption, you *cannot* use any of the lines governed by the assumption in subsequent lines of the proof. So, it is often wise to think a few lines ahead to avoid the need to duplicate lines that would be used in more than one assumption.

While you will most often use indirect or conditional proof with respect to the conclusion of an argument, you *can* use it regarding *any* statement. Remember, however, you will be able to draw conclusions that follow with validity from the augmented set of premises. So, if you assume $\sim p$ for indirect proof with an eye to conclude p, you will be able to conclude p only if the set of premises augmented by $\sim p$ is inconsistent. A practical consequence of this is that if the conclusion of an argument is a disjunction, for example, $p \lor q$, you should assume the denial of the disjunction for indirect proof. Why? You know that either p or q is entailed by the premises, but you don't know which is entailed. If you assumed only $\sim p$ for indirect proof, you might never reach a contradiction.

Sometimes indirect or conditional proofs are shorter than their direct counterparts. Usually they're longer, but many students find them easier since more effort is used in breaking compound statements into their simpler components than in using the various equivalences.

SUMMARY OF INDIRECT PROOF

1. Assume the denial of the proposition you wish to prove (A.I.P.).

2. Beginning with the line containing the assumption, indent and draw a vertical line to the left of each line in the scope of your assumption.

3. Use the assumption with earlier lines in the proof to draw conclusions.

4. When you have derived some statement p and its denial, $\sim p$, conjoin them and discharge your assumption by stating the proposition you wish to prove (the denial of your assumption for indirect proof).

5. Assumptions for indirect proof may be made within the scope of other assumptions for indirect or conditional proof, but the assumptions must be discharged in the reverse of the order in which they were made (last-in-first-out).

6. *Remember*: Conclusions reached within the scope of an assumption for indirect proof *cannot* be used to justify conclusions after the assumption has been discharged.

A FEW MORE RULES OF THUMB

1. If the conclusion is a conditional, start by assuming the antecedent of the conclusion for conditional proof (A.C.P.) and then assume the denial of the consequent for indirect proof (A.I.P.). This will allow you to establish the consequent by indirect proof and then obtain the conclusion a line later by conditional proof.

2. Use M.P., M.T., D.S., H.S., and Simp. to break down complex statements as far as possible.

3. Since it is generally helpful to break complex statements down into simpler components, if the conclusion is a disjunction, try proceeding by indirect proof.

4. Since it is generally helpful to break complex statements down into simpler components when using either conditional or indirect proof, it is wise to break premises down as far as possible before making any assumptions for conditional or indirect proof.

EXERCISES

I.   Construct an *indirect* proof for each of the following argument forms.

1. p
   $\therefore q \lor \sim q$

2. h
   $h \supset (m \lor a)$
   $a \supset \sim p$
   p
   $\therefore m$

3. $m \supset g$
   $g \supset a$
   $a \supset p$
   $p \supset i$
   m
   $\therefore i$

4. $p \supset q$
   $q \lor r$
   $p \lor \sim r$
   $\therefore q$

5. $\sim p \supset (o \bullet g)$
   $g \equiv p$
   $\therefore o \supset p$

6. $p \lor f$
   $p \supset (n \lor b)$
   $f \supset a$
   $\sim a \bullet \sim b$
   $\therefore n$

7. $p \supset [\sim q \lor (r \bullet s)]$
$\sim s \bullet q$
$\therefore \sim p$

8. $a \supset b$
$\sim (d \bullet \sim c)$
$a \lor (\sim c \bullet e)$
$\therefore b \lor \sim d$

9. $m \supset g$
$g \supset (c \lor h)$
$h \supset d$
$\sim d$
$c \supset a$
$\therefore \sim m \lor a$

10. $s \supset w$
$s \equiv (b \bullet y)$
$\sim w \supset b$
$\therefore w \lor \sim y$

II. Construct an indirect or conditional proof for each of the following. You may use both, if you wish.

11. $(m \bullet f) \supset (a \lor \sim c)$
$g \supset c$
$\sim f \supset j$
$\sim a \bullet g$
$\therefore \sim m \lor j$

12. $\sim f \supset (j \supset p)$
$p \supset (\sim a \lor m)$
$\therefore (\sim f \bullet j) \supset (a \supset m)$

13. $p \supset (\sim q \bullet r)$
$(q \lor \sim r) \supset s$
$\sim s \lor p$
$\therefore \sim q$

14. $(s \bullet w) \lor (b \bullet \sim y)$
$(s \supset b) \bullet (w \supset \sim y)$
$\therefore \sim y$

15. $n \equiv (h \lor s)$
$h \supset (b \bullet m)$
$s \supset e$
$\sim e \bullet n$
$\therefore b \bullet m$

16. $p \supset (q \lor r)$
$\sim r \supset s$
$\sim s \lor p$
$\therefore q \lor r$

17. $a \lor [g \bullet (\sim d \bullet \sim e)]$
$g \equiv e$
$\therefore \sim a \supset \sim (d \bullet \sim e)$

18. $(p \bullet \sim q) \supset (r \supset s)$
$p \bullet \sim s$
$\therefore \sim q \supset \sim r$

19. $(h \bullet m) \supset (k \bullet b)$
$(k \lor b) \supset (f \lor s)$
$h \bullet \sim s$
$\therefore m \supset f$

20. $p \bullet (q \lor \sim r)$
$(p \bullet \sim r) \supset s$
$(\sim s \lor \sim q) \supset r$
$\therefore q \lor (t \bullet \sim s)$

21. $a \supset (b \bullet \sim c)$
$\sim a \equiv b$
$\therefore a \supset d$

22. $p \supset q$
$(p \bullet q) \supset r$
$(p \bullet r) \supset s$
$\therefore p \supset s$

23. $[w \bullet (c \lor g)] \supset [g \equiv (o \supset r)]$
g
$g \supset (\sim r \bullet w)$
$\therefore \sim g \lor \sim o$

24. $p \equiv (q \lor \sim r)$
$\sim p \bullet \sim s$
$\therefore q \equiv s$

25. $\sim [p \equiv (q \lor \sim r)]$
$p \bullet \sim s$
$\therefore q \equiv s$

III. Construct an indirect or conditional proof for each of the following.

26. If Iowa Smith is the state's chief barber shop investigator and the Temple of Groom is the largest barber shop in the state, then either Smith is investigating illegal sales to a hair shirt company or he is investigating the use of illegal hair tonics. If Smith is investigating illegal sales to a hair shirt company, then the boys at St. Mort's Monastery will lose their shirts. If Smith is investigating the use of illegal hair tonics, then Baldilocks McCann has a hand in the affair. The boys at St. Mort's Monastery will not lose their shirts, and although Smith will find tainted moustache wax, Baldilocks McCann does not have a hand in the affair. Iowa Smith is the state's chief barber shop investigator. Therefore, the Temple of Groom is not the largest barber shop in the state. (*I, T, S, H, M, B, W*)

27. If Iowa Smith is investigating the Temple of Groom, then Baldilocks McCann has been spiking the hair tonic and Four Fingers O'Brien has his fingers in the till. If Four Fingers O'Brien has his fingers in the till, then he might lose another finger; and either Hannibal the cat has been drinking hair tonic or Milo the Kidder has not been telling bad jokes. If the fact that Milo the Kidder has been telling bad jokes implies that Four Fingers O'Brien has his fingers in the till, then Smith is in for the greatest adventure of his life. Iowa Smith is investigating the Temple of Groom. So, Smith is in for the greatest adventure of his life. (*I, B, F, L, H, M, S*)

28. Either the Temple of Groom is a front for hair smugglers, or business is going along at a good clip. If business is going along at a good clip, then Baldilocks McCann is a master barber. If Baldilocks McCann is a master barber, then Four Fingers O'Brien keeps a chair at St. Mort's and Milo the Kidder has lost his joke book even though Iowa Smith will not investigate the joint. But Iowa Smith will investigate the joint. So the Temple of Groom is a front for hair smugglers. (*T, B, M, O, K, I*)

29. Either Iowa Smith will investigate the Temple of Groom or Baldilocks McCann has developed a new hair grower, just in case Hannibal the cat has been used as a guinea pig. If Hannibal the cat has been used as a guinea pig, then the Society for the Prevention of Cruelty to Animals will be called in and Feline Alcoholics Anonymous will be concerned. If Feline Alcoholics Anonymous is concerned, then Four Fingers O'Brien has spiked the catnip. Iowa Smith will investigate the Temple of Groom. So Four Fingers O'Brien has spiked the catnip. (*I, B, H, S, F, O*)

30. If the Temple of Groom is a front for a smuggling operation, then Baldilocks McCann is the ringleader. If the Temple of Groom is the front for a smuggling operation and Baldilocks McCann is the

ringleader, then Four Fingers O'Brien will be implicated and Daphne Divine will need to find a different place to have her legs shaved. If Four Fingers O'Brien is implicated, then the boys at St. Mort's Monastery will need to find a new barber; and if the boys at St. Mort's Monastery will need to find a new barber, then Brother Boris will go to barber school. So if the Temple of Groom is the front for a smuggling operation, then Brother Boris will go to barber school unless Iowa Smith investigates. (*T, M, O, D, S, B, I*)

31. If Iowa Smith investigates the Temple of Groom but Virginia Johnson does not join in the investigation, then Baldilocks McCann will not be implicated or Milo the Kidder is calling the shots. If Milo the Kidder is calling the shots, then Virginia Johnson joins in the investigation. If Virginia Johnson joins in the investigation, then Lefty McLane is cutting more than hair and Hannibal the cat is going bald. So, if Lefty McLane is cutting more than hair and Milo the Kidder is calling the shots, then Virginia Johnson joins in the investigation. (*I, V, B, M, L, H*)

32. If Iowa Smith investigates the Temple of Groom and Virginia Johnson joins in the investigation, then if Four Fingers O'Brien is making moonshine in the back room, then Hannibal the cat has discovered the still. If Feline Alcoholics Anonymous enters the case, then Hannibal the cat has discovered the still. If Feline Alcoholics Anonymous enters the case, then either Lefty McLane is an undercover investigator or Milo the Kidder considers the whole affair a big joke. Milo the Kidder does not consider the whole affair a big joke, and both Iowa Smith investigates the Temple of Groom and Feline Alcholics Anonymous enters the case. So either Hannibal the cat has discovered the still or Lefty McLane is not an undercover investigator. (*I, V, O, H, F, L, M*)

33. If Baldilocks McCann is running a numbers racket, or Four Fingers O'Brien is making moonshine in the back room or Lefty McLane is bribing a judge, then the Temple of Groom is the front for illegal activities. Lefty McLane is not bribing a judge, just in case the Temple of Groom is a front for illegal activities and Iowa Smith investigates the joint. If Iowa Smith investigates the joint, then it is not the case that both Baldilocks McCann is running a numbers racket and Lefty McLane is bribing a judge. The Temple of Groom is not a front for illegal activities. So Iowa Smith investigates the joint and Virginia Johnson finds the entire case puzzling. (*B, F, L, T, I, V*)

34. If Lefty McLane is making moonshine and either Baldilocks McCann or Four Fingers O'Brien is a Treasury agent, then Smith's investigation will be foiled. If Smith's investigation is foiled, then Virginia Johnson will have the last laugh; and if Virginia Johnson

has the last laugh then the Governor will stop all investigations of barber shops. Lefty McLane is making moonshine and either Iowa Smith investigates the Temple of Groom or the Governor will not stop all investigations of barber shops. So if Baldilocks McCann is a Treasury agent, Iowa Smith will investigate the Temple of Groom. (*L, B, F, S, V, G, I*)

35. If both Baldilocks McCann and Four Fingers O'Brien are Treasury agents, then Iowa Smith will be convicted of tax evasion and Virginia Johnson will visit Smith in prison. Four Fingers O'Brien is not a Treasury agent, just in case either the Temple of Groom is a front for a federal investigation or Iowa Smith will be convicted of tax evasion. Baldilocks McCann is a Treasury agent. If Baldilocks McCann is a Treasury agent, then Milo the Kidder is a federal agent; and if Milo the Kidder is a federal agent, then Virginia Johnson will visit Smith in prison. If Iowa Smith will not be convicted of tax evasion, then Lefty McLane is not a federal agent; and if the Temple of Groom is the front for a federal investigation, then Lefty McLane is a federal agent. So Iowa Smith will be convicted of tax evasion. (*B, F, I, V, T, M, L*)

ESSENTIALS OF CHAPTER 7

In this chapter we introduced and explained the **method of deduction.**

In section 7.2, we defined **a formal proof of validity** for any given argument as: **a sequence of statements each of which is either a premise of that argument or follows from preceding statements of the sequence by an elementary valid argument, where the last statement of the sequence is the conclusion of the argument whose validity is being proved.** We defined **an elementary valid argument to be any argument that is a substitution instance of an elementary valid argument form.** We listed **nine elementary valid argument forms** to be used in constructing formal proofs of validity. The nine rules of inference can be used *only* on a whole line or two lines of a proof.

In sections 7.3 and 7.4, we strengthened the machinery for constructing formal proofs of validity by introducing the **Rule of Replacement, which permits us to infer from any statement the result of replacing any component of that statement by any other statement logically equivalent to the component replaced.** We introduced fifteen logically equivalent forms (under ten names) that can be substituted for each other *wherever* they occur in a proof.

In section 7.5 we introduced **the method of conditional proof**. When constructing a conditional proof, you *assume* a statement as an additional premise, use that statement with the other premises, and discharge the assumption by a conditional statement in which the assumption is the antecedent and the previous line of the proof is the consequent.

In section 7.6 we introduced **indirect proof**. Indirect proof is a variation on conditional proof. When constructing an indirect proof, you *assume* the denial of what you want to establish as an additional premise, use that statement with the other premises until you conclude both a statement and its denial—*any* statement and its denial. You conjoin the statement and its denial and discharge your assumption by stating the denial of the statement you assumed, that is, the statement you originally wished to prove.

QUANTIFICATION THEORY

8.1 WHEN PROPOSITIONAL LOGIC IS NOT ENOUGH

Consider a famous example of a valid deductive argument:

All humans are mortals.
Socrates is a human.
Therefore, Socrates is a mortal.

As we saw in Chapters 4 and 5, the first premise is a categorical proposition. The second premise and the conclusion are singular statements. Singular statements can be treated as universal propositions or particular propositions, as long as we do so consistently (5.3A). So, we can treat the argument as either an **AAA-1** or an **AII-1**. Both Venn diagrams and the rules for judging the validity of categorical syllogisms show that the forms **AAA-1** and **AII-1** are valid.

Now let's see if we can construct a proof for the argument. There are no sentential connectives, so each statement must be treated as a simple statement. So, we might represent the argument as:

$$A$$
$$B$$
$$\therefore C$$

No pair of simple statements entails the truth of another simple statement that is distinct from one of the premises. If you have any question, construct a reverse truth table in which you assume both premises are true and the conclusion is false. So, our symbolic representation of the argument is invalid. But we *know* that the argument itself is valid. What's the problem?

The problem is that the symbolic language for propositional logic does not adequately represent the structure of

> **ESSENTIAL** HINTS
>
> **A Note to Symbolphobes**
> Some of you might look at the new notation and panic. Don't! It's just a variation on what we've been doing for the last couple of chapters. We develop a way to represent categorical propositions, our old friends from Chapters 3–5. It *looks* imposing, but you'll catch on quickly. And once we get to proofs, you'll find that you spend more time doing *exactly* what we did in the last chapter than anything else. So, if you suffer from symbolphobia, take a few deep breaths. Relax. And prepare to have a lot of *fun!*

the argument. In order to represent the structure of the argument, we need to represent the *internal* structure of the propositions of which it is composed. To do this, we develop a symbolic language that represents the structure of categorical and singular propositions.

8.2 SYMBOLESE 102: THE LANGUAGE OF QUANTIFICATIONAL LOGIC

A. Singular Propositions, Subjects, and Predicates

Consider the statement, "Olaf is a cat." This is an example of a **singular proposition**. It concerns one object. There is a **subject term**, *Olaf*, and there is a **predicate term**, *cat*. The verb *is* connects the two. The predicate term names a property or characteristic of Olaf. One thing can have many properties. So, all the following might be true:

> Olaf is a cat.
> Olaf is a Siamese.
> Olaf is a nuisance.

Many things can have the same property; or, if you prefer, the predicate term can be true of many things. So, the following statements are also true:

> Turbo is a cat.
> Seal is a cat.
> Yumyum is a cat.

So, you can look at the form of a singular proposition as two blanks connected by a form of the verb *to be*:

> [subject term] is [predicate term]

You can put the name of any **individual**—whether it is a person, or an animal, or anything else—in the subject place. You can put the name of any property in the predicate place. The result will be a singular proposition.

The symbolic language we develop needs to represent subject terms (names of individuals) and predicates: the entire "[subject term] is a [predicate term]." Let's represent the names of individuals by the lowercase letters from *a* to *w*. So, the name *Olaf* could be represented by *o*. We shall call the names of individuals **individual constants**.

Let's represent predicates by the uppercase letters from *A* through *Z* followed by a blank that represents the subject term. So, the predicate "is a cat" could be represented by C. We shall call the names of predicates **predicate constants**. So, "Olaf is a cat" would be represented by Co.[1]

There are times when we want to talk about a predicate without talking about a particular individual of which it is true. For example, we might want to talk about some (unknown) thing of which the predicate "is a cat" is true. We represent these unknown things by **individual variables**, placeholders for individual constants. We shall use the letters x, y, and z as individual variables. So, the predicate, "_____ is a cat," might be represented as Cx. The expression Cx is read as "x is C." It is known as a **propositional function**. A propositional function may be defined as **an expression that (1) contains an individual variable and (2) becomes a statement when an individual constant is substituted for the individual variable.** Note that propositional functions are not propositions—they do not have truth values because they are grammatically incomplete. Any singular proposition is a *substitution instance* of a propositional function, the result of substituting an individual constant for the individual variable in that propositional function. Propositional functions that have only singular propositions as substitution instances—things such as Hx, Mx, Fx, Bx, Cx—are called **simple predicates**, to distinguish them from the more complex propositional functions we'll introduce shortly.

Similarly, sometimes we shall want to talk generally about predicates. We use uppercase Greek letters—usually phi (Φ) or psi (ψ)—as **predicate variables**.

So we may summarize the language of quantified logic as it applies to singular propositions as follows:

This sort of statement	could be symbolized
_____ is a cat	Cx
_____ is a human	Hx
_____ is a nuisance	Nx

This sort of statement	could be symbolized
Socrates is human	Hs
Protagoras is mortal	Mp
Socrates is snub-nosed	Ss
Aristotle is not snub-nosed	$\sim Sa$

This sort of statement	could be symbolized
Socrates is _____	Φs
Aristotle is _____	Φa
_____ is _____	Φx

---

[1]In this book we shall be concerned with only one-place predicates, such as "is a cat." If you take additional logic courses, you'll discover multiplace predicates or **relations**. These are represented in much the same way, but there are more individual constants involved. For example, the proposition, "John is to the left of Belinda," might be represented as Ljb; "Juanita is between Luis and Dmitri" might be represented as $Bjld$.

B. Universal and Particular Propositions

At this point we can represent the second premise and conclusion of the argument at the beginning of this chapter. "Socrates is a human" is *Hs*; "Socrates is mortal" is *Ms*. To represent the first premise, we need a way to represent universal propositions. To complete our language, we'll also need a way to represent particular propositions. So, let's start with some simple considerations.

Consider the statement, "Everything is puzzling." We deal with the predicate, *is puzzling*, in the manner discussed above. "_____ is puzzling" is symbolized as *Px*. How do we deal with *everything*? As you'll recall from Chapter 3, words such as *every* and *all* are universal quantifiers. So we need a symbol to represent words such as *every*, *all*, *everything*, and *anything*. We'll use an *x* in parentheses—(*x*)—to represent a universal quantifier.[2] This is called the **universal quantifier.** So (*x*)*Px* will represent "Everything is puzzling." The symbolic statement (*x*)*Px* can be read as "For all *x*, *Px*" or "For all *x*, *x* is *P*" or "Universal *x*, *Px*."

We also need a quantifier to represent particular propositions such as, "Some things are puzzling." We'll use a backward-*E* followed by an *x*—∃*x*—to stand for words indicating particularity, words such as *some* or *there is a* or *there is at least one*. This is called the **existential quantifier.** So (∃*x*)*Px* will represent "Some things are puzzling." The symbolic statement (∃*x*)*Px* can be read as, "There is an *x*, *Px*," "There is an *x*, such that *x* is *P*," or "Existential *x*, *Px*."

Now that we've introduced the quantifiers, we can turn to the standard form categorical propositions.

Categorical propositions assert relations among classes of things. As we saw in Chapter 3, there are four kinds of categorical propositions:

> Universal Affirmative: **A:** All *S* are *P*.
> Universal Negative: **E:** No *S* are *P*.
> Particular Affirmative: **I:** Some *S* are *P*.
> Particular Negative: **O:** Some *S* are not *P*.

Our translation of a universal affirmative proposition should be able to represent *all* true universal affirmative categorical propositions. The proposition, "All unicorns are one-horned horses," is true—it reflects the definition of *unicorn*. Since there are no unicorns, it must be understood as saying that *if* there were any unicorns, then they would be one-horned horses. Since there are no unicorns, the conditional is trivially true. Recognizing this fact, we may reasonably translate the proposition as follows:

$$(x)(Ux \supset Hx)$$

where *Ux* asserts, "*x* is a unicorn," and *Hx* asserts, "*x* is a one-horned horse."

---

[2]In some logic books, the universal quantifier is represented by an upside-down *A* followed by an *x*: (∀*x*).

Universal negative propositions can be understood analogously. "No dog is a cat" asserts that for anything, if it is a dog then it is not a cat. So, we may symbolize the proposition as follows:

$$(x)(Dx \supset \sim Cx)^3$$

In general, **when symbolizing a universal proposition, use a universal quantifier and treat the statement as a conditional.** So, the general form of a universal affirmative proposition is $(x)(\Phi x \supset \Psi x)$. The general form of a universal negative proposition is $(x)(\Phi x \supset \sim \Psi x)$.

Particular propositions are construed as conjunctions. "Some dogs are collies" means there is at least one thing that is both a dog and a collie. It's represented as follows:

$$(\exists x)(Dx \bullet Cx)$$

Similarly, "Some dogs are not collies" is represented as follows:

$$(\exists x)(Dx \bullet \sim Cx)$$

In general, **when diagramming a particular proposition, use a particular quantifier and treat the statement as a conjunction.** So, the general form of a particular affirmative proposition is $(\exists x)(\Phi x \bullet \Psi x)$. The general form of a particular negative proposition is $(\exists x)(\Phi x \bullet \sim \Psi x)$.

Just as grouping indicators are important in propositional logic, they are essential for our symbolization of categorical propositions. Grouping indicators show the **scope** of the quantifier. In the statement $(\exists x)(Px \bullet \sim Qx)$, both predicates are within the scope of the quantifier. They are **bound** by the quantifier. Binding variables in a propositional function converts the propositional function into a statement. If we have a statement of the form $(\exists x)Px \bullet \sim Qx$, only the Px is bound by the quantifier. In this case, $\sim Qx$ is a propositional function. As a propositional function—a predicate with an unbound variable—it has no truth value. As we saw above, one way in which a propositional function can be converted into a statement is to substitute an individual constant for its variable. We now should notice that when propositional functions are bound within the scope of a quantifier, the resulting formula is a statement and has a truth value.

---

[3]You might reasonably suggest that "No dog is a cat" means that there is not even one dog that is a cat. Such a proposition would be symbolized as $\sim(\exists x)(Dx \bullet Cx)$. As we'll see in the next section, $\sim(\exists x)(Dx \bullet Cx)$ is logically equivalent to $(x)(Dx \supset \sim Cx)$. We prefer to use $(x)(Dx \supset \sim Cx)$ to symbolize the universal negative since it provides a visual uniformity among the symbolizations of universal propositions.

C. And Sometimes the Statements are More Complex

Just as statements can become fairly complex in propositional logic, symbolic representations of categorical propositions can be composed of more than two predicate terms. Sometimes you'll be concerned with limited parts of the universe. For example, if you're given the statement, "Everyone who learns logic is wise," the word *everyone* indicates that you're concerned only with people. So, you introduce a predicate to represent people (Px), as well as one for logic learners (Lx) and one for wise things (Wx). Your statement would look like this:

$$(x)[(Px \bullet Lx) \supset Wx]$$

If the statement were "Someone who fishes is a boat owner," your symbolized statement would look like this:

$$(\exists x)[(Px \bullet Fx) \bullet Bx]$$

And, of course, there are the various other qualifications you found when dealing with propositional logic that can find their way into quantified statements:

Any long-haired dog is neither a cat nor a horse.

$$(x)[(Dx \bullet Lx) \supset {\sim}(Cx \lor Hx)] \quad \underline{or} \quad (x)[(Dx \bullet Lx) \supset ({\sim}Cx \bullet {\sim}Hx)]$$

Some cats are animals that sleep.

$$(\exists x)[Cx \bullet (Ax \bullet Sx)]$$

If Floyd is a philosopher then some philosophers are redheads.

$$Pf \supset (\exists x)(Px \bullet Rx)$$

Not all people who eat shrimp are boaters if and only if they're hunters.

$$(\exists x)[(Px \bullet Sx) \bullet {\sim}(Bx \equiv Hx)] \quad \underline{or} \quad {\sim}(x)[(Px \bullet Sx) \supset (Bx \equiv Hx)]$$

If all cats are mammals, then some large dogs are not reptiles.

$$(x)(Cx \supset Mx) \supset (\exists x)[(Dx \bullet Lx) \bullet {\sim}Rx]$$

Sometimes you'll have to think about what's being said before you can translate. Consider the statement, "All juniors and seniors are eligible for the scholarship." It's a universal proposition. Is the antecedent of the conditional a conjunction? It can't be, can it? By whatever criterion *your* school uses, no one is both a junior *and* a senior. So, the statement must be:

$$(x)[(Jx \lor Sx) \supset Ex]$$

And, of course, there are all those odd ways of making universal and particular statements that we examined in 5.3. So, "None but wise people are logicians" would be translated:

$$(x)[Lx \supset (Px \bullet Wx)]$$

"All citizens, except those under 18, are eligible to vote" would be translated:

$$(x)(Ux \supset \sim Vx) \bullet (x)(\sim Ux \supset Vx)$$

"Only some students are on the dean's list" would be translated:

$$(\exists x)(Sx \bullet Dx) \bullet (\exists x)(Sx \bullet \sim Dx)$$

And, of course, when there's no quantifier, you'll need to ask what quantifier would yield a true statement. For example, "Cats are mammals" probably means "All cats are mammals."

SUMMARY OF THE LANGUAGE OF QUANTIFICATIONAL LOGIC	
Ax, Bx, Cx, . . . , Zx	Predicates: names of properties
a, b, c, . . . , w	Constants: names of individuals
x, y, z	Variables ranging over individuals
Φ, Ψ	Variables ranging over predicates
$(x)(\Phi x \supset \Psi x)$	All Φ are Ψ. For all *x*, if *x* is Φ then *x* is Ψ.
$(x)(\Phi x \supset \sim \Psi x)$	No Φ are Ψ. For all *x*, if *x* is Φ then *x* is not Ψ.
$(\exists x)(\Phi x \bullet \Psi x)$	Some Φ are Ψ. There is an *x* such that *x* is Φ and *x* is Ψ.
$(\exists x)(\Phi x \bullet \sim \Psi x)$	Some Φ are not Ψ. There is an *x* such that *x* is Φ and *x* is not Ψ.

ENGLISH TO SYMBOLESE/SYMBOLESE TO ENGLISH DICTIONARY

Where Φ and Ψ are variables ranging over predicates and x, y, and z are variables ranging over individuals:

English to Symbolese

A (an)	A Φ is Ψ.	$(\exists x)(\Phi x \cdot \Psi x)$
A (an) . . . is not . . .	A Φ is not Ψ.	$(\exists x)(\Phi x \cdot \sim\Psi x)$
A few	A few Φ are Ψ.	$(\exists x)(\Phi x \cdot \Psi x)$
A few . . . are not . . .	A few Φ are not Ψ.	$(\exists x)(\Phi x \cdot \sim\Psi x)$
All	All Φs are Ψs.	$(x)(\Phi x \supset \Psi x)$
All except	All except Φ are Ψ.	$(x)(\Phi x \supset \sim\Psi x) \cdot (x)(\sim\Phi x \supset \Psi x)$
Almost all	Almost all Φ are Ψ.	$(\exists x)(\Phi x \cdot \Psi x) \cdot (\exists x)(\Phi x \cdot \sim\Psi x)$
Any	Any Φ is a Ψ.	$(x)(\Phi x \supset \Psi x)$
At least one	At least one Φ is Ψ.	$(\exists x)(\Phi x \cdot \Psi x)$
At least one . . . is not . . .		
	At least one Φ is Ψ.	$(\exists x)(\Phi x \cdot \Psi x)$
Diverse	Diverse Φ are Ψ.	$(\exists x)(\Phi x \cdot \Psi x)$
Diverse . . . are not . . .	Diverse Φ are not Ψ.	$(\exists x)(\Phi x \cdot \sim\Psi x)$
Every	Every Φ is a Ψ.	$(x)(\Phi x \supset \Psi x)$
Many	Many Φ are Ψ.	$(\exists x)(\Phi x \cdot \Psi x)$
Many . . . are not . . .	Many Φ are not Ψ.	$(\exists x)(\Phi x \cdot \sim\Psi x)$
No	No Φ is Ψ.	$(x)(\Phi x \supset \sim\Psi x)$
No	No Φ is Ψ.	$\sim(\exists x)(\Phi x \cdot \Psi x)$
None but	None but Ψs are Φs.	$(x)(\Phi x \supset \Psi x)$
None of	None of the Φs are Ψs.	$(x)(\Phi x \supset \sim\Psi x)$
Not all	Not all Φs are Ψs.	$(\exists x)(\Phi x \cdot \sim\Psi x)$
Not any	Not any Φ is Ψ.	$(x)(\Phi x \supset \sim\Psi x)$
Not any	Not any Φ is Ψ.	$\sim(\exists x)(\Phi x \cdot \Psi x)$
Not every	Not every Φ is Ψ.	$(\exists x)(\Phi x \cdot \sim\Psi x)$
Not only	Not only Ψ are Φ.	$(\exists x)(\Phi x \cdot \sim\Psi x)$
Not quite all	Not quite all Φs are Ψs.	$(\exists x)(\Phi x \cdot \Psi x) \cdot (\exists x)(\Phi x \cdot \sim\Psi x)$
Numerous	Numerous Φs are Ψs.	$(\exists x)(\Phi x \cdot \Psi x)$
Numerous . . . are not . . .		
	Numerous Φs are not Ψs.	$(\exists x)(\Phi x \cdot \sim\Psi x)$
Only	Only Ψs are Φs.	$(x)(\Phi x \supset \Psi x)$
Only some	Only some Φs are Ψs.	$(\exists x)(\Phi x \cdot \Psi x) \cdot (\exists x)(\Phi x \cdot \sim\Psi x)$
Several	Several Φs are Ψs.	$(\exists x)(\Phi x \cdot \Psi x)$
Several . . . are not . . .	Several Φs are not Ψs.	$(\exists x)(\Phi x \cdot \sim\Psi x)$
Some	Some Φs are Ψs.	$(\exists x)(\Phi x \cdot \Psi x)$
Some . . . are not . . .	Some Φs are not Ψs.	$(\exists x)(\Phi x \cdot \sim\Psi x)$
The	The Φ is a Ψ.	$(x)(\Phi x \supset \Psi x)$[4]
The only	The only Φ is a Ψ.	$(x)(\Phi x \supset \Psi x)$
There exists	There exists a Φ that is Ψ.	$(\exists x)(\Phi x \cdot \Psi x)$

---

[4]This is the way the word _the_ is used in "The dog is a mammal." It is _not_ the use of _the_ in "The present king of France is bald." The latter means that there is exactly one thing that is the present king of France and that thing is bald. The notation needed to represent such a statement goes beyond the scope of this book.

ENGLISH TO SYMBOLESE/SYMBOLESE
TO ENGLISH DICTIONARY (Continued)

There is a	There is a Φ that is Ψ.	$(\exists x)(\Phi x \bullet \Psi x)$
There exists a . . . that is not . . .		
	There exists a Φ that is not Ψ.	$(\exists x)(\Phi x \bullet \sim\Psi x)$
There is no . . . unless . . .		
	There is no Φ unless it is Ψ.	$(x)(\Phi x \supset \Psi x)$
Various	Various Φs are Ψs.	$(\exists x)(\Phi x \bullet \Psi x)$
Various . . . are not . . .	Various Φs are not Ψs.	$(\exists x)(\Phi x \bullet \sim\Psi x)$
Whatever	Whatever is Φ is Ψ.	$(x)(\Phi x \supset \Psi x)$

Symbolese to English

$(x)(\Phi x \supset \Psi x)$

> All Φs are Ψs.
> Any Φ is a Ψ.
> Every Φ is a Ψ.
> For any x, if x is Φ, then x is Ψ.
> None but Ψs are Φs.
> Only Ψs are Φs.
> The only Φ is a Ψ.
> The Φ is a Ψ.
> There is no Φ unless it is Ψ.
> Whatever is Φ is Ψ.

$(x)(\Phi x \supset \sim\Psi x)$

> For all x, if x is Φ, then x is not Ψ.
> No Φ are Ψ.
> None of the Φs are Ψs.
> Not any Φ is a Ψ.

$\sim(\exists x)(\Phi x \bullet \Psi x)$

> See $(x)(\Phi x \supset \sim\Psi x)$.

$(\exists x)(\Phi x \bullet \Psi x)$

> A Φ is Ψ.
>
> A few Φ are Ψ.
> At least one Φ is Ψ.
> Diverse Φ are Ψ.
> Many Φ are Ψ.
> Numerous Φs are Ψs.
> Several Φs are Ψs.
> Some Φs are Ψs.
> There exists a Φ that is Ψ.
> There is a Φ that is Ψ.
> There is an x such that x is both
> Φ and Ψ.
> Various Φs are Ψs.

$(\exists x)(\Phi x \bullet \sim\Psi x)$

> A Φ is not Ψ.
> A few Φ are not Ψ.

**ENGLISH TO SYMBOLESE/SYMBOLESE
TO ENGLISH DICTIONARY (*Continued*)**

$(\exists x)(\Phi x \cdot \sim\Psi x)$	At least one Φ is not Ψ.
	Diverse Φ are not Ψ.
	Many Φ are not Ψ.
	Not all Φs are Ψs.
	Not every Φ is Ψ.
	Not only Ψ are Φ.
	Numerous Φs are not Ψs.
	Several Φs are not Ψs.
	Some Φs are not Ψs.
	There exists a Φ that is not Ψ.
	There is a Φ that is not a Ψ.
	There is an x such that x is a Φ and x is not a Ψ.
	Various Φs are not Ψs.
$(x)(\Phi x \supset \sim\Psi x) \cdot (x)(\sim\Phi x \supset \Psi x)$	All except Φ are Ψ.
$(\exists x)(\Phi x \cdot \Psi x) \cdot (\exists x)(\Phi x \cdot \sim\Psi x)$	Almost all Φ are Ψ.
	Not quite all Φs are Ψs.
	Only some Φs are Ψs.

EXERCISES

I. Translate each of the following statements into the logical notation of propositional functions and quantifiers, in each case using the abbreviations suggested. Be sure each formula begins with a quantifier, *not* with a negation symbol.

1. Every aardvark is a mammal. (*Ax: x* is an aardvark; *Mx: x* is a mammal.)

2. Some aardvarks are not insects. (*Ax: x* is an aardvark; *Ix: x* is an insect.)

3. At least one monster is frightening. (*Mx: x* is a monster; *Fx: x* is frightening.)

4. No unicycles are black. (*Ux: x* is a unicycle; *Bx: x* is black.)

5. Some animals that eat corn are not raccoons. (*Ax: x* is an animal; *Cx: x* eats corn; *Rx: x* is a raccoon.)

6. Any marsupial is either a kangaroo or an opossum. (*Mx: x* is a marsupial; *Kx: x* is a kangaroo; *Ox: x* is an opossum.)

7. If Felicia drinks cocoa, then all students drink cocoa. (*f*: Felicia; *Cx: x* is a cocoa drinker; *Sx: x* is a student.)

8. Some students drink cocoa only if Felicia drinks cocoa. (*Sx: x* is a student; *Cx: x* is a cocoa drinker; *f*: Felicia.)

9. No dog that eats H*E*D dog food has bad breath. (*Dx: x* is a dog; *Ex: x* eats H*E*D dog food; *Bx: x* has bad breath.)

10. Any man who hates children and dogs cannot be all bad.

—W. C. Fields

   (*Mx: x* is a man; *Cx: x* hates children; *Dx: x* hates dogs; *Bx: x* can be all bad.)

11. Oswald likes dogs if and only if some professors like dogs. (*Dx: x* likes dogs; *Px: x* is a professor; *o:* Oswald.)

12. All professors like cats only if some professors like cats. (*Px: x* is a professor; *Cx: x* likes cats.)

13. If any professor likes cats, then Professor Hernandez likes cats. (*Px: x* is a professor; *Cx: x* likes cats; *h:* Professor Hernandez.)

14. All cats are friendly unless some cats are angry. (*Cx: x* is a cat; *Fx: x* is friendly; *Ax: x* is angry.)

15. Some dogs are mammals if and only if all dogs are vertebrates. (*Dx: x* is a dog; *Mx: x* is a mammal; *Vx: x* is a vertebrate.)

16. Any person is medically dead if and only if there is no detectable brain stem activity. (*Px: x* is a person; *Dx: x* is medically dead; *Bx: x* has detectable brain stem activity.)

17. All whole numbers are either even or odd. (*Wx: x* is a whole number; *Ex: x* is even; *Ox: x* is odd.)

18. Anything that is either sweet or crunchy is tasty. (*Sx: x* is sweet; *Cx: x* is crunchy; *Tx: x* is tasty.)

19. No man is an island if all men are social animals. (*Mx: x* is a man; *Ix: x* is an island; *Sx: x* is a social animal.)

20. All values are either subjective or objective, but objective values are dependent on subjective narratives. (*Vx: x* is a value; *Sx: x* is subjective; *Ox: x* is objective; *Nx: x* is dependent on subjective narratives.)

21. Peaches are good in vanilla ice cream, and nuts are good in chocolate ice cream, but butterscotch is good in both vanilla and chocolate ice cream. (*Px: x* is a peach; *Vx: x* is good in vanilla ice cream; *Nx: x* is a nut; *Cx: x* is good in chocolate ice cream; *Bx: x* is butterscotch.)

22. Some foods are edible only if they are cooked. (*Fx: x* is a food; *Ex: x* is edible; *Cx: x* is cooked.)

23. Any tall man is attractive if he is dark and handsome. (*Tx: x* is tall; *Mx: x* is a man; *Ax: x* is attractive; *Dx: x* is dark; *Hx: x* is handsome.)

24. Not all people who are wealthy are both educated and cultured. (*Px: x* is a person; *Wx: x* is wealthy; *Ex: x* is educated; *Cx: x* is cultured.)

25. Any person is a coward who deserts. (*Px: x* is a person; *Cx: x* is a coward; *Dx: x* deserts.)

II. Translate each of the following. Many of these translations require you to consider some of the less common quantifier-terms or to determine what quantifier is assumed when no quantifier is given.

26. Whales are not fish. (*Wx: x* is a whale; *Fx: x* is a fish.)
27. Movie ratings are not always accurate. (*Mx: x* is a movie rating; *Ax: x* is accurate.)
28. Fanatics are never right. (*Fx: x* is a fanatic; *Rx: x* is right.)
29. Only graduates can participate in the commencement. (*Gx: x* is a graduate; *Px: x* is a person who can participate in the commencement.)
30. Not every politician is honest. (*Px: x* is a politician; *Hx: x* is honest.)
31. Reporters are present. (*Rx: x* is a reporter; *Px: x* is present.)
32. Ambassadors are always dignified. (*Ax: x* is an ambassador; *Dx: x* is dignified.)
33. No Boy Scout cheats. (*Bx: x* is a Boy Scout; *Cx: x* cheats.)
34. Snakebites are sometimes fatal. (*Sx: x* is a snakebite; *Fx: x* is fatal.)
35. A child pointed his finger at the emperor. (*Cx: x* is a child; *Px: x* pointed his finger at the emperor.)
36. All that glitters is not gold. (*Gx: x* glitters; *Ax: x* is gold.)
37. None but the brave deserve the fair. (*Bx: x* is brave; *Dx: x* deserves the fair.)
38. Citizens of the United States can vote only in U.S. elections. (*Ex: x* is an election in which citizens of the United States can vote; *Ux: x* is a U.S. election.)
39. Not every applicant was hired. (*Ax: x* is an applicant; *Hx: x* was hired.)
40. Nothing of importance was said. (*Lx: x* is of importance; *Sx: x* was said.)

8.3   PROVING VALIDITY

In this section we extend the proof technique developed in Chapter 7 so we can use it with quantificational logic. Much of what we do will be *exactly* like what we did in Chapter 7. We introduce four rules of inference that will allow us to eliminate and introduce quantifiers. We also introduce a set of logically equivalent propositions that show the effect of moving a tilde across a quantifier. Once we have these rules and equivalences, we can prove the validity of the fifteen valid forms in traditional categorical logic as well as arguments whose structure is more complex than that of traditional syllogisms.[5]

---

[5]The latter are sometimes known as *asyllogistic* arguments.

The rules of inference and the equivalences falling under the rule of replacement in Chapter 7 are *not* directly applicable to quantified statements. So, if you're given:

$$(x)(Px \supset Qx)$$
$$\underline{(x)(Qx \supset Rx)}$$
$$\therefore (x)(Px \supset Rx)$$

you'd probably guess (correctly!) that hypothetical syllogism is involved in reaching the conclusion. But there are those (lovely?) quantifiers sitting outside the parentheses. Having a quantifier outside a set of parentheses is like having a tilde outside a set of parentheses in propositional logic: You can apply all the equivalences falling under the rule of replacement to the stuff inside the parentheses, but you can't apply the nine rules of inference as long as the tilde or the quantifier is outside of the parentheses.[6] So we can apply the nine rules of inference, we introduce four additional rules of inference that will allow us to eliminate and introduce quantifiers in proofs. Like the original nine rules of inference, *the rules of quantifier instantiation and generalization apply only to an entire line of the proof.*

The rule of **Universal Instantiation (U.I.)** allows you to go from a general statement to a particular case of it, an *instance*. It takes two forms: You can instantiate in terms of a constant, and you can instantiate in terms of a variable. Let the lowercase Greek letter *nu* (ν) be a variable that can be replaced by any *constant* ($a, b, c, \ldots, w$). Let x, y, and z be individual variables. The rule of universal instantiation may be stated as follows:

$$(x)\Phi x \qquad (x)\Phi x$$
$$\therefore \Phi\nu \qquad \therefore \Phi y$$

If x is always Φ, then *any* individual is Φ. So, choose your favorite constant—$a, b, c, \ldots, w$. It's Φ, too. We'll get to the reasons for a *second* version in a moment.

Example _____

All knights are warriors.
Sir Anthony Hopkins is a knight.
Therefore Sir Anthony Hopkins is a warrior.

_____

[6]The exception, of course, is when the entire statement *as it stands* can be used with another line of the proof.

A formal proof of this argument requires reference to Universal Instantiation:

1. $(x)(Kx \supset Wx)$
2. Ks
   $\therefore Ws$
3. $Ks \supset Ws$ 1, **U.I.**
4. Ws 2,3, M.P.

Since line 1 affirms the truth of the universal quantification of the propositional function $Kx \supset Wx$, we can, by Universal Instantiation, infer any desired substitution instance. Thus we get line 3, $Ks \supset Ws$, from line 1. Then, by *modus ponens*, we get the conclusion from lines 2 and 3.

To understand why there is a version of Universal Instantiation that is stated in terms of a variable, we need to look at it in conjunction with the rule of **Universal Generalization (U.G.)**, the rule that allows us to introduce a universal quantifier. The rule of Universal Generalization is stated as:

$$\Phi y$$
$$\therefore (x)\Phi x$$

Remember that rules of inference are truth-preserving: If the premise is true, the conclusion must be true as well. If we engaged in a universal generalization from a statement given in terms of a constant, there would be many times when the conclusion would be false. Consider the statement, "If Colin Powell were a secretary of state, then he is of Jamaican descent." The statement is true: Powell was U.S. secretary of state from 2001—2004, and he is of Jamaican descent. If you based a universal generalization on that statement, the conclusion, "All secretaries of state are of Jamaican descent," would be false. Henry Kissinger, Madeline Albright, and Condoleezza Rice are among the people who have been U.S. secretaries of state but are *not* of Jamaican descent.[7] So, you must generalize from a statement instantiated for a variable.

But what's going on here? The *only* way you can have a statement that is instantiated in terms of a variable is from Universal Instantiation. When you instantiate in terms of a variable, you are, in effect, moving the generality from the quantifier into the statement itself. It is this, and *only* this, that allows you to engage in universal generalization. And you shouldn't find that surprising. As we saw when looking at categorical syllogisms in Chapter 4, a universal

---

[7]If you generalized from one atypical case, your argument would commit the informal fallacy of converse accident (hasty generalization; see 2.3 P5). As we'll see in the next chapter, it would be a case of generalizing from very weak evidence.

conclusion follows with validity *only* from two universal premises.[8] So, if the conclusion is a universal proposition and the premises are consistent, the premises must be universal as well. So, when deciding whether to instantiate in terms of a constant or a variable, you should keep the conclusion in mind.

Example

All knights are warriors.
All talented actors are knights.
Therefore all talented actors are warriors.

A formal proof of this argument requires reference to Universal Generalization:

1. $(x)(Kx \supset Wx)$
2. $(x)(Tx \supset Kx)$
   $\therefore (x)(Tx \supset Wx)$
3. $Ky \supset Wy$ 1 U.I.
4. $Ty \supset Ky$ 2 U.I.
5. $Ty \supset Wy$ 4,3 H.S.
6. $(x)(Tx \supset Wx)$ 6 U.G.

From the premises we were able to deduce the statement $(Ty \supset Wy)$ by Universal Instantiation. Because y denotes any individual of which the statement is true, we know that *any* substitution instance must be true, and by Universal Generalization that all substitution instances must be true. Thus by Universal Generalization we get $(x)(Tx \supset Wx)$ from $(Ty \supset Wy)$.

> **ESSENTIAL** HINTS
>
> "Do we have to change from x to y?" you might ask. "Aren't variables simply variables?" This is largely a matter of taste and clarity. The rule of Universal Instantiation effectively allows you to drop the quantifier, and the rule of Universal Generalization allows you to reintroduce it. If *you* find it *clearer* to shift from x to y and back to x, do so. If not, you're still following the rule of Universal Instantiation if you instantiate in terms of x. **The *exception* is when you have a statement containing a propositional function.** In *that* case a bound variable *must* be replaced with a variable *not* found in the propositional function.

Where *nu* (ν) represents any individual constant $(a, b, c, \ldots, w)$, the rule of **Existential Instantiation (E.I.)** is stated as follows:

$$(\exists x)\Phi x$$
$$\therefore \Phi \nu$$

where ν is a constant new to the proof (**restriction**).

---

[8]Of course, *many* categorical syllogisms with universal premises and a universal conclusion are *invalid* because they break distribution rules, the rule against two negative premises, or the rule against a negative premise and an affirmative conclusion.

Keep in mind that an existential proposition asserts that there is at least one thing of which the statement is true. What you're doing when you instantiate is saying that Φ is true of some individual *a*, for example. You know *nothing* about the individual of which the statement is true *except* that the statement is true of it. This is why there is a restriction on Existential Instantiation. Let's say you have an argument with the premise, "Britney Spears is a singer" (*Ss*). If you had another premise that says, "Some singers are people known for singing Italian arias," $(\exists x)(Sx \bullet Kx)$, instantiating this premise for Britney Spears would yield the false statement, "Britney Spears is a singer who is known for singing Italian arias," $(Sx \bullet Kx)$. The restriction systematically prevents that kind of error. The restriction is necessary for our rules to be truth-preserving.

The restriction has a practical consequence: **Always instantiate existential propositions before you instantiate universal propositions. If there are several existential propositions, instantiate all of them—*each for a different constant*—before you instantiate any universal proposition.** You can, of course, instantiate each universal proposition several times, once for every constant for which you have instantiated an existential proposition.

Example _____

All knights are warriors.
Some talented actors are knights.   _____
Therefore some talented actors are warriors.

  1. $(x)(Kx \supset Wx)$
  2. $(\exists x)(Tx \bullet Kx)$
     ∴ $(\exists x)(Tx \bullet Wx)$
  3. $Ta \bullet Ka$ 2, **E.I.**

The existential quantification asserted in premise 2 is true if and only if it has at least one true substitution instance. As a result, by Existential Instantiation, we can assign any individual constant to $(Tx \bullet Kx)$ that has not been used before in the context. Thus by Existential Instantiation we get $(Ta \bullet Ka)$ from line 2. This is a necessary step toward deducing the conclusion. (We complete the proof below after introducing the rule of Existential Generalization.)

Where *nu* (v) represents any individual constant $(a, b, c, \ldots, w)$, the rule of **Existential Generalization (E.G.)** is stated as follows:

  $\Phi \nu$
  ∴ $(\exists x)\Phi x$

What this says is that if Φ is true of some constant—let's say *a*—then there is an *x* such that *x* is Φ. The singular statement tells you *which* one there is; the corresponding universal tells you that there is *at least* one thing without telling you *which* one.

Example _____

All knights are warriors.
Some talented actors are knights.
Therefore some talented actors are warriors.

1. $(x)(Kx \supset Wx)$
2. $(\exists x)(Tx \bullet Kx)$
   $\therefore (\exists x)(Tx \bullet Wx)$
3. $Ta \bullet Ka$ 2 E.I.
4. $Ka \supset Wa$ 1 U.I.
5. $Ka \bullet Ta$ 3 Com.
6. Ka 5 Simp.
7. Wa 4,6 M.P.
8. Ta 3 Simp.
9. $Ta \bullet Wa$ 8,7 Conj.
10. $(\exists x)(Tx \bullet Wx)$ 9 E.G.

Since line 9 has been correctly deduced, and since the existential quantification of a propositional function is true if and only if it has at least one true substitution instance, we can derive the conclusion, in line 10, by **ExistentialGeneralization (E.G.)**.

_____

To this point we have been concerned with rules that allow us to introduce and remove quantifiers. These are rules of inference. They apply *only* to an entire line of the proof. But just as there are equivalences falling under the rule of replacement in propositional logic, there is an additional rule falling under the rule of replacement in quantified logic. These equivalences are called **Quantifier Equivalence (Q.E.)**:

$$[\sim(x)\Phi x] \stackrel{\mathrm{T}}{=} [(\exists x)\sim\Phi x]$$
$$[(x)\sim\Phi x] \stackrel{\mathrm{T}}{=} [\sim(\exists x)\Phi x]$$
$$[(x)\Phi x] \stackrel{\mathrm{T}}{=} [\sim(\exists x)\sim\Phi x]$$
$$[(\exists x)\Phi x] \stackrel{\mathrm{T}}{=} [\sim(x)\sim\Phi x]$$

Quantifier equivalence might remind you of De Morgan's Theorems. Just as the negation of a disjunction is logically equivalent to the conjunction of the negation of each disjunct, when you move a tilde "across" a quantifier, a universal becomes a particular and a particular becomes a universal. The last two equivalences allow you to move a tilde across a quantifier without having to use double negation. If you have a tilde to the left of a quantifier, you *cannot* instantiate. The tilde to the left of the quantifier governs the whole line. So, you need to use quantifier equivalence before you can instantiate.

RULES OF INFERENCE: QUANTIFICATION			
NAME	**ABBREVIATION**	**FORM**	**EFFECT**
Universal Instantiation	**U.I.**	$(x)\Phi x$ $\therefore \Phi\nu$ (where ν is a constant) ***Or*** $(x)\Phi x$ $\therefore \Phi y$ (where y is an individual variable)	This rule eliminates a universal quantifier and replaces the variable with either a constant or a variable.
Universal Generalization	**U.G.**	Φy $\therefore (x)\Phi x$ (where y is an individual variable)	This rule introduces a universal quantifier. You can engage in a universal generalization *only* from a propositional function.
Existential Instantiation	**E.I.**	$(\exists x)\Phi x$ $\therefore \Phi\nu$ (where ν is a constant)	This rule eliminates an existential quantifier and replaces the variable with a constant.
Existential Generalization	**E.G.**	$\Phi\nu$ $\therefore (\exists x)\Phi x$ (where ν is a constant)	This rule introduces an existential quantifier. You can engage in existential generalization only from a statement given in terms of constants.

QUANTIFIER EQUIVALENCE
These statements can replace one another wherever they occur in a proof:
$[\sim(x)\Phi x] \stackrel{\mathrm{T}}{=} [(\exists x)\sim\Phi x]$ $[(x)\sim\Phi x] \stackrel{\mathrm{T}}{=} [\sim(\exists x)\Phi x]$ $[(x)\Phi x] \stackrel{\mathrm{T}}{=} [\sim(\exists x)\sim\Phi x]$ $[(\exists x)\Phi x] \stackrel{\mathrm{T}}{=} [\sim(x)\sim\Phi x]$

EXERCISES

I. In the following formal proofs the justification for some of the steps in each is missing. Identify the correct justification for each step that is missing.

1. 1. $(x)(Px \supset Sx)$
2. $(\exists x)(Px \bullet Tx)$
$\therefore (\exists x)(Tx \bullet Sx)$

3.	$Pa \cdot Ta$	2 (U.I., U.G., E.I., E.G.)?
4.	Pa	3 Simp.
5.	$Pa \supset Sa$	1 (U.I., U.G., E.I., E.G.)?
6.	Sa	4,5 M.P.
7.	$Ta \cdot Pa$	3 Com.
8.	Ta	7 Simp.
9.	$Ta \cdot Sa$	6,8 Conj.
10.	$(\exists x)(Tx \cdot Sx)$	9 (U.I., U.G., E.I., E.G.)?

2.

1.	$(x)(Nx \supset Mx)$	
2.	$(x)(Mx \supset Ox)$	
3.	Na	
	$\therefore Oa$	
4.	$Na \supset Ma$	1 (U.I., U.G., E.I., E.G.)?
5.	$Ma \supset Oa$	2 (U.I., U.G., E.I., E.G.)?
6.	$Na \supset Oa$	4,5 H.S.
7.	Oa	3,6 M.P.

II. In the following formal proof, the expressions that belong in some of the steps are missing. Identify the missing expression for each line based on the justification provided for the line.

3.

1.	$(x)(Kx \supset {\sim}Sx)$	
2.	$(\exists x)(Sx \cdot Wx)$	
	$\therefore (\exists x)(Wx \cdot {\sim}Kx)$	
3.	?	2 E.I.
4.	?	1 U.I.
5.	Sa	3, Simp.
6.	${\sim}{\sim}Sa$	5 D.N.
7.	${\sim}Ka$	4,6 M.T.
8.	$Wa \cdot Sa$	3 Com.
9.	Wa	8 Simp.
10.	$Wa \cdot {\sim}Ka$	7,9 Conj.
11.	?	10 E.G.

III. Construct formal proofs of the following arguments using the rules of influence for quantifiers.

4. $(x)(Dx \supset {\sim}Ex)$
$(x)(Fx \supset Ex)$
$\therefore (x)(Fx \supset {\sim}Dx)$

5. $(\exists x)(Jx \cdot Kx)$
$(x)(Jx \supset Lx)$
$\therefore (\exists x)(Lx \cdot Kx)$

6. $(\exists x)(Px \cdot {\sim}Qx)$
$(x)(Px \supset Rx)$
$\therefore (\exists x)(Rx \cdot {\sim}Qx)$

7. $(x)(Sx \supset {\sim}Tx)$
$(\exists x)(Sx \cdot Ux)$
$\therefore \exists x(Ux \cdot {\sim}Tx)$

8. $(x)(Vx \supset Wx)$
    $(x)(Wx \supset \sim Xx)$
    $\therefore (x)(Xx \supset \sim Vx)$

9. $(\exists x)(Yx \bullet Zx)$
    $(x)(Zx \supset Ax)$
    $\therefore (\exists x)(Ax \bullet Yx)$

10. $(x)(Fx \supset Gx)$
    $(\exists x)(Fx \bullet \sim Gx)$
    $\therefore (\exists x)(Gx \bullet \sim Fx)$

IV. Translate and construct a formal proof of validity for each of the following arguments using the suggested notations.

11. All dancers are exuberant. Some fencers are not exuberant. Therefore some fencers are not dancers. (Dx, Ex, Fx)

12. All jesters are knaves. No knaves are lucky. Therefore no jesters are lucky. (Jx, Kx, Lx)

13. Only pacifists are Quakers. There are religious Quakers. Therefore pacifists are sometimes religious. (Px, Qx, Rx)

14. No violinists are not wealthy. There are no wealthy xylophonists. Therefore violinists are never xylophonists. (Vx, Wx, Xx)

15. *ANNE:* No beast so fierce but knows some touch of pity.
    GLOUCESTER: But I know none and therefore am no beast.
    (Bx, Px, g)

    —William Shakespeare, *Richard the Third*, act 1, sc. 2

V. Each of the following is logically equivalent to an instance of one of the following four forms: $(x)(\Phi x \supset \Psi x)$, $(x)(\Phi x \supset \sim \Psi x)$, $(\exists x)(\Phi x \bullet \Psi x)$, or $(\exists x)(\Phi x \bullet \sim \Psi x)$. Use Quantifier Equivalence plus the other equivalences falling under the rule of replacement to determine to which each of the following is equivalent.

16. $\sim(\exists x)(Tx \bullet Rx)$

17. $\sim(x)(Px \supset \sim Sx)$

18. $\sim(\exists x)(Jx \bullet \sim Kx)$

19. $\sim(x)(Dx \supset Gx)$

20. $\sim(x)\sim(\sim Dx \bullet Ex)$

21. $\sim(x)(Cx \supset \sim\sim Dx)$

22. $\sim(\exists x)(\sim Gx \bullet \sim Hx)$

23. $\sim(x)(\sim Kx \lor \sim Lx)$

24. $\sim(\exists x)\sim(\sim Qx \lor Rx)$

25. $\sim(x)\sim(\sim Ux \bullet \sim Vx)$

VI. Construct a proof of validity for each of the following.

26. $(x)[(Px \bullet Qx) \supset Rx]$
    $(x)[(Qx \bullet Rx) \supset Sx]$
    $(\exists x)(Px \bullet \sim Sx)$
    $\therefore (\exists x)(Px \bullet \sim Qx)$

27. $(x)[(Px \supset Qx) \bullet (Rx \supset Sx)]$
    $\sim(x)(Tx \supset Qx)$
    $(x)(\sim Rx \supset Ux)$
    $\therefore (\exists x)[Tx \bullet (Px \supset Ux)]$

28. $(\exists x)(Px \bullet Qx)$
$(x)(Px \supset Rx)$
$(\exists x)(Sx \bullet \sim Rx)$
$\therefore (\exists x)(Qx \bullet Rx) \bullet (\exists x)(Sx \bullet \sim Px)$

29. $(x)(Gx \supset Qx)$
$(\exists x)(Px \bullet Qx) \supset (x)(Rx \supset Sx)$
$(\exists x)[Px \bullet (\sim Sx \bullet Gx)]$
$\therefore (\exists x)(Rx \supset \sim Hx)$

30. $(x)[Px \supset (Qx \vee Rx)]$
$(x)(Rx \supset \sim Tx)$
$\sim(x)(Sx \supset \sim Px)$
$\therefore (\exists x)[Sx \bullet (Tx \supset Qx)]$

31. $(x)[Px \supset (Qx \supset Rx)]$
$(\exists x)(Px \bullet Sx)$
$(\exists x)(\sim Rx \bullet Tx)$
$(\exists x)(Px \supset \sim Qx) \supset (x)(Sx \supset \sim Rx)$
$\therefore (\exists x)(Px \bullet \sim Qx)$

32. $(x)[(Px \bullet \sim Mx) \supset \sim Qx]$
$(\exists x)(Px \bullet Qx)$
$(\exists x)(Rx \bullet Sx)$
$(\exists x)(Mx \vee Tx) \supset (x)[Rx \supset (Tx \vee Vx)]$
$\therefore (\exists x)(Sx \bullet Vx)$

33. $(\exists x)(Qx \bullet \sim Tx)$
$(x)[Qx \supset (Tx \vee \sim Px)]$
$(\exists x)(\sim Tx \bullet Sx)$
$(\exists x)(Qx \bullet \sim Px) \supset (x)(Sx \supset Px)$
$\therefore (\exists x)(Sx \bullet \sim Qx)$

34. $(x)[(Px \vee Sx) \supset (Qx \bullet Rx)]$
$(x)(Rx \supset Tx)$
$(x)(Qx \supset \sim Tx)$
$(x)(\sim Px \supset Sx)$
$\therefore (x)(Sx \equiv Tx)$

35. $(x)[Px \supset (Qx \bullet Rx)]$
$(\exists x)(Sx \bullet \sim Rx)$
$(\exists x)(Px \bullet Tx)$
$[(\exists x)(Sx \bullet \sim Px) \bullet (\exists y)(Qy \bullet Ty)] \supset (\exists z)(Zz \bullet Fz)$
$(x)[Fx \supset (Px \lor \sim Zx)]$
$\therefore (\exists x)(Zx \bullet Px)$

8.4 CONDITIONAL AND INDIRECT PROOF

Constructing conditional and indirect proof in quantified logic follows the same procedure as in propositional logic. If you're going to do a conditional proof, you make an assumption for conditional proof, use it as an additional premise, and discharge the assumption with a conditional statement. If you're going to do an indirect proof, you assume the denial of the conclusion you wish to reach, use it as an additional premise until you have shown that both a statement and its denial follow from the augmented set of premises, conjoin the statement and its denial, and discharge the assumption by stating the conclusion you wished to reach (the denial of the denial of your assumption). You may construct a conditional proof within the scope of a conditional proof, but the last assumption made must be the first assumption discharged. You may construct an indirect proof within the scope of an indirect proof, but the last assumption made must be the first assumption discharged. You may construct indirect proofs within the scope of conditional proofs, and vice versa. Once an assumption is discharged, *none* of the conclusions drawn within the scope of the assumption can be use later in the proof. Let's look at some examples.

Consider the following argument:

$$(x)(Px \supset Qx)$$
$$(x)[Qx \supset (Rx \bullet \sim Sx)]$$
$$\therefore (x)(Px \supset Rx)$$

The conclusion is a universal statement. Look at the conclusion. If you do a conditional proof, you'll assume the antecedent of the propositional function in the scope of the conclusion's quantifier,[9] proceed until you obtain the consequent of the propositional function in the scope of the conclusion's

---

[9]That is, you'll assume Px. If you prefer changing the variable to y or z when instantiating a universal, then you'd assume Py or Pz and instantiate the universals in terms of the same variable.

quantifier, discharge your assumption, and generalize. Your proof will look like this:

$$1.\ (x)(Px \supset Qx)$$
$$2.\ (x)[Qx \supset (Rx \bullet \sim Sx)]$$
$$\therefore\ (x)(Px \supset Rx)$$

	3. Px	A.C.P.
	4. $Px \supset Qx$	1 U.I.
	5. $Qx \supset (Rx \bullet \sim Sx)$	2 U.I.
	6. Qx	4,3 M.P.
	7. $Rx \bullet \sim Sx$	5,6 M.P.
	8. Rx	7 Simp.
9. $Px \supset Rx$		3–8 C.P.
10. $(x)(Px \supset Rx)$		9. U.G.

There is a restriction on universal generalization that applies to conditional proof. **You are *not* allowed to introduce a propositional function as an assumption for conditional proof and then generalize with respect to that propositional function within the scope of the conditional proof.**

If you were constructing an indirect proof for the same argument, your assumption would be the denial of the conclusion. Your proof might look like this:

$$1.\ (x)(Px \supset Qx)$$
$$2.\ (x)[Qx \supset (Rx \bullet \sim Sx)]$$
$$\therefore\ (x)(Px \supset Rx)$$

	3. $\sim(x)(Px \supset Rx)$	A.I.P.
	4. $(\exists x)\sim(Px \supset Rx)$	Q.E.
	5. $\sim(Pa \supset Ra)$	4 E.I.
	6. $\sim(\sim Pa \lor Ra)$	5 Impl.
	7. $\sim\sim Pa \bullet \sim Ra$	6 De M.
	8. $Pa \bullet \sim Ra$	7 D.N.
	9. $Pa \supset Qa$	1 U.I.
	10. $Qa \supset (Ra \bullet \sim Sa)$	2 U.I.
	11. Pa	8 Simp.
	12. Qa	9,11 M.P.
	13. $Ra \bullet \sim Sa$	10,12 M.P.
	14. Ra	13 Simp.
	15. $\sim Ra \bullet Pa$	8 Com.
	16. $\sim Ra$	15 Simp.
	17. $Ra \bullet \sim Ra$	14, 16 Conj.
18. $(x)\ (Px \supset Rx)$		3–17 C.P.

As you might infer, when you're doing indirect proofs of arguments with consistent premises, you will *always* have at least one existential statement. In the proof we just did, the denial of the conclusion becomes an existential statement by Quantifier Equivalence. If the conclusion is an existential statement, it becomes a universal by Quantifier Equivalence. Consider the following:

1. $(x)(Px \supset Qx)$
2. $(\exists x)(Px \cdot Rx)$
∴ $(\exists x)(Qx \cdot Rx)$

	3. $\sim(\exists x)(Qx \cdot Rx)$	A.I.P.
	4. $(x)\sim(Qx \cdot Rx)$	3 Q.E.
	5. $Pa \cdot Ra$	2 E.I.
	6. $Pa \supset Qa$	1 U.I.
	7. $\sim(Qa \cdot Ra)$	4 U.I.
	8. Pa	5 Simp.
	9. Qa	6,8 M.P.
	10. $\sim Qa \lor \sim Ra$	7 De M.
	11. $\sim\sim Qa$	9 D.N.
	12. $\sim Ra$	10,11 D.S.
	13. $Ra \cdot Pa$	5 Com.
	14. Ra	13 Simp.
	15. $Ra \cdot \sim Ra$	14,12 Conj.
16. $(\exists x)(Qx \cdot Rx)$		3–15 I.P.

You can, of course, use conditional and indirect proof together, just as you did when doing propositional logic proofs.

1. $(x)(Px \supset Qx)$
2. $(x)(Qx \supset Rx)$
∴ $(x)(Px \supset Rx)$

	3. Px	A.C.P.
	4. $\sim Rx$	A.I.P.
	5. $Px \supset Qx$	1 U.I.
	6. $Qx \supset Rx$	2 U.I.
	7. Qx	5,2 M.P.
	8. Rx	6,7 M.P.
	9. $Rx \cdot \sim Rx$	8,4 Conj.
	10. Rx	4–9 I.P.
11. $Px \supset Rx$		3–10 C.P.
12. $(x)(Px \supset Rx)$		11 U.G.

Conditional and indirect proofs are often longer then direct proofs. Nonetheless, just as in propositional logic, the rules of conditional proof and indirect proof often make life considerably easier.

Rules of Thumb for Doing Quantified Conditional and Indirect Proofs

There are several points you might want to remember when doing conditional and indirect proofs:

1. If the conclusion is a universal statement, assume the propositional function that is the antecedent of the statement in the conclusion for conditional proof. Generally you *will not* want to assume a quantified statement: If it's quantified when you assume it, it has to be quantified when you discharge the assumption.

2. If you're trying to prove an existential statement, you'll probably want to use indirect proof.

3. If the conclusion is a conjunction, such as $(x)(Px \supset Qx) \bullet (\exists x)(Qx \bullet \sim Rx)$, you'll probably want to deal with each conjunct separately.

4. If the conclusion is a disjunction, such as $(x)(Px \supset Qx) \lor (\exists x)(Qx \bullet \sim Rx)$, you'll probably want to assume the denial of the *entire* conclusion.

5. If the conclusion is a conditional, such as $(x)(Px \supset Qx) \supset (\exists x)(Qx \bullet \sim Rx)$, you'll probably want to assume the antecedent (the universal statement) for conditional proof.

6. If the conclusion is a biconditional, such as $(x)(Px \supset Qx) \equiv (\exists x)(Qx \bullet \sim Rx)$, you'll probably want to do two conditional proofs, first assuming the left component to get the right component then assuming the right component to get the left component.

EXERCISES

Construct a conditional or indirect proof for each of the following.

1. $(x)[Px \supset (Qx \bullet Rx)]$
   $\therefore (x)(Px \supset Qx)$

2. $(x)(Px \supset Qx)$
   $(x)[(Qx \lor Sx) \supset \sim Rx]$
   $\therefore (x)(Px \supset \sim Rx)$

3. $(x)[Px \supset (Rx \lor \sim Sx)]$
   $(x)(Rx \supset \sim Sx)$
   $\therefore (x)(Px \supset \sim Sx)$

4. $(x)[(Px \bullet Qx) \supset Rx]$
$(x)(Px \supset Qx)$
$\therefore (x)[Px \supset (Rx \lor Sx)]$

5. $(x)[(Px \lor Qx) \supset (Rx \bullet Sx)]$
$(x)[Rx \supset (Qx \bullet \sim Sx)]$
$\therefore (x)(Qx \supset \sim Sx)$

6. $(\exists x)(Px \bullet Qx)$
$(x)[Px \supset (Rx \supset Sx)]$
$(x)[Qx \supset (\sim Rx \supset \sim Sx)]$
$\therefore (\exists x)[(Rx \bullet Sx) \lor (\sim Rx \bullet \sim Sx)]$

7. $(x)[(Px \bullet Qx) \supset Rx]$
$(\exists x)(Px \bullet \sim Rx)$
$\therefore (\exists x)\sim Qx$

8. $(x)[Px \supset (Qx \equiv Rx)]$
$(\exists x)(Qx \bullet \sim Rx)$
$\therefore (\exists x)\sim Px$

9. $(x)[Px \supset (Rx \lor \sim Sx)]$
$(\exists x)(Px \bullet \sim Rx)$
$\therefore (\exists x)(Px \bullet \sim Sx)$

10. $(x)(Px \supset Qx)$
$(x)(Qx \supset Px)$
$\therefore (x)(Px \equiv Qx)$

11. $(x)[(Px \lor Qx) \supset (Rx \bullet Sx)]$
$(x)[Rx \supset (Tx \lor \sim Px)]$
$\therefore (x)[Qx \supset (Px \supset Tx)]$

12. $(x)[(Px \bullet Qx) \supset (Rx \lor Sx)]$
$(x)[Rx \supset (Tx \bullet \sim Sx)]$
$(x)[Sx \supset (Tx \bullet \sim Rx)]$
$\therefore (x)[(Px \bullet Qx) \supset Tx]$

13. $(x)[Px \supset (Qx \equiv Rx)]$
$(\exists x)(Px \bullet Rx)$
$\therefore (\exists x)(Rx \bullet Qx)$

14. $(x)[(Qx \equiv Rx) \supset Px]$
$(\exists x)(\sim Px \bullet Rx)$
$\therefore (\exists x)(\sim Px \bullet \sim Qx)$

15. $(x)[(Qx \equiv Rx) \supset \sim Px]$
$\quad (x)(Px \supset Rx)$
$\quad \therefore (x)(Px \supset \sim Qx)$

16. $(x)[(Px \supset \sim Qx) \supset \sim(Px \lor Qx)]$
$\quad (x)(Qx \supset Rx)$
$\quad \therefore (x)(Px \supset Rx)$

17. $(x)[(Px \supset \sim Qx) \supset \sim(Px \lor Qx)]$
$\quad (x)(Qx \supset Rx)$
$\quad (x)(Rx \supset Qx)$
$\quad \therefore (\exists x)[(Px \supset Rx) \bullet (Rx \supset Px)]$

18. $(\exists x)[(Px \supset \sim Qx) \bullet (Px \supset \sim Rx)]$
$\quad (x)[\sim Px \supset \sim(\sim Qx \lor \sim Rx)]$
$\quad \therefore (\exists x)[(Qx \supset Rx) \bullet (Rx \supset Qx)]$

19. $(x)[Px \supset \sim(Qx \lor Rx)]$
$\quad (x)[\sim Px \supset \sim(\sim Qx \lor \sim Rx)]$
$\quad \therefore (x)(Qx \supset Rx)$

20. $(x)[Px \equiv \sim(Qx \lor Rx)]$
$\quad \sim(\exists x)[\sim Px \bullet (\sim Qx \lor \sim Rx)]$
$\quad \therefore (x)(Qx \equiv Rx)$

8.5 PROVING INVALIDITY

In this section, we develop a variation on reverse truth tables as a means of proving the invalidity in quantified logic. You'll recall (section 6.6) that when constructing a reverse truth table in propositional logic, you assume that the premises are true and the conclusion is false and consistently assign truth values to the simple statements in an attempt to make good on the assumption. If you could consistently assign truth values, you proved that the argument was invalid. If you could not, you proved that the argument was valid. In *quantified* logic, the technique can *only* be used to prove invalidity. We begin by setting the stage with a few remarks on the nature of quantified statements and adapting the reverse truth table technique to quantified logic.

If we're going to apply a truth table technique to quantified logic, we must begin by considering the truth conditions for quantified statements. A universal statement is true of all things. If a statement of the form $(x)\Phi x$ is true, then every substitution instance of x is true of Φ. Another way of putting this is:

$$(x)\Phi x \overset{\mathrm{T}}{\equiv} [\Phi a \bullet \Phi b \bullet \cdots \bullet \Phi w]$$

where a through w constitute all possible substitution instances of x.[10] An existential proposition is true of at least one thing. If a statement of the form $(\exists x)\Phi x$ is true, then a is Φ, or b is Φ, or some other substitution instance of x is Φ. Another way of putting this is:

$$(\exists x)\Phi x \overset{\mathrm{T}}{=} [\Phi a \lor \Phi b \lor \ldots \lor \Phi w]$$

When we construct a proof in quantified logic, we typically consider a universe or *domain of discourse*—the set of objects to which the argument refers—that is composed of all things. To show that an argument form is *invalid*, it is sufficient that there be one object in the universe—one substitution instance of the variables—such that all the premises are true and the conclusion is false. A specification of a domain of discourse plus a truth assignment to the predicates of the argument in that domain of discourse is called a *model*. So, we can consider models composed of varying numbers of objects, and we can specify their truth conditions.

In a domain of discourse in which there is exactly one individual,

$$(x)(\Phi x) \overset{\mathrm{T}}{=} \Phi a \overset{\mathrm{T}}{=} (\exists x)(\Phi x)$$

In a domain in which there are exactly two individuals,

$$(x)(\Phi x) \overset{\mathrm{T}}{=} [\Phi a \bullet \Phi b] \text{ and } (\exists x)(\Phi x) \overset{\mathrm{T}}{=} [\Phi a \lor \Phi b]$$

In a domain in which there are exactly three individuals,

$$(x)(\Phi x) \overset{\mathrm{T}}{=} [\Phi a \bullet \Phi b \bullet \Phi c] \text{ and } (\exists x)(\Phi x) \overset{\mathrm{T}}{=} [\Phi a \lor \Phi b \lor \Phi c]$$

Notice that, considered in their respective domains, these biconditionals are tautologies, and thus one component of the biconditional can be replaced by the other in arguments where those statements appear.

An argument involving quantifiers is invalid if there is a "possible universe" or model containing at least one individual such that the arguments' premises are true and its conclusion false in that model. For any invalid quantificational argument, it is possible to describe a model containing some definite number of individuals for which its logically equivalent truth-functional expansion can be proved invalid by the method of assigning truth values.

The procedure for proving the invalidity of an argument containing generalized propositions is the following:

1. Try a one-element model containing the individual a by writing the logically equivalent truth-functional argument for that model with respect to a.

---

[10]We do *not* mean, of course, that there are only twenty-three objects in the universe.

2. If the truth-functional argument can be proved invalid by assigning truth values to its component simple statements—a case in which all the premises are true and the conclusion is false—then you are finished; you have proved the original argument invalid. If not, go to Step 3.

3. If a one-element model *does not* show that the argument is invalid, try a two-element model containing the individuals *a* and *b*. If the original argument contains a universally quantified propositional function $(x)(\Phi x)$, use conjunction to join Φa and Φb. If the original argument contains an existentially quantified propositional function $(\exists x)(\Phi x)$, use disjunction to join Φa and Φb.

4. If this argument can be proved invalid by assigning truth-values to its component simple statements, then you are finished; you have proved the original argument invalid. If not, go to Step 5.

5. If a two-element model *does not* show that the argument is invalid, try a three-element model containing the individuals *a*, *b*, and *c*. And so on.

Example

$$(x)(Cx \supset Dx)$$
$$(x)(Ex \supset Dx)$$
$$\therefore (x)(Ex \supset Cx)$$

A one-element model containing the individual *a* would give us the following truth-functional argument, with respect to *a*:

$$Ca \supset Da$$
$$Ea \supset Da$$
$$\therefore Ea \supset Ca$$

Now construct a reverse truth table for an argument of this form. In this case, the antecedent of the conclusion must be true and the consequent false, and the truth values must be assigned consistently throughout.

$Ca \supset Da$	$Ea \supset Da$	$\therefore Ea \supset Ca$
F F	T T	T F
T	T	F

This shows that the model, and therefore the argument form, is invalid.

Sometimes a one-object universe will not show that an argument form is invalid, but a two-object universe will.

Examples

Consider the argument form:

$$(\exists x)(Dx \bullet Ex)$$
$$(\exists x)(Fx \bullet Ex)$$
$$\therefore (\exists x)(Dx \bullet Fx)$$

You start with a model consisting of exactly one object (*a*), and construct reverse truth tables. Since the conclusion will be a conjunction—there are three assignments of truth values that make it false—you will need to consider alternative assignments of truth values to the conclusion if the first does not show that the argument is invalid:

$$
\begin{array}{ccc}
Da \bullet Ea & Fa \bullet Ea & \therefore Da \bullet Fa \\
\text{(F/T)} \;\; \text{T} & \text{T} \quad \text{T} & \text{F} \quad \text{T} \\
\text{F} & \text{T} & \text{F} \\
\text{T} \quad \text{T} & \text{(F/T)} \;\; \text{T} & \text{T} \quad \text{F} \\
\text{T} & \text{F} & \text{F} \\
\text{(F/T)} \;\; \text{T} & \text{(F/T)} \;\; \text{T} & \text{F} \quad \text{F} \\
\text{F} & \text{F} & \text{F} \\
\end{array}
$$

A universe consisting of one object does not show that the argument form is invalid. Will a universe consisting of two objects do so? Yes.

$$
\begin{array}{cc}
(Da \bullet Ea) \lor (Db \bullet Eb) & (Fa \bullet Ea) \lor (Fb \bullet Eb) \\
\text{F} \quad \text{T} \qquad \text{T} \quad \text{T} & \text{T} \quad \text{T} \qquad \text{F} \quad \text{T} \\
\text{F} \qquad\qquad \text{T} & \text{T} \qquad\qquad \text{F} \\
\qquad \text{T} & \qquad \text{T} \\
\end{array}
$$

$$
\begin{array}{c}
\therefore (Da \bullet Fa) \lor (Db \bullet Fb) \\
\text{F} \quad \text{T} \qquad \text{T} \quad \text{F} \\
\text{F} \qquad\qquad \text{F} \\
\qquad \text{F} \\
\end{array}
$$

We now have a model in which all the premises are true and the conclusion is false. This shows that the argument form is invalid.

Now consider this one:

$$(\exists x)(Px \bullet \sim Qx)$$
$$(\exists x)(Px \bullet \sim Sx)$$
$$\therefore (x)(Sx \supset Qx)$$

Again, a one-element model will *not* show that the argument is invalid:

$$Pa \bullet \sim Qa \qquad Pa \bullet \sim Sa \qquad \therefore Sa \supset Qa$$
$$\quad\text{T}\quad\text{F} \qquad\quad\text{T}\quad\text{T/F} \qquad\quad\text{T}\quad\text{F}$$
$$\qquad\text{T} \qquad\qquad\quad\text{T} \qquad\qquad\quad\text{F}$$
$$\quad\text{T} \qquad\qquad\quad\text{F}$$

But a two-element model will show that the form is invalid:

$$(Pa \bullet \sim Qa) \lor (Pb \bullet \sim Qb) \quad (Pa \bullet \sim Sa) \lor (Pb \bullet \sim Sb)$$
$$\quad\text{T}\quad\text{F}\qquad\text{T}\quad\text{T}\qquad\text{T}\quad\text{T}\qquad\text{T}\quad\text{F}$$
$$\qquad\text{T}\qquad\qquad\text{F}\qquad\qquad\text{F}\qquad\qquad\text{T}$$
$$\qquad\text{T}\qquad\qquad\text{F}\qquad\qquad\text{F}\qquad\qquad\text{T}$$
$$\qquad\qquad\text{T}\qquad\qquad\qquad\qquad\text{T}$$
$$\therefore (Sa \supset Qa) \bullet (Sb \supset Qb)$$
$$\quad\text{T}\quad\text{F}\qquad\text{F}\quad\text{T}$$
$$\qquad\text{F}\qquad\qquad\text{T}$$
$$\qquad\qquad\text{F}$$

More complex (asyllogistic) arguments are proved invalid by the same procedure. Consider the following argument:

> Managers and superintendents are either competent workers or relatives of the owner.
> Anyone who dares to complain must be either a superintendent or a relative of the owner.
> Managers and foremen alone are competent workers.
> <u>Someone did dare to complain.</u>
> Therefore some superintendent is a relative of the owner.

This argument may be symbolized:

$$(x)[(Mx \lor Sx) \supset (Cx \lor Rx)]$$
$$(x)[Dx \supset (Sx \lor Rx)]$$
$$(x)(Mx \equiv Cx)$$
$$(\exists x)\,Dx$$
$$\therefore (\exists x)(Sx \bullet Rx)$$

and we can prove this invalid by describing a possible universe or model containing the single individual a; in that model, the above argument is logically equivalent to:

$$[(Ma \lor Sa) \supset (Ca \lor Ra)]$$
$$[Da \supset (Sa \lor Ra)]$$
$$(Ma \equiv Ca)$$
$$Da$$
$$\therefore (Sa \cdot Ra)$$

Assigning the truth value *true* to Ca, Da, Fa, and Ra, and the truth value *false* to Sa, yields true premises and a false conclusion. We have thereby shown that there is a model of the original argument in which the premises are true and the conclusion false, and thus the original argument is invalid.

EXERCISES

I.   Prove the invalidity of the following arguments.

1. $(x)(Sx \supset \sim Tx)$
$(x)(Tx \supset \sim Ux)$
$\therefore (x)(Sx \supset \sim Ux)$

2. $(\exists x)(Sx \cdot \sim Tx)$
$(x)(Ux \supset \sim Tx)$
$\therefore (x)(Ux \supset Sx)$

3. $(x)(Sx \supset \sim Tx)$
$(x)(Ux \supset \sim Tx)$
$\therefore (x)(Ux \supset \sim Sx)$

4. $(x)(Dx \supset \sim Ex)$
$(x)(Ex \supset Fx)$
$\therefore (x)(Fx \supset \sim Dx)$

5. $(x)(Gx \supset Hx)$
$(x)(Gx \supset Ix)$
$\therefore (x)(Ix \supset Hx)$

6. $(\exists x)(Jx \cdot Kx)$
$(\exists x)(Kx \cdot Lx)$
$\therefore (\exists x)(Lx \cdot Jx)$

7. $(x)(Px \supset \sim Qx)$
$(x)(Px \supset \sim Rx)$
$\therefore (x)(Rx \supset \sim Qx)$

8. $(x)(Sx \supset \sim Ux)$
$(x)(Tx \supset Ux)$
$\therefore (\exists x)(Ux \cdot \sim Sx)$

9. $(\exists x)(Vx \cdot \sim Wx)$
$(\exists x)(Wx \cdot \sim Xx)$
$\therefore (\exists x)(Xx \cdot \sim Vx)$

10. $(\exists x)(Yx \cdot Zx)$
$(\exists x)(Ax \cdot Zx)$
$\therefore (\exists x)(Ax \cdot \sim Yx)$

II.   Prove the invalidity of the following, in each case using the suggested notation.

11. No diplomats are extremists. Some fanatics are extremists. Therefore some diplomats are not fanatics. (Dx, Ex, Fx)

12. Some journalists are not kibitzers. Some kibitzers are not lucky. Therefore some journalists are not lucky. (Jx, Kx, Lx)

13. Some physicians are quacks. Some quacks are not responsible. Therefore some physicians are not responsible. (*Px, Qx, Rx*)

14. Some politicians are leaders. Some leaders are not orators. Therefore some orators are not politicians. (*Px, Lx, Ox*)

15. If anything is metallic, then it is breakable. There are breakable ornaments. Therefore there are metallic ornaments. (*Mx, Bx, Ox*)

III. Translate each of the following arguments into symbolic notation, in each case using the abbreviations suggested. Then either construct a formal proof of its validity or prove it invalid.

16. All problem-solvers and thinkers have minds. Computers are problem-solvers. Thus, computers have minds. (*Px, Tx, Mx, Cx*)

17. All horses are mammals. Some horses are pets. Thus, all pets are mammals. (*Hx, Mx, Px*)

18. All halibut are good eating. Some things that are good eating are vegetables. Thus, some halibut are vegetables. (*Hx, Gx, Vx*)

19. Bears are mammals. All pets are mammals. Thus, bears are pets. (*Px, Mx, Bx*)

20. Smart people are tall. All tall people wear clothes. Thus, smart people wear clothes. (*Sx, Tx, Cx*)

21. Popes are tall. All tall people are smart. Thus, Popes are smart. (*Px, Tx, Sx*)

IV. For each of the following, either construct a formal proof of validity or prove it invalid. If it is to be proved invalid, a model containing as many as three elements may be required.

22. $(\exists x)\{(Ex \cdot Fx) \cdot [(Ex \lor Fx) \supset (Gx \cdot Hx)]\}$
    $\therefore (x)(Ex \supset Hx)$

23. $(x)\{[Ix \supset (Jx \cdot {\sim}Kx)] \cdot [Jx \supset (Ix \supset Kx)]\}$
    $(\exists x)[(Ix \cdot Jx) \cdot {\sim}Lx]$
    $\therefore (\exists x)(Kx \cdot Lx)$

24. $(x)[(Mx \cdot Nx) \supset (Ox \lor Px)]$
    $(x)[(Ox \cdot Px) \supset (Qx \lor Rx)]$
    $\therefore (x)[(Mx \lor Ox) \supset Rx]$

25. $(x)[Wx \supset (Xx \supset Yx)]$
    $(\exists x)[Xx \cdot (Zx \cdot {\sim}Ax)]$
    $(x)[(Wx \supset Yx) \supset (Bx \supset Ax)]$
    $\therefore (\exists x)(Zx \cdot {\sim}Bx)$

26. $(\exists x)[Cx \cdot {\sim}(Dx \supset Ex)]$
    $(x)[(Cx \cdot Dx) \supset Fx]$
    $(\exists x)[Ex \cdot {\sim}(Dx \supset Cx)]$
    $(x)(Gx \supset Cx)$
    $\therefore (\exists x)(Gx \cdot {\sim}Fx)$

27. $(x)\{(Lx \lor Mx) \supset \{[(Nx \bullet Ox) \lor Px] \supset Qx\}\}$
$(\exists x)(Mx \bullet \sim Lx)$
$(x)\{[(Ox \supset Qx) \bullet \sim Rx] \supset Mx\}$
$(\exists x)(Lx \bullet \sim Mx)$
$\therefore (\exists x)(Nx \supset Rx)$

V. For each of the following, either construct a formal proof of its validity or prove it invalid, in each case using the suggested notation.

28. Teachers are either enthusiastic or unsuccessful. Teachers are not all unsuccessful. Therefore there are enthusiastic teachers. (Tx, Ex, Ux)

29. Argon compounds and sodium compounds are either oily or volatile. Not all sodium compounds are oily. Therefore some argon compounds are volatile. (Ax, Sx, Ox, Vx)

30. No employee who is either slovenly or discourteous can be promoted. Therefore no discourteous employee can be promoted. (Ex, Sx, Dx, Px)

31. There is nothing made of gold that is not expensive. No weapons are made of silver. Not all weapons are expensive. Therefore not everything is made of gold or silver. (Gx, Ex, Wx, Sx)

32. There is nothing made of tin that is not cheap. No rings are made of lead. Not everything is either tin or lead. Therefore not all rings are cheap. (Tx, Cx, Rx, Lx)

33. Some photographers are skillful but not imaginative. Only artists are photographers. Photographers are not all skillful. Any journeyman is skillful. Therefore not every artist is a journeyman. (Px, Sx, Ix, Ax, Jx)

34. Doctors and lawyers are professional people. Professional people and executives are respected. Therefore doctors are respected. (Dx, Lx, Px, Ex, Rx)

35. All cut-rate items are either shopworn or out of date. Nothing shopworn is worth buying. Some cut-rate items are worth buying. Therefore some cut-rate items are out of date. (Cx, Sx, Ox, Wx)

36. No candidate who is either endorsed by labor or opposed by the *Tribune* can carry the farm vote. No one can be elected who does not carry the farm vote. Therefore no candidate endorsed by labor can be elected. (Cx, Lx, Ox, Fx, Ex)

37. All logicians are deep thinkers and effective writers. To write effectively one must be economical if one's audience is general, and comprehensive if one's audience is technical. No deep thinker has a technical audience if he has the ability to reach a general audience. Some logicians are comprehensive rather than economical. Therefore not all logicians have the ability to reach a general audience. ($Lx, Dx, Wx, Ex, Gx, Cx, Tx, Ax$)

38. If anything is expensive it is both valuable and rare. Whatever is valuable is both desirable and expensive. Therefore if anything is either valuable or expensive then it must be both valuable and expensive. (*Ex, Vx, Rx, Dx*)
39. Gold is valuable. Rings are ornaments. Therefore gold rings are valuable ornaments. (*Gx, Vx, Rx, Ox*)
40. Socrates is mortal. Therefore everything is either mortal or not mortal. (*s, Mx*)

ESSENTIALS OF CHAPTER 8

In this chapter we have developed a symbolism to examine quantified propositions. This is a modification of the symbolic language of propositional logic.

We introduced the language in section 8.2. In our language, uppercase letters represent predicates, lowercase letters from a through w represent the names of individuals (constants), the letters x, y, and z are variables ranging over individuals, and the Greek letters Φ and ψ are variables ranging over predicates. We introduced the symbol (x) as the universal quantifier and the symbol $(\exists x)$ as the existential quantifier or particular quantifier.

In section 8.3 we introduced four additional rules of inference. The universal and existential instantiation rules allow you restate a quantified statement in terms of an individual. **Universal instantiation** allows you to restate a quantified statement in terms of an individual constant *or* an individual variable. **Existential instantiation** allows you to restate a quantified statement in terms of *only* an individual constant that is new to the proof. The **universal and existential generalization** rules allow you to introduce quantifiers. Given a statement asserted in terms of an individual *variable*, you can generalize to a universal proposition. Given a statement asserted in terms of an individual *constant*, you can generalize to an existential proposition. We also discussed **quantifier equivalence**. Quantifier equivalence falls under the rule of replacement. It says that when you move a tilde ($\sim$) across a quantifier, a universal quantifier becomes an existential quantifier, and an existential quantifier becomes a universal quantifier.

In section 8.4, we discussed conditional and indirect proof for quantified logic.

In section 8.5, we discussed using reverse truth tables to prove that an argument form in quantified logic is invalid.

CHAPTER NINE

INDUCTION

9.1 INTRODUCTION TO INDUCTION

The past six chapters focused on deductive arguments. It is impossible for the conclusion of a valid deductive argument to be false if its premises are true. So a sound deductive argument allows you to assert its conclusion with certainty.

No inductive argument is a valid deductive argument. So, even if the premises of an inductive argument are true, you cannot be certain that the conclusion is true. It's always possible for the conclusion of an inductive argument to be false. Inductive arguments are fallible. You can claim to know the truth of the conclusion of an inductive argument only with a certain degree of probability.

Nonetheless, the truth value of all contingent statements is known by induction. Most arguments you construct are inductive arguments. All knowledge of the natural world—including scientific knowledge—rests upon inductive inference. So, inductive arguments are of practical importance. Therefore, we need criteria to evaluate inductive arguments.

As we have seen, in the case of *deductive* arguments there are criteria that allow us *to determine conclusively* whether or not an argument form is valid. If an argument form is *invalid*, it might provide *some* evidence, but it cannot provide conclusive evidence for the truth of its conclusion. Some inductive arguments provide better evidence for the truth of their conclusions—they are *stronger*—than others. The criteria for evaluating inductive arguments are criteria that *tend to show* that an inductive argument is strong or weak. To see how this works, let's consider a paradigm of inductive argument, an argument by enumeration.[1]

---

[1]There are those who would claim that all inductive arguments are arguments by enumeration. If that were so, then the inductive/valid deductive argument distinction would not divide all arguments into one of two classes without remainder. Further, as we'll suggest below, arguments by enumeration are not so much as the most basic form of inductive argument.

You're sitting beside a lake observing swans. The first swan you see is white. The second swan you see is white. The third swan you see is white. You continue observing swans. The nth swan you see is white. You conclude that all swans are white. Your argument might be represented as follows:

> Swan #1 was observed to be white.
> Swan #2 was observed to be white.
> Swan #3 was observed to be white.
> . . .
> Swan #n was observed to be white.
> ∴ (probably) all swans are white.

Do you have good reason to accept your conclusion? No. Watching a bunch of swans on one lake on one day doesn't tell you a whole lot about all swans that did, do, or will exist anywhere. Could you strengthen the argument for your conclusion? Sure, you look at more swans. Does it make any difference at which swans you look? Sort of.

You reach an inductive generalization based upon a **sample**, a limited collection of objects of the kind under investigation. In some cases, the sample might be the complete collection: You could make a general claim based on an analysis of all of Shakespeare's plays, for example, assuming we have all of Shakespeare's plays. Often, as in the case of swans, the sample is very limited. So, if you increase the number of swans in your sample, the probability of the truth of the conclusion increases. But if you've been around animals for a while, you know there are variations in the appearances (and genetics) of animals in different areas. Rabbits are bigger and deer are smaller in Texas than they are in Virginia, for example. So, you want some **diversity** in your sample. And given what you know about genetic pools in other animals, you'll conclude that there is usually a correlation between genetic diversity and variations in geographical location. Further, the difference in geographical location probably needs to be significant.[2] So, if you made your initial observations in Minneapolis, Minnesota, a trip to the suburbs won't be enough. The chances of a genetic difference might be greater if you made observations in Charleston, South Carolina, Brownsville, Texas, and San Diego, California. But to do it right, you'd need to become a world traveler: Nicaragua, Brazil, Denmark, Italy, Russia, China, and Australia.

In Melbourne, Australia, you see a large black bird and ask your tour guide, "What kind of bird is that?" "That's a swan, mate. The Black Swan isn't

---

[2]You should notice that these considerations regarding the probable diversity of genetic makeup of swans in different areas is based on similarities between swans and other kinds of animals. There is genetic diversity among other kinds of animals that correlates with variations in geographical location. So, it is likely that there will be genetic variations in swans corresponding to geographical locations. This is an *argument by analogy*. We examine arguments by analogy beginning in the next section.

just a pub in London!" *One* observation of a swan that is not white shows that your conclusion, "All swans are white," is false. It's an **inductive counterexample**. An inductive counterexample is a case that is sufficient to show that the conclusion of an inductive argument is false. Your conclusion was a universal generalization. The observation of a black swan shows that the contradiction of your conclusion—"Some swans are not white"—is true.

The statement, "All swans are white," is a very **strong conclusion**. The strength of a conclusion is determined by the amount of evidence needed to show that the conclusion is false. One nonwhite swan is sufficient to show that the conclusion is false. Your evidence *might* be sufficient to show that a weaker conclusion is true, for example, "Most swans are white." To show *that* conclusion is false, you would need to show that over fifty percent of all swans are *not* white.

So, we may summarize the criteria for evaluating inductive arguments by enumeration as follows:

1. **As the number of objects taken into account increases, the generalization is strengthened.**
2. **The more diverse the sample is, the better the basis for the generalization is.**
3. **The stronger the conclusion is, the weaker the argument is.**

After our round-the-world-swan-sighting tour, do we have good reason to accept our now-weaker conclusion, "Most swans are white"? After all, we saw thousands of swans, and only a few hundred of them were Australian black swans. We have pretty good evidence that most presently-existing swans are white. But *most swans* means the majority of swans that exist now, that have existed, and that will exist. Our argument provides good evidence—but not conclusive evidence—that the majority of currently-existing swans are white. We cannot look at the colors of long-dead swans; the best we can do is read historical records, which are guaranteed to be incomplete. And future swans are something else again.

One of the reasons inductive arguments are important is that we use them to predict what will happen in the future. When you were a kid, you might have touched a hot stove a couple times, felt pain, and concluded that if you touched the stove again, you'd feel pain again. You've avoided stoves ever since—much to the glee of fast-food restaurants. Or you might have read several of J. K. Rowling's *Harry Potter* books, found each enjoyable, and looked forward to the release of the next one since you inferred that it would be enjoyable, too. Could you have been wrong? Sure. The story goes that Queen Victoria read one of Lewis Carroll's *Alice* books, liked it very much, and asked Carroll to dedicate his next book to her, which he did. That book was on the foundations of mathematics—which, I'm sure, was very enjoyable, even if

Queen Victoria might not have noticed.[3] Our assumption is that, at some level, the future will resemble the past. This assumption is called the **Principle of the Uniformity of Nature**. It is *assumed* in all our inductive arguments. In our swan argument, it functions as follows:

> The majority of past and present swans are (have been) white.
> The future will resemble the past.
> The majority of future swans will be white.

Over 250 years ago, the Scottish philosopher David Hume (1711–1776) asked whether the principle of the uniformity of nature can be known to be true.[4] He argued that the principle of the uniformity of nature is not self-evidently true: You can at least imagine what it would be like for one event to occur and not that which regularly follows it. Arguments from experience *assume* that the principle of the uniformity of nature is true. So, any argument from experience to support the principle of the uniformity of nature begs the question. All arguments are either arguments from self-evident premises or arguments from experience. Therefore, there is no argument showing that the principle of the uniformity of nature is true. Hence, there is no way to know that the principle is true. Hence, any inductive argument contains an implicit premise (the principle of the uniformity of nature) that is not known to be true. Notice, the principle of the uniformity of nature might *be* true, but it cannot be known to be such. So, there are grounds to doubt any inductive argument.

Of course, we always *assume* that the principle of the uniformity of nature is true: Organized life would be virtually impossible if we didn't. But even if the principle of the uniformity of nature is true, this doesn't mean that we can infer that just because most swans are and have been white, that most swans in the future will be white. Why? The principle of the uniformity of nature applies at a very fundamental level. Let's imagine that in 2255 there is an event that changes the genetic makeup of swans everywhere except in Australia. From 2255 onward, all non-Australian swans are blue. Let's assume blue swans are very prolific, and in the entire history of the world, blue swans outnumber white swans by two-to-one. Our generalization that most swans (past, present, and future) are white would be false. But this would be consistent with the principle of the uniformity of nature. Why? The color of swans is determined by genetic factors. It might be that all swans that have a certain gene α are white, whereas those that have a gene β are blue. The genetic explanation of the color is more basic than the apparent color itself. Indeed, the facts of genetics would allow us to explain the change.

---

[3]Lewis Carroll (Charles Lutwidge Dodgson) was a mathematician. So Queen Victoria's inference—the last book was about Alice's amusing adventures, so the next one will be too—might not have been based on a too simple application of the principle of the uniformity of nature; it might also have reflected too small a sample for her inference.
[4]David Hume, *An Enquiry Concerning Human Understanding* (1748), Section 4, Part II.

So, inductive arguments provide some, but not conclusive, evidence for their conclusions. Arguments concerning the future—and, therefore, all universal generalizations—assume the principle of the uniformity of nature, which cannot be proven to be true. The criteria for judging inductive arguments are *guidelines* for judging the relative strength of an inductive argument; they generally do *not* give you grounds for claiming conclusively that an argument is acceptable or unacceptable.

> **ESSENTIAL** HINTS
>
> In preindustrial England, there was a common white moth. The members of the same species of moth today are usually black. The change is explained by the principle of natural selection. As buildings became more covered with soot, the black members of the species had greater survival value: They could not be as easily seen by their natural enemies. So, moths with the gene for blackness reproduced; most of those with the gene for whiteness were killed.

In the remainder of this chapter we are going to examine arguments by analogy (9.2–9.3) and arguments to the best explanation as they're found in science and everyday life (9.5).

9.2   ARGUMENTS BY ANALOGY

Of the many kinds of inductive arguments, perhaps the one used most frequently is argument by analogy. **To draw an *analogy* between two or more entities is to indicate one or more respects in which they are similar.** *Analogical arguments* **conclude that two or more things are alike in some respect because they are alike in some other respect(s).** Since we use analogies even for such basic activities as classifying objects as objects of certain kinds, arguments by analogy are arguably the most basic kind of inductive argument. For example, one reason why whales are classified as mammals rather than fish is that they are like paradigmatic mammals—for example, dogs, cats, cows, humans—in more ways than they are like paradigmatic fish—for example, trout, bass, barracudas.[5]

Analogy is the basis of many kinds of ordinary reasoning. It uses past experience to predict what the future will hold. Since they are inductive, analogical arguments are not classified as valid or invalid; their conclusions have varying degrees of probability that are attached to them depending on factors discussed below. First, here are two examples of arguments by analogy.

> Some people look on preemployment testing of teachers as unfair—a kind of double jeopardy. "Teachers are already college graduates," they say. "Why should they be tested?" That's easy. Lawyers are college graduates and graduates of professional school, too, but they have to take a bar exam. And a number of other professions ask prospective members to prove that they know their stuff by taking and passing examinations: accountants, actuaries, doctors, architects. There is no reason why teachers shouldn't be required to do this too.[6]

---

[5]More recent ways to classify living things concern their genealogies.
[6]Albert Shanker, "Testing Teachers," *New York Times*, 8 January 1995.

CHARACTERISTICS OF ARGUMENT BY ANALOGY

Checkers and chess have lots of things in common. They are played on the same kind of board by two players who try to capture each other's pieces; they are both games; there is usually a winner and a loser; and they both have a set of rules that must be obeyed. Since checkers is an easy game to master, chess must be, too.

Checkers   Chess

This example illustrates some of the characteristics of argument by analogy as well as some of the ways such an argument might be refuted. Checkers and chess do indeed have all the characteristics mentioned in the premises in common. But they also have important differences, not the least of which is that chess has a greater variety of pieces each of which moves and captures opposing pieces in a different way. These differences make mastering chess more difficult than mastering checkers.

In this case the analogy asserted is that teachers are like other kinds of professionals (accountants, doctors, lawyers, etc.), and the argument is that because teachers are like these other professionals in given respects, teachers should have to take accreditation exams just as those other professionals do.

> We may observe a very great similitude between this earth which we inhabit, and the other planets—Saturn, Jupiter, Mars, Venus, and Mercury. They all revolve round the sun, as the earth does, although at different distances and in different periods. They borrow all their light from the sun, as the earth does. Several of them are known to revolve around their axis like the earth, and by that means, must have a like succession of day and night. Some of them have moons that serve to give them light in the absence of the sun, as our moon does to us. They are all, in their motions, subject to the same law of gravitation as the earth is. From all this similitude, it is not unreasonable to think that those planets may, like our earth, be the habitation of various orders of living creatures. There is some probability in this conclusion from analogy.[7]

Here the analogy is between the earth and the other planets in the solar system in terms of physical characteristics. The argument by analogy starts from this set of similarities as a premise, and concludes that since the earth has life, the other

---

[7]Thomas Reid, *Essays on the Intellectual Powers of Man*, Essay 1, 1785.

planets in the solar system probably have life, too. The author recognizes that this conclusion is only probable to some degree; an analogy in some respects is no guarantee that a further similarity exists, and there may be other factors that would decrease the probability we attach to the conclusion if we knew them.

It is important to note that there are many times when analogies are not used as arguments. The literary devices of metaphor and simile are obvious cases where analogy is not used to support a conclusion. For example, in the statement, "Lit from beneath by banks of floodlights, the church's two bell towers rose like stalwart sentinels above the building's long body,"[8] the comparison to sentinels describes the church's bell towers. Another important nonargumentative use of analogy is in explanation, when we use an analogy to compare something unfamiliar with something more familiar, for the sake of clarity rather than to prove a point. For example, a math teacher might explain how to do one problem by comparing it with another you already know how to do.

NONARGUMENTATIVE ANALOGY

At the beginning of the twentieth century, physicists used common knowledge of the sun and the planets as a picture to imagine how atoms and electrons act. The electrons were thought of as revolving around the nucleus in the way the planets revolved around the sun. Of course the physicists made sure that this picture was not to be taken literally, nor was it to be used as evidence that the atomic structure really worked the way the solar system did. They were using the analogy in an explanatory rather than in an argumentative way.

Every analogical inference proceeds from the similarity of two or more things in one or more respects to the similarity of those things in some further respect. The general form, or structure, of all analogical arguments is the following (where a, b, c, and d are any entities and P, Q, and R are any attributes or "respects" in which the entities are similar):

> a,b,c,d all have the attributes P and Q.
> a,b,c all have the attribute R.
> Therefore, d probably has the attribute R.

---

[8] Dan Brown, *The Da Vinci Code* (New York: Doubleday, 2003), p. 54.

In identifying, and especially in appraising, analogical arguments, it may be helpful to recast them into this form.

EXERCISES

The following passages contain analogies. Try to distinguish those that contain analogical arguments from those that make nonargumentative uses of analogy:

1. You will like the lasagna at this restaurant. You already tried their pizza, manicotti, and spaghetti, and you said you enjoyed each of them.

2. I once ate the meat of a cooked king cobra. It tasted a lot like chicken.

3. Your brother was a math major, had a GPA above 3.0, took this class in his junior year, and passed it with no problem. You are a math major, your GPA is above 3.0, and you are in your junior year, so you should pass this course with no problem.

4. It has been shown that listening to classical music improves the performance of humans, monkeys, apes, chickens, and pigs on intelligence tests. All these animals have at least two legs. Therefore, any animal with at least two legs will perform better on an intelligence test after listening to classical music.

5. Do you know what it's like getting a tooth pulled without any painkilling drugs? Well that's what it was like watching that awards show last night.

6. If you have ever been in love before and then broken up, then you know how hard it is to break up. So if you are ever in love again, take my advice and don't break up.

7. The Greeks created a great empire but then declined. The Romans created a great empire and also declined. So although the United States is now a great empire, it will also eventually decline.

8. "I'm not anti-Semitic, I'm just anti-Zionist" is the equivalent of "I'm not anti-American, I just think the United States shouldn't exist."

   —Benjamin Netanyahu, *A Place Among the Nations*
   (Bantam Books, 1993)

9. It is true that science has become so specialized, even a good education in basic science does not prepare one to be expert in all science. But the same is true of nonscientific pursuits. That historians, for example, have become experts in particular periods or areas (the history of the military, perhaps, or of science or economics) has not dissuaded us from teaching history.

   —Bruce J. Sobol, *Current Issues and Enduring Questions*
   (Boston: St. Martin's Press, 1990)

10. Talking about Christianity without saying anything about sin is like discussing gardening without saying anything about weeds.

    —The Rev. Lord Soper, quoted in *The New York Times*, 24 Dec 1998

11. Men and women may have different reproductive strategies, but neither can be considered inferior or superior to the other, any more than a bird's wings can be considered superior or inferior to a fish's fins.

    —David M. Buss, "Where is Fancy Bred? In the Genes or in the Head?"
    The New York Times, 1 June 1999

12. Thomas Henry Huxley, Charles Darwin's nineteenth-century disciple, presented this analogy: "Consciousness would appear to be related to the mechanism of the body simply as a collateral product of its working and to be completely without any power of modifying that working, as the steam whistle which accompanies the work of a locomotive is without influence upon its machinery."

13. Wittgenstein used to compare thinking with swimming: Just as in swimming our bodies have a natural tendency to float on the surface so that it requires great physical exertion to plunge to the bottom, so in thinking it requires great mental exertion to force our minds away from the superficial, down into the depth of a philosophical problem.

    —George Pitcher, *The Philosophy of Wittgenstein*

14. It is important that we make clear at this point what definition is and what can be attained by means of it. It seems frequently to be credited with a creative power; but all it accomplishes is that something is marked out in sharp relief and designated by a name. Just as the geographer does not create a sea when he draws boundary lines and says: "The part of the ocean's surface bounded by these lines I am going to call the Yellow Sea," so too the mathematician cannot really create anything by his defining.

    —Gottlob Frege, *The Basic Laws of Arithmetic*

15. Children in school are like children at the doctor's. He can talk himself blue in the face about how much good his medicine is going to do them; all they think of is how much it will hurt or how bad it will taste. Given their own way, they would have none of it. So the valiant and resolute band of travelers I thought I was leading toward a much hoped-for destination turned out instead to be more like convicts in a chain gang, forced under threat of punishment to move along a rough path leading nobody knew where and down which they could see hardly more than a few steps ahead. School feels like this to children: It is a place where *they* make you go and where *they* tell you to do things and where *they* try to make your life unpleasant if you don't do them or don't do them right.

    —John Holt, *How Children Fail*

9.3 APPRAISING ARGUMENTS BY ANALOGY

No argument by analogy is ever deductively valid, but some analogical arguments are more cogent than others. In this section we introduce criteria for evaluating arguments by analogy. They allow us to judge the relative strength of an argument by analogy.

The form of an argument by analogy is as follows: **If some number of objects all share a certain number of properties, then if all but one of those objects have some additional property, it is likely that the remaining object also has that additional property.**

Notice that there are four basic elements to an analogy. Let us call the **ground for the analogy** those objects having *all* the properties under consideration. So, if you have three objects, *A*, *B*, and *C*, each of which has properties *a*, *b*, and *c*, *A* and *B* also have property *d*, and the question is whether *C* also has property *d*, *A* and *B* are the ground for the analogy. Let us call the **objective extension of the analogy** the object compared to the ground of the analogy and which is known to have a number of properties in common with the objects in the ground. In the case above, *C* would be the objective extension. The **basis of an analogy** consists of those properties known to be common to the ground and the objective extension of the analogy. In the case above, *a*, *b*, and *c* are the basis of the analogy. The **problematic extension of an analogy** is that property common to objects in the ground not known to be a property of the objective extension. In the case above, the problematic extension is *d*.

Two commonplace examples will help show what factors make analogical arguments more (or less) effective. Suppose you choose to purchase a given pair of shoes because other pairs like it have given you satisfaction in the past; and suppose you select a dog of a given breed because other dogs of that same breed have exhibited the characteristics that you prize. In both cases analogical arguments have been relied upon. To appraise the strength of these sample arguments, and indeed all analogical arguments, six criteria may be distinguished.

1. Number of entities. If my past experience with shoes of a certain kind is limited to only one pair that I wore and liked, I will be disappointed with an apparently similar pair that I find flawed in unexpected ways. But if I have repeatedly purchased shoes just like those I liked, I may reasonably suppose that the next pair will be as good as the ones worn earlier. Several experiences of the same kind with the same kind of item will support the conclusion—that the purchase will be satisfying—much more than will a single instance. Each instance may be thought of as an additional entity, and the *number* of entities is the first criterion in evaluating an analogical argument.

In general, the larger the number of entities compared (the larger the ground for the analogy), the stronger the argument is. But there is no simple ratio between that number and the probability of the conclusion. Six happy experiences with golden retrievers, intelligent and sweet-tempered dogs, will lead you to conclude that the next golden retriever will be intelligent and sweet-tempered also. But the conclusion of the analogical argument having six instances in its premises will not be exactly three times as probable as a similar argument with two such instances in its premises. Increasing the number of entities is important, but other factors enter into the equation as well.

2. Number of similar respects. Among the instances mentioned in the premises, there may have been various similarities: Perhaps the shoes were of the same style, had the same price, and were made of the same sort of leather; perhaps the dogs were of the same breed, came from the same breeder at the same age, and so on. All the respects in which the instances mentioned in the premises are like one another, and also like the instance in the conclusion, increase the probability that the instance in the conclusion will have that further attribute at which the argument is aimed—giving great satisfaction in the case of the new shoes, being of a sweet disposition in the case of a new dog.

This criterion also is rooted in common sense: **The larger the number of respects in which the entity in the conclusion is similar to the entities in the premises (the more properties that are included in the basis), the more probable it is that the conclusion is true.** But again there is no simple numerical ratio between that conclusion and the number of similar respects identified.

3. Variety of the instances in the premises. If objects are similar in a number of ways, differences in characteristics among the objects mentioned can strengthen the analogy. If my previous purchases of those good shoes had been both from a department store and a specialty store, had been made both in New York and in California, and had been purchased by both mail order and direct sale, I may be confident that it is the shoes themselves and not their seller that accounts for my satisfaction. If my previous golden retrievers were both males and females, acquired both as puppies from breeders and as adults from the humane society, I may be more confident that it is their breed—not their sex or age or source—that accounts for my earlier satisfaction. **When a significant number of things are similar in a significant number of respects (when the ground and the basis are strong), differences among objects in the ground can *strengthen* the evidence for the conclusion of the analogy.**

4. Relevance. As important as the *number* of respects shared is the *kind* of respects in which the instances in the premises are like the instance in the conclusion. If the new pair of shoes, like the previous pairs, is purchased on a Tuesday, that is a likeness that will have no bearing on the satisfaction they give; but if the new pair, like all the previous pairs, had the same manufacturer, that will of course count heavily. **Respects add to the force of the argument when they are relevant, and a single highly relevant factor contributes more to the argument than a host of irrelevant similarities.**

Sometimes there will be disagreement about which attributes are relevant in establishing the likelihood of our conclusion. But the *meaning* of *relevance* itself is not in dispute. One attribute is relevant to another when it is connected to that other, when there is some kind of *causal relation* between them. That is why identifying causal connections of one kind or another is critical in analogical arguments, and why establishing such connections is often crucial in determining the admissibility of evidence, as relevant or irrelevant, in a court of law.[9]

Analogical arguments can be probable whether they go from cause to effect or from effect to cause. They can even be probable when the attribute in the premise is neither the cause nor the effect of the conclusion's attribute, provided both are the effect of the same cause. A doctor, noting the presence of a certain symptom in her patient, may predict another symptom accurately, not because either symptom is the cause of the other, but because they are jointly caused by the same disorder. The color of a car is irrelevant to its performance or reliability. The color might be relevant to a saleperson's ability to sell a car quickly.

5. Disanalogies. A *disanalogy* is a point of difference, a relevant respect in which objects in the ground for the analogy differ from those in the objective extension. Consider the example of the shoes. If the pair we plan to buy looks like those we had owned, but is much cheaper and made by a different company, those disanalogies will give us reason to doubt we'll be satisfied with the shoes.

What was earlier said about relevance is important here, too. Disanalogies undermine analogical arguments when the points of difference identified are relevant, causally connected to the outcome we are seeking. Investors often purchase shares of a stock mutual fund on the basis of its successful "track record," reasoning that since earlier purchases resulted in capital appreciation, a future purchase will do so as well. But if we learn that the person who had managed the fund during the period of its profitability has just been replaced, we confront a disanalogy substantially reducing the strength of that analogical argument.

Disanalogies weaken analogical arguments. They are often employed in *attacking* an analogical argument. As critics we may try to show that the case in the conclusion is different in important ways from the earlier cases, and that what was true of them is not likely to be true of it. In the law, where the uses of analogy are pervasive, some earlier case (or cases) will commonly be offered to a court as a precedent for deciding the case at hand. The argument is analogical. Opposing counsel will seek to *distinguish* the case at hand from the earlier cases; that is, counsel will seek to show that because there is some critical difference between the facts in the case at hand, and the facts in those earlier cases, they do not serve as good precedents in the present matter. If the differences are great, if the disanalogy is critical, it may succeed in demolishing the analogical argument that had been put forward.

Because disanalogies are the primary weapon against an analogical argument, whatever can ward off potential disanalogies will strengthen that argument. This explains why variety among the instances in the premises adds force to an argument, as noted in the third criterion. The more the instances in

---

[9]You might correctly infer that there is a connection between the third consideration and the fourth. When the objects in the ground for the analogy differ significantly in properties, the properties that are not common to them are not causally relevant.

the premises vary from one to another, the less likely it is that the critic can point to a relevant disanalogy between all of them and the conclusion that will weaken the argument. To illustrate: Kim Kumar comes to a university as a first year student; ten others from her secondary school had successfully completed studies at the same university. We may argue analogically that she is likely to succeed as well. If, however, all those other students are similar to one another in some respect that bears upon college study but *differ* from Kim in that respect—for example, having the good study and time-management skills that Kim lacks—that disanalogy will undermine the argument for Kim's success. But if we learn that the ten successful predecessors varied among themselves in many ways—in economic background, in family relations, in religious affiliation, and so on, those differences among them ward off such potential disanalogies. The argument for Kim's success is fortified—as we saw earlier—if the other students from her school mentioned in the premises do not resemble each other closely, but exhibit substantial variety.

A confusion must be avoided. The principle that disanalogies weaken analogical arguments is to be contrasted with the principle that differences among the premises strengthen such arguments. In the former, the differences are between the instances in the premises and the instance in the conclusion; in the latter differences are among the instances in the premises only. A disanalogy is a difference between the cases with which we have had experience and the case about which a conclusion is being drawn. In presenting the disanalogy as refutation we may say that conclusion is not warranted because circumstances in the critical case are not similar to circumstances in earlier cases. The analogy is said to be *strained*; the analogy *does not hold*. But when we point to dissimilarities among the premises we are strengthening the argument by saying, in effect, that the analogy has wide force, that it holds in cases like this and in other cases, and that therefore the respects in which the instances in the premises vary are not relevant to the matter with which the conclusion is concerned.

In sum: Disanalogies undermine an analogical argument; dissimilarities among the premises reinforce it. And both considerations are tied to the question of relevance: Disanalogies tend to show that there are relevant respects in which the case in the conclusion differs from those in the premises; dissimilarities among the premises tend to show that what might have been thought causally relevant to the attribute of interest is not relevant at all.

Notice that the very first criterion identified, pertaining to the *number* of entities among which the analogy is said to hold, is also linked to relevance. The greater the number of instances appealed to, the greater is the number of dissimilarities likely to obtain among them. Increasing the number of entities is therefore desirable—but as the number of entities increases, the impact of each additional case is reduced, since the dissimilarity it may provide is the more likely to have been provided by earlier instances—in which case it will add little or nothing to the protection of the conclusion from damaging disanalogies.

ARGUMENT BY ANALOGY

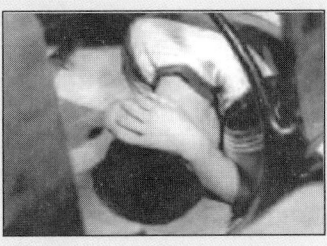

Here is an argument by analogy from a 1950s Civil Defense film.

"We all know the atomic bomb is very dangerous. Since it may be used against us, we must get ready for it, just as we are ready for many other dangers that are around us all the time. Fire is a danger. It can burn whole buildings if someone is careless. But we are ready for fires. We have a fine fire department to put out the fire, and you have fire drills in your school so you will know what to do. Automobiles can be dangerous too. They sometimes cause bad accidents. But we are ready. We have safety rules that car drivers and people who are walking must obey. Now we must be ready for a new danger, the atomic bomb." The argument has the following structure:

Fires are dangerous, automobiles are dangerous, and atom bombs are dangerous.
We can avoid the dangers of fires and automobiles by being ready and knowing what to do.
Therefore we can avoid the danger of atomic attack by being ready and knowing what to do.

This argument is vulnerable to many possible disanalogies. For one, although fires, automobiles, and atomic bombs do all pose dangers, the kinds of dangers they pose are not comparable. Atomic bombs are vastly more destructive than fires or automobiles. For another, the measures we can take to protect against accidental fires and automobile accidents are of known effectiveness. The measures proposed for protecting against atomic bomb attacks on the other hand are of unknown—and doubtful—effectiveness.

6. Claim that the conclusion makes. Every argument makes the claim that its premises give reasons to accept its conclusion. It is easy to see that the more one claims, the greater the burden of sustaining that claim, and that is true for every analogical argument. The *weakness or modesty of the conclusion relative to the premises* is critical in determining the merit of the inference.

If my friend gets 30 miles to the gallon from his new car, I may infer that were I to acquire a car of the same make and model, I would get at least 20 miles to the gallon. That conclusion is weak and therefore very probable. Were my conclusion much stronger—say, that I would get at least 29 miles to the gallon—it would be less well supported by the evidence I have. In general, **the weaker the conclusion the less burden is placed upon the premises and**

the stronger the argument; the stronger the conclusion the greater is the burden on the premises and the weaker the argument. Remember, the strength of the conclusion is determined by the ease with which it can be shown to be false.

An analogical argument is strengthened by reducing the strength of the conclusion on the basis of the premises affirmed, or by retaining the claim unchanged while supporting it with additional or more powerful premises. Likewise, an analogical argument is weakened if its conclusion is made stronger while its premises remain unchanged, or if the claim remains unchanged while the evidence in its support is found to exhibit greater frailty.

EXERCISES

I. For the following arguments by analogy, six alternative premises are suggested. Identify the analogy, and the argument that is based on it. Then, decide whether each of the alternative premises would strengthen or weaken the conclusion if added to the original argument. Identify the criterion that justifies your judgment in each case, and explain how that criterion applies.

1. Imagine two physicians discussing a patient: "The results of our tests revealed a low white blood cell count, low blood pressure, a rash on the abdomen, and loss of appetite. These are the classic symptoms found in every case of Rhett-Butler syndrome. Although this is a rare disease, there have been at least 1,000 recorded cases, and the disease has been found in both men and women. Therefore, we are going to prescribe the recommended treatment for this patient who probably has the disease."

   a. Suppose there had been only five recorded cases of those particular symptoms connected with the disease.

   b. Suppose the recorded cases had all been men and the current patient is a woman.

   c. Suppose two additional symptoms were found to hold between the current patient and the recorded cases.

   d. Suppose we noticed that all the recorded cases were of people who had a middle name, but this patient does not have a middle name.

   e. Suppose we find out that none of the recorded cases were people with Type-O blood, but that this patient has Type-O blood.

   f. Suppose the medical literature relates that only 70 percent of people with these specific four symptoms actually have the disease.

2. The actress Tragedia Comix has made eight movies—comedies and dramas—in the last ten years that have grossed, on average, over $200 million. Her newest movie, a comedy, is going to be released this month. It, too, will probably gross over $200 million.

   a. Suppose Tragedia had been in sixteen movies instead of eight that grossed over $200 million.

   b. Suppose only Tragedia's dramatic films, not her comedies, had grossed over $200 million.

   c. Suppose the previous movies had dealt with both historical and contemporary subjects, and that the new movie has a contemporary setting.

   d. Suppose all of the previous movies were released over the summer, as the new movie will be.

   e. Suppose the previous movies were all made in the United States, whereas the new movie was made elsewhere.

   f. Suppose the conclusion is that the new movie will gross exactly $200 million.

3. A faithful alumnus, heartened by State's winning its last four football games, decides to bet his money that State will win its next game, too.

   a. Suppose that since the last game, State's outstanding quarterback was injured in practice and hospitalized for the remainder of the season.

   b. Suppose that two of the last four games were played away, and that two of them were home games.

   c. Suppose that, just before the game, it is announced that a member of State's Chemistry Department has been awarded a Nobel Prize.

   d. Suppose that State had won its last six games rather than only four of them.

   e. Suppose that it has rained hard during each of the four preceding games, and that rain is forecast for next Saturday, too.

   f. Suppose that each of the last four games was won by a margin of at least four touchdowns.

4. Although she was bored by the last few foreign films she saw, Charlene agrees to go to see another one this evening, fully expecting to be bored again.

   a. Suppose that Charlene also was bored by the last few American movies she saw.

   b. Suppose that the star of this evening's film has recently been accused of bigamy.

   c. Suppose that the last few foreign films seen by Charlene were Italian, and that tonight's film is Italian as well.

   d. Suppose that Charlene was so bored by the other foreign films that she actually fell asleep during the performance.

   e. Suppose that the last few foreign films she saw included an Italian, a French, an English, and a Swedish film.

   f. Suppose that tonight's film is a mystery, whereas all of those she saw before were comedies.

5. Bill has taken three history courses and found them very stimulating and valuable. So he signs up for another one, confidently expecting that it, too, will be worthwhile.

   a. Suppose that his previous history courses were in ancient history, modern European history, and American history.

   b. Suppose that his previous history courses had all been taught by the same professor that is scheduled to teach the present one.

   c. Suppose that his previous history courses all had been taught by Professor Smith, and the present one is taught by Professor Jones.

   d. Suppose that Bill had found his three previous history courses to be the most exciting intellectual experiences of his life.

   e. Suppose that his previous history courses had all met at 9:00 a.m., and that the present one is scheduled to meet at 9:00 a.m., also.

   f. Suppose that, in addition to the three history courses previously taken, Bill also had taken and enjoyed courses in anthropology, economics, political science, and sociology.

II. Analyze the structures of the analogical arguments in the following passages and evaluate them in terms of the six criteria that have been explained.

6. If you cut up a large diamond into little bits, it will entirely lose the value it had as a whole; and an army divided up into small bodies of soldiers, loses all its strength. So a great intellect sinks to the level of an ordinary one, as soon as it is interrupted and disturbed, its attention distracted and drawn off from the matter in hand: For its superiority depends upon its power of concentration—of bringing all its strength to bear upon one theme, in the same way as a concave mirror collects into one point all the rays of light that strike upon it.
    —Arthur Schopenhauer, "On Noise"

7. Every species of plant or animal is determined by a pool of germ plasm that has been most carefully selected over a period of hundreds of millions of years. We can understand now why it is that mutations in these carefully selected organisms almost invariably are detrimental. The situation can be suggested by a statement made by Dr. J. B. S. Haldane: My clock is not keeping perfect time. It is conceivable that it will run better if I shoot a bullet through it; but it is much more probable that it will stop altogether. Professor George Beadle, in this connection, has asked, "What is the chance that a typographical error would improve *Hamlet?*"
    —Linus Pauling, *No More War!*

8. The philosopher Metrodorus of Chios, who lived in the fourth century B.C., was greatly interested in the heavenly bodies. He wrote: "To consider the Earth as the only populated world in infinite space is as absurd as to assert that in an entire field of millet, only one grain will grow."

9. If a single cell, under appropriate conditions, becomes a person in the space of a few years, there can surely be no difficulty in understanding how, under appropriate conditions, a cell may, in the course of untold millions of years, give origin to the human race.
    —Herbert Spencer, *Principles of Biology*

10. Just as the bottom of a bucket containing water is pressed more heavily by the weight of the water when it is full than when it is half empty, and the more heavily the deeper the water is, similarly the high places of the earth, such as the summits of mountains, are less heavily pressed than the lowlands are by the weight of the mass of the air. This is because there is more air above the lowlands than above the mountain tops; for all the air along a mountainside presses upon the lowlands but not upon the summit, being above the one but below the other.
    —Blaise Pascal, *Treatise on the Weight of the Mass of the Air*

11. One cannot require that everything shall be defined, any more than one can require that a chemist shall decompose every substance. What is simple cannot be decomposed, and what is logically simple cannot have a proper definition.
    —Gottlob Frege, "On Concept and Object"

12. Opposing legislation that would restrict handgun ownership in the United Kingdom, the husband of Queen Elizabeth II reasoned as follows:

    Look, if a cricketer, for instance, suddenly decided to go into a school and batter a lot of people to death with a cricket bat, which he could do very easily, are you going to ban cricket bats?
    —Prince Philip, the Duke of Edinburgh,
    in an interview on the BBC, 19 December 1996

9.4   EXPLANATIONS AND HYPOTHESES

Explanations answer the questions "Why?" or "How?" Explanations increase our understandings of the world. When we don't know why something happened, we propose a **hypothesis**. A hypothesis is a proposed answer to a question or solution to a problem. The hypothesis, if true, would explain why the **phenomenon**, the event or circumstance to be explained, is as it is.

In this section, we examine the criteria for evaluating explanations. We discuss the criteria for evaluating hypotheses. We examine how the criteria apply in various circumstances and examine several cases. In applying these criteria you assume that the hypothesis has all the properties you look for in *any* discourse. (a) The hypothesis must not merely redescribe the phenomenon in other words. (b) The hypothesis must be free from ambiguities. (c) The hypothesis must be consistent; it must not entail self-contradictory statements. (d) The hypothesis and the predictions made on the basis of the hypothesis must be precise.

Hypotheses explain why a phenomenon is as it is. Hypotheses provide the basis for **predictions** and **retrodictions**. A prediction is a claim that some phenomenon will occur in a specified set of circumstances. A retrodiction is a claim that some phenomenon has occurred in a specified set of circumstances. Retrodictions are common in historical studies. Predictions and retrodictions provide the basis for testing a hypothesis. So, the first criterion for the adequacy of a hypothesis is:

H1: A hypothesis must be testable

How do you test a hypothesis?

Assume one morning I get into my car, turn the key, and nothing happens. Why won't my car start? I propose a hypothesis: The battery is dead. If the battery is dead, this would explain why the car won't start. If I'm going to test my hypothesis, there must be a procedure. Knowing a bit about cars, I propose the following conditional:

> If the battery is dead and I connect my battery by jumper cables to the battery of a functioning car, then my car will start.

So, I connect jumper cables between my car and my son's car, start his car, and try to start mine. *Voilà!* The car starts. Have I discovered the cause of my problem? Probably. Although we'll see there are additional considerations that strengthen the evidence, the test tends to **confirm** my hypothesis. The evidence tends to show that my hypothesis is true. It reflects the second criterion for the acceptability of a hypothesis:

H2: If predictions based upon a hypothesis are true, this tends to show that the hypothesis is true

Hypotheses are cheap. The only hypotheses that are valuable are those that can be tested. For example, if my hypothesis had been, "The gods of General Motors are frowning upon me this morning," I could not have tested the hypothesis. But the value of the hypothesis is not primarily in the fact that I made a prediction that worked. The value of the hypothesis is in the fact that if my prediction had failed, I would have shown that the hypothesis is false. Remember, I *do not* know that the problem is with the battery. All I know is that, *if the hypothesis is true*, then the test procedure will result in a functioning car. The test procedure, when successful, provides some evidence that the battery was dead. You're arguing from the effect (the running car) to the supposed cause (the dead battery). It is a case of affirming the consequent.[10]

What happens if the car does *not* start? Then I have shown that the hypothesis is false. It's a case of *modus tollens*. The argument goes like this:

> If the battery is dead and I connect my battery by jumper cables to the battery of a functioning car, then my car will start.
> The car did not start.
> _____
> So, (by *modus tollens*) it is not the case that both the battery is dead and I have connected my jumper cables to the battery of a functioning car.
> _____
> So, (by De Morgan's theorem) either the battery is not dead or I have not connected by jumper cables to the battery of a functioning car.
> I have connected by jumper cables to the battery of a functioning car.
> _____
> So, (by Double Negation and Disjunctive Syllogism) the battery is not dead.

This is sufficient to **falsify** the hypothesis, that is, to show that the hypothesis is false.[11] Notice that since there is no procedure to test the hypothesis, "The gods of General Motors are frowning upon me," it is impossible to falsify that hypothesis.

A third criterion for evaluating a hypothesis is:

H3: A hypothesis is more probably true if it has a broader explanatory scope, that is, if it explains more phenomena than alternative hypotheses.

Before rousing my son from his sonorous slumbers to start his car, I might ask whether my hypothesis will explain more than the fact that my car won't start. Knowing a bit a about the electrical system of the car, I propose a number of hypotheses.

> If the battery is dead and I turn on the lights, then the lights will not shine.
> If the battery is dead, I turn the switch to "auxiliary," and turn on the radio, then the radio will not work.
> If the battery is dead, I turn the switch to "on," and try to lower my electric windows, then the windows will not go down.
> If the battery is dead, I turn the switch to "auxiliary," and turn on the windshield wipers, then the windshield wipers will not work.

I do the appropriate tests. Each prediction is realized. These tests, together with the jumper cable test, reflect **consilience**. Consilience is the tendency of several forms of inductive evidence to point to the same conclusion.

---

[10]The problem might not have been that the battery was dead. For example, it might have been that the terminals on the battery were corroded, and while connecting the jumper cables I scraped off enough corrosion for the connections to be made.

[11]At least, it is sufficient in this simple case. In a complicated case, such as a hypothesis that is related to a scientific theory, predictive failure shows that either the hypothesis *or* some element of the theory is false. We'll look at examples of this below.

In practice, this criterion is particularly important when a hypothesis will explain an **anomaly**, a fact that cannot be explained on the basis of an accepted hypothesis or theory. The explanation of an anomaly together with any other facts that could be explained on the basis of an earlier hypothesis is often a basis for claiming the new hypothesis to be superior to the old one.

You should notice that throughout this example I have been concerned *only* with the assumption that the battery was dead. I *could* have had a more complex hypothesis; for example, the battery is dead and the fuel pump is not functioning. My dead-battery hypothesis was simpler in the sense that it involves fewer theoretical assumptions. Generally speaking,

H4: If either of two hypotheses will explain a phenomenon and one involves fewer theoretical assumptions, the hypothesis that involves fewer assumptions is more probably true.

This is sometimes known as the **Principle of Parsimony** or **Ockham's Razor** for the thirteenth-century English philosopher who championed the principle. The principle of parsimony, like considerations of scope, tends to unify our understanding of a phenomenon or a collection of phenomena. Further, the smaller the number of theoretical assumptions, the easier it is to falsify the hypothesis (theory). So, if it is possible to explain why my car won't start on the basis of a dead battery alone, that is more probably the cause than a dead battery *and* something else. A more interesting case is this. If it is possible to explain all psychological phenomena on the basis of physiological phenomena (states of the nervous system), it is likely that a physiological explanation of psychological states is true.

You also should notice that my hypotheses did not occur in a vacuum. Like almost anyone who has driven a car for a few years, I know a little bit about how they work. I know, for example, that cars are *not* powered by squirrels running on a treadmill. My hypotheses were consistent with theories of automotive mechanics. Generally,

H5: A hypothesis is more probably true if it is consistent with the best theoretical explanations available.

This requires a couple of remarks. (1) The theory guides you regarding what are *probably* relevant hypotheses. I might know little about the workings of cars, but I know that when it doesn't start it's usually either a problem with the electrical system or the fuel system. I might also know that a dead battery is one of the most common reasons a car won't start. So, I start there. (2) Theories explain. If there is a widely confirmed theory—a theory in electronics, or chemistry, or mechanics, etc.—and it explains why your hypothesis is reasonable, you have reason to believe that your hypothesis is true. As we'll see below, one of the grounds on which hypotheses are accepted is that they fit into an established theoretical framework. This is a matter of theoretical consistency. (3) Theoretical explanations are conservative. If there is already an explanation of a phenomenon, a novel explanation must be shown to be superior to the accepted theory on the basis of the other criteria for accepting a hypothesis. In particular, it must explain something that the accepted theory does not explain.

There is one more theoretical virtue that should be mentioned, a virtue that I cannot tie to my dead-battery case.

H6: A hypothesis is more probably true if it is fruitful, that is, if it predicts previously unknown phenomena.

A hypothesis is fruitful if it correctly predicts previously unknown phenomena. Among the phenomena predicted by Einstein's General Theory of Relativity was that light rays near massive bodies appear to be bent. This prediction could be tested during a solar eclipse. During a solar eclipse the moon blocks the sun's light and stars very close to the sun's edge become visible. It is the light from these stars that passes through the sun's gravitational field. If Einstein's General Theory is correct, then it should correctly predict the apparent position of these stars during a solar eclipse. Observations made during a total eclipse in 1919 showed that the apparent positions of the stars were exactly as Einstein had predicted. His theory was fruitful.

Since we propose hypotheses to solve everyday problems, let's start with a few cases of trouble-shooting before turning to the confirmation of scientific theories.

We engage in trouble-shooting every day. For many people, it is an integral part of their daily jobs—they call it "diagnosis." When trouble-shooting, criteria **H1**, **H2**, and **H5** play the principal roles, with **H3** playing a subordinate role. Typically, you're looking for *one* cause of the phenomenon, so **H4** (simplicity) is implicit. For example, assume you walk into your apartment one evening and turn on a lamp. Nothing happens. Immediately a number of hypotheses come to mind, any one of which would explain why the lamp won't work:

1. The electricity is off in the city.
2. The electricity is off to your house.
3. The bulb burned out.
4. The switch is broken.
5. There is a short in the cord.

Each of these is based on your theoretical understanding of how lamps work (**H5**). If you have evidence that is inconsistent with the hypothesis, the hypothesis must be rejected. You glance out the window and notice that the street lights are on, as are the lights in the house next door. So, (1) is rejected. You click on the switch on another lamp. Behold, there was light! So, (2) is rejected. Given your experience with light bulbs, (3) is the favored hypothesis.

So you test the hypothesis (**H1**). You change the bulb. It still doesn't work. So, you reject (3). Now things become serious. To test (4) you'd have to go to a store to buy a new switch, and then install it. So, you might skip (4) and go to (5). If there is a short in the cord, *sometimes* that causes the circuit-breaker to click off. So, you test that hypothesis by visiting the breaker-box (**H3**). The breaker is on. If there is a short in the cord, *sometimes* jiggling the cord in various ways causes the lamp to flicker. You try it, and nothing happens. So, you're relatively confident that the problem is in the switch. You replace the switch and install the original bulb. The lamp works. So, the problem was the switch, right?

One day, while listening to my favorite tape, my boom box stopped. My experiences with boom boxes suggested three hypotheses.

1. There is a short in the electrical cord.
2. There is a short inside the machine, either (a) in the tape player or (b) at some other place in the machine.
3. The belt running the tape player broke.

I did an easy test. I flipped the switch from "tape" to "radio" and heard the appropriate noises. This tended to show that there was not a short in the cord (not hypothesis 1) and that there was not a short in some part of the machine distinct from the tape recorder (not hypothesis 2b). Of course, I've had experience with power cords. I know that *sometimes* a short in a power cord can be reconnected by a gentle nudge, which could have happened when I turned on the radio. So, I nudged, twisted, and tugged on the power cord a few times. The radio stayed on. I had better reason to believe that the problem was not in the power cord (not hypothesis 1). So, I was reduced to hypotheses (2b) and (3). If it was an electrical short in the tape player, I'd have to buy a new machine. *I* don't know how to find electrical shorts or defective transistors. My favorite stereo repair-person's motto is, "I don't fix boom boxes, since it would be cheaper for you to buy a new one." But testing hypothesis (3) was easy. After letting the boom box sit for a few days—there are always warnings about electrical build-up, so one must be careful!—I opened the back. The belt was broken. So, I installed a new belt, closed the back, and popped in a tape. The tape player ran, but the tape didn't sound quite right. Why was that? There were three hypotheses:

1. The heads are dirty. (They hadn't been cleaned for some time.)
2. The tape was bad.
3. I'd messed up the repairs.

Cleaning the heads made no difference. So, I put in a newish, commercially-produced tape. Things sounded find. So, I concluded (a) the problem with the boom box had been a broken belt, (b) I'd solved the problem by replacing the belt, and (c) there is at least one defective tape in my house.

In each of these cases we've considered alternative hypotheses. We rejected hypotheses when the predictions we made on the basis of them proved false. When the predictions we made on the basis of a hypothesis were true, we took that as a reason for believing the hypothesis was true. It is important to be open to alternative hypotheses when diagnosing the cause of a problem.

One day I was walking across my deck when I experienced a sharp pain in my foot and noticed blood flowing from a wound. I put a band-aid on the wound and thought little of it—except when I walked. Since the nails holding down the boards on my deck had worked their way up, I assumed I'd caught the head of a nail with my heel. My tetanus shots were up-to-date, so I wasn't concerned. After a few days, the wound became filled with pus. The medical book I consulted was very illuminating: "If a wound becomes filled with pus, you should visit a doctor." So, I visited my doctor and stated my nail hypothesis. I also mentioned that in some of the pus that had oozed out there appeared to be gray flecks. "Could the large grayish spot in the wound be a wooden sliver?" "No," he said, "that's just the infection." He prescribed an antibiotic salve and pills.

Was the doctor right? Yes and no. After a few days on the pills, there was no more pus. So, I assume the wound had been infected. The large grayish spot remained. It also felt as if I was walking on a small board. After a couple weeks, I clipped away the dead skin and removed a large gray piece of wood. I'm convinced that stating my nail-hypothesis blinded the doctor to alternatives.

EXERCISES

For each of the following, state a hypotheses or a series of hypotheses that would explain why the phenomenon occurs. Develop a test procedure to determine which hypothesis is most likely correct. Explain why you place confidence in your procedure.

1. It's 10:00 in the morning. You missed the test in your 8:00 class. You intended to go, but did not hear your alarm clock. How did that happen?

2. Assume you own a HP Inkjet printer. Recently you've noticed that the documents you print often are smeared. There are lines of ink where there should not be such lines. You consult the manual, and it suggests three possible causes. (1) The ink jets are clogged. (2) You are using the wrong paper. (3) Ink has accumulated on various parts of the printer, and needs to be washed off with warm water. You're using the same kind of paper you've always used. How would you test the hypotheses?

3. The toilet in your apartment occasionally "runs." You flush it, and everything is fine, but about an hour later there is the sound characteristic of the tank filling, a sound which lasts for about thirty seconds. The tank never overflows. You examine the objects inside the tank and conclude that the problem is with either (1) the float, (2) the flush valve, (3) the tank ball, or (4) the ball seat (the gasket under the tank ball). You know that the tank ball is raised when you flush. The tank fills until the float reaches a certain level, at which point the flush valve closes. How would you determine the probable cause of the problem?

4. You taped a movie on your VCR. After watching the movie, you popped the cassette out and put it away. You did not rewind, since you wanted to tape another movie in a few days. When you taped the second movie you discovered that the tape had rewound a bit, and in taping the second movie, you'd taped over the last minute or two of the previous movie. You are puzzled. You'd programmed the VCR to tape two T.V. shows on the same night—with an hour between the end of the first and the beginning of the second—there had been no problem. What probably happened? How can you prevent such problems in the future?

5. Your automatic drip coffee maker occasionally pours coffee grounds into the carafe. When it does so, the coffee filter had collapsed. Usually there is no problem. Usually when you're done, the wet filter is neatly sticking to the sides of the basket. You usually have problems with grounds in your coffee only when you're near the bottom of your box of filters and the filter doesn't sit neatly in the basket with its sides uniformly along the sides of the basket. How can you solve the problem?

9.5 ARGUMENTS TO THE BEST EXPLANATION

Cases of trouble-shooting provide illustrations of arguments to the best explanation. You propose alternative hypotheses which, if true, would explain the phenomenon. You test them. When you reach the desired result, you figure your hypothesis was correct. Trouble-shooting assumes the don't-mess-with-success approach to choosing the best explanation. If you're successful, doesn't that mean your hypothesis was correct? No. Sometimes by "fixing" one thing, you inadvertently change something else that was the actual cause of the problem. We've all "fixed" something at one time or another, only to find that the problem reappears a few days or weeks later. This suggests that the hypothesis we accepted was false or that our explanation of the phenomenon was incomplete. Replacing a blown fuse might explain why your toaster won't work. But if you pop a slice of bread in the toaster and the result is blowing another fuse, you would need to find out why the circuit is overloaded.

Knowledge develops slowly over time. We propose and test hypotheses. Hypotheses are explained in terms of more general hypotheses or **theories**. An explanatory theory consists of a number of well-confirmed, interrelated hypotheses which explain phenomena of a certain kind. More general hypotheses or statements of natural law explain the less general hypotheses. Theories unify diverse phenomena. They are broad in scope (**H3**). So, let's look at the possible explanations of an airplane crash and some cases confirming scientific hypotheses.

On August 2, 1947, the British airliner *Stardust* left Buenos Aires, Argentina. It's destination was Santiago, Chili. It never arrived. The experienced crew of four contacted air traffic control in Santiago four minutes before it was due to arrive, suggesting that it was on course. It sent another message in Morse code, "S.E.N.D.E.C." When the tower requested clarification, the same message was sent twice more. Then the plane disappeared. This was a period before commercial flights were tracked by radar and before there were radio guidance systems. It was a period when air-to-ground communications could be made only in Morse code except when a plane was very close to its destination.

An air search was undertaken. Nothing was found. This led to various hypotheses. (1) Sabotage was suggested. It was suggested that this would also explain the disappearance of two other planes from the same airline within months of each other (**H3**). (2) Since one of the passengers on the plane was a messenger of King George VI, and since Britain and Argentina were not on good terms at the time, it was suggested that the plane had been blown up. (3) And there was the UFO hypothesis: The plane had been abducted by aliens. This, it was said, might also explain *Stardust*'s mysterious final message (**H3**).

None of the explanations was very good. If the plane had been sabotaged or blown up, you would expect that some remnants of the plane would be found. None was. There is a further problem with sabotage. If the plane had been sabotaged—if there had been a conspiracy to destroy the plane—the hypothesis would be plausible only if there were evidence of a conspiracy. Conspiracy theories are very popular. Historians say that conspiracy theories usually make for bad history. If there is a conspiracy, you need to show that various people worked together toward a specific end. To show that this is *possible*, there must be a way for the conspirators to communicate. You would expect some of the conspirators to be in the same area at the same time. Without evidence that the conspirators met together, it is *improbable* that there was a conspiracy. Even if the alleged conspirators were acquaintances and met together, one has no ground for claiming that there *probably* was a conspiracy unless there is further evidence. Written evidence (letters and papers) or known active participation in the act itself is evidence of a conspiracy. Given these considerations, there is good evidence of conspiracies to assassinate President Lincoln and to destroy the World Trade Center Towers. There is far less evidence that there was a conspiracy to assassinate President Kennedy.[12] There was *no* evidence of a conspiracy to sabotage the *Stardust*. No possible conspirators were identified. There was no physical evidence of sabotage, since the plane literally disappeared. The sabotage hypothesis was pure speculation.

The UFO hypothesis is dubious on theoretical grounds. Plausible explanations are always conservative. They are based on the best available theories (**H5**). Alien beings do not fit into current scientific accounts of the world. Further, introducing alien life-forms into explanatory theories would yield a far more complicated theory than is currently available. So, considerations of simplicity (**H4**) suggest that *if* the phenomenon could be explained without the introduction of extraterrestrials, it would be a superior explanation by criteria **H4** and **H5**. Further, although the UFO hypothesis might explain other odd phenomena (**H3**)—crop circles, accounts of alien abduction by the alleged victims, strange lights in the sky, etc.—it was not testable (**H1**) nor could it provide the basis for predictions (**H2**) in the case of the *Stardust*. The UFO hypothesis was pure speculation.

Fifty-three years after its disappearance, pieces of the *Stardust* and some human remains were found on Mount Tupangato, fifty miles from Santiago. This called the UFO hypothesis further into question. An expedition by the Chilean army found about ten percent of the plane in an area about one kilometer square. The spread of the wreckage was *inconsistent* with what should have been found if the plane had been destroyed by a bomb, which called hypotheses related to sabotage further into doubt. Further, the damage to the propellers indicated that the plane had flown directly into the mountain.

Finding the wreckage fifty miles off course at the bottom of a glacier on one of Chile's highest peaks raised a number of questions. How could the plane have been that far off course? Was the place the wreckage was found the place that the plane crashed?

A World War II fighter had been discovered in Greenland under 250 feet of ice. It had been deserted there with five other planes, and as the snows accumulated, the plane was frozen into the Greenland glacier. If the *Stardust* had crashed higher on the mountain, the wreckage eventually would have become part of the glacier. Glaciers move down mountains by gravitational attraction. As the glacier reaches more temperate areas of the mountain, it melts, thereby disgorging the objects it contains. So, investigators framed the hypothesis that the *Stardust* crashed high on the mountain, caused an avalanche, and became part of the glacier. The hypothesis can be tested by determining whether—as is predicted—more pieces of the plane and remains of the passengers and crew will be found at the bottom of the glacier in coming years. So, the

---

[12]One reason for this is a dispute regarding facts. Were all the shots fired from the textbook depository building, or were some shots fired from the grassy knoll? If shots were fired from several places, there would be *some* evidence of a conspiracy, but it would be consistent with the facts to claim that there were independent plots to kill the President.

hypothesis is testable (**H1**) by predicting events that will occur (**H2**) in the future. Further, it is consistent with the best scientific theory available (**H5**). And if it is correct, it explains something else as well (**H3**). The area near the top of Mount Tupangato was scanned for wreckage after the *Stardust* disappeared. Nothing was seen. Loud noises and shocks in glacial regions often cause avalanches. So, it is quite probable that crashing a plane into a glacier would cause an avalanche, covering the wreckage. This would explain why searchers flying over the area in 1947 saw no signs of the wreckage. So, on criteria **H1**, **H2**, **H3**, and **H5**, it is superior to the speculative hypotheses introduced in the aftermath of the disappearance. In addition, it is a theoretically simpler hypothesis than any of the alternatives (**H4**). So, it is currently the best explanation of the disappearance of *Stardust*. But that doesn't explain why the plane was fifty miles off course.

August 2, 1947, was a stormy day. On stormy days, pilots fly above the clouds. The *Stardust* was a converted Lancaster bomber. It was one of the most powerful airplanes of its time, and therefore capable of flying over high mountains. The jet stream flows at high altitudes above storms. The jet stream was unknown in 1947. So, the effects of the jet stream were not a part of navigational calculations made on the *Stardust*. This would explain the navigational error. Is it the only explanation? No, but it's probably the best explanation. Can you explain why?

Of course, none of this explains the mysterious Morse code message, "S.E.N.D.E.C.," which remains a mystery.[13]

Let's turn to some scientific discoveries and see how the criteria were used to confirm the hypotheses. Consider Marie Curie's discovery of radium.

Madam Curie. By the early nineteenth century, both physics and chemistry followed a mathematical model. Laws of nature, such as Newton's laws of motion, were described mathematically. Mathematical equations must be balanced. After Henri Becquerel discovered that uranium is radioactive, the use of an electrometer allowed scientists to determine the amount of radiation given off by a sample of uranium of a given size. Marie Curie developed an interest in uranium and examined samples of pitchblende, a uranium ore. The equations did not balance. Given the amount of uranium in the ore and other known components, the radioactivity was higher than it should have been. This was the occasion for Madame Curie's hypothesis that there was another, unknown, radioactive element in pitchblende, an element she called radium. Her hypothesis provided the basis for a prediction and test procedure (**H1**). If she could purify the uranium ore, she would be able to isolate an element with properties that would explain why the equations did not balance. Her hypothesis was simple. She *initially* contended that the difference in radioactivity could be explained by the presence of one element (**H4**). Pierre and Marie Curie spent three years extracting one decigram (1/10 gram) of pure radium from several

---

[13]For a more complete discussion of the *Stardust*, see *http://www.pbs.org/wgbh/nova/vanished/resources.html* and follow the links.

tons of pitchblende. Her hypothesis had to be revised, however. There were two elements that accounted for the difference in radioactivity. Several months before isolating radium, they isolated polonium, which was also unknown at the time. Since her prediction was true, this tended to confirm her hypothesis (**H2**). Her hypothesis was fruitful (**H6**). As her later work confirmed, it extended the domain of inquiry in numerous directions, including medicine.

But the confirmation of her hypothesis is not merely a case of extracting the elements from several tons of pitchblende. It also involved showing the place of her discovery within on-going scientific theory (**H5**). On-going theory provided the basis for claiming that her radium hypothesis was plausible even before she isolated the element.

The periodic table of the elements, developed by Dmitri Ivanovich Mendeleyev in the late nineteenth century, provided a systematic understanding of the known elements. This allowed Mendeleyev to predict the existence and chemical properties of gallium, germanium, and scandium in 1871, elements that were subsequently discovered. It also allowed Marie Curie to place radium within a general scheme and to describe its chemical properties in a systematic way. This **external consistency**, that is, consistency between claims made by Madam Curie's hypothesis for which there appeared to be evidence and the ongoing theoretical assumptions of the science of the time, was partially responsible for the acceptance of the discovery of polonium and radium.

Barry Marshall. There are times when a hypothesis is contrary to "common knowledge"—and, therefore seems to violate **H5**—but turns out to be true. In some cases, there are alternative explanatory models, and the issue is whether an explanatory model that has been successful in some other area can be extended to the case under examination.

Consider gastric ulcers (ulcers of the stomach). Twenty years ago, little was known of their cause.

> A stomach ulcer is a raw spot, often about 30mm (more than one inch) wide, that develops in the lining of the stomach. The exact cause of such ulcers is not known. There is evidence, however, that irritation of the stomach lining from bile juices from the duodenum is sometimes a factor.[14]

The cause of ulcers was assumed to be some combination of genetic and environmental factors,[15] and either stress or how persons react to stress was assumed to contribute to the occurrence of ulcers.[16] The typical treatment for ulcers was antacids and rest. About 95 percent of those so treated relapsed within two years.

---

[14]Jeffrey R. M. Kunz, editor-in-chief, *The American Medical Association Family Medical Guide* (New York: Random House, 1982), p. 465.

[15]Editors of *Prevention* Magazine Health Books, *Everyday Health Tips: 2000 Practical Hints for Better Health and Happiness* (Emmaus, PA: Rodale Press, 1988), p. 19.

[16]Sharon Faelton, David Diamond, and the Editors of *Prevention* Magazine, *Take Control of Your Life: A Complete Guide to Stress Relief* (Emmaus, PA: Rodale Press, 1988), pp. 205–8.

Enter Drs. Barry Marshall and J. Robin Warren. In 1982, Drs. Marshall and Warren studied biopsies of 100 ulcer patients and found the presence of bacteria resembling *Campylobacter* in 87 percent of them. They never found such bacteria in patients without ulcers or gastritis (a common precursor of ulcers). They proposed the hypothesis that the bacteria were the cause of ulcers in at least the overwhelming majority of patients. Through a literature search, Marshall discovered that as early as 1893 scientists had known of the presence of bacteria in the stomach, and a 1940 article indicated that the over-the-counter drug bismuth seemed to heal some ulcers. Eventually he discovered that a regimen of bismuth and antibiotics cured ulcers—without a relapse within two years—in about 75 percent of all patients. Convincing the medical community, however, took nearly another decade.[17]

Notice the initial problem. There was a widely accepted account of the cause of ulcers. Marshall's hypothesis was inconsistent with that. So, on the basis of **H5**, it was deemed improbable. On the other hand, the germ-theory-of-disease has proven very fruitful since the time of Pasteur (**H6**). Since Marshall's hypothesis was closely tied to a fruitful *general* theory, it should be deemed probable (**H5**). In theory, these two considerations regarding **H5** might be expected to cancel one another. In practice, any hypotheses that are contrary to "common knowledge" face an uphill battle. The cause of this seems to be based more on what might be called "psychological inertia" than purely theoretical considerations.[18]

Marshall's hypothesis was that ulcers, like many other diseases, are caused by bacteria. If the hypothesis is true and the correct combination of antibiotics could be found, then patients treated with the antibiotics will be cured of ulcers (**H1**). The results of the tests were favorable (**H2**), indeed, more favorable than the standard treatment for ulcers. His hypothesis is no more complex than the stress hypothesis (**H4**). And the scope of the hypothesis is broader than the stress hypothesis (**H3**). Marshall's hypothesis explains why a certain bacterium is found in the stomach when, and only when, one has ulcers or gastritis. It was only after Marshall convinced others to engage in clinical trials, and the results of those trials were consistent with Marshall's, that his hypothesis was accepted.

Barbara McClintock. Now consider an issue in the sociology of science. Barbara McClintock (1902–1992) was an American geneticist who won the 1983 Nobel Prize in physiology for her work on plant genetics. Throughout her career, her research focused on the genetics of maize (*Zea mays*). Her early work was very well-received. Her early papers are among the classics of genetic theory. In 1944, she began an investigation on unstable mutations in maize. Her

---

[17]For some of the details of Marshall's research, see Suzanne Chazin, "The Doctor *Who* Wouldn't Accept No," *Reader's Digest*, October 1993, pp. 119–24, as well as the medical journal articles cited therein.
[18]A physicist once told me that the acceptance of quantum mechanics depended upon the death of a generation of physicists who were trained prior to the introduction of quantum mechanics.

hypothesis was that some mutations arise, not from the gene on the DNA strand that is usually associated with the trait, but from adjacent genes. Her hypothesis was new. It was radical. And it was ignored for over a decade.

Why was her work ignored? Consider three hypotheses: (1) McClintock was a victim of gender discrimination. (2) Her hypothesis was implausible. (3) No one cared. Which of these provides the best explanation and why? To answer this question, we need to look at a few more historical facts.

Seen within its historical context, McClintock's hypothesis was theoretically implausible (**H5**). She presented her hypothesis in a paper in 1951. At that time, most genetic research focused on fruit flies and bacteria, notably *E. coli*. At the time, it was assumed that any genetic modification that occurred in fairly simple organisms was paralleled in more complex organisms, such as maize. Further, it was a *fundamental assumption* of genetic research that genetic information in DNA was not subject to modification except by means of mutation. McClintock's research was not only focused on a less-than-popular subject (maize), it also flew in the face of the fundamental working assumption of genetic research at the time.

In the early 1960s, François Jacob and Jacque Monod argued that protein synthesis in bacteria is not regulated by the structural DNA gene itself, but by two genes lying adjacent to the structural gene. This was a rejection of the fundamental assumption of a decade earlier, and it brought McClintock's work into the mainstream of genetic research.

So what is the best explanation of McClintock's temporary fall from scientific grace? Is it (1) that she was a woman in a field dominated by men, and she was, therefore, a victim of gender discrimination? Let us grant the unhappy fact that women, particularly in certain fields, are victims of discrimination. But the discrimination hypothesis explains neither the widespread acceptance of McClintock's early work nor her subsequent acclaim. Hence, hypothesis (1) does *not* seem to be the best explanation of the temporary rejection of the work McClintock undertook in the 1940s and 1950s. Is it (2) that her hypothesis was deemed implausible? This certainly is at least part of the explanation. Her hypothesis flew in the face of a fundamental assumption of genetic research at the time. In this respect, McClintocks's hypothesis is like Marshall's ulcer hypothesis. Given the state of knowledge when the hypothesis was proposed, it was implausible. This explains why McClintock's hypothesis was rejected. It also explains why it ultimately was accepted. In the early 1960s, her hypothesis regarding the genetic behavior of maize was shown also to explain the genetic behavior of bacteria. Her hypothesis provided the best available explanation of the genetic behavior of both kinds of organisms, and with this the assumption that the information on the DNA strand was not subject to modification was rejected. So this would seem to be a better explanation than (1) for two reasons. First, it explains both why her hypothesis was initially rejected but ultimately accepted. Second, the history of science provides many examples of cases in which the acceptance of the correct hypothesis requires a significant period of time and a shift in some of the underlying theoretical assumptions.

Is it a better explanation than (3) that no one cared? It would seem so. Certain discoveries that were later deemed significant were ignored for a period of time. Alexander Fleming announced his discovery of penicillin in 1929. It was ignored for a decade. The potential importance of penicillin was recognized only when World War II loomed on the horizon. McClintock's hypothesis was purely theoretical. By itself her hypothesis would not save lives, it would not produce a better hybrid corn, it would not have any immediate economic or humanitarian effects. It was a hypothesis that would be of interest *only* to those involved in genetic research—and they were all looking in a different direction, because McClintock's hypothesis was inconsistent with the leading theoretical assumptions in the genetics of the time. For these reasons, hypothesis (2) seems to provide the best explanation for McClintock's temporary fall from scientific grace.

There is a common analogy between problem-solving and a jigsaw puzzle. When the pieces of a jigsaw puzzle fit together, you've got the desired picture. Similarly, it is said, when the bits and pieces of evidence fit together—when you have an explanation that accounts for all the evidence—it has to be right. The analogy is imperfect. If there were a jigsaw puzzle that could be put together several ways to form several different pictures, it would be closer, since you can never be certain that your explanation is correct—there are *always* alternative explanations. Nonetheless, if you follow the criteria for evaluating arguments to the best explanation and you are willing to continually revise your conclusions as more evidence becomes available, you should be able to reach increasingly probable conclusions.

> **ESSENTIAL** HINTS
>
> Mystery readers should recognize that arguments to the best explanation are the common coin of fictitious detectives. Colin Dexter's Inspector Morse mysteries give wonderful examples of proposing and testing—sometimes rather outrageous—hypotheses and continually honing them in an attempt to figure out whodunit. *The Wench is Dead* is particularly nice, insofar as it concerns a murder committed over a hundred years earlier. Jeffrey Deaver's *The Bone Collector* and other Lincoln Rhyme novels are also good reads that exemplify arguing to the best explanation.

EXERCISES

1. Why is the following passage from the chapter, "The Science of Deduction," in Sir Arthur Conan Doyle's *A Study in Scarlet* better described as an argument to the best explanation than as a case of deduction?

   Sherlock Holmes remarks: "I have a lot of special knowledge which I apply to the problem, and which facilitates matters wonderfully. Those rules of deduction laid down in that article which aroused your scorn are invaluable to me in practical work. Observation with me is second nature. You appeared to be surprised when I told you, on our first meeting, that you had come from Afghanistan."
   "You were told, no doubt."

"Nothing of the sort. I knew you came from Afghanistan. From long habit the train of thoughts ran so swiftly through my mind that I arrived at the conclusion without being conscious of intermediate steps. There were such steps, however. The train of reasoning ran, 'Here is a gentleman of a medical type, but with the air of a military man. Clearly an army doctor, then. He has just come from the tropics, for his face is dark, and that is not the natural tint of his skin, for his wrists are fair. He has undergone hardship and sickness, as his haggard face says clearly. His left arm has been injured. He holds it in a stiff and unnatural manner. Where in the tropics could an English army doctor have seen much hardship and got his arm wounded? Clearly in Afghanistan.' The whole train of thought did not occupy a second. I then remarked that you came from Afghanistan, and you were astonished."

2. Why is the following an argument to the best explanation?

"The radiator fan is not working," he told me after about fifteen seconds. He showed it to me and explained that ordinarily it only comes on when start-and-stop city driving makes the engine overheat.
"Could it be a blown fuse?"
"Could be," he said. But he ruled that out by trying a new one, which did no better than the old one. He said, "Hold on," and fetched a pen-type probe, which he used to test the plug that connected the fan to the electrical system. "You got fire to the fan," he told me, "so it looks like it's the fan itself that's shot."

> —Daniel Quinn, *Ishmael: An Adventure of the Mind and Spirit*
> (New York: Bantam/Turner Books, 1992), p. 258

3. Using the criteria for evaluating arguments to the best explanation, evaluate the following:

Far Eastern influences permeated the Beatles recordings from 1965 to 1967 like the pungent aroma of incense. George Harrison introduced the droning sounds of the sitar into Beatles' compositions. For the first time, the Beatles experimented with backward recordings and introduced metaphysical themes. However, not everyone was happy with the sudden change in the group.
The American public, it seemed, refused to allow change in its heroes. If there really was change in the Beatles, there had to be a reason for it. After the release of the Beatles' albums from 1967 to 1969, these adoring fans of the past became inquisitors of the present. A scapegoat was demanded, and when the "Paul is dead" rumors surfaced in October 1969, those fans, filled with insecurity, were only too eager to search for the clues that provided the answer for this strange changes in the Beatles' behavior.
The answer was obvious: Paul McCartney had indeed died, and an imposter had taken his place.

> —R. Gary Patterson, *The Walrus Was Paul: The Great Beatle Death Clues*
> (New York: Fireside Books, 1998), p. 37

4. In 1962, General Dynamics, a company that recently had suffered serious financial setbacks, was awarded a multibillion dollar contract to develop a tactical fighter plane for the navy. Its primary competitor was Boeing. In an elaborate evaluation process throughout 1961 and 1962,

Boeing's design was consistently chosen by the military. The Navy was strongly opposed to the General Dynamics design. In this passage from his *The Dark Side of Camelot* (Boston: Little Brown, 1997, pp. 316–318) Seymour M. Hersh provides a possible explanation of the choice. Do you believe it constitutes the *best* explanation? Why or why not?

Jack Kennedy's womanizing had repeatedly put his career at risk, but until now the potential loss had always been his. The affair with Exner posed a much broader danger: to the well-being of the nation's security. The Kennedy–Exner relationship apparently became known in the late summer of 1962 to the General Dynamics Corporation, one of two defense firms intensely competing for the right to manufacture a new generation of air force and navy combat plane known as the TFX (Tactical Fighter Experimental). General Dynamics may have used that knowledge to win the contract and force the government to spend billions of dollars to build a navy version of TFX that many in the military knew would not work.

J. Edgar Hoover's lunch in March 1962 with Jack Kennedy had not left the FBI director reassured enough to stop the Los Angeles field office from continuing its round-the-clock surveillance of Exner's apartment from a nearby undercover observation post. Hoover's hunch paid off in an unexpected way late on August 7, 1962, when the FBI's William Carter watched as two young men climbed onto a balcony at Exner's apartment on Fontaine Avenue, in west Los Angeles; one man watched as the other slid open a glass door and entered. After fifteen minutes or so—more than enough time to sort through records or install a wiretap—the pair fled. . . . "We were absolutely stunned," Carter told me. . . .

Carter's role in the Exner break-in ended at that point. His supervisors did not tell him that within three days they tracked the break-in team to a getaway car rented by a former FBI special agent named I. B. Hale, of Fort Worth, Texas. The two men who entered Exner's apartment were identified by the FBI as Hale's twin sons, Bobby and Billy, twenty-one years old. I. B. Hale, who died in 1971, was in charge of security for General Dynamics.

At the time of the break-in, the company's chances of winning the immensely lucrative TFX contract were precarious, as the men running General Dynamics were only too aware. To improve the company's odds, nothing could be ruled out in the summer of 1962, including the utilization of a high-priced former FBI agent who might be in a position to accumulate information on the Kennedy administration. The Hale family's criminal entry into Judith Campbell Exner's apartment, . . . , raises an obvious question: Was Jack Kennedy blackmailed by a desperate corporation?

5. In 1692 in Salem Village, Massachusetts, a number of young women brought charges of witchcraft against numerous women and men in the village and the surrounding area. Nineteen people were convicted of and hung for the crime of witchcraft.

    Below are three explanations of the phenomenon. Using the criteria for evaluating a hypothesis, which is the best explanation of that phenomenon? Why? If you are uncertain, explain how you would go about determining what the best explanation is.

(1) Cotton Mather (1663–1728) was the son of Increase Mather and grandson of John Cotton and Richard Mather. A third-generation Puritan, Cotton Mather was noted for both his theological studies and his interests in science. In 1692, he published a book entitled *On Witchcraft*. The book is a compilation of numerous theories on witchcraft and the identification of witches. Among the characteristics he lists as showing that a person is probably a witch are the following: (a) the testimony of the person(s) bewitched, (b) unusual body marks, (c) cursing and living a "lewd and naughty kind of Life," (d) inconsistent testimony, (e) pacts with the devil and rejection of divine worship, (f) certain gestures, (g) talking to their familiars (cats and other animals), (h) possessing pictures and dolls, (i) periods of ecstasy, and (j) confessing their own witchcraft and denouncing others as witches. All those convicted of witchcraft exhibited *some* of these characteristics. The accused were witches.

(2) The playwright Arthur Miller (1915–2005; attended the University of Michigan) proposed an alternative explanation in his play *The Crucible* (1953). This was written during the period of the McCarthy Hearings, a period when numerous notable people were called before the Senate to answer to charges of being Communists or Communist sympathizers. Miller suggested that there was a parallel to witchcraft trials. He wrote:

The Salem tragedy, which is about to begin in these pages, developed from a paradox. It is a paradox in whose grip we still live, and there is no prospect yet that we will discover its resolution. Simply, it was this: For good purposes, even high purposes, the people of Salem developed a theocracy, a combine of state and religious power whose function was to keep the community together, and to prevent any kind of disunity that might open it to destruction by material or ideological enemies. It was forged for a necessary purpose and accomplished that purpose. But all organization is and must be grounded on the idea of exclusion and prohibition, just as two objects cannot occupy the same space. Evidently the time came in New England when the repressions of order were heavier than seemed warranted by the dangers against which the order was organized. The witch-hunt was a perverse manifestation of the panic which set in among all classes when the balance began to turn toward greater individual freedom. (*The Crucible*, Act I [New York: Penguin Books, 1954], pp. 6–7.)

(3) Mary L. Starkey (B.A. and M.A. from Boston University) was a journalist who taught at schools including the University of Connecticut at New London. Her book, *The Devil in Massachusetts: A Modern Enquiry into the Salem Witch Trials* (New York: Doubleday Anchor Books, 1949) attributed the phenomenon to hysteria.

There was nothing new, nothing peculiar to Salem Village in the outbreak. Similar examples of mass hysteria and on a far more enormous scale had occurred repeatedly in the Middle Ages, and always like this one, in the wake of stress and social disorganization, after wars or after an epidemic of the Black Death. There had been the Children's Crusades, the Flagellantes, the St Vitrus' Dance, and again and again there had been outbreaks of witchcraft. Sweden had recently had one, and on such a scale as to make what was going on in Salem Village look trivial.

Nor has susceptibility to "demonic possession" passed from the world. A rousing religious revival will bring out something like what Salem Village was experiencing; so will a lynching, a Hitler, so will a dead motion-picture star or a live crooner. Some of the girls were no more seriously possessed than a pack of bobby-soxers on the loose. The affliction was real enough, deserving of study and treatment, but not of the kind of study and treatment it was about to receive.

In the long run what was remarkable here was less the antics of the girls than the way the community responded to them. It was the community — extended in time to include the whole Bay Colony — that would in the end suffer the most devastating attack of possession, and not only the ignorant, but the best minds. The nearly universal belief in devils and witches could not alone explain the capitulation of reason which took place. The fact was that the commonwealth, no less than the girls, craved its Dionysiac mysteries. A people whose natural instincts had long been repressed by the severity of their belief, whose security had been undermined by anxiety and terror, continued longer than could be borne, demanded their catharsis. Frustrated by the devils they could not reach, they demanded a scapegoat and a full-scale lynching. And they got it.

Yet surely no one was "plotting," least of all the hapless Mary [Warren]. The community at large had become bewitched, magistrates no less than the girls — bewitched by a kind of mad hypnosis, expressed in panic on the one hand and crusading fervour on the other. At such moments, the voice of reason always sounds like blasphemy, and dissenters are of the devil. The wonder was not that Mary's defection was denounced, but that it should have been treated with mercy. (*The Devil in Massachusetts*, pp. 46–47, 102)

6. In the late 1960s, Erich von Däniken published a book entitled, *Chariots of the Gods? Unsolved mysteries of the past*. His hypothesis was that various historical mysteries—the building of the pyramids, certain biblical accounts (such as the exodus from Egypt and Ezekiel's chariot ride into heaven), accounts of giants, etc.—could be explained by the visitation of extraterrestrial beings. This would also explain the various UFO "sightings" that were common in the 1950s and 1960s. His account has two virtues not found in religious accounts. (1) His account is possible, given our scientific knowledge of the universe. Ezekiel's supposed chariot ride, for example, is not consistent with a scientific understanding of the universe. (2) Extraterrestrials, although mysterious beings, would fit into a purely naturalistic account of the world. Däniken's hypothesis is simpler than explaining some events on the basis of a religious hypothesis and most events on the basis of science. Is this sufficient to deem Däniken's hypothesis probable?

7. Between 1844 and 1848 numerous women at the Vienna General Hospital died shortly after childbirth. The cause of death was called childbed fever. The hospital had two maternity divisions. In the First Division, 8.8 percent of mothers died of childbed fever between 1844 and 1847. In the Second Division, only 2.33 percent died of childbed fever during the same period. Medical students were trained in the First Division. Midwives were trained in the Second Division. Ignaz Semmelweis (1818–1865) was charged with investigating the phenomenon.

   There were numerous hypotheses. (1) It was simply an epidemic. But this would explain neither why it was more prevalent in the First Division than in the Second, nor why the death rate from childbed fever was lower among those giving birth outside the hospital than among those giving birth in the First Division. (2) Overcrowding and poor ventilation were proposed hypotheses, but there were no differences regarding these factors between the First and Second Divisions. (3) It was suggested that the examination techniques of medical students were rough, but the techniques did not differ from those of the midwives in the Second Division, and injuries resulting naturally from the birth process were more extensive than those caused by the examinations. (4) In the First Division, but not the Second, priests offering last rites were preceded by an attendant ringing a bell. The bell-ringing practice was stopped with no change in death rates. (5) In the First Division, women delivered on their backs. In the Second Division, women delivered on their sides. Changing the delivery position in the First Division resulted in no change in death rates.

   In 1847, one of Semmelweis's colleagues died. The symptoms of his final illness corresponded to those of childbed fever. Prior to the illness, the colleague's hand had been punctured by a scalpel while performing an autopsy. The medical students regularly dissected cadavers before attending to the women in the First Division. Semmelweis proposed a new hypotheses and a test. The hypothesis was that the students were carriers of an infectious material from the cadavers. He tested the hypotheses by requiring medical students to wash their hands in a solution of chlorinated lime before making examinations. In 1848, the death rate in the First Division dropped to 1.27 percent, compared to 1.33 percent in the Second Division.

   Why was Semmelweis's hypothesis more probably true than the alternatives?

8. There is an area off the southeastern coast of the United States popularly known as the Bermuda Triangle. It is an area noted for unexplained disappearances of ships, small boats, and aircraft. A popular explanation of the disappearances claims the missing craft are spirited away by extraterrestrial beings. The U.S. Navy suggests the mysterious disappearances can be explained by environmental factors. They cite the following. (1) The

Bermuda Triangle is one of two places on earth where magnetic compasses do not point north. They can be off by as much as 20°. The second place which exhibits the same phenomenon is an area off the coast of Japan known as the "Devil's Sea." The Devil's Sea is also known for disappearances. (2) The Gulf Stream is strong in the Triangle, which would explain the rapid disappearance of the craft. (3) Weather patterns are violent and unpredictable in the Triangle. (4) A significant number of the craft which disappeared were pleasure craft, which suggests human error may have played a significant role in the disappearance of the craft.

Which is the better explanation? Why?

9. In 1857, Louis Pasteur attempted to discover why some batches of wine and beer turned bad. At the time, wine was produced by crushing grapes in vats and simply allowing the juice to ferment. The process differed from brewing beer insofar as beer could be brewed only if yeast were added from a previously successful batch. A generation before Pasteur, there was good evidence that yeast was some kind of living being. His studies of beer brewing showed that the amount of yeast in the batch increased greatly until the sugar was consumed, then fermentation stopped. He concluded that the presence of yeast was necessary for the production of alcohol, and his hypothesis was that "bad" batches of beer and wine were caused by unwanted microorganisms. He did parallel studies on the souring of milk. Later in life he developed vaccines to fight anthrax and rabies.

Prior to Pasteur, diseases were believed to be caused by chemical reactions and little was understood about the role of microorganisms in brewing. Explain why Pasteur's hypothesis that fermentation is the result of the actions of microorganisms can be deemed "fruitful."

10. A friend of mine believes in astrology. He said that when he was young, an astrologer had constructed his horoscope, and the predictions had been exceptionally accurate. It had predicted that he would fight in a war, which he did. It predicted that he would have two children, a boy and a girl, which he did. It predicted that he would move away from his homeland, which he did.

It is unquestionable that *some* astrological predictions come true. Taking the criteria for confirming a hypothesis into account, what reasons are there to believe that astrology does *not* provide the best explanation of the events in my friend's (or anyone's) life?

ESSENTIALS OF CHAPTER 9

Inductive arguments provide evidence that their conclusions are probably true. Unlike valid deductive arguments with true premises, no inductive argument shows conclusively that its conclusion is true.

We briefly examined **arguments by enumeration** in 9.1. The strength of an argument by enumeration is increased by a larger **sample**, the objects that provide the basis for the conclusion, and a more **diverse** sample. The diversity of a sample is determined by the different places in time and space from which the sample is drawn. Finally, the stronger the conclusion is, the weaker the evidence is that supports that conclusion. The strength of a conclusion is determined by the ease with which one can find a **counterexample** to it. An inductive counterexample shows that a conclusion is false. For example, the statement, "All swans are white," is a very strong claim, since finding only one nonwhite swan would be a counterexample sufficient to show that the claim is false.

We examined arguments by analogy in 9.2–9.3. Analogies are based on comparisons among things. An **argument by analogy** claims that because two or more things are similar in a certain number of respects, and all but one of those objects has an additional property, it is likely that the remaining object also has that property. There are six criteria for evaluating arguments by analogy:

1. The greater the number of things compared (the larger the ground for the analogy), the stronger the evidence is for the conclusion.
2. The more respects in which the objects compared are similar (the larger the basis is for the analogy), the stronger the evidence is for the conclusion.
3. When a significant number of things are similar in a significant number of respects (when the ground and the basis are strong), differences among objects in the ground can *strengthen* the evidence for the conclusion of the analogy.
4. Respects add to the force of the argument when they are relevant, and a single highly relevant factor contributes more to the argument than a host of irrelevant similarities.
5. Disanalogies weaken analogical arguments.
6. The weaker the conclusion—the more difficult it is to prove the conclusion false—the less burden is placed upon the premises and the stronger the argument; the stronger the conclusion, the greater is the burden on the premises and the weaker the argument.

In sections 9.4–9.5, we examined explanations and arguments to the best explanation. There are six criteria for evaluating hypotheses:

H1: A hypothesis must be testable.

H2: If predictions based upon hypothesis are true, this tends to show that the hypothesis is true.

H3: A hypothesis is more probably true if it has a broader explanatory scope, that is, if it explains more phenomena than alternative hypotheses.

H4: If either of two hypotheses will explain a phenomenon and one involves fewer theoretical assumptions, the hypothesis that involves fewer assumptions is more probably true.

H5: A hypothesis is more probably true if it is consistent with the best theoretical explanations available.

H6: A hypothesis is more probably true if it is fruitful, that is, if it predicts previously unknown phenomena.

These criteria are used not only to judge whether an individual hypothesis is probably true, they are also used to judge between alternative hypotheses to determine which of two or more hypotheses provides the best (most probable) explanation of a phenomenon. Arguments to the best explanation are common in the sciences and ordinary life.

Truth trees provide a way to determine whether any argument in propositional logic is valid and to demonstrate the validity of valid arguments in quantified logic. Like truth tables, the procedure is purely mechanical: If you follow the procedure correctly, you can demonstrate the validity of an argument without developing proof strategies. It is like reverse truth tables and indirect proofs insofar as it assumes the denial of the conclusion (the assumption that the conclusion is false) as an additional premise.

A.1 PROPOSITIONAL LOGIC

The procedure is straightforward. The premises constitute the **trunk** of the tree.

1. Append the *denial* of the conclusion to the trunk of the tree.
2. Apply the following rules to break compound statements down into their simple components. In doing so, you're forming **branches** from the trunk. The results are placed on *every open branch below* the statement. As you apply the rules, place a checkmark (✓) beside each compound statement to which you've applied a rule.

BRANCHING RULES FOR TRUTH TREES			
Conditional $p \supset q$ / \\ $\sim p$　q	Conjunction $p \bullet q$ p q	Disjunction $p \vee q$ / \\ p　q	Biconditional $p \equiv q$ / \\ p　$\sim p$ q　$\sim q$
Negation of a Conditional $\sim(p \supset q)$ p $\sim q$	Negation of a Conjunction $\sim(p \bullet q)$ / \\ $\sim p$　$\sim q$	Negation of a Disjunction $\sim(p \vee q)$ $\sim p$ $\sim q$	Negation of a Biconditional $\sim(p \equiv q)$ / \\ $\sim p$　p q　$\sim q$
Erase all double tildes (~~)			

3. Read back *up* the branch and trunk to see whether there is both a simple statement and its denial.

4. If a continuous path from the branch *up* the tree contains *both* a simple statement and its denial, close the branch by placing an *X* at the bottom of the branch. Nothing more is to be added to a closed branch.

5. If any branch remains open and there is a compound statement to which the rules have not been applied, check the statement (✓) and apply the rule, appending the results to *every* open branch *below* it.

6. If all the branches close, the argument is valid. If the rules have been applied to all the compound statements in the tree and any branches remain open, the argument is invalid.

By looking at a few examples, the procedure will become clear.

Here is how you prove the validity of disjunctive syllogism by means of a truth tree. The form of a disjunctive syllogism is:

$$p \lor q$$
$$\sim p$$
$$\therefore q$$

Begin by appending the denial of the conclusion to the trunk of the tree:

$$p \lor q$$
$$\sim p$$
$$\therefore q$$
$$\sim q$$

Now apply the rule for a disjunction to the first premise. This will give you a split branch with p on the left branch and q on the right branch:

$$✓p \lor q$$
$$\sim p$$
$$\therefore q$$
$$\sim q$$
$$/ \setminus$$
$$p \quad q$$

Starting at the bottom of the tree, trace up each branch to see whether you have a simple statement and its denial. Tracing up the left branch, you have both p and $\sim p$. Tracing up the right branch, you have both q and $\sim q$.

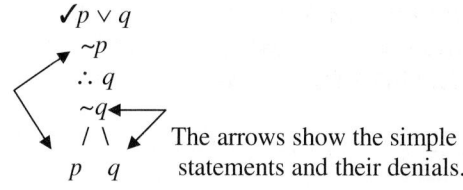

The arrows show the simple statements and their denials.

Whenever you have a statement and its denial in a single branch, you place an
X at the bottom of the branch and declare it closed.

$$\checkmark p \lor q$$
$$\sim p$$
$$\therefore q$$
$$\sim q$$
$$/ \; \backslash$$
$$p \quad q$$
$$X \quad X$$

Since all the branches are closed, the truth tree shows that the argument is valid.

If the argument form is invalid, such as denying the antecedent, not all the
branches on the tree will close. The form of denying the antecedent is:

$$p \supset q$$
$$\sim p$$
$$\therefore \sim q$$

Append the denial of the conclusion to the trunk:

$$p \supset q$$
$$\sim p$$
$$\therefore \sim q$$
$$\sim\sim q$$

Since we have a double-tilde, we erase it and then apply the rule for the
conditional:

$$\checkmark p \supset q$$
$$\sim p$$
$$\therefore \sim q$$
$$q$$
$$/ \; \backslash$$
$$\sim p \quad q$$

In this case neither branch closes. You *do not* have a p to close the branch with
a $\sim p$ at the bottom; you do not have a $\sim q$ to close the branch with q at the bottom. If *any* branch remains open when the rules have been applied to all the
compound statements in an argument, the argument in invalid. So, denying
the antecedent is invalid.

So far we have looked at fairly simple arguments. The procedure is the
same when arguments become more complex. Consider:

$$p \supset (q \bullet r)$$
$$\sim r \lor s$$
$$\therefore \sim(p \bullet \sim s)$$

Append the denial of the conclusion and erase the double-tildes:

$$p \supset (q \bullet r)$$
$$\sim r \lor s$$
$$\therefore \sim(p \bullet \sim s)$$
$$(p \bullet \sim s)$$

Now you apply the rules to all the compound statements. *It makes no logical difference where you begin,* so let's begin with the first premise and work down. The rule for the conditional gives us a split branch with $\sim p$ on the left branch and $(q \bullet r)$ on the right branch:

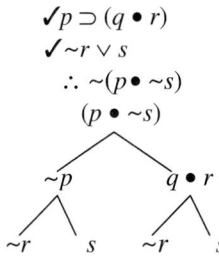

There is no p on which the $\sim p$ would close, and the statement on the right branch is compound. So neither branch of the tree closes.

If we continue down the trunk of the tree, we'll diagram the second premise next. This is the rule for disjunction. We'll need to append a split branch to every open branch:

$$\checkmark p \supset (q \bullet r)$$
$$\checkmark \sim r \lor s$$
$$\therefore \sim(p \bullet \sim s)$$
$$(p \bullet \sim s)$$

We trace up the tree from each of the open branches. There is not an r above on any branch that has a $\sim r$. There is not a $\sim s$ above on any branch that has an s. So, no branches close.

Next we can apply the rule for conjunction to $(p \bullet \sim s)$. This yields a straight branch on every open branch below it:

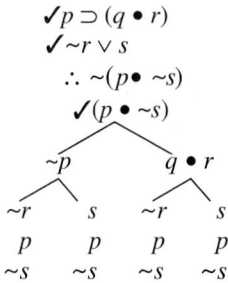

This time some branches close. Tracing the *p* up in the left-most branch, we find a ~*p*, so that branch closes. Tracing the ~*s* up on the second branch from the left, we find both a ~*s* and an *s*, so that branch closes. Tracing up the simple statements on the third branch from the left, we do not find the denial of any of the simple statements, so the branch remains open. On the right-most branch, we find both ~*s* and *s*, so we can close the branch. So, now our tree looks like this:

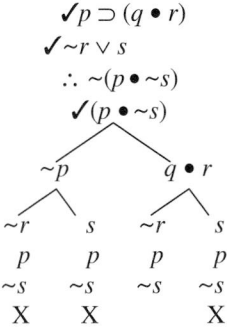

You will notice that there is one compound statement to which a rule has not been applied, namely, *q* • *r*. So, we apply the rule for conjunction to that statement and append the result to the open branch below it:

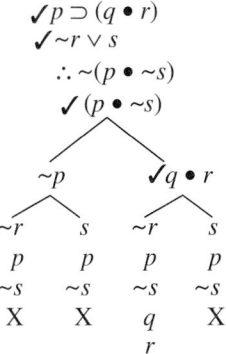

Now you trace the *r* at the bottom of the branch up and you find a ~*r*. So, the branch closes. So the argument form is valid:

$$\checkmark\, p \supset (q \bullet r)$$
$$\checkmark\, {\sim}r \vee s$$
$$\therefore {\sim}(p \bullet {\sim}s)$$
$$\checkmark\, (p \bullet {\sim}s)$$

$$
\begin{array}{cccc}
 & {\sim}p & & \checkmark\, q \bullet r \\
{\sim}r & s & {\sim}r & s \\
p & p & p & p \\
{\sim}s & {\sim}s & {\sim}s & {\sim}s \\
X & X & q & X \\
 & & r & \\
 & & X &
\end{array}
$$

As we mentioned above, the order in which you apply the rules to the premises, the denial of the conclusion, and the resulting compound statements makes no *logical* difference. So, there is nothing wrong with the tree we just did. But as arguments become more complex, life is easier if you keep your trees "pruned." If you apply rules resulting in straight branches (conjunction, negation of a conditional, and negation of a disjunction) before the other rules, there will be fewer branches. As you become more familiar with the rules, you'll also choose to apply split-branching rules to statements that will allow you to close one of the branches quickly. So, the truth tree for the argument above could have looked like this:

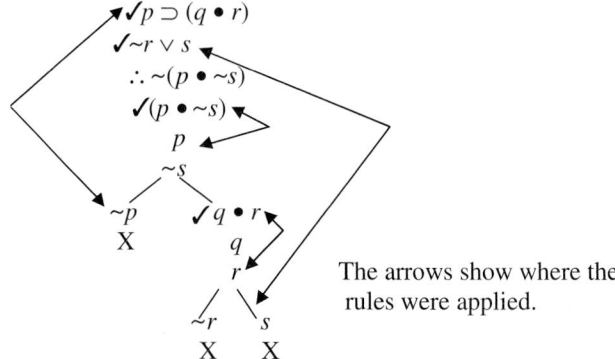

The arrows show where the rules were applied.

Exercises

Do exercises 1–34 in Chapter 6, Section 5.

A.2 QUANTIFICATIONAL LOGIC

Truth trees for quantificational logic use the rules for propositional logic in conjunction with three additional rules that concern quantifiers. Once the quantifiers are gone, you do *exactly* what you did when constructing truth trees for propositional logic. There are two differences, however. First, since you'll be *instantiating* quantified statements, that is, restating the proposition in terms of a constant $(a, b, c, \ldots, w)$, there will be times that you will instantiate a given quantified proposition for more than one constant. Secondly, if a truth tree for an argument in quantified logic closes, the tree shows that the argument is valid. If a truth tree *doesn't* close, that *does not* show that the argument is invalid. To demonstrate that a quantified argument is invalid you need to follow the procedures in Chapter 8, Section 5.

To see why we need more rules and how those rules work, let's focus on the following arguments:

$$(x)(Mx \supset Px)$$
$$(\exists x)(Sx \bullet Mx)$$
$$\therefore (\exists x)(Sx \bullet Px)$$

$$(x)(Mx \supset Px)$$
$$(x)(Sx \supset Mx)$$
$$\therefore (x)(Sx \supset Px)$$

Quantifier Negation

We begin as we always begin a truth tree by appending the denial of the conclusion to the tree. So, if the conclusion is $(\exists x)(Sx \bullet Px)$, we append
$\sim(\exists x)(Sx \bullet Px)$ to the trunk of the tree. If the conclusion is $(x)(Sx \supset Px)$, we
append $\sim(x)(Sx \supset Px)$ to the trunk of the tree. As we'll see shortly, you can
instantiate a statement *only* when the quantifier governs the entire statement.
If you have a tilde to the left of a quantifier, you need to move it across the
quantifier before you can instantiate. **Quantifier negation tells you that when
you move a tilde across a quantifier, a universal quantifier (x) becomes an
existential quantifier $(\exists x)$, and an existential quantifier $(\exists x)$ becomes a
universal quantifier (x).** So, you place a checkmark (✓) beside the statement
to which you apply quantifier negation, and write the resulting statement
immediately below it.

> **Examples**
>
> $$(x)(Mx \supset Px)$$
> $$(\exists x)(Sx \bullet Mx)$$
> $$\therefore (\exists x)(Sx \bullet Px)$$
> $$✓\sim(\exists x)(Sx \bullet Px)$$
> $$(x)\sim(Sx \bullet Px)$$
>
> $$(x)(Mx \supset Px)$$
> $$(x)(Sx \supset Mx)$$
> $$\therefore (x)(Sx \supset Px)$$
> $$✓\sim(x)(Sx \supset Px)$$
> $$(\exists x)\sim(Sx \supset Px)$$

Existential Instantiation

When you construct a truth tree for quantified logic, *all* the variables are
replaced with constants, that is, names of individuals $(a, b, c, \ldots, w)$. **The rule
of Existential Instantiation allows you to replace a variable in an existential
statement with a constant that is *new to the truth tree*.** The constant *must* be
new to the truth tree. Why? Let's say you were given the statement, "Some
U.S. Secretaries of State were accomplished pianists." That statement is true of
Condoleezza Rice; it is not true of former Secretary of State Colin Powell. The
choice of the constant is arbitrary: You don't know to whom it applies, but to
whomever it applies the resulting statement will be true. The restriction to a
new constant means that you instantiate existential statements *before* you
instantiate universal statements for the same constant. So, you check the existential statement and introduce a new constant. If you're instantiating for a,
you place a small a over the checkmark ($\overset{a}{✓}$) to show that you have instantiated
it for the constant a.

Examples

$$(x)(Mx \supset Px)$$
$$\cancel{\mathscr{V}}(\exists x)(Sx \bullet Mx)$$
$$\therefore (\exists x)(Sx \bullet Px)$$
$$\checkmark \sim(\exists x)(Sx \bullet Px)$$
$$(x)\sim(Sx \bullet Px)$$
$$Sa \bullet Ma$$

Since the second premise is an existential statement, you instantiate *that* statement *before* you instantiate any of the universal statements.

$$(x)(Mx \supset Px)$$
$$(x)(Sx \supset Mx)$$
$$\therefore (x)(Sx \supset Px)$$
$$\checkmark \sim(x)(Sx \supset Px)$$
$$\cancel{\mathscr{V}}(\exists x)\sim(Sx \supset Px)$$
$$\sim(Sa \supset Pa)$$

Since the result of using quantifier negation on the conclusion of the argument is an existential statement, you instantiate *that* statement *before* you instantiate any of the universal statements.

Universal Instantiation

The rule of Universal Instantiation allows you to replace a variable in a universal statement with *any* constant. So, if you've instantiated your existential statement for *a*, you check the universal statement for *a* ($\mathscr{V}$), and replace the variables with *a*.

Examples

$$\cancel{\mathscr{V}}(x)(Mx \supset Px)$$
$$\cancel{\mathscr{V}}(\exists x)(Sx \bullet Mx)$$
$$\therefore (\exists x)(Sx \bullet Px)$$
$$\checkmark \sim(\exists x)(Sx \bullet Px)$$
$$\cancel{\mathscr{V}}(x)\sim(Sx \bullet Px)$$
$$Sa \bullet Ma$$
$$Ma \supset Pa$$
$$\sim(Sa \bullet Pa)$$

$\mathscr{V}(x)(Mx \supset Px)$
$\mathscr{V}(x)(Sx \supset Mx)$
$\therefore (x)(Sx \supset Px)$
✓$\sim(x)(Sx \supset Px)$
$\mathscr{V}(\exists x)\sim(Sx \supset Px)$
$\sim(Sa \supset Pa)$
$Ma \supset Pa$
$Sa \supset Ma$

Now you proceed exactly as you did when doing truth trees in propositional logic. To keep the tree well-pruned, you'll apply rules yielding a straight branch before you apply rules yielding a split branch and close those branches that contain a statement and its denial.

Examples_____

$\mathscr{V}(x)(Mx \supset Px)$
$\mathscr{V}(\exists x)(Sx \bullet Mx)$
$\therefore (\exists x)(Sx \bullet Px)$
✓$\sim(\exists x)(Sx \bullet Px)$
$\mathscr{V}(x)\sim(Sx \bullet Px)$
✓$Sa \bullet Ma$
✓$Ma \supset Pa$
✓$\sim(Sa \bullet Pa)$
Sa
Ma
/ \
$\sim Ma$ Pa
X / \
$\sim Sa$ $\sim Pa$
X X

$\mathscr{V}(x)(Mx \supset Px)$
$\mathscr{V}(x)(Sx \supset Mx)$
$\therefore (x)(Sx \supset Px)$
✓$\sim(x)(Sx \supset Px)$
$\mathscr{V}(\exists x)\sim(Sx \supset Px)$
✓$\sim(Sa \supset Pa)$
✓$Ma \supset Pa$
✓$Sa \supset Ma$

$$Sa$$
$$\sim Pa$$
$$/\quad\backslash$$
$$\sim Ma\quad Pa$$
$$/\;\backslash\quad X$$
$$\sim Sa\quad Ma$$
$$X\quad\quad X$$

Both trees close. So, both arguments are valid.

If there are several existential propositions, you will need to instantiate each one for a different constant. If the same argument contains a single universal proposition, you might instantiate that proposition more than once.

Example

Consider the argument:

$$(\exists x)(Px \bullet Qx)$$
$$(\exists x)(Qx \bullet \sim Rx)$$
$$(x)[Px \supset (Sx \bullet Rx)]$$
$$\therefore (\exists x)(Px \bullet Sx) \bullet (\exists x)(Qx \bullet \sim Px)$$

Notice that the conclusion is a conjunction of existential propositions. Appending the denial of the conjunction will eventually result in a split branch. If you want to keep your tree pruned, you'll probably want to instantiate the premises and apply rules to the instantiated premises before you apply a rule to the denial of the conclusion. Here's one way to do the tree:

$$\overset{a}{\checkmark}(\exists x)(Px \bullet Qx)$$
$$\overset{b}{\checkmark}(\exists x)(Qx \bullet \sim Rx)$$
$$\overset{b}{\checkmark}\overset{a}{\checkmark}(x)[Px \supset (Sx \bullet Rx)]$$
$$\therefore (\exists x)(Px \bullet Sx) \bullet (\exists x)(Qx \bullet \sim Px)$$
$$\sim[(\exists x)(Px \bullet Sx) \bullet (\exists x)(Qx \bullet \sim Px)]$$
$$\checkmark Pa \bullet Qa$$
$$\checkmark Qb \bullet \sim Rb$$
$$Pa$$
$$Qa$$
$$Qb$$
$$\sim Rb$$

$$\checkmark Pa \supset (Sa \bullet Ra) \quad \text{Notice, we have instantiated}$$
$$Pb \supset (Sb \bullet Rb) \quad \text{the universal for both } a \text{ and } b.$$

```
                ✓Pa ⊃ (Sa • Ra)     Notice, we have instantiated
                 Pb ⊃ (Sb • Rb)      the universal for both a and b.
                     /  \
                  ~Pa     ✓Sa • Ra
                   X          Sa
                              Ra
                            /  \
                        ~Pb     ✓Sb • Rb
                       / \          Sb
                      /   \         Rb
                     /     \         X
          ✓~(∃x)(Px • Sx)     ✓~(∃x)(Qx • ~Px)
          ᵃ∀(x)~(Px • Sx)     ᵇ∀(x)~(Qx • ~Px)
            ✓~(Pa • Sa)          ✓~(Qb • ~Pb)
              /  \                  /  \
           ~Pa    ~Sa           ~Qb     Pb
            X      X             X       X
```

Notice that since the branches formed from the denial of the conclusion contained universals, we could instantiate them for anything. By instantiating one branch for *a* and the other for *b*, we were able to close the tree. If we had instantiated both for *a*, the right-hand branch also would have had to be instantiated for *b* to close.

Exercises

Construct truth trees for numbers 4–10 and 26–35 in Chapter 8, Section 3.

ESSENTIALS OF THE APPENDIX

Truth trees provide a mechanical way to determine whether any argument in propositional logic is valid and to show that any valid argument in quantified logic is valid.

In propositional logic append the denial of the conclusion to the premises to form the trunk of the tree. Use the following rules to turn compound statements into straight and split branches:

BRANCHING RULES FOR TRUTH TREES			
Conditional $p \supset q$ $/ \ \backslash$ $\sim p \quad q$	Conjunction $p \bullet q$ p q	Disjunction $p \vee q$ $/ \ \backslash$ $p \quad q$	Biconditional $p \equiv q$ $/ \ \backslash$ $p \quad \sim p$ $q \quad \sim q$
Negation of a Conditional $\sim(p \supset q)$ p $\sim q$	Negation of a Conjunction $\sim(p \bullet q)$ $/ \ \backslash$ $\sim p \quad \sim q$	Negation of a Disjunction $\sim(p \vee q)$ $\sim p$ $\sim q$	Negation of a Biconditional $\sim(p \equiv q)$ $/ \ \backslash$ $\sim p \quad p$ $q \quad \sim q$
Erase all double tildes ($\sim\sim$)			

If each branch on the resulting tree closes—if it contains both a statement and its denial—the tree shows that the argument is valid; if any branch remains open, it shows that the argument is invalid.

The procedure in quantificational logic is similar, but it requires three additional rules, rules to move negation signs across quantifiers and to eliminate quantifiers. Quantifier negation tells you that when you move a tilde across a quantifier, a universal quantifier (x) becomes an existential quantifier $(\exists x)$, and an existential quantifier $(\exists x)$ becomes a universal quantifier (x). The rule of Existential Instantiation allows you to replace a variable in an existential statement with a constant that is *new to the truth tree*. The rule of Universal Instantiation allows you to replace a variable in a universal statement with *any* constant. When using the instantiation rules, you check the compound statement for a constant $(a, b, c, \ldots, w)$. A new constant *must* be introduced any time you use the rule of existential instantiation. A universal proposition can be instantiated for *any* constant, and may be instantiated for several constants in the same tree. You then use the rules to break compound statements into simple statements. If all the branches of the tree close—if each branch contains a statement and its denial—the tree shows that the argument is valid. If one or more branches of a tree for a quantified argument *does not* close, however, this *does not* show that the argument is invalid.

SOLUTIONS TO THE ODD-NUMBERED PROBLEMS

Chapter 1 Solutions

1.3 ARGUMENTS, PREMISES, AND CONCLUSIONS

1. P: A well regulated militia being necessary to the security of a free state.
   C: The right of the people to keep and bear arms shall not be infringed.

3. P: My porridge is all gone!
   C: Someone must have eaten it.

5. P: Everything is in color.
   C: This can't be Kansas.

7. P: Snow is white.
   P: This stuff is not white.
   C: This stuff is not snow.

9. P: We have class on Monday, Wednesday, and Friday.
   P: Today is Monday.
   C: We must have class today.

11. P: You never change the oil in your car.
    P: You never check the coolant.
    C: You can expect engine trouble soon.

13. P: We are sinners all.
    C: Forbear to judge.

15. P: God is love.
    C: He that loveth not knoweth not God.

17. P: Legalized abortion leads to fewer "unwanted" babies being born.
    P: Unwanted babies are more likely to suffer abuse and neglect and are therefore more likely to be criminally involved in later life.
    C: Abortion should be legalized.

19. P: Accusations [of sexual harassment] are based on "impact" not intention.
    C: The accused is guilty if the accuser believes him to be guilty.

1.4 ARGUMENTS AND EXPLANATIONS

Part I

1. Argument
3. Explanation of why people are getting into cults.
5. Explanation of the drop in computer prices.
7. Explanation of why I get headaches.
9. Argument: the conclusion is the last proposition.

1.4 Part II

11. Argument
13. Argument
15. This is an explanation of why traditionally Cupid is painted blind, and thus an explanation of why it is that so much conduct, under the influence of love, is not rational.

17. Argument to support the claim that increasing incarceration rates do not result in decreasing crime rates. There is also an explanation of why few crimes result in imprisonment.

19. Explanation of why Mason refused to sign the Constitution.

1.5 RECOGNIZING ARGUMENTS

A. Premise- and Conclusion-Indicators

1. P: Genes and proteins are discovered, not invented.
   P: Inventions are patentable, discoveries are not.
   C: Protein patents are intrinsically flawed.

3. P: In Midtown the bedrock's close to the surface.
   C: In Midtown the aquifers are close to the surface.

5. P: Economic inequality is correlated with political instability.
   P: Economic inequality is correlated with violent crime.
   P: Economic inequality is correlated with reduced life expectancy.
   P: There is no moral justification for chief executives being paid hundreds of times more than ordinary employees.
   C: The wealth gap is a bad thing and should be decried.

7. P: Married people are healthier and more economically stable than single people.

P: Children of married people do better on a variety of indicators.

C/P: Marriage is a socially responsible act.

Implicit P: Socially responsible acts should be rewarded.

C: There ought to be some way of spreading the principle of support for marriage throughout the tax code.

9. P: Today is Thursday.

C/P: You didn't wait until Sunday.

P: If approval were certain and the vote only a matter of form, you would have waited until Sunday to tell me.

C: It is not the case that approval is certain and the vote a matter of form.

P: Today is Thursday.

C/P: You didn't wait until Friday evening services.

P: If approval were likely but not absolutely certain, you would probably mention it when next you happened to see me, which would be Friday evening at the services.

C: Approval is not likely but not absolutely certain.

P: If it looked as though the vote were uncertain or even likely to go against me, you would not want to mention it Friday evening for fear of spoiling the Sabbath.

P: You did not want to spoil the Sabbath.

C: So your coming tonight can only mean that you have reason to believe I will not be reappointed.

1.5   D. Unstated Propositions—Part I

1. P: Federal racial set-asides will be upheld by the Supreme Court only where there is convincing evidence of past discrimination against minorities by the Federal government.

P: But for almost 20 years the Federal government has been discriminating in favor of minority contractors, not against them.

C: Federal minority preferences in procurement are doomed.

3. P: Driving without a seatbelt is dangerous. (reformulated question)

P: Statistics show you are ten times more likely to be injured in an accident if you are not wearing a seat belt.

P: In our state you can get fined $100 if you are caught not wearing one.

C: You ought to wear one even if you are driving a short distance.

5. P: If marriage is based on trust then the saying, "If you are not with the one you love, love the one you are with," is not good advice for a happy marriage. (rephrased rhetorical question)

C: "Absence makes the heart grow fonder" is good advice for a happy marriage.

7. P: If future scientists find a way to signal back in time, their signals would have reached us already.

P: Their signals have not reached us.

C: Future scientists did not find a way to signal back in time.

9. P: Insofar as a man fulfills his obligation to make himself the author of his decisions, he will . . . deny that he has a duty to obey the laws of the state *simply because they are the laws.*

C: There can be no resolution of the conflict between the autonomy of the individual and the putative authority of the state.

1.5   D. Unstated Propositions—Part II

11. P: The dominant characteristic of sprawl is that each component of a community—housing, shopping centers, office parks, and civic institutions—is segregated, physically separated from the others, causing the residents of suburbia to spend an inordinate amount of time and money moving from one place to the next.

P: Nearly everyone drives alone.

C: Even a sparsely populated area can generate the traffic of a much larger traditional town.

13. P: There are disturbing patterns of abuse in sports at institutions of higher education, especially at some big-time programs.

P: These patterns are grounded in institutional indifference, presidential neglect, and the growing commercialization of sport combined with the urge to win at all costs.

Subconclusion: On too many campuses big-time revenue sports are out of control.

C: All of the positive contributions that sports make to higher education are threatened.

15. P: Genes produce enzymes.

P: Enzymes influence neurochemical processes in the brain.

P: Neurochemical processes in the brain are what cognitive (i.e., intellectual) functions depend on.

C: It would be dumbfounding if intellectual function were without genetic influence.

17. P: The diminutive capital held by the lower strata of the middle class does not suffice for the scale on which modern industry is carried on, and is swamped in the competition with the largest capitalists.

P: The specialized skills of the lower strata of the middle class are rendered worthless by new methods of production.

Subconclusion: The lower strata of the middle class gradually will sink into the proletariat.

C: The proletariat is recruited from all classes of the population.

19. P: In certain cases income for institutions of higher education from government-financed programs is based on total expenses charged to students by the institution.

Subconclusion: Cuts in tuition can reduce institutional income from government-financed aid programs.

Hidden premise: Institutions of higher education are disinclined to do anything that will reduce their incomes.

C: There is a built-in disincentive for institutions of higher education to lower their tuition costs.

1.9 Analyzing Arguments

1. P: Artistic creations are precious commodities.

P: We support artists by purchasing their creations.

P: Taking someone's artistic creation without paying for it deprives the artist of a deserved royalty.

P: Lacking a reasonable royalty the artist cannot survive.

C: Therefore, we should prosecute people who steal copyrighted material.

3. P: (1) If you get dressed slowly, then we shall be late for the party.

P/C: (2) If we are late to the party, we shall have to stay until the end of the party.

P: (3) If we are late for the party and leave early, the host will not think we were glad to go to the party, but we want the host to think we were glad to go to the party.

P: (4) If we stay until the end of the party, then we shall be late to your mother's party.

P: (5) If we are late to your mother's party, then your mother will not think you love her anymore.

C: (6) If you get dressed slowly, then your mother will not think you love her anymore.

Implicit conclusions:

C: (7) If you get dressed slowly, we shall have to stay until the end of the party.

C: (8) If you get dressed slowly, then we shall be late to your mother's party.

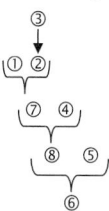

5. P: (1) Texas added more people to prisons in the 1990s than New York's entire prison population.

C: (2) (and the premise of the argument that follows): If prisons are a cure for crime, Texas should have mightily outperformed New York from a crime control standpoint.

P: (3) From 1990 to 1998, the decline in New York's crime rate exceeded the decline in Texas's crime rate by 26 percent.

C: (4) An over-reliance upon prisons as a cure for crime is futile.

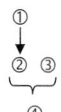

1.10 Complex Argumentative Passages

1. ① Since you are going to have to work for a living for most of your life, ② you should get into an occupation that you enjoy. ③ Of course, it is not always possible to correctly predict how you will like a certain occupation. ④ Sometimes a career looks good from the outside, but when you actually do it for awhile it loses its appeal. ⑤ Getting a broad education allows you to gain general skills applicable to many careers. ⑥ Sometimes specializing too early locks you into a field that you may not like later on in life. ⑦ These are some of the reasons why getting a liberal arts education can be a good decision.

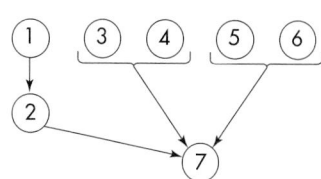

3. ① Paternal and maternal genes can be antagonistic to one another. Consider pregnancy. ② In most mammals, the mother's body regards the embryo as an intruder, and ③ tries to limit the demands it places on her resources. ④ The father, of course, does not bear the young and so ⑤ is unaffected by such considerations. His genetic interest is unambiguous: to stimulate the embryo's growth and to shield it from the mother's defenses. Thus ⑥ only males contribute the genes that foster the growth of the protective organ known as the placenta; ⑦ females do not. ⑧ Uniparental mouse eggs, created from the genes of the mother alone, develop into normal embryos, but the embryos lack a placenta and so ⑨ do not flourish.

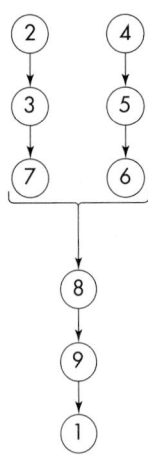

5. Consider why the federal government is involved in student lending. ① It is in the national interest to have an educated populace. ② On average, college graduates earn almost twice the annual salary of high school graduates. ③ The cost of the nation's investment in the education of student borrowers is recouped many times over through increased productivity and greater earnings. ④ By making a college education possible for millions of Americans, federally sponsored student loans produce a

tremendous return for the U.S. Treasury and for students, whose incomes—and tax payments—are greatly increased with their college degrees. ⑤ But most college students are not creditworthy borrowers. ⑥ The typical student is cash poor, ⑦ owner of few if any assets that could be used as collateral and ⑧ often earns too little to be considered a good credit risk. ⑨ If such a borrower could get a loan, in all likelihood it would carry a high interest rate—high enough to lead many students to decide not to go on to higher education. That is why ⑩ student loans are backed by federal money and the interest charged on those loans is capped.

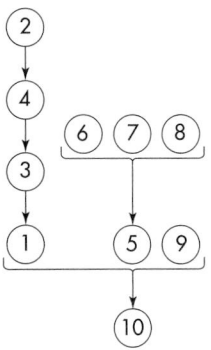

7. One of the most difficult problems associated with quantum research is how to observe subatomic particles in their natural states without affecting them—observing them non-destructively, so to speak. ① It's very difficult for two reasons. ② First, atoms and subatomic particles are the smallest constituents of matter. Since ③ any medium used to observe them emits energy of its own ④ that energy of the observing medium must affect the energy of the observed particles. ⑤ Second, in isolation, atomic components exist in two quantum states simultaneously—particles and waves. ⑥ It's as if they were packets of statistical probability. ⑦ Only when they interact with other components do they display one manifestation or the other.

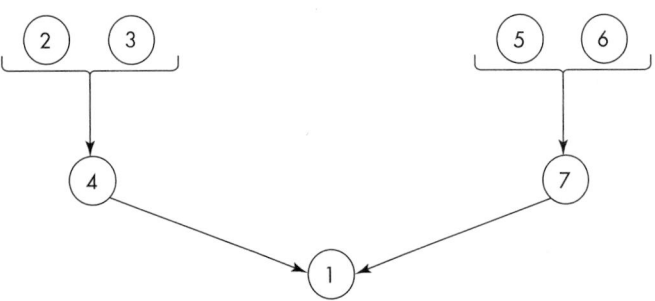

9. ① Eliminating a tax on marriage sounds like a great idea. But ② it is also a sound idea to set higher rates on wealthier people and ③ to tax families with the same total income no matter how their income is split between spouses. ④ No tax code can satisfy these three goals simultaneously. ⑤ Two people whose individual incomes are low enough to be taxed at 15 percent can, under a progressive code, hit the 28 percent bracket when their incomes are combined. ⑥ Congress can eliminate the marriage tax, but only by sacrificing progressivity.

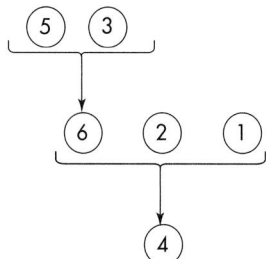

Chapter 2 Informal Fallacies

2.2 FALLACIES OF RELEVANCE
Part I

1. Appeal to Pity
3. Appeal to Illegitimate Authority
5. Personal Attack, circumstantial
7. Appeal to Force
9. Appeal to Force
11. Irrelevant Conclusion
13. Irrelevant Conclusion
15. Irrelevant Conclusion
17. Appeal to Emotion
19. Irrelevant Conclusion
21. Appeal to Emotion
23. Appeal to Emotion
25. Personal Attack, abusive; also Appeal to Emotion
27. Appeal to Ignorance
29. Appeal to Illegitimate Authority

2.2 Part II

31. Personal Attack, circumstantial, although Mr. Welch believed that the attack on GE was based on a false premise.
33. Appeal to Ignorance and an appeal to the fears of the readers.
35. Whether this is an *inappropriate* appeal to authority is certainly a disputable matter. Freud was a great thinker, whose understanding of the human psyche and its needs was penetrating and often very wise. But whether Freud's judgment regarding the "impossibility" or implausibility of religious belief by enlightened moderns is authoritative is not at all clear. It may be that with regard to religious beliefs, his authority, as a great psychoanalyst and theorist, dissolves, and that in this sphere the appeal to his writings is fallacious.

2.3 FALLACIES OF PRESUMPTION

1. False Cause
3. Complex Question
5. Suppressed Evidence
7. False Dichotomy
9. False Cause
11. Begging the Question
13. Accident, or False Cause
15. Converse Accident. The generalization that most people like fighting and adventure-packed computer games is a hidden premise here and is being applied illegitimately to a case it does not necessarily govern.
17. False Dichotomy
19. This is a case of stereotyping: people without jobs are assumed to be unconcerned with justice. In virtue of applying a generalization too broadly, this commits the fallacy of accident.
21. False Cause
23. False Dichotomy
25. False Cause. It is altogether unlikely that the involvement of the Federal Government in public education (a process found unavoidable because of the long-continued failings of many state and local governments) is itself the cause of the large number of functional illiterates in America.

2.4 FALLACIES OF AMBIGUITY
Part I

1. Composition
3. Equivocation
5. Amphiboly
7. Equivocation
9. Amphiboly

2.4 Part II

11. Composition
13. Equivocation

15. Amphiboly

2.4 Part III

17. Equivocation on *this*.

19. Division

2.4 Part IV

21. Appeal to Force

23. Appeal to Emotion (snob appeal)

25. Appeal to Emotion

27. False Cause

29. Complex Question

31. Amphiboly

33. There is no fallacy: Colonel Oakdale has the credentials that make him an authority on fuses.

35. Appeal to Force

37. Appeal to Pity

39. Irrelevant Conclusion (straw person)

41. False Dichotomy

43. Personal Attack

45. Composition

47. Appeal to Emotion

49. Appeal to Force

51. Accident

53. False Cause (slippery slope)

55. Equivocation on *euthanasia/youth in Asia*

57. Complex Question

59. Irrelevant Conclusion (straw person)

61. Appeal to Authority

63. Begging the Question

65. Division

67. Appeal to Pity

69. False Cause

71. This is a delightful stew of fallacies, the primary ingredients being begging the question, false cause, and sophistical irrelevant conclusion. But Miss Alabama was no doubt very charming.

73. An appeal to emotion of the baldest kind. As in much advertising, one is here urged to do something simply because "everybody" else is doing it.

75. Although this passage contains some verbal abuse, the argument is fallacious as a sophistical irrelevant conclusion: that many folks are careless or foolish enough to kill themselves and others with automobiles, is no proof whatever that their protests against nuclear power are wrongheaded.

77. The premise says that religion is important, and that mysticism is part of religion. The conclusion asserts that mysticism is therefore important. But this is to infer a property of the part from a property of the whole, and so it commits the fallacy of division.

79. If this is taken to be an argument—that the question of our immortality is the most intelligible of all questions because it is the most important of all questions—it is plainly fallacious, a sophistical irrelevant conclusion, a great *non sequitur*. But the passage may not have been intended as an argument so much as an assertion that the question of immortality is both exceedingly important and perfectly intelligible.

Chapter 3 Categorical Propositions

3.2 Categorical Propositions and Classes

1. **A proposition** Subject Term: game shows; Predicate Term: intellectually stimulating shows

3. **E proposition** Subject Term: parrot; Predicate Term: my grandfather

5. **O proposition** Subject Term: zodiac signs; Predicate Term: lucky signs

7. **O proposition** Subject Term: jokes; Predicate Term: funny things

9. **E proposition** Subject Term: life form; Predicate Term: a closed thermodynamic system

11. **O proposition** Subject Term: parrot; Predicate Term: my grandmother

13. **E proposition** Subject Term: dogs that are without pedigrees; Predicate Term: candidates for blue ribbons in official dog shows sponsored by the American Kennel Club

15. **O proposition** Subject Term: drugs that are very effective when properly administered; Predicate Term: safe remedies that all medicine cabinets should contain

3.3 Symbolism and Venn Diagrams for Categorical Propositions

1. **A proposition**
$B\overline{H} = 0$

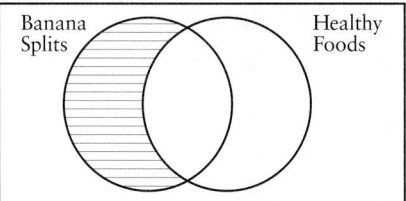

3. **E proposition**

$HS = 0$

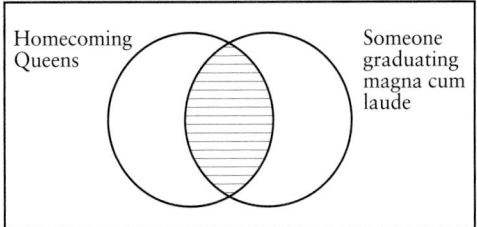

11. **E proposition**

$DP = 0$

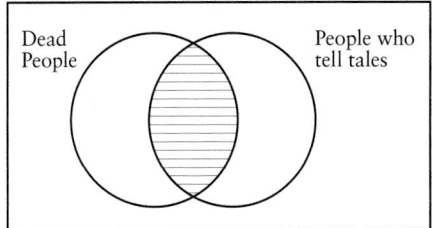

5. **A proposition**

$P\overline{F} = 0$

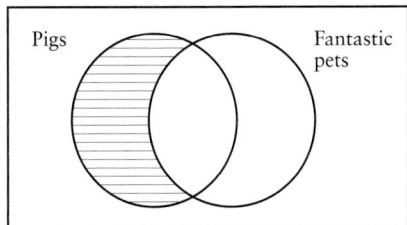

13. **A proposition**

$T\overline{C} = 0$

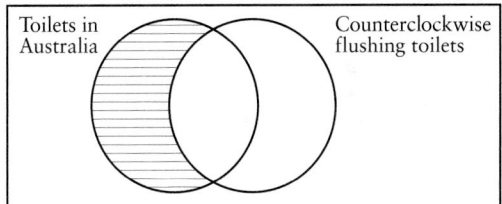

7. **I propositions**

$OD \neq 0$

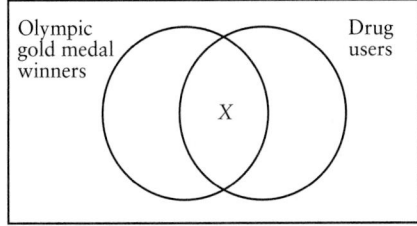

15. **E proposition**

$PA = 0$

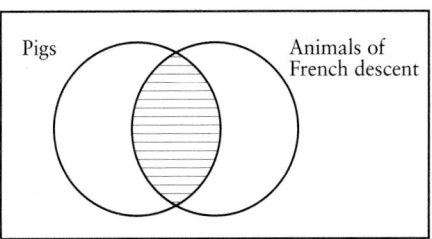

9. **A proposition**

$K\overline{P} = 0$

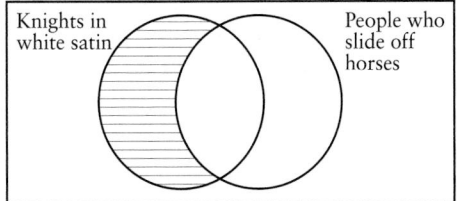

17. **A proposition**

$T\overline{O} = 0$

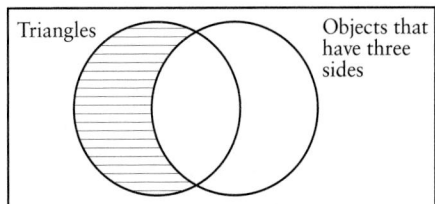

19. O proposition

$M\overline{P} \neq 0$

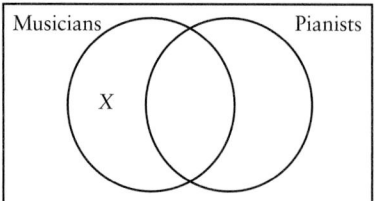

21. E proposition

$MP = 0$

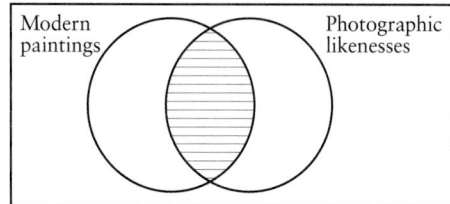

23. O proposition

$P\overline{S} \neq 0$

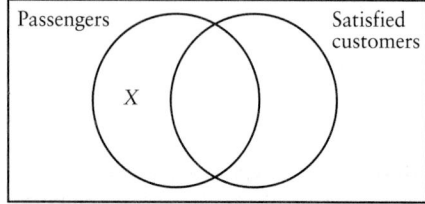

25. A proposition

$P\overline{M} \neq 0$

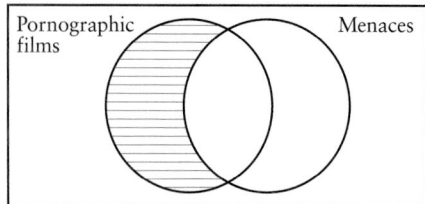

3.4 DISTRIBUTION

1. **A proposition** SUBJECT TERM *sweet-toothed teenagers* is distributed; PREDICATE TERM *dentists' best friends* is undistributed.

3. **E proposition** SUBJECT TERM *chlorinated swimming pool* is distributed; PREDICATE TERM *an algae-free thing* is distributed.

5. **E proposition** SUBJECT TERM *stuffed turkeys* is distributed; PREDICATE TERM *vegetarians' delights* is distributed.

7. **E proposition** SUBJECT TERM *puppy* is distributed; PREDICATE TERM *a big dog* is distributed.

9. **O proposition** SUBJECT TERM *things* is undistributed; PREDICATE TERM *things that are clear* is distributed.

11. **A proposition** SUBJECT TERM *artificial intelligence (AI) algorithms* is distributed; PREDICATE TERM *abstract entities that are unaware of what they are* is undistributed.

13. **I proposition** SUBJECT TERM *members of the military-industrial complex* is undistributed; PREDICATE TERM *mild-mannered people to whom violence is abhorrent* is undistributed.

15. **A proposition** SUBJECT TERM *new labor-saving devices* is distributed; PREDICATE TERM *major threats to the trade union movement* is undistributed.

3.6 THE ARISTOTELIAN SQUARE OF OPPOSITION AND IMMEDIATE INFERENCES

Part I

1. Some spiders are not nine-legged creatures.

3. There is no opposition between the two statements, since the predicates differ.

5. You can infer the truth of the statement, "Some rocket scientists are not slow thinkers."

7. True: They're subcontraries.

9. You can make no inference regarding the superaltern of the statement.

3.6 Part II

11. If **a** is true, then **b** is false (it's the contrary of **a**), **c** is true (it's the subaltern of **a**), and **d** is false (it's the contradictory of **a**). If **a** is false, all you can infer is that its contradictory, **d**, is true.

13. If **a** is true, all you can infer is that its contradictory, **d**, is false. If **a** is false, you can infer that its contradictory, **d**, is true; its subcontrary, **b**, is true; and its superaltern, **c**, is false.

3.8 LOGICAL EQUIVALENCE AND IMMEDIATE INFERENCES

Part I

1. "Some results of plastic surgery are things beyond belief."

Converse: Some things beyond belief are the results of plastic surgery.

Obverse: Some results of plastic surgery are not non-things beyond belief.

Contrapositive (not logically equivalent): Some non-things beyond belief are non-results of plastic surgery. It does not pick out the same class of things as the contraponend.

3. "No VCRs are easy-to-program things."

Converse: No easy-to-program things are VCRs.

Obverse: All VCRs are non-easy-to-program things.

Contrapositive (not logically equivalent): No non-easy-to-program things are non-VCRs. The contraponend claims that there is nothing that is in both the subject and predicate classes, while the contrapositive claims there is nothing that is in the complement of both classes.

5. "No chocolate candy bars are things good for your complexion."

Converse: No things good for your complexion are chocolate candy bars.

Obverse: All chocolate candy bars are non-things good for your complexion.

Contrapositive (not logically equivalent): No non-things good for your complexion are non-chocolate candy bars. The contrapositive obverts to (stated in a more colloquial way): All things that are not good for your complexion are chocolate candy bars. The class of things not good for your complexion includes more than chocolate candy bars, so the contrapositive is not equivalent to the given statement.

7. "All cigarettes are carcinogenic things."

Converse (not logically equivalent): All carcinogenic things are cigarettes. This is false, since some cancer-causing objects are not cigarettes.

Obverse: No cigarettes are noncarcinogenic things.

Contrapositive: All noncarcinogenic things are noncigarettes.

9. "All UFOs are unidentified flying objects." Here we need to draw a distinction. Properly speaking, *UFO* is an acronym for *unidentified flying object*. So understood, the statement says, "All UFOs are UFOs," that is, the subject and predicate terms are the same, so you could convert as well as obvert and contrapose. If you understand *UFO* to mean extraterrestrial flying object (EFO), that is, "All EFOs are unidentified flying objects," the converse would be, "All unidentified flying objects are EFOs," which is false: There are often unidentified blips on air traffic control radar, and they seldom (if ever) turn out to be EFOs. Of course, the obverse, "No EFOs are non-unidentified (= identified) flying objects" and the contrapositive, "All non-unidentified flying objects are non-EFOs" would be logically equivalent to "All EFOs are unidentified flying objects."

3.8 Part II

11. "No reckless drivers who pay no attention to traffic regulations are people who are considerate of others": logically equivalent.

13. "Some warm-blooded animals are not reptiles": It is not logically equivalent.

3.8 Part III

15. "Some clergy are nonabstainers."

3.8 Part IV

17. "Some nonofficers are not nonsoldiers." Logically equivalent.

19. "All non-objects not more than four feet high are non-things weighing fewer than 50 pounds." Logically equivalent.

3.8 Part V

21. True on both interpretations: It's the contrapositive of the given.

3.8 Part VI

23. False on the Aristotelian interpretation (convert the given then contrapose the corresponding **A** proposition, the contrary of the given). On the Boolean interpretation, where we introduce no existential assumptions, the truth value is undetermined.

25. True on the Aristotelian interpretation. Undetermined on the Boolean interpretation.

3.8 Part VII

27. "All martyrs were nonsaints" obverts to "No martyrs were saints," which converts to "No saints were martyrs," which is the contradictory of the given. If the given is true, the statement is false on either interpretation.

29. Undetermined on either interpretation.

3.8 Part VIII

31. "No merchants are nonpirates" obverts to "All merchants are pirates," which is the contradictory of the given, and therefore false on both interpretations.

33. "No pirates are nonmerchants" obverts to "All pirates of merchants." Neither the given nor the universal affirmative converts. So, you cannot restate both statements with the same subject and predicate terms. So, the truth value is undetermined on both interpretations.

35. "No merchants are nonpirates" obverts to "All merchants are pirates," which is the contradictory of the given, and therefore false on both interpretations.

Chapter 4 Categorical Syllogisms

4.1 STANDARD FORM CATEGORICAL SYLLOGISMS

Part I

1. The major term is *gentlemen*. The minor term is *gamblers*. **EAE-1**

3. The major term is *vans*. The minor term is *automobiles*. **EAE-3**

5. The major term is *chess players*. The minor term is *Wookies*. **AAA-1**

7. The major term is *inkblots*. The minor term is *butterflies*. **AOO-2**

9. The major term is *examples of Indian art*. The minor term is *living room decorations*. **AEE-4**

11. The major term is *snake pits*. The minor term is *places in the Bronx*. **EIO-4**

13. The major term is *elevators*. The minor term is *claustrophobic places*. **AAI-1**

15. The major term is *undated documents*. The minor term is *unimportant documents*. **EEE-3**

4.1 Part II

17. Some objects of worship are fir trees.

    All fir trees are evergreens.

    ∴ Some evergreens are objects of worship.
    IAI-4

19. Some juvenile delinquents are products of broken homes.

    All juvenile delinquents are maladjusted individuals.

    ∴ Some maladjusted individuals are products of broken homes.
    IAI-3

4.2 THE NATURE OF SYLLOGISTIC ARGUMENTS

1. Form: **EEI–4**. Refutation:

   No elephants are Republicans.

   No Republicans are Democrats.

   ∴ Some Democrats are elephants.

3. Form: **AII-4**. Refutation:

   All dogs are mammals.

   Some mammals are cats.

   ∴ Some cats are dogs.

5. Form: **AAA–2**. Refutation:

   All ducks are birds.

   All geese are birds.

   ∴ All geese are ducks.

7. Form: **AAA-4**. Refutation:

   All jelly beans are things made of sugar.

   All things made of sugar are things attractive to young people.

   ∴ All things attractive to young people are jelly beans.

9. Form: **EEA-1**. Refutation:

   No polar bears are seals.

   No buzzards are polar bears.

   ∴ All buzzards are seals.

11. Form: **EAA-2**. Refutation:

    No ravens are cows.

    All holsteins are cows.

    ∴ All holsteins are ravens.

13. Form: **OEI-4**. Refutation:

    Some mammals are not dogs.

    No dogs are reptiles.

    ∴ Some reptiles are mammals.

15. Form: **AOO-1**. Refutation:

    All mammals are vertebrates.

    Some fish are not mammals.

    ∴ Some fish are not vertebrates.

4.3 VENN DIAGRAM TECHNIQUE FOR TESTING

Part I

1. **AEE–1**
   All M are P,
   No S are M.
   No S are P.

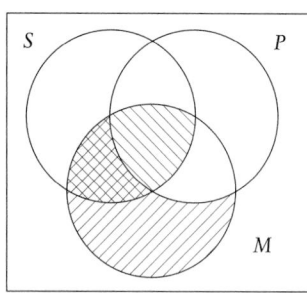

Invalid

3. **AAA–4**
   All P are M.
   All M are S.
   All S are P.

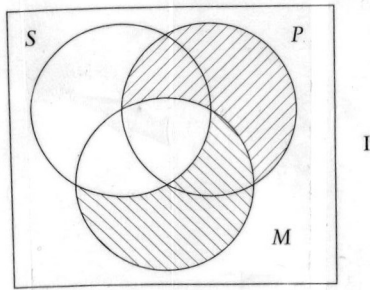

Invalid

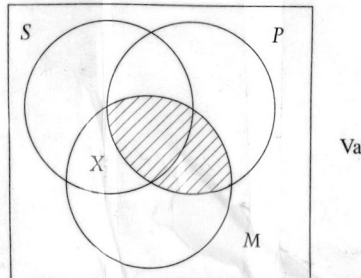

Valid

5. OAO–3
Some M are not P.
All M are S.
Some S are not P.

4.3 Part II

11. Some philosophers are mathematicians.
All scientists are mathematicians.
∴ Some scientists are philosophers.

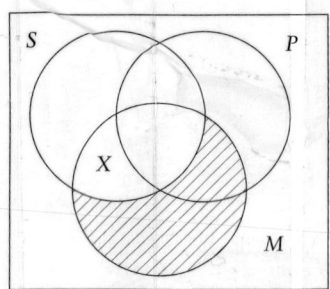

Valid

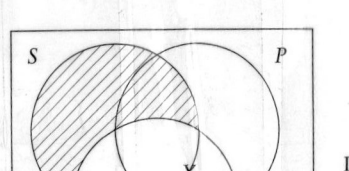

Invalid

7. AOO–1
All M are P.
Some S are not M.
∴ Some S are not P.

13. No pleasure vessels are underwater craft.
All underwater craft are submarines.
∴ No submarines are pleasure vessels.

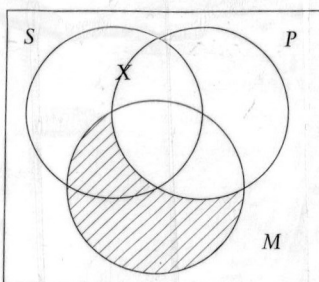

Invalid

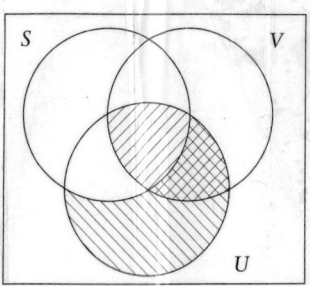

Invalid

9. EIO–3
No M are P.
Some M are S.
∴ Some S are not P.

15. All labor leaders are liberals.
No weaklings are liberals.
∴ No weaklings are labor leaders.

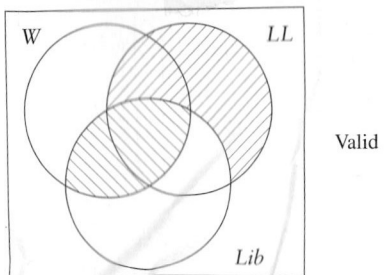

Valid

17. Some flowers are not trees.
All roses are flowers.
∴ No roses are trees.

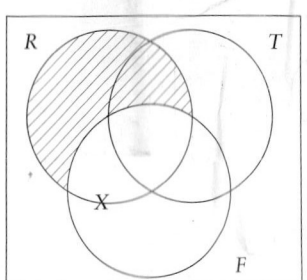

Invalid

19. All moose are large animals.
Some elephants are not moose.
∴ Some elephants are large animals.

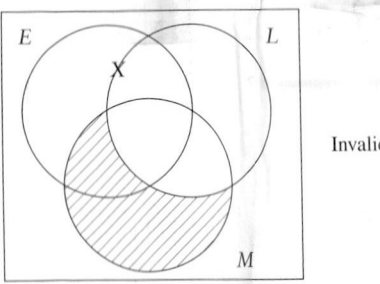

Invalid

21. Some prodigious persons are people who live a balanced life.
Some people who live a balanced life are not eccentrics.
∴ All eccentrics are prodigious persons.

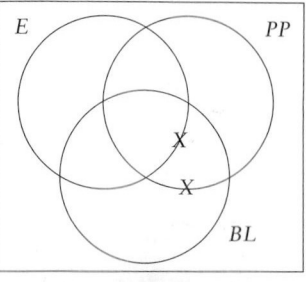

Invalid

23. All elephants are large animals.
No mice are large animals.
∴ No mice are elephants.

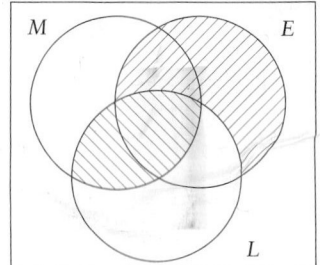

Valid

25. All candy makers are people who like licorice.
Some chocoholics are not candy makers.
∴ Some chocoholics are people who like licorice.

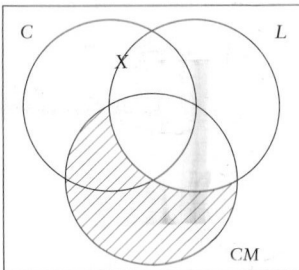

Invalid

27. All successful authors are coffee addicts.
No kindergartners are successful authors.
∴ Some kindergartners are coffee addicts.

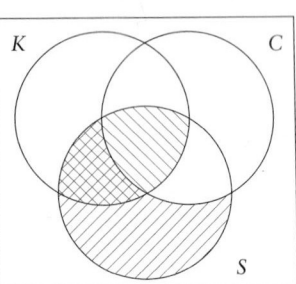

Invalid

5.3 B. Categorical Propositions with Adjectives or Adjectival Phrases as Predicates

1. All people who are Muhammad Ali are the greatest people. *or* Some people who are Muhammad Ali are the greatest people.

3. All people who are my doctor are people who are out of time. *or* Some people who are my doctor are people who are out of time.

5. All astronauts are courageous people.

7. Some houses are not houses built for families of six or more.

9. All Swedish meatballs are meatballs made from beef and pork.

5.3 C. Categorical Propositions with Verbs Other Than the Standard Form Copula *To Be*

1. All people who are Muhammad Ali are people who sting like a bee. *or* Some people who are Muhammad Ali are people who sting like a bee.

3. All people who are my doctor are people who didn't follow my doctor's advice. *or* Some people who are my doctor are people who didn't follow my doctor's advice.

5. All cows are things that eat grass.

7. All people who are the person to my left are people who have bad breath. *or* Some people who are the person to my left are people who have bad breath.

9. All stained houses are houses that fade after a few years.

5.3 D. Categorical Propositions in Nonstandard Order

1. All boxers are people who worship Muhammad Ali.

3. All doctors are people who have their faults.

5. All times are times when you have the poor with you.

7. All people who enter here are people who should abandon hope.

9. No Chevy Cavalier is a Corvette.

5.3 E. Categorical Propositions with Nonstandard Quantifiers

1. Some great boxers are not boxers of the caliber of Muhammad Ali.

3. No doctor is in. *or* Some doctor is a person who is not in.

5. Some problem in this set is not a difficult problem.

7. All people who went to last night's game are people who saw an exciting finish.

9. All dogs are mammals.

5.3 F. Exclusive Propositions

1. All people who can enter here are people who know geometry.

3. All monkeys with their own book series are monkeys that are identical with Curioius George.

5. All people who figure out how to translate *none but* are clever people.

7. All horses are mammals.

9. All people in this class who find exclusive propositions amusing are people identical with Katrina.

5.3 J. More Complex Quantifiers

1. All cats are curious animals.

3. Some preachers are not boring speakers.

5. All logicians are people who analyze arguments.

7. All times are times when you have to look at the bright side of life.

9. Some people are people who have lived to regret a misspent youth.

11. No person who faces the sun is a person who sees his or her shadow.

13. All people who know their own limitations are happy people.

15. All soft answers are answers that turn away wrath.

17. All nonscoundrels are people who can be expected to tell the truth, and no scoundrels are people who can be expected to tell the truth.

19. Some exercises in this section are exercises that could be challenging.

5.4 UNIFORM TRANSLATION

Part I

1. No time is a time when Susan eats her lunch at her desk.

3. All cases of errors being tolerated are cases of errors resulting from honest mistakes.

5. All places where he chooses to walk are places where he walks.

7. All places were she may happen to be are places where she tries to sell life insurance.

9. All times are times when the lights are on.

5.4 Part II

11. All predicables are things that come in contradictory pairs.

   No names are things that come in contradictory pairs.

   ∴ No names are predicables.

   AEE-2

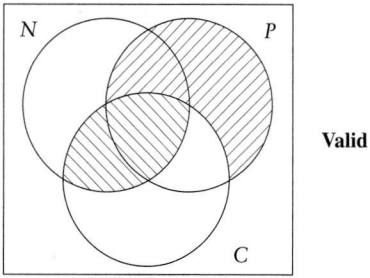

Valid

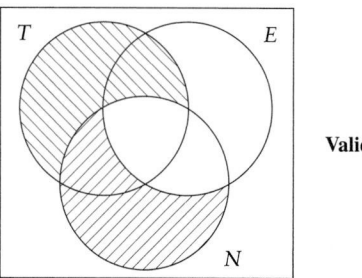

Valid

13. All pairs of persons who contradict each other are pairs of persons who cannot both be lying.

   The pair of persons who are identical with the first and third natives is a pair of persons who contradict each other.

   The pair of persons who are identical with the first and third natives is a pair of persons who cannot both be lying.

   The singular premise and conclusion allow you to treat it as an **AAA-1** or an **AII-1**.

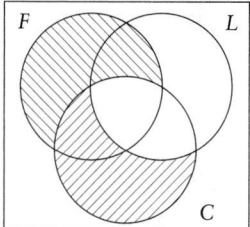 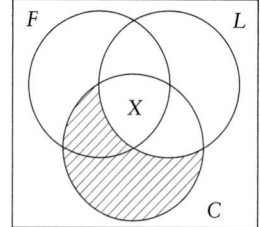

Valid

15. All people are thinkers.

   All bridge players are people.

   ∴ All bridge players are thinkers.

   AAA–1

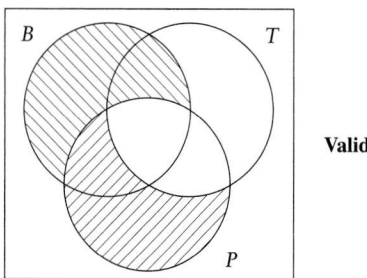

Valid

17. All fightings against neighbors are evil actions.

   All fightings against the Thebans are fightings against neighbors.

   ∴ All fightings aginst the Thebans are evil actions.

   AAA-1

19. All times when Cynthia compliments Henry are times when Henry is cheerful.

   This time is a time when Henry is cheerful.

   This time is a time when Cynthia compliments Henry.

   The minor premise and conclusion are singular, so the syllogism can be treated as either an **AAA-2** or as an **AII-2**.

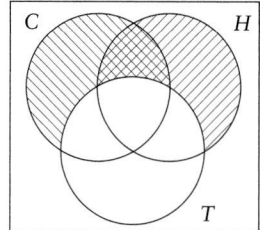 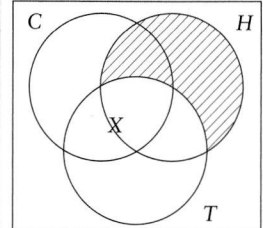

Invalid:
Rule 2, Fallacy of Undistributed Middle

21. All trains not stopping at the station are trains that are the express train.

   The last train was a train not stopping at the station.

   The last train was a train that is the express train.

   The minor premise and conclusion are singular propositions, so the syllogism can be treated as either an **AAA-1** or an **AII-1**.

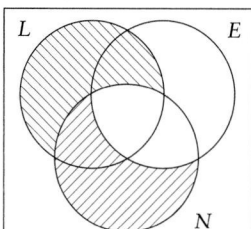 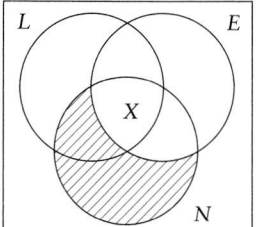

Valid

23. Some men are handsome creatures.

    All vile creatures are men.

    ∴ Some vile creatures are handsome creatures.

    IAI-1

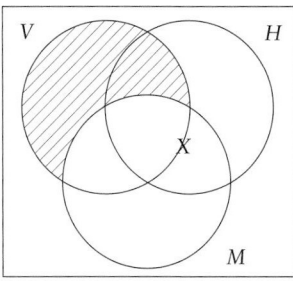

Invalid: Rule 2,
Undistributed Middle

25. All penniless persons were convicted persons.

    Some guilty persons were not convicted persons.

    ∴ Some guilty persons were not penniless persons.

    AOO–2

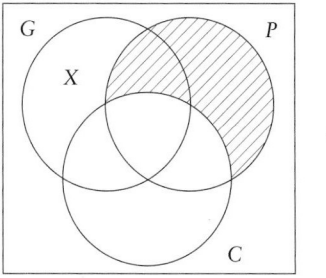

Valid

5.5 ENTHYMEMES

1. All refined people are honest people.

   Hal is a refined person.

   ∴ Hal is an honest person.

3. All people who are safe drivers are people whose insurance rates are low.

   Susanna is a person who is a safe driver.

   Susanna is a person whose insurance rates are low.

5. Hal is a thing that is a computer.

   All things that are computers are things that do not lie.

   ∴ Hal is a thing that does not lie.

7. All things that are always in motion are things that are immortal.

   The soul through all her being is a thing that is always in motion.

   ∴ The soul through all her being is a thing that is immortal.

9. All people who believe that all that exists is spiritual are idealists.

   I am a person who believes that all that exists is spiritual.

   ∴ I am an idealist.

11. The premise and conclusion are singular propositions. So, they both could be stated as either universal affirmative or particular affirmative propostions. In either case, the major premise must be a universal affirmative. So, the syllogism is:

    All times when fish do not bite are times following rain.

    (All/Some) This time is a time when fish do not bite.

    ∴ (All/Some) This time is a time following rain.

    The *problem*, as anyone who fishes will tell you, is that the assumed premise is false, alas!

13. No enthymemes are complete arguments.

    This argument is an enthymeme.

    ∴ This argument is not a complete argument.

15. No sinner is one who should cast the first stone.

    All persons here are sinners.

    ∴ No person here is one who should cast the first stone.

17. All responsibilities are things dreaded by most men.

    All liberties are responsibilities.

    ∴ All liberties are things dreaded by most men.

19. All things that help bring buyers and sellers together are things that perform a vital function in almost any society.

    All advertisements are things that help bring buyers and sellers together.

    ∴ All advertisements are things that perform a vital function in almost any society.

Chapter 6 Symbolic Logic

6.2 SYMBOLESE 101: THE LANGUAGE OF PROPOSITIONAL LOGIC

Part I

1. T	3. F	5. F	7. T	9. F
11. T	13. T	15. T	17. F	19. F
21. T	23. T	25. F		

6.2 Part II

27. T	29. T	31. T	33. T	35. F
37. T	39. T	41. T	43. F	45. F
47. F	49. F			

6.2 Part III

51. F	**53.** F	**55.** INDET.	**57.** T
59. INDET.	**61.** T	**63.** F	
65. T	**67.** T	**69.** T	
71. F	**73.** T	**75.** INDET.	

6.2 Part IV

77. $R \supset T$	**79.** $S \vee L$
81. $S \equiv K$	**83.** $J \equiv {\sim}Y$
85. ${\sim}(B \supset W)$	**87.** $L \supset {\sim}W$
89. ${\sim}(S \bullet D)$	**91.** ${\sim}Y \bullet {\sim}A$ *or* ${\sim}(Y \vee A)$
93. $M \equiv (J \bullet A)$	**95.** $(L \vee T) \bullet Z$
97. $L \supset (G \vee M)$	**99.** $(R \supset F) \vee C$
101. $(B \vee M) \supset {\sim}G$	**103.** $(M \bullet B) \supset H$
105. ${\sim}O \supset ({\sim}S \vee C)$	**107.** $(S \vee {\sim}I) \supset (W \bullet R)$
109. $(B \supset G) \supset (H \equiv R)$	
111. $({\sim}T \supset H) \bullet {\sim}(T \supset {\sim}H)$	
113. ${\sim}(S \supset J) \bullet ({\sim}C \supset B)$	
115. $L \supset [N \vee (M \equiv O)]$	
117. $(C \supset D) \supset {\sim}(N \supset L)$	
119. $C \supset [B \supset (H \supset N)]$	
121. ${\sim}(F \vee A) \supset (B \vee {\sim}D)$	

123. $(N \equiv D) \equiv [J \supset (B \supset S)]$
125. $(L \supset N) \supset [(I \vee J) \supset G]$

6.3 Truth Tables as Tools for Analyzing Compound Propositions

Part I

1. $p \supset {\sim}q$

p	q	${\sim}q$	$p \supset {\sim}q$
T	T	F	F
T	F	T	T
F	T	F	T
F	F	T	T

3. $(p \vee q) \supset {\sim}q$

p	q	$p \vee q$	${\sim}q$	$(p \vee q) \supset {\sim}q$
T	T	T	F	F
T	F	T	T	T
F	T	T	F	F
F	F	F	T	T

5. $(p \equiv {\sim}q) \supset ({\sim}q \supset {\sim}p)$

p	q	${\sim}q$	$p \equiv {\sim}q$	${\sim}p$	${\sim}q \supset {\sim}p$	$(p \equiv {\sim}q) \supset ({\sim}q \supset {\sim}p)$
T	T	F	F	F	T	T
T	F	T	T	F	F	F
F	T	F	T	T	T	T
F	F	T	F	T	T	T

7. $(p \supset {\sim}p) \equiv [q \supset (p \bullet {\sim}q)]$

p	q	${\sim}p$	$p \supset {\sim}p$	${\sim}q$	$p \bullet {\sim}q$	$q \supset (p \bullet {\sim}q)$	$(p \supset {\sim}p) \equiv [q \supset (p \bullet {\sim}q)]$
T	T	F	F	F	F	F	T
T	F	F	F	T	T	T	F
F	T	T	T	F	F	F	F
F	F	T	T	T	F	T	T

9. $({\sim}p \vee q) \equiv ({\sim}q \bullet r)$

p	q	r	${\sim}p$	${\sim}p \vee q$	${\sim}q$	${\sim}q \bullet r$	$({\sim}p \vee q) \equiv ({\sim}q \bullet r)$
T	T	T	F	T	F	F	F
T	T	F	F	T	F	F	F
T	F	T	F	F	T	T	F
T	F	F	F	F	T	F	T
F	T	T	T	T	F	F	F
F	T	F	T	T	F	F	F
F	F	T	T	T	T	T	T
F	F	F	T	T	T	F	F

11. $\sim(\sim p \equiv q) \cdot (\sim q \supset r)$

p	q	r	$\sim p$	$\sim p \equiv q$	$\sim(\sim p \equiv q)$	$\sim q$	$\sim q \supset r$	$(\sim p \equiv q) \cdot (\sim q \supset r)$
T	T	T	F	F	T	F	T	T
T	T	F	F	F	T	F	T	T
T	F	T	F	T	F	T	T	F
T	F	F	F	T	F	T	F	F
F	T	T	T	T	F	F	T	F
F	T	F	T	T	F	F	T	F
F	F	T	T	F	T	T	T	T
F	F	F	T	F	T	T	F	F

13. $[\sim p \lor \sim(\sim q \cdot \sim r)] \lor p$

p	q	r	$\sim r$	$\sim q$	$\sim q \cdot \sim r$	$\sim(\sim q \cdot \sim r)$	$\sim p$	$\sim p \lor \sim(\sim q \cdot \sim r)$	$[\sim p \lor \sim(\sim q \cdot \sim r)] \lor p$
T	T	T	F	F	F	T	F	T	T
T	T	F	T	F	F	T	F	T	T
T	F	T	F	T	F	T	F	T	T
T	F	F	T	T	T	F	F	F	T
F	T	T	F	F	F	T	T	T	T
F	T	F	T	F	F	T	T	T	T
F	F	T	F	T	F	T	T	T	T
F	F	F	T	T	T	F	T	T	T

15. $\sim[(p \lor \sim q) \cdot r] \lor \sim s$

p	q	r	s	$\sim q$	$p \lor \sim q$	$(p \lor \sim q) \cdot r$	$\sim[(p \lor \sim q) \cdot r]$	$\sim s$	$\sim[(p \lor \sim q) \cdot r] \lor \sim s$
T	T	T	T	F	T	T	F	F	F
T	T	T	F	F	T	T	F	T	T
T	T	F	T	F	T	F	T	F	T
T	T	F	F	F	T	F	T	T	T
T	F	T	T	T	T	T	F	F	F
T	F	T	F	T	T	T	F	T	T
T	F	F	T	T	T	F	T	F	T
T	F	F	F	T	T	F	T	T	T
F	T	T	T	F	F	F	T	F	T
F	T	T	F	F	F	F	T	T	T
F	T	F	T	F	F	F	T	F	T
F	T	F	F	F	F	F	T	T	T
F	F	T	T	T	T	T	F	F	F
F	F	T	F	T	T	T	F	T	T
F	F	F	T	T	T	F	T	F	T
F	F	F	F	T	T	F	T	T	T

6.3 Part II

17. $B \bullet (C \vee \sim D)$

B	C	D	$\sim D$	$C \vee \sim D$	$B \bullet (C \vee \sim D)$
T	F	F	T	T	T

19. $A \bullet B$

A	B	$A \bullet B$
T	T	T

21. $A \bullet \sim B$

A	B	$\sim B$	$A \bullet \sim B$
T	T	F	F

23. $B \bullet (A \vee D)$

A	B	D	$A \vee D$	$B \bullet (A \vee D)$
T	T	F	T	T

25. $[B \supset (C \vee D)] \bullet (A \equiv B)$

A	B	C	D	$C \vee D$	$B \supset (C \vee D)$	$A \equiv B$	$[B \supset (C \vee D)] \bullet (A \equiv B)$
T	T	F	F	F	F	T	F

6.3 Part III

27. $B \supset Y$

B	Y	$B \supset Y$
T	F	F

29. $(X \supset Y) \supset Z$

X	Y	Z	$X \supset Y$	$(X \supset Y) \supset Z$
F	F	F	T	F

31. $(X \supset Y) \supset C$

X	Y	C	$X \supset Y$	$(X \supset Y) \supset C$
F	F	T	T	T

33. $[(A \supset B) \supset C] \supset Z$

A	B	C	Z	$A \supset B$	$(A \supset B) \supset C$	$[(A \supset B) \supset C] \supset Z$
T	T	T	F	T	T	F

35. $[A \supset (B \supset Y)] \supset X$

A	B	X	Y	$B \supset Y$	$A \supset (B \supset Y)$	$[A \supset (B \supset Y)] \supset X$
T	T	F	F	F	F	T

37. $[(A \supset Y) \supset B] \supset Z$

A	B	Y	Z	$A \supset Y$	$(A \supset Y) \supset B$	$[(A \supset Y) \supset B] \supset Z$
T	T	F	F	F	T	F

39. $[(A \bullet X) \vee (\sim A \bullet \sim X)] \supset [(A \supset X) \bullet (X \supset A)]$

A	X	$A \bullet X$	$\sim A$	$\sim X$	$\sim A \bullet \sim X$	$(A \bullet X) \vee (\sim A \bullet \sim X)$	$A \supset X$	$X \supset A$
T	F	F	F	T	F	F	F	T

$(A \supset X) \bullet (X \supset A)$	$[(A \bullet X) \vee (\sim A \bullet \sim X)] \supset [(A \supset X) \bullet (X \supset A)]$
F	T

6.3 Part IV

41. $X \supset Q$

X	Q	$X \supset Q$
F	T	T
F	F	T

43. $(P \bullet A) \supset B$

A	B	P	$P \bullet A$	$(P \bullet A) \supset B$
T	T	T	T	T
T	T	F	F	T

45. $(P \bullet X) \supset Y$

X	Y	P	$P \bullet X$	$(P \bullet X) \supset Y$
F	F	T	F	T
F	F	F	F	T

47. $(P \supset X) \supset (X \supset P)$

X	P	$P \supset X$	$X \supset P$	$(P \supset X) \supset (X \supset P)$
F	T	F	T	T
F	F	T	T	T

49. $[(P \supset B) \supset B] \supset B$

B	P	$P \supset B$	$(P \supset B) \supset B$	$[(P \supset B) \supset B] \supset B$
T	T	T	T	T
T	F	T	T	T

51. $(X \supset P) \supset (\sim X \supset Y)$

X	Y	P	$X \supset P$	$\sim X$	$\sim X \supset Y$	$(X \supset P) \supset (\sim X \supset Y)$
F	F	T	T	T	F	F
F	F	F	T	T	F	F

53. $\sim(A \bullet P) \supset (\sim A \vee \sim P)$

A	P	$A \bullet P$	$\sim(A \bullet P)$	$\sim A$	$\sim P$	$\sim A \vee \sim P$	$\sim(A \bullet P) \supset (\sim A \vee \sim P)$
T	T	T	F	F	F	F	T
T	F	F	T	F	T	T	T

55. $[P \supset (A \vee X)] \supset [(P \supset A) \supset X]$

A	X	P	$A \vee X$	$P \supset (A \vee X)$	$P \supset A$	$(P \supset A) \supset X$	$[P \supset (A \vee X)] \supset [(P \supset A) \supset X]$
T	F	T	T	T	T	F	F
T	F	F	T	T	T	F	F

6.4 Tautologous, Contradictory, and Contingent Statement Forms

Part I

1. $[p \supset (p \supset q)] \supset q$

p	q	$[p \supset (p \supset q)] \supset q$
T	T	T T **T**
T	F	F F **T**
F	T	T T **T**
F	F	T T **F**

Contingent statement

3. $[(p \supset \sim q) \supset p] \supset p$

p	q	$[(p \supset \sim q) \supset p] \supset p$
T	T	F F T **T**
T	F	T T T **T**
F	T	T F F **T**
F	F	T T F **T**

Tautology

5. $p \cdot \sim p$

p	p $\cdot$	$\sim p$
T	**F**	F
F	**F**	T

Contradiction

7. $p \lor q$

p	q	$p \lor q$
T	T	**T**
T	F	**T**
F	T	**T**
F	F	**F**

Contingent

6.4 Part II

9. $(p \supset q) \equiv (\sim q \supset \sim p)$

p	q	$(p \supset q)$	$\equiv$	$(\sim q \supset \sim p)$
T	T	T	**T**	F T F
T	F	F	**T**	T F F
F	T	T	**T**	F T T
F	F	T	**T**	T T T

Tautology

11. $[p \cdot (q \lor r)] \equiv [\sim((\sim q \cdot \sim r) \lor \sim p)]$

p	q	r	$[p \cdot (q \lor r)]$	$\equiv$	$[\sim((\sim q \cdot \sim r)$	$\lor$	$\sim p)]$
T	T	T	T T	**T**	T F FF	F	F
T	T	F	T T	**T**	T F FT	F	F
T	F	T	T T	**T**	T T FF	F	F
T	F	F	F F	**T**	F T TT	T	F
F	T	T	F T	**T**	F F FF	T	T
F	T	F	F T	**T**	F F FT	T	T
F	F	T	F T	**T**	F T FF	T	T
F	F	F	F F	**T**	F F TT	T	T

Tautology

13. $p \equiv (p \lor p)$

p	$p \equiv (p \lor p)$
T	**T** T
F	**T** F

Tautology

15. $p \supset [(p \supset q) \supset q]$

p	q	$p \supset [(p \supset q) \supset q]$
T	T	**T** T T
T	F	**T** F T
F	T	**T** T T
F	F	**T** T F

Tautology

17. $p \supset [\sim p \supset (q \lor \sim q)]$

p	q	$p \supset [\sim p \supset (q \lor \sim q)]$
T	T	**T** F T T F
T	F	**T** F T T T
F	T	**T** T T T F
F	F	**T** T T T T

Tautology

19. $[p \supset (q \supset r)] \supset [(p \supset q) \supset (p \supset r)]$

p	q	r	$[p \supset (q \supset r)] \supset [(p \supset q) \supset (p \supset r)]$
T	T	T	T T **T** T T T
T	T	F	F F **T** T F F
T	F	T	T T **T** F T T
T	F	F	T T **T** F T F
F	T	T	T T **T** T T T
F	T	F	T F **T** T T T
F	F	T	T T **T** T T T
F	F	F	T T **T** T T T

Tautology

6.4. Part III

21. $(p \supset q) \equiv (\sim p \supset \sim q)$

p	q	$(p \supset q)$	$\equiv$	$(\sim p$	$\supset$	$\sim q)$
T	T	T	**T**	F	T	F
T	F	F	**F**	F	T	T
F	T	T	**F**	T	F	F
F	F	T	**T**	T	T	T

Not a tautology

23. $[p \supset (q \supset r)] \equiv [q \supset (p \supset r)]$

p	q	r	$[p \supset (q \supset r)] \equiv [q \supset (p \supset r)]$
T	T	T	T T **T** T T
T	T	F	F F **T** F F
T	F	T	T T **T** T T
T	F	F	T T **T** T F
F	T	T	T T **T** T T
F	T	F	T F **T** T T
F	F	T	T T **T** T T
F	F	F	T T **T** T T

Tautology

25. $p \equiv [p \vee (p \supset q)]$

p	q	$p \equiv [p \vee (p \supset q)]$
T	T	**T** T T
T	F	**T** T F
F	T	**F** T T
F	F	**F** T T

Not a tautology

27. $p \equiv [p \vee (q \vee \sim q)]$

p	q	$p \equiv [p \vee (q \vee \sim q)]$
T	T	**T** T T F
T	F	**T** T T T
F	T	**F** T T F
F	F	**F** T T T

Not a tautology

29. $[p \vee (q \bullet r)] \equiv [(p \vee q) \bullet (p \vee r)]$

p	q	r	$[p \vee (q \bullet r)] \equiv [(p \vee q) \bullet (p \vee r)]$
T	T	T	T T **T** T T T
T	T	F	T F **T** T T T
T	F	T	T F **T** T T T
T	F	F	T F **T** T T T
F	T	T	T T **T** T T T
F	T	F	F F **T** T F F
F	F	T	F F **T** F F F
F	F	F	F F **T** F F F

Tautology

6.5 Truth Tables as a Test for Validity of Arguments

Part I

a. 3 has *a* as a substitution instance and is the specific form of *a*.

c. 4 is the specific form of *c*.

e. 10 is the specific form of *e*.

g. 8 is the specific form of *g*.

i. 12 is the specific form of *i*.

k. 4 has *k* as a substitution instance.

m. 3 has *m* as a substitution instance.

1.

p	q	$p \supset q$	$\sim q$	$\sim p$	$\sim q \supset \sim p$
T	T	T	F	F	T
T	F	F	T	F	F✓
F	T	T	F	T	T
F	F	T	T	T	T

Valid

3.

p	q	$p \bullet q$	p
T	T	T	T
T	F	F	T
F	T	F	F✓
F	F	F	F✓

Valid

5.

p	q	p	$p \supset q$
T	T	T	T
T	F	T	F✓
F	T	F	T
F	F	F	T

Invalid

7.

p	q	$(p \vee q)$	$\supset$	$(p \bullet q)$	$(p \supset q)$	$\bullet$	$(q \supset p)$
T	T	T	T	T	T	T	T
T	F	T	F	F	F	F	T
F	T	T	F	F	T	F✓	F
F	F	F	T	F	T	T	T

Valid

9.

p	q	$p \supset q$	$\sim q$	$\sim p$
T	T	T	F	F✓
T	F	F	T	F✓
F	T	T	F	T
F	F	T	T	T

Valid

13.

p	q	r	$p \supset (q \supset r)$	$p \supset q$	$p \supset r$
T	T	T	T	T	T
T	T	F	F	T	F✓
T	F	T	T	F	T
T	F	F	T	F	F✓
F	T	T	T	T	T
F	T	F	T	T	T
F	F	T	T	T	T
F	F	F	T	T	T

Valid

11.

p	q	r	$p \supset q$	$p \supset r$	$q \vee r$
T	T	T	T	T	T
T	T	F	T	F	T
T	F	T	F	T	T
T	F	F	F	F	F✓
F	T	T	T	T	T
F	T	F	T	T	T
F	F	T	T	T	T
F	F	F	T	T	F✓

Invalid

15.

p	q	r	$p \supset (q \supset r)$	$q \supset (p \supset r)$	$(p \vee q) \supset r$
T	T	T	T	T	T
T	T	F	F	F	F✓
T	F	T	T	T	T
T	F	F	T	T	F✓
F	T	T	T	T	T
F	T	F	T	T	F✓
F	F	T	T	T	T
F	F	F	T	T	T

Invalid

17.

p	q	r	s	$(p \supset q) \bullet (r \supset s)$	$\sim q \vee \sim s$	$\sim p \vee \sim s$
T	T	T	T	T T T	F F F	F F✓ F
T	T	T	F	T F F	F T T	F T T
T	T	F	T	T T T	F F F	F F✓ F
T	T	F	F	T F T	F T T	F T T
T	F	T	T	F F T	T T F	F F✓ F
T	F	T	F	F F F	T T T	F T T
T	F	F	T	F F T	T T F	F F✓ F
T	F	F	F	F F T	T T T	F T T
F	T	T	T	T T T	F F F	T T F
F	T	T	F	T F F	F T T	T T T
F	T	F	T	T T T	F F F	T T F
F	T	F	F	T F T	F T T	T T T
F	F	T	T	T T T	T T F	T T F
F	F	T	F	T F F	T T T	T T T
F	F	F	T	T T T	T T F	T T F
F	F	F	F	T F T	T T T	T T T

Valid

19.

p	q	r	s	p ⊃ (q ⊃ r)	(q ⊃ r) ⊃ s	p ⊃ s	
T	T	T	T	T T	T T	T	
T	T	T	F	T T	T F	F✓	
T	T	F	T	F F	F T	T	
T	T	F	F	F F	F T	F✓	
T	F	T	T	T T	T T	T	
T	F	T	F	T T	T F	F✓	
T	F	F	T	T T	T T	T	
T	F	F	F	T T	T F	F✓	
F	T	T	T	T T	T T	T	
F	T	T	F	T T	T F	T	
F	T	F	T	T F	F T	T	
F	T	F	F	T F	F T	T	
F	F	T	T	T T	T T	T	Valid
F	F	T	F	T T	T F	T	
F	F	F	T	T T	T T	T	
F	F	F	F	T T	T F	T	

21.

p	q	(p ∨ q) ⊃ (p • q)	~(p ∨ q)	~(p • q)	
T	T	T T T	F	F✓	
T	F	T F F	F	T	
F	T	T F F	F	T	
F	F	F T F	T	T	Valid

23.

p	q	r	s	(p • q) ⊃ (r • s)	(p • q) ⊃ [(p • q) • (r • s)]	
T	T	T	T	T T T	T T	
T	T	T	F	T F F	F✓ F	
T	T	F	T	T F F	F✓ F	
T	T	F	F	T F F	F✓ F	
T	F	T	T	F T T	T F	
T	F	T	F	F T F	T F	
T	F	F	T	F T F	T F	
T	F	F	F	F T F	T F	
F	T	T	T	F T T	T F	
F	T	T	F	F T F	T F	
F	T	F	T	F T F	T F	
F	T	F	F	F T F	T F	
F	F	T	T	F T T	T F	
F	F	T	F	F T F	T F	
F	F	F	T	F T F	T F	
F	F	F	F	F T F	T F	Valid

6.5 Part II

25.

p q	p ⊃ q	q ⊃ p	p ∨ q
T T	T	T	T
T F	F	T	T
F T	T	F	T
F F	T	T	F✓

Invalid

27.

p q r	p ⊃ (q ∨ ~r)	q ⊃ ~r	p ⊃ ~r
T T T	T	F	F✓
T T F	T	T	T
T F T	F	T	F✓
T F F	T	T	T
F T T	T	F	T
F T F	T	T	T
F F T	T	T	T
F F F	T	T	T

Valid

29.

C D	(C ∨ D) ⊃ (C • D)	C • D	C ∨ D
T T	T	T	T
T F	F	F	T
F T	F	F	T
F F	T	F	F✓

Valid

31.

G H	(G ∨ H) ⊃ (G • H)	~(G • H)	~(G ∨ H)
T T	T	F	F✓
T F	F	T	F✓
F T	F	T	F✓
F F	T	T	T

Valid

33.

O	P	Q	(O ∨ P) ⊃ Q	Q ⊃ (O • P)	(O ∨ P) ⊃ (O • P)
T	T	T	T	T	T
T	T	F	F	T	T
T	F	T	T	F	F✓
T	F	F	F	T	F✓
F	T	T	T	F	F✓
F	T	F	F	T	F✓
F	F	T	T	F	T
F	F	F	T	T	T

Valid

6.5 Part III

35. D ⊃ (E ⊃ F)
   E
   ∴ D ⊃ F

D	E	F	D ⊃ (E ⊃ F)	E	D ⊃ F
T	T	T	T	T	T
T	T	F	F	T	F✓
T	F	T	T	F	T
T	F	F	T	F	F✓
F	T	T	T	T	T
F	T	F	T	T	T
F	F	T	T	F	T
F	F	F	T	F	T

Valid

37. M ⊃ (N ⊃ O)
   N
   ∴ O ⊃ M

M	N	O	M ⊃ (N ⊃ O)	N	O ⊃ M
T	T	T	T	T	T
T	T	F	F	T	T
T	F	T	T	F	T
T	F	F	T	F	T
F	T	T	T	T	F✓
F	T	F	T	T	T
F	F	T	T	F	F✓
F	F	F	T	F	T

Invalid

39. $R \supset (A \vee U)$
   $\sim A$
   $\therefore \sim U \supset \sim R$

R	A	U	R⊃(A∨U)	~A	~U	⊃	~R
T	T	T	T	T	F	F	T	F
T	T	F	T	T	F	T	F✓	F
T	F	T	T	T	T	F	T	F
T	F	F	F	F	T	T	F✓	F
F	T	T	T	T	F	F	T	T
F	T	F	T	T	F	T	T	T
F	F	T	T	T	T	F	T	T
F	F	F	T	F	T	T	T	T

Valid

6.6 INCOMPLETE AND REVERSE TRUTH TABLES

A. Incomplete Truth Tables

1.

p	q	p⊃~q	q	~p
T	T	F F	T	F✓
T	F		F	F✓
F	T			T
F	F			T

Valid

3.

p	q	p∨~p	q•(p•q)
T	T		T T
T	F	T F	F✓ F
F	T		F✓ F
F	F		F✓ F

Invalid

5.

p	q	r	p⊃(q∨~r)	~q	p⊃~r
T	T	T		F	F✓ F
T	T	F			T T
T	F	T	F F F	T	F✓ F
T	F	F			T T
F	T	T			T F
F	T	F			T T
F	F	T			T F
F	F	F			T T

Valid

7.

p	q	r	p	p⊃(q•~r)	r
T	T	T			T
T	T	F	T	T T T	F✓
T	F	T			T
T	F	F			F✓
F	T	T			T
F	T	F			F✓
F	F	T			T
F	F	F			F✓

Invalid

9.

p	q	r	s	p•[(q∨r)⊃s]	~s∨~p	~q	•	~r
T	T	T	T		F F F	F	F✓	F
T	T	T	F	F T F	T T F	F	F✓	F
T	T	F	T		F F F	F	F✓	T
T	T	F	F	F T F	T T F	F	F✓	T
T	F	T	T		F F F	T	F✓	F
T	F	T	F	F T F	T T F	T	F✓	F
T	F	F	T		F F F	T	T	T
T	F	F	F	T F T	T T F	T	T	T
F	T	T	T			F	F✓	F
F	T	T	F			F	F✓	F
F	T	F	T			F	F✓	T
F	T	F	F			F	F✓	T
F	F	T	T			T	F✓	F
F	F	T	F			T	F✓	F
F	F	F	T			T	T	T
F	F	F	F			T	T	T

Invalid

6.6 B. Reverse Truth Tables

1. Assume: T   T   F
        p q $\therefore p \equiv q$
        T   (F/T)   T F
                  F
     (F/T)   T   F T
              F   **Valid**

3. Assume: T   T   F
    $(p \bullet q) \bullet r$ $p \vee \sim r$ $\therefore q$
    T (F/T) T   T   T   T   F
      F   F
        F   T   **Valid**

5. Assume:
             T   T   F
    $(p \supset q) \vee r$ $r \supset \sim p$ $\therefore q$
    F F   T T   F   F
    T   T
      T
               Invalid

7. Assume: T   T   F
    $p \equiv (r \supset \sim q)$ $\sim p \supset r$ $\therefore \sim q \bullet p$
    F   T   T   F T   T F
          F   T   F
         F   T   F
    T
               Invalid

9. Assume: T   T   F
    $p \equiv (r \supset \sim q)$ $\sim p \supset r$ $\therefore \sim q \supset p$
    (F/T) T   F   F T   F F
        T   T   T
        T   T   F
    F
              Valid

11. $p \vee (q \equiv \sim r)$ $r \bullet (p \vee \sim q)$ $\therefore p \equiv \sim q$
    T   T   T   T   T   T   T   T
        F   F   F
        F   T   F
      T   T   **Invalid**

13. $p \supset [q \vee (r \bullet s)]$ $p \vee \sim s$ $q \vee \sim r$ $\therefore \sim p \vee q$
    T   F   T   T   T   F   F   (T/F)   T F
       T   T   F   F
      T   T   F   F
      T   **Valid**

                            Invalid

15. $p \equiv [\sim q \bullet (r \equiv s)]$ $p \vee \sim s$ $\sim q \bullet r$ $\therefore \sim p \bullet s$
  T   F T T   T   T   F T   T T
    T   T   F T   F
     T   T   T   F
  T

17. $p \vee [q \supset (\sim r \equiv s)]$ $\sim p \supset \sim s$ $(p \bullet \sim s) \supset r$ $\therefore \sim p \supset q$
  F   F   T F   F   F   F F   T   F F
    F   T   T   T   T
    F   T   F   F
    T   T   T
    T   **Invalid**

19. $p \vee [q \supset (\sim r \equiv s)]$ $\sim p \supset t$ $\sim p \equiv (\sim t \supset s)$ $(\sim p \vee s) \supset \sim t$ $\therefore \sim s \vee t$
  F   F   T T   F   (F/T) F   F   T   F T   F   T F
    F   T   T   T   T   F
     F   F   T   T   F
    T   T   T
  T   **Valid**

Chapter 7 The Method of Deduction

7.2 FORMAL PROOFS OF VALIDITY

Part I

1. C.D.
3. Add.
5. M.T.
7. M.P.
9. M.P.
11. M.T.
13. Conj.
15. C.D.

7.2 Part II

17. 1. $I \supset J$
    2. $J \supset K$
    3. $L \supset M$
    4. $I \vee L$
    $\therefore K \vee M$
    5. $I \supset K$ 1,2 H.S.
    6. $(I \supset K) \bullet (L \supset M)$ 5,3 Conj.
    7. $K \vee M$ 6,4 C.D.

19. 1. $(A \vee B) \supset C$
    2. $(C \vee B) \supset [A \supset (D \equiv E)]$
    3. $A \bullet D$
    $\therefore D \equiv E$
    4. A 3 Simp.
    5. $A \vee B$ 4 Add.
    6. C 1,5 M.P.
    7. $C \vee B$ 6 Add.
    8. $A \supset (D \supset E)$ 2,7 M.P.
    9. $D \equiv E$ 8,4 M.P.

7.2 Part III

21. 1. $D \supset E$
    2. $D \bullet F$
    $\therefore E$
    3. D 2 Simp.
    4. E 1,3 M.P.

23. 1. $P \bullet Q$
    2. R
    $\therefore P \bullet R$
    3. P 1 Simp.
    4. $P \bullet R$ 3,2 Conj.

25. 1. $Y \supset Z$
    2. Y
    $\therefore Y \bullet Z$
    3. Z 1,2 M.P.
    4. $Y \bullet Z$ 2,4 Conj.

27. 1. $\sim(K \bullet L)$
    2. $K \supset L$
    $\therefore \sim K$
    3. $K \supset (K \bullet L)$ 2 Abs.
    4. $\sim K$ 3,1 M.T.

29. 1. $(Z \bullet A) \supset (B \bullet C)$
    2. $Z \supset A$
    $\therefore Z \supset (B \bullet C)$
    3. $Z \supset (Z \bullet A)$ 2 Abs.
    4. $Z \supset (B \bullet C)$ 3,1 H.S.

31. 1. $(K \supset L) \supset M$
    2. $\sim M \bullet \sim(L \supset K)$
    $\therefore \sim(K \supset L)$
    3. $\sim M$ 2 Simp.
    4. $\sim(K \supset L)$ 1,3 M.T.

33. 1. $A \supset B$
    2. $A \vee C$
    3. $C \supset D$
    $\therefore B \vee D$
    4. $(A \supset B) \bullet (C \supset D)$ 1,3 Conj.
    5. $B \vee D$ 4,2 C.D.

35. 1. $(M \supset N) \bullet (O \supset P)$
    2. $N \supset P$
    3. $(N \supset P) \supset (M \vee O)$
    $\therefore N \vee P$
    4. $M \vee O$ 3,2 M.P.
    5. $N \vee P$ 1,4 C.D.

7.2 Part IV

37. 1. $(H \supset I) \bullet (H \supset J)$
    2. $H \bullet (I \vee J)$
    $\therefore I \vee J$
    3. H 2 Simp.
    4. $H \vee H$ 3 Add.
    5. $I \vee H$ 1,4 C.D.

39. 1. $Q \supset R$
    2. $R \supset S$
    3. $\sim S$
    $\therefore \sim Q \bullet \sim R$
    4. $\sim R$ 2,3 M.T.
    5. $\sim Q$ 1,4 M.T.
    6. $\sim Q \bullet \sim R$ 5,4 Conj.

41. 1. $\sim X \supset Y$
    2. $Z \supset X$
    3. $\sim X$
    $\therefore Y \bullet \sim Z$
    4. Y 1,3 M.P.
    5. $\sim Z$ 2,3 M.T.
    6. $Y \bullet \sim Z$ 4,5 Conj.

43. 1. $(H \supset I) \bullet (J \supset K)$
    2. $K \lor H$
    3. $\sim K$
    $\therefore I$
    4. H 2,3 D.S.
    5. $H \supset I$ 1 Simp.
    6. I 5,4 M.P.

45. 1. $(T \supset U) \bullet (V \supset W)$
    2. $(U \supset X) \bullet (W \supset Y)$
    3. T
    $\therefore X \lor Y$
    4. $T \lor V$ 3 Add.
    5. $U \lor W$ 1,5 C.D.
    6. $X \lor Y$ 2,5 C.D.

7.2 Part V

47. 1. $(K \lor L) \supset (M \lor N)$
    2. $(M \lor N) \supset (O \bullet P)$
    3. K
    $\therefore O$
    4. $(K \lor L) \supset (O \bullet P)$ 1,2 H.S.
    5. $K \lor L$ 3 Add.
    6. $O \bullet P$ 4,5 M.P.
    7. O 6 Simp.

49. 1. $A \supset B$
    2. $C \supset D$
    3. $A \lor C$
    $\therefore (A \bullet B) \lor (C \bullet D)$
    4. $A \supset (A \bullet B)$ 1 Abs.
    5. $C \supset (C \bullet D)$ 2 Abs.
    6. $[A \supset (A \bullet B)] \bullet [C \supset (C \bullet D)]$ 4,5 Conj.
    7. $(A \bullet B) \lor (C \bullet D)$ 6,3 C.D.

51. 1. $[(A \lor B) \supset C] \bullet [(X \bullet Y) \supset Z]$
    2. $\sim C$
    3. $(A \lor B) \lor (Y \supset X)$
    4. $\sim X$
    $\therefore \sim Y \lor (X \equiv Y)$
    5. $(A \lor B) \supset C$ 1 Simp.
    6. $\sim(A \lor B)$ 5,2 M.T.
    7. $Y \supset X$ 3,6 D.S.
    8. $\sim Y$ 7,4 M.T.
    9. $\sim Y \lor (X \equiv Y)$ 8 Add.

7.2 Part VI

53. 1. $(B \supset P) \bullet (P \supset \sim L)$
    2. $T \supset L$
    3. $B \lor T$
    $\therefore P \lor L$
    4. $B \supset P$ 1 Simp.
    5. $(B \supset P) \bullet (T \supset L)$ 4,2 Conj.
    6. $P \lor L$ 5,3 C.D.

55. 1. $A \supset B$
    2. $(A \bullet B) \supset (C \lor D)$
    3. $(C \lor D) \supset \sim E$
    4. $(A \supset \sim E) \supset F$
    $\therefore F$
    5. $A \supset (A \bullet B)$ 1 Abs.
    6. $A \supset (C \lor D)$ 5,3 H.S.
    7. $A \supset \sim E$ 6,3 H.S.
    8. F 4,7 M.P.

57. 1. $(G \supset L) \bullet (\sim T \supset J)$
    2. $G \bullet T$
    3. $\sim L$
    $\therefore (J \bullet G) \lor (\sim L \supset T)$
    4. G 2 Simp.
    5. $G \lor \sim T$ 4 Add.
    6. $L \lor J$ 1,5 C.D.
    7. J 6,3 D.S.
    8. $J \bullet G$ 7,4 Conj.
    9. $(J \bullet G) \lor (\sim L \supset T)$ 8 Add.

59. 1. $(L \supset G) \bullet (H \supset X)$
    2. $(P \supset S) \bullet (M \supset D)$
    3. L
    4. $(G \lor S) \supset (B \supset C)$
    5. $\sim C$
    $\therefore \sim B$
    6. $L \supset G$ 1 Simp.
    7. $P \supset S$ 2 Simp.
    8. $(L \supset G) \bullet (P \supset S)$ 6,7 Conj.
    9. $L \lor P$ 3 Add.
    10. $G \lor S$ 8,9 C.D.
    11. $B \supset C$ 4,10 M.P.
    12. $\sim B$ 11,5 M.T.

61. 1. H
   2. $H \supset (M \bullet S)$
   3. $H \supset (C \bullet K)$
   4. $(M \bullet C) \supset L$
   5. $L \supset (P \vee R)$
   6. $\sim P$
   7. $R \supset D$
   $\therefore D$
   8. $M \bullet S$ 2,1 M.P.
   9. $C \bullet K$ 3,1 M.P.
   10. M 8 Simp.
   11. C 9 Simp.
   12. $M \bullet C$ 10,11 Conj.
   13. $(M \bullet C) \supset (P \vee R)$ 4,5 H.S.
   14. $P \vee R$ 13,12 M.P.
   15. R 14,6 D.S.
   16. D 7,15 M.P.

7.3 The Rule of Replacement (1)

Part I

   1. De M.
   3. Dist.
   5. De M.
   7. D.N.
   9. Dist.

7.3 Part II

11. 1. $(p \bullet q) \vee (r \bullet s)$
   2. $[(p \bullet q) \supset t] \bullet (s \supset w)$
   $\therefore t \vee w$
   3. $[(p \bullet q) \vee r] \bullet [(p \bullet q) \vee s]$ 1 Dist.
   4. $[(p \bullet q) \vee s] \bullet [(p \bullet q) \vee r]$ 2 Com.
   5. $(p \bullet q) \vee s$ 4 Simp.
   6. $t \vee w$ 2,5 C.D.

13. 1. $\sim p \vee (q \vee \sim r)$
   2. $\sim\sim(p \bullet r)$
   $\therefore q \vee \sim(t \bullet \sim s)$
   3. $\sim p \vee (\sim r \vee q)$ 1 Com.
   4. $(\sim p \vee \sim r) \vee q$ 3 Assoc.
   5. $\sim(p \bullet r) \vee q$ 4 De M.
   6. q 5,2 D.S.
   7. $q \vee \sim(t \bullet \sim s)$ 6 Add.

15. 1. $p \vee (q \bullet s)$
   2. $\sim q$
   3. $p \supset s$
   $\therefore \sim\sim s$
   4. $(p \vee q) \bullet (p \vee s)$ 1 Dist.
   5. $p \vee q$ 4 Simp.
   6. $q \vee p$ 5 Com.
   7. p 6,2 D.S.
   8. s 7,3 M.P.
   9. $\sim\sim s$ 8 D.N.

17. 1. $p \supset q$
   2. $(q \bullet p) \supset (r \vee s)$
   3. $\sim r$
   4. $s \supset r$
   $\therefore \sim p$
   5. $\sim s$ 4,3 M.T.
   6. $\sim r \bullet \sim s$ 3,5 Conj.
   7. $\sim(r \vee s)$ 6 De M.
   8. $\sim(q \bullet p)$ 2,7 M.T.
   9. $\sim(p \bullet q)$ 9 Com.
   10. $p \supset (p \bullet q)$ 1 Abs.
   11. $\sim p$ 10,9 M.T.

19. 1. $\sim p \vee (q \bullet \sim r)$
   2. $\sim(p \bullet r) \supset \sim[r \bullet (s \vee t)]$
   $\therefore \sim(r \bullet t)$
   3. $(\sim p \vee q) \bullet (\sim p \vee \sim r)$ 1 Dist.
   4. $(\sim p \vee \sim r) \bullet (\sim p \vee q)$ 3 Com.
   5. $\sim p \vee \sim r$ 4 Simp.
   6. $\sim(p \bullet r)$ 5 De M.
   7. $\sim[r \bullet (s \vee t)]$ 2,6 M.P.
   8. $\sim r \vee \sim(s \vee t)$ 7 De M.
   9. $\sim r \vee (\sim s \bullet \sim t)$ 8 De M.
   10. $(\sim r \vee \sim s) \bullet (\sim r \vee \sim t)$ 9 Dist.
   11. $(\sim r \vee \sim t) \bullet (\sim r \vee \sim s)$ 10 Com.
   12. $\sim r \vee \sim t$ 11 Simp.
   13. $\sim(r \bullet t)$ 12 De M.

7.3 Part III

21. 1. $A \bullet \sim B$
   $\therefore \sim B$
   2. $\sim B \bullet A$ 1 Com.
   3. $\sim B$ 2 Simp.

23. 1. $A \vee (B \bullet C)$
   $\therefore A \vee B$
   2. $(A \vee B) \bullet (A \vee C)$ 1 Dist.
   3. $A \vee B$ 2 Simp.

25. 1. $E \supset (G \lor H)$
2. $(\sim G \bullet \sim H)$
∴ $\sim E$
3. $\sim(G \lor H)$ 2 De M.
4. $\sim E$ 1,3 M.T.

27. 1. $(A \supset B) \bullet (C \supset D)$
2. $C \lor A$
∴ $B \lor D$
3. $A \lor C$ 2 Com.
4. $B \lor D$ 1,3 C.D.

29. 1. $(A \bullet B) \supset C$
∴ $(A \bullet B) \supset [C \bullet (A \bullet B)]$
2. $(A \bullet B) \supset [(A \bullet B) \bullet C]$ 1 Abs.
3. $(A \bullet B) \supset [C \bullet (A \bullet B)]$ 2 Com.

31. 1. $B \bullet (C \bullet D)$
∴ $C \bullet (D \bullet B)$
3. $(C \bullet D) \bullet B$ 1 Com.
4. $C \bullet (D \bullet B)$ 3 Assoc.

33. 1. $(E \bullet F) \supset (G \bullet H)$
2. $F \bullet E$
∴ $G \bullet H$
3. $E \bullet F$ 2 Com.
4. $G \bullet H$ 1,3 M.P.

35. 1. $[(A \lor B) \bullet (A \lor C)] \supset D$
2. $A \lor (B \bullet C)$
∴ D
3. $[A \lor (B \bullet C)] \supset D$ 1 Dist.
4. D 3,2 M.P.

7.3 Part IV

37. 1. $A \lor \sim(B \lor C)$
∴ $A \lor \sim B$
3. $A \lor (\sim B \bullet \sim C)$ 1 De M.
4. $(A \lor \sim B) \bullet (A \lor \sim C)$ 3 Dist.
5. $A \lor \sim B$ 4 Simp.

39. 1. $(P \lor Q) \lor R$
2. $\sim Q$
∴ $P \lor R$
3. $(Q \lor P) \lor R$ 1 Com.
4. $Q \lor (P \lor R)$ 3 Assoc.
5. $P \lor R$ 4,2 D.S.

41. 1. $(N \lor O) \bullet (N \lor P)$
2. $\sim N$
∴ O
3. $N \lor (O \bullet P)$ 1 Dist.
4. $O \bullet P$ 3,2 D.S.
5. O 4 Simp.

43. 1. $\sim(\sim U \bullet \sim P)$
2. $\sim U$
∴ P
3. $\sim\sim(U \lor P)$ 1 De M.
4. $U \lor P$ 3 D.N.
5. P 4,2 D.S.

45. 1. $E \lor (F \bullet G)$
∴ $E \lor G$
2. $E \lor (G \bullet F)$ 1 Com.
3. $(E \lor G) \bullet (E \lor F)$ 2 Dist.
4. $E \lor G$ 3 Simp.

7.3 Part V

47. 1. $p \bullet (q \bullet r)$
∴ r
2. $(p \bullet q) \bullet r$ 1 Assoc.
3. $r \bullet (p \bullet q)$ 2 Com.
4. r 3 Simp.

49. 1. $\sim p \supset \sim q$
2. q
∴ p
3. $\sim\sim q$ 2 D.N.
4. $\sim\sim p$ 1,3 M.T.
5. p 4 D.N.

51. 1. $p \lor (q \lor r)$
2. $\sim q$
∴ $p \lor r$
3. $(p \lor q) \lor r$ 1 Assoc.
4. $(q \lor p) \lor r$ 3 Com.
5. $q \lor (p \lor r)$ 4 Assoc.
6. $p \lor r$ 5,2 D.S.

53. 1. $(p \supset q) \bullet (r \supset s)$
2. $p \lor (q \bullet r)$
∴ $q \lor s$
3. $p \lor (r \bullet q)$ 2 Com.
4. $(p \lor r) \bullet (p \lor q)$ 3 Dist.
5. $p \lor r$ 4 Simp.
6. $q \lor s$ 1,5 C.D.

55. 1. $\sim[(p \lor q) \lor r]$
∴ $\sim q$
2. $\sim(p \lor q) \bullet \sim r$ 1 De M.
3. $\sim(p \lor q)$ 2 Simp.
4. $\sim p \bullet \sim q$ 3 De M.
5. $\sim q \bullet \sim p$ 4 Com.
6. $\sim q$ 5 Simp.

57. 1. $(p \supset q) \bullet (q \supset p)$
  $\therefore (p \supset p) \bullet (q \supset q)$
  2. $p \supset q$ 1 Simp.
  3. $(q \supset p) \bullet (p \supset q)$ 1 Com.
  4. $q \supset p$ 3 Simp.
  5. $p \supset p$ 2,4 H.S.
  6. $q \supset q$ 4,2 H.S.
  7. $(p \supset p) \bullet (q \supset q)$ 5,6 Conj.

59. 1. $\sim[p \lor (q \bullet r)]$
  2. r
  $\therefore \sim q$
  3. $\sim p \bullet \sim(q \bullet r)$ 1 De M.
  4. $\sim(q \bullet r) \bullet \sim p$ 3 Com.
  5. $\sim(q \bullet r)$ 4 Simp.
  6. $\sim q \lor \sim r$ 5 De M.
  7. $\sim r \lor \sim q$ 6 Com.
  8. $\sim\sim r$ 2 D.N.
  9. $\sim q$ 7,8 D.S.

61. 1. $p \lor \sim(q \lor r)$
  2. $\sim(\sim p \bullet q) \supset s$
  3. $s \supset w$
  $\therefore (s \bullet w) \lor (t \bullet z)$
  4. $(\sim\sim p \lor \sim q) \supset s$ 2 De M.
  5. $(p \lor \sim q) \supset s$ 4 D.N.
  6. $p \lor (\sim q \bullet \sim r)$ 1 De M.
  7. $(p \lor \sim q) \bullet (p \lor \sim r)$ 6 Dist.
  8. $p \lor \sim q$ 7 Simp.
  9. s 5,8 M.P.
  10. $s \supset (s \bullet w)$ 3 Abs.
  11. $s \bullet w$ 10,9 M.P.
  12. $(s \bullet w) \lor (t \bullet s)$ 11 Add.

63. 1. $(p \bullet q) \lor (\sim p \bullet \sim q)$
  $\therefore (\sim p \lor q) \bullet (\sim q \lor p)$
  2. $[(p \bullet q) \lor \sim p] \bullet [(p \bullet q) \lor \sim q]$ 1 Dist.
  3. $(p \bullet q) \lor \sim p$ 2 Simp.
  4. $[(p \bullet q) \lor \sim q] \bullet [(p \bullet q) \lor \sim p]$ 2 Com.
  5. $(p \bullet q) \lor \sim q$ 4 Simp.
  6. $\sim p \lor (p \bullet q)$ 5 Com.
  7. $(\sim p \lor p) \bullet (\sim p \lor q)$ 6 Dist.
  8. $(\sim p \lor q) \bullet (\sim p \lor p)$ 7 Com.
  9. $\sim p \lor q$ 8 Simp.
  10. $\sim q \lor (p \bullet q)$ 5 Com.
  11. $(\sim q \lor p) \bullet (\sim q \lor q)$ 10 Dist.
  12. $\sim q \lor p$ 11 Simp.
  13. $(\sim p \lor q) \bullet (\sim q \lor p)$ 9,12 Conj.

65. 1. $(p \bullet q) \lor (p \bullet r)$
  2. $\sim(\sim q \bullet \sim r) \supset t$
  3. $\sim t \lor (x \bullet z)$
  $\therefore (x \lor a) \bullet (x \lor z)$
  4. $\sim\sim(q \lor r) \supset t$ 2 De M.
  5. $(q \lor r) \supset t$ 4 D.N.
  6. $p \bullet (q \lor r)$ 1 Dist.
  7. $(q \lor r) \bullet p$ 6 Com.
  8. $q \lor r$ 7 Simp.
  9. t 5,8 M.P.
  10. $\sim\sim t$ 9 D.N.
  11. $x \bullet z$ 3,10 D.S.
  12. x 11 Simp.
  13. $x \lor (a \bullet z)$ 12 Add.
  14. $(x \lor a) \bullet (x \lor z)$ 13 Dist.

7.4 THE RULE OF REPLACEMENT (2)

Part I

1. Equiv.
3. Exp.
5. Equiv.
7. Exp.
9. Impl.
11. Assoc.
13. Equiv.
15. Dist.

7.4 Part II

17. 1. $(M \lor N) \supset (O \bullet P)$
  2. $\sim O$
  $\therefore \sim M$
  3. $\sim O \lor \sim P$ 2 Add.
  4. $\sim(O \bullet P)$ 3 De M.
  5. $\sim(M \lor N)$ 1,4 M.T.
  6. $\sim M \bullet \sim N$ 5 De M.
  7. $\sim M$ 6 Simp.

19. 1. $A \supset B$
  2. $B \supset C$
  3. $C \supset A$
  4. $A \supset \sim C$
  $\therefore \sim A \bullet \sim C$
  5. $A \supset C$ 1,2 H.S.
  6. $(A \supset C) \bullet (C \supset A)$ 5,3 Conj.
  7. $A \equiv C$ 6 Equiv.
  8. $(A \bullet C) \lor (\sim A \bullet \sim C)$ 7 Equiv.
  9. $\sim A \lor \sim C$ 4 Impl.
  10. $\sim(A \bullet C)$ 9 De M.
  11. $\sim A \bullet \sim C$ 8,10 D.S.

7.4 Part III

21. 1. A
2. $\sim B \supset \sim A$
$\therefore B$
3. $A \supset B$ 2 Trans.
4. B 3,1 M.P.

23. 1. C
2. $(C \bullet D) \supset E$
$\therefore D \supset E$
3. $C \supset (D \supset E)$ 2 Exp.
4. $D \supset E$ 3,1 M.P.

25. 1. $Q \supset [R \supset (S \supset T)]$
2. $Q \supset (Q \bullet R)$
$\therefore Q \supset (S \supset T)$
3. $(Q \bullet R) \supset (S \supset T)$ 1 Exp.
4. $Q \supset (S \supset T)$ 2,3 H.S.

27. 1. $W \supset X$
2. $\sim Y \supset \sim X$
$\therefore W \supset Y$
3. $X \supset Y$ 2 Trans.
4. $W \supset Y$ 1,3 H.S.

29. 1. $F \equiv G$
2. $\sim(F \bullet G)$
$\therefore \sim F \bullet \sim G$
3. $(F \bullet G) \vee (\sim F \bullet \sim G)$ 1 Equiv.
4. $\sim F \bullet \sim G$ 3,2 D.S.

31. 1. $(S \bullet T) \vee (U \bullet V)$
2. $\sim S \vee \sim T$
$\therefore U \bullet V$
3. $\sim(S \bullet T)$ 2 De M.
4. $U \vee V$ 1,3 D.S.

33. 1. $(A \vee B) \supset (C \vee D)$
2. $\sim C \bullet \sim D$
$\therefore \sim(A \vee B)$
3. $\sim(C \vee D)$ 2 De M.
4. $\sim(A \vee B)$ 1,3 M.T.

35. 1. $(M \supset N) \bullet (\sim O \vee P)$
2. $M \vee O$
$\therefore N \vee P$
3. $(M \supset N) \bullet (O \supset P)$ 1 Impl.
4. $N \vee P$ 3,2 C.D.

37. 1. $(Y \supset Z) \bullet (Z \supset Y)$
$\therefore (Y \bullet Z) \vee (\sim Y \bullet \sim Z)$
2. $Y \equiv Z$ 1 Equiv.
3. $(Y \bullet Z) \vee (\sim Y \bullet \sim Z)$ 2 Equiv.

39. 1. $(J \bullet K) \supset [(L \bullet M) \vee (N \bullet O)]$
2. $\sim(L \bullet M) \bullet \sim(N \bullet O)$
$\therefore \sim(J \bullet K)$
3. $\sim[(L \bullet M) \vee (N \bullet O)]$ 2 De M.
4. $\sim(J \bullet K)$ 1,3 M.T.

7.4 Part IV

41. 1. $\sim B \vee (C \bullet D)$
$\therefore B \supset C$
2. $(\sim B \vee C) \bullet (\sim B \vee D)$ 1 Dist.
3. $\sim B \vee C$ 2 Simp.
4. $B \supset C$ 3 Impl.

43. 1. $H \bullet (I \bullet J)$
$\therefore J \bullet (I \bullet H)$
2. $(H \bullet I) \bullet J$ 1 Assoc.
3. $J \bullet (H \bullet I)$ 2 Com.
4. $J \bullet (I \bullet H)$ 3 Com.

45. 1. $Q \supset (R \supset S)$
2. $Q \supset R$
$\therefore Q \supset S$
3. $(Q \bullet R) \supset S$ 1 Exp.
4. $Q \supset (Q \bullet R)$ 2 Abs.
5. $Q \supset S$ 4,3 H.S.

47. 1. $W \bullet (X \vee Y)$
2. $\sim W \vee \sim X$
$\therefore W \bullet Y$
3. $(W \bullet X) \vee (W \bullet Y)$ 1 Dist.
4. $\sim(W \bullet X)$ 2 De M.
5. $W \bullet Y$ 3,4 D.S.

49. 1. $G \supset H$
2. $H \supset G$
$\therefore (G \bullet H) \vee (\sim G \bullet \sim H)$
3. $(G \supset H) \bullet (H \supset G)$ 1,2 Conj.
4. $G \equiv H$ 3 Equiv.
5. $(G \bullet H) \vee (\sim G \bullet \sim H)$ 4 Equiv.

7.4 Part V

51. 1. $\sim A$
$\therefore A \supset B$
2. $\sim A \vee B$ 1 Add.
3. $A \supset B$ 2 Impl.

53. 1. $E \supset (F \supset G)$
$\therefore F \supset (E \supset G)$
2. $(E \bullet F) \supset G$ 1 Exp.
3. $(F \bullet E) \supset G$ 2 Com.
4. $F \supset (E \supset G)$ 3 Exp.

55. 1. $K \supset L$
  $\therefore K \supset (L \lor M)$
  2. $(K \supset L) \lor M$ 1 Add.
  3. $(\sim K \lor L) \lor M$ 2 Impl.
  4. $\sim K \lor (L \lor M)$ 3 Assoc.
  5. $K \supset (L \lor M)$ 4 Impl.

57. 1. $(Q \lor R) \supset S$
  $\therefore Q \supset S$
  2. $\sim(Q \lor R) \lor S$ 1 Impl.
  3. $(\sim Q \bullet \sim R) \lor S$ 2 De M.
  4. $S \lor (\sim Q \bullet \sim R)$ 3 Com.
  5. $(S \lor \sim Q) \bullet (S \lor \sim R)$ 3 Dist.
  6. $S \lor \sim Q$ 5 Simp.
  7. $\sim Q \lor S$ 6 Com.
  8. $Q \supset S$ 7 Impl.

59. 1. $W \supset X$
  2. $Y \supset X$
  $\therefore (W \lor Y) \supset X$
  3. $\sim X \supset \sim W$ 1 Trans.
  4. $\sim X \supset \sim Y$ 2 Trans.
  5. $X \lor \sim W$ 3 Impl.
  6. $X \lor \sim Y$ 4 Impl.
  7. $(X \lor \sim W) \bullet (X \lor \sim Y)$ 5,6 Conj.
  8. $X \lor (\sim W \lor \sim Y)$ 7 Dist.
  9. $(\sim W \lor \sim Y) \lor X$ 8 Com.
  10. $\sim(W \bullet Y) \lor X$ 9 De M.
  11. $(W \lor Y) \supset X$ 10 Impl.

7.4 Part VI

61. 1. p
  2. $\sim p \lor q$
  $\therefore q$
  3. $p \supset q$ 2 Impl.
  4. q 3,1 M.P.

63. 1. $p \equiv q$
  2. $\sim q$
  $\therefore \sim p \bullet \sim q$
  3. $(p \supset q) \bullet (q \supset p)$ 1 Equiv.
  4. $p \supset q$ 3 Simp.
  5. $\sim p$ 4,2 M.T.
  6. $\sim p \bullet \sim q$ 5,2 Conj.

65. 1. $(p \supset q) \bullet (r \supset s)$
  2. $\sim q \lor \sim s$
  $\therefore \sim p \lor \sim r$
  3. $(\sim q \supset \sim p) \bullet (r \supset s)$ 1 Trans.
  4. $(\sim q \supset \sim p) \bullet (\sim s \supset \sim r)$ 3 Trans.
  5. $\sim q \lor \sim s$ 4,2 C.D.

67. 1. $p \supset q$
  2. $\sim\sim p$
  $\therefore \sim\sim q$
  3. $\sim q \supset \sim p$ 1 Trans.
  4. $\sim\sim q$ 3,2 M.T.

69. 1. $p \supset (q \lor \sim s)$
  $\therefore p \supset [p \supset (\sim s \lor \sim\sim q)]$
  2. $p \supset (\sim q \supset \sim s)$ 1 Impl.
  3. $p \supset (\sim\sim s \supset \sim\sim q)$ 2 Trans.
  4. $p \supset (\sim s \lor \sim\sim q)$ 3 Impl.
  5. $(p \bullet p) \supset (\sim s \lor \sim\sim q)$ 4 Taut.
  6. $p \supset [p \supset (\sim s \lor \sim\sim q)]$ 5 Exp.

71. 1. $p \equiv q$
  2. $\sim p \supset r$
  $\therefore \sim q \supset r$
  3. $(p \supset q) \bullet (q \supset p)$ 1 Equiv.
  4. $p \supset q$ 3 Simp.
  5. $\sim q \supset \sim p$ 4 Trans.
  6. $\sim q \supset r$ 5,2 H.S.

73. 1. $\sim p$
  2. $\sim p \supset \sim s$
  $\therefore \sim(\sim r \supset \sim q) \supset \sim s$
  3. $\sim s$ 2,1 M.P.
  4. $\sim s \lor (\sim r \supset \sim q)$ 3 Add.
  5. $s \supset (\sim r \supset \sim q)$ 4 Impl.
  6. $\sim(\sim r \supset \sim q) \supset \sim s$ 5 Trans.

75. 1. $q \supset \sim p$
  2. $p \equiv q$
  3. $\sim\sim p \supset (\sim q \supset r)$
  $\therefore \sim\sim p \supset r$
  4. $\sim\sim p \supset \sim q$ 1 Trans.
  5. $\sim\sim p \supset (\sim\sim p \bullet \sim q)$ 4 Abs.
  6. $(\sim\sim p \bullet \sim q) \supset r$ 3 Exp.
  7. $\sim\sim p \supset r$ 5,6 H.S.

7.4 Part VII

77. 1. $(G \supset \sim H) \supset I$
  2. $\sim(G \bullet H)$
  $\therefore I \lor \sim H$
  3. $(\sim G \lor \sim H) \supset I$ 1 Impl.
  4. $\sim(G \bullet H) \supset I$ 3 De M.
  5. I 4,2 M.P.
  6. $I \lor \sim H$ 5 Add.

79.
1. $[(Y \bullet Z) \supset A] \bullet [(Y \bullet B) \supset C]$
2. $(B \lor Z) \bullet Y$
∴ $A \lor C$
3. $(Z \lor B) \bullet Y$ 2 Com.
4. $Y \bullet (Z \lor B)$ 3 Com.
5. $(Y \bullet Z) \lor (Y \bullet B)$ 4 Dist.
6. $A \lor C$ 1,5 C.D.

81.
1. $M \supset N$
2. $M \supset (N \supset O)$
∴ $M \supset O$
3. $M \supset (M \bullet N)$ 1 Abs.
4. $(M \bullet N) \supset O$ 2 Exp.
5. $M \supset O$ 3,4 H.S.

83.
1. $\sim B \lor [(C \supset D) \bullet (E \supset D)]$
2. $B \bullet (C \lor E)$
∴ D
3. B 2 Simp.
4. $\sim\sim B$ 3 D.N.
5. $(C \supset D) \bullet (E \supset D)$ 1,4 D.S.
6. $(C \lor E) \bullet B$ 2 Com.
7. $C \lor E$ 6 Simp.
8. $D \lor D$ 5,7 C.D.
9. D 8 Taut.

85.
1. $(M \supset N) \bullet (O \supset P)$
2. $\sim N \lor \sim P$
3. $\sim(M \bullet O) \supset Q$
∴ Q
4. $(\sim N \supset \sim M) \bullet (O \supset P)$ 1 Trans.
5. $(\sim N \supset \sim M) \bullet (\sim P \supset \sim O)$ 4 Trans.
6. $\sim M \lor \sim O$ 5,2 C.D.
7. $\sim(M \bullet O)$ 6 De M.
8. Q 3,7 M.P.

7.4 Part VIII

87.
1. $\sim(F \lor \sim A)$
∴ A
2. $\sim F \bullet \sim\sim A$ 1 De M.
3. $\sim\sim A \bullet \sim F$ 2 Com.
4. $\sim\sim A$ 3 Simp.
5. A 4 D.N.

89.
1. $U \supset C$
2. $L \lor U$
3. $\sim L$
∴ C
4. U 2,3 D.S.
5. C 1,4 M.P.

91.
1. $F \supset W$
∴ $(F \bullet S) \supset W$
2. $\sim F \lor W$ 1 Impl.
3. $(\sim F \lor W) \lor \sim S$ 2 Add.
4. $\sim F \lor (W \lor \sim S)$ 3 Assoc.
5. $\sim F \lor (\sim S \lor W)$ 4 Com.
6. $(\sim F \lor \sim S) \lor W$ 5 Assoc.
7. $\sim(F \bullet S) \lor W$ 6 De M.
8. $(F \bullet S) \supset W$ 7 Impl.

93.
1. $(T \lor C) \supset (V \bullet P)$
2. $P \supset O$
3. $\sim O$
∴ $\sim T$
4. $\sim P$ 2,3 M.T.
5. $\sim P \lor \sim V$ 4 Add.
6. $\sim V \lor \sim P$ 5 Com.
7. $\sim(V \bullet P)$ 6 De M.
8. $\sim(T \lor C)$ 1,7 M.T.
9. $\sim T \bullet \sim C$ 8 De M.
10. $\sim T$ 9 Simp.

95.
1. $D \lor (I \bullet S)$
2. $(D \supset L) \bullet (L \supset S)$
∴ S
3. $(D \lor I) \bullet (D \lor S)$ 1 Dist.
4. $(D \lor S) \bullet (D \lor I)$ 3 Com.
5. $D \lor S$ 4 Simp.
6. $S \lor D$ 5 Com.
7. $\sim\sim S \lor D$ 6 D.N.
8. $\sim S \supset D$ 7 Impl.
9. $(L \supset S) \bullet (D \supset L)$ 2 Com.
10. $D \supset L$ 2 Simp.
11. $L \supset S$ 9 Simp.
12. $\sim S \supset L$ 8,10 H.S.
13. $\sim S \supset S$ 12,11 H.S.
14. $\sim\sim S \lor S$ 13 Impl.
15. $S \lor S$ 14 D.N.
16. S 15 Taut.

7.4 Part IX

97.
1. $(M \supset T) \bullet (\sim M \supset H)$
2. $M \lor (H \equiv A)$
3. $\sim T$
$\therefore A \bullet (T \supset H)$

4. $\sim T \lor H$	3 Add.
5. $T \supset H$	4 Impl.
6. $M \supset T$	1 Simp.
7. $\sim M$	6,3 M.T.
8. $H \equiv A$	2,7 D.S.
9. $(H \supset A) \bullet (A \supset H)$	8 Equiv.
10. $H \supset A$	9 Simp.
11. $(\sim M \supset H) \bullet (M \supset T)$	1 Com.
12. $\sim M \supset H$	11 Simp.
13. H	12,7 M.P.
14. A	10,13 M.P.
15. $A \bullet (T \supset H)$	14,5 Conj.

99.
1. $(H \lor C) \bullet [(R \lor \sim D) \supset V]$
2. $R \supset (C \supset D)$
3. $V \supset (H \supset T)$
4. $\sim T$
$\therefore D \lor C$

5. $(V \bullet H) \supset T$	3 Exp.
6. $\sim(V \bullet H)$	5,4 M.T.
7. $\sim V \lor \sim H$	6 De M.
8. $V \supset \sim H$	7 Impl.
9. $H \lor C$	1 Simp.
10. $\sim\sim H \lor C$	9 D.N.
11. $\sim H \supset C$	10 Impl.
12. $V \supset C$	8,11 H.S.
13. $[(R \lor \sim D) \supset V] \bullet (H \lor C)$	1 Com.
14. $(R \lor \sim D) \supset V$	13 Simp.
15. $(R \lor \sim D) \supset C$	14,12 H.S.
16. $\sim(R \lor \sim D) \lor C$	15 Impl.
17. $(\sim R \bullet \sim\sim D) \lor C$	16 De M.
18. $(\sim R \bullet D) \lor C$	17 D.N.
19. $C \lor (\sim R \bullet D)$	18 Com.
20. $(C \lor \sim R) \bullet (C \lor D)$	19 Dist.
21. $(C \lor D) \bullet (C \lor \sim R)$	20 Com.
22. $C \lor D$	21 Simp.
23. $D \lor C$	22 Com.

101.
1. $P \supset [Q \supset (R \supset S)]$
2. $R \bullet P$
3. $(S \supset T) \bullet (T \supset \sim S)$
$\therefore \sim Q$

4. $S \supset T$	3 Simp.
5. $(T \supset \sim S) \bullet (S \supset T)$	3 Com.
6. $T \supset \sim S$	4 Simp.
7. $S \supset \sim S$	4,6 H.S.
8. $\sim S \lor \sim S$	7 Impl.
9. $\sim S$	8 Taut.
10. $P \bullet R$	2 Com.
11. P	10 Simp.
12. $Q \supset (R \supset S)$	1,11 M.P.
13. $(Q \bullet R) \supset S$	12 Exp.
14. $(R \bullet Q) \supset S$	13 Com.
15. $R \supset (Q \supset S)$	14 Exp.
16. R	2 Simp.
17. $Q \supset S$	15,16 M.P.
18. $\sim Q$	17,9 M.T.

103.
1. $A \supset C$
2. $(A \bullet C) \supset (G \lor J)$
3. $(E \lor D) \supset H$
4. $A \lor M$
5. $M \supset E$
$\therefore J \lor (G \lor H)$

6. $A \supset (A \bullet C)$	1 Abs.
7. $A \supset (G \lor J)$	6,2 H.S.
8. $\sim(E \lor D) \lor H$	3 Impl.
9. $(\sim E \bullet \sim D) \lor H$	8 De M.
10. $H \lor (\sim E \bullet \sim D)$	9 Com.
11. $(H \lor \sim E) \bullet (H \lor \sim D)$	10 Dist.
12. $H \lor \sim E$	11 Simp.
13. $\sim\sim H \lor \sim E$	12 D.N.
14. $\sim H \supset \sim E$	13 Impl.
15. $\sim E \supset \sim M$	5 Trans.
16. $\sim H \supset \sim M$	14,15 H.S.
17. $\sim\sim A \lor M$	4 D.N.
18. $\sim A \supset M$	17 Impl.
19. $\sim M \supset \sim\sim A$	18 Trans.
20. $\sim M \supset A$	19 D.N.
21. $\sim H \supset A$	16,20 H.S.
22. $\sim H \supset (G \lor J)$	21,7 H.S.
23. $\sim\sim H \lor (G \lor J)$	22 Impl.
24. $H \lor (G \lor J)$	23 D.N.
25. $(H \lor G) \lor J$	24 Assoc.
26. $J \lor (H \lor G)$	25 Com.
27. $J \lor (G \lor H)$	26 Com.

105.
1. $(A \supset B) \bullet (C \supset D)$
2. $(A \bullet C) \supset (D \supset E)$
3. $\sim E \bullet C$

$\therefore \sim A \bullet (B \lor D)$

4. $\sim E$	3 Simp.
5. $C \bullet \sim E$	3 Com.
6. C	5 Simp.
7. $(C \bullet A) \supset (D \supset E)$	2 Com.
8. $C \supset [A \supset (D \supset E)]$	7 Exp.
9. $A \supset (D \supset E)$	8,6 M.P.
10. $(A \bullet D) \supset E$	9 Exp.
11. $\sim(A \bullet D)$	10,4 M.T.
12. $\sim A \lor \sim D$	11 De M.
13. $A \supset \sim D$	12 Impl.
14. $(C \supset D) \bullet (A \supset B)$	1 Com.
15. $C \supset D$	14 Simp.
16. D	15,6 M.P.
17. $\sim\sim D$	16 D.N.
18. $\sim A$	13,17 M.T.
19. $D \lor B$	16 Add.
20. $B \lor D$	19 Com.
21. $\sim A \bullet (B \lor D)$	18,20 Conj.

7.4. Part X

107.

1. $(H \supset P) \bullet (S \supset W)$

$\therefore (H \bullet S) \supset (P \bullet W)$

2. $H \supset P$	1 Simp.
3. $(H \supset P) \lor \sim S$	2 Add.
4. $(\sim H \lor P) \lor \sim S$	3 Impl.
5. $\sim H \lor (P \lor \sim S)$	4 Assoc.
6. $\sim H \lor (\sim S \lor P)$	5 Com.
7. $(\sim H \lor \sim S) \lor P$	6 Assoc.
8. $\sim(H \bullet S) \lor P$	7 De M.
9. $(S \supset W) \bullet (H \supset P)$	1 Com.
10. $S \supset W$	9 Simp.
11. $(S \supset W) \lor \sim H$	10 Add.
12. $\sim H \lor (S \supset W)$	11 Com.
13. $\sim H \lor (\sim S \lor W)$	12 Impl.
14. $(\sim H \lor \sim S) \lor W$	13 Assoc.
15. $\sim(H \bullet S) \lor W$	14 De M.
16. $[\sim(H \bullet S) \lor P] \bullet [\sim(H \bullet S) \lor W]$	8,15 Conj.
17. $\sim(H \bullet S) \lor (P \bullet W)$	16 Dist.
18. $(H \bullet S) \supset (P \bullet W)$	17 Impl.

109.

1. G

$\therefore H \lor \sim H$

2. $G \lor \sim H$	1 Add.
3. $\sim H \lor G$	2 Com.
4. $H \supset G$	3 Impl.
5. $H \supset (H \bullet G)$	4 Abs.
6. $\sim H \lor (H \bullet G)$	5 Impl.
7. $(\sim H \lor H) \bullet (\sim H \lor G)$	6 Dist.
8. $\sim H \lor H$	7 Simp.
9. $H \lor \sim H$	8 Com.

7.5 CONDITIONAL PROOF

1.

1. $p \lor q$
2. $\sim p$

$\therefore r \supset q$

3. r	A.C.P.
4. q	1,2 D.S.
5. $r \supset q$	3-4 C.P.

3.

1. p
2. $(p \bullet q) \supset r$

$\therefore \sim r \supset \sim q$

3. $\sim r$	A.C.P.
4. $\sim(p \bullet q)$	2,3 M.T.
5. $\sim p \lor \sim q$	4 De M.
6. $\sim\sim p$	1 D.N.
7. $\sim q$	5,6 D.S.
8. $\sim r \supset \sim q$	3-7 C.P.

5.

1. $(p \bullet q) \supset r$
2. $p \supset q$

$\therefore (s \bullet p) \supset r$

3. $s \bullet p$	A.C.P.
4. $p \bullet s$	3 Com.
5. p	4 Simp.
6. q	2,5 M.P.
7. $p \bullet q$	5,6 Conj.
8. r	1,7 M.P.
9. $(s \bullet p) \supset r$	3-8 C.P.

7.

1. $p \supset q$
2. $\sim r \supset \sim q$

$\therefore p \supset (p \supset r)$

3. p	A.C.P.
4. p	A.C.P.
5. q	1,3 M.P.
6. $q \supset r$	2 Trans.
7. r	6,5 M.P.
8. $p \supset r$	4-7 C.P.
9. $p \supset (p \supset r)$	3-8 C.P.

9.

1. $[p \bullet (q \lor r)] \supset s$
2. $\sim q \supset r$
3. $\sim p \supset r$

$\therefore \sim r \supset (q \bullet s)$

4. $\sim r$	A.C.P.
5. $\sim\sim p$	3,4 M.T.
6. p	5 D.N.
7. $\sim\sim q$	2,4 M.T.

8. q	7 D.N.
9. $q \lor r$	8 Add.
10. $p \bullet (q \lor r)$	6,9 Conj.
11. s	1,10 M.P.
12. $q \bullet s$	8,11 Conj.
13. $\sim r \supset (q \bullet s)$	4-12 C.P.

11. 1. $(p \supset q) \bullet (r \supset s)$
$\therefore (p \lor r) \supset (q \lor s)$

2. $p \lor r$	A.C.P.
3. $q \lor s$	1,2 C.D.
4. $(p \lor r) \supset (q \lor s)$	2-3 C.P.

13. 1. $\sim(p \bullet q)$
2. $\sim q \supset r$
3. $\sim r \lor p$
$\therefore r \equiv p$

4. r	A.C.P.
5. $\sim\sim r$	4 D.N.
6. p	3,5 D.S.
7. $r \supset p$	4-6 C.P.
8. p	A.C.P.
9. $\sim p \lor \sim q$	1 De M.
10. $\sim\sim p$	8 D.N.
11. $\sim q$	9,10 D.S.
12. r	2,11 M.P.
13. $p \supset r$	8-12 C.P.
14. $(r \supset p) \bullet (p \supset r)$	7,13 Conj.
15. $r \equiv p$	14 Equiv.

15. 1. $p \supset (q \bullet s)$
2. $\sim q \lor s$
3. $(q \bullet s) \supset (r \supset t)$
4. $\sim t$
$\therefore \sim p \lor (t \equiv r)$

5. p	A.C.P.
6. $q \bullet s$	1,5 M.P.
7. $r \supset t$	3,6 M.P.
8. $\sim t \lor r$	4 Add.
9. $t \supset r$	8 Impl.
10. $(t \supset r) \bullet (r \supset t)$	9,7 Conj.
11. $t \equiv r$	10 Equiv.
12. $p \supset (t \equiv r)$	5-11 C.P.
13. $\sim p \lor (t \equiv r)$	12 Impl.

17. 1. $p \supset [(q \bullet r) \supset s]$
2. $\sim s$
3. $p \bullet q$

$\therefore \sim r$

4. r	A.C.P.
5. p	3 Simp.
6. $q \bullet p$	3 Com.
7. q	6 Simp.
8. $[(q \bullet r) \supset s]$	1,5 M.P.
9. $q \bullet r$	7,4 Conj.
10. s	8,9 M.P.
11. $s \lor \sim r$	10 Add.
12. $\sim r$	11,2 D.S.
13. $r \supset \sim r$	4-12 C.P.
14. $\sim r \lor \sim r$	13 Impl.
15. $\sim r$	14 Taut.

19. 1. $p \equiv (q \lor r)$
2. r
3. $(p \bullet r) \supset (s \lor t)$
4. $\sim t$
$\therefore s$

5. $\sim s$	A.C.P.
6. $\sim s \bullet \sim t$	5,4 Conj.
7. $\sim(s \lor t)$	6 De M.
8. $\sim(p \bullet r)$	3,7 M.T.
9. $\sim(r \bullet p)$	8 Com.
10. $\sim r \lor \sim p$	9 De M.
11. $\sim\sim r$	2 D.N.
12. $\sim p$	10,11 D.S.
13. $[p \supset (q \lor r)] \bullet [(q \lor r) \supset p]$	1 Equiv.
14. $[(q \lor r) \supset p] \bullet [p \supset (q \lor r)]$	13 Com.
15. $(q \lor r) \supset p$	14 Simp.
16. $\sim(q \lor r)$	15,12 M.T.
17. $\sim q \bullet \sim r$	16 De M.
18. $\sim r \bullet \sim q$	17 Com.
19. $\sim r$	18 Simp.
20. $r \lor s$	2 Add.
21. s	20,19 D.S.
22. $\sim s \supset s$	5-21 C.P.
23. $s \lor s$	22 Impl.
24. s	23 Taut.

7.6 Indirect Proof

Part I

1. 1. p
$\therefore q \lor \sim q$

2. $\sim(q \lor \sim q)$	A.I.P.
3. $\sim q \bullet \sim\sim q$	2 De M.
4. $q \lor \sim q$	2-3 I.P.

3. 1. $m \supset g$
    2. $g \supset a$
    3. $a \supset p$
    4. $p \supset i$
    5. m
    $\therefore i$

	6. $\sim i$	A.I.P.
	7. g	1,5 M.P.
	8. a	2,7 M.P.
	9. p	3,8 M.P.
	10. i	4,9 M.P.
	11. $i \bullet \sim i$	10,6 Conj.
12. i		6-11 I.P.

5. 1. $\sim p \supset (o \bullet g)$
    2. $g \equiv p$
    $\therefore o \supset p$

	3. $\sim(o \supset p)$	A.I.P.
	4. $\sim(\sim o \vee p)$	3 Impl.
	5. $\sim\sim o \bullet \sim p$	4 De M.
	6. $\sim p \bullet \sim\sim o$	5 Com.
	7. $\sim p$	6 Simp.
	8. $o \bullet g$	1,7 M.P.
	9. $g \bullet o$	8 Com.
	10. g	9 Simp.
	11. $(g \supset p) \bullet (p \supset g)$	2 Equiv.
	12. $g \supset p$	11 Simp.
	13. p	12,10 M.P.
	14. $p \bullet \sim p$	13,7 Conj.
15. $o \supset p$		3-14 I.P.

7. 1. $p \supset [\sim q \vee (r \bullet s)]$
    2. $\sim s \bullet q$
    $\therefore \sim p$

	3. p	A.I.P.
	4. $\sim q \vee (r \bullet s)$	1,3 M.P.
	5. $\sim s$	2 Simp.
	6. $q \bullet \sim s$	2 Com.
	7. q	6 Simp.
	8. $\sim\sim q$	7 D.N.
	9. $r \bullet s$	4,8 D.S.
	10. $s \bullet r$	9 Com.
	11. s	10 Simp.
	12. $s \bullet \sim s$	11,5 Conj.
13. $\sim p$		3-12 I.P.

9. 1. $m \supset g$
    2. $g \supset (c \vee h)$
    3. $h \supset d$

    4. $\sim d$
    5. $c \supset a$
    $\therefore \sim m \vee a$

6. $m \supset (c \vee b)$		1,2 H.S.
	7. $\sim(\sim m \vee a)$	A.I.P.
	8. $\sim\sim m \bullet \sim a$	7 De M.
	9. $\sim\sim m$	8 Simp.
	10. $\sim a \bullet \sim\sim m$	8 Com.
	11. $\sim a$	10 Simp.
	12. m	9 D.N.
	13. $c \vee h$	6,12 M.P.
	14. $\sim c$	5,11 M.T.
	15. h	13,14 D.S.
	16. $\sim h$	3,4 M.T.
	17. $h \bullet \sim h$	15,16 Conj.
18. $\sim m \vee a$		7-17 I.P.

7.6 Part II

11. 1. $(m \bullet f) \supset (a \vee \sim c)$
    2. $g \supset c$
    3. $\sim f \supset j$
    4. $\sim a \bullet g$
    $\therefore \sim m \vee j$

	5. $\sim(\sim m \vee j)$	A.I.P.
	6. $\sim\sim m \bullet \sim j$	5 De M.
	7. $\sim j \bullet \sim\sim m$	6 Com.
	8. $\sim j$	7 Simp.
	9. $\sim\sim f$	3,8 M.T.
	10. f	9 D.N.
	11. $\sim\sim m$	6 Simp.
	12. m	11 D.N.
	13. $m \bullet f$	12,10 Conj.
	14. $a \vee \sim c$	1,14 M.P.
	15. $\sim a$	4 Simp.
	16. $\sim c$	14,15 D.S.
	17. $\sim g$	2,16 M.T.
	18. $g \bullet \sim a$	4 Com.
	19. g	18 Simp.
	20. $g \bullet \sim g$	19,17 Conj.
21. $\sim m \vee j$		5-20 I.P.

13. 1. $p \supset (\sim q \bullet r)$
    2. $(q \vee \sim r) \supset s$
    3. $\sim s \vee p$
    $\therefore \sim q$

	4. q	A.I.P.
	5. $q \vee \sim r$	4 Add.
	6. s	2,5 M.P.

7. $\sim\sim s$	6 D.N.	
8. p	3,7 D.S.	
9. $\sim q \bullet r$	1,8 M.P.	
10. $\sim q$	9 Simp.	
11. $q \bullet \sim q$	4,10 Conj.	
12. $\sim q$	4-11 I.P.	

15.
1. $n \equiv (h \lor s)$		
2. $h \supset (b \bullet m)$		
3. $s \supset e$		
4. $\sim e \bullet n$		
$\therefore\ b \bullet m$		
5. $\sim e$	4 Simp.	
6. $n \bullet \sim e$	4 Com.	
7. n	6 Simp.	
8. $[n \supset (h \lor s)] \bullet [(h \lor s) \supset n]$	1 Equiv.	
9. $\sim(b \bullet m)$	A.I.P.	
10. $\sim h$	2,9 M.T.	
11. $\sim s$	3,5 M.T.	
12. $\sim h \bullet \sim s$	10,11 Conj.	
13. $\sim(h \lor s)$	12 De M.	
14. $n \supset (h \lor s)$	8 Simp.	
15. $\sim n$	14,13 M.T.	
16. $n \bullet \sim n$	7,15 Conj.	
17. $b \bullet m$	9-16 I.P.	

17.
1. $a \lor [g \bullet (\sim d \bullet \sim e)]$		
2. $g \equiv e$		
$\therefore\ \sim a \supset \sim(d \bullet \sim e)$		
3. $\sim a$	A.C.P.	
4. $g \bullet (\sim d \bullet \sim e)$	1,3 D.S.	
5. g	4 Simp.	
6. $(\sim d \bullet \sim e) \bullet g$	4 Com.	
7. $\sim d \bullet \sim e$	6 Simp.	
8. $\sim e \bullet \sim d$	7 Com.	
9. $\sim e$	8 Simp.	
10. $(g \supset e) \bullet (e \supset g)$	2 Equiv.	
11. $g \supset e$	10 Simp.	
12. e	11,5 M.P.	
13. $e \lor \sim(d \bullet \sim e)$	12 Add.	
14. $\sim(d \bullet \sim e)$	13,9 D.S.	
15. $\sim a \supset \sim(d \bullet \sim e)$	3-14 C.P.	

19.
1. $(h \bullet m) \supset (k \bullet b)$	
2. $(k \lor b) \supset (f \lor s)$	
3. $h \bullet \sim s$	
$\therefore\ m \supset f$	

4. m	A.C.P.	
5. $\sim f$	A.I.P.	
6. h	3 Simp.	
7. $\sim s \bullet h$	3 Com.	
8. $\sim s$	7 Simp.	
9. $\sim f \bullet \sim s$	5,8 Conj.	
10. $\sim(f \lor s)$	9 De M.	
11. $\sim(h \bullet m)$	1,10 M.T.	
12. $\sim h \lor \sim m$	11 De M.	
13. $\sim\sim h$	6 D.N.	
14. $\sim m$	12,13 D.S.	
15. $m \bullet \sim m$	4,14 Conj.	
16. f	5-15 I.P.	
17. $m \supset f$	5-16 C.P.	

21.
1. $a \supset (b \bullet \sim c)$		
2. $\sim a \equiv b$		
$\therefore\ a \supset d$		
3. $(\sim a \supset b) \bullet (b \supset \sim a)$	2 Equiv.	
4. a	A.C.P.	
5. $b \bullet \sim c$	1,4 M.P.	
6. b	5 Simp.	
7. $(b \supset \sim a) \bullet (\sim a \supset b)$	3 Com.	
8. $b \supset \sim a$	7 Simp.	
9. $\sim\sim a$	4 D.N.	
10. $\sim b$	8,9 M.T.	
11. $b \lor d$	6 Add.	
12. d	11,10 D.S.	
13. $a \supset d$	4-12 C.P.	

23.
1. $[w \bullet (c \lor g)] \supset [g \equiv (o \supset r)]$		
2. g		
3. $g \supset (\sim r \bullet w)$		
$\therefore\ \sim g \lor \sim o$		
4. $\sim(\sim g \lor \sim o)$	A.I.P.	
5. $\sim\sim(g \bullet o)$	4 De M.	
6. $g \bullet o$	5 D.N.	
7. $o \bullet g$	6 Com.	
8. o	7 Simp.	
9. $\sim r \bullet w$	3,2 M.P.	
10. $\sim r$	9 Simp.	
11. $w \bullet \sim r$	9 Com.	
12. w	11 Simp.	
13. $g \lor c$	2 Add.	
14. $c \lor g$	13 Com.	
15. $w \bullet (c \lor g)$	12,14 Conj.	
16. $g \equiv (o \supset r)$	1,15 M.P.	

17. $[g \supset (o \supset r)] \bullet [(o \supset r) \supset g]$ 16 Equiv.
18. $g \supset (o \supset r)$ 17 Simp.
19. $o \supset r$ 18,2 M.P.
20. r 19,8 M.P.
21. $r \bullet \sim r$ 20,10 Conj.
22. $\sim g \vee \sim o$ 4-21 I.P.

25. 1. $\sim[p \equiv (q \vee \sim r)]$
2. $p \bullet \sim s$
$\therefore q \equiv s$
3. p 2 Simp.
4. $\sim s \bullet p$ 2 Com.
5. $\sim s$ 4 Simp.
6. $\sim\{[p \bullet (q \vee \sim r)] \vee [\sim p \bullet \sim(q \vee \sim r)]\}$ 1 Equiv.
7. $\sim[p \bullet (q \vee \sim r)] \bullet \sim[\sim p \bullet \sim(q \vee \sim r)]$ 6 De M.
8. q A.C.P.
9. $\sim[p \bullet (q \vee \sim r)]$ 7 Simp.
10. $\sim p \vee \sim(q \vee \sim r)$ 9 De M.
11. $p \supset \sim(q \vee \sim r)$ 10 Impl.
12. $\sim(q \vee \sim r)$ 11,3 M.P.
13. $\sim q \bullet \sim\sim r$ 12 De M.
14. $\sim q$ 13 Simp.
15. $q \vee s$ 8 Add.
16. s 15,14 D.S.
17. $q \supset s$ 8-16 C.P.
18. $\sim s \vee q$ 5 Add.
19. $s \supset q$ 18 Impl.
20. $(q \supset s) \bullet (s \supset q)$ 17,19 Conj.
21. $q \equiv s$ 20 Equiv.

7.6 Part III

27. 1. $I \supset (B \bullet F)$
2. $(F \supset L) \bullet (H \vee M)$
3. $(M \supset F) \supset S$
4. I
$\therefore S$
5. $\sim S$ A.I.P.
6. $B \bullet F$ 1,4 M.P.
7. $F \bullet B$ 6 Com.
8. F 7 Simp.
9. $\sim(M \supset F)$ 3,5 M.T.
10. $\sim(\sim M \vee F)$ 9 Impl.
11. $\sim\sim M \bullet \sim F$ 10 De M.
12. $\sim F \bullet \sim\sim M$ 11 Com.
13. $\sim F$ 12 Simp.
14. $F \bullet \sim F$ 8,13 Conj.
15. S 5-14 I.P.

29. 1. $(I \vee B) \equiv H$
2. $H \supset (S \bullet F)$
3. $F \supset O$
4. I
$\therefore O$
5. $\sim O$ A.I.P.
6. $\sim F$ 3,5 M.T.
7. $\sim F \vee \sim S$ 6 Add.
8. $\sim S \vee \sim F$ 7 Com.
9. $\sim(S \bullet F)$ 8 De M.
10. $\sim H$ 2,9 M.T.
11. $[(I \vee B) \supset H] \bullet [H \supset (I \vee B)]$ 1 Equiv.
12. $(I \vee B) \supset H$ 11 Simp.
13. $I \vee B$ 4 Add.
14. H 12,13 M.P.
15. $H \bullet \sim H$ 14,10 Conj.
16. O 5-15 I.P.

31. 1. $(I \bullet \sim V) \supset (\sim B \vee M)$
2. $M \supset V$
3. $V \supset (L \bullet H)$
$\therefore (L \bullet M) \supset V$
4. $L \bullet M$ A.C.P.
5. $M \bullet L$ 4 Com.
6. M 5 Simp.
7. V 2,6 M.P.
8. $(L \bullet M) \supset V$ 4-7 C.P.

33. 1. $[B \vee (F \vee L)] \supset T$
2. $\sim L \equiv (T \bullet I)$
3. $I \supset \sim(B \bullet L)$
4. $\sim T$
$\therefore I \bullet V$
5. $\sim(I \bullet V)$ A.I.P.
6. $\sim I \vee \sim V$ 5 De M.
7. $[\sim L \supset (T \bullet I)] \bullet [(T \bullet I) \supset \sim L]$ 2 Equiv.
8. $\sim L \supset (T \bullet I)$ 7 Simp.
9. $\sim T \vee \sim I$ 4 Add.
10. $\sim(T \bullet I)$ 9 De M.
11. $\sim\sim L$ 10,8 M.T.
12. $\sim[B \vee (F \vee L)]$ 1,4 M.T.
13. $\sim B \bullet \sim(F \vee L)$ 12 De M.
14. $\sim B$ 13 Simp.
15. $\sim(F \vee L) \bullet \sim B$ 13 Com.
16. $\sim(F \vee L)$ 15 Simp.
17. $\sim F \bullet \sim L$ 16 De M.
18. $\sim L \bullet \sim F$ 17 Com.
19. $\sim L$ 18 Simp.
20. $\sim L \bullet \sim\sim L$ 19,11 Conj.
21. $I \bullet V$ 5-20 I.P.

35. 1. $(B \bullet F) \supset (I \bullet V)$
2. $\sim F \equiv (T \lor I)$
3. B
4. $(B \supset M) \bullet (M \supset V)$
5. $(\sim I \supset \sim L) \bullet (T \supset L)$
∴ I

	6. $\sim I$	A.I.P.
	7. $\sim I \supset \sim L$	5 Simp.
	8. $\sim L$	7,6 M.P.
	9. $(T \supset L) \bullet (\sim I \supset \sim L)$	5 Com.
	10. $T \supset L$	9 Simp.
	11. $\sim T$	10,8 M.T.
	12. $[\sim F \supset (T \lor I)] \bullet [(T \lor I) \supset \sim F]$	2 Equiv.
	13. $\sim F \supset (T \lor I)$	12 Simp.
	14. $\sim T \bullet \sim I$	11,6 Conj.
	15. $\sim (T \lor I)$	14 De M.
	16. $\sim\sim F$	13,15 M.T.
	17. F	16 D.N.
	18. $B \bullet F$	3,17 Conj.
	19. $I \bullet V$	1,18 M.P.
	20. I	19 Simp.
	21. $I \bullet \sim I$	20,6 Conj.
22. I		6-21 I.P.

Chapter 8 Quantification Theory

8.2 SYMBOLESE 102: THE LANGUAGE OF QUANTIFICATIONAL LOGIC

Part I

1. $(x)(Ax \supset Mx)$
3. $(\exists x)(Mx \bullet Fx)$
5. $(\exists x)[(Ax \bullet Cx) \bullet \sim Rx]$
7. $Cf \supset (x)(Sx \supset Cx)$
9. $(x)[(Dx \bullet Ex) \supset \sim Bx]$
11. $Do \equiv (\exists x)(Px \bullet Dx)$
13. $(\exists x)(Px \bullet Cx) \supset Ch$
15. $(\exists x)(Dx \bullet Mx) \equiv (x)(Dx \supset Vx)$
17. $(x)[Wx \supset (Ex \lor Ox)]$
19. $(x)(Mx \supset Sx) \supset (x)(Mx \supset \sim Ix)$
21. $(x)(Px \supset Vx) \bullet \{(x)(Nx \supset Cx)$
      $\bullet (x)[Bx \supset (Vx \bullet Cx)]\}$
23. $(x)\{(Tx \bullet Mx) \supset [(Dx \bullet Hx) \supset Ax]\}$
25. $(x)[(Px \bullet Dx) \supset Cx]$

8.2 Part II

27. $(\exists x)(Mx \bullet \sim Ax)$
29. $(x)(Px \supset Gx)$
31. $(\exists x)(Rx \bullet Px)$
33. $(x)(Bx \supset \sim Cx)$

35. $(\exists x)(Cx \bullet Px)$
37. $(x)(Dx \supset Bx)$
39. $(\exists x)(Ax \bullet \sim Hx)$

8.3 PROVING VALIDITY

Part I

1. line 3 is by E.I.
line 5 is by U.I.
line 10 is by E.G.

8.3 Part II

3. line 3: $Sa \bullet Wa$
line 4: $Ka \supset \sim Sa$
line 10: $(\exists x)(Wx \bullet \sim Kx)$

8.3 Part III

5. 1. $(\exists x)(Jx \bullet Kx)$
2. $(x)(Jx \supset Lx)$
∴ $(\exists x)(Lx \bullet Kx)$

3. $Ja \bullet Ka$	1 E.I.
4. Ja	3 Simp.
5. $Ka \bullet Ja$	3 Com.
6. Ka	5 Simp.
7. $Ja \supset La$	2 U.I.
8. La	7,4 M.P.
9. $La \bullet Ka$	8,6 Conj.
10. $(\exists x)(Lx \bullet Kx)$	9 E.G.

7. 1. $(x)(Sx \supset \sim Tx)$
2. $(\exists x)(Sx \bullet Ux)$
∴ $(\exists x)(Ux \bullet \sim Tx)$

3. $Sa \bullet Ua$	2 E.I.
4. $Sa \supset \sim Ta$	1 U.I.
5. Sa	3 Simp.
6. $\sim Ta$	4,5 M.P.
7. $Ua \bullet Sa$	3 Com.
8. Ua	7 Simp.
9. $Ua \bullet \sim Ta$	8,6 Conj.
10. $(\exists x)(Ux \bullet \sim Tx)$	9 E.G.

9. 1. $(\exists x)(Yx \bullet Zx)$
2. $(x)(Zx \supset Ax)$
∴ $(\exists x)(Ax \bullet Yx)$

3. $Ya \bullet Za$	1 E.I.
4. $Za \supset Aa$	2 U.I.

5. Ya 3 Simp.
6. $Za \bullet Ya$ 3 Com.
7. Za 6 Simp.
8. Aa 4,7 M.P.
9. $Aa \bullet Ya$ 8,5 Conj.
10. $(\exists x)(Ax \bullet Yx)$ 9 E.G.

8.3 Part IV

11.   1. $(x)(Dx \supset Ex)$
    2. $(\exists x)(Fx \bullet \sim Ex)$
    $\therefore$ $(\exists x)(Fx \bullet \sim Dx)$
    3. $Fa \bullet \sim Ea$ 2 E.I.
    4. $Da \supset Ea$ 1 U.I.
    5. Fa 3 Simp.
    6. $\sim Ea \bullet Fa$ 3 Com.
    7. $\sim Ea$ 6 Simp.
    8. $\sim Da$ 4,7 M.T.
    9. $Fa \bullet \sim Da$ 5,8 Conj.
    10. $(\exists x)(Fx \bullet \sim Dx)$ 9 E.G.

13.   1. $(x)(Qx \supset Px)$
    2. $(\exists x)(Rx \bullet Qx)$
    $\therefore$ $(\exists x)(Px \bullet Rx)$
    3. $Ra \bullet Qa$ 2 E.I.
    4. $Qa \supset Pa$ 1 U.I.
    5. Ra 3 Simp.
    6. $Qa \bullet Ra$ 3 Com.
    7. Qa 6 Simp.
    8. Pa 4,7 M.P.
    9. $Pa \bullet Ra$ 8,5 Conj.
    10. $(\exists x)(Px \bullet Rx)$ 9 E.G.

15.   1. $(x)(Bx \supset Px)$
    2. $\sim Pg$
    $\therefore$ $\sim Bg$
    3. $Bg \supset Pg$ 1 U.I.
    4. $\sim Bg$ 3,2 M.T.

8.3 Part V

17.   1. $\sim(x)(Px \supset \sim Sx)$
    2. $(\exists x)\sim(Px \supset \sim Sx)$ 1 Q.E.
    3. $(\exists x)\sim(\sim Px \vee \sim Sx)$ 2 Impl.
    4. $(\exists x)\sim\sim(Px \bullet Sx)$ 3 De M.
    5. $(\exists x)(Px \bullet Sx)$ 5 D.N.

19.   1. $\sim(x)(Dx \supset Gx)$
    2. $(\exists x)\sim(Dx \supset Gx)$ 1 Q.E.
    3. $(\exists x)\sim(\sim Dx \vee Gx)$ 2 Impl.
    4. $(\exists x)(\sim\sim Dx \bullet \sim Gx)$ 3 De M.
    5. $(\exists x)(Dx \bullet \sim Gx)$ 4 D.N.

21.   1. $\sim(x)(Cx \supset \sim\sim Dx)$
    2. $\sim(x)(Cx \supset Dx)$ 1 D.N.
    3. $(\exists x)\sim(Cx \supset Dx)$ 2 Q.E.
    4. $(\exists x)\sim(\sim Cx \vee Dx)$ 3 Impl.
    5. $(\exists x)(\sim\sim Cx \bullet \sim Dx)$ 4 De M.
    6. $(\exists x)(Cx \bullet \sim Dx)$ 5 D.N.

23.   1. $\sim(x)(\sim Kx \vee \sim Lx)$
    2. $(\exists x)\sim(\sim Kx \vee \sim Lx)$ 1 Q.E.
    3. $(\exists x)\sim\sim(Kx \bullet Lx)$ 2 De M.
    4. $(\exists x)(Kx \bullet Lx)$ 3 D.N.

25.   1. $\sim(x)\sim(\sim Ux \bullet \sim Vx)$
    2. $(\exists x)(\sim Ux \bullet \sim Vx)$ 1 Q.E.

8.3 Part VI

27.   1. $(x)[(Px \supset Qx) \bullet (Rx \supset Sx)]$
    2. $\sim(x)(Tx \supset Qx)$
    3. $(x)(\sim Rx \supset Ux)$
    $\therefore$ $(\exists x)[Tx \bullet (Px \supset Ux)]$
    4. $(\exists x)\sim(Tx \supset Qx)$ 2 Q.E.
    5. $(\exists x)\sim(\sim Tx \vee Qx)$ 4 Impl.
    6. $(\exists x)(\sim\sim Tx \bullet \sim Qx)$ 5 De M.
    7. $(\exists x)(Tx \bullet \sim Qx)$ 6 D.N.
    8. $Ta \bullet \sim Qa$ 7 E.I.
    9. Ta 8 Simp.
    10. $\sim Qa \bullet Ta$ 8 Com.
    11. $\sim Qa$ 10 Simp.
    12. $(Pa \supset Qa) \bullet (Ra \supset Sa)$ 1 U.I.
    13. $Pa \supset Qa$ 12 Simp.
    14. $\sim Pa$ 13,11 M.T.
    15. $\sim Pa \vee Ua$ 14 Add.
    16. $Pa \supset Ua$ 15 Impl.
    17. $Ta \bullet (Pa \supset Ua)$ 9,16 Conj.
    18. $(\exists x)[Tx \bullet (Px \supset Ux)]$ 17 E.G.

29.   1. $(x)(Gx \supset Qx)$
    2. $(\exists x)(Px \bullet Qx) \supset (x)(Rx \supset Sx)$
    3. $(\exists x)[Px \bullet (\sim Sx \bullet Gx)]$
    $\therefore$ $(\exists x)(Rx \supset \sim Hx)$
    4. $Pa \bullet (\sim Sa \bullet Ga)$ 3 E.I.
    5. $Gx \supset Qx$ 1 U.I.
    6. Pa 4 Simp.
    7. $(\sim Sa \bullet Ga) \bullet Pa$ 4 Com.
    8. $\sim Sa \bullet Ga$ 7 Simp.
    9. $Ga \bullet \sim Sa$ 8 Com.

10. Ga — 9 Simp.
11. Qa — 5,10 M.P.
12. $Pa \cdot Qa$ — 6,11 Conj.
13. $(\exists x)(Px \cdot Qx)$ — 12 E.G.
14. $(x)(Rx \supset Sx)$ — 2,13 M.P.
15. $Ra \supset Sa$ — 14 U.I.
16. $\sim Sa$ — 8 Simp.
17. $\sim Ra$ — 15,16 M.T.
18. $\sim Ra \lor \sim Ha$ — 17 Add.
19. $Ra \supset \sim Ha$ — 19 Impl.
20. $(\exists x)(Rx \supset \sim Hx)$ — 19 E.G.

31.
1. $(x)[Px \supset (Qx \supset Rx)]$
2. $(\exists x)(Px \cdot Sx)$
3. $(\exists x)(\sim Rx \cdot Tx)$
4. $(\exists x)(Px \supset \sim Qx) \supset (x)(Sx \supset \sim Rx)$
∴ $(\exists x)(Px \cdot \sim Qx)$
5. $Pa \cdot Sa$ — 2 E.I.
6. $\sim Rb \cdot Tb$ — 3 E.I.
7. $Pb \supset (Qb \supset Rb)$ — 1 U.I.
8. $(Pb \cdot Qb) \supset Rb$ — 7 Exp.
9. $\sim Rb$ — 6 Simp.
10. $\sim (Pb \cdot Qb)$ — 8,9 M.T.
11. $\sim Pb \lor \sim Qb$ — 10 De M.
12. $Pb \supset \sim Qb$ — 11 Impl.
13. $(\exists x)(Px \supset \sim Qx)$ — 12 E.G.
14. $(x)(Sx \supset \sim Rx)$ — 4,13 M.P.
15. $Sa \supset \sim Ra$ — 14 U.I.
16. $Sa \cdot Pa$ — 5 Com.
17. Sa — 16 Simp.
18. $\sim Ra$ — 15,17 M.P.
19. $Pa \supset (Qa \supset Ra)$ — 1 U.I.
20. Pa — 5 Simp.
21. $Qa \supset Ra$ — 19, 20 M.P.
22. $\sim Qa$ — 21,18 M.T.
23. $Pa \cdot \sim Qa$ — 20,22 Conj.
24. $(\exists x)(Px \cdot \sim Qx)$ — 23 E.G.

33.
1. $(\exists x)(Qx \cdot \sim Tx)$
2. $(x)[Qx \supset (Tx \lor \sim Px)]$
3. $(\exists x)(\sim Tx \cdot Sx)$
4. $(\exists x)(Qx \cdot \sim Px) \supset (x)(Sx \supset Px)$
∴ $(\exists x)(Sx \cdot \sim Qx)$
5. $Qa \cdot \sim Ta$ — 1 E.I.
6. $Qa \supset (Ta \lor \sim Pa)$ — 2 U.I.
7. Qa — 5 Simp.
8. $Ta \lor \sim Pa$ — 6,7 M.P.
9. $\sim Ta \cdot Qa$ — 5 Com.

10. $\sim Ta$ — 9 Simp.
11. $\sim Pa$ — 9,10 D.S.
12. $Qa \cdot \sim Pa$ — 7,11 Conj.
13. $(\exists x)(Qx \cdot \sim Px)$ — 12 E.G.
14. $(x)(Sx \supset Px)$ — 4,13 M.P.
15. $\sim Tb \cdot Sb$ — 3 E.I.
16. $\sim Tb$ — 15 Simp.
17. $Sb \cdot \sim Tb$ — 15 Com.
18. Sb — 17 Simp.
19. $Sb \supset Pb$ — 14 U.I.
20. Pb — 19,18 M.P.
21. $\sim\sim Pb$ — 20 D.N.
22. $Qb \supset (Tb \lor \sim Pb)$ — 2 U.I.
23. $\sim Tb \cdot \sim\sim Pb$ — 16,21 Conj.
24. $\sim (Tb \lor \sim Pb)$ — 23 De M.
25. $\sim Qb$ — 22,24 M.T.
26. $Sb \cdot \sim Qb$ — 18,25 Conj.
27. $(\exists x)(Sx \cdot \sim Qx)$ — 26 E.G.

35.
1. $(x)[Px \supset (Qx \cdot Rx)]$
2. $(\exists x)(Sx \cdot \sim Rx)$
3. $(\exists x)(Px \cdot Tx)$
4. $[(\exists x)(Sx \cdot \sim Px) \cdot (\exists y)(Qy \cdot Ty)] \supset$
   $(\exists z)(Zz \cdot Fz)$
5. $(x)[Fx \supset (Px \lor \sim Zx)]$
∴ $(\exists x)(Zx \cdot Px)$
6. $Sa \cdot \sim Ra$ — 2 E.I.
7. $Pa \supset (Qa \cdot Ra)$ — 1 U.I.
8. $\sim Pa \lor (Qa \cdot Ra)$ — 7 Impl.
9. $\sim Pa \lor (Ra \cdot Qa)$ — 8 Com.
10. $(\sim Pa \lor Ra) \cdot (\sim Pa \lor Qa)$ — 9 Dist.
11. $\sim Pa \lor Ra$ — 10 Simp.
12. $Pa \supset Ra$ — 11 Impl.
13. Sa — 6 Simp.
14. $\sim Ra \cdot Sa$ — 6 Com.
15. $\sim Ra$ — 14 Simp.
16. $\sim Pa$ — 12,15 M.T.
17. $Sa \cdot \sim Pa$ — 13,16 Conj.
18. $(\exists x)(Sx \cdot \sim Px)$ — 17 E.G.
19. $Pb \cdot Tb$ — 3 E.I.
20. Pb — 19 Simp.
21. $Tb \cdot Pb$ — 19 Com.
22. Tb — 21 Simp.
23. $Pb \supset (Qb \cdot Rb)$ — 1 U.I.
24. $Qb \cdot Rb$ — 23,20 M.P.
25. Qb — 24 Simp.
26. $Qb \cdot Tb$ — 25,22 Conj.
27. $(\exists y)(Qy \cdot Ty)$ — 26 E.G.
28. $(\exists x)(Sx \cdot \sim Px) \cdot (\exists y)(Qy \cdot Ty)$ — 18,27 Conj.
29. $(\exists z)(Zz \cdot Fz)$ — 4,28 M.P.

30. $Zc \bullet Fc$	29 E.I.
31. Zc	30 Simp.
32. $Fc \bullet Zc$	30 Com.
33. Fc	32 Simp.
34. $Fc \supset (Pc \lor \sim Zc)$	5 U.I.
35. $Pc \lor \sim Zc$	34,33 M.P.
36. $\sim Zc \lor Pc$	35 Com.
37. $Zc \supset Pc$	36 Impl.
38. Pc	37,31 M.P.
39. $Zc \bullet Pc$	38,31 Conj.
40. $(\exists x)(Zx \bullet Px)$	39 E.G.

$$Q.E.D.$$

8.4 CONDITIONAL AND INDIRECT PROOF

1.
1. $(x)[Px \supset (Qx \bullet Rx)]$	
$\therefore (x)(Px \supset Qx)$	
2. Px	A.C.P.
3. $Px \supset (Qx \bullet Rx)$	1 U.I.
4. $Qx \bullet Rx$	3,2 M.P.
5. Qx	4 Simp.
6. $Px \supset Qx$	2-5 C.P.
7. $(x)(Px \supset Qx)$	6 U.G.

3.
1. $(x)[Px \supset (Rx \lor \sim Sx)]$	
2. $(x)(Rx \supset \sim Sx)$	
$\therefore (x)(Px \supset \sim Sx)$	
3. Px	A.C.P.
4. $Px \supset (Rx \lor \sim Sx)$	1 U.I.
5. $Rx \supset \sim Sx$	2 U.I.
6. $Rx \lor \sim Sx$	4,3 M.P.
7. $\sim Sx \lor Rx$	6 Com.
8. $Sx \supset Rx$	7 Impl.
9. $Sx \supset \sim Sx$	8,5 H.S.
10. $\sim Sx \lor \sim Sx$	9 Impl.
11. $\sim Sx$	10 Taut.
12. $Px \supset \sim Sx$	3-11 C.P.
13. $(x)(Px \supset \sim Sx)$	12 U.G.

5.
1. $(x)[(Px \lor Qx) \supset (Rx \bullet Sx)]$	
2. $(x)[Rx \supset (Qx \bullet \sim Sx)]$	
$\therefore (x)(Qx \supset \sim Sx)$	
3. Qx	A.C.P.
4. $(Px \lor Qx) \supset (Rx \bullet Sx)$	1 U.I.
5. $Rx \supset (Qx \bullet \sim Sx)$	2. U.I.
6. $Qx \lor Px$	3 Add.
7. $Px \lor Qx$	6 Com.
8. $Rx \bullet Sx$	4,7 M.P.

9. Rx	8 Simp.
10. $Qx \supset \sim Sx$	5,9 M.P.
11. $\sim Sx \bullet Qx$	10 Com.
12. $\sim Sx$	11 Simp.
13. $Qx \supset \sim Sx$	3-12 C.P.
14. $(x)(Qx \supset \sim Sx)$	13 U.G.

7.
1. $(x)[(Px \bullet Qx) \supset Rx]$	
2. $(\exists x)(Px \bullet \sim Rx)$	
$\therefore (\exists x)\sim Qx$	
3. $\sim(\exists x)\sim Qx$	A.I.P.
4. $(x)Qx$	Q.E.
5. $Pa \bullet \sim Ra$	2 E.I.
6. Pa	5 Simp.
7. $\sim Ra \bullet Pa$	6 Com.
8. $\sim Ra$	7 Simp.
9. $(Pa \bullet Qa) \supset Ra$	1 U.I.
10. Qa	4 U.I.
11. $Pa \bullet Qa$	6,10 Conj.
12. Ra	9,11 M.P.
13. $Ra \bullet \sim Ra$	12,8 Conj.
14. $(\exists x)\sim Qx$	3-13 I.P.

9.
1. $(x)[Px \supset (Rx \lor \sim Sx)]$	
2. $(\exists x)(Px \bullet \sim Rx)$	
$\therefore (\exists x)(Px \bullet \sim Sx)$	
3. $Pa \bullet \sim Ra$	2 E.I.
4. $\sim(\exists x)(Px \bullet \sim Sx)$	A.I.P.
5. $(x)\sim(Px \bullet \sim Sx)$	Q.E.
6. $Pa \supset (Ra \lor \sim Sa)$	1 U.I.
7. $\sim(Pa \bullet \sim Sa)$	5 U.I.
8. Pa	3 Simp.
9. $\sim Pa \lor \sim\sim Sa$	7 De M.
10. $\sim\sim Pa$	8 D.N.
11. $\sim\sim Sa$	9,10 D.S.
12. $Ra \lor \sim Sa$	6,8 M.P.
13. $\sim Ra \bullet Pa$	3 Com.
14. $\sim Ra$	13 Simp.
15. $\sim Sa$	12,14 D.S.
16. $\sim Sa \bullet \sim\sim Sa$	15,11 Conj.
17. $(\exists x)(Px \bullet \sim Sx)$	4-16 I.P.

11.
1. $(x)[(Px \lor Qx) \supset (Rx \bullet Sx)]$	
2. $(x)[Rx \supset (Tx \lor \sim Px)]$	
$\therefore (x)[Qx \supset (Px \supset Tx)]$	
3. Qx	A.C.P.
4. Px	A.C.P.
5. $(Px \lor Qx) \supset (Rx \bullet Sx)$	1 U.I.
6. $Px \lor Qx$	4 Add.

| | 7. $Rx \supset Sx$		5,6 M.P.
| | 8. Rx		7 Simp.
| | 9. $Rx \supset (Tx \lor \sim Px)$		2 U.I.
| | 10. $Tx \lor \sim Px$		9,8 M.P.
| | 11. $\sim Px \lor Tx$		10 Com.
| | 12. $Px \supset Tx$		11 Impl.
| | 13. Tx		12,4 M.P.
| 14. $Px \supset Tx$		4-14 C.P.
15. $Qx \supset (Px \supset Tx)$		3-15 C.P.
16. $(x)[Qx \supset (Px \supset Tx)]$		15 U.G.

13. 1. $(x)[Px \supset (Qx \equiv Rx)]$
2. $(\exists x)(Px \bullet Rx)$
∴ $(\exists x)(Rx \bullet Qx)$

| 3. $\sim(\exists x)(Rx \bullet Qx)$	A.I.P.
| 4. $(x)\sim(Rx \bullet Qx)$	3 Q.E.
| 5. $Pa \bullet Ra$	2 E.I.
| 6. Pa	5 Simp.
| 7. $Ra \bullet Pa$	5 Com.
| 8. Ra	7 Simp.
| 9. $Pa \supset (Qa \equiv Ra)$	1 U.I.
| 10. $Qa \equiv Ra$	9,6 M.P.
| 11. $\sim(Ra \bullet Qa)$	4 U.I.
| 12. $\sim Ra \lor \sim Qa$	11 De M.
| 13. $Ra \supset \sim Qa$	12 Impl.
| 14. $\sim Qa$	13,8 M.P.
| 15. $(Qa \supset Ra) \bullet (Ra \supset Qa)$	10 Equiv.
| 16. $(Ra \supset Qa) \bullet (Qa \supset Ra)$	15 Com.
| 17. $Ra \supset Qa$	16 Simp.
| 18. Qa	17,8 M.P.
| 19. $Qa \bullet \sim Qa$	18,14 Conj.
20. $(\exists x)(Rx \bullet Qx)$	3-19 I.P.

15. 1. $(x)[(Qx \equiv Rx) \supset \sim Px]$
2. $(x)(Px \supset Rx)$
∴ $(x)(Px \supset \sim Qx)$

| 3. Px	A.C.P.
| 4. $(Qx \equiv Rx) \supset \sim Px$	1 U.I.
| 5. $Px \supset Rx$	2 U.I.
| 6. Rx	5,3 M.P.
| 7. $\sim\sim Px$	3 D.N.
| 8. $\sim(Qx \equiv Rx)$	4 M.T.
| 9. $\sim[(Qx \bullet Rx) \lor (\sim Qx \bullet \sim Rx)]$	8 Equiv.
| 10. $\sim(Qx \bullet Rx) \bullet \sim(\sim Qx \bullet \sim Rx)$	9 De M.
| 11. $\sim(Qx \bullet Rx)$	10 Simp.
| 12. $\sim(Rx \bullet Qx)$	11 Com.
| 13. $\sim Rx \lor \sim Qx$	12 De M.
| 14. $\sim\sim Rx$	6 D.N.
| 15. $\sim Qx$	13,14 D.S.
16. $Px \supset \sim Qx$	3-15 C.P.
17. $(x)(Px \supset \sim Qx)$	16 U.G.

17. 1. $(x)[(Px \supset \sim Qx) \supset \sim(Px \lor Qx)]$
2. $(x)(Qx \supset Rx)$
3. $(x)(Rx \supset Qx)$
∴ $(\exists x)[(Px \supset Rx) \bullet (Rx \supset Px)]$

| 4. $\sim(\exists x)[(Px \supset Rx) \bullet (Rx \supset Px)]$	A.I.P
| 5. $\sim(\exists x)(Px \equiv Rx)$	4 Equiv.
| 6. $(Pa \supset \sim Qa) \supset \sim(Pa \lor Qa)$	1 U.I.
| 7. $Qa \supset Ra$	2 U.I.
| 8. $Ra \supset Qa$	3 U.I.
| 9. $(\sim Pa \lor \sim Qa) \supset \sim(Pa \lor Qa)$	6 Impl.
| 10. $\sim(Pa \bullet Qa) \supset \sim(Pa \lor Qa)$	9 De M.
| | 11. Pa	A.C.P.
| | 12. $Pa \lor Qa$	11 Add.
| | 13. $\sim\sim(Pa \lor Qa)$	12 D.N.
| | 14. $\sim\sim(Pa \bullet Qa)$	9,13 M.T.
| | 15. $Pa \bullet Qa$	14 D.N.
| | 16. $Qa \bullet Pa$	15 Com.
| | 17. Qa	16 Simp.
| | 18. Ra	7,17 M.P.
| 19. $Pa \supset Ra$	11-18 C.P.
| | 20. Ra	A.C.P.
| | 21. Qa	8,20 M.P.
| | 22. $Qa \lor Pa$	21 Add.
| | 23. $Pa \lor Qa$	22 Com.
| | 24. $\sim\sim(Pa \lor Qa)$	23 D.N.
| | 25. $\sim\sim(Pa \bullet Qa)$	9,24 M.T.
| | 26. $Pa \bullet Qa$	25 D.N.
| | 27. Pa	26 Simp.
| 28. $Ra \supset Pa$	20-27 C.P.
| 29. $(Pa \supset Ra) \bullet (Ra \supset Pa)$	19,28 Conj.
| 30. $Pa \equiv Ra$	29 Equiv.
| 31. $(\exists x)(Px \equiv Rx)$	30 E.G.
| 32. $(\exists x)(Px \equiv Rx) \bullet \sim(\exists x)(Px \equiv Rx)$	31,5 Conj.
33. $(\exists x)[(Px \supset Rx) \bullet (Rx \supset Px)]$	4-32 I.P.

19. 1. $(x)[Px \supset \sim(Qx \lor Rx)]$
2. $(x)[\sim Px \supset \sim(\sim Qx \lor \sim Rx)]$
∴ $(x)(Qx \supset Rx)$

| 3. Qx	A.C.P.
| 4. $Px \supset \sim(Qx \lor Rx)$	1 U.I.
| 5. $\sim Px \supset \sim(\sim Qx \lor \sim Rx)$	2 U.I.
| 6. $Qx \lor Rx$	3 Add.
| 7. $\sim\sim(Qx \lor Rx)$	6 D.N.
| 8. $\sim Px$	4,7 M.T.
| 9. $\sim(\sim Qx \lor \sim Rx)$	5,8 M.P.
| 10. $\sim\sim(Qx \bullet Rx)$	9 De M.
| 11. $Qx \bullet Rx$	10 D.N.
| 12. $Rx \bullet Qx$	11 Com.
| 13. Rx	12 Simp.
14. $Qx \supset Rx$	3-13 C.P.
15. $(x)(Qx \supset Rx)$	15 U.G.

8.5 Proving Invalidity

Part I

1. $Sa \supset \sim Ta \quad Ta \supset \sim Ua \quad \therefore Sa \supset \sim Ua$
   T F F   T   T   T   T
       T   F   F
     T   T   F

3. $Sa \supset \sim Ta \quad Ua \supset \sim Ta \quad \therefore Ua \supset \sim Sa$
   T F   T   F   T   T
    T   T   F
   T   T   F

5. $Ga \supset Ha \quad Ga \supset Ia \quad \therefore Ia \supset Ha$
   F F   F   T   T   F
     T   T   T

7. $Pa \supset \sim Qa \quad Pa \supset \sim Ra \quad \therefore Ra \supset \sim Qa$
   F   T   F   T   T   T
      F   F   F
    T   T   F

9. $(Va \bullet \sim Wa) \vee (Vb \bullet \sim Wb) \ (Wa \bullet \sim Xa) \vee (Wb \bullet \sim Xb) \therefore (Xa \bullet \sim Va) \vee (Xb \bullet \sim Vb)$
   T   T   T   F   T   F   F   F   F   T   F   T
     F   T   T   T   F   F
     F   T   T   F   F   F
       T   T

8.5 Part II

11. $(x)(Dx \supset \sim Ex) \quad Da \supset \sim Ea \quad Fa \bullet Ea \quad \therefore Da \bullet \sim Fa$
   $(\exists x)(Fx \bullet Ex)$ F   T   T T   F   T
   $\therefore (\exists x)(Dx \bullet \sim Fx)$ F   T   F
               T   F

13.

$(\exists x)(Px \bullet Qx)$
$(\exists x)(Qx \bullet \sim Rx)$
$\therefore (\exists x)(Px \bullet \sim Rx)$

$(Pa \bullet Qa) \quad \vee \quad (Pb \bullet Qb) \quad (Qa \bullet \sim Ra) \quad \vee \quad (Qb \bullet \sim Rb) \quad \therefore (Pa \bullet \sim Ra) \quad \vee \quad (Pb \bullet \sim Rb)$
  T T   F T   T   T   T   F   T   T   F   F
   T   F   F   T   F   T
       T   F   T   F   F
               T   F

15. $(x)(Mx \supset Bx)$
   $(\exists x)(Ox \bullet Bx)$
   $\therefore (\exists x)(Ox \bullet Mx)$

   $Ma \supset Ba \quad Oa \bullet Ba \quad \therefore Oa \bullet Ma$
    F T   T T   T   F
      T   T   F

8.5 Part III

17. $(x)(Hx \supset Mx)$
   $(\exists x)(Hx \bullet Px)$
   $\therefore (x)(Px \supset Mx)$

$(Ha \supset Ma) \bullet (Hb \supset Mb) \ (Ha \bullet Pa) \vee (Hb \bullet Pb) \therefore (Pa \supset Ma) \bullet (Pb \supset Mb)$
  F F   T T   F T   T T   T   F   T T
    T   T   F   T   F   T
       T   T   F

19. $(x)(Bx \supset Mx)$
$(x)(Px \supset Mx)$
$\therefore (\exists x)(Bx \bullet Px)$

$Bx \supset Mx$	$Px \supset Mx$	$\therefore Bx \bullet Px$
F F	F F	F F
T	T	F

21.
1. $(x)(Px \supset Tx)$
2. $(x)(Tx \supset Sx)$
$\therefore (x)(Px \supset Sx)$
3. $Px \supset Tx$ — 1 U.I.
4. $Tx \supset Sx$ — 2 U.I.
5. $Px \supset Sx$ — 3,4 H.S.
6. $(x)(Px \supset Sx)$ — 5 U.G.

8.5 Part IV

23.
1. $(x)\{[Ix \supset (Jx \bullet \sim Kx)] \bullet [Jx \supset (Ix \supset Kx)]\}$
2. $(\exists x)[(Ix \bullet Jx) \bullet \sim Lx]$
$\therefore (\exists x)(Kx \bullet Lx)$
3. $(Ia \bullet Ja) \bullet \sim La$ — 2 E.I.
4. $Ia \bullet Ja$ — 3 Simp.
5. $[Ia \supset (Ja \bullet \sim Ka)] \bullet [Ja \supset (Ia \supset Ka)]$ — 1 U.I.
6. $Ia \supset (Ja \bullet \sim Ka)$ — 5 Simp.
7. Ia — 4 Simp.
8. $Ja \bullet \sim Ka$ — 6,7 M.P.
9. Ja — 8 Simp.
10. $\sim Ka \bullet Ja$ — 8 Com.
11. $\sim Ka$ — 10 Simp.
12. $[Ja \supset (Ia \supset Ka)] \bullet [Ia \supset (Ja \bullet \sim Ka)]$ — 5 Com.
13. $Ja \supset (Ia \supset Ka)$ — 12 Simp.
14. $Ia \supset Ka$ — 13,9 M.P.
15. $\sim Ia$ — 14,11 M.T.
16. $Ia \lor (\exists x)(Kx \bullet Lx)$ — 7 Add.
17. $(\exists x)(Kx \bullet Lx)$ — 16,15 D.S.

25.
1. $(x)[Wx \supset (Xx \supset Yx)]$
2. $(\exists x)[Xx \bullet (Zx \bullet \sim Ax)]$
3. $(x)[(Wx \supset Yx) \supset (Bx \supset Ax)]$
$\therefore (\exists x)(Zx \bullet \sim Bx)$
4. $Xa \bullet (Za \bullet \sim Aa)$ — 2 E.I.
5. Xa — 4 Simp.
6. $(Za \bullet \sim Aa) \bullet Xa$ — 4 Com.
7. $Za \bullet \sim Aa$ — 6 Simp.
8. Za — 7 Simp.
9. $\sim Aa \supset Za$ — 7 Com.
10. $\sim Aa$ — 9 Simp.
11. $Wa \supset (Xa \supset Ya)$ — 1 U.I.
12. $(Wa \bullet Xa) \supset Ya$ — 11 Exp.
13. $(Xa \bullet Wa) \supset Ya$ — 12 Com.
14. $Xa \supset (Wa \supset Ya)$ — 13 Exp.
15. $Wa \supset Ya$ — 14,5 M.P.
16. $(Wa \supset Ya) \supset (Ba \supset Aa)$ — 3 U.I.

17. $Ba \supset Aa$ — 16,15 M.P.
18. $\sim Ba$ — 17,10 M.T.
19. $Za \bullet \sim Ba$ — 8,18 Conj.
20. $(\exists x)(Zx \bullet \sim Bx)$ — 19 E.G.

27.
1. $(x)\{(Lx \lor Mx) \supset \{[(Nx \bullet Ox) \lor Px] \supset Qx\}\}$
2. $(\exists x)(Mx \bullet \sim Lx)$
3. $(x)\{[(Ox \supset Qx) \bullet \sim Rx] \supset Mx\}$
4. $(\exists x)(Lx \bullet \sim Mx)$
$\therefore (\exists x)(Nx \supset Rx)$
5. $La \bullet \sim Ma$ — 4 E.I.
6. La — 5 Simp.
7. $(La \lor Ma) \supset \{[(Na \bullet Oa) \lor Pa] \supset Qa\}$ — 1 U.I.
8. $La \lor Ma$ — 6 Add.
9. $[(Na \bullet Oa) \lor Pa] \supset Qa$ — 7,9 M.P.
10. $[(Oa \supset Qa) \bullet \sim Ra] \supset Ma$ — 3 U.I.
11. $\sim Ma \bullet La$ — 5 Com.
12. $\sim Ma$ — 11 Simp.
| 13. $Na \bullet Oa$ — A.C.P.
| 14. $(Na \bullet Oa) \lor Pa$ — 13 Add.
| 15. Qa — 9,14 M.P.
16. $(Na \bullet Oa) \supset Qa$ — 13-15 C.P.
17. $Na \supset (Oa \supset Qa)$ — 16 Exp.
18. $(Oa \supset Qa) \supset (\sim Ra \supset Ma)$ — 10 Exp.
19. $Na \supset (\sim Ra \supset Ma)$ — 17,18 H.S.
| 20. Na — A.C.P.
| 21. $\sim Ra \supset Ma$ — 19,20 M.P.
| 22. $\sim \sim Ra$ — 21,12 M.T.
| 23. Ra — 22 D.N.
24. $Na \supset Ra$ — 20-23 C.P.
25. $(\exists x)(Nx \supset Rx)$ — 24 E.G.

8.5 Part V

29. $(x)[(Ax \lor Sx) \supset (Ox \lor Vx)]$
$(\exists x)(Sx \bullet \sim Ox)$
$\therefore (\exists x)(Ax \bullet Vx)$

$(Aa \lor Sa) \supset (Oa \lor Va)$	$Sa \bullet \sim Oa$	$Aa \bullet Va$
F T F T	T F	F T
T T	T	F
T	T	

31.
1. $(x)(Gx \supset Ex)$
2. $(x)(Wx \supset \sim Sx)$
3. $(\exists x)(Wx \bullet \sim Ex)$
$\therefore (\exists x)[\sim (Gx \lor Sx)]$
4. $Wa \bullet \sim Ea$ — 3 E.I.
5. Wa — 4 Simp.
6. $\sim Ea \bullet Wa$ — 4 Com.
7. $\sim Ea$ — 6 Simp.

8. $Ga \supset Ea$ 1 U.I.
9. $Wa \supset \sim Sa$ 2 U.I.
10. $\sim Ga$ 8,7 M.T.
11. $\sim Sa$ 9,4 M.P.
12. $\sim Ga \bullet \sim Sa$ 10,11 Conj.
13. $\sim(Ga \vee Sa)$ 12 De M.
14. $(\exists x)[\sim(Gx \vee Sx)]$ 13 E.G.

33. 1. $(\exists x)[Px \bullet (Sx \bullet \sim Ix)]$
2. $(x)(Px \supset Ax)$
3. $(\exists x)(Px \bullet \sim Sx)$
4. $(x)(Jx \supset Sx)$
∴ $(\exists x)(Ax \bullet \sim Jx)$
5. $Pa \bullet \sim Sa$ 3 E.I.
6. Pa 5 Simp.
7. $\sim Sa \bullet Pa$ 5 Com.
8. $\sim Sa$ 7 Simp.
9. $Ja \supset Sa$ 4 U.I.
10. $\sim Ja$ 9,8 M.T.
11. $Pa \supset Aa$ 2 U.I.
12. Aa 11,6 M.P.
13. $Aa \bullet \sim Ja$ 12,10 Conj.
14. $(\exists x)(Ax \bullet \sim Jx)$ 13 E.G.

35. 1. $(x)[Cx \supset (Sx \vee Ox)]$
2. $(x)(Sx \supset \sim Wx)$
3. $(\exists x)(Cx \bullet Wx)$
∴ $(\exists x)(Cx \bullet Ox)$
4. $Ca \bullet Wa$ 3 E.I.
5. Ca 4 Simp.
6. $Wa \bullet Ca$ 4 Com.
7. Wa 6 Simp.
8. $Ca \supset (Sa \vee Oa)$ 1 U.I.
9. $Sa \supset \sim Wa$ 2 U.I.
10. $Sa \vee Oa$ 8,5 M.P.
11. $\sim\sim Wa$ 7 D.N.
12. $\sim Sa$ 9,11 M.T.
13. Oa 10,12 D.S.
14. $Cx \bullet Ox$ 5,13 Conj.
15. $(\exists x)(Cx \bullet Ox)$ 15 E.G.

37. $(x)[Lx \supset (Dx \bullet Wx)]$
$(x)\{Wx \supset [(Gx \supset Ex) \bullet (Tx \supset Cx)]\}$
$(x)[(Dx \supset Ax) \supset \sim Tx]$
$(\exists x)[Lx \bullet (Cx \bullet \sim Ex)]$
∴ $(\exists x)(Lx \bullet \sim Ax)$

$La \supset (Da \bullet Wa)$ $Wa \supset [(Ga \supset Ea) \bullet (Ta \supset Ca)]$
  T T T T   T   F F   F T
          T   T   T
  T   T
          T

$(Da \bullet Aa) \supset \sim Ta$ $Lx \bullet (Cx \bullet \sim Ex)$
  T T T   F   T T   T T   F
    T   T   T   T
          T   T
  ∴ $La \bullet \sim Aa$
    T T
      F
      F

39. 1. $(x)(Gx \supset Vx)$
2. $(x)(Rx \supset Ox)$
∴ $(x)[(Gx \bullet Rx) \supset (Vx \bullet Ox)]$
| 3. $Gx \bullet Rx$ A.C.P.
| 4. Gx 3 Simp.
| 5. $Rx \bullet Gx$ 3 Com.
| 6. Rx 5 Simp.
| 7. $Gx \supset Vx$ 1 U.I.
| 8. Vx 7,4 M.P.
| 9. $Rx \supset Ox$ 2 U.I.
| 10. Ox 9,6 M.P.
| 11. $Vx \bullet Ox$ 8,10 Conj.
12. $(Gx \bullet Rx) \supset (Vx \bullet Ox)$ 3-11 C.P.
13. $(x)[(Gx \bullet Rx) \supset (Vx \bullet Ox)]$ 12 U.G.

Chapter 9 Induction

9.2 ARGUMENTS BY ANALOGY

1. Analogical argument. The speaker is using an analogy to support the claim that you'll like the lasagna.

3. Analogical argument. The evidence of a variety of animals is used to support the conclusion.

5. Nonargumentative use of analogy.

7. Analogical argument. The conclusion is that the United States will eventually decline, and the reason is that similar empires have declined in the past.

9. Analogical argument. The conclusion is that, in spite of increasing specialization in science, we ought not discontinue teaching science.

11. Analogical argument. The conclusion is that it makes no sense to claim that either male or female reproductive strategies are superior to the other.

13. Nonargumentative use of analogy.

15. Nonargumentative use of analogy.

9.3 APPRAISING ARGUMENTS BY ANALOGY

Part I

1. a. Less probable; criterion 1, number of entities decreased.

b. Less probable; criterion 5, there is now an important disanalogy between the instances in the premises and the instance in the conclusion.

c. More probable; criterion 2, greater number of respects of similarity between the instances in the premises and the instance in the conclusion.

d. No change; criterion 4, the difference is not relevant.

e. Less probable; criterion 5, this is possibly an important disanalogy between the cases (unless we have other reasons to think that blood type is irrelevant).

f. Less probable; criterion 6, the conclusion is bolder than the new medical information warrants.

3. a. Less probable; criterion 5, an important disanalogy has arisen.

b. More probable; criterion 3, more dissimilarity among the cases mentioned in the premises.

c. Neither; criterion 4, the additional premise is not relevant.

d. More probable; criterion 1, the number of entities increased.

e. More probable; criterion 2, the number of respects of similarity increased.

f. More probable; criterion 6, the conclusion is weaker.

5. a. More probable; criterion 3, more dissimilarity among the premises.

b. More probable; criterion 2, an additional important respect has been added.

c. Less probable; criterion 5, an important disanalogy has been introduced.

d. More probable; criterion 6, the added premise renders the conclusion relatively more modest.

e. Neither. But, although the hour is not relevant to the substance of the course, Bill may know that he is more alert and/or appreciative early in the morning, in which case another significant respect may have been added, and the conclusion becomes more probable on criterion 2.

f. More probable; criterion 1, since all those courses mentioned are social sciences, the number of entities has been increased by the additional of the premise.

9.3 Part II

7. The conclusion, that genetic mutations are almost invariably detrimental, is supported by an analogy between genes and clocks. It is possible that a bullet will cause my clock to run better, but much more likely that it will cause it to run less well; similarly, a genetic mutation in a well-adapted animal is more likely to cause detriment than benefit. The additional analogy of a typographical error improving *Hamlet* introduces additional entities between which the analogy holds, and hence strengthens the conclusion. But overall the conclusion is not strongly supported by either (or both) of these analogies because there are many important disanalogies between organisms and clocks (or plays). But perhaps the analogies are meant mainly to illustrate, rather than to prove, the principle that changes to a working system are more likely to be detrimental than beneficial to its functioning, which does seem to be correct in general.

9. The analogy is weak, and therefore the conclusion is weak. The analogy is weak because cells "become" a human being in a much different way than they "become" a whole human population; that is, there is a significant disanalogy between the cases compared.

11. The analogy between chemical and logical decomposition is fairly strong. Clearly there are big differences between chemicals and sentences, but those differences are not relevant to the question of decomposition. What matters is that there are simples involved, and that simples cannot be divided. If it is true that chemical and logical analysis ultimately arrive at simples, then it is true that not everything can be defined if definition is taken to mean something like showing what parts the definiendum is composed from.

9.4 Explanations and Hypotheses

1. You'd probably propose a series of hypotheses: (1) The electricity was off, so the alarm didn't make its normal noise. (2) I forgot to set the alarm clock. (3) Either the alarm or the clock is off by twelve hours. (4) My roommate played a practical joke on me. If you have an electric alarm clock, and the electricity was off, you'll probably see a flashing number on the display. If you don't see that, you'll probably see whether the alarm was set. If it was, you'll check to see whether the a.m. and p.m. designations are correct for both the clock and the alarm. If they're both right, you'll probably talk with your roommate.

3. It's probably not the float or the valve, since the float rises when it's flushed and at a point engages the flush valve, stopping the water flow. The flush valve engages when the water level—and with it the float—drops, which gives more reason to

believe it's either the ball or the ball seat. You might check the ball to see if there are any irregularities, or you might simply change it to see if that corrects the problem—flush balls are relatively inexpensive and easy to change. If that doesn't do it, you'll conclude it's the ball seat, which requires removing the tank. Have fun!!!

5. You might propose a number of hypotheses. Filters at the bottom of the box might generally be defective, but that wouldn't explain why there are sometimes problems with filters higher in the stack, and, given the manufacturing and packaging processes, it would be puzzling that defective filters were *always* at the bottom of the box. If you compare the cases that work with the problematic cases, you'll notice that when there is no problem, the filter is wet and sticking to the sides of the basket. So, you propose the hypothesis that wetting the filter before adding the grounds will solve the problem and test the hypothesis. If, after doing this a few times, there are no grounds in the coffee, you've probably solved the problem.

9.5 ARGUMENTS TO THE BEST EXPLANATION

1. There is no deduction. Holmes shows how the assumption that Watson was in Afghanistan explains a number of observable properties.

3. The hypothesis would explain the changes in the Beatles's behavior, but it was implausible insofar as there is incontrovertible evidence (fingerprints and DNA testing) showing that Paul McCartney is still alive.

5. Mather's witch hypothesis is least good since we can *now* explain the behavior of the young women in other ways, as we can virtually any other phenomena that were once attributed to witchcraft. The choice between Miller's hypothesis and Starkey's hysteria hypothesis is more difficult. The hysteria hypothesis explains other, similar phenomena, as does Miller's societal evolution hypothesis. They are, in fact, compatible. The choice between the two would need to be made on the basis of the fruitfulness of each in predicting and explaining other historical phenomena.

7. The transfer of infectious materials hypothesis was best because it was testable, the test yielded the predicted outcome, and it was fruitful: It could be used to predict causes of other diseases.

9. Pasteur's hypothesis explained fermentation on the basis of the effects of living beings. It placed serious doubt on the chemical explanation of disease that was prevalent at the time. It was fruitful insofar as it allowed him to predict that human diseases were also the result of the actions of microorganisms.

Appendix: Truth Trees

APPENDIX, SECTION 1: PROPOSITIONAL LOGIC

1.
$$\checkmark p \supset q$$
$$\therefore \sim q \supset \sim p$$
$$\checkmark \sim (\sim q \supset \sim p)$$
$$\sim q$$
$$p$$
$$/ \quad \backslash$$
$$\sim p \quad q$$
$$X \quad X \qquad \text{Valid}$$

3.
$$\checkmark p \bullet q$$
$$\therefore p$$
$$\sim p$$
$$p$$
$$q$$
$$X \qquad \text{Valid}$$

5.
$$p$$
$$\therefore p \supset q$$
$$\sim (p \supset q)$$
$$p$$
$$\sim q \qquad \text{Invalid}$$

7.
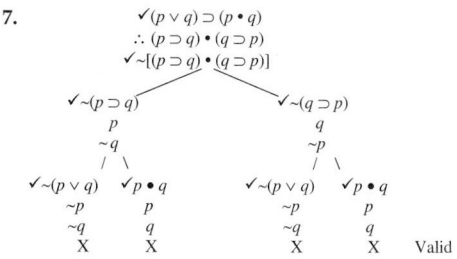

9.
$$\checkmark p \supset q$$
$$\sim q$$
$$\therefore \sim p$$
$$p$$
$$/ \quad \backslash$$
$$\sim p \quad q$$
$$X \quad X \qquad \text{Valid}$$

11.   ✓$p \supset q$
        ✓$q \supset r$
        ∴ $q \lor r$
        ✓$\sim(q \lor r)$
            $\sim q$
            $\sim r$
            $/ \, \backslash$
        $\sim p$ q
        $/ \, \backslash$ X
    $\sim q$ r
        X   Invalid

13. ✓$p \supset (q \supset r)$
        ✓$p \supset q$
        ∴ $p \supset r$
        ✓$\sim(p \supset r)$
            p
            $\sim r$
            $/ \, \backslash$
        $\sim p$ q
        X $/ \, \backslash$
            $\sim p$ ✓$(q \supset r)$
            X $/ \, \backslash$
                $\sim q$ r
                X   X   Valid

15.   ✓$p \supset (q \supset r)$
        $q \supset (p \supset r)$
        ∴ $(p \lor q) \supset r$
        ✓$\sim[(p \lor q) \supset r]$
                ✓$p \lor q$
                $\sim r$
            $\sim p$ $q \supset r$
                            $/ \, \backslash$
                            $\sim q$ r
                            $/ \, \backslash$ X
        $\sim q$ ✓$p \supset r$ $\sim q$ ✓$p \supset r$
        $/ \, \backslash$ $/ \, \backslash$ $/ \, \backslash$ $/ \, \backslash$
        p q $\sim p$ r p q $\sim p$ r
        X   X $/ \, \backslash$ X   X $/ \, \backslash$ X
                p q p q
                X   X   X   Invalid

17. ✓$(p \supset q) \bullet (r \supset s)$
        ✓$\sim q \lor \sim s$
        ∴ $\sim p \lor \sim s$
        ✓$\sim(\sim p \lor \sim s)$
            p
            s
            ✓$p \supset q$
            $r \supset s$
            $/ \, \backslash$
        $\sim p$ q
        X $/ \, \backslash$
            $\sim q$ $\sim s$
            X   X   Valid

19. ✓$p \supset (q \supset r)$
        ✓$(q \supset r) \supset s$
        ∴ $p \supset s$
        ✓$\sim(p \supset s)$
            p
            $\sim s$
            $/ \, \backslash$
        $\sim p$ ✓$q \supset s$
        X $/ \, \backslash$
            $\sim q$ s
            $/ \, \backslash$ X
    ✓$\sim(q \supset r)$ s
        q X
        $\sim r$
        X   Valid

21. $(p \lor q) \supset (p \bullet q)$
        ✓$\sim(p \lor q)$
        ∴ $\sim(p \bullet q)$
        $(p \bullet q)$ p
            q
            $\sim p$
            $\sim q$
            X   Valid

23.   ✓$(p \bullet q) \supset (r \bullet s)$
        ∴ $(p \bullet q) \supset [(p \bullet q) \bullet (r \bullet s)]$
        ✓$\sim\{(p \bullet q) \supset [(p \bullet q) \bullet (r \bullet s)]\}$
            ✓$p \bullet q$
            $\sim[(p \bullet q) \bullet (r \bullet s)]$
                p
                q
                $/ \, \backslash$
        ✓$\sim(p \bullet q)$ ✓$(r \bullet s)$
            $/ \, \backslash$ r
        $\sim p$ $\sim q$ s
        X   X
    ✓$\sim(p \bullet q)$ ✓$\sim(r \bullet s)$
        $/ \, \backslash$ $/ \, \backslash$
    $\sim p$ $\sim q$ $\sim r$ $\sim s$
        X   X   X   X   Valid

25.   ✓$p \supset q$
   ✓$q \supset p$
   ∴ $p \vee q$
   ✓$\sim(p \vee q)$
     $\sim p$
     $\sim q$
     $\diagup\ \diagdown$
   $\sim p$ q
   $\diagup\ \diagdown$ X
   $\sim q$ p
        X   Invalid

27.   ✓$p \supset (q \vee \sim r)$
   ✓$q \supset \sim r$
   ∴ $p \supset \sim r$
   ✓$\sim(p \supset \sim r)$
        p
        r
       $\diagup\ \diagdown$
    $\sim q$ $\sim r$
   $\diagup\ \diagdown$ X
   $\sim p$ ✓$q \vee \sim r$
    X $\diagup\ \diagdown$
        q $\sim r$
        X   X   Valid

29. $(C \vee D) \supset (C \bullet D)$
   ✓$C \bullet D$
   ∴ $C \vee D$
   ✓$\sim(C \vee D)$
      $\sim C$
      $\sim D$
       C
       D
       X   Valid

31.   .   ✓$(G \vee H) \supset (G \bullet H)$
   ✓$\sim(G \bullet H)$
   ∴ $\sim(G \vee H)$
   ✓$G \vee H$
      $\diagup\ \diagdown$
   ✓$\sim(G \vee H)$ ✓$(G \bullet H)$
     $\sim G$ G
     $\sim H$ H
     $\diagup\ \diagdown$ $\diagup\ \diagdown$
    G H G H
    X   X $\diagup\ \diagdown$ $\diagup\ \diagdown$
        $\sim G$ $\sim H$ $\sim G$ $\sim H$
         X   X   X   X   Valid

33.
   ✓$(O \vee P) \supset Q$
   $Q \supset (O \bullet P)$
   ∴ $(O \vee P) \supset (O \bullet P)$
   $\sim[(O \vee P) \supset (O \bullet P)]$
     ✓$O \vee P$
     ✓$\sim(O \bullet P)$
        $\diagup\qquad\qquad\diagdown$
      O P
      $\diagup\ \diagdown$ $\diagup\ \diagdown$
    $\sim O$ $\sim P$ $\sim O$ $\sim P$
       X$\diagup\ \diagdown$ $\diagdown$ X
   ✓$\sim(O \vee P)$ Q ✓$\sim(O \vee P)$ Q
     $\sim O$ $\sim O$
     $\sim P$ $\sim P$
      X   X
       $\diagup\ \diagdown$ $\diagup\ \diagdown$
     $\sim Q$ ✓$O \bullet P$ $\sim Q$ ✓$O \bullet P$
      X O X O
           P P
           X   X   Valid

Appendix, Section 2: Quantificational Logic

5.   ⊘$(\exists x)(Jx \bullet Kx)$
   ⊘$(x)(Jx \supset Lx)$
   ∴ $(\exists x)(Lx \bullet Kx)$
   ✓$\sim(\exists x)(Lx \bullet Kx)$
   ⊘$(x)\sim(Lx \bullet Kx)$
      ✓$Ja \bullet Ka$
        Ja
        Ka
      ✓$Ja \supset La$
       $\diagup\ \diagdown$
     $\sim Ja$ La
       X   ✓$\sim(La \bullet Ka)$
            $\diagup\ \diagdown$
          $\sim La$ $\sim Ka$
            X   X

7.   ⊘$(x)(Sx \supset \sim Tx)$
   ⊘$(\exists x)(Sx \bullet Ux)$
   ∴ $(\exists x)(Ux \bullet \sim Tx)$
   ✓$\sim(\exists x)(Ux \bullet \sim Tx)$
   $(x)\sim(Ux \bullet \sim Tx)$
      ✓$Sa \bullet Ua$
        Sa
        Ua
      ✓$Sx \supset \sim Ta$
       $\diagup\ \diagdown$
     $\sim Sa$ $\sim Ta$
       X   ✓$\sim(Ua \bullet \sim Ta)$
            $\diagup\ \diagdown$
          $\sim Ua$ Ta
            X   X

9.
$$\not{\mathscr{V}} (\exists x)(Yx \bullet Zx)$$
$$\not{\mathscr{V}}(x)(Zx \supset Ax)$$
$$\therefore (\exists x)(Ax \bullet Yx)$$
$$\checkmark \sim(\exists x)(Ax \bullet Yx)$$
$$(x)\sim(Ax \bullet Yx)$$
$$\checkmark Ya \bullet Za$$
$$Ya$$
$$Za$$
$$\checkmark Za \supset Aa$$
$$\diagup \diagdown$$
$$\sim Za \quad Aa$$
$$X \quad \checkmark \sim(Aa \bullet Ya)$$
$$\diagup \diagdown$$
$$\sim Aa \quad \sim Ya$$
$$X \quad X$$

27. $\not{\mathscr{V}}(x)[(Px \supset Qx) \bullet (Rx \supset Sx)]$
$$\checkmark \sim(x)(Tx \supset Qx)$$
$$(x)(\sim Rx \supset Ux)$$
$$\therefore (\exists x)[Tx \bullet (Px \supset Ux)]$$
$$\checkmark \sim(\exists x)[Tx \bullet (Px \supset Ux)]$$
$$\not{\mathscr{V}}(x)\sim[Tx \bullet (Px \supset Ux)]$$
$$\not{\mathscr{V}}(\exists x)\sim(Tx \supset Qx)$$
$$\checkmark \sim(Ta \supset Qa)$$
$$Ta$$
$$\sim Qa$$
$$\checkmark \sim[Ta \bullet (Pa \supset Qa)]$$
$$\diagup \diagdown$$
$$\sim Ta \quad \checkmark \sim(Pa \supset Qa)$$
$$X \qquad Pa$$
$$\sim Qa$$
$$\checkmark(Pa \supset Qa) \bullet (Ra \supset Sa)$$
$$\checkmark Pa \supset Qa$$
$$Ra \supset Sa$$
$$\diagup \diagdown$$
$$\sim Pa \quad Qa$$
$$X \quad X$$

29. $\not{\mathscr{V}}(x)(Gx \supset Qx)$
$$\checkmark(\exists x)(Px \bullet Qx) \supset (x)(Rx \supset Sx)$$
$$\not{\mathscr{V}}(\exists x)[Px \bullet (\sim Sx \bullet Gx)]$$
$$\therefore (\exists x)(Rx \supset \sim Hx)$$
$$\checkmark \sim(\exists x)(Rx \supset \sim Hx)$$
$$\not{\mathscr{V}}(x)\sim(Rx \supset \sim Hx)$$
$$\checkmark Pa \bullet (\sim Sa \bullet Ga)$$
$$Pa$$
$$\checkmark \sim Sa \bullet Gx$$
$$\sim Sa$$
$$Ga$$
$$\checkmark Ga \supset Qa$$
$$\diagup \diagdown$$
$$\sim Ga \quad Qa$$
$$X \quad \diagup \diagdown$$

$$\diagup \qquad \diagdown$$
$$\checkmark \sim(\exists x)(Px \bullet Qx) \quad \not{\mathscr{V}}(x)(Rx \supset Sx)$$
$$\not{\mathscr{V}}(x)\sim(Px \bullet Qx) \quad \checkmark Ra \supset Sa$$
$$\checkmark \sim(Pa \bullet Qa) \qquad \diagup \diagdown$$
$$\diagup \diagdown \qquad \sim Ra \quad Sa$$
$$\sim Pa \quad \sim Qa \qquad | \quad X$$
$$X \quad X \quad \checkmark \sim(Ra \supset \sim Ha)$$
$$Ra$$
$$Ha$$
$$X$$

31. $\not{\not{\mathscr{V}}}(x)[Px \supset (Qx \supset Rx)]$
$$\not{\mathscr{V}}(\exists x)(Px \bullet Sx)$$
$$\not{\not{\mathscr{V}}}(\exists x)(\sim Rx \bullet Tx)$$
$$\checkmark(\exists x)(Px \supset \sim Qx) \supset (x)(Sx \supset \sim Rx)$$
$$\therefore (\exists x)(Px \bullet \sim Qx)$$
$$\checkmark \sim(\exists x)(Px \bullet \sim Qx)$$
$$\not{\mathscr{V}}(x)\sim(Px \bullet \sim Qx)$$
$$\checkmark Pa \bullet Sa$$
$$Pa$$
$$Sa$$
$$\checkmark Pa \supset (Qa \supset Ra)$$
$$\diagup \diagdown$$
$$\sim Pa \quad \checkmark(Qa \supset Ra)$$
$$X \quad \checkmark \sim(Pa \bullet \sim Qa)$$
$$\diagup \diagdown$$
$$\sim Pa \quad Qa$$
$$X \quad \diagup \diagdown$$
$$\sim Qa \quad Ra$$
$$X \quad \diagup \diagdown$$
$$\checkmark \sim(\exists x)(Px \supset \sim Qx) \quad \not{\mathscr{V}}(x)(Sx \supset \sim Rx)$$
$$\not{\not{\mathscr{V}}}(x)\sim(Px \supset \sim Qx) \quad \checkmark Sa \supset \sim Ra$$
$$\checkmark \sim Rb \bullet Tb \qquad \diagup \diagdown$$
$$\sim Rb \qquad \sim Sa \quad \sim Ra$$
$$Tb \qquad X \quad X$$

$$\checkmark \sim(Pb \supset \sim Qb)$$
$$Pb$$
$$Qb$$
$$\checkmark Pb \supset (Qb \supset Rb)$$
$$\diagup \diagdown$$
$$\sim Pb \quad \checkmark Qb \supset Rb$$
$$X \qquad \diagup \diagdown$$
$$\sim Qb \quad Rb$$
$$X \quad X$$

33. ⌐∀(∃x)(Qx • ~Tx)
⌐∀⌐∀(x)[Qx ⊃ (Tx ∨ ~Px)]
⌐∀(∃x)(~Tx • Sx)
✓(∃x)(Qx • ~Px) ⊃ (x)(Sx ⊃ Px)
∴ (∃x)(Sx • ~Qx)
✓~(∃x)(Sx • ~Qx)
⌐∀(x)~(Sx • ~Qx)
✓Qa • ~Ta
Qa
~Ta
Qa ⊃ (Ta ∨ ~Pa)
/　＼
~Qa　✓Ta ∨ ~Pa
X　/ ＼
Ta　~Pa
X　/ ＼
✓~(∃x)(Qx • ~Px)　⌐∀(x)(Sx ⊃ Px)
⌐∀(x)~(Qx • ~Px)　✓~Tb • Sb
✓~(Qa • ~Pa)　~Tb
/ ＼　Sb
~Qa　Pa　✓Qb ⊃ (Tb ∨ ~Pb)
X　X　✓Sb ⊃ Pb
/ ＼
~Sb　Pb
X　✓~(Sb • ~Qb)
/ ＼
~Sb　Qb
X　/
~Qb　✓(Tb ∨ ~Pb)
X　/ ＼
Tb　~Pb
X　X

35. ⌐∀(∀ x)[Px ⊃ (Qx • Rx)]
(∀ ∃x)(Sx • ~Rx)
(∀ ∃x)(Px • Tx)
✓[(∃x)(Sx • ~Px) • (∃y)(Qy • Ty)] ⊃ (∃z)(Zz • Fz)
(∀ x)[Fx ⊃ (Px ∨ ~Zx)]
∴ (∃x)(Zx • Px)
✓~(∃x)(Zx • Px)
(∀ x)~(Zx • Px)
✓Sa • ~Ra
Sa
~Ra
✓ Pa ⊃ (Qa • Ra)
/
~Pa　✓Qa • Ra
✓Pb • Tb　Qa
Pb　Ra
Tb　X
✓ Pb ⊃ (Qb • Rb)

~Pb　✓Qb • Rb
X　Qb
Rb

✓~[(∃x)(Sx • ~Px) • (∃y)(Qy • Ty)]　⌐∀(∃z)(Zz • Fz)
/ ＼　✓Zc • Fc
✓~(∃x)(Sx • ~Px)　✓~(∃y)(Qy • Ty)　Zc
⌐∀(x)~(Sx • ~Px)　⌐∀(x)~(Qy • Ty)　Fc
~(Sa • ~Pa)　~(Qb • Tb)　✓Fc ⊃ (Pc ∨ ~Zc)
/ ＼　/ ＼　/ ＼
~Sa　Pa　~Qb　~Tb　~Fc　✓Pc ∨ ~Zc
X　X　X　X　X　/ ＼
Pc　~Zc
✓~(Zc • Pc)　X
/ ＼
~Zc　~Pc
X　X

Argument Against the Person, Fallacy of: An argument commits the informal fallacy of argument against the person (*ad hominem*) if, in replying to an argument, it attacks the arguer rather than the argument. There are three varieties of argument against the person. (1) An abusive argument against the person attacks the arguer's character. (2) A circumstantial argument against the person appeals to some circumstances in which the arguer finds himself or herself as a reason to discredit the argument. (3) A *tu quoque* focuses on inconsistencies between an argument and the arguer's actions. The fallacy of argument against the person is an informal fallacy of relevance, 54–57

Argument form: An argument form is an array of symbols exhibiting logical structure. It contains statement variables but no statements, such that when statements are consistently substituted for the statement variables, the result is an argument 137–38, 221–22; common invalid argument forms, 227–28; common valid argument forms, 225–27; truth tables and, 221–30

Aristotelian logic: Aristotelian logic is the traditional account of syllogistic reasoning, in which certain interpretations of categorical propositions are presupposed. In particular, universal propositions are assumed to have existential import. In this regard, it is contrasted with the modern symbolic or Boolean interpretation of categorical propositions, 113, 115–20

Aristotle, 100

Association (Assoc.): Association is an expression of logical equivalence falling under the Rule of Replacement. According to it $[p \lor (q \lor r)]$ may be replaced by $[(p \lor q) \lor r]$ and vice versa; and $[p \bullet (q \bullet r)]$ may be replaced by $[(p \bullet q) \bullet r]$ and vice versa, 258

Authority, Fallacy of Appeal to Illegitimate: An argument commits the informal fallacy of appeal to illegitimate authority (*ad verecundiam*) if it appeals to someone or something as an authority on a particular subject who is not an authority on that subject. Appeals to illegitimate authority are informal fallacies of relevance, 51–54

Begging the question: An argument commits the fallacy of begging the question (*petitio principii*) if it assumes as a premise what it sets out to prove as its conclusion. This can occur when: (1) The conclusion of the argument is merely a restatement of the premise; (2) In a chain of arguments, the conclusion of the last argument is a premise of the first (circular argument); or (3) The premise of an argument uses terms that assume what is asserted in the conclusion (question-begging epithet). Begging the question is an informal fallacy of presumption, 70–71

Biconditional Proposition, or Biconditional Statement: A biconditional is a compound statement or proposition that asserts that its two component statements have the same truth value, and therefore are materially equivalent. It is so named because, since the two component statements are either both true or both false, they must imply one another. A biconditional statement form is symbolized by $p \equiv q$, which may be read as "*p* if and only if *q*," 197. *See also* **Material Equivalence**.

Boolean Interpretation: The Boolean interpretation is the modern interpretation of categorical propositions adopted in this book. It is named after the English logician George Boole (1815–1864). On the Boolean interpretation, universal propositions (**A** and **E** propositions) do *not* have existential import, 113–14, 129

Categorical Proposition: A categorical proposition is a proposition that can be analyzed as being about classes, or categories, affirming or denying that one class, *S*, is wholly or partially included in some other class, *P*. Four standard forms of categorical propositions are traditionally distinguished: **A:** Universal affirmative propositions (all *S* are *P*); **E:** Universal negative propositions (no *S* are *P*); **I:** Particular affirmative propositions (some *S* are *P*); **O:** Particular negative propositions (some *S* are not *P*), 100–135; classes and, 100–105; symbolism and Venn diagrams for, 106–9; translating into standard form, 168–81

Categorical Syllogism: A categorical syllogism is a deductive argument consisting of three categorical propositions that contain exactly three terms, each of which has the same meaning throughout the syllogism, and each of which occurs in exactly two of the propositions, 136; Venn diagram technique for testing, 143–51; rules for testing, 152–59. *See also* **Disjunctive Syllogism; Hypothetical Syllogism; Syllogistic Argument**.

Circular Argument. *See* **Begging the Question**.

Class: The collection of all objects that have some specified characteristic in common, 83–86, 100

Classical logic. *See* **Aristotelian logic**.

Commutation (Com.): Commutation is an expression of logical equivalence falling under the Rule of Replacement that permits the valid reordering of the components of conjunctive or disjunctive statements. According to commutation, $(p \lor q)$ and $(q \lor p)$ may replace one another, as may $(p \bullet q)$ and $(q \bullet p)$, 258

Complement, or Complementary Class: The complement of a class is the collection of all things that do not belong to that class, 125

Complex argumentative passages, 36–40

generalization) when a general claim—whether universal or statistical—is reached on the basis of insufficient evidence, particularly when the sample on which the generalization is based is atypical. Converse accident is an informal fallacy of presumption, 73–74, 85–86

Copula: A copula is any form of the verb *to be* that serves to connect the subject term and the predicate term of a categorical proposition, 102

Corresponding propositions: Propositions with the same subject and predicate terms that agree in quality but differ in quantity are called corresponding propositions, 134

De Morgan's Theorem (De M.): De Morgan's theorem is an expression of logical equivalence falling under the Rule of Replacement that permits the mutual replacement of the negation of a disjunction by the conjunction of the negations of the disjuncts: $\sim(p \lor q) \overset{T}{\equiv} (\sim p \bullet \sim q)$; and that permits the mutual replacement of the negation of a conjunction by the disjunction of the negations of the conjuncts: $\sim(p \bullet q) \overset{T}{\equiv} (\sim p \lor \sim q)$, 219–20

Deduction: Deduction is one of two major types of argument traditionally distinguished, the other being induction. A deductive argument claims to provide conclusive grounds for its conclusion. If a deductive argument is *valid*, it is impossible for its premises to be true and its conclusion false, 24–25, 136–329

Denying the Antecedent: Denying the antecedent is a formal fallacy. It is so named because the nonconditional premise in the argument, not-*p*, denies the antecedent rather than the consequent of the conditional premise. Symbolized as: $p \supset q$, $\sim p$, $\therefore \sim q$, 46, 227–28, 236

Disanalogy: In an analogical argument, a disanalogy is a point of difference between the cases mentioned in the premises and the case mentioned in the conclusion, 341–42

Disjunct: A disjunct is a component of a disjunction, 195

Disjunction: A disjunction is a truth-functional connective meaning *or*. When disjunction is taken to mean that at least one of the disjuncts is true and that they may both be true, it is called a *weak* or *inclusive* disjunction and is symbolized by the wedge, $\lor$. When disjunction is taken to mean that at least one of the disjuncts is true and that at least one of them is false, it is called a *strong* or *exclusive* disjunction. Exclusive disjunction is symbolized as: $(p \lor q) \bullet \sim(p \bullet q)$. Unless there are good reasons to believe that a statement is intended as an exclusive disjunction, disjunctions are treated as weak disjunctions, 195–96

Disjunctive Statement Form: A disjunctive statement form is a statement form symbolized as: $p \lor q$. Its substitution instances are disjunctive statements, 195–96

Disjunctive Syllogism (D.S.): Disjunctive syllogism is a rule of inference. It is a valid argument form in which one premise is a disjunction, another premise is the denial of the first disjunct, and the conclusion is the truth of the second disjunct. Symbolized as: $p \lor q$, $\sim p$, $\therefore q$, 222, 247

Distribution (Dist.): Distribution is an expression of logical equivalence falling under the Rule of Replacement. Distribution allows the mutual replacement of specified pairs of symbolic expressions. In symbolic form:
$$[p \bullet (q \lor r)] \overset{T}{\equiv} [(p \bullet q) \lor (p \bullet r)];$$
$$[p \lor (q \bullet r)] \overset{T}{\equiv} [(p \lor q) \bullet (p \lor r)].$$

Distribution (in categorical logic): In categorical logic, a term is distributed if it refers to an entire class of objects. The *subject* term of an **A** proposition is distributed. *Both* terms of an **E** proposition are distributed. *Neither* term of an **I** proposition is distributed. The *predicate* term of an **O** proposition is distributed, 258–59

Division, Fallacy of: An argument commits the informal fallacy of division if it illegitimately claims that a term that is true of a whole is true of a part or a term that is true of a class of things is true of a member of that class. Division is an informal fallacy of ambiguity, 85–86

Dot: The symbol for conjunction, $\bullet$. A statement of the form $p \bullet q$ is true if and only if both p and q are true, 194

Double Negation (D.N.): Double negation is an expression of logical equivalence falling under the Rule of Replacement asserting that the double negation of a statement p is logically equivalent to p. Symbolized as: $p \overset{T}{\equiv} \sim\sim p$, 219

E Proposition. *See* **Universal Negative Proposition**.

Elementary Valid Argument Form: An elementary valid argument form is any one of a set of specified deductive argument forms that serves as a rule of inference and that may therefore be used in constructing a formal proof of validity, 245–47

Emotional Appeal, Fallacy of: An argument commits the informal fallacy of emotional appeal (*ad populum*) if it takes the fact that believing that a proposition is true makes one "feel good" is a sufficient reason to believe that it is true. Emotional appeal is a fallacy of relevance, 57–58

Enthymeme: An enthymeme is an argument that is incompletely stated, the unstated part of it being taken for granted, 18–20, 184–88

Enumeration. *See* **Induction by Enumeration**.

Equivocation, Fallacy of: An argument commits the informal fallacy of equivocation if there is a shift in the meaning of a word or phrase in the course of an argument. Equivocation is an informal fallacy of ambiguity, 79–80

Exceptive Proposition: An exceptive proposition is a proposition asserting that all members of some class, with the exception of the members of one of its subclasses, are members of some other class. Exceptive propositions are compound because they assert both a relation of class inclusion and a relation of class exclusion. For example, "All persons except employees are eligible" is an exceptive proposition in which it is asserted both that "All nonemployees are eligible" and that "No employees are eligible," 178

Exclusive (or Strong) Disjunction. *See* **Disjunction**.

Exclusive Premises, Fallacy of: A categorical syllogism commits the formal fallacy of exclusive premises if it has two negative premises, 156

Exclusive Proposition: An exclusive proposition is a categorical proposition which asserts that the predicate applies exclusively to the subject named. For example, "None but generals wear stars," asserts that the predicate term, *wearing stars*, applies only to generals ("All officers who wear stars are generals"), 175–76

Existential Fallacy: A categorical syllogism on the Boolean interpretation of categorical logic commits the existential fallacy if it concludes that a particular proposition is true on the basis of two universal premises. The existential fallacy applies *only* on the Boolean interpretation of categorical logic, 157

Existential Generalization (E.G.): Existential generalization is a rule of inference in quantification theory that says that from any true substitution-instance of a propositional function we may validly infer the existential quantification of the propositional function. Where v is an individual constant, Φ is a predicate variable, and x is an individual variable, existential generalization is symbolized as: $\Phi v, \therefore (\exists x)\Phi x$, 310

Existential Import: Existential import is an attribute of those categorical propositions which normally assert the existence of objects of some specified kind. Particular propositions (**I** and **O** propositions) always have existential import; thus the proposition, "Some dogs are obedient," asserts that there are dogs. Whether universal propositions (**A** and **E** propositions) have existential import is an issue on which the Aristotelian and Boolean interpretations of propositions differ, 113–14

Existential Instantiation (E.I.): Existential instantiation is a rule of inference in quantification theory that says that we may validly infer from the existential quantification of a propositional function the truth of its substitution instance with respect to any individual constant that does not occur earlier in that context. Where a is an individual constant *new to the proof*, Φ is a predicate variable, and x is an individual variable, existential instantiation is symbolized as: $(\exists x)\Phi x, \therefore \Phi a$, where a is new to the proof, 309–10

Existential Presupposition: In Aristotelian logic, existential presupposition is the blanket presupposition that all classes referred to in a proposition have members, 113

Existential Quantifier: The existential quantifier ($\exists$) is a symbol in modern quantification theory which indicates that any propositional function immediately following it has some true substitution instance; "$(\exists x)Fx$" means "there exists an x that is F," 298

Explanation: An explanation is a statement that answers the question Why? or (sometimes) How? In a scientific explanation, you typically deduce a description of the phenomenon to be explained from a natural law and a statement of antecedent conditions, 5, 7–9, 347–61

Exportation (Exp.): Exportation is an expression of logical equivalence falling under the Rule of Replacement. It permits the mutual replacement of statements of the form $(p \cdot q) \supset r$ by statements of the form $p \supset (q \supset r)$, that is $[(p \cdot q) \supset r] \overset{\text{T}}{\equiv} [p \supset (q \supset r)]$, 265

Fallacies of Ambiguity. *See* **Ambiguity, Fallacies of**.

Fallacies of Presumption. *See* **Presumption, Fallacies of**.

Fallacies of Relevance. *See* **Relevance, Fallacies of**.

Fallacy: A fallacy is a mistake in reasoning. It is a type of argument that may seem to be correct, but that proves upon examination not to be so. Fallacies may be formal or informal, 46–48

False Cause, Fallacies of: An argument commits the informal fallacy of false cause when it identifies something as a cause which is *not* a cause. A *slippery slope fallacy* occurs when there is a chain of alleged causes and at least one of the causal claims is false. In a slippery slope argument, the situation described first is usually fairly mundane, but things become progressively worse as you slide down the slope. False cause fallacies are informal fallacies of presumption, 68–70

False Dichotomy, Fallacy of: A false dichotomy is a disjunctive syllogism with a false disjunctive premise.

Induction by Enumeration: Induction by enumeration is a type of inductive generalization in which the premises are instances in which phenomena of two kinds repeatedly accompany one another in certain circumstances, from which it is concluded that phenomena of those two kinds always or usually accompany one another in such circumstances, 330–34

Inductive Generalization: Inductive generalization is the process of arriving at general or universal propositions from the particular facts of experience, 330–34

Inference: Inference is a mental process by which one proposition is arrived at and affirmed on the basis of one or more other propositions assumed as the starting point of the process, 3. *See also* **Immediate Inference**.

Inference, Rules of: In deductive logic, the rules of inference are rules that may be used in constructing formal proofs of validity, comprising a set of elementary valid argument forms, a Rule of Replacement, and a set of rules for introducing and eliminating quantifiers, 247

Instantiation: In quantification theory, instantiation is the process of substituting an individual constant or an individual variable for a variable in a general statement. It is a rule that allows you to state an *instance* of a general proposition, 307, 309

Interwoven arguments, 34

Invalid: An argument form is invalid if it is possible for all of its premises to be true and its conclusion to be false. It is a *formal* characteristic, that is, a characteristic of an argument form, 24

Irrelevant Conclusion: An argument commits the informal fallacy of irrelevant conclusion (*ignoratio elenchi; non sequitur*) when it draws a conclusion that is *not* suggested by the premises. Two common varieties are red herring and straw person. Red herring: A red herring is a reply to an argument that diverts attention from the issue. Straw person: A straw person argument is a reply to an argument that attacks an allegedly unstated premise (when that premise is *not* assumed) or distorts the conclusion and attacks the distorted version of the conclusion, 60–62

Limitation, Conversion by and Contraposition by: On the *Aristotelian* interpretation of categorical logic, given the truth of an **A** proposition, you can infer the truth of the corresponding **I** proposition and convert it. This is conversion by limitation or conversion by subalternation. On the *Aristotelian* interpretation of categorical logic, given the truth of an **E** proposition, you can infer the truth of the corresponding **O** proposition and contrapose it. This is

contraposition by limitation or contraposition by subalternation, 125, 130

Logical Equivalence: Two propositions are logically equivalent if they are true and false under the same conditions, 121–31, 216–20, 258, 265

Major Premise: In a standard-form categorical syllogism, the major premise is the premise that contains the major term, 136

Major Term: The major term of a categorical syllogism is the predicate term of the conclusion when the conclusion is given in standard form, 136

Material Equivalence: Material equivalence is a truth-functional relation (symbolized by the tribar, $\equiv$). Two statements are materially equivalent if and only if they have the same assignments of truth values for all assignments of truth values to their simple components. Materially equivalent statements always materially imply one another, 197. *See also* **Logical Equivalence**.

Material Equivalence (Equiv.): Material equivalence is the name of a logical equivalence falling under the Rule of Replacement that allows one to introduce or eliminate the tribar ($\equiv$). Symbolized as:

$$(p \equiv q) \stackrel{\mathrm{T}}{\equiv} [(p \supset q) \bullet (q \supset p)] \text{ and}$$
$$(p \equiv q) \stackrel{\mathrm{T}}{\equiv} [(p \bullet q) \vee (\sim p \bullet \sim q)], 265$$

Material Implication: Material implication is a truth-functional relation (symbolized by the horseshoe, ($\supset$) that connects two statements. A statement of the form $p \supset q$ is true *except* when p is true and q is false, 196–97

Material Implication (Impl.): Material implication is a logical equivalence falling under the Rule of Replacement that permits the mutual replacement of statements of the form "$p \supset q$" by statements of the form "$\sim p \vee q$," 265

Middle Term: In a standard-form categorical syllogism, the middle term is the term that appears in both premises but does not appear in the conclusion, 136

Minor Premise: In a standard-form categorical syllogism, the minor premise is the premise that contains the minor term, 136

Minor Term: In a categorical syllogism, the minor term is the subject term of the conclusion when the conclusion is given in standard form, 136

Modus Ponens (M.P.): Modus ponens is one of the nine elementary valid argument forms. It is a rule of inference according to which, if the truth of a conditional premise is assumed, and the truth of the antecedent of that premise is also assumed, we may conclude that the consequent of the premise is true. Symbolized as: $p \supset q, p, \therefore q$, 225, 226, 247

propositions that are claimed to provide grounds or reasons for accepting the truth of the conclusion, 3

Presumption, Fallacies of: The fallacies of presumption occur when an argument makes presuppositions unwarranted by the context, 66–67. *See also* **Accident; Begging the Question; Complex Question; Converse Accident; False Cause; False Dichotomy; Suppressed Evidence**.

Proposition: A proposition or statement is what is typically asserted using a declarative sentence, and hence is always either true or false—although its truth or falsity may be unknown, 1; exceptive, 178; exclusive, 177–78; existential, 310; nonstandard-form, 165–83; quantified, 295–326; sentences and, 1; singular, 169–70, 296–97; subject–predicate, 101–5; unstated, 18–20. *See also* **Categorical Proposition; Standard-form Categorical Proposition**.

Propositional Function: In quantification theory, a propositional function is an array of symbols that includes at least one unbound variable. A propositional function is converted into a proposition if either the variables are replaced by individual constants or the variables are bound by a quantifier, 297

Punctuation for Symbolic Logic: The punctuation marks for symbolic logic are the parentheses, brackets, and braces that are used in symbolic language to render a string of symbols unambiguous in meaning, 197–200

Quality: Quality is an attribute of every categorical proposition. It is determined by whether the proposition *affirms* or *denies* some form of class inclusion. Every categorical proposition is affirmative in quality or negative in quality, 102–3

Quantification theory, 295–329; asyllogistic inference and, 306, 325; existential quantifier and, 298; proving invalidity and, 321–26; proving validity and, 306–19; quantified propositions and, 296–304; singular propositions and, 296–97; subject–predicate propositions and, 296–99

Quantifier: In categorical logic, the quantifier tells you the number of objects about which the proposition makes a claim. The three quantifiers in standard-form categorical propositions are *all*, *no*, and *some*. In quantificational logic, the quantifiers are the symbols that show whether the statement is a universal (x) or existential $(\exists x)$ 102, 298

Quantity: Quantity is an attribute of every categorical proposition, determined by whether the proposition refers to *all* members or only to *some* members of the class designated by its subject term. Thus every categorical proposition is either universal in quantity or particular in quantity, 102

Red Herring. *See* **Irrelevant Conclusion**.

Reducing the Number of Terms in a Categorical Syllogism: You reduce the number of terms in a categorical syllogism by eliminating synonyms and the names of complementary classes from a syllogism to ensure that it contains exactly three terms. This is part of the process of translating a syllogism into standard form to test it for validity, 165–67

Reduction to Standard Form: Reduction to standard form is the restatement of the premises and conclusion in categorical syllogisms so that each statement is a standard form categorical proposition and so that there are exactly three terms in the argument. This is also called translation to standard form, 168–81

Refutation by Logical Analogy: An invalid deductive argument can be shown invalid by a refutation by logical analogy. To refute the argument, you present an argument with the same form but which has premises that are obviously true and a conclusion that is obviously false, 141–42

Relevance, Fallacies of: Fallacies of relevance are those informal fallacies committed when the premises of an argument are not relevant to its conclusion and therefore cannot establish the truth of that conclusion, 45–63. *See also* **Argument Against the Person, Fallacy of; Authority, Fallacy of Appeal to Illegitimate; Emotional Appeal, Fallacy of; Force, Fallacy of Appeal to; Ignorance, Fallacy of Appeal to; Irrelevant Conclusion, Fallacy of; Pity, Fallacy of Appeal to**.

Replacement, Rule of: The rule of replacement is a principle of inference asserting that all the logically equivalent expressions falling under it may replace each other wherever they occur in a proof, 257–61, 265–71

Rules of Inference: The rules of inference are rules that permit valid inferences from statements assumed as premises. The nine rules plus the rule of replacement are rules of inference, 245–51

Self-contradictory Statement Form: A self-contradictory statement form is a statement form all of whose substitution instances are false, 215, 242

Sentence: A sentence is a unit of language that expresses a complete thought; a sentence may express a proposition, but it is distinct from the proposition it may be used to express, 1–3

Sentential Logic: Sentential logic (also called propositional logic) is a system of deductive logic that is based upon the relations among propositions, 191. *See also* **Symbolic Logic**.

Sentential Variables: Sentential variables are the lower case letters from p through w which stand for propositions in sentential (propositional) logic, 223

The rules of inference and equivalences falling under the rule of replacement are as follows:

ELEMENTARY VALID ARGUMENT FORMS:	LOGICALLY EQUIVALENT EXPRESSIONS:
1. Modus Ponens (M.P.): $p \supset q,\ \ p,\ \therefore q$	**10. De Morgan's Theorems** (De M.): $\sim(p \bullet q) \stackrel{\mathsf{T}}{=} (\sim p \vee \sim q)$ $\sim(p \vee q) \stackrel{\mathsf{T}}{=} (\sim p \bullet \sim q)$
2. Modus Tollens (M.T.): $p \supset q,\ \ \sim q,\ \therefore \sim p$	**11. Commutation** (Com.): $(p \vee q) \stackrel{\mathsf{T}}{=} (q \vee p)$ $(p \bullet q) \stackrel{\mathsf{T}}{=} (q \bullet p)$
3. Hypothetical Syllogism (H.S.): $p \supset q,\ \ q \supset r, \therefore p \supset r$	**12. Association** (Assoc.): $[p \vee (q \vee r)] \stackrel{\mathsf{T}}{=} [(p \vee q) \vee r]$ $[p \bullet (q \bullet r)] \stackrel{\mathsf{T}}{=} [(p \bullet q) \bullet r]$
4. Disjunctive Syllogism (D.S.): $p \vee q,\ \ \sim p,\ \therefore q$	**13. Distribution** (Dist.): $[p \bullet (q \vee r)] \stackrel{\mathsf{T}}{=} [(p \bullet q) \vee (p \bullet r)]$ $[p \vee (q \bullet r)] \stackrel{\mathsf{T}}{=} [(p \vee q) \bullet (p \vee r)]$
5. Constructive Dilemma (C.D.): $(p \supset q) \bullet (r \supset s),\ p \vee r,\ \therefore q \vee s$	**14. Double Negation** (D.N.): $p \stackrel{\mathsf{T}}{=} \sim\sim p$
6. Absorption (Abs.): $p \supset q,\ \ \therefore p \supset (p \bullet q)$	**15. Transposition** (Trans.): $(p \supset q) \stackrel{\mathsf{T}}{=} (\sim q \supset \sim p)$
7. Simplification (Simp.): $p \bullet q,\ \_ \therefore p$	**16. Material Implication** (Impl.): $(p \supset q) \stackrel{\mathsf{T}}{=} (\sim p \vee q)$
8. Conjunction (Conj.): $p, q,\ \_ \therefore p \bullet q$	**17. Material Equivalence** (Equiv.): $(p \equiv q) \stackrel{\mathsf{T}}{=} [(p \supset q) \bullet (q \supset p)]$ $(p \equiv q) \stackrel{\mathsf{T}}{=} [(p \bullet q) \vee (\sim p \bullet \sim q)]$
9. Addition (Add.): $p, \therefore p \vee q$	**18. Exportation** (Exp.): $[p \supset (q \supset r)] \stackrel{\mathsf{T}}{=} [(p \bullet q) \supset r]$
	19. Tautology (Taut.): $p \stackrel{\mathsf{T}}{=} (p \vee p)$ $p \stackrel{\mathsf{T}}{=} (p \bullet p)$

RULES OF INFERENCE: QUANTIFICATION

NAME	ABBREVIATION	FORM	EFFECT
Universal Instantiation	**U.I.**	$(x)\Phi x$ $\therefore \Phi\nu$ (where ν is a constant) ***Or*** $(x)\Phi x$ $\therefore \Phi y$ (where y is an individual variable)	This rule eliminates a universal quantifier and replaces the variable with either a constant or a variable.
Universal Generalization	**U.G.**	Φy $\therefore (x)\Phi x$ (where y is an individual variable)	This rule introduces a universal quantifier. You can engage in a universal generalization *only* from a propositional function.
Existential Instantiation	**E.I.**	$(\exists x)\Phi x$ $\therefore \Phi\nu$ (where ν is a constant *new to the proof*)	This rule eliminates an existential quantifier and replaces the variable with a constant.
Existential Generalization	**E.G.**	$\Phi\nu$ $\therefore (\exists x)\Phi x$ (where ν is a constant)	This rule introduces an existential quantifier. You can engage in existential generalization only from a statement given in terms of constants.

QUANTIFIER EQUIVALENCE

These statements can replace one another wherever they occur in a proof:

$$[\sim(x)\Phi x] \stackrel{\text{T}}{=} [(\exists x)\sim\Phi x]$$

$$[(x)\sim\Phi x] \stackrel{\text{T}}{=} [\sim(\exists x)\Phi x]$$

$$[(x)\Phi x] \stackrel{\text{T}}{=} [\sim(\exists x)\sim\Phi x]$$

$$[(\exists x)\Phi x] \stackrel{\text{T}}{=} [\sim(x)\sim\Phi x]$$